THE
INDIVIDUAL DELINQUENT

PATTERSON SMITH REPRINT SERIES IN
CRIMINOLOGY, LAW ENFORCEMENT, AND SOCIAL PROBLEMS

A listing of publications in the SERIES *will be found at rear of volume*

PUBLICATION NO. 85: PATTERSON SMITH REPRINT SERIES IN
CRIMINOLOGY, LAW ENFORCEMENT, AND SOCIAL PROBLEMS

THE
INDIVIDUAL DELINQUENT

A TEXT-BOOK

OF

DIAGNOSIS AND PROGNOSIS FOR ALL CONCERNED IN UNDERSTANDING OFFENDERS

BY

WILLIAM HEALY, A.B., M.D.

DIRECTOR OF THE PSYCHOPATHIC INSTITUTE, JUVENILE COURT, CHICAGO
ASSOCIATE PROFESSOR MENTAL AND NERVOUS DISEASES, CHICAGO POLICLINIC

Montclair, New Jersey

PATTERSON SMITH

1969

SBN 87585-085-5

Library of Congress Catalog Card Number: 69-16238

TO

MRS. W. F. DUMMER

Give therefore thy servant an understanding heart to judge thy people.

SOLOMON'S PRAYER, I Kings, iii. 9.

Socrates : And yet, O my friend, if true opinion in law courts and knowledge are the same, the perfect judge could not have judged rightly without knowledge.

PLATO : *Theætetus.*

There is only one principle in penology that is worth any consideration: it is to find out why a man does wrong and make it not worth his while.

DEVON : *The Criminal and the Community.*

The only way to stop us is to find out who and what we are, and what we're good for. Then you've got to make punishment severe enough or opportunities good enough for us. You don't do either of these now.

Statement of an unjailed expert criminal.

Bei uns soll dann aber erst der Zweck unserer Arbeit; eine gesunde, psychologisch begründete Kriminalpolitik beginnen und alles in unserem Streben muss dem einen Ziele untergeordnet sein: Kriminalpolitik auf richtig erkannter Kriminalätiologie.

GROSS : *Aufsätze.*

PREFACE

It has been a joy to direct for five years the important scientific task which finds expression in the present volume. Our work has been done under favoring auspices and, indeed, with the constant stimulus of a kindly reception. For advice in early planning, and for later counsel, I am deeply grateful to many. My acknowledgments made in an already published schedule for data (24)[1] and in a monograph on mental tests (70) are to be repeated. To my coworkers acknowledgment is also due. Their names are connected with their special contributions.

The organization of the Juvenile Psychopathic Institute is set forth in Appendix B. Miss Julia C. Lathrop, as one of the originators, is indissolubly connected with the research. Several of our advisory council and others have given expert assistance. There has always been encouragement from the wise outlook of Judge Merritt W. Pinckney, who ever urges better understanding of the cases coming before him. Elsewhere we have received the heartiest welcome from jurists and others who cherish the vision of rational treatment for the delinquent.

To the ideals of Mrs. W. F. Dummer we have felt the utmost devotion and responsibility. Her financial support has been only part of her effect on the work.

We should be unjust to our feelings if we did not gratefully acknowledge the fine-spirited coöperation of the many practical workers who handled the delinquents we studied. They have been on the firing-line of effort.

To the dear friends who have aided in the literary preparation of this volume the gratitude of all who benefit by their emendations is due.

The statement of our findings has gradually assumed the scope of a text or reference book, the first on the subject. We hope for our science the growth that other sciences have experienced;

[1] Throughout this work, both in the text and foot-notes, the full-face numerals in parentheses refer to detailed mention in the Bibliography, Appendix A, of the particular works of the authors indicated.

there is great necessity for further research, but extensions and modifications are to be embodied only as their truth is assured.

It would take long to specify the parts of our subject with which people of various affairs should be familiar. Judges, other court officers, including lawyers, and institutional authorities, should have a particularly well-rounded knowledge of the whole field. Without the most thoughtful observation a great deal is hidden from view, as may be easily appreciated by consideration of our cases and causal types. (Some suggestion of the special bearings of special types as seen in court work is given in § 139.) Psychologists, physicians, religious leaders, school people, and, not least of all, parents, should be in possession of many of our fundamental facts. All who have to deal with offenders need the utmost possible understandings of human beings.

WILLIAM HEALY.

WINNETKA, ILLINOIS,
September, 1914.

CONTENTS

BOOK ONE
GENERAL DATA

CHAPTER I

CHAPTER II

CHAPTER III

CHAPTER IV

ix

CHAPTER V

CHAPTER VI

CHAPTER VII

CHAPTER VIII

CHAPTER IX

CHAPTER X

BOOK TWO
CASES, TYPES, CAUSATIVE FACTORS

CHAPTER I

CHAPTER II

CHAPTER III

CHAPTER IV

CHAPTER V

CHAPTER VI

CONTENTS

CHAPTER XIV

CHAPTER XV

CHAPTER XVI

CHAPTER XVII

CHAPTER XVIII

CHAPTER XIX

CHAPTER XX

CHAPTER XXI

CHAPTER XXII

CHAPTER XXIII

CHAPTER XXIV

CHAPTER XXV

CHAPTER XXVI

CHAPTER XXVII

LIST OF PLATES

BOOK ONE
GENERAL DATA

THE INDIVIDUAL DELINQUENT

CHAPTER I

INTRODUCTION

§ 1. Presentation of Results. § 2. Our Research into Genetics and Dynamics. § 3. Delinquency and Abnormality not Synonymous. § 4. Scheme of Presentation. § 5. Practical Aspects of the Study. § 6. To Whom this Study Should Appeal. § 7. Legal Dicta *vs.* Scientific Studies. § 8. Constructive Values for the Law. § 9. Scientific Data Indispensable for Treatment.

§ 1. **Presentation of Results.** — Out of deep consideration of hard-won facts this work is produced. In view of the failure of the past and of the present effectively to handle anti-social conduct, and in the light of the enormous expense of criminality, standing in striking contrast to recent progress in many other fields of human endeavor, there seems the utmost justification for research work in the underlying causations of delinquency.[1]

It has been called to our attention again and again that there is astonishingly little in the literature of criminology which is directly helpful to those who have to deal practically with offenders. Of general theory there is no lack, but when we come to that study of the individual which leads to clear understanding and scientific treatment, there is almost no guidance. The field covered by this volume, which is developed from the findings in many well-rounded case-studies, has only been touched heretofore in spots. Pioneering has stimulated deepest endeavor, but pleasure in it is tempered by the realization that fewer mistakes might have been made had there been more scientific foundations upon which to build. Through appreciation expressed, we know that some service has been rendered

---

[1] "Crime" and "delinquency" are used in this work as overlapping and practically synonymous terms. "The Individual Delinquent" may be either a young offender or an older criminal. The criminal is a person found guilty of a crime. Criminalism may be the action of a person not yet a criminal. Criminalistics is the study of criminalism.

3

by our development of mental tests and methods of case study, and it is hoped that the present elaboration of the whole subject will prove of much further value.

§ 2. **Our Research into Genetics and Dynamics.** — Our studies, for reasons enumerated later, have purposely for the most part been confined to youthful recidivists. We have dealt with a formative period for the sake of learning the structural growth of whole delinquent careers. Since knowledge of growth processes is always important for understanding the fully developed state, we feel assured that we have a definite contribution to make to the anatomy of delinquency in general. Of course, study and discussion of older criminals will always be needed; knowledge of consequences is necessary even for the predictabilities with which we concern ourselves so much. But far more important for the science and practice of criminology is the study of beginnings. Just because the delinquent's character is the result of a long-continued process of growth, one needs to regard him as the product of forces, as well as the sum of his present constituent parts; one must study him dynamically as well as statically, genetically as well as a finished result. This side of criminology has heretofore received very little attention.

§ 3. **Delinquency and Abnormality not Synonymous.** — We would make it clear here and elsewhere that we have not the slightest inclination to place delinquents as such in the list of abnormal individuals. Selection of our cases has not been made by their possession of a given quality; all along we have been simply searchers for *any* driving forces. Review of our case studies will plainly show this. Nor has our aim been the development of any philosophical system or scientific theory concerning delinquency or delinquents. In view of the immense complexity of human nature in relation to complex environmental conditions it is little to us even if no set theory of crime can ever be successfully maintained. Such statements as, "Crime is a disease," appear dubiously cheap in the light of our experience. Altogether our task has been not so much gathering material for generalizations, as ascertainment of the methods and the facts which will help towards the making of practical diagnoses and prognoses.

§ 4. **Scheme of Presentation.** — The general survey of the subject, which is frequently undertaken in an introduction, can

4

well be omitted here, because the relationship between the previous development of the science and our work frequently crops out in the opening chapters. Of historical surveys of criminology there are a plenty, of polemics anent the theory of criminal law there are altogether too many, of statistics leading to general explanations and theories there are interesting and scholarly analyses. For our own part we leave these almost entirely alone. What material we studied, why we chose this material, what methods we used and what viewpoint we assumed in projecting our study and in obtaining our data, what attitude we found most serviceable in reaching the individual, each of these will be set forth in its place. At all times we have felt ourselves concerned solely with the endeavor to ascertain the best way in which the interests of the individual and of society can be conserved by the regulation of tendencies to misconduct. In our writing we have maintained the same mental attitude, in order that there shall be a presentation of the workable methods and possibilities of diagnosis and prognosis in cases of delinquency.

In our chapter on methods we have introduced a general survey of the procedure for the adequate study of a delinquent. Such a sketch was not to be found elsewhere. It is a feature of the work about which there is always much inquiry. Enough references are given for filling out the details so that the chapter may be used as a chart for the elaboration of studies. Many items of inquiry taken from the fields of anthropology and sociology are enumerated. A schema for the entire examination is offered. The psychological method is gone into with detailed explanation because of its great interest and the recency of its development.

Following the acquirement of separate facts from the study of the individual case, we see great advantage in the careful grouping of them for the purpose of drawing safe inferences. We regard this logical use of the findings as the strongest feature of our procedure. Familiarity with our method of summarizing cases, and with our card system of causative factors will make this point stand out sharply. The chapter on conclusions speaks for itself. Our main conclusion is that every case will always need study by itself. When it comes to arraying data for the purpose of generalization about relative values of causative factors we experience difficulty; it is not easy to see how any systematic order can be followed. The concatenation of factors making for

5

delinquency leads now in this direction and now in that. The statistical method has been carried by us only so far as common sense would warrant, and we have tried to make neither this nor any other form of interpretation a fetish.

§ 5. **Practical Aspects of the Study.** — It is to our concrete studies, with the accompanying exposition of groups and types, that we specially ask attention. If one had space and skill, many of these histories could be portrayed with the force and interest of clever romance. Even in their synoptic form some will command deep interest. Particularly for the reader who wishes to gain general understanding is this part of the work to be recommended. No precept concerning the value of a professional understanding of the whole problem of delinquency can be so powerful as this actual setting forth of the facts.

The handling of a delinquent in any way is an important affair for society. Our findings show how vital it is that the handling should be entrusted to intelligent people, capable of understanding a human individual, and charged with a feeling of grave public duty. We see every need of insisting on this matter of understanding all along the line. It begins with parents, for they should comprehend at least the main phenomena of child life, and should guard the mental and moral sources of weal and woe. Ultimately, as many a judge has insisted, the problem of crime must hark back to parental guardianship. Unfortunately, however, cases are seen too late to educate parents, while of course many parents, by reason of innate defect or other circumstances, have never been educable in this matter.

§ 6. **To Whom this Study Should Appeal.** — But there are many besides parents who fail to understand the foundations on which delinquent careers are built. Teachers, pastors, and physicians, to whom the laity go so frequently for advice on mental and moral questions, have not always adequate knowledge of the springs of conduct. These things are not taught as yet in theological and medical schools, and are only just finding a place in psychological departments of universities and teachers' colleges. It would seem, however, that the phase of applied psychology which has to do with human behaviour should be essential in all these disciplines.

Our outlining of concrete case-studies should appeal to all who deal with delinquency under the law. Judges, and especially juvenile court judges, ought to gain the fullest possible acquaintance with types and causes. To this end instruction in at least the fundamentals of social adjustment needs to be carried back to the law schools — for what is learned as a standard branch of one's profession makes deep impress. Perhaps if there was a more intellectual outlook upon the problem, and the intricacies of the human individual were shown to be as captivatingly interesting as the solution of a case in civil law, judges would enter with more zest and better preparation into this field.

One would argue for a similar instruction among the ancillaries to modern court work; probation officers, and officials of detention institutions of all kinds. They come in closest contact with the individual offender, and the former can often study him in his own environment. They, especially, should know the possibilities and limitations of constructive efforts. A movement for the better achievement of reformatory work is now at hand, but only can advance far by introducing among institutional workers acquaintance with the scientific verities of the mental and moral life. As a basis for supplying the vaguely felt need for individualization of treatment in institutions comprehension of the genetics of misbehavior is a prime necessity.

§ 7. **Legal Dicta** *vs.* **Scientific Studies.** — We are acutely aware of the full many problems and perhaps legal obstacles which may be involved in applying to the field of criminal law and procedure the principles and facts we are setting forth in this work. We would not presume to make a statement of the special bearings of such problems, but it is plainly to be seen that here are difficulties implicating much profounder issues than those which arise within the field of penology. However, actual existence of legal obstacles does not automatically prove either their own fundamental worth or their irrevocability. Legal dicta represent merely certain conceptions of ways in which to deal with some social exigencies, and these conceptions, so far as criminal law is concerned, always have been built up in default of attempt to trace fundamental issues and causes, and entirely without study of the ultimate efficiency of adopted measures. Realization of these historical facts forces doubt, to put it mildly, of the omniscience of existing codes.

§ 8. **Constructive Values for the Law.** — Precisely here, it would seem, might arise one of the greatest values of such a work as ours, by suggesting to those who deal with criminal law some rational principles for its criticism, and some possibilities for its

7

development along lines of more efficient human service. Certainly the facts we have to show clearly indicate that from knowledge of the springs of conduct in the offender we may hope a thousand times more reasonably for a wise adjustment of his case than from the application of artificial legal rules and punishments. It is quite beside the mark to say that the individual must be sacrificed to the public welfare, or to say, with John Stuart Mill, that the aim of punishment under the law is curative, albeit the administration of it is painful. The fact is that, let the aim of the law be what it may, the actual effect of carrying out legal measures is frequently anything but curative. Might not the law, however, be vastly more curative if understandings of beginnings and foundations of misconduct in general, and knowledge of them as existing in the individual career, were made the business of those who administer treatment under the law? The investigation of these fundamentals in the offender's case may never be a part of the lawyer's or the jurist's work, but surely general acquaintance with them and with the possibilities of their bearing upon particular cases should be a required qualification of any one who sits in legal judgment. Can social treatment — a main business of the law — ever be really learnedly or efficiently prescribed without adapting it closely to the fundamental facts and possibilities of the given case? The letter of the law must not stand as a shibboleth preventing better adjustment of affairs in the field of delinquency.

§ 9. **Scientific Data Indispensable for Treatment.** — In fine, there may be gathered from our work as a whole every reason for the deepest conviction that only through logical, scientific study of the individual can there be any reasonable expectation of amendment in most delinquent careers. Those who have to do with the judging and treatment of offenders must reckon with such methods and facts as we present, if they would rank as intelligent workmen.

8

CHAPTER II

ORIENTATIONS

§ 10. **Our Main Point of View.** — To ascertain from the actualities of life the basic factors of disordered social conduct has been the deliberate plan of our work. Our orientations, inasmuch as they have been developed by careful reflection, should prove of worth to the student.

After formulation of the plan, the next step was discovery of a vantage ground from which to gain accurate information concerning the forces which drive towards delinquency. Nothing would seem to be easier in such an endeavor than in the library chair to gather descriptive histories and biographical statements;[1] but it was soon clear that the merely anecdotal nature of the available material precluded scientific results. The truth is that the literature offers almost nothing in the way of studies of delinquents which meet the requirements of recently developed science. In fact, one finds even no trail distinctly blazed to the goal of competent studies. Our only course was to devote, with generous assistance, years of hard work to winning the facts while serving in the field. Meanwhile the methods and tools of study had, many of them, to be developed.

§ 11. **General Data for Delimiting the Field of Study.** — In exploring the field, certain manifest possibilities and certain in-

---

[1] Something of this sort has been undertaken; for example, there is a good deal of biographical material, gathered often from German newspaper reports, in Wulffen's (2) two volume work on the psychology of the criminal. Also van Dijck (168) has collected from literary sources many biographies of criminals, classified them by offenses, and attempted the comparative sizing up of their personal attributes.

9

surmountable barriers were soon perceived in various quarters. These possibilities and limitations will stand out clearly by consideration of the following points:

(a) *By reason of their number and the seriousness of their offenses, repeated offenders (recidivists) have the greatest significance for society.* In this country we have only immature statistics on this point, but penologists accord in their opinion that conditions are much the same here as in Germany and England. The Blue Book (40) of 1912 gives the English figures for 1910. Out of 168,260 convictions during that year, 104,171 had received at least one previous conviction; 12,133 had been convicted above 20 times previously. Of the 11,337 convictions for the more serious offenses tried at the assizes and quarter sessions, 7,997, or seventy per cent., had been previously convicted. The importance of recidivists, and of all that makes them what they are, is thus clearly determined.

(b) *Practically all confirmed criminals begin their careers in childhood or early youth.* The fact of this remarkable early development of a definite tendency towards criminality was soon clear to us, both through observable trends in young offenders, and through the life histories of older delinquents. Experienced penologists all verify the fact of extremely early beginnings. The deplorable dearth of productive criminal statistics in this country can here again be offset only by figures from abroad where, after all, conditions are fairly comparable. Despite many opinions and references which could be offered as minor corroborations, the only extensive researches found are the following: In connection with the early impulse given to the reformatory movement in England during the conferences of 1851, 1853 and 1861 a number of direct observations were reported. Clay in a communication to the Earl of Shaftesbury stated that he had found that 58 per cent. of criminals are already dishonest before they are 15 years old, that 14 per cent. become so between 15 and 16, and that all of them have shown their anti-social tendencies before they are 19 or 20. Elliott stated at the Birmingham meeting in 1863, " Of the 1000 prisoners examined by me, 395 had beeen convicted before they were out of their teens. The great majority of professional thieves have been engaged in their careers almost from infancy." Another writer, cited by Morrison (54), states, " It is an ascertained fact that there is scarcely an habitual criminal in the county of Staffordshire who has not been imprisoned as a child."[1] Even more important is the thorough research of Matz (56), who investigated the prison population of the province of Pommern. He found that in 70 per cent. the first imprisonment had been inflicted before the 21st year, and that of the repeated offenders by far the greater number had received their first punishment before the 17th year. It must be remembered that here Matz is speaking not of the commission of the first offense, but of receiving the first punishment.

Although his figures are based on studies of a particular class of criminals, the chapter on age as an etiological factor in crime in the recent statistical work by Goring (160), shows out clearly these same points. It appears that the principal age for recruiting into the ranks of criminal life is between 15 and 20, as judged by the first convictions of 2204 English habitual offenders. And here again it is only the first punishment, not the first offense that is recorded.

(c) *The determinants of delinquent careers are the conditions of youth.* This conclusion is a corollary from the well-established findings set forth in the preceding paragraph. Now if these early causes, either external or internal, are to be accurately ascertained, there must be first-hand acquaintance with them; the phenomena should be studied when they are active.

(d) *In youth prime causative factors stand out much more clearly than they do later.* Many adventitious elements, such as the effects of alcoholism, morphinism, years of social degradation, the evil results of imprisonment, and the never-to-be-forgotten inexorable laws of mental habit render difficult the later appreciation of beginnings.

(e) *Knowledge of developmental conditions is important.* Many of the conditions of mind and body which stand in intimate relationship to criminalism can be ascertained only through inquiry into early illnesses and other untoward circumstances. Such knowledge is rarely to be obtained except during the youth of the offender. Then family life is more apt to be intact, and

---

[1] An excerpt from Clay's paper may be found in Morrison's book (54) on crime. Rylands' interesting work (55) makes a special point of this whole topic of juvenile beginnings; it is from this that Elliott is quoted. In his admirable little volume on the psychology of the criminal, Pollitz (8) devotes an instructive chapter to the age when delinquent careers are started. Kinberg (161) the eminent Swedish authority, in the absence of complete national statistics, states that in Sweden the maximum frequency of immoral crimes, arson, and grand larceny occurs in the age group of 15–18 years.

11

memories of elders are keener. Working with adult offenders in courts and institutions makes us quickly realize how little the average person knows of his own developmental history.

(f) *Data about family traits, early characteristics, and environment may be worth much for explanation of the offender's tendencies.* Both for positive and negative values, the careful student of the delinquent is most desirous of ascertaining the facts of heredity and of early formative conditions. These possible determinants of the career can best be known also when details and general aspects are not dim in the past.

(g) *Disingenuousness of the offender is a barrier.* For this reason it is important in the ascertainment of whole groups of causes to approach the delinquent in the years of naïveté. With the development of reserve and self-containment characteristic of the adult, and particularly of the adult who feels himself antagonistic to society, there is often difficulty in getting at some vital points. Our chapter and case histories on mental conflicts show the worth of knowing formative influences at the time when they can most easily be brought to the surface.

(h) *The best rewards of therapeutic efforts are from working with youth.* Experimental endeavor is frequently necessary in adjusting the affairs of the offender, and this is comparatively difficult in the case of the adult. When the delinquent is young, relatives have not usually acquired the hopeless attitude so often seen later. Then they sometimes can be wakened from their neglect and failure, and can be urged to try constructive measures. At that age the state agencies and other organizations take a more hopeful view, and render more intelligent aid. Both for the human interest and for the scientific elucidation of fundamentals, one would demand alteration of circumstances during a period when the individual was still plastic.

§ 12. **Best Age for Study.** — Notwithstanding our emphasis on youthful beginnings, never would we in the least discourage the study of older offenders. Much practical social improvement, both in courts and institutions, waits for the development of such work. One of our reasons for undertaking prolonged and intimate study of young offenders was, in truth, establishment of a better understanding of the types and possible social adjustments of older delinquents. Man is but a child with a little larger growth; and genetic fundamentals are the logical forbears of etiology and diagnosis in later years. Conversely, mature types present diagnostic pictures in characterology which suggest by deduction the genetic processes. This retracing the steps of a career is not only explanatory, but sometimes has an almost forgotten therapeutic value.

Partial studies of older offenders have been discussed by me elsewhere (29). The value of what is done in any given situation depends upon fulfilment of immediate needs, and upon scientific contributions apperceived in their true relationship. Of the making of fragmentary researches we have said, "There can be no scientific danger in this, provided there is not the unwarranted jumping at conclusions and indulgence in theorizing from insufficient premises, both as to the nature of 'the criminal' and of crime, which has unfortunately characterized very much of the criminology of the past. The snapshot diagnosis, that categorizing of individuals as belonging to some type, without adequate study of the make-up or the possibilities of the individual, can only lead to immature decisions and interference with the development of a science of adjustment."

§ 13. **Our Study of Recidivists.** — The repeated offender we have spoken of above as especially jeopardizing society, is early to be discerned as such. During even our juvenile court work, for recidivism is rampant here as elsewhere, we have seen that one of the most valid distinctions that could practically and scientifically be offered is between the repeater and the offender for a single time. There are many types of each, but psychologically the great distinguishing mark seems to be that the non-repeater finds in the outcome of his deed sufficient reason for future refraining. Our working definition is simple: The repeated offender is that individual who in spite of reprimands, warnings, probation or punishment proceeds to further anti-social deeds. Usually in our cases what has been offered in the way of retribution has emanated from police and juridical sources. However, I should not care to hinge the classification on that fact, for some of the worst repeated offenders one has ever seen, including young adults, have managed through family protection to escape prior contact with the courts.

While discussing the repeated offender it should parenthetically be said that no judgment is here passed on the comparative viciousness or sinfulness of his conduct. In fact, we are not at all inclined to state in general that misconduct punishable under the law is necessarily worse than many other vices **and**

13

meannesses. The social results of various sorts of improper conduct about which there are no laws at all may be a hundred times more disastrous than certain misdeeds of which the law takes special cognizance.

§ 14. **Group of Cases Studied and Our Approach to their Problems.**—Our studies as finally summarized deal with a group of 1000 repeated offenders selected from the total number of cases seen, on the basis of repetition of offense plus sufficiency of data. As will be later seen, 823 of these have been used for comparative study of causative factors. Most of the subjects have been adolescents; the average age between 15 and 16 years. Sometimes younger children have been observed and occasionally young adults. We have made a specialty of seeing youthful "problem cases," those in which previous efforts, sometimes even including definitive reformatory training, have proved useless for checking anti-social tendencies.

Offenders have been brought to us from many sources, mostly through the officials of the juvenile court who have been desirous of getting light on their different cases. Almost all have been seen in connection with relatives, but of course a few have had no immediate family. Credit should be rendered to the numerous parents, clergymen, and school people who have sought to avert an evil career by seeking scientific knowledge of the case. This coöperation has been great encouragement to arduous effort.[1]

Occasionally cases have been studied elsewhere than in Chicago, and enough insight has been gained into the workings and material of courts in other places to see that the problems are those of human nature, and vary but little with the locality. Diagnosis of cases belonging to the simpler groups, such as the obviously feebleminded, has been easy, and much more time has thus been left for study of other types. This latter has often meant, as may be estimated from some of the cases cited in this volume, expending a total of days of work on a single individual.

[1] The unexpectedly ready response, both on the part of the offender and his relatives, has been, after all, the most markedly encouraging feature of our work. In no cases had there been previously any thorough-going attempt to study causation, and such effort is nearly always appreciated. In some cases it awakened vigorous apperceptive interest, once to the extent that the examination alone caused the cure. The young man turned to his mother and asked her if she thought he was "off" in any way because he behaved so badly. He said he would show her differently, and from that time on he has been a reformed character. Very frequently, through hearing of our work, parents of children of many ages have themselves first sought us out.

Without didactically prescribing such intensive application as necessary for other investigators, we ourselves have found it imperative for the establishment of some hitherto unelaborated types of delinquent causation. However, we hardly see, even in the light of increased knowledge, how the work in certain cases, as where a deep-rooted mental conflict existed, could have been done in shorter time. As to such earnest effort being worth the time or energy expended we can say a little something about the practical economics involved.

§ 15. **Social and Scientific Values of Deeper Studies.**—Even leaving out the tremendous human side, which really should give the first impulsion towards activity in this field, it is clear to us that the saving to society from averting criminal careers is immense. Taking the outcome of only a few cases we have adjusted by scientific study, enough profit has accrued readily to equal the expenses of our institute during its five years. Other saving from corresponding work done under court auspices may be very great. One has known a trial based on psychopathic accusations and fairly estimated to have cost the state $15,000, which might have been wholly avoided through the application of scientific diagnosis.

The prime motive for our research into beginnings and causative factors we have ever felt to be the establishment of scientific laws of predictability upon which all sorts of treatment could be rationally planned. With the accumulation of data it also stands out clearly that the ascertainment of causative factors in the individual is fundamental, not only for the application of practical therapy, but also for the gathering of any statistics and the framing of any classifications which can be safely utilized. In our chapter on conclusions and results we offer a careful statement of the relative dangers and values of dealing with isolated facts of causation, while all through these pages will be found echoes of our insistence on the ultimate validity of only thoroughgoing studies of the individual.

§ 16. **Historical Orientation of Our Standpoint.**—Our relation to prior development of criminology should be summarily reviewed, though with attempt to avoid the polemic which invasion of the realms of this largely theoretical science always seems to incite. It is quite fair to speak of most previous works on this subject as theoretical, for their marshalling of statistical and individual facts often may be likened to the gathering of

15

building stones for an edifice of opinions already designed. Not only have many theories been published at great length, but volumes have, in turn, been written in review of them.[1] Too much splendid effort has been deliberately busied with these theoretical inquiries for us to turn such studious opinions lightly aside.

One who derives his first interest in the problem of delinquency, as did the author, from the neurological clinic, and whose first teachers were the works of Lombroso, Ferri, and Talbot, need hardly be considered as prejudiced against the Italian positivist school. To these early masters of individual study we still offer all praise as pioneers. And so far as our relations to the so-called anthropological school are concerned, Ellis is right in combating the constant attributing to it of set opinions, because no such school really exists. Anthropology, the science of man, must be ever growing with the growth of human knowledge, and can not be held to the limitations of set opinions.

§ 17. **Ascertained Facts Overwhelm the Theories.** — Our experience is simply that we found the facts too much for the theories. Through the detailed study of cases, under good conditions for getting at the essentials, the path of preconceived etiology and classification was seen beset with difficulties. The intricacies of causations appeared manifold. It was then that the plan of making straight for the facts, all the facts available, showed itself of significant worth to us. Pigeon-holes and categories could remain unused if we had to damage our facts to fit them in. It was clearly evident that classification by crimes leads only in special instances to knowledge of the criminal; that statistics of seasons, and races, and head-measurements, and alcoholism, and so on, mean almost nothing for the fundamental understanding of the individual case; that epileptic and atavistic theories could not be substantiated by case histories; that refinements of psycho-physical measurements sometimes used on criminals need a tremendous amount of over-

---

[1] Mentioning only the important reviews, we have "Modern Theories of Criminality," by De Quiros| (121), "Individualization of Punishment," by Saleilles (123), and the eminently well-balanced "Penal Philosophy," by Tarde (5). Crammed full of the data used for building theories, is Havelock Ellis's "The Criminal" (124). Aschaffenburg (1) also handles carefully the contentions of the different schools. Most noteworthy is the collection of fourteen volumes, "Kritische Beiträge zur Strafrechtsreform" (125), in which every phase of the conceptual bases of criminal law is treated in the fashion of true Teutonic scholarship.

16

hauling before they can be regarded as valid for conclusions;[1] that the elders, who spoke so glibly of "the criminal" as a born type, had not the means of investigating whether he was not rather a born defective, and a criminal through accident of environment.

This last consideration alone is enough to make the student look askance at all the older classifications. The statistics that we are offered concerning criminals, whether about their deeds, their ears, their religious faith, or what not, are presented without knowledge of essential facts, such as whether or not they were mentally defective; and thus lead us nowhere for purposes of practical treatment. We see segregated in institutions the feebleminded with just these stigmatized skulls and palates and ears. We find well-developed stigmata sometimes in those who are morally normal.[2] So it seems that by virtue of education or social protection, such marked individuals need not become criminals. In the light of these facts and of the constructive possibilities of our own findings we have become certain that the development of mental tests and psychological analysis is doing more towards the establishment of true theories and of practical classifications of criminals than all other methods of study combined. In the past there has been great mistaking of incidentals for essentials.

It seems that we have not entirely avoided polemic in showing

[1] As a paradigm for criticism on some of the older conclusions, one might review the data on "Physical Insensibility of Criminals," well summarized by Ellis (124, pp. 123–140). Since this phenomenon has been so often asserted and commented on, the following points should be known. First, we are offered no evidence that the findings were not obtained largely by testing mental defectives, notoriously insensible, who were secondarily criminals. Only correlation with mental tests would show this. Next, there is, as Ellis acknowledges, considerable disagreement in the findings. Finally, the methods of testing insensibility involve some very grave sources of possible error. Miss Kellor (127, p. 52) has neatly shown some of the difficulties which she experienced. We so appreciated, by long experience in the neurological clinic, the impediments to safe judgment where stoicism and other subjective elements were involved, that from the first, testing for the pain sense was omitted by us as a routine procedure.

[2] In this country where so little comparative anthropometry has been undertaken we should not forget the careful researches of Channing and Wissler (128), and of Boas (129). The former show the most common classical stigma to be only slightly more prevalent in some mentally abnormal types than in normal individuals. The latter demonstrate the great influence which environment may have upon the most stable of bodily measurements — a most important fact for those to meet who in anywise correlate criminality as such with anthropometric measurements. Just now there is newly before us the monumental work of Goring (160) who, better than any one, proves from his extensive studies of the physique of English convicts the nonexistence of a criminal anthropological type.

our evolution of opinion as we progressed in the study of cases and methods. We should do every justice to the fathers, particularly to Lombroso, whose chief glory it was to insist on understanding the individual preliminary to handling his case. So far as the theories are concerned, we would in agreement cite Aschaffenburg (1, p. 177): " As often as a new field of criminal anthropological investigation has been attacked, the same thing has been repeated. First, assertion is made that a certain form of deviation is characteristic of the criminal. Then it is proved that the same phenomena are found in non-criminals, and finally, it is shown that these anomalies are somewhat more frequent in criminals."

§ 18. **Our Empirical Method.** — We resolved to classify, then, etiologic or diagnostic facts only according to what we should find. If no scheme was followable, or much overlapping was shown, that could not be helped. To apply by rule of thumb either the simple four-fold scheme of Bianchi (276), or the recent elaboration of Ingegnieros (131), or any other *a priori* classification, would be to disregard the complexity of causation which can be found in every case. We early ascertained that the facts needed one classification of mental findings, another of physical conditions, another of environmental background, and so on. The outcome was the discovery of combined types of causations and individual peculiarities that often fit the criminal into no system. Any classification according to theories of epileptoidism, of atavism, or of other biological causation, would end in the mere giving of a name; whereas a complete survey of the facts leads through the realization of a many-sided etiology to adequate conception of diagnosis, prognosis and treatment. All this may be seen concretely elaborated in our chapter on conclusions and in our presentation of cases and types.

§ 19. **Newer Methods of Study.** — In relating our methodology to that of the past we may add that, starting from no criminological theory, our attempt has been to obtain all the available facts by combination of all methods which bid fair to offer explanatory results. The more recent conceptions of individual study carry one far beyond external and anthropometric details. The introduction of psychological tests for estimation of the mental potential is as new and valuable as the application of those analytical methods which throw light on covert mental mechanisms and the startling effects, unsuspected or apparently

18

unrelated, of early experience. To compare these improved methods, which bring to the surface such an increased number of facts, with the older modes of study, as applied to Marie Schneider (*vide* Ellis, **124**, p. 7 ff.) or to Jesse Pomeroy (*vide* Folsom, **60**), is like comparing many of the mechanical advances of the day with those of a generation or two ago.

§ 20. **Follow-Up Observations Necessary.**—We are impressed with the necessity for much follow-up work in the establishment of scientific principles. It is not enough, certainly at this stage of the development of the science of individual study, if it ever will be, merely to say that here is a given human equipment with certain powers and with such-and-such background of experience. One has to venture a prognosis under various possible social circumstances, and then to follow up year by year to see if what one has said about this given type or case needs revision as the result of changed conditions. Only by such a method of self-criticism and prolonged observation can the observer or his science grow. It is a fact that in our work this longitudinal study has in many cases demanded a record of several scores of pages, and the spending of considerable energy in personal observation. However, this was the way to set about it, and we have come to see that neither we nor other investigators can make such a contribution to the principles of our science as shall ever do away with the necessity for (*a*) careful personal study of each offender, and (*b*) testing the value of measures carried out, always by the criteria of future results.

§ 21. **Insoluble Problem of Legal Responsibility.** — It is frequent in the general discussion of delinquency to deal specifically with the problem of legal responsibility.[1] Many times it has been made the center of argument, and yet if one watches the concrete issues appearing every day in court, and endeavors

---

[1] The psychological and social aspects of responsibility, as a basis for legal adjudications, are treated in the following recent notable contributions. Parson (**190**) in a dissertation, summarizes the best authorities and interprets them according to the scientific principle that most human action is response to stimuli. McConnell (**191**) also covers much ground in his work, which takes in both the legal and social standpoints. A paper by Jones (**192**) led to an unusually thorough discussion by medical psychologists of the border line of responsibility. The modern scientific viewpoint of attenuated criminal responsibility is finely treated in synopsis by Wagner von Jauregg (**193**), the scholarly Austrian neurologist, and a review of the literature on the subject is given by Gottschalk (**375**). Sibenaler of Bordeaux (**194**) presents a careful study of juvenile responsibility and age of moral discernment. A remarkably pithy symposium is contributed to by Engelen (**226**) Kahl (**227**), and Mezger (**228**).

fair-mindedly to gather information bearing upon the problem
of dealing with offenders, he cannot avoid the conclusion that
the practical question of responsibility is not the core of the problem. If responsibility has been, as Tarde asserts, the pivot
upon which penal philosophy has heretofore revolved, then it
seems clear that what has been called penal philosophy should
be replaced by something much more human, more economic
in the long run, and more efficient for reformation.

And then the criteria of responsibility involve so much that
is intricate, uncertain, and metaphysical, and are themselves
properly subject to variations by reason of environmental and
disease conditions, by reason of innate defects and differences
in social suggestibility, that, for the purposes of general discrimination and the development of a general standardization,
they are thoroughly impracticable. Our case studies contain
many proofs of this point.

Some of the greatest thinkers have found the problem insoluble. Mercier (148), one of the latest and best-known writers on
the subject, finally gives up the whole question (to be sure, he
does not accede to the idea of gradations of responsibility, and
does not allow for psychological discoveries made by modern
methods of testing) and wants decision relegated to the common
sense of a jury of untrained men. Can anything be more significant of the difficulties which stand in the way of a satisfactory
solution of dealing with criminals by standard laws and artificial rules applicable to all persons alike?

§ 22. **Responsibility a Dispensable Criterion.** — But the saving grace of it all is that when one invades the field, and sees
clearly the issues at stake, it at once becomes plain that to face
this long-maintained point of view is not at all necessary. The
light of better things for the future is seen to lie in an entirely
different direction, and in dealing with the practical question
of social welfare, we are early constrained to leave the path that
ends in the dilemma of responsibility or irresponsibility.

Concerning an alternative idea, that of a continental sociological school, to center the problem of punishment on criminal
intent — the state of mind in which, or the purpose with which
the act was done — almost the same ground might be taken as
in regard to responsibility.[1] This idea is the nucleus of a pro-

---

[1] A scholarly volume by Allfeld (158) is devoted to discussion of the plan
of meting out the penalty according to the intent. This author opposes any

posed system which cannot, on account of the many practical difficulties, nearly cover the field of treatment of the offender.

§ 23. **Our Study Largely Characterology.**—As a last word in this chapter, we may say that much of our study might be termed *characterology*,[1] to adopt the appellation of several authors. As students of character, we are dealing with the motives and driving forces of human conduct and, since conduct is directly a product of mental life, we immediately become involved in individual and differential psychology. This relationship of mental life to conduct is, however, a subject important enough to be treated in a separate chapter.

general scheme elaborated on such a basis, although he acknowledges its good points.

[1] The word characterology was introduced at least as early as 1862. Bahnsen's (62) essays on the subject appeared then. Wulffen (2) has a chapter on this branch of anthropology, and Stern (79) also uses the word. John Stuart Mill used the more euphonious term, ethology.

CHAPTER III

THE INDIVIDUAL

§ 24. **Dynamic Center of the Problem.**—The dynamic center of the whole problem of delinquency and crime [1] will ever be the individual offender.

§ 25. **Definite and Practical Knowledge of the Individual is Necessary.**—It is impossible to get away from the fact that no general theories of crime, sociological, psychological or biological, however well founded, are of much service when the concrete issue, namely the particular offense and the individual delinquent, is before those who have practically to deal with it. The understanding needed is just that craved by Solomon — the understanding of the one who has actually to deal with people, the one who formally is the therapeutist. It does not require prolonged observation of any treatment of the offender to realize what knowledge will prove of most worth in the procedure; one quickly perceives that it must be information concerning characteristic variations of physical and psychical equipment, concerning laws of mental mechanics, and the influence of the various forms of experience on various types of mankind. From this arises scientific and common-sense appreciation of the relation of antecedent to consequent in the life history of the individual offender whose actions and person are to be dealt with.

Collected statistics and groups of facts concerning criminality are offered from time to time as the bases upon which measures of public policy may be erected. So far, however, there has been

---

[1] The terms "delinquency" and "crime," or "criminality," will be used throughout our work as synonymous. There is no logical line of demarcation of meaning, in European terminology the words are interchangeable. In our country "delinquency" and "delinquent," because of their seemingly less harsh connotation, are applied to youthful offenders. For the vital reasons given above we have concerned ourselves most largely with the study of youthful offenders and have chosen for our title the less offensive term.

astonishingly little written into social ordinances as the result of much labor expended in the effort to determine the general facts of crime. There may be several reasons for this. Sometimes the criminologist, even of wide renown, has allowed himself to become almost obsessed by theories and doctrines which have led for the most part only to controversy. But perhaps the greatest cause for slight effect upon legislation and other practical procedure may be found in the fact that when face to face with the complications of the actual case many of the generalizations of criminology are seen to crumble away.

§ 26. **Weakness of General Causation Theories.** — Nothing is shown by our data more convincingly than the predictable inadequacy of social measures built upon statistics and theories which neglect the fundamental fact of the complexity of causation, determinable through study of the individual case. Many of the works on social misconduct deal with what is often denominated 'general causation,' and attempt to establish geographical, climatological, economic and many other correlations. Much of this is interesting and even seductive, intellectually, and it is true that there are some relationships, such as that between alcoholism and crime, well enough verified to justify social alteration. But that many of these suggested correlations contain only half-truths, one is constrained to believe after prolonged attempt to gather in all available facts in many individual cases. To illustrate a couple of these ' general causation ' inferences, we might take the failure of the treatment of drunkards during the last decade under the English Inebriate Acts. It was soon found that the projected curative measures, proposed without any adequate estimation of the personal equipment of those who would come under treatment, could not combat, for example, innate mental deficiencies. In other words, many of the great army of topers are such because of their feeblemindedness, and it is that, and not the ingestion of alcohol, which must be fundamentally reckoned with. For another illustration, we may take the findings, often alluded to, that several forms of crime are more prevalent in certain seasons of the year. Sex assault and violence are notably more frequent during hot weather; is it then safe to assert summer temperature as the main cause? One might well ask, is there not rather a lowering of moral inhibitions during that season through the excess of alcoholic beverages then ingested? The above are two of the very simplest instances of the neglect to ascertain the complexities in the causation of crime.[1] Studies of individual cases, and final summary analysis of these cases, such as we present in the latter part of this work, form the only way of arriving at the truth. Results of such work make the investigator exceedingly chary of theories built upon the consideration of single causes.

§ 27. **Thorough Study Means Balancing of Factors.**—Thorough study of individual cases does not imply that we shall always find the main cause of the offender's tendency in his own make-up — it merely implies the logical balancing of causative factors. One has seen an extensive family chart exhibited as proof that criminalism is inherited, because of its springing up in several side lines. But in addition to the chart the investigator possessed information that the various persons showing delinquent tendencies all lived in an atrocious environment. The facts not plotted on the chart could be used to show, if we took them also by themselves, that in this family criminalism was uniformly the result of bad social circumstances. On the other hand, it may be conditions in the home, or other environmental agents, which at first sight loom large. But then one finds other individuals in the same family turning out well, *vide* § 108, others on the same street or with the same associates who do not become criminals. Complicating the argument again, we may discover grave delinquent tendencies appearing in some one member of the most upright families, while, contrariwise, we have occasionally found all the numerous immediate descendants of a terrible drunkard successfully arising in full strength of character from the squalor in which he placed them. So it goes; to single out and blame this or that specific condition, without proceeding by the scientific process of elimination and attempting to rule out other possible causes, will not lead far towards real solutions. Indeed, without well-rounded studies of the pivotal facts in the particular case it ensues that " experience is fallacious and judgment difficult."

§ 28. **Growth of Idea of Studying the Offender.** — The idea

---

[1] As an example of the bare collection of minute data concerning the social and biological background of a group of offenders, which omits many of the psychological possibilities, and fails to analyze the relative bearings of the total facts in the respective cases, we might cite Gruhle's recent book (147). Here even an extreme application of the statistical method fails to demonstrate its value when applied to only 105 cases.

that the individual must be carefully studied in order that crime may be ameliorated has been steadily growing since the day of Lombroso. The humanitarian efforts of John Howard were evidence of the appreciation of the needs of offenders as individual human beings; the view of Lombroso was that of the scientific man who sees in this field the inexorable laws which govern man's nature and environment. It makes little difference which theoretical view of penology is held; the problem of society ever is to handle a given offender satisfactorily. Recently the Japanese authority, Oba (51), a strong believer in the necessity of meeting evil by evil, maintains that at the beginning of the handling of the offender there must be the most exact research into the characteristics and conditions of both him and his family. In his plans for effectively dealing with recidivism this writer insists that only through such a method could the punishment be made proportionate to the guilt — and that is a prime necessity in his scheme.

§ 29. **The Problem of Personality.** — Clear comprehension of the make-up of human personality will prove a gain to the student of our subject. A person is not fairly to be regarded merely as the soul and body of the moment. It is only our own temporal limitations which prevent us from seeing people as they really are — as products of the loom of time. Every individual is partly his ancestors, and partly the result of his developmental conditions, and partly the effects of many reactions to environment, and to bodily experiences, and even of reactions to his own mental activities. An ideal description of a human person would refer each trait or condition to its proper source. Most serviceable to us is the conception of the individual as the product of conditions and forces which have been actively forming him from the earliest moment of unicellular life. To know him completely would be to know accurately these conditions and forces; to know him as well as is possible, all of his genetic background that is ascertainable should be known. The interpretations that may be derived from acquaintance with the facts of ancestry, ante-natal life, childhood development, illnesses and injuries, social experiences, and the vast field of mental life, lead to invaluable understandings of the individual and to some idea of that wonderful complex of results which we term personality.

CHAPTER IV

THE MENTAL BASES OF DELINQUENCY

§ 30. Conduct an Expression of Mental Life.   § 31. Practical Bearings of
the Psychological Viewpoint.   § 32. Importance of Mental Abnormality.
§ 33. Psychological Standpoint Taken Alone is Unsafe.   § 34. Specific
Features of Mental Life Underlying Delinquency.

§ 30. Conduct an Expression of Mental Life. — All conduct
is directly an expression of mental life. Immediately back of the
action is the idea, or the wish, or the impulse, existing as mental
content. Of course many actions have no representation in
consciousness, either before or after performance, but nevertheless they are just as truly controlled by mental processes.
One starts to walk down the street, thereby engaging in public
conduct, and continues to walk, and finally stops; all without
the slightest thought about this succession of acts. Yet every
part of the performance has been impelled by operations of the
mind, that part of the mind which, fortunately for our ability
to pay attention to other things, is subconscious. Proof of all
this is found in the normal power to produce similar action as
consciously controlled behavior; to see, as it were, how it was done.
More evidence on the same point is derived from our ready recollection that actions arose from mental activity which at the moment of action was not above the threshold of consciousness.
We remember how we walked down the street and that the
walking was carried out at the bidding of our desires, although
we did not at the time formulate this sequence. Altogether, a
great deal of mental life at any given moment is subconscious,
and a great deal of conduct which appears for the moment uncontrolled, nevertheless is directly dependent on subconscious
mental activity.

Even conduct in the pathological mental states which supervene during the varied conditions of epilepsy or insanity is just
as truly the direct outcome of mental activity, although not
controlled by the conscious will, and frequently not in the least
representable at any time in consciousness. The anti-social
actions of such periods are the fault of the disordered mental

26

mechanism which at the time precludes normal conscious mental life. Disordered though the higher mentality may then be, some parts of the mind are actively at work creating conduct.[1] We can be sure of this through the easy determination of hallucinations and morbid ideations and impulsions which are often discernible in such cases.

In its physiological aspect conduct may be traced back to origins which, reasoning from the well-established correlation of brain-cell activity with mental life, show also the mental processes back of the deed. Conduct may be readily stated in terms of muscular action; the latter activity, in turn, is propagated by currents of nervous force which, for all such complicated processes, are known to arise from the coördinated energy of cerebral cells. The parts of the brain involved are the higher levels, those which we know are correlated with mental phenomena rising on occasion above the threshold of consciousness. So it seems that all analysis of the dynamics back of conduct leads directly to contemplation of mental activity.

§ 31. **Practical Bearings of the Psychological Viewpoint.** — However, for the pragmatic ends of this work, one would not be satisfied with any *a priori* considerations alone, however logically fundamental, in the study of the causative factors of delinquency. To be suited for our purposes, such a line of approach as the above must present tangible evidences of practical worth. It must appear that by deliberately turning our studies towards the phenomena of mental life, paths will be discovered to amendment of the moral situation. The psychological point of view, if it fail in this, must be discarded as not inherently essential.

---

[1] On several occasions I have had the opportunity of attempting with intelligent subjects, analysis of criminalistic behavior enacted during a previous aberrational period. A woman of fine character, who in her attacks of insanity, for which she had to be confined, was very prone to commit violence, said she always knew at the time it was wrong, but something stronger than her reason impelled her. Another particularly high-minded woman, who in ephemeral outbreaks of her psychoses made attempts at murder which she finally accomplished, said the voice which she heard at the time was so commanding that it seemed to be the word of God. An epileptic young man (§ 256) who during one of his whim-controlled, almost automatic states nearly perpetrated a most heinous crime — wrecking a passenger train — has since frequently discussed it. His consciousness, judging by his memory of the event and by witnesses to his actions at almost the same time, seems to have been narrowed to the one impulse and the cunning scheming for its satisfaction. Clear though it is that the fellow was not right mentally at the time, he has always felt that, since his action followed an idea, the deed was mentally controlled, and from the evidence of his memory, he never has been inclined to assert his own actual irresponsibility. This is another example of the great difficulty of adjudication according to criteria of responsibility.

In taking up the actual problem of the sources of delinquency it was apparent that just this method of approach afforded the quickest and clearest understanding, the surest interpretation, and by far the greatest promise of success; and altogether was a much less difficult path to follow than might be expected. Our own case studies have gradually led us to the overwhelming conclusion that, for practical purposes, what we particularly want to know about the offender are the immediate mental antecedents of his conduct.

Misconduct is only a branch of conduct in general; and nowhere can the relationships between conduct and mental life be perceived better than in studying the immediate causations of social misdoing. The robbery was preceded by the mental presentation, the plan; the assault followed upon the mental reaction of anger to the displeasing pictures which the spoken word brought up; the temptation was followed because the idea of immediate satisfaction was not counterbalanced just then by conscious representation of consequences. Thus illustrations might be indefinitely multiplied of how a mental process immediately precedes conduct.

Hence it is clear that *whatever* influences the individual towards offense must influence first the mind of the individual. It is only because the bad companion puts dynamically significant pictures into the mind, or because the physical activity becomes a sensation with representation in psychic life, or the environmental conditions produce low mental perceptions of one's duty towards others, that there is any inclination at all towards delinquency.

So true is this that, through application of the methods of individual study, it soon becomes apparent that really the only safe way to ascertain the driving forces which make for social offense is to get at the mental mechanisms antecedent to the behavior in question.

Not reckoning with the mental factor leads to many errors in the drawing of conclusions. The force of the actual findings is the strongest argument against the student of delinquency becoming an externalist, an investigator merely of outward and overt circumstances. If the facts are taken all together the following sorts of complications are to be found: The family life may have been faulty, but it was actually the influence of certain pernicious experiences which made recurrent imagery that has consciously or subconsciously driven to offense. Study of heredity may show wanderers in a family line, but in this member of the family it was a hidden mental conflict about a terrible secret that led to the running away from home. We came to know this because we brought the conflict to light, and the light cured both it and the running away. In another case frightful crowding of the home could not be blamed except that it induced ideas and mental pictures which led straight to bad conduct.

Such facts, and what is brought out by differential psychology, give some suggestion as to why other persons in the same family, or house, or street, or gang, have not turned to delinquency. These comparisons should be ever a barrier to the acceptance of general social or biological theories of crime. Realization of the mental factors must prevent our giving credit to mouth-filling declarations that crime is an atavistic phenomenon, or a disease, or that "the criminal" belongs to this or that human sub-species — declarations in which definition is bought for too cheap an intellectual outlay.

§ 32. **Importance of Mental Abnormality.** — Turning now to abnormal mental traits and conditions correlated with delinquency, we have further corroboration of mental life standing to conduct as antecedent to consequent. The part insanity plays in the production of social disturbance is too obvious to need illustration. Border-line individuals with their morbid, overwhelming impulses and compulsions are also well recognized as having a mental equipment prone to develop delinquency. Showing mostly negative aspects we have the mental defectives. In them it is not so much that their actual concepts give rise to delinquency, as that through their lack of judgment and counterbalancing power, influences and suggestions coming either from their own physical selves or from the external world, lead to impulses and pictures which determine the misdeed.

Therefore, even in these abnormal individuals it is clearly improbable that peculiar palates, or insensitive finger tips, or queerly-shaped heads will ever be found in any such close relationship to delinquency as are the mental phenomena we discuss. With full respect for those who earliest apprehended the problem of the delinquent as an individual, we nevertheless see the utter inadequacy of work which did not, first and foremost, determine the offender's mental content, his mental traits, pecu-

29

liarities and abilities. Vastly important though social and biological backgrounds are, yet they must take at least second place
to these more immediate causative factors of delinquency.

We have previously insisted on the impossibility of applying
in all cases the criterion of responsibility as definable in the law.
We believe this matters little because cases can be satisfactorily
handled from other standpoints. But as students of mental life
we are forced to unequivocally commit ourselves to the opinion
that many individuals who commit misdeeds have abnormal
impulsions, or are temporarily or chronically weak in the powers
of self-control. This is the basis for the idea of lessened moral
responsibility which accords truly with the facts. We may call
the attention of the reader to our studies of types primarily defective in self-control (§ 281), types of those affected by adolescent impulsions (§§ 316, 336), of those assailed by the curious
phenomena of the epilepsies (§ 253), of menstrual mental disorders (§ 310), of senile failures of inhibition (§ 163), and so on.
When one has surveyed such groups as these, two practical conclusions must be drawn; one, that there often is prodigious
difficulty in defining legal responsibility, and, next, that these
cases, for their own welfare and for the protection of society,
need appropriate physical, educational, or even disciplinary
treatment under highly individualized surveillance.

§ 33. **Psychological Standpoint Taken Alone is Unsafe.**—We
will not attempt to review the opinions of the several criminologists who upon *a priori* grounds have already declared themselves for the psychological point of view.[1] We can do better
by presenting the facts gleaned from life studies which lead us
directly to the same position. The concrete argument is to be
read in almost every page of our case histories. Mental and
moral problems may there be seen to merge.

---

[1] The psychological point of view in the study of individual delinquents
is well stated by Bechterew (**63**). His program is based upon the distinction
between general and individual factors in the development of delinquency,
and involves an actual study of the criminal's personality. It is strange that
in the literature of criminology there are so many works designated "psychology of the criminal," which nevertheless deal with psychology in only
the most indirect way, without development of a methodology, and which
really set us onward very little towards a better understanding of the mental
mechanisms standing as immediate precursors of delinquent conduct. For a
general statement of "such a pragmatic applied psychology as will deal with
all states of mind that might possibly be involved in the determination and
judgment of crime" no one can afford to neglect the work of Gross (**64**). He
gives a long list of authors who have written from the standpoint of psychology, and includes in his text many of their best ideas.

Notwithstanding all this I fully recognize that there are many cases in which sole dependence on the psychological standpoint would be a grave mistake. Repeatedly I have asserted the opinion, still held, that it is very difficult to decide which is in general the most important investigatory vantage ground — social, medical, or psychological. The point is clear, however, that one can most surely and safely arrive at remedial measures through investigation of the mental factors.

There is no doubt that certain groups of physicians and educators will best understand the importance of the above truths — physicians who have been especially engaged with psychiatric and neurological problems, and educators who are interested in applied psychology. Sociologists and psychologists have nowadays rapidly growing conceptions of the value of individual study.[1] Those who under the law have to deal with offenders are, however, foremost in needing to understand fundamentals. And if it be intimated that these issues are too abstruse, we should feel justified in asserting that those who have not the capacity to appreciate these things are certainly not fitted to pass judgments on delinquents or hold authority over them.

§ 34. **Specific Features of Mental Life Underlying Delinquency.**—This chapter, dealing with the general survey of the mental bases of delinquency, is hardly the proper place in which to offer specific details. Not that the fundamentals are too technical, but that they are best presented in connection with concrete findings. The study of actual cases is imperative for understanding the part which mental life plays in the production of misconduct. It may be useful here, however, to itemize some of those features of mental life which study shows directly underlie delinquency. Perusal of concrete instances in the second part of this volume will lead to completer understanding of what is now merely enumerated. The proof of the validity of the psychological data will often be found in the actual outcome of the case as predicted in accordance with them.

We may find existing as bases of delinquency any of the following:

---

[1] There can be no question but that applied psychology is in the infancy of a mighty growth, and that our field is in large part its field. Writing on the control of mental life, Yerkes (**284**) says, "the prediction, modification and direction of psychological processes is an unescapable task of psychology." That this is a view somewhat opposed to that of many older psychologists certainly does not bespeak for it any the less fruitfulness.

Mental dissatisfactions; those developed from cravings of no special moral significance in themselves, or even from unfulfilled creditable ambitions.

Criminalistic imagery, sometimes fairly obsessional, which persists, and is strong enough to impel misconduct.

Irritative mental reactions to environmental conditions, seeking expression or relief in misdoing.

The development of habits of thought involving persistent criminalistic ideas and reactions.

Adolescent mental instabilities and impulsions.

Mental conflicts, worries or repressions concerning various experiences or matters of mental content. These sometimes interfere with that smooth working of the inner life which fosters socially normal conduct. The misdeed here, too, may be a relief phenomenon.

The chronic attitude of the offender representing himself to himself as one, like Ishmael, whose hand shall be against every man and every man's hand against him. The remarkable phenomenon of anti-social grudge may be included here.

Mental peculiarities or twists which are agents in the production of anti-social conduct, but which do not overwhelm the personality enough to warrant us in grading the subject as aberrational.

Aberrational mental states : — all the way from fully-developed psychoses to temporary or border-line psychotic conditions.

Mental defect in any of the several forms described in our special chapter on the subject.

CHAPTER V

WORKING METHODS

§ 35. General Survey of Working Methods.   § 36. The Observer and His Attitude.   § 37. Privileged Communication.   § 38. Previous Training of Observer.   § 39. Age of Examinee.   § 40. Types for Study.   § 41. Sources of Information.   § 42. Place of Observation.   § 43. Extent of Study of a Case.   § 44. Office and Equipment.   § 45. Assistants.   § 46. Interview and Examination.   § 47. Records.   § 48. **Schedule of Data Concerning Delinquents.**   I. Family History.   II. Developmental History.   III. History of Environment.   IV. Mental and Moral Development.   V. Anthropometry.   VI. Medical Examination.   VII. Psychological Examination: (A) Records of Tests.   (B) Records of Psychological Analysis.   VIII. Delinquency.   IX. Diagnostic Summary.   X. Follow-up Records.   XI. Subsidiary Records.   § 49. **Medical Methods.**

§ 35. **General Survey of Working Methods.**—Our conception of working methods starts from the premises that a sound procedure for understanding and treatment of delinquency is only to be found in a well-rounded survey of the individual delinquent and the driving forces of his career. To this end there must be made first a cross-section study of the offender, just as complete as is practicable, including data derived from the standpoints of social, medical and psychological investigations. From such a cross-section the diagnosis must be derived by thoughtful consideration, and the prognosis or predictabilities carefully rendered. The prognosis should be offered with a view to the several possibilities that loom up for the given case. After this should come, whenever conditions permit, the valuable checking up of predictions as set over against results, especially with scrutiny of the working of some trial scheme which has been suggested as of worth. This follow-up work is often of great benefit, primarily, to the offender whose treatment is in this way supervised and who is sensible of the interest taken in him as an individual; secondarily, to the examiner and other observers who may grow by the accumulation of their own data and judgments; and finally, for the development of the whole nascent science. Back of the technological details of methods are the following practical considerations which are of great import for the success of the investigation.

33

§ 36. The Observer and His Attitude.

Of first importance is the suitableness of the person to undertake this oftentimes difficult research. He, or she, must have a temperament or an attitude of mind calculated to develop friendly coöperation with the offender and his relatives, to say nothing of those who, under the law, or otherwise, will have to do with the offender's treatment. I should no more expect good results from an unsuited examiner, whatever his background of training, than I should anticipate the production of an appropriate architectural design from an inartistic, though well-trained draughtsman. It is simply a matter of common-sense observation that some persons are much better equipped in spirit to bring out the best in others, and that is a prime necessity in this working situation. Everyday recognition of the differences in talents, sympathies, understandings and innate impulses should lead to greater discrimination in selecting physicians and psychologists fitted for this work than has been recommended [1] for the eligibility of judges for the criminal and juvenile courts.

The only attitude to be assumed with much profit is that of shrewd, but sympathetic inquiry into an unsolved problem. We have insisted that the examiner should have no special nose for the pathological, and should be entirely willing to survey all the facts, and to be guided in his conclusions by no special bias. The question for him must be: What is the cause in this person or in his experience, and how can it be altered? The investigation is seldom an affair merely of objective psychology or medical testing. The impersonal effort of those methods is usually inadequate. The work is much more like that of the modern neurologist, or rather psycho-neurologist, who uses both psychological and physiological inquiry in his study of patients. The successful attitude combines that of the specialist with that of the family physician.

Often I have stated the following fact, which has become increasingly apparent to me. Just as soon as the offender and

---

[1] For the whole needs of the situation, it will be instructive to read the conclusions of Gross (64) in his keen study of the general psychological aspects of criminal procedure and of the personalities involved. Resolutions passed embodying the high authority of the International Prison Congress of 1910, meeting at Washington, offer also much food for thought in their urgent demand for special temperamental and technical qualifications on the part of judges and others who deal with beginning criminal careers.

his relatives realize that there is some one who takes the attitude of the friendly family physician, to whom they can go with their secret troubles, the case frequently undergoes the most remarkable transformation from the fighting aspect actually seen in the court room, or while the interested ones are in contact with the police or other authorities of the law.

The opening of the interview with some such friendly and reasonable statement as the following has been found in itself to have a rationalizing effect. One may say: "Well, you people do seem to have a difficult affair on your hands with this boy. Let's sit down and talk it all over, and study it out together — how it all began and what's going to happen. I'm at your service. Did you ever think it all out carefully?"

As we have previously said, it is certain that often ours has been the first really inquiring approach that has ever been made to this individual and his problem. The response is nearly always gratifying. The attitude of all concerned becomes much the same as when the family physician makes a complete study and inquiry into the possible causes for an obscure ailment or defect. We get accounts of characteristics, and environments, and forebears, and other antecedents, and even histories of offenses unknown to the authorities, that throw often a great, new light on what should be done with and for the offender. Just this alone shows how vastly necessary it is to have, as in any other business-like endeavor, the attitude that wins success.

§ 37. Privileged Communication.

It is apparent from the above that the procedure involves a very different approach and obligation from that of the examining detective who, according to classic account, prefaces his interrogatory with, "You know that anything you say can be used against you." Our States differ in their legislation on the point of privileged communication. To be sure, the question very rarely comes up, for practically always recommendation can be made to the judge or officer or institutional worker, without specific enumeration of family and personal affairs.

A great deal that is most valuable in this work can never be done successfully except when the attitude and obligations of the family physician are assumed by the observer. The offender and his family must have appreciation of the good offices at their

35

service. The point of privileged communication may occasionally have to be made clear, or the statement made that what is revealed by the family or the offender is not a matter of court record. Personally, in most cases I am in favor of an open discussion with the interested ones as to what the judge ought to know. This frankness helps towards general rationality, and is usually met by a satisfactory response.

§ 38. Previous Training of Observer.

A question frequently asked is whether a physician or psychologist is best fitted for the work. This is a difficult question, and the answer always depends on the exigencies of the given situation. Undoubtedly, much the best personal equipment is to be found in the combination of medical, including clinical, training, with previous instruction in normal psychology, and actual experience in studying abnormal mental types. For the giving of tests, preparation in the modern field of practical differential psychology is essential.[1] When a person trained in both lines cannot be obtained, certain facts stand out clearly. Both the medical and psychological work must be done in each case. The work of the physician can usually be secured most easily. And then, except where actual pathological conditions are found, the physical examination is by far the shortest. So it may be wise in some circumstances to put a clinical psychologist in charge of the work. When there is use of the physician's findings, there must be complete coöperation in the interpretation of the significance of the data. The psychologist must have had practical acquaintance with abnormal and defective mental types, in order clearly to discern them during the process of the psychological examination. The studies of neurotic and border-line cases by the psychoneurologists have developed such understanding of mental mechanisms that their methods are absolutely essential to the equipment of all who would deal with certain of the most interesting and hopeful phases of delinquent tendencies.

There is much room for the work of intelligent and well-trained women in this field. Especially the objective psychological

[1] Definite qualifications for those who professionally handle delinquents have been set forth perhaps best by Kinberg (52). He shows what demands have been made and what opportunities offered for special knowledge in Europe. For the prison physician he recommends, as indispensable, training in both normal and abnormal psychology, plus some months of experience in both a hospital for the insane and a criminological institute.

work, namely, the giving of the tests, can be done successfully by them. Rather less well are they fitted for the other parts of the work. The reason for this is, of course, that men and boys are not going to reveal much of their inner troubles to women. Occasionally even the girls state that what they have to say can only be said to the " doctor." Both directly and indirectly, unpleasant features of sex life are discovered persistently cropping out in the experiences of offenders, and they have to be met in scientific spirit. Very frequently has one heard from parents or the offender the introductory question, " Are you the doctor? " before the feeling is engendered that it is proper to tell all the facts. Women should calculate upon these unpleasant features before entering the work.

Physicians are not only valuable in this field because they have knowledge of pathological conditions, but also because of their acquaintance with physiological norms. Here, as in school work, they may be of service for this reason. This seems to be forgotten by those who maintain that the profession can only offer advice about disease.

It is very different, of course, in the case of psychologists who, for the most part, have had little training in the study of abnormal individuals. In the interest of both sciences it should be remembered that the discovery of pathological conditions has very frequently led to differential knowledge of normal structure and conditions. This is proving as true where mental structure and functions are thrown into new light during the investigatory process of psycho-analysis or during the progress of a psychosis as it was in the development of knowledge of cardiac physiology or the anatomy of the spinal cord.

A matter that lies midway between the considerations of this section and the next, concerns the difference between the adult and the child type of mind. There is collected as yet altogether too little information on this point, but we see many indications why we should reckon on this difference when giving various tests. The examiner, in general, should not take it for granted, when he is passing social judgment on an offender's capacity, that experience with one type of individual can without modification be safely applied to another. What is true of ages is true, to some extent, when working with different social conditions or classes. Glueck (283) points this out as clearly bearing on the problem of the mentally defective immigrant. A level of mental

37

capacity quite sufficient to keep a ditch digger within the limits
of good behavior would probably lead to much misconduct where
environmental demands and temptations were greater. Especially until we get further differential norms established the examiner should have personal experience with different ages and
social groups.

§ 39. Age of the Examinee.

We have spoken previously of the advantage of seeing a case
as early as possible in the beginning of the criminal career, for
explanatory as well as therapeutic reasons. It has been suggested
to us that the age at which we have taken delinquents (the average age has been nearly 16 years) is too late. If all is true that
has been stated about the early genesis of character formation
as elicited by the many investigators in the field of psychological
analysis, we are surely somewhat behind. It may be seen in
our case studies that the strange beginnings of the criminal impulse may often be discovered in young childhood. Common
sense, too, would teach us that the earlier the case is studied, the
better for constructive purposes.

On the other hand, every case, at every age, is a problem that
requires study, if any real solution is to be worked out. Sometimes the beginnings can be taken into account very little. Then
occasionally conditions which lead to delinquency, for instance
senility, may supervene upon a previous background of good
citizenship and normality. The genesis in these instances is not
far to seek. Our final dictum, then, must be that in nearly every
case the earliest possible study will be followed by the best results. But every case of delinquency needs adjustment, at whatever age appearing, and should be investigated, even if habit or
alcohol or environment are adventitious factors, in themselves
difficult to grapple with.

§ 40. Types for Study.

Elsewhere we have committed ourselves to the opinion that it
is the repeated offender who particularly needs study. As seen
in the juvenile and adult courts, there are those who have been
merely transgressors of the moment; breaking ordinances, or
misdoing in such other ways that the possession of criminal
tendencies is not in the least betokened. Nobody would allege
it worth while to spend the time and energy necessary for the

careful study of such offenders. It is true also that certain crimes for which long sentences are imposed, either on account of the money values involved, or the injuries received, have been committed by offenders under peculiar stress, such as might overtake many an ordinarily law-abiding citizen. It is usually quite unnecessary to study these delinquents, except for the opinion which might be desired by a board of pardons, or by a prisoners' aid society, which might wish vocationally or otherwise to aid them.

We must most sincerely discredit any notion that our methods of study are primarily developed to discern the pathological. While one always realizes that the recognition and the segregation of the insane, feebleminded, or epileptic criminal is of immense import to society, yet the discovery of some capacity, or adaptabillty, or mental conflict, upon which to base therapeutic measures for the checking of a criminal career is an occasion of much greater satisfaction. Repeated offenders of all types, then, especially form proper subjects for thorough-going inquiry.

§ 41. Sources of Information.

The shrewdness which we have insisted on as a part of the general attitude of the observer implies a sufficient skepticism. Entirely undesirable is that brutal suspicion so frequently seen in police and prison officials, justified more or less by the usual prevaricating retort to coarse inquiry. It is better apparently to believe a great deal, and preserve one's kindly attitude, than to spoil one's service in the case. The skepticism required is that of the scientist who asks at least a reasonable amount of corroboration. To this end other sources of information than the offender are requisite in the vast majority of cases. Some offenders' accounts of themselves and their surroundings have such veridical flavor that they can be in fairness accepted; here the corroboration comes from the examiner's own experience.

Relatives are to be seen whenever possible. We have found surprisingly little difficulty in getting them to come. The idea that some one was trying to take an intelligent interest in their family problem has generally been sufficient to arouse coöperation. It must be confessed that at first, however, it has been necessary to stimulate interest and show some background for optimism in the situation. With us the introduction to parents has perhaps most frequently come through officers of the law, and the kindly efforts of policemen and probation officers can not be too highly praised in this connection. Officers have themselves sometimes been long acquainted with the family and can offer much in the way of sidelights derived from their visits to the household. Teachers, and school principals, and religious leaders are all to be drawn on for the facts. When the offender is held in a place of detention various observations, sometimes very shrewd ones, are made by the officials there. How much visitation to the home or other environment is to be made for the purpose of specific inquiry depends upon the circumstances surrounding the study.

§ 42. Place of Observation.

Often when a center for the study of delinquents is established the location will be predetermined. With us a certain amount of choice was enjoyed, which led to offer of the service of our Institute to the court where studies could not only best be made, but best be acted upon. Although choice is not usually to be had, yet a few words about the comparative advantages of different situations are worth while.

I credit Kauffmann (81) and Holmes (66), critical students of criminology, with wise discernment when they so emphatically state that the place really to study the criminal is in the open. But yet how difficult must this be when we wish to apply the methods of an objective psychology, for instance. Desirable though their recommendations would seem, we have yet to become acquainted, even through these authors, with any adequate well-rounded researches carried out " in the open."

Certain points which seemed to stand out clearly at first, appear even stronger as time goes on. The offender must approach you willingly before you can do anything for him. Now, when will he exhibit this willingness? Certainly not when he is " on the outs," and feeling it quite unlikely that he will recommit offenses or at least be caught again. No, the golden moment is when he feels himself to be a problem, and his relatives feel it, and all want a promising solution of the difficulty. It is after he has been caught, and while he is either detained or on probation, and has not already been sentenced that is the best time of all for inquiry. Then parents will come many miles in search of a solution, not by any means always desiring the softest outcome for the offender. Then the offender will himself strive hardest to achieve with the " doctor " some fundamental explanation of the causes of his delinquent tendencies. For many reasons this is the opportune moment for gathering information from many sources. The wise judge perceives this, and often holds a case in abeyance, that he may have the gathered facts laid before him, or at least have definite recommendations from well-informed sources.

Immediately after the trial, when hope is abandoned, and the spirit evinced is that of taking the medicine and gritting the teeth, one finds that very little can then be gained by study. Relatives are usually tired of the case and evade inquiry. There is little use then in making any approach, unless the offender be on probation and the question arises as to what constructive measures can be carried out for his reformation. Under these circumstances also a favorable point of entrance into the problem can be utilized.

But in institutional life there are certain other advantages accruing from possible studies that make them decidedly worth while. We should hardly agree with Holmes that the worst place in the world to study an offender is in prison, unless he means by prison something entirely different from our reformatories, where prisoners most desirable to be studied are congregated. Here not only cross-section studies may be made, but also a longitudinal observation can be undertaken. How does the individual thrive, for instance, under this or that discipline, or treatment, or education, or encouragement? Many questions which the observer is unable to answer from his laboratory in a court building can be determined there. On the other hand, the reformatory or penitentiary observer is confronted with an unfortunate paucity of prior history and opportunity to have carried out various measures of social alteration with a view to moral therapy. The former drawback can, in varying measure, be obviated by the efforts of competent field workers, who have the possible opportunity of bringing to the physician or psychologist invaluable information, when families themselves cannot be seen at the institution. Field workers from institutions of the industrial school type can accomplish more than those from reformatories, for the reason, mentioned above, that the families of younger individuals are more often found intact and interested.

41

§ 43. Extent of Study of a Case.

Concerning the length of time or extent of effort necessary for working up a single case, the objections we have occasionally heard are likely to be repeated. The best answer we can make to the objectors, who are frequently officials of the law, is Socratic in form. Is it not true that a vast deal of time, days and even weeks, is spent in preparation for and trial of merely one feature of a case, namely, the question of the guilt of the accused? Is not this true sometimes even in the trial of repeated offenders? If, under the law, the resources of society are thus liberally spent,[1] does it not ill behoove those who see such facts to criticize any prolongation of individual study which may lead to knowledge of measures indispensable for satisfactory treatment of the case? Is not efficient treatment a feature of the total procedure to which the question of guilt is but a preliminary? John X, for example, is a reformatory graduate. This is well known, but it may require many days of work to connect him by evidence with a recent burglary, and secure a verdict. How much more important, however, to study him so that there may be the fullest scientific determination of the possibilities of efficient treatment.

It is easy to see that there is great variation in the time necessary to be spent in the study of different types. In an hour or an hour and a half one can determine the fact of the simpler forms of feeblemindedness, and with intelligent relatives get a sufficiently accurate notion of the causation through history of heredity or development. With corroborative evidence from school people, or officers of the law, or others who are working in the field, that may be sufficient diagnosis in this, the simplest type of case. But when it comes to digging out the very essential facts in border-line cases, or in normal individuals, where certain mental or environmental experiences have been paramount causative factors, the length of time is altogether a different matter. The equivalent of whole days of study, perhaps not all done at once, is frequently necessary for accurate determination of just those facts upon which effective treatment must be founded. After our prolonged experience, I see no way to avoid

---

[1] The average cost of obtaining one conviction in this country is about $1500. Boies' (286) figures on this have been reaffirmed by Moore (287), who writes me that his own calculations have been based on the total convictions for 1912 in the most populous county in New Jersey.

this, if work is to be done which shall stand professional criticism.

The time is, of course, part of the expense, but even so considered, there must not be any shortening of it that shall lead to inefficiency. In any given situation there is apt to be some calculation of the number of individuals that ought to be seen. No one can plan out work upon this basis. The proper question is, what number can be competently studied, and that can only be determined as the work advances in any given field. It is argued in some quarters that even superficial study will help out of the mess that results from undiscriminating judgments and treatments. This contention is undoubtedly true, and is inspired by a practical situation that must be met. On the other hand, it is indubitably a fact, as was suggested to me by keen thinkers at the inception of our own work, that to study a dozen cases of varying type, with a thoroughness that shall lead to scientific understanding of the bases of conduct, is to make a far greater contribution than to have studied a thousand superficially.

Outside of the actual time spent on study, including the taking of first notes, there must be allowed time for the dictation and review of such extensive records as alone can provide for the future development of safe conclusions in the case. The after study and summary of these records, in the form of a practical statement of the data which stand behind the prognostic conclusions, is another time-consuming effort.

The up-shot of all this is, that the observer must be allowed sufficient time to do good work, and his official studies should not be so crowded as to drown out good scientific achievement. The habit we have in this country of overwhelming a good man in public or institutional life with executive duties, has had a notoriously bad result for the progress of our own social conditions. In this new field it ought to be avoided. With superficial studies of the individual, nobody, especially the critics from the side of the law, will be satisfied. Our summarized studies and causative factor cards, *vide infra*, will show how thorough scientific work leads to practical issues. But just these terse and definite charts of causes and predictabilities can only be developed upon the basis of studies sufficiently prolonged.

§ 44. Office and Equipment.

There is little that needs to be said about the office itself
except that several small rooms make the best arrangement,
and that quiet is absolutely essential. A vast deal of time and
effort is economized if interfering entrances and outside noises
are avoided. Here, as elsewhere, the direct and quick response
can best be obtained through appreciation of the psychological
economics of attention. To keep the mind of the examinee, or
the relative, upon the subject in hand, means many minutes
saved in the course of the day. To the same end the appurte-
nances of the office should be of the simplest form, and altogether
non-distractive. One distance of 20 feet with good light upon a
wall for preliminary examination of vision is essential. It is
only in rare instances that the dark room of the oculist is available.

One cannot be too careful in dealing with delinquent women
and girls, even though in the friendly attitude of the family physician, which in this country is almost an unviolated relationship.
I have maintained that there should be absolutely no possibility
of criticism, and a third person must always be present during an
interview, or at least just outside a glass partition, when an interview with a delinquent girl or woman is taking place.

The equipment of medical apparatus hardly needs to be mentioned. It will vary according to the needs of given circumstances.
In cosmopolitan centers, such as we have been working in, all
of the special work has been done in hospitals or in the offices of
specialists. All that has been needed with us has been the apparatus for first examination of the eyes, nose, throat, ears, etc.,
which shall lead to the individual being sent to a specialist when
necessary. Routine examination of the body in general can be
done with very little equipment. Accurate scales and a standard
for measuring height are essentials. Simple apparatus for taking
some anthropometric data is also requisite, but we early conceived and have later confirmed, the advisability of not emphasizing this. If there is any suspicion that the work is connected
with measuring for identification there is an immediate revulsion
of feeling which will often spoil the entire interview. Consequently one must keep out of sight the few instruments necessary for the gathering of such facts as are of real significance and

not obtrude the measuring process in any way. Anything that savors of merely medical work proves to be acceptable, but there must not be the least flavor of police methods.

The laboratory equipment on the psychological side has been a source of much discussion, and we ourselves early obtained advice from the most competent authorities. Several of the best psychologists insisted there was no indication that work with the complicated apparatus found in psychological laboratories bore in any way on our problem, so their advice was not to fit our laboratory with any such apparatus. It was evident that therein might lie an element of diversion from perception of the direct issues. While many forms of apparatus are imposing as exhibitory mechanical features it has always been my feeling that the presence of these would be to a certain extent deceptive, at least to others, and perhaps to ourselves. As to the desirability of certain deceptions, such as are deliberately intended in many a physician's office, I have little comment to offer. It is barely possible that they are occasionally justifiable. Matters of special research can well be undertaken and apparatus, imposing or otherwise, directly obtained for the purpose.

There can be no doubt that this work demands laboratory methods and special apparatus. The essentials are that one must have the literature and the material for giving a large variety of practical mental tests. What we have found necessary in our work, will be seen by consulting the section on psychological examination. There must be a full line of tests for the estimation of various abilities and mental functions, and for the grading of various psycho-physical powers, and the gauging of the individual response to certain age norms and other standards. One hopes to see in the future much more development of these important testing methods, particularly in the line of studying vocationl aptitudes. Most of this apparatus is simple and can be made by those who are accurate at such work. However, we would call attention to the fact that we have seen repeatedly some of our own tests used with much lack of appreciation of fundamental purposes, because of inaccuracy of construction. The safest way for those who are not adepts in working up such material, is to get apparatus from the standard makers.[1] The equipment,

---

[1] For convenience to the reader we may mention that C. H. Stoelting Co., 125 North Green Street, Chicago, make much of the psychological apparatus used in this country, and deal in the material used in our tests.

although not occupying much space, is made up of many pieces and must include blank forms for the accurate recording of results. The cost of the entire material is comparatively small.

§ 45. Assistants.

It is obvious what a large part the personal element plays in this work, and it must be clear that, however large an office force it is possible to have, there is always a great deal that cannot be relegated to assistants. The principal observer in each case has a hold on the individual, the value of which cannot be overestimated even for scientific purposes. For instance, in follow-up work it is rarely that the progress of a case, especially when any such subtle factor as mental conflict be present, can be accurately determined by a second person. Many parts of the objective examination, however, be they medical or psychological, may be performed by another examiner. The total results should be brought together and estimated by the one who has had most relation to the case. The working possibilities of assistants will have to be developed according to the exigencies of any given situation. Sometimes the foregoing method will seem best; at another time the entire working up of an individual case by a single observer will prove safest.

We have been surprised to find that one of the most particular portions of the work was the interviewing of relatives. Just the right attitude has to be assumed in this. They frequently feel that they have to see the head of the office, because it is his name that has been mentioned to them as the one who is to be interested in their family trouble. As I have elsewhere mentioned, the facts of developmental history and family life are frequently so explanatory that it is most necessary to get the best possible approach to those who can give this information. The whole working out of the problem is much the same as in the office of some famous physician who has assistants. Nobody who goes there is satisfied without saying his most intimate word to the chief. Advice and prognosis are valued most highly when they come from the master. Just what training is required for assistants depends upon what work is going to be demanded of them, and hence is not a matter for general statement.

For the scientific success of work done in many situations, particularly in institutions, field work is essential. I have found reason at times to be surprised at the great values contained in reports from field workers who are especially fitted by training and natural adaptation to this style of work. They can get hold of medical, social, educational and other information which is invaluable for the understanding of the individual. It requires a rare combination of shrewdness, friendliness, and scientific training to form a good field worker.[1]

Success of the entire work depends largely upon the accuracy and completeness with which records are kept, and one assistant must be a secretary who can intelligently take charge of this. This person must be on hand directly after an interview in order that every detail of importance may be accurately recorded when it is perfectly fresh in the mind of the observer. The work of this secretary will have a great deal to do with both the scientific and practical success accruing from the results of individual study.

§ 46. The Interview and Examination.

A tactful approach to the individual delinquent is in many cases a matter of deep concern, inasmuch as upon it depends success or failure. Over and over from relatives and others we have heard of the difficulty in getting their problem individual to come and see us. It seems to be hard to get it understood that because there is delinquency there must be need of study. The answer is given, "There's nothing the matter with me. I know what I'm doing." So it comes about that a collateral explanation is offered. "We want you to go to see the doctor to find out if you are healthy," or, "We want to find out what you are best fitted for." This latter explanation indeed makes a truthful form of entrance that we have come to use most frequently as offering the chance of developing the greatest amount of interest. The question of vocational diagnosis is really a part of almost every young person's thoughts, however crudely apperceived. The old examiners in phrenology thrived on the general desire for this information. So when a young man or boy is studied, one of the best ways to begin the interview, or to get him to come at all, is to state that you are going to make a study of his special abilities — which, indeed, is the truth.

[1] To those interested in the development of such work I would recommend as a paradigm the records of field work made for the trustees of the Massachusetts Training Schools under the planful efforts of Miss Burleigh and Miss Cree.

The part of the study to enter upon at first depends upon what seems to afford the best opportunity to elicit the examinee's interest. If the vocational approach has been made, then tests for various abilities are usually given at first. From these one can work off either into the medical examination, or the tests for general intelligence, or into the story of the life career and its influences. In all this, tact is of great service and one learns to develop an elastic method which best of all subserves scientific as well as practical interests. It is useless to talk of giving the tests in any certain order, because interests differ, and the one unvarying condition that should pervade the entire study is that of securing interest and attention.

This means that an interview may have to be broken and continued on another day. Flagging attention or actual tire demand this. We should unhesitatingly recommend the advantage of several interviews in order to see the individual in as many moods as possible. We should have made failures in many a prognosis had we relied, for instance, upon a single recalcitrant interview, or for that matter upon a most promising outlook that had developed merely upon the spur of the moment, and was based upon unusual manifestations in the individual's conduct.

Interviews should always be undertaken alone with the examinee, and preferably with only one of his relatives at a time. The presence of both husband and wife will not infrequently lead to the interviewer not getting just exactly the facts he is looking for. Friction is very frequently discoverable in the families of delinquents, and from one side of the house at a time can one best obtain the facts. Then again, stories of family ailments and troubles are not going to be retailed as the professional man wishes them, in the presence of other people. Indeed, the fact is certain from experience that even the child prefers to be alone with the " doctor " when telling his troubles.

It has been suggested by some observers, e. g., Binet, that a stenographer should be present to take down the subject's remarks during his work with tests. We should not at all agree to this at any stage. There should be no onlooker or any third person even surreptitiously taking notes when one is dealing with a delinquent. We have come to feel that even the Binet tests are given much more freely when the psychologist is alone with the examinee. To a considerable extent the same question comes up when the interviewer himself takes the words in shorthand.

People all look askance when they know what they are saying is being taken down word for word. Of course it is absolutely necessary to take notes in order that there shall be records, preferably verbatim records, for scientific purposes alone, of much that is said in all of these various interviews. We have tried several methods, and are convinced that by far the best scheme is to make little jottings of words and phrases and facts in an apparently careless and irregular fashion while sitting at one's desk, and then immediately after the interview to dictate as nearly as possible the actual words used. After a little practice one uses all sorts of abbreviations that really make up an individual shorthand system, and from these one can later dictate accurately the essence of interviews lasting an hour or more. This scheme works very well with us, and rarely arouses any comment from the interviewed.[1]

§ 47. Records.

Not so very long ago, in the critical attempt to develop better methods of studying the insane, it was quite generally found that the older forms of records, in which a few impressions were jotted down about the patient from time to time were quite inadequate. This has also been found true of individual studies along educational lines and in other fields of endeavor. Such ineffective superficiality should be avoided from the start in the building up of our new science. We need accurate and full records of

---

[1] No better illustration of the value of an understanding attitude and a rational technic can be given than the following report of an actual occurrence with us. A young woman of 18, being studied by a certain psychologist said, after several tests had been performed well, "Is n't it funny I'm not a bit afraid with you, and I was so frightened the other day with that other lady." It then appeared that she had already been examined and the verdict given that she was defective. She went on to say, "Well, the doctor sat there first and stared at me. That made me nervous. I got so embarrassed. I guess I really did act like a fool. I don't know what I did say to them. Then two ladies came in, and once when I answered some question, I saw the lady that was talking to me look at them and laugh. After that I got mad, and I did not try. I just felt like I did not want to say anything."

In the course of the Binet series the free association test was given, which calls for 60 words in 3 minutes. The girl gave the 60 words in about 2 minutes, and when comments on her good record were made she said, "I'm glad you think I can do something, because I gave only 25 words the other day. Oh, I know because I saw her write it down. She had the paper right there where I could see it. My probation officer told me I did wrong because I had the mind of a little child."

The story of this girl, who by Binet and other tests was found positively not to grade now as a defective, contained a great lesson for us. We saw the unfavorable bearings which suspicious scrutiny, others being present, and a visible record of tests may have on results.

facts and modifying collateral circumstances, and we want complete accounts of results of introspection on the part of the offenders. Samples of phraseology and direct statements of points of view should be carefully set down. The golden mean will always be to preserve the essential while not burdening our records with trivialities. What has been found useful in the working up of the best case studies in hospitals for the insane has served as an example to us. The formulation of case study methods by Dr. Adolf Meyer (**67**) was a previous step that helped us much on our way.

The form of the records, aside from the actual contents, one finds to be of importance. The temptation is always to start with some schedule on which certain items are enumerated. The development of such a method obviously is based on the fact that one can put down in a word the answer to such specific questions as age and nationality. But trouble soon arises because one finds a set form not fluid enough to answer the requirements except on simple facts. As one cannot answer some questions by yes or no, so one cannot scientifically record many facts in three words, or even in a line or two. For example, the formulated query may be concerning measles. Now answering this yes or no means very little, for measles may be an entirely insignificant fact on account of innocuousness of the attack, or it may have been accompanied by or may have left in its train conditions which rightfully require much space scientifically to describe. The observer working with a set form tends to feel that a plus or minus sign is sufficient, and may entirely neglect the qualifications which may be significant in every answer. So while we ourselves started with some five large sheets of formulated inquiry, we have now entirely adopted the typewritten page, with its more natural and more scientific statement of the facts.

Every sheet that records an inquiry should state who the inquirer was, and in the case of records of hear-say facts must give an evaluation of the sources of information. No student of the psychology of testimony can be willing to neglect this important precaution. We can take two mothers, for instance, coming to us, one of whom by virtue of natural endowment, or educational background, is qualified to give us a fundamentally correct story of the developmental history of her child, and the main characteristics of her family line. The next woman might

well be a poor unfortunate from whose loquacity we might safely
gather only a few general conclusions. Yet if personalities were
not commented upon, the record of one would stand of equal
value with the other, and as for the length of report, the loqua-
cious one might easily outstrip the other. It is always important
to estimate, as far as possible, good will and qualifications for
accurate report. Of course, in the interview with the offender
these points stand out all through as of great import.

A statement of the general format of our case study records,
as at present constituted after several years of experience and
outside criticism, may prove helpful. Mr. W. F. Dummer,
from his standpoint as a skillful business man, has at various
times given us very practical aid in the development of our system. Our main records are kept on sheets of uniform size to
fit in a 9 x 11 inch filing cover, which may be of the usual folder
design, or if more stiffness is desired may be made of cardboard
— in either case to fit in an upright filing case where the name
or number is prominently displayed. The only printed forms
are the sheet for medical examination (on which plus and minus
signs, and the like, are recorded in the usual professional style),
and some of the records of psychological tests, mentioned in the
proper place. A color scheme of sheets for different types of
information is most useful. For instance, information derived
from the family may be on pink, the offender's own statement
on white, and so on. Where there are many sheets of typewriting, as there must be in the study of some of the difficult cases,
this color scheme aids future survey of the records. Frequently
we will have an officer's introductory statement, then the mother's
story, which may cover several closely typewritten pages, then
perhaps other points which have been learned from the father
or other relatives, from a pastor or school teacher. Then there is
the offender's own long story about himself — a story that may
be told in continuous chapters when he has been seen in different
interviews — then the medical examination, and scoring of
psychological results, covering probably a good many sheets.
(We record the latter on a different kind of paper.) Next we
come to a registered summary of the facts and possibilities drawn
up from the first study, or when an opinion is first rendered.
This is an affair of several paragraphs, as shown in the specimen
below, and in its attempt to relate antecedent and consequent
is to be regarded as the most important record. (The summary

51

is written on a distinctively colored sheet.) Finally come the sheets pertaining to the follow-up work, in which other examinations, or interviews, or conclusions, are recorded properly on their corresponding color sheets. The records are headed, "Mother's Story," "Father's Story," "Officer's Story," "Own Story," "Court Record," "Record from Industrial School," etc. We give all this in detail because of the many inquiries we have received about our form of record.

Over and beyond the main sheets there are subsidiary records for various purposes. If the main records are kept according to number then there must be an alphabetical card system which may contain a few general facts of identification, and of disposition of the case, and perhaps a few facts for statistical purposes. Card systems can be worked up on any basis, and are of the utmost scientific value as giving easy opportunity for survey of the facts. Card systems, for instance, of heredity, of medical findings, of environmental causes and the like might be developed. Uniquely valuable with us has been the development of a card system of specific causative factors — a system which has called forth much favorable comment (*vide infra*).

Beyond all these general considerations there is the great problem of desirable information. We are frequently asked for a statement of what information we look for, and what we have found the most valuable. An enumeration of items for inquiry is largely demanded. Since we have maintained that the best method of recording is to have no form at all, but to use typewritten sheets, it is clear that a schedule of desirable data must exist somewhere — either at the inquirer's side or in his mind. The latter is preferable, but implies, of course, considerable familiarity with the many points of value. To facilitate inquiry we have twice gotten out a schedule of data appearing as reports of Committee A [1] of the American Institute of Criminal Law and Criminology (**68, 69**). The first report was a statement of numerous items of inquiry, developed from our own experience and from the advice of numerous authorities, and classified under

[1] American Institute of Criminal Law and Criminology. Report of Committee A: System] for Recording Data Concerning Criminals. — "Investigation of an effective system for recording the physical and moral status and the hereditary and environmental conditions of delinquents, and in particular of the persistent offender; the same to contemplate, in complex urban conditions, the use of consulting experts in the contributory sciences." The first bulletin, although issued in a large edition, has long been out of print.

general headings.   The second report, omitting the enumeration of separate items, showed further possibilities in the development of a constructive and useful form of record.

On the following pages will be found the good points of both reports.   It should be clear that we have never found it possible to get anything like all the scheduled items answered.   It would be unlikely even under the best possible family conditions.   But most of the items of information, as stated, are desirable, and by the use of the schedule to form sweeping inquiries, a great many of them are actually obtainable.

§ 48.   Schedule of Data Concerning Delinquents.

A system can well be developed under the following eleven heads:

   I. FAMILY HISTORY — especially all aspects of heredity.
   II. DEVELOPMENTAL HISTORY — including antenatal conditions.
   III. ENVIRONMENT.
   IV. MENTAL AND MORAL DEVELOPMENT.
   V. ANTHROPOMETRY — including photography.
   VI. MEDICAL EXAMINATION — particularly from a neurologic and psychiatric standpoint.
   VII. PSYCHOLOGICAL — (a) Mental testing; (b) Psychological analysis.
   VIII. DELINQUENCY.
   IX. DIAGNOSTIC AND PROGNOSTIC SUMMARY.
   X. FOLLOW-UP RECORDS.
   XI. SUBSIDIARY RECORDS.

I.

FAMILY HISTORY.

Offender's Name.   Date.
Address.
Age.   Birthplace.
Sources of Information.

1. Racial and national characteristics of forebears.   For both father and mother give,
   (a) name.
   (b) age.
   (c) birthplace.
   (d) race.
   (e) years in the U. S.
   (f) language spoken at home.

53

2. Marital conditions in the family.
>   (a) legitimacy.
>   (b) parents living together, divorced, remarried.
>   (c) age of each parent at birth of this child.
>   (d) consanguinity.

3. Industrial and financial history of the family in its general bearings on the problem.
>   (a) occupation of father now and previously, occupational contact with poisons.
>   (b) occupation of mother as a child, later, during this pregnancy, and since child was born.
>   (c) earnings of father and mother.
>   (d) earnings — how used.
>   (e) other support of family.

4. Account of siblings (a convenient term for brothers and sisters taken together).
>   (a) schedule of siblings in order of birth, including miscarriages, giving sex and age of each; give causes of death.

5. Abuse of alcohol or drugs by father and mother before conception and by mother during pregnancy.
>   (a) include in this a study of either parent as an alcohol or a drug habitué.
>   (b) tea and coffee in excess.
>   (c) tobacco in excess or any tobacco smoking on the part of the mother.

6. Specific defects or diseases of father and mother, particularly such as may have debilitated germ plasm or affected embryo, and including hereditary diseases.
Particularly consider father and mother in relation to the following:
>   (a) condition as child.
>   (b) general diseases.
>   (c) blind or deaf.
>   (d) sexual diseases: syphilis and gonorrhea.
>   (e) nervous and mental diseases: particularly convulsions, epilepsy, periodic headache, neurasthenia, nervous prostration.
>   (f) ever insane: diagnosis and length of attack.
>   (g) feebleminded: grade of amentia.
>   (h) deformed.
>   (i) ever in hospital or sanitarium: for what. ·

7. Mental aberrations or defects on the part of the forebears; peculiar traits of disposition in the family. For grandparents, uncles and aunts specify whether paternal or maternal, and consider the following:
>   (a) consanguinity.
>   (b) general diseases.
>   (c) nervous and mental disorders.
>   (d) peculiar traits of disposition.
>   (e) ever in institution, and if so why.

8. Mental and physical defects or diseases in siblings which may throw light on hereditary tendencies.
  (a) general diseases.
  (b) nervous and mental disorders.
  (c) peculiar traits of disposition.
  (d) ever in institution, and if so why.

9. Mental, moral and other traits in ancestors, siblings, and ancestral side lines.

For father and mother and siblings give,
  (a) mental traits and talents.
  (b) mental peculiarities as children.
  (c) mental peculiarities as adults.
  (d) schooling.
  (e) ability to speak, read and write English or other language.
  (f) moral or immoral traits and habits.

For grandparents, uncles and aunts give,
  (a) mental peculiarities.

For any member of the family give,
  (a) court or institutional record.
  (b) death and cause.
  (c) longevity.
  (d) suicide.

For family as a whole give,
  (a) relief received — public or private charities.
  (b) social station in relation to the past, showing tendency of the family to go morally or socially up or down.

II.

DEVELOPMENTAL HISTORY.

1. Conditions of disease, use of intoxicants, or debility of either parent directly prior to conception.

2. Antenatal conditions of health, hygiene and occupation of mother during pregnancy.

3. Mental condition of mother during pregnancy, including aberrations, worries, shock. Note illegitimacy and its effects.

4. Injury or accident to mother during pregnancy.

5. Attempted abortion.

6. Birth.
  (a) full term.
  (b) instrumentation, operation, difficult labor, difficulty in resuscitation, deformity of head, weight and size at birth, or any other peculiarity.

7. Infancy and Childhood.
  (a) full history of all diseases or nutritional disturbances, including anything in the way of convulsions or disturbances of consciousness.

55

(b) developmental defects or deformities.
(c) defects in special senses.
(d) injuries, especially to head.
(e) chronological development — age of crawling, walking, running, teething, talking, going to school.
(f) mental aberrations, defects, disposition and traits.
(g) use of tea, coffee, tobacco, alcohol and drugs.
(h) sex habits in detail, if possible.
(i) fright or shock.
(j) habits of sleep.
(k) age and peculiarities of onset of puberty, menstruation.
(l) adolescent instabilities or peculiarities, both mental and physical.
(m) later health history.
(n) comparison of development with other members of family.
(o) enuresis.
(p) somnambulism, night terrors, etc.

III.

HISTORY OF ENVIRONMENT.

1. Changes of living through immigration. Other residential changes.
2. Effect of various languages used in the family.
3. Effect of disordered marital conditions. Harmony in family.
4. Education and mental disposition of parents which may influence child in environment.
5. Housing and financial conditions in detail.
6. Recreational facilities. Occupation outside of school hours.
7. Family control, and influence of neglect. Mother working or away from home.
8. Companionship. Opportunities afforded by relatively good or bad association. Amusements in detail.
9. Opportunities for religious culture.
10. Occupational opportunities. Character of places worked in.
11. Institutional life in detail.
12. Efforts to assist individual before or after custody.
13. If married, complete history of home life.

IV.

MENTAL AND MORAL DEVELOPMENT.

1. School history in detail with individual's own reaction towards it.
(a) duration of attendance; why left.
(b) grade reached.

56

(c) public, sectarian or private schools attended.

(d) knowledge of English; was foreign language used in the school.

(e) much absence; why.

(f) teacher's report; scholarship — deportment — general impression.

(g) child's impressions of school.

(h) studies; which was child best in or worst in.

(i) was child ever regarded as subnormal; ever studied by a child study department.

2. Effect of companionship, beginning with earliest associations.

3. Were bad companions voluntarily sought or were associations forced?

4. Character of associations with the opposite sex.

5. History and character of reading.

6. Use and development of special talents, in music, art, mechanics, athletics, etc.

7. Occupation or employment history, with detailed account of success or failure.

8. History of the home life and the development of the individual in it.

9. General behavior, with detailed characteristics.

10. Disposition and mental traits. Detailed history of any changes taking place in these.

11. Habits with regard to alcohol, tobacco, drugs, sex, etc.

12. Effect of coming into the hands of the law.

13. The effect of incarceration, sentence, or probation.

14. The effect of institution as compared with the opportunities and training while there.

V.

Anthropometry.

The high hopes of leaders of the anthropometric school of criminologists not having been fulfilled, especially with regard to our American population, the detailed work to be done in this field with prospect of valuable results is, according to our best authorities, decidedly limited.[1] In study of the young offender perhaps developmental tendencies are worthy of the most attention. To be especially noted are — Time of appearance of menstruation and its characteristics; Time of appearance of hair on the pubes and on the face;[2] Time and degree of development of the breasts; Time and peculiarity of eruption of the various teeth; Studies of the growth curves of height and weight. In addition and more particularly for all ages are to be recorded: Com-

[1] Since writing the above, Goring's classic anthropometrical study (160) of English convicts has appeared. He gives us the most authoritative statement of the narrow limitations of that field that has yet appeared.

[2] Crampton's (229) methods of recording the degree of pubescence offer the best approach to a standard. His work should be consulted.

plexion and color of hair; Peculiarities of physiognomy; The well-
known stigmata of degeneracy — especially those of head, ears, eyes,
palate, teeth, hands and feet; Weight; Height; Chest size and capacity; A few careful measurements of the head, taking principally the
circumference, the biparietal and antero-posterior diameters and
allowing for or eliminating measurement of hair as much as possible.
Besides such determining of the status of the body and its parts, tests
and measurements may be made of motor functioning, particularly of
strength and control.

Criminal characteristics are frequently not marked in photographs
of an offender's face taken in repose, and it has been amply proven that
differentiation of even the feebleminded from the normal cannot be
made by a study of such photographs. It has been suggested that
since skillful observers frequently make diagnosis of mental defect by
studying motor phenomena, not only of the whole body, but of the
face in action, that possibly some clue to the character and mental
status of the individual might be gained by developing a photographic
method of recording instantaneous impressions of, say, response in the
facial expression to various intellectual and emotional stimuli. Moving film pictures have also been suggested for this purpose.

Striking characteristics of physiognomy and expression, including
facial action, are always impressive and legitimately find place in the
summarized final impressions of the offender. But the whole subject
is difficult to generalize on. A study of Mantegazza (**282**) gives little
help for our purpose. There has been overexaggeration of facial and
cranial criminal types, as Goring (**160**) very clearly shows by his
photographic profiles.

Use of the algometer and the ergograph, instruments for making
psycho-physical measurements of the pain sense and fatigue respectively, have been frequently recommended for the study of criminals.
But their application, though interesting, proves of exceedingly little
value as compared with many other examination methods which we
mention.

VI.

Medical Examination.

Family History (complete record under section I).

Personal History: special attention to convulsions, epilepsy, petit
mal, sexual habits and diseases, alcoholism, excess of tobacco, drug
taking, sleep.

Present Ailments.

Examination:
- (a) personal cleanliness — vermin, etc.
- (b) weight, height.
- (c) development.
- (d) nutrition.
- (e) deformity.
- (f) attitude.

(*g*)   expression.
(*h*)   speech.
(*i*)   thyroid gland.
(*j*)   nose.
(*k*)   throat.
(*l*)   thoracic viscera; heart, lungs.
(*m*) abdominal viscera.
(*n*)   teeth; special attention to Hutchinson teeth, carious and impacted conditions.
(*o*)   temperature — pulse — blood — urine.
(*p*)   genital organs.
(*q*)   trophic conditions; muscle — skin — bones.
(*r*)   functions of digestion, circulation, etc.
(*s*)   Mental (very important):
  (1) perceptions: hallucinations, illusions, clouding of consciousness, etc.
  (2) association processes.
  (3) attention.
  (4) judgment: delusions, orientation, etc.
  (5) memory.
  (6) emotions: many abnormal variations.
  (7) abnormal physical sensations.
  (8) physical control.
  (9) mental control.
  (10) moral control.
(*t*)   Cranial Nerves:
  I.
  II. vision — visual fields — optic discs.
  III. IV. VI. pupillary form and reactions — strabismus — ocular movements — nystagmus — ptosis— diplopia.
  V. motor — sensory.
  VII. paralysis — tics.
  VIII. hearing — subjective auditory disturbances.
  IX. X. XI. XII.
(*u*) Sensory:
  (1) headache.
  (2) vertigo.
  (3) pain.
  (4) tactile sense.
  (5) temperature sense.
  (6) joint sense.
  (7) vibratory sense.
  (8) paræsthesias.
(*v*)   Motor:
  (1) upper extremity.
  (2) lower extremity.
  (3) trunk.
  (4) coördination.

(v) Motor — *continued*
    (5) tremor.
    (6) gait.
    (7) tonicity.
(w) Reflexes:
    (1) conjunctival.
    (2) palatal.
    (3) pharyngeal.
    (4) abdominal — upper, lower, right, left.
    (5) cremasteric.
    (6) plantar.
    (7) jaw.
    (8) arm.
    (9) knee jerks.
    (10) ankle jerks.
    (11) micturition.
    (12) defecation.

VII.

PSYCHOLOGICAL EXAMINATION.

A.

The records of psychological tests are for the most part made at the moment of testing. It is essential that they be so recorded that interpretation of them later, even by others, is easy. Standardization of records, that there may be uniformity at different times and between different workers, is a great desideratum. A summary of the observer's impressions, gained during the period of testing, both from general behavior, as well as from the tests themselves, should quickly be written up in order that no vital points be omitted. The mere numerical statement of time or of other elements of performance by no means covers the ground. A keen observer learns much and ought to record much that is not to be stated in figures.

Records of tests are of use not alone for immediate judgment on the characteristics of the individual, but also for future studies on the value of the tests themselves. Then, too, we need to further our understanding of general reaction types of individuals as gauged by performance on given tests according to age, according to general levels of ability, and according to performance on other tests. Good records that provide for such comparisons may be the foundation of valuable discoveries. As showing what can be developed, the ledger-like sheet, devised by Mr. W. F. Dummer, for our data and published in our monograph, "Tests for Practical Mental Classification," (70) is a good example. Here ruled columns and colored lines make the several comparisons of results mentioned above an easy matter, since they appear on one page. The original scoring sheet should be permanently filed with the subject's record, and can be referred to for statistical estimation of any given point.

B.

The important studies which may be undertaken of hidden mental worries and conflicts, of recurrent imageries, and mental attitudes, and half-forgotten mental experiences, many of which underlie misconduct, also require careful recording. One of the most promising features of investigation lies before us here, and all accuracy is required that we go not astray in developing it. Verbatim records of essential passages are demanded by their importance, and particularly should we be able to read and understand at any time by what associative processes previous thoughts and experiences have been brought to mind in the interview. The value of recording all this will better be seen when the topic of psychological analysis is discussed, and perhaps even more when corresponding case histories are read.

VIII.

DELINQUENCY.

(a) Description of special acts and types of misconduct.
(b) The cause of delinquency in the opinion of relatives and friends.
(c) Attitude of delinquent towards court, probation, institution, etc.
(d) Official record, police, court, institutional.

IX.

DIAGNOSTIC SUMMARY.

The mere registration of information must be followed, for the vital aims of individual diagnosis and prognosis, by a careful summary of such facts as positively bear upon the case. These facts ought to clearly focus upon the point at issue, namely, the delinquent behavior, and in the light of their significance the outlook under various environmental conditions often becomes plain. Predictability, which is the aim of any science of dynamics is here, too, the end in view.

The summary, leading up to its outcome in prognosis, can be built up in several ways, but to insure healthy self-criticism and ultimate professional respect it must be inclusive of all the main contributory factors. A systematic method of approach is essential. A scheme used satisfactorily in court work and passed upon by a number of eminent scientific men develops its theme in five paragraphs as follows: Here is the individual with (1) such-and-such physical characteristics, and (2) such-and-such mental abilities and mental traits, who (3) committed such-and-such types of delinquent acts. There are (4) in the background such-and-such conditions of defective heredity, pathological development, injuries, early teachings of immoral conduct, bad personal habits, lack of educational opportunity, or what not. In the light (5) of his being what he is physically and mentally and having this background, we can offer, on the basis of known pre-

dictabilities, such-and-such a prognosis if such-and-such treatment
is afforded in such-and-such an environment. (Always to be included
here are the old environment and other alternatives open.)

How cases have been actually worked up by this logical method
is shown in the examples to be found under § 87 in our chapter on
methods.

X.

FOLLOW-UP RECORDS.

After the making of studies leading up to the first transcribed
opinion there is often some opportunity for following up the case.
We have insisted above on the value of this latter work, and the records
gained should be kept in accordance with the dignity of the proceeding. Items of information should be written in uniform style with
the case record — at least one sheet to a date, with statement of the
sources of information, the circumstances of examination and so on.
Frequently upon request, or as a matter of self-criticism, secondary
opinions or prognoses are rendered, and should be written upon the
colored paper devoted to impressions and summaries.

XI.

SUBSIDIARY RECORDS.

Card systems or charts for statistical purposes, and the graphic
representation of findings are extremely valuable and may be developed in various ways. Our weight chart, as given in another
chapter, and the well-known heredity chart, illustrated below, are
examples. For scientific evaluation of the related facts of inheritance,
a card system, showing for each individual offender the various findings besides the superficial one of criminalism in the family, items
which could not be plotted on a chart, was of the greatest service for
the avoidance of misinterpretation. Card systems of record lend
great aid to the rapid sorting and enumeration of facts which are
vital to a clear survey of the general situation. The use of different
colored cards for different classes of cases or facts also promotes clear
perception.

Our gradual development of a card system of causative factors has
proved one of our strongest points of methodology, and has received
wide commendation as a measure of great practical value. By the
use of this system one is bound to evolve more than ever the spirit
of deep reflection. It certainly forms the only safe basis for the building of statistics of causation, but above all, in its presentation of the
relative values of causative factors, it may be of the greatest service
for the adjustment of circumstances immediately concerning the
offender. For both these ends the development of such a comparative
record of causations should be most carefully developed. Study shows
all cases of delinquency to be complex in origin. However, it is usually

not difficult to determine that one factor is of greater importance than any of the others.   Yet while this conclusion may be with fairness determinable, the proportionate value of the remaining factors proves frequently to be much less distinguishable.   The main factor is written above the top line of a card and the others follow below in their best arrangeable order.

We have been speaking of the presentation of the total facts when well-rounded study could be made of probable sources of origin. But if study of the delinquent is undertaken, for example, in an institution where there are distinct hiatuses in the available information, any card system dealing with causations should clearly denote the insufficiency to guard against immature conclusions.

Exemplars of causative factor cards are as follows and many others may be seen inserted in the case studies.

Home conditions.   John Doe, 15 yrs.
    Large family.   Case 163.
    Poor control.
    Poverty.

    Bad Companions.

        Lack healthy mental interests,
            occupational or recreational.

           Sex habits with other boys.

              Stimulants.   Tea $+$, $+$.

Former truancy.
Runaway.   Mental:
Petty stealing.   Class C.

Mentality.   Moron.   John Doe, 14 yrs.
                                   Case 597.

    Injuries.
        Two severe fractures skull in drunken brawls.

        Family conditions atrocious.

            Father A. and C.
            3 brothers notorious C.

Vagrancy.
Cruelty.   Mental:
Stealing.   Class K.

63

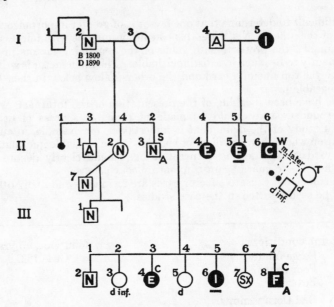

HYPOTHETICAL FAMILY CHART SHOWING THE NOW GENERALLY
ADOPTED USE OF SYMBOLS

KEY TO HEREDITY CHART.

(The symbols may be put on the sheet with rubber stamps or in the
form of pasters, which may be readily obtained.)

Male. Female.

□ ○ No Data.

Other letters used in or around
the squares or circles are:

A Alcoholic.
B Blind.
D Deaf.
M Migraneous.
N Normal.
Ne. Neurotic.
P Paralytic.
Sx. Sexually Immoral.
S Syphilitic.
T Tubercular.
W Wanderer or confirmed run-
away.

E **E** Epileptic.

F **F** Feebleminded.

I **I** Insane.

C **C** Criminalistic.

NUMERALS.

Above the line — Order in the line of birth.
Above the square or circle — Individual reference number.

Below the square or circle — Age at time of death or date of birth
or death.

In squares or circles — Number of individuals of that sex.

Roman numerals at side denote the generation.

SMALL LETTERS.

b — Born.   † or (d) — Died or dead.
† or (d) inf. — Died in infancy.   m — Married.

LINES.

Solid — Connects married individuals and fraternities.
Dotted — Not married or illegitimate.

SYMBOLS.

☞   Shows patient at institution where chart is made.
●   Miscarriage or stillbirth.
—   Under institutional care (place under symbol).

§ 49. Medical Methods.

There is little to further be said about methods. The immensely
important means of physical identification find no place in our
work. Over and beyond the usual medical findings there are
certain anthropometric data, e.g., developmental anomalies in
adolescence, which are sometimes of utmost importance for the
estimation of the primary causes of delinquency. The medical
examiner should carefully register those as suggested in our
schedule. On account of so much being found negative in the
examinee, who does not usually come as a patient, a half-hour
medical examination is all that avails much in the ordinary run
of court cases. But when definite indications are met, such as
existence of special sense defect, or actual disease, or when certain classes of offenses are under consideration, such as exhibitionism in old men, a thorough examination is essential. A report
from a competent and careful specialist is highly desirable in
many of these instances.

Physical examination of wayward girls and women should
be undertaken by a skillful woman physician. Gynecological
anomalies and ailments are frequent conditions of grave causative importance, and should be carefully studied and remedied.
In those places where a competent woman physician is not

65

available, the work may be done, as in private practice, with a nurse always present.

Diseases and other defective conditions of the genito-urinary system, and syphilis being present in proportionately such a large number of offenders, and leading by local irritation and by deteriorative conditions almost directly to the production of further misconduct, call for much attention and treatment.

Examination of girls for virginity as a basis for their moral classification is, from our observations in many cases, to be greatly deprecated and I have especially urged parents against it. Contrary to common opinion, I do not believe the evidence of actual penetration, the accident of a moment, to be necessarily of great weight for moral prognosis. Of course, if the attitude of society towards sex morality centers around this materialistic consideration, the girl herself is through reflection of general sentiment going to regard her future as hopeless after such an event. The vulgar opinion of outcomes in such cases is strengthened by social discouragement and recklessness induced by just the common idea. But fortunately we have been able, even among the sordid material of court work, to see another side — involving as another viewpoint for prognosis, the psychological or spiritual life. From watching the result of treatment over years we are convinced that many a girl with a record of scores of physical contacts has essentially the clean mind that under better environmental circumstances, promises well for good living. And, contrariwise, there are girls who have not experienced complete sexual contact, whose minds nevertheless are so charged with mental imagery and desires concerning sexual things that the prognosis for their conduct, without closest segregation and supervision, is inevitably bad. To decide the disposition of the case by the physical finding is to overlook the deeper facts which form the real basis of predictability, and, unhappily, is often to do grave injustice to a human career.

Psychiatric investigation, so important in selected cases of delinquency, consists of methods too technical to be elaborated here. The general outline of investigation is sketched under the head of medical examination in our schedule, but in its study of mental states belongs properly to the field of abnormal psychology, which, to be sure, has been largely preëmpted by medical men. The psychiatrist, in dealing with aberrational individuals, should always study them both from the standpoint of their

66

physical functions or defects, any of which may be causing the aberrant mental manifestations, and from the side of the mental life itself. This latter involves use of tests, some of which are found mentioned in our following enumeration of psychological tests, and by analysis of mental workings as evidenced in conversation and conduct. We are not called on to discuss psychiatric methods, they are dealt with fully in many other text books. It is very clear that judgment by means of tests, or otherwise, as to the possible existence of those abnormal states which constitute insanity, is often a matter only for those with a highly technical training and experience.

CHAPTER VI

WORKING METHODS — *Continued*

Psychological Methods.   § 50. General Statement Concerning Psychological Methods.   § 51. (A) Anamnesis.   § 52. (B) Method of Giving Mental Tests.   § 53. (C) The Mental Tests.   § 54. A Plan of Psychological Inquiry.   § 55. Our Development of Performance Tests.   (a) *Tests for Levels of General Intelligence.*   § 56. Binet Tests.   (b) *Tests for School Work.*   § 57. Interpretation of Educational Tests.   (c) *Tests for Special Abilities and Functions.*   § 58. Special Capacities and Tests for Them.   § 59. Memory Powers.   § 60. Ability to Give Testimony.   § 61. Powers of Attention.   § 62. Motor Coördination.   § 63. Associative Processes.   § 64. Perception of Form and Color Relationships.   § 65. Learning Ability.   § 66. Ability to Profit by Experience.   § 67. Language Ability.   § 68. Arithmetical Ability.   § 69. Mental Representation and Analysis.   § 70. Foresight and Planfulness.   § 71. Perception (Visual) and Analysis.   § 72. Judgment and Discrimination.   § 73. Suggestibility.   § 74. Will Power.   § 75. Apperception.   § 76. Moral Discrimination.   § 77. Following Instructions. Vocational Tests.   § 78. Special Abilities.   § 79. Mental Content and Interests.

Psychological Methods.

§ 50. General Statement Concerning Psychological Methods. — Under the head of psychological methods in general we are constrained to speak again of certain very important preconsiderations. In psychological work with offenders, not obviously insane or feebleminded, we are bound, in getting at either the intelligence, capabilities, mental functionings, or mental content, to be engaged very largely in a subtle process of observation and inquiry. In considering the scientific exactness of the results, we must remember that there are many delicate possibilities of variation ever present. These occur through the many varying conditions of the investigator, the one investigated, and the medium of investigation — especially if the latter be verbal and interrogatory. On account of all this there should be much self-conscious preparation on the part of the observer for the avoidance of all possible interference with the accurate determination of facts. As Ribot (**71**) says, " The method of inquiry cannot become a true auxiliary to psychology unless criticism, too frequently neglected, is accorded the rôle which it deserves. Criticism must be two-fold — of the procedure and of the response."

Foremost must come criticism of the observer's temperamental qualities and attitude. We would hardly again emphasize this point, especially in the light of its neglect in the literature, if our actual observation did not vouch for its importance. In a chapter on methods, one of the best authorities, Stern (**79**), starts from the fact that in any case of investigation, there must always be a chain of three elements, namely, the observer, the material used during observation, and the observed. It may be that, since so very few psychologists have dealt largely with the offender, there has been too little professional observation of the general difficulties caused mainly by the extreme emotional conditions presented by those under study. This lack of experience may be the reason why there is so little expressed realization of the grave necessity for the examining psychologist's being able sympathetically to sink his own personality for the needs of the inquiry. This, however, is keenly appreciated in some quarters. Devon (**6**) asserts, "As for the assessment of the mental characters of prisoners, the value of it will largely depend upon the ability of the examiner to place himself in touch with them." We ourselves have over and again witnessed success or failure, of which we could give striking anecdotes, in the court room, or the home, or school, or psychological laboratory — by judge, parent, probation officer, teacher or psychologist — dependent upon just this ability or inability to get in touch with the individual. An examiner or teacher who would attempt to bulldoze the person tested into giving good results is on a par with the judge who shows anger to the powerless wretch before him, or the parent who summarily thrashes his child.

It may be that in the mind of the psychologist is the general idea that with proper criticism of method will come apperception by the observer of the needs of his own relationship to the situation. The point, however, sometimes needs expressly stating. Binet (**74**) in many places has made clear his conception of the requisite personal bearing and method of the examiner. Goddard (**75**) thinks, "The attitude of the examiner is all important." The point of personality is simply this; it is an indispensable condition for success in the investigation that the observer be easily able to bend to the occasion, so that the most vital facts concerning the offender are obtained for the understanding of him.

Now concerning the other party to the investigation, only a

little needs to be said, but this is most important as a general review. The offender may present any of a great number of varying qualities; fatigue, ennui, quick comprehension, trickiness, sullenness, response to stimulation, friendliness, and in fact most of the entire list of mental traits described in such richness by Partridge (**18**). Such of these exhibited conditions as may be unfortunate for the purposes of the examination have to be carefully reckoned with and ameliorated, if possible, and always finally evaluated in reference to the results on tests. That coöperation which is met in testing the friend who is interested in science, or in testing the good school child who is doing exercises every day at the bidding of his teacher, is not always easily duplicated in the offender. Partridge (**18**, p. 113) says, " The study of the emotional life is probably the most important chapter in the study of individuality, for not only are the emotions the foundation of all the practical life, but they enter into the abstract intellectual functions in various ways." If this be true, then important indeed is taking into account the affective states in those who exhibit such wide variation in them as do offenders.

The penumbra of emotional conditions is never shown more clearly about various phases of mental life than in this study of the mental phenomena of delinquents, *vide* § 236. Before potential mental activities reach expression in word or deed they may meet obstructions in mind, body, or environment that prevent their full development and normal appearance. He who fails to reckon on the various possible stimulative or inhibitive conditions at work inside or outside the offender fails to have the first requisite for understanding the results of tests or of other inquiry.

Next, the conditions surrounding the inquiry; here everything should be conducive to winning the coöperation of the subject. The needs of his personality should be met by arrangement of the general features of the laboratory, and by the method of presentation of tests. The psychologist who stated that all he wanted was the facts, not the personality, and the one who said that any given minute of time in an examination had equal value with another minute, forgot that mental phenomena are not to be observed as one observes the dropping of a weight during an experiment in physics, or as one observes the movements of the eye at a word of command. Essential facts of mental life are not to be picked up, like pebbles on the shore, with indifferent mood.

§ 51. A. Anamnesis of Mental Traits.

We have already indicated under the head of schedule of data concerning Mental and Moral Development, § 48, that the inquiry into past life should include facts of psychological interest. Under favoring circumstances such investigation may well go much farther. We are primarily students of personality. Whatever light the mental history of the individual throws on his present personality should be highly welcomed. Sometimes one's services are invoked by intelligent parents and sometimes there is access to the school people who knew the offender. Under these circumstances the anamnesis can be widely extended in regard to mental traits.

In the giving of mental tests we may learn much about the individual's capacity to meet certain situations, but many sections of the emotional life are not even tapped in the process. Now so far as conduct is concerned, we have every reason to see over and again from our case studies that it is just these emotional reactions towards conditions which are not artificially presentable that have most significance for us. The best guide to such a study is that offered by Hoch.[1] We cannot afford space for all the details of his carefully-thought-out inquiry, but the main headings will give an indication of its scope:

I. Traits relating essentially to the intelligence, the capacity for acquiring knowledge, the judgment, etc.

II. Traits relating essentially to the out-put of energy.

III. Traits relating essentially to the subject's estimation of himself.

IV. Adaptability towards the environment.

    (a) The more striking traits which on their abnormal side interfere in a rather general and striking way with contact with the environment.

    (b) Traits which in a more specific but in a less obvious way interfere with contact with the environment.

    (c) Traits which show to what extent the subject lays bare to others his real self.

---

[1] A guide to the descriptive study of the personality by Hoch and Amsden (265) gives us a schedule produced from ripe consideration of the subject. While this guide is primarily introduced to psychiatrists, still, on account of the mental bases of conduct, it has much value for us. It should be carefully reviewed by every student of criminalistic behavior. In its philosophical presentation of the subject it is of vastly more use for us than any bare enumeration of mental traits, such as is found in "The Trait Book" (*vide* Davenport, 277) issued by the Eugenics Record Office.

71

(d) Traits which in normal proportions are useful qualities, but in exaggerated form interfere with efficiency.

(e) Traits which show a tendency to actively shaping situations, or the reverse.

(f) Traits showing the attitude towards reality.

V. Mood.

VI. Instinctive demands, traits which are more or less clearly related to the sexual instinct.

    (a) Friendship.

    (b) Attachment to members of the family.

    (c) Attitude towards the other sex.

        (1) General.

        (2) Specific sexual demands.

        (3) General traits derived from sexual instinct or reactions against its assertions.

VII. General interests.

VIII. Pathological traits.

In reviewing the above it is interesting to note how many of these points are brought out in a good family and developmental history, as ordinarily given by interested and intelligent parents. But the value of the inquiry is clearly added to by some categorical arrangement of the facts. As finally summarized, the main issues must be presented in the psychological impressions or psychogram, of which we speak later.

§ 52. B. Method of Giving Mental Tests.

The desiderata in testing offenders are obvious. The results of the best possible efforts of the subject are desired for comparison with norms that, in turn, have been established by stimulating the best efforts of those who are known to be willing to coöperate. It seems clear that the fundamental basis of standardization must be comparisons of efforts of individuals who have done their best. All else is secondary; measurement of quantities, qualities and time of work presupposes this best effort. If the best was not obtained, then evaluation of the output, since we desire to predict, is of little value. Many times now have we learned by experience the significance of this fact.

The surroundings and the examiner must elicit, on the part of the subject, attention, interest, friendliness, understanding, and secure him from distractions and fatigues.

Simplicity, if not actual bareness of the room, is desirable. There should be no exhibition of apparatus, or of instruments or tests, except as such exhibition may prove valuable for the awakening of interest. We have seen, however, a prior survey of testing material arouse desire for action, and we have by explanation of the nature of the scientific work with tests, brought around many a doubtfully coöperating adult. Many times my stop watch has proved valuable in awakening appreciation and in arousing competitive spirit. A cursory exhibition of tests which look interesting, but which are quickly put out of sight, will prove, of course, a stimulus to all.

Records as they are made are quickly thrown aside in an off-hand way without discussion. The performances of others are not to be mentioned or shown. Only in rare cases is anything but encouragement given, and that is generally offered in liberal doses. Still, occasionally, appreciation of a failure and the carelessness it implies, will stimulate to better effort on other tests. The order of giving tests varies with the capacity of the subject, and according to necessity for arousing interest and attention and for preventing fatigue. More than one sitting is usually necessary, except for the testing of the clearly feebleminded, or those who are so capable that the work is done with great rapidity.

In the presentation of each test standard procedures should prevail as far as is conducive to the desideratum, namely, the exertion of the best possible efforts. In the giving of the tests, as well as in the interpretation of the results, much shrewd common sense, as well as acquaintance with technic, should come into play. I mean this sort of thing; suppose the standard presentation of, say, our Construction Test A, calls for one statement: "Here is a frame, and these five pieces will exactly fill all the spaces in it, if you get them in correctly. Do it as quickly as you can." Now an examinee, through some emotional condition or non-understanding of some word, may not fully take in the nature of the test. It is clearly important precisely for the standardization of his efforts that there be appreciation of his difficulty, and that he get a fair start through complete understanding of the task. It is just because of such practical points as this that conditions must be carefully watched and gauged in the light of common sense. Whipple (78), in his general rules for the conduct of tests, curiously implies in one important sentence how necessary shrewd judgment is for all this work, much as one would like to eliminate conditional variations and personal equations. He says, "No test should be undertaken until the

73

subject is perfectly clear as to what is required of him." If only one could know when another's comprehension is perfectly clear! However, Whipple when elsewhere asserting the great value of adventitious observation while recording tests, clearly concedes our point.

The general nature of tests for intelligence and special capacities, such as are serviceable for the study of the offender, may be profitably discussed for a moment, together with some general methods of procedure and interpretation. It must be remembered that nearly all of these tests call for a much more complex mental activity and response than is measured by the typical psychological laboratory instruments, where visual perceptions and the like are finely discriminated and timed. We are dealing with differential human psychology; and as Stern (79) says, "Differential psychology is not based on minute analysis of mental phenomena and determination of general laws, but upon the delineation of individual peculiarities." [1] Elsewhere the same author adds, "And so we come to the important methodological conclusion that under certain circumstances the general psychological exactness of an experiment may stand in inverse proportion to its worth for differential psychology." [2] These considerations call for no lessening of the attempt at precision in the procedure of giving tests, but they do give room for introduction of the thought that precision, under such complex conditions, may rest in other things than uniformity of the spoken word or time of exposure of the test.

In the interpretation of the scoring of tests the same points come out. I agree with Goddard (80), who after a series of conferences on methods, speaking of the Binet tests, says, "But the most serious objection to a time limit comes from the fact that it makes the whole test a stereotyped, rigid, mathematical procedure, which, in the last analysis, reduces the whole method to an absurdity." In some of our own tests, for instance, Construction Test A, wide time limits must be allowed, in all common sense, before discriminating for or against the performer. The

---

[1] "Die differentielle Psychologie geht nicht aus auf feinste Analyse psychischer Phänomene und Feststellung allgemeiner Gesetze sondern auf Charakteristik individueller Besonderheiten."

[2] "Und so kommen wir zu dem methodologisch wichtigen Schluss, dass unter Umständen die generell psychologische Exaktheit eines Experimentes in umgekehrter Proportionalität zu seinem differentiellepsychologischen Symptomwert stehen kann."

fact that John did the test in 15 seconds is really no proof that he
is so much better in the very qualities the test is devised to estimate than Jim who did it in 35 seconds.   John's comprehension
of the spoken word may have been quicker.   We used the accent
and phraseology with which he was familiar; we struck an encouraging note in meeting him; he has heard this morning that
he will be released next week; the first piece he picked up at once
appeared directly over its place in the frame, and the other pieces
followed fortuitously into their correct places.   Really we have
no right to call John more intelligent in method or truer in form
perception than Jim who is downcast, and slow at understanding
words, and who accidentally put the first piece in the wrong
place, where it deceptively seemed to fit.   He then placed the
other pieces, but had to retrace his steps, learning, however,
quickly by experience, and showing after all just as good perception as John.   No, it is clear that very much more has to be
registered than the time, or any other numerically recordable
element, in order to form a fair judgment of the ability of the
two.

§ 53.   C.   The Mental Tests.

Before mentioning specific tests and their import, we should
indicate how our selection of tests arose.   Here we can neither
go into the theory of psychological tests nor consider individual
and differential psychology as a special discipline.[1]   It will
suffice to show the immediate rational background of our psychological method.

Prior to making a selection, or undertaking the production
ourselves, of any tests, we attempted carefully to formulate, with
all possible criticism, the definition of our problem.   We saw
ourselves as students of the causations of delinquency, directly
meeting the mental bases of action, those that we have indicated
in our chapter on the subject.   With the next step we saw that
we must ascertain those peculiar mental characteristics, and
potentialities, and functionings, and content, which might be
correlated with the fact of the offender's delinquency.   We

[1] For extensive discussion of these we would refer to William Stern's able
work, "Differentielle Psychologie" (**79**), where the foundations as well as the
superstructure of the science find detailed treatment.   Any careful student in
this field should become acquainted with this fundamental work; its survey
of principles and methods and literature on specific problems and tests is
unsurpassed.

needed the mental measurements for those traits or functionings which first, from a common-sense point of view, would seem likely to stand in some sort of relationship to the mental background of misconduct. No findings were to be passed upon lightly as indicating discovery of the causative agents of delinquency, but naturally with the realization of the intimate relationship between mind and deed, one would first turn in the investigation of causes to those phenomena which lie obviously linked together. Of prime importance, then, should always be construction of a PSYCHOGRAM of the offender, namely, a studied estimate of his mental qualities and conditions, including both the strengths and weaknesses.

Now for the studying of all possible mental conditions and qualities great stretches of time would be required, and then, of course, many things might be investigated which would stand in no known relationship to delinquency. For the practical psychologist — der Menschenkenner, who does not begin by asking in the fashion of the psychiatrist, " What psychosis is this person suffering from " — Kauffmann (81) states the problem to be, " Just why does this offender commit these offenses." One might carefully investigate auditory perceptions, or spacial judgments, or muscle fatiguability and so on, but none of these seems to give rational promise of any correlation with delinquency, or offers more probability of explanation than the study of finger-tip perceptions and ear measurements of an older criminology. There must from the start be selection of studies of such mental structure and function as offer most return in the way of direct explanation of our prime phenomenon, anti-social conduct. To illustrate. A wider view than that of the old criminology leads us to note the fact that some individuals, who are mentally dull, are as insensitive as certain notorious criminals studied for sensory discrimination. Now, the background of insensitivity in both types may be general mental incapacity, which was almost never tested in those criminals, and which is known in other cases to stand in close causal relationship to crime. Then, on the other hand, one only needs to take an unselected group of criminals under the best conditions, namely, when they are young, to find that most of them are normally sensitive in all directions, mentally and physically. The direction of the more valuable investigations may be perceived as indicated by such considerations as these.

§ 54. **A Plan of Psychological Inquiry.** — Close reasoning on this whole subject from our own first findings and in the light of many conferences with able specialists, led to the following formulation of a plan for psychological inquiry;

1. What is the subject's mental ability, independent, so far as ascertainable, of the results of formal education? This should be estimated in terms of strength or weakness of
> *(a) the subject's general ability or general intelligence (if such a thing as general intelligence there be).*
> *(b) the subject's special abilities — selecting for investigation here those abilities or functions which, since we are dealing with social conduct, seem most likely to be related to social action, success, or failure;*

2. What has been the result of formal education, interpreted in the light of its conditions and extent?

3. Does the individual suffer from aberrational mental functionings, whether border-line or fully-developed psychoses?

4. What are the individual's preponderating mental interests, as stated in terms of mental content, imagery, ideation and the like?

5. Has the individual important peculiar characteristics, particularly of emotional or moral life, leading to impulsive or other abnormal action?

6. Has the individual suffered earlier experiences, mental or environmental, which have, through the arousal of inner conflicts, complexes, inhibitions or resistances, interfered with the satisfactory, smooth and healthy working of mental life? This is peculiarly, in modern terminology, a study of mental mechanisms.

We can at once see that mental tests are imperative for answering the queries advanced in 1 and 2. They may at times detect the facts in answer to question 3, and when given under the form of bare interrogation help to determine 4. Some expert investigators also use certain tests at times to help in the solution of 6, but that is altogether a highly technical matter. The range of interests indicated in this scheme of inquiry shows at once the necessity for keeping well within the bounds, since all studies must be limited, of attempt to answer the most important questions.

So far as inquiry 3, namely, into aberrational tendencies, is concerned, we may at once say again that discussion of test material for this purpose is outside our province. At first indication of the fact we pass the problem into the field of special inquiry where special tests and special literature [1] are used in development of the subject's pathogram.

---

[1] The most noteworthy literature on psycho-pathological tests consists of Sommer's text book (**82**), Gregor's manual (**83**), and the recent work by

§ 55. **Our Development of Performance Tests.** — The wisdom of developing our tests along lines befitting our eminently practical aims has been well proven. The early advice of a number of the foremost American psychologists to avoid complicated apparatus or mechanical devices in the establishment of a psychological laboratory, accorded with our own first survey of the necessities and ends of the work. The initial investigation showed the important fact that no set of mental tests existed at all adequate to give the desired information about the capabilities of delinquents. It was soon found that offenders range in mental capacity all the way from imbeciles to those who seem to excel the ordinary person of their age in ability and information. We had then to evolve practical methods for estimating range of ability, except for children under 10 to 12, and for the definitely feebleminded. In work with these two latter classes the system of Binet has all along been found extremely valuable, especially since for the feebleminded it has been so generally adopted as a criterion of mental development.

We have tried and discarded many tests which have been offered, or which we have devised, because of their failure as tests or the failure of their results to meet the practical ends of the above inquiry. We have no space in this work technically to describe all the tests we have found available, but they may at least be enumerated in connection with the types of information that they give about the characteristics of mental life. Our own first set of tests has been described by us at length in a separate monograph (**70**) and the others we have selected are described (see the respective references) elsewhere. We see no reason to regret further development of new tests. In fact, as is shown, we have welcomed all those which seemed to have peculiar and direct import for our studies.[1] In this matter our point of view is not that of those who mainly have at heart the science of mental life as such; we need the higher lights and deeper shadows of mental processes. We hope for much more standardization of all sorts of tests, but find, as yet, no evidence of the value of

---

Franz (**84**); the last is in English. Each gives descriptions of tests valuable beyond the realm of psychotic manifestations.

[1] We highly commend sets of tests published by Sommer from Giessen — recently called the Giessen tests — by Rossolimo (**278**), by de Sanctis and Jastrow (*vide* Whipple, **78**). There has been interesting further development of the performance test idea with concrete material in the immigrant service by Gwyn (**376**) and Knox (**377**).

very close work with numerical norms when dealing with diagnosis and predictabilities. One has only to review Whipple's Manual (78) to see how often, after a test has been found to bring out differential high lights, further attempts at refinement of measurements by it have resulted in critical discovery of modifying influences that invalidate more minute conclusions. Our selection of a point of view for the attack of our psychological problem was guided in this matter by the best psychological authority, and our appreciations of a practical methodology have grown apace.

(a) Tests for Levels of General Intelligence.

§ 56. **The Binet Tests.** — The most widely used system of tests is that of Binet.[1] We have had long experience with this so-called "Measuring Scale of Intelligence," and find it of great value within certain well-defined limits. The gist of the method is its application of the idea that mental development, like bodily growth, shows distinct accretions from year to year. Just where measurement of these accretions can stop is a moot question. By application of this system to older mental defectives, they can be gauged by the age standards of young children and spoken of in terms of so many years of mental growth or of retardation.

We may at present leave out of consideration tests for years above 12, because psychologists with the greatest experience[2] feel now that the tests for the later years are uncertain. As a matter of fact a good many of us feel the same about the five tests

[1] Alfred Binet and Th. Simon about 1904 began the standardization with public school children of various tests most of which they had devised. They published (85) in 1905 a first set of tests which appeared in 1908 in the form of a system of tests graded for ages up to 13 years. A final revision appeared in 1911, still more formally laid out, with five tests for each year up to 10, and then five tests for 12 years, 15 years, and for adult intelligence. There have been various short summary presentations of the system in English, notably by Goddard (86), Kuhlmann (91), and Whipple (78), but the only actual translation of the tests and of directions for giving them is that of Town (87), who presents the 1911 article of Binet and Simon. Revisions of the system have been attempted by Goddard (88), Kuhlmann (89), and Terman and Childs (90). The full description of these tests, particularly as given in Dr. Town's work, is now so available that we need give no space to their enumeration.

[2] At the 1913 meeting of the American Association for the Study of the Feebleminded there was general expression of the uncertainty involved in the use of any tests which have thus been developed for grading intelligence for years above the 12-year limit. Binet's tests for this are found quite unfair, and both Goddard and Kuhlmann at this time asserted lack of faith in even their own revisions of tests for those upper ages.

for 12 years. But for children under ten, and for defectives who range as low as ten, there can be no doubt that this scheme of gauging intelligence by age levels is of the utmost practical usefulness, and is one of the greatest contributions made to the science of psychography. To be able to say to the judge, or to any one with the power to take action, that the offender of 23 chronologically is mentally an individual of 10 years, puts the whole matter in an enticingly clear light.

The trouble, however, with just this scoring of the intelligence by these comparatively few tests is that many facts may be left out of the evaluation. This kind of a psychogram, measuring the mentality on a given numerical basis, tells little about the many other conditions of mental structure and function which should be known. Especially should one understand, in order to do the best for the individual, whether or not there are special disabilities, or special capabilities, or aberrational tendencies. The numerical method forms too easy an evaluation of the human mind with its complexities and manifold potentialities. Many times we have seen this demonstrated. The Binet scale may not reveal what might be of vast importance for society to know concerning the individual. We refer to our case studies for many evidences of the fact.

One of the most difficult phases of the use of this scale is found in its application to a cosmopolitan population. Occasionally with a good interpreter safe results can be obtained, but the difficulties are obvious. The system was built up for a homogeneous people, and largely turns in many ways upon the ability to use and understand language. And then the system is unfair in its high grading of those who are, on the one hand, glib in the use of language and, on the other hand, it grades too low those whose performances on other tests may not be down on a par with their inability to use words well.

Those who think that this scale measures general ability apart from schooling and other advantages should read Binet himself on this subject. He goes so far as to say that the scale as he produced it embodies the norm for schools of Paris in the poorer districts. He finds that easy circumstances are correlated with higher intellectual development, the pupils of a private school, for instance, showing an average of a year and a half advance on his norms. The findings are always to be interpreted in the light of physiological conditions and of influence of past poverty and other experiences. Binet would have been one of the first to agree to this.

Much more might be said in praise or in adverse criticism, but we have practically covered the principal non-technical points. The fact is that the scale is really a valuable measure of the lower general levels of intelligence. It will have to be revised ultimately for our conditions, although there is surprisingly little difficulty with the use of it in this country. The idea of this system will continue to hold good.

(b) Tests for School Work.

§ 57. **Interpretation of Educational Tests.** — Testing the results of formal education is always of interest and value and, of course, is the common way of evaluating the individual's ability. There is logic in the notion that if a child has been going to school for a certain number of years, and has failed to learn what has been taught during that period, and has failed to advance with children of his class, that this is an indication of personal defect. But yet in the light of certain possibilities one would ask for an indulgent attitude in this matter. When we consider variabilities in teaching powers, and in the interest which may be aroused in school work, or when we think how the necessary attitude for learning may be counteracted by bad companions, or learning abilities lessened by bad hygiene, sensory defect, or poor nutrition, it makes us hesitate about summarily interpreting the fact of retardation. Any one who has observed month-long failure in school work because of the distraction of bad company, or because of impotent teaching in a room where there are three times as many pupils as there should be, or because of improper nourishment, feels keenly this whole problem. Though arithmetic is found to be done abominably, or reading is atrocious, the burden of proof is still on the observer who denominates the pupil as mentally defective. The point is capable of demonstration, and may require two methods; the giving of a wide range of other tests, and instruction under the best possible conditions, including remedy of physical defects.

Tests to be given for school work are easily enough selected. They should not have an age basis, but call for the appreciation of facts and processes that have actually been taught. There is considerable variation in different school systems, as, for

81

instance, the age at which arithmetic is taught, and one must be correspondingly guarded in tests. A very practical point seems obvious, although it is not at first remembered. The likelihood of school teaching being retained is in inverse proportion to the length of time the individual has been away from school, unless practice has been continued in school subjects, and both these circumstances must be carefully taken into account.

(c) Tests for Special Abilities and Functions.

§ 58. **Special Capacities and Tests for Them.** — It will be quickly seen that our selection of tests under the following heads embodies, whenever possible, the idea of performance with other material than language. The use of language is of course the most important of all human activities in the development of civilization, and gauging of the individual's ability in this direction is highly desirable. But there are many other abilities and disabilities which should be studied in their relation to needs and opportunities that the social order presents. Again we will refer to our case histories as showing in strong light and shade the variations in language ability, and the curious misinterpretations and unfortunate results which have developed from not understanding the whole mental make-up of the offender. Many vocations call for performance without words, and in seeking an estimation of the possibilities of social success by tests this must be kept clearly in the examiner's mind.

Some of the special qualities studied by our range of tests are, of course, more fundamental than others, but one does not pass judgment on relative values for the individual, if one is wise, without making a well-rounded investigation and learning the possibilities of vicarious activity on the part of other functions. It is the tests taken altogether, we feel, that give us a basis for sound practical judgment — a judgment leading very often to the establishment of helpful measures, or in other instances to the greater protection of society. Many fine points of psychological research are purposely neglected, but we think a finer point, in another sense, is keeping constantly in view the development of a fair psychogram of the individual for the purpose of actually doing something for him.

§ 59. **Memory Powers.** — Of course the powers of memory and recall, conscious and subconscious, are involved in every single test that is offered. Memory of movements, and space relationships and images, are part and parcel of our entire being from the day of birth or even before it. The bases and beginnings of memory are not to be tested. The ability to succeed in certain efforts which largely involve memory processes, and which are of social import can, however, be gauged by performance on tests. Without resolving the process used into the various memory types, visual, auditory, motor, etc., we can offer important types of tasks and gauge ability thereby. For instance, the capacity for remembering what has been read by one's self is of great social import. We can gauge this by a fair enough test, such as our Test XII,[1] where an interesting standard passage is given for reading and recall. It boots little that we cannot separate in this task visual perception, storing of images, recall of sounds for the response, and so on. The task is one that we are all called on to do in practical life without knowledge of the component parts of the mental process. (This statement will serve as a text for explanation of the principle involved in most of our other tests.) The test mentioned is for the powers of memory of visually presented verbal material.

In just the same way the powers of recall from auditory verbal presentation can be tested. Capacities in this direction may not be quite so important in modern civilization as the former powers, but still are vastly worth gauging for assessment of the subject's chances to succeed under many conditions. Test XIII covers this point.

The so-called memory span, the amount that can be taken in at one time and remembered, may be obviously a function of importance in various ways. This quantitative measurement is not always correlated with general intelligence. Various ways of testing the auditory or visual powers by this method will occur to psychologists. The memory span for numbers [2] as presented by the spoken word, or on the printed page as visually presented numerals, offers perhaps the simplest form of test. Norms of performance have been carefully established. The

---

[1] Reference will be made throughout this work to the numbers given in our Monograph on tests (70). We have found reason to describe shortly and to illustrate in the following pages some of these tests. We earnestly counsel that no work with them be undertaken without exact knowledge of the tests and standard methods of presentation. Also *vide* § 82.

[2] Many psychologists have busied themselves with this interesting form of immediate rote memory. Especially to be commended is the work of Smedley (92). Whipple (78) gives a good description of the method.

bearing of this test upon gauging certain vocational aptitudes is clear.

The visual memory for form, also vocationally important, can be estimated in a number of ways, the easiest of which is the use of a couple of geometrical figures of special import which have been extensively used, following the publication of Binet. We describe them as Test VII. Even here it is difficult to estimate visual memory powers *per se*, for it is quite easy to discern some subjects introducing elements of motor memory in their efforts on the test.

Not only immediate memory should be tested, but also the power of longer retention — an ability that is perhaps as important as the other. Some passage of interest may be read or some nonsense syllables learned, and then recall is asked for on another day. For the purposes of our testing we and our advisers have felt that it was better to ask for the memory of passages which included a logical presentation of its subject, and which preferably should be of a nature to appeal in interest to the learner. The will to coöperate and put forth the best effort is not going to be brought out in offenders by asking them to memorize nonsense syllables and perform other feats of rote memory. In the case of testing for retention, it is only fair to find out how much conscious endeavor to renew the memory there had been in the interval. The performance of one who has been able to call to mind many times the test during the interval, is not to be compared with the production of the one who has been constantly subjected to environmental distraction.

§ 60. **Ability to Give Testimony.**—In recent years no psychological test has aroused so much interest as a certain one which involves very largely the powers of memory. I speak of the so-called "Aussage" or Testimony Test — the ability of the observer to recall, immediately or at a future time, a scene or action that has been presented. No one has done so much to develop the study of this socially important subject as Stern, and with him, and following him, there have been numerous observers,[1] who have convinced at least the judiciary of Ger-

---

[1] In Germany an entire periodical edited by Stern (**93**) is devoted to the psychology of testimony, and the other literature on the subject is already immense. A good selection of the important contributions is to be found in Stern's text book (**79**, p. 423). At a number of conferences of psychologists and jurists this important topic has been dwelt upon and laboratory tests have been prepared. An interesting account of some of them has

many that in this psychological investigation there was matter of vital import to certain phases of social life. Outside of any question of good will or intent the result of an examination on the witness-stand depends most largely on sheer abilities of recall. These abilities vary not only according to the distance in time from the observed event, but also according to certain special types of powers possessed in greatly varying quantity and quality by different subjects. Nor is this ability by any means always correlated with general intelligence. A very simple way of testing some of the abilities in this direction is presented in our Test VI, and is copied from Stern's method of presenting a picture of a familiar subject and asking for a description of it, proceeding then to a cross-examination for the details presented in it. Frequently the results of this test are indifferent, but then again they demonstrate remarkable abilities or weaknesses which may be corroborated in other ways.

§ 61. **Powers of Attention.** — Observations of the ability of the subject to attend, are properly made all through the process of testing, and should form part of the observer's report — another evidence of the necessity of the use of general judgment for the psychogram. When it comes to testing directly the powers of attention, various methods suggest themselves. We have ourselves occasionally created distractions, such as we know are ordinarily effective during mental tasks, and in some instances have gained thereby valuable knowledge. We learned a good deal about a certain bookish lad by finding out that revealing the works of a stop watch beside him did not divert his attention from reading. When we consider how large a part the interest of the individual, either positive or negative, plays in his power to withstand distraction, we see that measurements of anything except gross divergencies may be difficult. Possibly, however, only those are of any importance for us. Our judgment from general observations in giving a series of other tests has usually seemed sufficient to us, but sometimes specific information is desirable. For diagnostic purposes, it must be carefully remembered that observed attention to one type of activity may be quite at variance with possible attention in another field.

been given by Münsterberg (95), and Whipple (96) has made a special point of gathering the literature on the subject. He who reads Münsterberg should follow it up by perusing Wigmore's (97) scholarly presentation of certain counterfindings.

A widely-used type of test involves largely the question of attention to visual perceptions. In several forms it is very simple to give. One well-standardized test calls for the selection and cancellation as rapidly as possible of given letters or numerals as presented on a sheet where they are mixed with other symbols. One of these demands the crossing of all A's on a sheet of closely printed letters.[1]

In the interpretation of results here, as in the case of those derived from a number of other tests, we believe that the psychogram developed for our purposes should not deal too closely with numerical calculations, but rather with more important characterizations. We should be especially interested in some such determination as that the subject was slow and accurate, or was speedy and accurate.

§ 62. **Motor Coördination.** — Testing the motor coördinating abilities is well worth doing in every case, because when disturbances are found they are important, from neurological, vocational, and educational standpoints. The neurologist always gives well-known tests, particularly those with the eyes shut, in order to see whether certain functions of the nervous system are intact. Coördination of the motor with the visual perceptive functions is also important to test. We have with satisfaction used a test where the subject taps as rapidly as possible in succeeding half-inch squares without touching the lines or missing the squares. Information of value has been found out in numerous cases by this method. Testing by means of other and more complicated methods, particularly with the use of electrical apparatus, where the individual attempts steadily to hold a stylus in a given space without causing the ringing of a bell, is well known. Most of the apparatus can be very easily installed in a simple laboratory. Our tapping sheet, Test XVI, has so far answered our purposes.

§ 63. **Associative Processes.** — Testing the rapidity and accuracy of associative processes brings us very close to estimation of the essential working powers of the mind in general. All of the separate items of our total mental content are connected in a stream of thought by links of association; one calls up the other because it is in some way related to it. Now study of the

---

[1] Whipple in his Manual, under the title of Test XXVI, Cancellation, describes various tests primarily adapted to estimate attention as applied to visual perception.

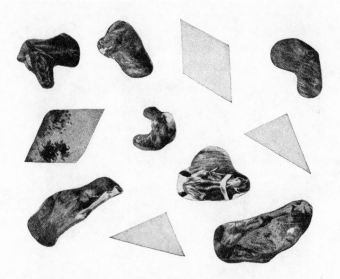

A PICTURE FORM-BOARD — OUR TEST I

An example of a test in which form and color perceptions, some apperceptions,
and methods of trial and success are brought out.

rapidity and rational accuracy of these links gives us a clue to fundamental strengths and weaknesses. Study of them is peculiarly valuable for knowledge of the existence of a number of psychological conditions.

The only direct way in which to know the associative process is through the medium of language. Where a foreign language has been used extensively by a subject in school or at home, that must be taken into account in the interpretation of certain of the tests given for association. We have tried a number of methods which have not proved available. The following seem to be of most worth.

The so-called uncontrolled continuous association is where the individual is told to say all the words he can as rapidly as possible, or when he is told to follow the same method, but after the giving of a stimulus word. By this means not only the rapidity of response may be gauged, as in one of the Binet tests for 12 years, but also the range of information and interests may be sometimes discerned.

Controlled association may be tested both for rapidity and accuracy. The subject is asked to give as rapidly as possible a word that means exactly the opposite to the word given, and the time is taken in fifths of seconds by a stop watch. If the language factor can be fairly ruled out of the case, the rapidity of correct association in this test gives one of the best indications that we have of any form of native ability. Our Test XV, Antonyms, offers a standard list of words. Much work on this test has been done by Norsworthy (99) and others. It affords one of the easiest ways to study mental reaction times. (Latterly we use a better standardized list.)

Another form of this test is to give a word, and call for another word naming the class to which the stimulus word belongs. Studies of accuracy and rapidity have been made for such a standard set of words by Norsworthy. This test has much less significance for us than the antonym method.

§ 64. **Perception of Form and Color Relationships.** — Form perceptions are tested in their very primary relationships by the so-called Form Board Test, which is seen in many institutions for the feebleminded. Goddard has attempted to standardize the apparatus. It will hardly be found useful except for those mental defectives who are usually segregated as such before they become arrant offenders. Perception of form relationships enters into our Test I, and also into our Construction Tests, which are illustrated on the accompanying plates.

It is very difficult to distinguish between native and acquired abilities in working with these tests. Training of children in kindergarten work, or with geometrical figures, undoubtedly affects profoundly their abilities.

Perception of color relationship is perhaps of less importance vocationally. Although for some time in the beginning of our own researches we looked fairly carefully for major defects of color vision, we found not a single case. There has been some suggestion in the past of the relationship of this defect to criminalism. Our results would not justify our going farther in the study of a possible correlation that had no warranted *a priori* basis, nor grounds in observed fact.

§ 65. **Learning Ability.** — Learning ability for words as ordinarily presented may be tested as described, § 59, under the topic of Memory. Perhaps more exact determinations of native learning ability may be tested in other ways; meaningless lists of words may be memorized and so on. We have advisedly confined ourselves in this matter to the study of the ability of the subject to learn the arbitrary association of a set of symbols with numerals. In the form we present as Test VIII there is found a variation on some ideas proffered earlier by a number of psychologists. Learning ability in more complicated relationships, as shown by the results gained from the use of a number of our other tests, is a matter of rather obvious estimation.

§ 66. **Ability to Profit by Experience.** — One of the commonest remarks concerning the unsuccessful, repeated offender is that the individual does not seem to be able to profit by experience. Now, of course, this profiting by experience in social situations implies not only learning powers, but also the elements of attention, memory, apperception and what not, that go to make it possible consciously to represent a situation in the light of past related ideas and experiences. There are thus many circumstances and conditions which affect the total social result, but it is certainly important to note, if possible, whether the individual has the innate power to make any such combination of mental activities. Several of our tests, which involve the manipulative performance of a task, the solution of which is usually not obvious, are calculated to demonstrate something of the individual's ability to profit by the results of what he has

PLATE II

CONSTRUCTION TEST A

An example of a test which demonstrates planfulness and the powers of
learning by experience. The illustration shows the test as
presented, as completed, and two types of error.

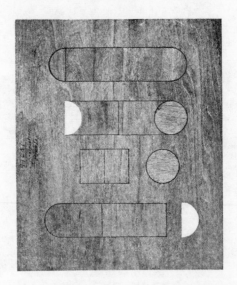

Plate III

Construction Test B

Another test for planfulness and learning by the method of trial and
success. The illustration shows the test as presented, and
one example of error in placing the pieces.

done previously in the performance. In the doing of our Construction Tests III and IV, this point is sometimes brought out most remarkably. Other estimations might be made by observing the procedure on tests which involve more of the puzzle idea — in fact to a clear-headed person the solution of a puzzle involves exactly this type of work, namely, making a trial and profiting by one's success or error. We have tried a number of puzzles, but for our purposes have found very little satisfaction in their use, because so many other elements were involved in working with them. One probably valuable form of test for this purpose, as some one has suggested, might embody the electrical wiring of a simple switchboard or a little system of bells in which the inner combination of wires could not be seen.

An exceedingly ingenious test, unfortunately taking up much space, was devised by G. V. Hamilton (112), to study in animals and human beings of low capacity the ability to profit by simple experience. The ingenuity of his device offers much food for thought. It is quite possible that the same principles might be used for methods which could be evolved to apply to institutional inmates. For the description of the apparatus we must refer the reader to the original article, but may say here that it consists of a room with one entrance and several exits, only one of which was opened at the time. The one that would be opened at the time of a given trial varied according to a scheme which could be learned by the results of previous trials. The direct results of errors and successes are very clearly appreciated in this test — a quality making for its validity.

§ 67. **Language Ability.** — On account of its practical importance in the many ways which crop out in our case studies, particularly in the groups concerned with special mental abilities or disabilities, and with pathological liars, language ability should be definitively evaluated. By general observations during the giving of the tests, many of which deal directly with language, and during the interview, enough of an estimate can be made practically to classify the individual, or at least to get first impressions of any peculiar language characteristics. In any case, further tests with reading, and estimation of the vocabulary, and the flow of ideas, can be made as necessary. For the summarized psychological impressions, in cases where the abilities are remarkable on account of richness or poverty of language powers, judgment should be made on the rapidity of speech, choice of words, formation and consequentiality of ideas. If innate inability to read or write is discovered, that matter should be specially investigated by methods familiar to neurologists ·and educational psychologists.

§ 68. **Arithmetical Ability.** — The ability to deal with number relationships, a capacity that can be isolated for practical purposes, although thoroughly complex in its elements, when it appears to be below par should be investigated as a possible cause of trouble in the individual's career. It is an issue of sufficient importance, as we have on occasion found, to be taken carefully by itself. Psychologists will study the weakness, and endeavor to find if due to innate disability or to poor teaching, to find if it exists for concrete or only abstract numerical items, whether it is dependent on weak auditory or visual functions, defective memory span, and so on. Some of these facts may stand so closely related to the welfare of the individual that they are correlated with delinquency.

§ 69. **Mental Representation and Analysis.** — The ability to represent in terms of various imageries a given situation to one's self, and to revolve it over in the mind, seeing its different parts, and mentally commenting on their comparisons and relationships, is one of the most valuable of human faculties. It is an ability that greatly makes for social success or failure, even to the point of giving that understanding which is the best prophylaxis of delinquency. A group of tests of increasing difficulty we have used with much satisfaction — our numbers IX and X, namely, the Cross Line Tests, and XI, the Code Test — appears to bring out the possession of just this quality. These tests involve spacial and numerical relationships, and require the mental representation of a simple form scheme, and analysis of the parts as the whole is mentally viewed through use of imagery. On these tests, usually regarded by adults as easy, some curious results may be observed from many offenders who are not feebleminded.

In many other ways this important ability may be estimated; a social situation involving moral sanctions may be orally presented, as is done by ethical and religious preceptors, and an analysis required. This latter constitutes a complex test of comprehension. We offer a couple of interesting orally presentable situations, Test XXI (Moral Judgment § 76), but warn that interpretation of results should be made with much circumspection. The varying mental elements often, though not always, interfere with final safe conclusions.

§ 70. **Foresight and Planfulness.** — It was Thorndike who long ago said to us, that if weakness in any one particular ability were, *a priori*, to be selected as most likely to stand often at the root of criminalism, it would be the lack of foresight. Perhaps the facts, if they were determinable, might confirm this suspicion, but it appears to be a very difficult matter to check up with accuracy the powers of foresight, so much do they vary in different fields of thought and action. Certainly foresight has much to do with planfulness, and the latter can be partially tested in various ways. From our construction tests we can frequently obtain a good register of planning ability. In the handling of our mechanical box, which is offered for perceptual analysis (*vide* § 71), the planning or lack of it may be noted. Just so with many other tests; notes can be made on the question at many points of the performance. A test that commands interest, and which involves some visual perception, much mental representation, and analysis of the representation, and is directly calculated to demonstrate planning ability, is offered by Terman (**113**). A baseball is supposed to be lost in a circular, grassy field and the subject is asked to think over the situation and plan and diagram the most economical possible route to be taken over the field in search of the ball. Nothing can be easier than the giving of this test and the results obtained are often valuable.

We early considered games as demanding planning and foresight. The only available one, on account of its universality, has seemed to be checkers or draughts. Of course, if this game has not been played often enough to offer the subject opportunity for gaining skill in it, the test is not available. But when we ascertain this to have been the case we can use it as a test. The most important result, as in the case of any performance, is when we have the positive proof of ability. Under our Test XX we consider the conditions of proof. When ability has not been shown, we must, to be fair, feel sure that effort was made.

§ 71. **Perception (Visual) and Analysis.** — We have made an effort to develop means of estimating the combination of visual perceptive and analytic functions. A mechanical box, our Test V, (see illustration) was gradually evolved, in which the task could be easily perceived and then analyzed and solved by

91

studying the sequence of steps required. This test is undoubtedly of some value for vocational diagnosis. This same combination of powers is less directly involved in the performance of other tests, such as our Construction and Cross Line Tests.

§ 72. **Judgment and Discrimination.** — Judgment has to be displayed notably in the performance of a number of the tests, particularly those mentioned in the preceding paragraph. As exercised either through direct or indirect discrimination, we can test judgment in several ways. The sorting of a series of weights in the Binet ten-year test, and the asking for judgment on the length of slightly different lines are good examples. Both these tests can be carried to any desirable extent. The Binet eight-year question about the difference between remembered objects gives suggestion for the development of further and harder questions that involve the same type of judgment. Ziehen (**114**, p. 28) developed earlier this method of determining the ability to discriminate mentally represented material, and the difference test is sometimes called Ziehen's test.

A number of other tests of perceptual and sensory judgment or discrimination are available, beginning with the simple tests of neurologists for anomalies of nervous conductivity. Whipple (**78**) in a chapter on tests of sensory capacity, and Franz (**84**) in his chapter on sensation give many tests which can be applied without the use of exceedingly complicated apparatus. The discrimination which is under discussion in this paragraph is supposed to involve very little of the feature of mental representation. But as a matter of fact, what really constitutes pain or brightness or pleasantness, forms in itself a matter of judgment on the part of the subject. The data collectable by these tests do not belong to the simple anthropometric categories where they were earlier placed. Perhaps some of these tests will be shown later to have considerable worth for the study of offenders, but at present we feel justified in mostly passing them by.

An interesting judgment test, first developed for vocational ends, is described by Münsterberg (**111**). It consists in the rapid visual perceptive judgment upon and sorting of cards, which present varying numbers of special letters mixed among other members of the alphabet. Judgment is formed as to which letter preponderates and the card is sorted accordingly. Accuracy and time are recorded. We see clearly from this test that some

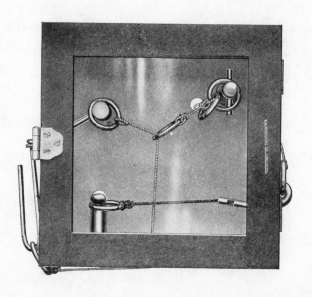

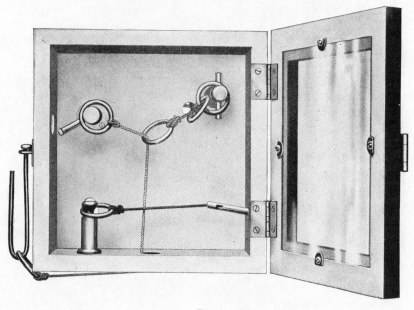

PLATE IV

A PUZZLE BOX — OUR TEST V

An example of a concrete problem to be reasoned out from perceived
relationships.   Each step to the solution, namely, opening
the box, is plainly visible.

fair characterizations of the examinee may be formed, but the establishment of numerical coefficients worked up on the combination of varying quantities of time and accuracy is to be looked upon as dangerously artificial.

§ 73. **Suggestibility.** — Many tests for estimating suggestibility by the sensory illusion type of test (looking for false interpretation of perceptions, such as those of warmth and weight) have been worked out, but are hardly to be considered desirable for study of the offender unless carefully undertaken and interpreted by a technician. They offer little for a practical psychogram.

On the other hand, tests of suggestibility where personal influence is a factor, are obviously of considerable import in the study of the delinquent.[1] Binet wisely laid much stress on personal influences in suggestibility, and even introduced a test of resistance to suggestion into his series, putting it into the 12-year group because he considered at that age level there was first developed, on the average, resistance to suggestion. (Psychologists working with the "Aussage" test have concluded that there are very great differences between resistance to personal suggestion at different ages in the giving of testimony.) Binet says heedlessness and lack of attention may cause falling into the trap. This, as we see it, is exactly how in social life certain individuals from empty-headedness or lapses of will receive criminalistic suggestions. The individual through certain negative aspects of his mental life is more passive and suggestible than he might otherwise be. Proved suggestibility in one field, however, does not necessarily imply suggestibility in another. Another point is that deliberate persuasion, with its straightforward attempt to change judgment, is to be very properly separated in test work and in judgments of social conduct, from either direct or indirect suggestion.

We have always seen many reasons for doubting whether we could reproduce conditions that would lead to accurate determination of the individual's practical suggestibility in social situations. Our § 331 on Social Suggestibility should be care-

---

[1] This most captivating psychological problem, individual suggestibility (we deliberately omit consideration of hypnosis and other abnormal conditions, and also the psychology of crowds), should be looked into by every careful student of offenders. Very many partial contributions have been offered, but the most desirable works with which to become acquainted are those of Binet (**100** and **101**), O. Lipmann (**102**) and Sidis (**17**).

fully perused in this connection. We can see at least that if the individual, with the determined bracing of his will and judgment that is frequently seen in the examiner's office, shows normal or even more than the ordinary resistance to various types of suggestion, it by no means signifies that he will not succumb outside to social temptations. Unpredictable though this point is, we probably can, with some degree of accuracy, prognosticate from the converse findings — for instance, it seems certain that those who show undue acceptance of indirect or direct suggestion with us are often those who notoriously exhibit the same qualities socially.

In this whole matter of personal suggestion it should always be remembered that suggestibility within moderate limits is a perfectly normal quality of mind, and that people of the highest character and attainments show the phenomenon. We have never made a specialty of developing these tests, seeing plainly the unsatisfactoriness and difficulty of safe interpretation for the psychogram. We perceive, however, that some types of tests bear good fruit. Suggestibility in testimony has long been a subject of discussion and many of the contributions to the " Aussage" or testimony problem (§ 60) deal with it. An easy method of introducing experimental suggestion into our own testimony test (Test VI) is to ask, during cross-examination of the subject about what the picture reveals, whether certain things have been seen which are not there. Our suggestive inquiry concerns such items as might well be in the picture. We have uniformly told the subject at the beginning of the cross-examination that many things would be inquired for, some of which were there and some not there. For the purposes of a harder test this verbal precaution might be left out, as it is during the examination of the witness on the stand by the shrewd lawyer. In our responses, we find, according to the facts of normal suggestibility mentioned above, much must be often interpreted as neutral. But occasionally such an egregious example of suggestibility is seen, even when the individual is not feebleminded, or such sturdy and well-judged responses are obtained, that the test proves of much worth for our psychological impressions of the individual.

From our series of repeated offenders we have selected the cases of seven who, being mentally normal, have very markedly shown themselves to be extraordinarily suggestible socially (§ 331), and have compared their results on the Aussage test. None

of these was diagnosed lower than having fair mental ability.
In these cases from 4 to 7 of our standard suggestions were used
when asking for a report on the picture. We found that in three
of these cases no suggestions whatever were accepted. One accepted 2 suggestions, two accepted 3, and in one instance the
individual proved extremely suggestible, falling in with no less
than 5 of the points. As an average this shows far more than
normal suggestibility. The youngest of the group was 14, and
at this age we find the norm for our suggestions is not more than
1 accepted. But the extreme variations show that averages are
of little import. The outstanding facts are that in some cases
of extreme social suggestibility no positive result whatever (vide
§ 331) was shown on the "Aussage" test, while in others there was
distinct correlation between the two. Indeed, in a couple of
cases our suspicions of the true nature of the social difficulty
were first aroused by the findings in this test. But, in
general, the conditions of laboratory quiet are very different
from those of the coercion which so often obtains in social
comradeship.

The story of the individual's social reactions as revealed by
himself or his relatives and friends occasionally brings out the
point of social suggestibility very strongly. We have many
records containing remarkable examples of statements, even by
subjects themselves, in regard to their being unduly influence-
able by other individuals or groups of individuals. This is simply
one more indication of the fact that if the social test could be applied, which would tell us the individual's actual response under
environmental conditions, we should have one of the best of
psychological tests. The report that we can get, even at second
hand, of the performance under some of these living conditions
has its import, particularly in the matter of suggestibility, for
the psychogram.

§ 74. **Will Power.** — Whatever may be the equivalent of the
phrase " weakness of will power " in correct psychological terminology (the barest study will show that it implies numerous
defective conditions of mind and body), it is used in the every-
day characterization of offenders, with common-sense, forceful
significance. We may get direct indications of the strength of
this faculty, also, while carrying the subject through a series of
tests. There are great difficulties in testing the will as such, except in aberrational cases. No test has been devised that has

yet received sufficient trial of its validity for discernment of
types and comparative strength of will.

A most commendable effort in this direction is the simple
but ingenious test of Guy C. Fernald (**104**). Here there is attempt to measure will power through making observations of
conscious, long-continued muscular effort, namely, standing
easily on the toes. The important distinction which Fernald
makes between this and ergographic work, is that the latter is
primarily a measure of fatigue, the muscles giving out long before
the will does; while in his test the strength of the muscles involved is so great that the discontinuance of the task is always
brought about by breaking down of the will. This Achievement
Capacity Test, as it is called, deserves in its original form, or in
modification, much trial in suitable laboratories, such as those
in reformatories, where plenty of time is available. Whoever
uses it, however, should remember the numerous *a priori* criticisms which have been offered, to the effect that the personal
interest and good intention of the subject are greatly involved.
It might be just the one who would say, "To thunder with the
test," after doing it a little while, who would unremittingly
exert his will to some personally desired end. But after all, *a
priori* criticism is not always found valid when practically working with tests.

§ 75. **Apperception.** — One of the highest intellectual faculties is that of recognition of the relationship of part to part in a
given event, or situation, or in a sequence of ideas or perceptions.
This process of apperception, according to the complexities involved, involves combining mental material, directly presented
as perception, with what is already in the mental content. The
person with so-called quick perceptions, or good understanding,
is the one who has apperceptive ability in full measure. According to Ebbinghaus (**105**), whose scheme for verbally testing the
power to discern relationships between separate ideas has been
given wide recognition, we have in the performance of tests
which call out the above powers, the opportunity of getting an
estimate of general intelligence. Of course all of our tests call
out to some degree the ability to put what is already in the mind
together with what is immediately presented, but any test
which more directly serves to estimate this important ability is
altogether worth while. The Ebbinghaus Completion Test requires the insertion of words or syllables for the completion of the

PLATE V —PICTORIAL COMPLETION TEST. A test for apperceptive ability. The pieces which belong in the squares are mixed with forty other pieces, all the same size, representing a variety of objects. From these selection is made to fill the spaces. The picture is highly colored.

sense of a passage from which various parts have been omitted.[1] The subject has to draw on his stock of words and ideas about the relationships of things for the performance of this Completion Test. For our purposes, although we see the great value of estimating some of the powers called forth by these completion tests, certain of the requirements are clearly adventitious. It is the same old trouble; there is involved in this form of test, through its use of language, entirely too much dependence on the acquaintance with words and particularly with language as visually presented. In testing apperception in this way subjects who have had the advantage of much language training, have an immense advantage, which is unfair for our general study of offenders.

It occurred to me that perhaps the valuable central idea of the completion test might be utilized without involving the medium of language. Our Test II, originally designed to bring out this point, has been found too easy and so has been discarded. More recently a picture representing ten easily recognizable activities and events was constructed, and from it ten squares of equal size were cut so that on each piece was a part essential to the meaning. Then on forty other pieces, all of the same size and fitting into any of the square holes, were drawn objects that could be put in place only with injury to the meaning of the picture. Some of the wrong pieces are not so wrong as others. Some may cover part of the meaning. We designate errors as partial and complete, or logical and illogical. The total fifty pieces represent a stock of ideas from which to draw to complete the meaning of the picture. This test (see illustration) arouses much interest, and from a clearly bad or clearly good performance of it very definite conclusions as to apperceptive ability may be drawn.[2]

Testing apperceptive ability by jokes has been suggested, but not much developed as yet. It is a scheme that offers promise

[1] Texts of all degrees of difficulty may be contrived for the giving of this test. Several may be found in the original article of Ebbinghaus, also as used by Wiersma (**107**), but those are all in German. Terman (**106**) worked up a couple of forms and has done something to standardize them.

[2] This picture has been developed since we published our monograph on tests. For a technical description of it, with directions for giving, and an account of the norms established, *vide* Healy (**378**). The skill of the artist, Mrs. Eleanor Manierre, was necessary to the success of this undertaking. Her experience in illustrating children's books was just what was found necessary for the evolution of the test. Much gratitude is due her for her interested efforts.

of results when undertaken by means of well-selected pictures.[1]
Binet's test for nonsense statements in the ten-year group is
along the same line. Anderson is using for the same purpose tests for interpretation of proverbs and of verbal ideational
analogies.[2]

§ 76. **Moral Discrimination.** — In forming impressions of
the offender, one would naturally feel the importance of the
actual capacity for moral judgment. Of all the mental furniture,
the power to discriminate between right and wrong would seem
to be most essential for well-doing. Undoubtedly of greatest value
to know would be the mental procedure in the face of an active
moral issue. Unfortunately, the only thing open to ordinary
testing is the general ideational potentiality, and that by no
means reveals the procedure that actually takes place in a living situation. The capacity is not the same thing as the practice in the realm of moral decisions. The tyro will realize that
by questioning the answer will generally be obtained that stealing and assault and so on are pernicious deeds, as considered in
the abstract, and will also realize that the answer gives no criterion of what the subject's judgment will be in the face of opportunity or provocation.

However, the powers of general moral judgment and particularly of the comprehension of moral issues involved in a
given situation, are sometimes important to appreciate. F. C.
Sharp (**110**) has done interesting work with non-offenders on this
subject of moral discrimination, and we have utilized, in modification, in our Test XXI, some of his methods. A short narra-
tion involving some points of ethical judgment is orally presented,
and a discriminating response is called for.

Professor Sharp's concise rendering of the problems is something
as follows:

(1) In a Russian city last year there lived a man who could get no
work. He had for a neighbor a sick widow with two little children,
who were starving. The poor man took some bread that did not belong to him from a baker's shop, because he could get it in no other
way and gave it to the widow and her children. Did he do right or
wrong?

(2) A settlement was once besieged by a large body of Indians be-

---

[1] An article on testing intelligence by means of jokes from "Die Fliegende
Blätter" has appeared, *vide* bibliography, Testing Intelligence (**379**).

[2] These tests are used by Dr. V. V. Anderson of the Municipal Court,
Boston. Results on them have not yet been published.

cause the chief thought that one of the white men had done him an injury, though he really had not done so. The chief sent word to the captain of the village that if the man was given up to him he would go away, but if not he would burn the village and kill the people. The captain and the people knew that if the Indians attacked them they would be very likely to capture the settlement and, at least, would kill a good many. They also knew that their fellow citizen was innocent and that to give him up meant torture and death for him.

What was the right thing for the captain of the village to do and why?

What would you have done if you had been captain?

We see at once many difficulties in interpretation of the answers, and have to confess that in only comparatively few instances has the response proved of distinct worth. Occasionally strong types are met with, either showing much appreciation of ethical sanctions, or clearly belittling the canons of social morality, and then only is interpretation fair. One grave trouble is in noting whether all the details of the situation have been comprehended. On cross-examination we have sometimes found absence of realization of some of the facts mentioned. The test then turns out to be, as we mentioned above, one of comprehension or mental representation of a situation verbally presented.

An ingenious test for ethical discrimination has been evolved by Guy Fernald (109). He uses ten slips of paper, each having printed on it a few words describing tersely some offense, or ambition or meritorious act. The task is to sort these in the order of their moral significance. The idea is good, but through the use of only a few words the lack of sufficient connotation and explanation leaves great possibilities of variation in the comprehension of the significance of the deed. At our suggestion Fernald has developed illustrations representing the same deeds with, of ·course, a vast increase of the detailed significant background of fact and meaning. (Moving pictures represent manifold possibilities in this direction.) Another trouble in this test is with the standard of norms. The deed may be considered obviously from the legal, the conventional ethical, the religious, or the personal emotional standpoint. For instance, the killing of a moose may be looked at from the standpoint of a hungry woodsman, of a game warden, or of a nature-lover like Thoreau. The student of the evolution of morals would have much to say

on this whole question. Still another trouble, and one that we
have found peculiarly in our own situation, is in the language
factor. In our population the understanding of the written word
in any given language varies too greatly for the idea of complete
comprehension of even these short sentences to be safely used
as an established norm. Perhaps this test may be worked up
past some of these difficulties.

§ 77. **Following Instructions. Vocational Tests.** — One of
the oldest tests used by neurologists in the diagnosis of general
mental powers, is that of the ability to follow instructions.
Usually the directions for three simple tasks were given together,
orally. The results of the performance gave important indications,
even though the mental process involved was unresolved. Binet
took this same idea in extremely simple form for one of the seven-
year tests. It is obvious that desirable elaboration of this method
could be introduced for vocational or general ability diagnosis.

In instances where information for vocational diagnosis in a
broad sense, as between fitness for being a field laborer and an
office clerk, was desirable, we have used the following test, which
may be regarded as an example of its kind. Our Test XIV, see
illustration, consists of a mechanical box to be opened by careful manipulations following verbal instructions. The form of
the test arouses competitive interest; the performance always
gives some indication of general ability and some specific knowledge of fitness for certain kinds of accurate work.

Other tests could readily be devised if vocational diagnosis
in any given study of the offender was desirable, and how extremely desirable it may be can be seen from contemplation of
some of our case studies. We are certain that diagnosis of occupational aptitude should properly be a careful part of the study
of the delinquent, because of the frequent relationship between
vocational dissatisfaction and social misconduct. The development of this whole line of work promises much, but as yet it is
nearly a virgin field. The best vocational bureaus themselves
advisedly await the production of really dependable methods
of diagnosis and prediction at the hands of practical psychologists.

§ 78. **Special Abilities.** — On account of their importance,
and also because they are not always to be considered in a vocational light, special abilities may be dwelt on apart from the
matter of the previous section. Tests for special abilities may be

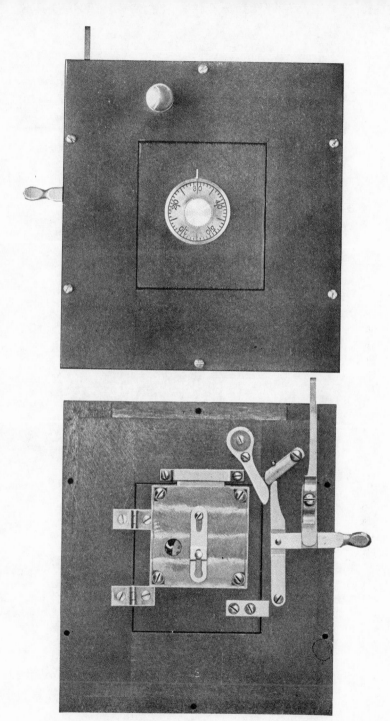

PLATE VI

AN INSTRUCTION BOX—OUR TEST XIV

Example of a vocational test. The box can only be opened by
accurately following each step of the instructions given.

presented and, naturally, in the form of selected tasks. What emphasis to place on the possession of special talents may be gathered from the relevant facts presented in our practical study of delinquents. The need for self-expréssion forms in some persons the soil from which misconduct springs. The first abilities that come to the reader's mind are, no doubt, those connected with the artistic world, where the peculiar mental traits connected with genius and ardent desire for self-expression are so well recognized. The mere desire to shine in any of these fields may be exotic, however, and bespeak no corresponding natural faculty. The only way to determine such ability is to have people competent in the artistie world sympathetically conduct a special test. Even if discovered, the presence of artistic ability, as we know only too well, does not guarantee freedom from delinquency; but that full exercise of native talents does bring about immensely favorable changes in some careers we also have reason to know.

Other special abilities may be more easily reckoned with. A boy may have capacity for mechanical pursuits, powers he has never had a chance to know he possessed, and which may prove his saving grace. Not a few girls with real histrionic ability have become delinquent in the search for self-expression. Their abilities and desires might have been recognized and utilized, in ways quite normal and moral, and quite apart from the public theatre.

I am not sure but that I should include under this head of special abilities the peculiar sagacities and capacities which make for success in the great out-door world. The capacity of a man for solitude and hardship, and for overcoming the difficulties of nature, and the ability keenly to observe and reason on natural phenomena, and the desire for large freedom, and for long stretches of muscular activity, mark a man as having peculiar adaptabilities just as much as do his possession of qualities which will make him an artist. While these traits are hardly open to laboratory testing, another field of trial may be found in the larger world, from which we can gather, after all, many facts for our psychogram.

Knowledge of special abilities in the field of imagination may be worth testing for. Simple devices, such as the well-known inkblot test, *vide* Binet (115) and Whipple (78, p. 430), where the subject is asked what he can imagine a certain irregular blot looks

101

like, have been used. Much more important, of course, is the use
of imagination in the artistic and literary fields. Recognition of
the latter is possible by obvious methods, and has led to successful careers. The writing of a story which has been read some days
previously may be demanded, and if the subject is told to give
full sway to his powers, the possession of imagination can usually
be determined from one such production. We have had reason
to recognize practical connection, at first not obvious, between
the possession of the imaginative faculty and a tendency to delinquency. It is Stemmermann (117) who tells of a delinquent who
long continued his career of swindling and misrepresentation,
until he found expression for his imaginative powers in the field
of journalism.

A familiar field for use of the imagination in the modern world
is that of invention. It might be more or less easy to test abilities in this direction, and one would certainly like to see something
of this sort done. Terman (118) has suggested a simple way of
bringing out what might be called the first principles of this ability. His test consists of the offering of five sets of chains of three
links each. The subject is asked to figure out how these could
all be welded into one chain with breaking and welding only
three of the links. By such methods, carried to any desired complexity, no doubt a great deal of the subject's power of imagination and invention could be learned.

§ 79. **Mental Content and Interests.** — A questionnaire calculated to bring out the quantity and quality of general information in a number of branches of human knowledge frequently
reveals much of importance. As the result of our special inquiries, Test XXII, we have at times wondered if this was not
one of the most important of tests, because of its revelation of
the paucity of healthy mental interests to be found in mentally
normal offenders. Of this more in our case studies. The idea is
not new. Whipple (119) has published a " Range of Information Test " for high school and college students, consisting of one
hundred words for definition, belonging to various fields of human
knowledge. One would venture to say that the use of this test
would give considerable accurate information about abilities
and interests. Simpler lists of words could be gotten up, such as
Terman (120) has developed for his revision of the Binet scale.
We should strongly counsel the use of this method, realizing that
it should be modified to suit the circumstances found in any

given place where work with offenders was to be carried out. The mere vocabulary tests of Whipple and of Terman are hardly as direct as the questionnaire method we have used. Asking for definitions may frighten the subject from full self-expression, whereas if one asks him sympathetically to tell all he knows about a steam engine, or professional baseball, or the civil war, you may soon arouse interest which in turn may give clue to abilities that often, for the sake of preventing a delinquent career, should be practically tested and utilized.

CHAPTER VII

WORKING METHODS — *Concluded*

§ 80 (D) Interpretation of Mental Tests. § 81. Enumeration of Disturbing Conditions. § 82. Norms on our Own Tests. § 83. Dangers of Insufficient Data. § 84. (E) Classification from Tests. § 85. (F) Psychoanalysis. § 86. (G) Psychological Impressions; The Psychogram.. § 87. Summarizing of Case.

§ 80. D. Interpretation of Mental Tests.

To present a detailed statement concerning the interpretation of psychological tests, their standards, norms and variabilities, is here quite out of our province. For technical instruction in all these points special works must be consulted, and no one is qualified to work in this field without professional training. All that we purpose to give here is some guidance for those who are psychologically inclined and wish to make some general interpretation for themselves of the results of the tests as set forth in our case studies. For them the following statement of norms will suffice for such conclusions as are justifiable.

Psychology is in its infancy as an applied science, and, as may be gathered from the foregoing pages, the work of studying abilities and functions by means of tests is one of the more recent developments. On account of this we have had not only to select, but also to develop tests, and then, what was even more arduous, to establish some standards of norms for the group of individuals we work with.

Much space might be occupied by discussion of the possibilities, limitations, and pitfalls of developing and applying standards, but all that is really necessary to state here comes under two points; First, we are thoroughly convinced that some sort of standards must be worked up for each given situation or social group in which tests are applied. Second, unless there be remarkable uniformity of school training, environmental background and emotional conditions, such as obtain readily in testing students in a college laboratory, interpretation of answers, types and times of performance can only, in all fairness, be made within wide limits. The many variabilities possible in the performance of an individual as seen, for instance, in court work, with all the complications of life bearing on the given result, as well as the variations depending on social opportunities, we have given some hint of on other pages.

§ 81. **Enumeration of Disturbing Conditions.** — It may serve the purpose of illustrating our particular theme here to give a bare enumeration of the disturbing conditions, many of them at first not at all plainly perceived, which may produce a performance in the tests leading to error in diagnosis of ability. The principal interferences we have noted are: (a) The various peculiar mental states supervening in cases which later proved to be epileptic. (b) The irregular mental states of hystericals. (c) Choreic mental conditions, especially when the symptoms are confined, as they occasionally are, to the psychical sphere. (d) Any of the tremendously varying mental conditions seen in mild manic-depressive conditions. (e) Deliberate deception (very rare). (f) Sheer laziness, as occasionally seen. (g) Complete recalcitrancy, sometimes combined with deception. (h) Temporary dullness on account of excessive sex practices. (i) Bashfulness or other inhibitory emotions. (j) Environmental conditions, e. g. effect of a warm afternoon or a close room. (k) Fatigue on the part of the examinee. (l) Fatigue on the part of the examiner. (m) Dullness from narcotics or aberration from stimulants. (n) Dullness from general physical conditions, such as anemia, exhaustion from recent illness, over-exercise. (o) The effects of special sensory defects; these are too obvious to need detailed mention. (p) Emotional conditions resulting from incrimination, from being charged — whether rightly or not — with offense (*vide* § 315).

Fortunately, however, when the above conditions are taken into account there is extraordinarily little difficulty in the interpretation of most results as bearing on the question of general classification of the individual in the broad, but useful categories set forth in the next section, and in ascertainment of those special abilities and disabilities which we find are of much concern for those who would seriously attempt to treat delinquency according to its causes. At no time do we expect to see mental performances set forth for a general group, such as ours, with such numerical precision that one who has not taken counsel of experience with the causes of variability can safely interpret them. But given scientific training in this direction, and the

105

experience which common sense would dictate is necessary in such a situation, so that the many causes of variability are as far as possible reckoned with, then, we find by observation of new workers in the field, interpretation is comparatively easy.

§ 82. **Norms on Our Own Tests.** — The following statement shows what may be expected on our own group of tests from individuals who are to be considered as normal, or as of ordinary ability, among the general social group which one meets in studying delinquents in a large cosmopolitan center. There is not the slightest reason to think that this normal differs to any extent from the normal of a city school in the same community. It does, however, naturally differ from that of a selected group, for example, the pupils in a high-grade private school.[1] Binet declared the same difference for his tests. What is subnormal or feebleminded in our group we generally find has been regarded as the same by the public school people. Since we deal mostly with older individuals, we may say that what we schedule as ordinary or fair in ability, is the equipment possessed by the young person who shows himself qualified to succeed under the requirements of employment which call for what we might roughly denominate average intelligence. Other things being equal, the members of this group had usually proved themselves capable of passing one school grade a year.

Smaller type is used for the statements of norms, in uniformity with the record of results as given in the case studies. Technical signs are used for minutes and seconds. Interpretation of the Binet tests is spoken of above. Fuller description of the following tests is to be found in our Monograph (**70**).

Test I. (Illustrated on Plate I.)   Beginning at about **7** years any mentally normal child should be able to do this test in its entirety — many 2 years younger do it. The time naturally varies a great deal. A bright 5th grade group, ranging about 11 years, averaged 1' 43"; a kindergarten group averaged 3' 16". There is purposely a great deal of difference in the difficulty of working with the triangles and putting the other pieces in place. Of the normal kindergarten group 14 per cent. failed on these triangles, none on the other pieces. The triangles

---

[1] An extended study of performance on a number of our tests, partly combined with the Binet system, has been made by Dr. Clara Schmitt (to be published later). She particularly compared the results on our general group of offenders with those gained from the pupils in a certain large private school, notable for the high character of its work and attended by children from unusually intelligent families. Some of her results are embodied in our statement of norms.

are put in place by most children of 12 or under by a trial and error method; very few plan the approach to the problem. The other pieces, however, most often are at once apperceived in their true relationship — 9 out of 27 kindergarten children put them in place without error. As we have said in another place, this test is given to interest and to get a first general measure of the individual and is not suited for close methods of scoring.

Test II. Special Picture Puzzle. Even at kindergarten age normal children are able to do this correctly, though usually with many trials. Average time, then, 3′ 15″. At 10 years, 33 per cent. did the test without any errors, although 18 per cent. still made from 3 to 10 errors. The time then averaged 2′ 22″. We have latterly given up the test as too simple for the ages we work with. Our Completion Test, *vide infra*, takes its place.

Test III. Construction Test A. This is one of our more important tests. (Illustration, Plate II.) No normal person over 8 or 9 years should fail to do it in 5′. At 12 years we find great variation in the time, showing very distinct differences in ability. Some grasp and plan the task very readily, performing it in 12″ to 15″; nearly all of those normal mentally getting it done in 2′. To be considered as done well it should be done within these limits, and without replacing pieces in obviously impossible positions. Of course a planned method is better than trial and error, but some get through with it rapidly by quickly perceiving the possibilities of the latter. The number of moves used depends, of course, on the method. Estimation of the method is certainly more important than the time, within the above limits. The least possible number of moves is 5.

The private school group all succeeded from 2d grade up, with a gradual diminution of the average time, which in the 2d grade was 2′ 7″; 33 per cent. failed in the 1st grade, even with 10′ trial, and 23 per cent. in the 2d grade. Beginning with the 4th grade 50 per cent. did it by planning. None in this school did any better than many of the best in the group of offenders.

Test IV. Construction Test B. (Illustration, Plate III.) This is similar in idea to the preceding test, but for most is much harder. It should be done in 10′ by all normal persons from 12 years on. Most of our normal 12-year-old offenders do it in from 1′ to 3′, but even when older persons exceed such time limits it can hardly be maintained as evidence of low ability. Again in this it is the method that is most valuable to note — particularly the attitude of planning, as put over against taking the chances on trial and error, and particularly as against the repetition of impossibilities. This, namely, the ability to profit by experience, is registered with certainty in the number of moves made. Errors to the extent of 10 or 15 indicate little, but beyond that there is carelessness or actual inability to think out the situation. There are 11 pieces to put in — thus normally the task should be done in at least 26 moves. Occasionally a slap-dash method done by a bright person involves more moves, but only seldom. It should be remembered that a planful attack may be very slow.

107

The private school group made no failures after the 4th grade. The average time then was 2′ 10″, and that was not decreased in 2 higher grades. In fact, at 11 years the performance was as good as it was for 2 years later. This type of result, both here and in the preceding test, is characteristic. We see our brighter young offenders doing these two tests quite as well as any of the private school group, or as well as adults. These two tests are more definitely ability than age tests.

Test V. Puzzle Box. (See Plate IV.) Nearly all of our offenders above 12 years who have ordinary ability can open this box, well inside of 10′, but very occasionally such a one may fail. Since a considerable time may be rationally spent in studying the situation involved in the test, the time, unless very rapid or very slow, hardly counts for much. There is every invitation to plan the task, and of course with increasing years there is the tendency to do so. It is difficult to say how many errors are allowable — it is easier to judge of the method by observing whether the correct steps are interspersed with errors, which should not be. Upwards of 2 or 3 errors before doing step one makes the probability quite against planfulness. Very often there is a combination of trials with some later planning. Miss Schmitt estimated that 39 per cent. of our offenders between 12 and 16 years, who showed no school retardation, did the test by planning, but 11 per cent. failed entirely. It is not uncommon, however, for a girl to take very little interest in this test, usually so inviting for a boy.

The private school group made no failures above the 4th grade. Average time was steadily lowered to 6th grade, the highest worked with, and then it was 3′ 54″. Planning then was done by 70 per cent.

Test VI. Testimony from a Picture. (See page 85.) The interpretation of this test lies largely along common-sense lines. Beginning with 8 years, bright persons can give a good account of the picture, bringing out most of the main points on cross-questioning, if not on free recital. An ordinary good account as heard from our offenders is to give 12 or 15 items on free recital, and perhaps 8 or 10 more on inquiry. More than 2 or 3 erroneous details is a bad record, as is also to accept more than 2 suggestions. General interpretations of absent or excessive suggestibility, and of memory failures are obvious. So, too, are the extraordinarily straightforward or dramatic accounts sometimes registered. There is the greatest variation in ability to testify and this shows itself early — many a bright child of 10 has correct and vivid pictures, not excelled by others of greater age. (For further comment on results in this test see §§ 60, 73, 331.)

Test VII. Visual Memory of Geometrical Figures. (See page 84.) This should be done correctly by all from 10 years who have normal visual memory, as Binet states, but great variations in ability to draw well are, of course, noticeable.

Test VIII. Learning Arbitrary Associations. (See page 88.) This test is done exceedingly well by even young children who have normal ability. Beginning certainly with the 10th year we should expect, even among our offenders who are normal, the task to be done with at the most 1 or 2 errors.

In the private school group 55 per cent. of 1st grade children did it without any error, 70 per cent. in 2d grade, 80 per cent. in 3rd grade, and 86 per cent. in 4th grade.

Test IX. Cross Line Test A. (See page 90.) This is done by nearly all normal persons correctly, either at first or second trial, by the age of 10. It is an easy task for most, even at the first attempt. In the private school group there were no total failures above the 2d grade — a total failure meaning four trials without success. In the 3d grade 90 per cent. got it at first trial, and at the 5th grade all of them. Beginning at the 6th grade all of our offenders got it right at first trial.

Test X. Cross Line Test B. (See page 90.) This is on the same order as the preceding test, but is more difficult. It should be done by normal persons above 12 years, certainly on the second trial. Each trial follows demonstration of ability to draw the whole figure from memory — this is the same as in giving Test IX. The private school pupils all did it at first trial in the 6th grade; 94 per cent. at first or second trial in 5th grade; 84 per cent in the 4th grade. No final failure (after the fourth trial) was first noted in 4th grade. No final failure among our offenders was first noted at 6th grade. Between the ages of 11 and 15, judging mental ability normal by absence of school retardation, only 4 per cent. of our offenders made a total failure, whereas 41 per cent. of those who were retarded 2 years or more totally failed. This is a test which the adult type of mind finds much easier — as differentiating the faculty of mental analysis from mere memory.

Test XI. Code Test. (See page 90.) This is one of our most difficult tests, requiring good powers of concentration and analysis. Many persons who prove themselves able to cope with the world in the ordinary simpler walks of life do not accomplish this test with less than 3 or 4 errors. To do the task without errors shows some good mental powers. The average numbers of errors was 3 at 6th grade in the private school group. It is probably fair to say that the person of ordinary ability above 14 years in our offending group should do this test with at most 4 errors, out of the possible 11. More errors are made by those who come in our group of poor in ability, though not distinctly subnormal; and fewer errors by those of marked good ability. In working with offenders on such a test which requires prolonged effort and does not long appeal to the mentally lethargic, whether temporary or chronic cases of mental debility, the interpretation of partial failure is not always obvious, and needs the critical comparison of results on other tests.

Test XII. Visual Verbal Memory. (See page 83.) The passage consists of 20 details which follow in definite logical sequence. Beginning with 3d grade pupils — ages 9 or 10 — there is much more difference between types of individual response to this test, than between response by ages. At 10 years the results average nearly as good as for later years. In the private school group 86 per cent. in the 5th grade gave the sequence quite correctly, and 72 per cent. gave from 15 to 19 details, while 13 per cent. gave the entire 20 details. The latter result, however, is peculiarly high, for only 4 per cent. of the 6th grade did as well, and none in the 4th grade. Our offenders above 12 years of age and of ordinary ability nearly always give correctly the general logical sequence, and at least 12 of the details are recalled with accuracy.

Test XIII. Auditory Verbal Memory. (See page 83.) In this test there are 12 details. Every one knows the facility with which bright young children learn a passage by ear, so we are not surprised to find in the private school group 88 per cent. in the 2d grade remembered at least 9 details with much accuracy of sequence. Below that, the sequence was very defective. At the 4th grade all got 9 details or better, 25 per cent. got all the details, and the sequence was almost perfect. In our group of offenders of ordinary ability above 10 years we should expect at least 9 items remembered in logical sequence.

Test XIV. Instruction Box. (See Plate VI.) This test should be done correctly at the second trial by all above 14 years, unless there is distinct misunderstanding of the figures on the dial, — and even then there is a fault of perception. Failure to open the box after being shown twice, would make us question very carefully whether the person should be recommended at all for office or shop work.

Test XV. Antonym or Opposites Test. (See page 87.) Interpretation on this test is only fair where there has been a normal chance of becoming acquainted with the English language. Under such conditions it becomes a very interesting, and occasionally important measure of the rapidity of associations. For the ages above 10 years there is no marked increase in ability to quickly respond. We expect in our offenders of ordinary ability, response in average time of at least 2″ and with certainly not more than 2 or 3 errors. The private school group at 4th grade gave average time 2″, and 61 per cent. no errors; in the 6th grade, time 1.6″, and 87 per cent. no errors.

Test XVI. Motor Coördination Test. (See page 86.) Above 12 years old we expect from individuals of ordinary ability at least 60 squares tapped in 30″ with not more than 3 or 4 errors. Various physical conditions, of course, prevent good performance.

Tests XVII, XVIII, XIX. Writing, Arithmetic, and Reading. The interpretation of these when schooling has been good is obvious; the performance should be up to grade. Unfortunately, it is very difficult to say that schooling has been suited to the needs of some pupils, especially those with specialized defects of sensory or intellectual faculties.

Test XX. Checkers. This test has been rarely given, but when a game is played with care and foresight it is a sure indication of certain very good mental qualities — powers of analysis and foresight.

Test XXI. Reaction to Moral Questions. (See page 98.) This test, rather infrequently given by us, may show both some indication of powers of comprehension of a situation verbally presented, and powers to analyze an ethical problem. The comprehension and

110

analysis, irrespective of the exact solution offered, is most important. From our group of offenders above 12 years, ordinary in ability, we get reasonable answers, with some show of analysis of the situation as correctly represented in their own mind.

Test XXII. Information. (See page 102.) The correct interpretation of answers to the questions given is obviously dependent on environmental conditions as well as on mental ability, but a well-rounded inquiry in either case serves as an indication of absence or presence of those normal, healthy mental interests and opportunities which are so important as a preventive of criminalistic ideas and imageries.

Test XXIII. Pictorial Completion Test. (See Plate V.) At 11 years this test should be readily accomplished with not more than 1 or 2 final errors, and certainly not more than 1 illogical error. Most of our group of normal offenders by 11 years do better than this, and even some at 10 years do as well. With age there seems to be no marked average increase of ability. The median or average performance for all in the group of those ordinary in ability above 10 years, is 1 final error and no illogical error.

The private school group does just about the same — at 11 years the mark is set which, for at least 2 ensuing years, is not passed. In this school, however, a good many below 11 years are able to do the test without error, great variations occurring. The median error above 10 years is the same as for the offenders.

The average time is about 3' and this does not vary greatly for ages above 11 years. The erratic performance often seen in psychosis cases has seemed very notable; indeed, hardly any other test has proved so indicative of the aberrational tendencies, but, no doubt, some of the really insane could perform the test readily. We have seen no feeble-minded person, as yet, able to do it without error, although, on account of the variance of special abilities which we so much insist on, two or three have come within limits we prescribe as normal. Looking over the brightest subjects at Vineland we found a young man of 21 — Binet age of 10 — said to be perhaps the nearest to normal of any boy in the institution, who accomplished the test with only 1 logical error, but he took 16' for the task. Then one of the brighter girls, 16 years old, — Binet age 11 — made only one logical error, and did it in 3' 30". Both of these came very near to apperceiving all the relationships depicted in the test; all the others of even this brightest group fell much behind these performances, and none of our feebleminded offenders has done so well.

§ 83. **Dangers of Insufficient Data.** — As a last word on interpretation we may warn against drawing conclusions from insufficient data as, for instance, the findings on a single test, or without taking into consideration physical and environmental conditions. In working with any group of considerable size, curious variations, perhaps on a single test, will be found which must be interpreted for the individual person or in the light of peculiar conditions. Then one must not forget the whole question of specialized defects and special abilities, which we have concretely illustrated in their proper place.

§ 84. E. Classification from Tests.

We have had surprisingly little trouble with the classification of cases in the scale of mental ability and peculiarity as given below. Perhaps that is because no preconceived standpoint was taken, and divisions were not forced. We waited until the data on about 250 offenders had accumulated, and then the results of psychological tests were sorted by the method of allowing them to fall into what seemed to be natural classes. This first work was done with the help of outsiders who could not be prejudiced by acquaintance with the cases. The classification, with more exact definitions and some modifications, has stood the test of time. In my course to professional people, working with disguised synoptic case studies replete with abbreviations, both instructor and students have been surprised at the facility with which a practical diagnosis could be rendered, corresponding with the original classification made years before.

It must be strictly understood that such a classification is only one part of the psychogram and, indeed, in some cases does not even cover all the facts which can be learned from the giving of tests. For instance, the possession of special capacities or disabilities, and of peculiar traits of character, which may be learned during the laboratory examination, is not accounted for in this scheme, and must be added to the psychogram. Of course, one would always like to know more of the individual than is expressed in such categorical terms, but sometimes it is difficult to get a chance to minutely study individual peculiarities. I should always insist, however, that an examination which did not go far enough to enable the observer to place the offender in one of these rough classifications was entirely inadequate for the purposes of even first impressions. As a matter of fact, in our regular court work we have seldom encountered a case which we could not study to this extent.

With slight modification from the original statement in our monograph on tests, the scheme of classification stands as follows:

A. Considerably above ordinary in ability and information — the latter estimated with reference to age and social advantages.

B. Ordinary in ability and information — the latter estimated with reference to age and social advantages.

C. Native ability fair and formal educational advantages fair or good, but very poorly informed.

D. Native ability fair and formal educational advantages fair or good.

E. Native ability distinctly good, but formal educational advantages poor.

F. Native ability fair and formal educational advantages poor.

G. Native ability poor and formal educational advantages poor.

H. Native ability poor and formal educational advantages good or fair.

I. Dull, perhaps from ascertained physical causes, including some cases of epilepsy.

J. Subnormal mentality — considerably more educability than the feebleminded.

K. Moron.

L. Imbecile.

M. Psychoses.

For accurate understanding some comment on the above is needed. It will be seen that above the group of subnormal there are only three large subdivisions, the supernormals, the ordinary or fair, and the poor in ability. There is some overlapping of definition, especially in the middle group, but we have found it very difficult to avoid this. Those who are graded as fair are simply those who do not make such a well-rounded presentation of themselves as to be called quite up to the ordinary, while yet one would hesitate to denominate them poor. Consideration of any such point brings us at once to the main question — what forms our standard of norms for the different classes? To this we can only reply, that we must work by the rough averages of the social situation in which we find ourselves. Any one who attempts to do otherwise and engage in finer calculations will find untold intricacies. Let us remember that all mental classification is social classification — even the insane man is one who is first noticeable for not doing as others do. Let us remember Binet's acknowledgment, that children of the bourgeoisie grade no less than a year and a half above his published norms. After all, the practical question is best answered by the fact that psychologically trained workers coming to our Institute as assistants from time to time have found little or no difficulty or disagreement with others in

113

using the above classification. Finer distinctions would bring trouble.

Our estimation, "Formal educational advantages poor," includes no implication of cause, it may be due to chronic truancy or to faulty environment. What we mean by mental subnormality is set forth with some attempt at exactness in our chapter on Mental Defect. The class entitled, "Dull, perhaps from physical causes," is intended to form a temporary pigeon-hole for the class of cases that Witmer (142) and Holmes (141) have done so much to emphasize. On many of these only a tentative statement is possible. Perhaps with remedy of the physical conditions there will be a show of mental betterment, or perhaps not. Physical causes include general poor physical conditions, over-use of narcotics and stimulants, bad sex habits, arrested development, and epilepsy. All this is set forth, too, in connection with our chapter on Mental Defect. It should be remembered from the start that epilepsy may be correlated with anything from supernormality to idiocy and insanity, and that sometimes an apparent mental defect may clear up under successful treatment for this disease.

Our classification into mental groups above subnormality is made largely on a social basis — that is, our classification in a general way is determined by the averages of the class of individuals we see. It is obvious that if one were to take the findings on tests for a picked and successful social class, the averages would be much higher than for a lower social group. We have had to get not only our own results, but to establish our general norms, and for the latter we have purposely allowed a wide range of findings. For example, interpretation one way or another of five or ten seconds more or less on certain performance tests, when the total task takes on the average forty or fifty seconds, seems to us of little value because of the many incidental causes of variation which come in. Our so-called B Class consists of individuals who do not make an exceptionally good or bad performance and who, as a rule, have been able to keep up to their school grade if they have had the social opportunity to do so. We have clearly noted the fact that some individuals who have grouped in this class might, if gauged by certain exceptional family and social standards, be considered almost subnormal individuals. For instance, we have seen a boy whose performance on school work and on tests was up to the average of our general group, but who

114

when measured by the unusual mental performances of his exceedingly brilliant family seemed and indeed was designated a subnormal individual.

So it comes about that the study of any human individual by a mere process of classification and registering results on tests without reference to the relationship of abilities or disabilities to environment, lacks in the common-sense elements which must be introduced into any investigation which would fundamentally deal in predictabilities, treatments, and preventions.

§ 85. F. Psychoanalysis.

One would prefer a term other than psychoanalysis for the heading of this section, a term which savored less of highly technical considerations and which would not suggest acrid disputations on theories which have been built up from the use of this method. Appreciation of the vital principles involved in the method is not confined to one school, in spite of the recent tendency to fit the term psychoanalysis into the mold of one particular scheme of interpretation. Again, in this matter we are not concerned with general theories. We want facts which can be used for understanding a given case.

This method in varying measure is available for the study of offenders, and in accordance with well-known curative principles brilliant results may ensue. Our interest in the psychoanalytic method has been only aroused by the common-sense explanations and therapeutic results it has given us. The application to the study of misconduct is a natural evolution, although its main use lately has centered about treatment of the psychoneuroses. Indeed, some of the best technicians speak of it as being fundamentally a study of motives, and this fact is brought out even more strongly in the title of a recently started periodical, "The Psychoanalytic Review — a Journal Devoted to the Understanding of Human Conduct" (132). From all this it is seen that we may perhaps best adopt the general term psychoanalysis, even if we omit very much of the matter discussed under that head. Many of the facts and some of the principles of this rapidly developing branch of psychological science are still *sub judice*, and others we are not at all sure concern us in our study of offenders.

In developing the simplest statement about the technic and usefulness of this method for our work we draw at various points

115

upon the voluminous literature.[1] From this we soon learn that the whole structure of the psychoanalytic method rests upon one foundation — that for explanation of all human behavior tendencies we must seek the mental and environmental experiences of early life. If one traces back the driving forces of conduct in any normally minded individual, one finds their first springs so far away that the intervening links of relationship are not quickly perceived. Up through the aisles of time the mental individual has progressed by steps that are now forgotten, and by paths which may have been dimmed to consciousness in the passing. The psychoanalytic method, first and foremost, invokes retracing the steps which progressively formed the whole character; hence it bespeaks utmost value for students of social misconduct.

It is clear that the technic of the method must take account of facts and laws conditioning the activity of mental processes. Of prime importance is the discovery that tracing connected mental experiences soon leads to that huge portion of the life of the individual not for the moment in consciousness. Many times the chains of causal nexus lead in and out of subconscious life; some links of experience stand out clear and sharp above the threshold of realization, and other linked groups of activities remain below. Some psychologists have laid much stress on the structure of that vast world of mentality which is not naïvely perceived as being

---

[1] I am accustomed to ask my students to get, in all fairmindedness, their first acquaintance with psychoanalysis through sympathetic exposition. Putnam's paper on "Etiology and Treatment of Psychoneuroses" (**133**) and Meyer's (**153**) discussion of fundamental issues form splendid first statements for any one. White's monograph on "Mental Mechanisms" (**134**) gives a sound presentation of many bearings interesting to the general reader. For a simple historical presentation Freud's own lectures (**135**) at Clark University are to be highly recommended. A clear-cut protest against certain criticisms is found in Putnam's "Comments on Sex Issues" (**136**). A much more technical and thorough presentation of the whole subject is found in Hitschmann's "Freud's Theory of the Neuroses" (**137**), recently translated. Brill's "Psychanalysis" (**138**) is calculated to offer a free general statement of the whole subject. Jones (**139**) has written brilliantly of many phases, and we would especially recommend here his essays on educational subjects. Much of the literature in German is very difficult and is scattered in various periodicals and in separate works. The deep student of the subject will only be satisfied with original sources. A painstaking survey of the important findings, with much original observation, devoted to the purposes of pedagogy, comes recently from the pen of the pastor and teacher, Óskar Pfister (**140**). For a review of the literature see the edition of Hitschmann mentioned above. Notwithstanding tomes of argumentation, there has been really very little constructive criticism of Freud's development of technic. As a possible example of the latter, reference should be made to Sidis's (**145**) various articles. However, he and many other critics use the general methods of psychoanalysis.

part of one's individuality; the technic of psychoanalysis has come, on the other hand, to reckon closely with its dynamics. Latent memories must be called up; one never realizes how much of the forgotten, once conscious past, or even of the unconsciously experienced past there is that can be remembered.

The term psychogenesis is frequently used in discussion of tendencies traceable by psychoanalytic methods. This term implies that the given tendency spoken of as originating in the mind sprang from reactions which were essentially mental activities. The reactions, of course, are either to environmental experiences, direct or indirect, or to other mental experiences. The important facts of psychogenesis are, then, only to be learned through knowledge of the dynamics, the laws of mental activity, which condition conscious and subconscious reactions. The user of this psychoanalytic method has constantly to work with active consequential relationships. No other part of psychological study is so keenly alive to the actual forces of mental life.

The exponents of psychoanalysis have ever alleged, despite superficial criticism to the contrary, that original reaction to experience was partly determined by structural conditions derived from hereditary or congenital sources. The following seems a fair statement of psychical genetics. From early environmental experiences, reacting on the original organism, arose a reactive tendency, a character. From now on all future behavior reactions must have a three-fold parentage — the new experience (opportunity we called it above in thinking of our offenders), the innate functional potentialities of the individual, and the reactive tendency or character already formed. Which one of these mainly engenders any given act of conduct it may be very hard to determine, but two things are sure — innate conditions are unalterable and new experiences are always crowding in. Concerning the reactive tendency, that is the business of psychoanalysis. Thus we see how much of the field of characterology psychoanalysis may possibly cover.

Induced introspection is the principal method of psychoanalysis. The subject in an atmosphere of perfect calm is asked to remember, to remember; letting the machinery of associated processes have full sway in pulling up for inspection each link of the chain of mental causation which reaches gradually into the past. There are really many chains, and skilled guidance is needed for keeping the right one centered in the field of view. Many links, of course, are unimportant and can be rapidly passed by. Tangles are met which must be straightened out, if possible, and sometimes there are interferences, technically known as resistances, to be overcome. In these hindrances perhaps the machinery fails to work well because of deep-set and hardly conscious lack of desire to cooperate. So quietness and good will, skilled questioning without undue suggestion, and, above all, sympathetic understanding, are indispensable to the inquiry.

Some have tried to develop other ways of getting acquainted with the facts of mental life locked up for the moment in subconsciousness. There has been considerable advocacy of Jung's (142) method of using association reactions to stimulus words. Putnam terms this a sort of concentrated conversation. So far we have not found this scheme pregnant with results for our study of offenders. Then comes the vastly disputed field of interpretation of symbols and of dreams. We ourselves see at the present youthful stage of development of the psychoanalytic method, no reason in our department of study to deal much with these disputed points.[1] The technic best suited for work with offenders undoubtedly is that of uncontrolled or free association, simply guiding the subject in the bringing of his related experiences up to consciousness.

Many of the limitations and the possibilities of the application of this method will at once occur to the reader. Without good will nothing can be accomplished, but often, however, good will can be created. If the inquirer is willing to spend sympathetically so much effort in the services of the subject, that in itself should be a bid for his good will. If one reads of the long months over which interviews continue in the difficult cases handled by the neurologists, discouragement for this method of study ensues. But we can offer a contribution on both the above points that puts a different face on the matter. In the first place, we have found that in working with individuals near the beginning of their careers the essential facts are much more easily obtainable. Perhaps this is because in the formative years the subjects themselves are more naïve and pliant, and are looking forward to possible changes in their careers; and certainly it must be partly because the important facts of origin are nearer the surface of mental life. As

---

[1] We have no sympathy with the grotesque fabrication of symbolisms, such as have been offered for the interpretation of the phenomena of "kleptomania," *vide* Stekel (143), and it is only fair to state that the most authoritative exponents of psychoanalysis decry this exaggerated effort.

the years go on, more and more strata of experience are deposited in the memory, and deeper are buried the beginnings of character tendencies; it is harder, for geological reasons, as it were, to pull up the facts into consciousness. Then, too, difficulties arise as side issues in the form of pride, grudge, hopelessness and establishment of mental habits.

It is repeatedly urged that mental flexibility is necessary for the therapeutic success of psychoanalysis, and that consequently age and unintelligence are barriers. We have purposely worked for the most part with adolescents. With children we have often found it possible to get the needed information in a few interviews, although even at this age rare cases have been met which showed undoubted mental conflict problems in the background, while our efforts proved unavailing for ascertainment of the facts. In working with adolescents, we have found vast differences of reaction in different individuals, and in relation to the time which has elapsed since the vital experience occurred. In some of the older cases we perceive at once the difficulties that the neurologists encounter; careers are set which probably could at one time have been modified. Very much more work will have to be done with adult offenders before anything like a final estimate can be given of the value of the method as a whole for this particular class. In the case of the comparatively young and intelligent adult delinquent, we find evidences ourselves that the value is great, and note corroboration of this in the literature, *vide* Pfister (**140**). For faults of conduct it may not be necessary to go so deeply as for faults of nervous function, with which most psychoanalysts have been engaged. At any rate, with much less work than they have generally prescribed, we have achieved knowledge of facts, and reached the eminently satisfactory therapeutic results outlined in some of our sample case studies.

This simple review of the method and intent of psychoanalysis is not satisfactory without some word of what is revealed by the use of the method. Full of meaning for us are the following main discoveries: Very much that is formative of character does not appear above the surface. Active interreactions of mental elements may be all unconsciously the motive forces of conduct. Experiences which come to the individual with a great deal of emotional context are likely to cause the greatest amount of reaction. As through life in general so here, experiences, either inner or outer, related to sex life, in the broadest sense, show the

119

strongest and subtlest reactions. Mental shock, psychic trauma, is produced frequently by experiences of which dearest relatives may be ignorant. These traumata are experienced most frequently in young childhood. Mental conflicts occur on the basis of either outward experiences, physical sensations, or pure ideation, at ages so early as to be unsuspected. These conflicts may be entirely repressed, but do not thereby lose their force and significance for the formation of character tendencies. Repression of that which naturally needs expression is followed by reaction, which may vent itself mostly in the organism or show as anomalies of conduct. The cause of habit formations of many sorts is deeper than appears on the surface, many of them being vicarious expressions of hidden and even unconscious impulses to action. Much more might be said, but the above is sufficient to indicate the scope of the findings of psychoanalysis, aside from an involvement of technical issues.

For our specific ends the general points mentioned above offer much, but in addition one can add that early mental experiences and strange, altogether hidden, mental conflicts have arranged the destinies of many a chronic offender. We are not at all convinced that the sole source of mental conflict is some experience with the sex instinct; there are other causes of emotional disturbance which strike deeply into the mental organism. Taking cases as they come, we find an immense amount of inner mental disturbance at the background of stealing and other delinquencies. Such disturbance often forms an attitude of mind showing itself either as grudge, or hopelessness, or as a tendency to seek relief in misconduct, — all directly leading to a delinquent career.

The therapeutic effects of the application of the psychoanalytic method to the study of offenders prove in some instances nothing short of brilliant. Such results would warrant from every standpoint the expenditure of much effort. The success has always been alleged to be largely due to the mere exploration itself, the bringing to consciousness of the causal steps, which were not known before to exist as such. It is just the bringing of the facts to light, say some, that does the good. And in our experience it does seem sometimes as if the subject, in pulling up parts of his mental past and seeing their connections, does say to himself, " That's so; now I know why I did this thing." Any of us can have this explanatory experience by applying the analysis to every day phenomena, such as memory lapses and slips of the tongue, which the psychoanalyst shows us have deeper roots in our prior mental life than would naturally be expected. Now it is to be readily conceived that self-consciousness of the origin of a fault might prove the first step, and perhaps a long one, towards its cure.

By merely showing to the subject, through hauling up the contents of his own mental reservoirs, what his failure is based on, may not prove sufficient, if environmental or physical conditions, which serve as two of the three instigating causes, are still irritating as of old. Various reasons will readily suggest themselves why this should be so. Habits and thoughts and tendencies of years' standing are not to be lightly overcome if nothing but added knowledge is to stand up against them. Re-education and helpful new interests from the outside are also frequently necessary. For energies which previously found outlet in socially undesirable behavior, " substitution " must be made possible by discovery of a junction point where now, by conscious volition, shunting on to another track can take place. More of this, however, and more of the whole subject will be appreciated by study of the concrete issues. We purposely refrain from introducing more technical considerations and terminology. We resist also the temptation to illustrate here the simple points mentioned in this our little primer of psychoanalysis, and ask the reader carefully to study the living facts as given in our chapter on Mental Conflicts.

§ 86. G. Psychological Impressions. The Psychogram.

Logically, the development of the psychogram should be considered here, but as a matter of fact this ground has nearly all been covered before. In the first part of our discussion on mental tests (§ 54) we formulated our plan of inquiry, and the answer to the problems there propounded forms exactly the psychogram. What is needed is a statement of all psychological points which offer a likelihood of bearing on delinquency. Under the six headings given in § 54 the field is plotted. Close statement of the psychological diagnosis is of course desirable.[1] For in-

[1] With the development of our science more and more attention is going to be paid to writing up a psychogram. The best general reference work for the student on this subject is the volume by Stern (**79**), from which valuable ideas may be drawn. From several quarters has come the suggestion that comparative evaluation of mental traits and qualities be stated according

stance, if the individual is a specialized defective, what is the nature of his defect, and so on.

The first psychological impressions should be carefully written immediately after the observational work has been done. The later statement, after all the case material has been worked up, forms the final impressions or psychogram. Sometimes for formulation of this a page or two of typewriting is necessary, but sometimes only a paragraph is required in its proper place on the sheet which represents the final summarizing of the case.

§ 87. Summarizing of Case.

Under the head of Diagnostic Summary, in our § 48 on records, we gave the outline of a logical scheme. In the five paragraphs we propose to present all of the salient facts which in any way focus upon the problem of delinquency. This is not at all for enumerative purposes, but is to be strictly regarded as a study of antecedent and consequent, both in the past and in the future. The form of this scheme was a gradual development, and has proven so far to be much the best form for rational presentation of the accumulated facts that we have ever seen. In fact, we cannot over-emphasize the value that accrues both to the studied individual and to the observer from this type of studious representation of the case. By this method of selecting apparent causative factors we can keep ourselves freest from the tendency unscientifically to attribute everything to a single cause, and from otherwise drawing unsafe conclusions. The only rational way to proceed is to investigate all probable sources and then fairly and squarely to set the facts down in relationship one to the other. As Devon says, " Mere discovery

to a numerical scale. For instance, Rossolimo (**278**) has a scheme for indicating the comparative strength of psychic processes on a decimal scale — the unit being the highest known manifestations. In the Trait Book of Davenport (**277**) we find it recommended to assign grades to mental qualities on a scale of five units, in which one and five (the lowest and highest grades) are assigned to the best or the worst found in study of 1000 cases of the whole population; the grades two and four, distinctly above or below the ordinary, are for results obtained on the average in one out of 50 cases. Grade three is for the *ordinary*. Van Dijck (**168**) in his psychobiographical studies of criminals uses a system of plus and minus signs. Woods (**279**) in researches into the personal characteristics of royalty proceeds on a basis of ten points for each quality. Other minor studies known to us have the same basis. We would counsel in our field extreme caution in the use of this method, at least for a long time to come, until there has been established a very much greater body of information on norms, even of special classes of persons, than has yet been gathered.

of facts means nothing unless they are shown to have causal connection with delinquency."

Nothing should make all these points clearer than the careful perusal of actual summaries of cases. We append herewith some examples for this purpose.

Mrs. A. C.   No. 000.   March 3, 1905.
    Age 35.
    Physically in very good general condition. Strong and vivacious. Good color. Seven months pregnant.
    Mentally: psychosis — for details see psychological impressions.
    Delinquencies: misrepresentation; swindling; neglecting family.
    Causative factors: (*a*) heredity. Comes from a family notorious for alcoholism and general bad behavior, but no insanity known. (*b*) puerperal conditions. We have the account of a prior attack of mental excitation at about the time of the birth of another child; (*c*) alcoholism, as indulged in during the last few months.
    The *outlook* for this case is temporarily poor, but perhaps good in the long run, since she now shows characteristics quite changed from those of her normal self. She should be immediately taken care of in some hospital and without the excitement of a trial for insanity. We referred her to the Mental Hygiene Society. The welfare of the unborn child is to be thought of as well as of the mother's own well-being.

John Doe. Age 16.   No. 111.   Sept. 26, 1908.
    Physically: very good general condition. Strong, active boy, slouchy type. Sex development, adult.
    Mentally, high-grade feebleminded — Moron.
    Delinquencies consist in earlier truancy — was once in institution on account of this; general mean behavior earlier at home; recent vicious sex assault upon a boy.
    Causative factors: (*a*) mentality as above. The boy has been in an institution for the feebleminded for a couple of years; (*b*) lack of family control. The father was rather an irresponsible character and the family has broken up; (*c*) proportionate sex over-development and (*d*) alcohol. Up to the day of the assault this boy had been doing quite well at work, but he was given whiskey to drink and the offense quickly followed. (The causation of the mental defect was never satisfactorily obtained. The father was previously a drinking man, but now holds a good position. The mother is long since dead. She was said to have had some education.)
    The *outlook* is altogether bad in a community where he can get alcohol. He might do well on a farm where he was free from temptation to drink. He has succeeded industrially since leaving the school for the feebleminded over a year ago. Under the circumstances he should be returned.

Adele B.   Age 15.   No. 222.   March 8, 1907.

This girl is magnificently endowed *physically*. She is strong and well and has a considerable measure of good looks. She had an early puberty and is much over-developed in sex characteristics for her age. We note a rather mask-like expression, typical of some prostitutes.

Mentally, this girl has distinctly good ability and has a very good range of interests. She belongs in our B class. Is rather a suggestible type. Considering her advantages she has read many good books. She has a distinctly refined attitude towards her delinquencies, as shown in her manner of relating them.

Delinquencies: excessive sex immorality since she was ten years old. She has already been once in a reformatory school.

Causative factors: (*a*) heredity. Father alcoholic. Mother immoral. Maternal uncle criminalistic; (*b*) mother's influence. She has been flagrantly immoral herself and has made light of this girl's transgressions, if she has not deliberately urged them; (*c*) early maturity and magnificent physique.

Prognosis: notwithstanding this girl's bad background in heredity and environmental conditions, she shows certain qualities which speak in favor of her reformation. Her good mental ability and good interests, and her refined behavior are encouraging. Her physical over-development at present rather speaks against her chances, but she may develop self-control. Her suggestibility may be used to her advantage. This is a case in which better environment under good personal influences may produce an entirely different result from that of the past. She is probably worth doing much for.

Mary Doe.   Age 18.   No. 333.   Sept. 26, 1911.

Physical: Very well developed and nourished. Pleasant features and expression. No sensory defects of importance. Examination otherwise negative.

Mental: Notwithstanding the fact that this girl never got beyond third grade, we find her to have quite fair mental ability. We were astonished to see her good performance on some tests. She has good mental control and is well oriented in all ways. She has much motor dexterity. Not the slightest evidence of aberrancy found, although her relatives say she must be crazy to do what she has done. Mental diagnosis; good ability with exceedingly poor educational advantages.

Delinquencies: Repeated stealing over a considerable period in department stores where she has been employed. At one time she was stealing by a system which she had evolved.

Causative factors: (*a*) heredity. Parents are dead, but from other relatives we gain nothing but negative evidence. The whole family have good reputation; (*b*) developmental history. This, except for ordinary children's ailments, is negative; (*c*) environmental conditions during childhood were not especially good on account of poverty which in turn was caused by much illness in the family. However, we do not know this has direct bearing; (*d*) much more important is the fact that the girl had exceedingly poor educational advantages on account of frequent changes of abode and being kept at home on account of family illness; from this has come (*e*) a dearth of healthy mental interests. The girl is a great reader, but only of the cheapest literature and the sensational daily newspapers; (*f*) probably the most important factor is due to mental conflict over sex affairs. She has had no guiding hand and ever since her childhood has been hearing of these things from bad sources. Many of her occupational acquaintances tell her of the easy money they make in these ways and are able to indulge in dress and pleasures which are beyond her. Apparently she has always rejected the advances which had naturally come to her as an attractive girl among immoral associates, but has thought much about it. (Note her own story.) As a definite reaction to this, she has got to stealing; (*g*) bad companions.

The *outlook* we should consider distinctly good under different environmental conditions and if some good woman will give her a helping hand. The mental mechanism back of her misconduct has been frequently observed by us and the best of results have been obtained when constructive measures have been offered under probation. Change of occupation, friendship with some woman competent to become her confidant, adviser and helper, and development of healthy mental interests we feel sure will do what is needed.

CHAPTER VIII

STATISTICS [1]

§ 88. **The Basis of Valuable Statistics.** — By far the most important statistics of causation, indeed almost the only ones worth deep consideration, are those gathered from well-rounded study, enumeration, and analysis of the factors which stand in direct logical relationship to delinquency in the individual. One might easily pick out all sorts of isolated facts, for example, defective eyesight, or low family wages, and show them to have certain correlations with delinquency. However, even if the correlations show higher than for non-delinquents, their significance is not in the least proven without the establishment of

---

[1] A pertinent inquiry, partially answered above, would be, why in a text book there is so little space given to statistics from other sources. Putting aside the question of the comparison of foreign statistics with American conditions, we may say that nowhere could be found, except on special points, what was needed for the elucidation of our problem, namely, that of gaining understanding of the individual. Perhaps Gruhle (**147**) comes the nearest, but this author stops far short of putting together all that might have been known about the small group he studied. We insist again that statistics on isolated facts are, in general, unsafe for us. Many case histories scattered in recent German literature contain just the type of information we ourselves have gathered, but except in dealing with certain small classes no figures for groups have been discovered. The clearing of the ground by the statistics gained from just such work as that of Goring (**160**), which throws a great light on some single vital point, is most important.

norms for the social groups from which the delinquent came, particularly if, when it comes to facing actual cases, other factors are found which stand in vastly more direct relationship to the delinquency. The offender with bad eyesight, from a family of poor earners, may be the victim of obsessional mental imagery, or of character-destroying habits, or mental defects — any one of which conditions is known to produce delinquent tendencies with or without bad eyesight and poverty. Then, on the contrary, plenty of individuals from poorly-paid families or with bad eyesight have not at all turned towards delinquency. Thus the only efficient method of gathering highly valuable statistics of delinquent causation is to proceed by scheduling evaluated facts as they are discerned through study of the individual offender.

The enumerative results offered in this chapter have nearly all been produced according to the criticism of values offered above. Our first gathering of statistics, three or four years ago, by the accumulation of isolated facts, in the manner of the prevailing methods of criminology, led to nothing serviceable for a scientific and practical study of delinquency, such as was our aim. The lesson learned from this attempt was that we ought not to proceed along any such scientifically dangerous path. The critique of methods used in working up the individual case for diagnosis and prognosis is fundamental for the production of essentially valuable statistics. Since our early abortive attempt, we have entirely enumerated the factors by first setting them in rough chronological order, as they apparently produced the career of the offender, afterwards estimating them as far as possible in their relative importance. A survey of the method is to be obtained by study of the case summaries (§ 87) and the card system of causative factors. We regard the establishment of these modes of procedure as one of our best contributions.

§ 89. **Characteristics of Our Group of Cases.** — Our figures are based on the study of 1000 repeated offenders (Group I) seen during the years 1909 to 1914. We early conceived the value of dealing for all enumerative purposes with a homogeneous group. The phenomenon of recidivism appeared so striking that it was used as the criterion for selection of the series of cases. Judgment as to recidivism was based on the grounds already given in the Introduction. Many facts might be tabulated for the whole 1000, and some of these are elaborated in the succeed-

127

ing tables, but careful after-criticism has led to the judgment
that 823 cases only (Group II), are to be regarded as studied
sufficiently well by the completer methods we have insisted on,
to be used for satisfactory comparison of causative factors. Then
in our special study of heredity, for reasons given below (§ 116),
there was further selection of 668 cases (Group III).

For the most part the values of the facts speak for themselves.
Taken as a whole, the chief importance of the comparative statistics of causative factors undoubtedly lies in their urgent call
for just the type of study upon which the statistics themselves
were built. The number of cases is too small from which to
draw many statistical conclusions. To be sure, the changes
might be rung on various groups of facts, many of which we have
not even introduced, but to no more purpose than when the same
type of work has been done in other quarters. Some few tables,
such as the age-weight charts, are significant, but we are ever
inclined to caution about the specific application of even major
findings to the individual case, unless they are in the given instance shown to be probable causative influences. Interesting
though it is, for example, to note the physical over-development
of girl offenders, one must logically hesitate to give excess of
physique as a factor unless there is good reason to consider it
as a causal antecedent in the actual instance. Tables showing high
correlations between offense and antecedent merely indicate the
direction in which to look for causes; they do not prove the
existence of any cause in any case.

Early in this volume we dwelt on our choice of ages for study.
Our observations cover offenders from 6 years, at which age
we have noted several cases of strongly developed delinquent
tendencies, to adult life. We have purposely busied ourselves
with only a few above 20 years; there are, of course, comparatively few recidivists under 10; so our total material clusters
well about the average age, which is $15\frac{1}{2}$ years.

The proportion of sexes studied by us is about the ratio of
juvenile offenders as they come before a cosmopolitan court.
It represents no selection by us; we have always taken cases
as they have been brought.

Indeed, our material for enumeration has not been selected by
us in any way except on the basis of backsliding. The choice
by others who bring cases to us involves simply the fact of the
offender being a " problem case," the solution of which by the

ordinary methods of family treatment or court decree was not readily to be discerned.   (Non-repeaters have been seen by us, but they have been studied much less thoroughly, and have never been placed in our series, except when later they may have become recidivists.)   Selection of " problem cases " for us has involved, without question, our seeing a somewhat unduly large number of cases of mental abnormality.   However, even such cases hardly present the difficult problems which other more normally minded individuals sometimes offer, and this fact has made somewhat for the balancing of our material.   Taking it altogether, notwithstanding years of experience with our large material, I hesitate even to suggest exact figures on percentages of types which come before juvenile or other courts.[1]

§ 90.   **Interpretation of Statistical Findings.** — For the interpretation of many general statistics, local conditions of economic welfare, nationality, police regulation, truancy, consumption of alcohol and so on, should be taken into account.   My observations would lead me to believe, for instance, that vastly more delinquency could be attributed to poverty in London than in Chicago, that far slighter offenses lead to police interference in New England than in the West, that truancy is rare in certain German cities, and so on.   A word about our not finding poverty to be a very large causative factor is here in order.   Local conditions of relative financial welfare in Chicago constitute part of the explanation — in clinical and court experience here one rarely indeed sees the physical evidences of poverty which simply abound in some European cities.   Then, on the other hand, in contravention of the first impulse to attribute much to poverty, one finds either other members of the same poor family

---

[1] Here it is of interest to compare certain findings and statements of Goddard (**151**) and his helpers, drawn from the observation of small groups in courts by the Binet system.   Since we have largely avoided first offenders, and undoubtedly have seen most of the easily discernible mental defectives appearing in court during our connection with it, our results are certainly not to be taken as fair indications of total percentages, and yet they range lower than Goddard's estimation.   (A very careful research on large numbers by Dr. Augusta Bronner, that has been going on for some time, is showing nothing like the large numbers of defectives that have been alleged to appear in juvenile courts.)   Observation of a very large unselected group of offenders, such as Britton (*vide* Churchill and Britton, **150**) made in his study of physical conditions, is absolutely the only logical basis of percentages, and even then the figures may only prove true for the given locality.   In this connection, again, I should urge the weakness of isolated facts, even though so apparently valuable as those obtained by the Binet tests.   For more on this point of judgment by mental tests alone, note our chapter on Mental Defect.

living righteously, or that the poverty itself arose from an anterior factor, such as alcoholism or mental defect, which often is the progenitor of both poverty and delinquency.

As being of greatest importance, we shall first present our enumeration of causative factors, — under their general heads, and then as analyzed in detail.[1] The latter will include the findings concerning the equipment of offenders, both mental and physical. Then will come the table of offenses, and finally statistics and charts of facts which have significance for students of criminology in general. The latter are given for what they are worth; some of them point one way and some another. Certain of the special findings, for instance, those on heredity, deserve to carry great weight.

It will be seen in our studies of types of causation that we fully recognize the fact that certain important factors in the production of delinquency, such as mental habit, imagery, etc., are hardly at all open to enumeration. *Statistics will never tell the whole story.*

§ 91. Group II. Summary of Causative Factors by Groups and Totals in 823 Cases — 560 Males, 263 Females.

Groups of Causative Factors.	Number of times appeared to be main factor.	Number of times appeared to be minor factor.	Total number of times appeared as factor.
Mental abnormalities and peculiarities	455	135	590
Defective home conditions, including alcoholism	162	394	556
Mental conflict (*vide infra*)	58	15	73
Improper sex experiences and habits	46	146	192
Bad companions	44	235	279
Abnormal physical conditions, including excessive development .	40	233	273
Defects of heredity		502	502
Defective or unsatisfied interests, including misuse or nonuse of special abilities	16	93	109
Defective early developmental conditions		214	214

[1] For most of the work in arraying and enumerating our collected facts and summaries of findings, we are deeply indebted to Miss Frances Porter, who has with much intelligence and painstaking effort carried out a prolonged task.

Mental shock		3	3
Deliberate choice	1		1
Sold by parent	1		1
Use of stimulants or narcotics . . .		92	92
Experiences under legal detention .		15	15
Educational defects extreme . . .		20	20
	823	2097	2920

Reference to the tables of analyzed groups of factors will be necessary before complete understanding of the above summary can be obtained. However, the numerical proportions of the various groups, even in their bareness, are of great interest.

There is undoubtedly some unfairness about the relativity of the times mental conflict appears as a cause. During our first two years we were not nearly so alive to the discovery of this factor because, although we early listed it as a factor, we desired longer observation of typical cases before feeling justified in spending the long time in study that most cases of the kind demand. To a less degree this same criticism could be made against the number of times we discovered the influence of bad sex experiences and habits; occasionally these facts are carefully hidden, but, after all, not so often as one would suspect.

The totals of analyzed minor factors will not agree with the group totals of minor factors, because under one group head several registerable conditions may be factors and yet are only counted once. For example, under home conditions in a single case we may have alcoholism, poverty and marked lack of parental control; these are enumerated separately under the head of analyzed home conditions, but in the summary appear registered altogether as simply one case where home conditions were defective.

§ 92. Group II. Analysis of Mental Abnormalities and Peculiar Mental Characteristics.

	Number of times appears as a major factor.	Number of times appears as a minor factor.
Defective types:		
Poor native mental ability	6	5
Mental subnormality	66	2
Feeblemindedness — moron	87	

131

Feeblemindedness — imbecile   5

Dull, perhaps from ascertained physical causes,
  including some cases of epilepsy 28   5

Specialized defects, including defect in self-
  control 16   8

Aberrational types:

Epileptic mentality — variable 60   3

Hysteria — with well-marked mental manifestations 12   2

Psychoses:

Paranoia   4

Dementia precox   6

Juvenile paresis   1

Manic depressive insanity   2

Confusional excitement during pregnancy . .   1

Major psychoses not further classified by us   . 34

Minor psychoses not further classified by us
  — this includes some cases of so-called menstrual psychosis 17   **1**

Adolescent or pubertal, temporary psychoses .   4

Choreic psychoses   2

Traumatic psychoses   3

Hypomania; constitutional excitement . . .   2

Amnesic fugues   1

Temporary psychoses   3

Peculiar mental characteristics:

Adolescent instability, marked cases 30   61

Social suggestibility extreme   9   6

Love of adventure extreme   5   5

Marked sensual type   6   10

Constitutional inferiority, including marked neurasthenic and psychopathic types 20   2

Extreme stubborn, reckless, self-assertive type .   3   3

Marked criminalistic impulses on unanalyzed
  mental basis 12

Extreme laziness, in spite of very good physical
  and mental endowment   1

Hypersensitiveness   2   1

High mental ability — only in connection with
  unsatisfied interests   3   2

Obsessed by mental imagery   1   5

Racial characteristics extreme, negro, Indian,
  or both   3   5
                                        ———
                                        455

Definitions of the terms used above in enumerating defective
types will be found best in the chapter on case studies of Mental

Defect. A considerable number of the psychosis cases could not be finally diagnosed in the time at our disposal; indeed, later inquiry at the hospitals for the insane to which some of the offenders had been sent often brought forth only a tentative statement. (For the non-professional reader we should state that many cases of insanity have to go through a considerable period of evolution before they can be ultimately classified according to categories at present available.) Mental confusion, hebetude, delusions, or other break-down of function forced the recognition of a psychosis; the giving of a name would have added nothing explanatory, and scientifically was most often inadmissible. Cases of insanity with very well marked symptoms very evidently are recognized and handled as such before they get into court primarily as offenders. Many of those seen by us may be said to have had comparatively masked characteristics. So far as recounting symptoms may be concerned, we have found mostly weakened functions with slowness, confusion, and inaccuracy of mental reactions. Delusional states are less frequent, as are also the excited conditions. To obtain correct ideas of the correlation of different types of insanity with delinquencies, the records of the population of penal institutions, of general hospitals for the insane, as well as for the criminal insane, would have to be studied for this purpose.

For our definitions and the significance of the various minor psychoses and peculiar mental characteristics, reference should be made to our case studies. The nature of the work has led to our seeing an unusually large number of not only border-line, but also of temporary, pubertal or adolescent and other minor psychoses. We get also major psychoses in their earlier evolution, when the outcome is not determinable. No doubt a certain few of those classified above as minor psychoses will develop into full-fledged cases of insanity — at least such has been our experience in the past. The figures in the above analysis of mental causative factors do not agree with certain totals given in our psychological classification, *vide* § 103, because of the fleeting or minor nature of some psychotic manifestations. This has led sometimes to our classification of the subject as belonging to another mental category than that of being a victim of psychosis.

§ 93. Group II. **Analysis of Defective Home Conditions.**

	Major.	Minor.
Quarreling and other irritative conditions	26	78
Members of family at home alcoholic, immoral, or criminalistic	62	95
Poverty	4	59
Lack of home control through		
gross ignorance	2	10
illness	2	26
father away much		6
mother working out	21	32
sheer inability of parents to control	11	68
family not immigrated		3
Parental neglect excessive	7	31
Family broken up	20	35
No home, plus		
street life		1
wandering life		4
child changed about in institutions and boarding places	2	17
Immoral home environment	5	23
	162	

§ 94. Group II. **Analysis of Mental Conflicts.**

	Major.	Minor.
About sex matters	43	12
About parentage	7	2
Cause unknown	4	
About home conditions		2
Cause unknown, but extreme development of anti-social grudge	4	3
About superstitious folk-lore belief		1
About social significance of own physical defects		1
	58	

§ 95. Group II. **Analysis of Improper Sex Experiences.**

	Major.	Minor.
Extremely early improper learning or experiencing sex life	34	73
Masturbation in excess	12	75
Sex perversions (regarded as antecedent to other offense; elsewhere themselves registered as offense)		11
Sex attraction by negro men		1
	46	

§ 96. Group II. Bad Companions.

No analysis is needed of the figures under the heading of bad companions. It is obvious that bad companionship may have been sometimes within the family circle, but most often elsewhere. Sometimes bad companions were of about the same age, and of the same sex, and sometimes the reverse.

§ 97. Group II. Analysis of Abnormal Physical Conditions.

	Major.	Minor.
General excessive over-development for age	4	33
Marked over-development of sex characteristics for age	5	18
Puberty markedly premature	9	53
Excessively poor general development	7	42
Very poor nutrition	3	24
Puberty much delayed		8
General poor physical condition	5	23
Anemia	5	7
Heart disease	1	6
Excessive enlargement of thyroid	1	2
Diseases or defects in nose and throat	10	41
Excessively carious teeth	3	19
Marked defective vision	13	72
Marked defective hearing	1	13
Phimosis	5	5
Local irritative conditions of genitals	1	5
Venereal disease		1
Pregnancy		1
Ptosis		1
Defective control of bladder		3
Deaf-mutism	1	1
Stammering in excess	2	4
Headaches in excess	3	11
General nervous manifestations (neurotic types)	2	15
Gynecological ailment		1
Chorea		3
Epilepsy		1
Ring worm		1
Tuberculosis		2
Recent injury		1
Migraine		1
Boyish type of physique in girl		1

It is only when physical conditions have appeared themselves directly as causes, irrespective of mental conditions, that we have

135

included them in the above enumeration. For example, epilepsy was a factor in the delinquency of one individual who did not have any accompanying mental symptoms, and thus it is counted as a physical cause. Then ring worm caused the rejection of a boy from school and his consequent life with bad street companions. Of course, in many more cases than given above, carious teeth were found, but only in the 22 instances could the condition be counted in any way related to the delinquency. It is the same with defective vision, and other conditions. The number of instances in which phimosis was a factor will to some appear very small, but it is as we have found it with very careful observation. Venereal disease is very common among the young women we have seen, but in itself could only be regarded as a causative factor in one case. Pregnancy once was a factor when there was an accompanying minor psychosis. Possession of a boyish type of physique was an incentive in one case to the girl pursuing a life of adventure, suitably attired as a boy.

In this group the total of even the major causative factors does not agree with the total given in the summary (§ 91); an offender whose physical conditions may be regarded as responsible for his career is most often suffering from more than one defective condition.

§ 98. Group II. Analysis of Defective and Unsatisfied Interests.

	Major.	Minor.
Lack of general healthy mental interests	9	53
Lack of healthy recreational interests		7
School or vocational dissatisfaction	6	24
Dissatisfaction with racial religion	1	
Excessive interest in moving picture shows		9
Social life of saloons		1
Exciting literature		2
Excitement of revival meeting		1
Excessive interest in theatres		1
	16	

I have no doubt that our findings set forth in the above group will arouse criticism. One would certainly believe off-hand that the influence of low types of picture shows, theatres, of bad newspapers and other pernicious literature could be much more surely traced than is shown in our figures. One cannot doubt that they really do have much more influence than our figures would indicate, but it is altogether a difficult matter to make any kind of a trustworthy estimation of such subtle factors. One feels that frequently the matter is better stated by saying that there is a lack of healthy interests, and that these other things have come in to fill up the vacuum. Upon this whole subject it is easy to offer impressionistic conclusions, but specific data and proofs are hard to get. A very interesting point is in regard to saloon influences, for it is quite evident that the social life of saloons, which has been made so much of, does not begin to get in its work until after 17 or 18 years of age. If we had not been so scrupulously careful in regard to the individual facts of influence, much greater emphasis would be placed on both the negative and positive factors listed numerically. For instance, if one were to judge by the findings on our Information Test, one would say there was overwhelming evidence of the paucity of healthy mental interests being a large general factor. On this point, our chapter and case studies where lack of healthy mental interests is set forth as a cause of delinquency, should be read.

§ 99.　Group II.　Analysis of Defective Early Developmental Conditions.

	Major	Minor
Antenatal:		
Congenital syphilis		26
Mother sickly or poor condition		34
Mother severely ill		6
Mother much worried		16
Mother much abused, generally by drunken husband		31
Mother alcoholic		6
Mother morphinist		2
Mother old		4
Father old		1
Attempted abortion		4
Mother insane		1
Severe mental shock to mother		3
One of twins		3
Mother destitute		8
Mother working very hard		4
Natal:		
Markedly premature birth		5
Very difficult labor		18
Postnatal:		
Much illness in general		28
Very severe early illness		18
Epilepsy in childhood		9

137

Severe convulsions in childhood	15
Severe head injury	21
Early malnutrition severe	6
Impacted teeth, very severe	2
Severe accident	1
Severe rheumatism	1
Mastoid infection severe	3
Gonorrhea severe	1
Early paralysis	4
Severe "brain fever"	5
Severe "meningitis"	5
Severe chorea	7

As in the case of defective heredity, so here the factor never appears as major, because the more immediate cause is the condition or peculiarity of mind or body that defective hereditary or defective developmental factors leave in their train. The diagnosis of congenital syphilis was usually made from somatic findings. The laboratory tests have only recently been at our disposal. There is little doubt that a somewhat larger number would have proved positive to tests.

§ 100. Group II. Analysis of Mental Shock.

	Major	Minor
Fright in riot and massacre		2
From killing companion accidentally		1

§ 101. Group II. Analysis of Stimulants and Narcotics.

	Major	Minor
Alcohol		22
Excessive tea or coffee		43
Tobacco in excess		60

§ 102. Group II. Experiences under Legal Detention.

In most cases where experiences under legal detention have been a readily ascertained cause of delinquency, we have been sorely tempted on account of the virulence of the cause to ascribe to it the major part. If it were not that chronologically some other cause had antedated the first offense one would feel justified in doing this. Altogether we must acknowledge that our separation into major and minor factors of delinquent careers breaks down at this point. However, we are unquestionably far under-shooting the mark in our slight ascribing of crime to this cause. For the varied details of what we mean by experiences under legal detention our case studies on this subject should be read.

(From this point we deal with enumerations concerning our series of 1000 young repeated offenders, setting forth facts which stand by themselves, irrespective of whether or not they have relationship to ascertained causation.)

§ 103. **Group I. Statistics of Psychological Classification of 1000 Young Repeated Offenders.**

A. Considerably above ordinary in ability and information, — the latter estimated with reference to age and social advantages   31
B. Ordinary in ability and information, — the latter estimated with reference to age and social advantages . . .   267
C. Native ability fair and formal educational advantages fair or good, but very poorly informed   69
D. Native ability fair and formal educational advantages fair or good   69
E. Native ability distinctly good, but formal educational advantages poor   22
F. Native ability fair and formal educational advantages poor   123
G. Native ability poor and formal educational advantages poor   40
H. Native ability poor and formal educational advantages good or fair   53
I. Dull, perhaps from ascertained physical causes, including some cases of epilepsy   79
J. Subnormal mentality — considerable more educability than the feebleminded   81
K. Moron   89
L. Imbecile   8
M. Psychosis   69

                                                                            ———
                                                                            1000

Some explanation of the above classification has been given in the chapter on Methods. In our numerical studies of these 1000 cases, percentages are obvious. Since the classification necessarily, for practical purposes, has to have a place both for the categories of mental ability and of aberration, there is some overlapping which is not shown in the table. For instance, a choreic, or epileptic, or dissipated individual may be well up to the ordinary in ability and still have shown temporary aberrational tendencies which led to delinquency. If the psychotic manifestations were past at the time we studied him, our logical classification was according to demonstrated ability — although so far as causation was concerned we carefully reckoned in the aberration. Then in other instances there may be, as a continuous condition, a slight

139

aberrational tendency superimposed on quite fair ability. Such a case might be classified, for example, as D plus M. As is also well known, a feebleminded person may be insane; thus we get K plus M. Our clue to classification, as given in the above table, has been the most predominant mental classification of the individual. We may call attention to this table, with its overlapping of facts in the sphere of mental attributes, as showing another example of the danger of inferring causative factors from the bare isolated facts of a set classification.

It will be noted that, leaving out all the cases with any appearance of doubt, and all cases where we observed the subject in a temporarily dull or aberrational condition, we found 67.4 per cent. that should be regarded without question as mentally normal. Of the 7.9 per cent. dull from physical causes, we have found some making extraordinary improvement with the cessation of bad habits or rectification of bodily ailments. Others for whom nothing was done or could be done, eventually may be graded lower. In the course of years, changes, either up or down, in the classification of some of the subnormals also may well be made. As beyond peradventure feebleminded, we found about 10 per cent., but the figure will be increased as some of the younger in the lower groups fail to advance with age. The group of psychoses has already shown a number of cases of cures and we may expect more. Further discussion of these cases and classes may be found in our chapters on mental defects and the psychoses.

§ 104.   Group I.   Offenses of 1000 Young Repeated Offenders.

(Not only as charged in court, but as obtained from the story of parents and others.)

(a) Of 694 Male Offenders.

Stealing 455
    Including stealing automobiles, robbing from mail boxes, etc.
Burglary 54
    Means breaking and entering. Ordinary sneaking into stores, or homes, even through a window, is counted merely as stealing.
Pickpocket 11
    Only counted as such when distinctly professional tendencies shown in this line.
Hold-ups 6
    There is much disproportion of this offense before 17 years and afterwards, as shown by comparison with records of courts for adults.

Forging 12
Truancy 225
    Only marked cases. Staying away from school a day or two
    infrequently, not counted.
Loafing 71
    Marked cases of refusal to work while living at home.
Vagrancy 14
    This always means wandering and loafing and not living at
    home.
Runaway 261
    This means going away from home and staying more than over
    night and usually more than once.
Sleeping out at night 85
    This usually means staying in barns or hallways or in vacant
    houses, generally in the neighborhood of the home.
General incorrigibility 92
    This includes quarrelsomeness, excessive disobedience, imperti-
    nence, mischievous conduct, and disturbance of many kinds at
    home and in school. When this type of conduct occurs in a place
    of employment the individual is discharged, and, of course, not
    complained of.
Lying 104
    Only when very excessive and when a notorious characteristic of
    the individual has this been counted.
False accusations 5
    Only recorded when of an excessive and dangerous sort.
Obtaining or attempting to get money under false pretenses . . 11
    Only marked cases, including various schemes of misrepresenta-
    tion. Includes some vicious cases; for instance, "black-hand"
    schemes.
Begging 7
    In Chicago only extreme cases of this kind are brought to court,
    and only when misrepresentation is involved.
Bad temper 21
    Only recorded when excessive manifestations.
Violence 40
    Only when a very marked characteristic. It may be either at-
    tacks on person or property.
Cruelty 11
    Either to children or animals.
Fighting with weapons 42
    Ordinary street fights of boys not included. This category means
    much more serious offenses.
Carrying concealed firearms 11
Destructiveness 21
    Of a malicious type.
Attempt to wreck train 2
Setting fires 11
"Flipping" moving trains 4

141

Desertion from navy   1
Gambling   14
    Only when excessive.
Alcoholism   24
    In our study of young offenders, this complaint of alcoholism gen-
        erally means the use of intoxicating beverages quite beyond
        moderate standards of family life. In many cases it also implies
        intoxication.
Use of cocaine   1
Use of opium   1
    The use of these drugs by young people is regarded as a delin-
        quency, but, of course, only the excessive cases are brought to
        court.
Sex offenses with the opposite sex   33
    In only this number of cases have boys under 17 been reported so
        delinquent. Adults are not usually charged with this offense
        unless there is assault, etc.
Masturbation   32
    Reported as delinquency only when very excessive.
Sex perversion   29
    This includes various sorts of homosexual and other perversions.
Sex assault   15
    This includes a few cases of homosexual assault.
Obscenity   10
    Only counted when excessive characteristic.
Murder   2
    As a rule we have purposely refrained from studying sensational
        murder cases. Murderers generally have careers behind them that
        are best studied at earlier stages.
Accessory to murder   1
Attempted homicide   1
Attempted suicide   4
Exhibitionism   4
    This has been reported as a delinquency only when not done as a
        childish performance. It means a flagrant offense by an older
        individual and in a more public manner.

(b) Of 306 Female Offenders.

Sex offenses with the opposite sex   180
    In many other cases where the charge has been "staying out
        nights" or "runaway" there has been grave suspicion of sex
        delinquency, but not proven.
Masturbation   22
    Regarded as delinquency only in excessive cases.
Sex perversions   9
    Homosexual, etc.
Stealing   97
Obtaining money under false pretenses   5

This includes swindling and begging plus swindling. Begging, as such, rarely brought into court.

Begging 1
Burglary 1
Forging 6
Lying 80
   Only when this is a very notorious characteristic of the individual is this made part of the charge.
False accusations 16
   Only when very serious charges have been brought, elaborated and persisted in.
Runaway 76
Sleeping out nights 33
   This usually means staying out somewhere in the neighborhood, sleeping in barns, hallways or vacant places.
Truancy 23
   Only when a very repeated offense is this counted.
Pretending to be employed 19
   Under this category are the cases where individuals have been living at home, pretending to work in the daytime while really loafing elsewhere.
Bad temper 18
   Only when excessive is this recorded.
Violence 16
   Includes attacks on both person and property.
Incorrigibility 39
   This includes quarrelsomeness, excessive disobedience, impertinence, mischievous conduct, and disturbances of many kinds at home and at school. When this type of conduct occurs in a place of employment, of course the individual is discharged and not complained of.
Attempted homicide 3
Attempted infanticide 1
Attempted suicide 9
Threatened suicide 2
   This only counted when repeated excessively and causing much trouble.
Setting fire 3
Cruelty to children 1
Alcoholism 8
   The mere fact of a girl's indulging regularly in alcohol is regarded as a delinquency, but intoxication is frequently the result in girls.
Smoking 1
   This reported as a delinquency only when excessive. In fact, in this case it was a habit of years' standing.
Obscenity 13
   Only very marked cases reported as a delinquency.
Sex assault 1

In explanation of the above table of delinquencies the following points should be made: Numerical comparison of offenses is of peculiar interest for the study of the beginnings of delinquent careers, hence we have confined our attention to the 1000 young repeated offenders we have all along used as a basis for statistics. Much more extensive statistics could have been compiled from juvenile court records, but it is well known that the short wording of a court charge most frequently does not represent the whole facts of delinquency. In our cases great care has been used to get an account of the offenses in detail, and this has been comparatively easy for us in our direct dealings with parents and others interested in the case.

In comparing the delinquencies of males and females certain differences stand out clearly from the numerical comparisons above. We have attempted for this purpose to have our classes of offenses cover analogous conduct for both sexes. The set categories of the law or of the criminological literature have not been followed. We have attempted to go farther than this and get the direct first-hand facts and to present them without attention to set terminology.

It is most interesting to note the differences in the charges of offense for the two sexes, either as set forth in court, or as a general social consideration. The attitude of society varies mostly in offenses against the person. Seduction of a boy by a female is never charged in court. Exhibitionism by girls is a very frequent phenomenon, but no charge of that nature has been observed. Smoking is regarded as vastly more of a delinquency in girls than it is in boys. This is also true of staying out late at night, or away from home. Staying out late nights is a common charge for both sexes, but without other delinquencies it is hardly to be regarded as an offense. It is practically never charged as a sole delinquency. Standards in different families in regard to such things as a child staying away from home over night, or in regard to drinking vary greatly.

§ 105. Group I. Statistics of Weight Correlated with Age.

For the interpretation of physical conditions as the cause of delinquency in any given case, we all along insist on the close scrutiny of them as related to other possible causes. Discovery of the poor nutrition or defective eyesight of an offender does not mean

GIRLS — MENTALLY NORMAL

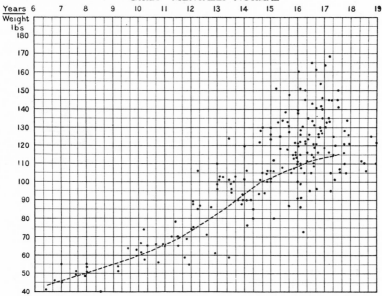

GIRLS - MENTALLY ABNORMAL

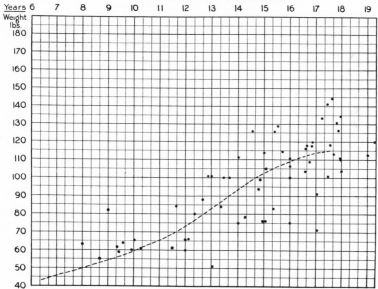

PLATE VII

AGE-WEIGHT CHARTS

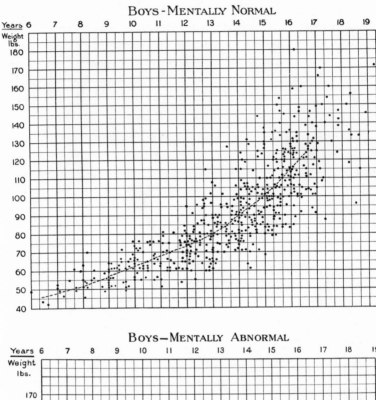

BOYS-MENTALLY NORMAL

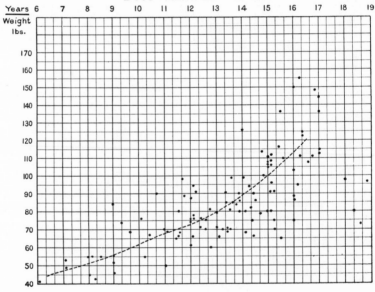

BOYS—MENTALLY ABNORMAL

PLATE VIII

AGE-WEIGHT CHARTS

that either of these faulty conditions should necessarily be regarded as the responsible factor. But in massing the collected facts, conclusions of great interest emerge. For many summed-up details there is no fair norm to compare with; for example, we cannot compare our findings on defective eyesight with any standard for the general population, but in the case of development or nutrition as judged by weight and age we have as fair a chance to compare massed facts with a standard norm as can be obtained.

We would immediately insist that both our findings and the norms are to be interpreted only for the United States — one can be very sure from observations abroad that the same findings would not obtain there. Then the interpretation of under-size should properly include knowledge of how many families and nationalities normally under the average in size are represented. To a less degree this might be true of over-size, if the accompanying charts did not show clearly the immense sex difference, even when the normal curve is plotted for the sexes separately.

The discrepancy between the physique of boy and girl offenders is remarkable — that between the mentally normal and abnormal is to be expected. The difference between the sexes can perhaps best be appreciated by realizing that on the charts for the mentally normal almost exactly 50 per cent. of the boys are on each side of the curve of averages, while no less than 73 per cent. of the girls range in weight above normal. The meaning of over-development in studies of delinquent causation is discussed in §§ 142, 188 ff.

The charts easily explain themselves. The curve of norms has been taken from Burk's (189) study of massed data concerning 69,000 American young people. The averages made from this largest group study of growth seems unquestionably the best with which to compare our offenders. We could have obtained a great many more age-weight records of delinquents to plot on our charts, but decided to confine ourselves to our own homogeneous and carefully studied series. Norms have been developed only up to 16 or 17 years, so there was no use plotting cases above that age.

§ 106. Group I. Statistics of "Stigmata of Degeneracy."

Well-marked stigmata were found in 133 of the 1000 cases as follows:

Anomalies of external ear	67
Anomalies of palate and jaws	63
Anomalies of shape of head. (Including facial asymmetry)	55
Anomalies of teeth	5
Body asymmetry	5
Anomalies of eye	4
Gynecomastia	2
Anomalies of hands	2
Supernumerary mammae	1

Defects of teeth usually ascribed to congenital syphilis were found in 40 cases. Most of these were typical Hutchinsonian forms. Minor defects of enamel, small " erosions " of undoubted congenital origin, are not counted in the above.

It should be distinctly understood that those structural anomalies which, it has well been said, could be found by careful examination on almost every human body, have altogether been left out of count. The stigmata recorded were decidedly obvious to an experienced medical examiner. In illustration we note that the following are the types of defect given in our records: Ear anomalies were; completely adherent lobule, crumpled helix, excessive Darwinian tubercle, flattened — relatively formless ear, and other marked malformations. The dental anomalies were supernumerary teeth, completely absent teeth, etc. Misplacement that was due to crowding is not enumerated. (Of course, an expert student of dental development would have discovered much that we missed in the way of minor data.) Chest and body asymmetry was not counted unless it appeared to be due to congenital malformation — spinal curvatures and the many sequelae of rickets are not stigmata. Anomaly of the hands means hypertrophy of a digit, and the like.

The writer offers the above facts without comment, except to state that if the cases of mental abnormality were taken out of our series, the proportion of marked stigmata would be little, if any, larger than in the general population.[1]

---

[1] We are fully cognizant of the possibilities of a prolonged discussion at this point, but we can see no good coming out of it. The fact that Knecht (**164**) found 20 per cent. of 1274 German criminals with malformed ears, and that 5 per cent. had cleft palate, and that 14 per cent. of the European prostitutes

§ 107. Group I. **Epilepsy Among 1000 Repeated Offenders.**

The diagnosis of epilepsy was made on the finding that the offender suffered from convulsions with loss of consciousness and other well-recognized accompaniments of the seizures, or from the characteristic phenomena of *petit mal*. No subdivision according to the newer conceptions of epilepsy was attempted, but the possibility of hysteria was frequently taken into consideration. Convulsions in early childhood were not counted as epileptic unless there was good positive evidence. Following the above rules we found.

Epilepsy . . . . 67 cases.
Possible epilepsy — in these cases there were evidences
strongly suggestive of major or minor epilepsy, but on account of incomplete history the diagnosis could not be
made with certainty . . . . 18 cases.

Then in the immediate families, including grandparents, uncles and aunts (blood relatives), we learned of epilepsy in:

29 cases where the offender was epileptic.
53 cases where the offender was not known to be epileptic.

Not all the cases of epilepsy are ranged under the head of aberrational types — in some of them the disease appeared to be merely incidental to their otherwise determined mental and moral life.

examined by Tarnowsky (**165**) had cleft palate, whereas we found not a single case of cleft palate among our repeaters; the fact that Talbot (**166, 167**) found stigmata twice as frequent among the inmates of Pontiac and Elmira as among non-criminals — all this simply leads us back to the point we made in our chapter on Orientation, namely, that all these physical signs may possibly better be correlated with mental defect and also with nutritional and even environmental conditions than with criminalism, as such. The definition of degeneracy as an embryonic nutritional defect is sufficient to clear the theoretical ground for these latter-day considerations.

§ 108. Group I. **Numerical Family Table in 1000 Cases of Repeated Delinquency.**

No. of living children in family	Only one de-linquent	Two delin-quents	Three delin-quents	Four delin-quents	Five delin-quents	Six delin-quents	Charac-ter of others unknown
	No. of instances	No. of instances	No. of instances	No. of instances	No. of instances	No. of instances	No. of instances
1	119	. .	. .	. .	. .	. .	. .
2	111	26	. .	. .	. .	. .	6
3	117	21	12	. .	. .	. .	12
4	86	24	14	6	. .	. .	12
5	86	22	11	4	4	. .	11
6	46	17	12	3	3	. .	14
7	32	10	5	6	. .	. .	4
8	24	6	8	1	1	. .	6
9	16	5	4	. .	1	1	5
10	5	5	1	1	. .	. .	2
11	2	. .	4	. .	. .	. .	2
12	. .	1	. .	. .	. .	. .	. .
13	. .	. .	. .	. .	. .	. .	1
Family unknown	. .	. .	. .	. .	. .	. .	42
	644	137	71	21	9	1	117

From the above table we see among other points that there were
119 cases in which the delinquent was the only child;
48 cases in which all the children were delinquent in family of more than one.
525 cases in which only one was delinquent in a family of more than one.

The significance of the above figures is great for any who would attribute to family conditions alone the largest share in the causation of delinquency. They must reckon with the fact that in so many cases where there are several children only one has become criminalistic. Then those who draw other conclusions, e. g., that the conditions which surround an only child specially make for delinquency, must take note of our relatively small figures on that correlation. Sometimes, however, conditions peculiar to the family, either environmental or hereditary, must be entirely responsible, as can be seen from the instances when several children, or even all the children are delinquent. It is clear that our statistics do not all point one way, and that they emphasize once more the logical need for well-rounded individual study of cases.

§ 109. Group I. Family Conditions of 1000 Young Repeated Offenders.

One parent (usually father) deserted	86
Parents separated	114
Both parents dead	57
Father dead	87
Mother dead	154
	498

In the above cases there are:

Foster parents or two step-parents in	20 cases.
Step-father or foster father in	105 cases.
Step-mother or foster mother in	109 cases.
In the 1000 cases mother works away from home in	165 cases.

§ 110. Group I. Illegitimacy in 1000 Repeated Offenders.

Parents born in the U. S. (white)	7
Parents born in the U. S. (colored)	5
Parents, one negro, one white	3
Parents, German	5
Parents, Italian	1
Parents, unknown nationality	5
	26

These figures would seem very small as compared with many foreign statistics. Perhaps had we accurately known all the facts (to be obtained with difficulty from some of our shifting population) rather larger figures would have been obtained, but not very much larger.

§ 111. Group I. Birthplace of Offenders.

United States	783	France	2
United States (negro)	27	Sweden	1
Russia (Jewish)	33	Denmark	1
Poland	29	Slavonia	1
Italy	22	Norway	1
Germany	16	Croatia	1
Austria	13	Bulgaria	1
England	12	Galicia	1

149

Roumania	5	Greece	1
Canada { English	5	Switzerland	1
Canada { French	2	Unknown	33
Bohemia	3		
Scotland	3		1000
Ireland	3		

§ 112. Group I. Birthplace of Parents of 1000 Repeated Offenders.

United States	233	Denmark	3
United States (negro)	42	Hungary	2
Poland	109	Slavonia	2
Germany	77	Belgium	1
Italy	59	Wales	1
Ireland	54	Spain	1
Bohemia	28	Croatia	1
Austria	17	Galicia	1
Sweden	16	Bulgaria	1
England	12	Russia (Jewish)	70
Scotland	10	Parents foreign born, but	
France	8	from different countries .	74
Lithuania	8	Mother U. S. and father	
Norway	7	foreign	41
Canada { French	6	Father U. S. and mother	
Canada { English	4	foreign	18
Roumania	5	Unknown	85
Holland	4		
			1000

For fair interpretation of the above statistics of nationality the cosmopolitan character of the people of Chicago must be taken into account, although there are several reasons why the proportions of nationalities or races of offenders as seen by us may not agree with census percentages. In the case of Jews, for instance, we have studied more than a fair proportion because of the splendidly organized Jewish efforts to look after the delinquents as well as the dependents of their own race, and the desire of their workers to have individuals studied and handled with the greatest efficiency. For opposite reasons we should be unlikely to see an equal proportion of certain other races and nationalities.

It would be difficult to present comparable statistics on account of the selective ages of those we have enumerated — the majority being beyond school age but under 21 — but the following figures give some indication of our city conditions: In Chicago the native white population of native-born parents is only about 20 per cent.; the native whites of foreign or mixed parentage number

150

about 41 per cent.; the foreign-born whites are 35 per cent., and the negroes 2 per cent. of the total population. The only court figures available in Chicago are those of the Juvenile Court where 14,183 delinquents (boys under 17, girls under 18) were seen in the ten years, 1899 to 1909. The parentage of these showed in about the following percentages: American whites, 14.5; American negro, 4; Foreign, 69.5; Unknown, 12 (*vide* Breckenridge and Abbot **318**, p. 57).

§ 113. Group 1. **Previous Institutional Life.**

We had thought of stating in detail the figures concerning the previous residence of offenders in institutions, but the information we get from case studies leads us to see definite unfairness in this. We might say, what is the truth, that 18 per cent. of our Chicago male offenders had been in a certain correctional institution, and another percentage had been in some other institution. But picking out such an isolated fact, without analysis of the mentality and the later environmental conditions of these offenders, leads to no safe conclusion as to the efficacy of these institutions. The same point came up when I was asked my opinion about certain narrower statistics; the working up of the after-careers of graduates of Elmira Reformatory. Unless one knows the physical and mental equipment of the individual, and consequently what chance he has to succeed in the world, no fair gauge of the possibilities of reformatory work can be obtained from following his career. What they say at Elmira, might be said of any other good institution which attempts reform: " Give us reformable material, and we can reform." The same might be said concerning the work of probation and parole officials. So we have deliberately left out these statistics, which, without thorough contemplation of the individual handled, mean little indeed.

§ 114. Group I. **Religion.   Education.**

Similar complications and many more would arise if one presented statistics of the religious creeds of offenders. One would have to compare the figures with the local membership in various churches and with a number of other modifying facts. It will suffice to say that the figures would. leave little room anywhere for self-satisfaction or for sectarian controversy. It is quite evident that formal religious training has not prevented delinquency in many of our cases, when other strong personal or environmental

conditions were not, as such, squarely met. Participation in religious education and religious communion has been quite general
among our offenders, but of course the answer given by pastors of
all congregations is that these have had the word, but not caught
the spirit. Occasionally in certain unstable types there is a
tendency to religious emotionalism and anti-social conduct at
the same time. It is curious that in not over a dozen cases have
we heard expressions of formed irreligious opinions. I should
be far from asserting that religious life does not sustain against
the provocations and temptations of alcoholism, poverty, bad
social companionship, or even that it does not offset some bad
effects of certain minor aberrational tendencies, but certain it is
that, through not taking into account these other backgrounds
of delinquency, such religious experience as most of our offenders
have had has not proved thus sustaining. Many a parish would
be bettered if the fundamental sources of misconduct were studied,
enumerated, and treated in a scientific spirit.

Our figures on education are only of negative value. Practically every one of our native born, and most of our foreigners,
has had a chance in our school system. That the school system
has not fitted the needs of every one goes without saying. Some
significant points concerning this are to be gleaned from our
case studies. Otherwise, we may say that illiteracy arising through
lack of opportunity plays no important part in the production
of delinquency as we have seen it in our city population.

§ 115. Group I. **Alcoholism of Parents in 1000 Cases.**

Occasionally intoxicated:
Father 129
Mother 9
Both father and mother 12
Rather frequently intoxicated:
Father 118
Mother 5
Both father and mother 4
Excessive drinking and intoxication:
Father 25
Mother 8
Both father and mother 1
                                                    ———
                                                    311

Distinctly moderate drinking of alcoholic beverages has not
been counted at all in the above figures.

§ 116. Statistics on Heredity.

Our statistical findings on heredity are of especial theoretical and practical interest because they are based on studies which included all ascertainable causal factors in each case. For our main study of the facts,[1] out of our 1000 cases of repeated offenders, 668 only (Group III) were found to have data sufficient to justify the conclusion that we could fairly evaluate the causal factors, having at the same time probable knowledge of whether or not there was a criminalistic tendency in the immediate family. This study was centered on the problem of the direct inheritance of criminalistic tendencies as such. In 271 cases there was good evidence that no prior criminalistic tendency in the family existed. In 245 other cases epilepsy, or some grade of mental defect, was present. (In order to be absolutely fair in this matter, the group of subnormals — see our chapter on Mental Defect for definitions — and those with special mental defects, were enumerated together with the feebleminded and epileptic.) In these cases there was such an obvious mental or physical basis for delinquency that they could be left out of account, whatever their inheritance showed. The remaining 152 cases were neither mentally defective nor epileptic, and did show other criminalistic persons in the direct family.

The positive group of 152 cases would seem undoubtedly large enough to bring out some facts proving the inheritance of criminalistic tendencies as such, if this trait is inheritable. But these facts fail to materialize. The predominating causative factors as obtained from careful individual study in these 152 cases have been scheduled as:

Offender distinctly psychopathic or neuropathic, with heredity
of this type 42
Offender victim of faulty developmental factors with serious
sequelae   3
Cases in which the environment was extremely faulty — similar
to that causing delinquency where there is no criminalistic
heredity. (It is interesting to note that in many of these cases
the faulty environment is undoubtedly the result of defective

---

[1] Dr. Edith R. Spaulding spent several months in collating our data. Her results have been recently published (162). In their dealing with the variety of data obtained from well-rounded individual studies they form one of the most important contributions to this subject.

physical or mental conditions on the part of parents, even
 when there is no proof of defective transmission to the child) . 61
Cases in which there is some inheritance of defect plus very bad
 developmental conditions or faulty environment 17
Cases in which bad environment is combined with faulty developmental factors 2
Cases in which, aside from criminalistic tendencies, there are
 peculiar mental characteristics, not traceable to inheritance . 3
Cases in which the factors are so complicated that they cannot
 be discriminated in value for the individual case; however,
 these are factors of importance outside of criminalistic heredity 9
Cases not included in the above 15

——
152

By elimination this leaves, then, 15 cases in which to search
further for criminalistic inheritance as such. In every one of these,
however, other predominant factors than mere inheritance of
criminalistic impulses could be made out. Peculiar outbursts
of temper, hypersexualism as a prevailing trait, premature
puberty, lack of general mental and moral energy, excess of
energy, and lack of normal mental and moral inhibitions, each
figures as the main cause of delinquency in the individual. Sometimes these traits could be traced in the inheritance and sometimes not. All of them might make for delinquency, and do so
make in other cases, even if there are no other criminals in the
family. Dr. Spaulding in resolving these data for us, calls attention to the fact that at least the last two traits enumerated could,
in a good environment, easily be factors making for genius.

(The proportion of 31 per cent. of alcoholism, noted previously
in our total figures, more than obtains all through this series
of cases with criminalism in the family. In 6 of the last 15 cases
cited there was alcoholism to excess on the part of parents; and
in 86 out of the total 152, that is in 56 per cent., parents were
alcoholics.)

Altogether there seems to be no proof whatever from our extensive material that there is such a thing as criminalistic inheritance apart from some otherwise significant physical or
mental trait, which in the offender and his forbears, forms the
basis of delinquency.[1]

---

[1] In our chapter where we give cases showing heredity as a cause, there
may be found illustrations and enumeration of what is discoverable, outside
the well-known inherited background for many cases of mental disease and
defect.

When it comes to the question of indirect inheritance we have an entirely different statement to make. Our summary of causative factors by groups showed that in 823 cases, Group II, heredity appeared as a minor factor no less than 502 times. This means that while in no case could we feel justified in denominating heredity the immediate and main factor of delinquency, yet in 61 per cent. distinct defects in the family antecedents were noted. (The reader should be reminded that in the normal, non-criminal population a goodly number of family defects might be discovered, but, of course, nothing approaching this large percentage.)

To enumerate in heredity, a matter apart from the above narrower study, the various defects which have been considered as possible factors in the indirect development of delinquency will prove a matter of general interest, although it must be distinctly understood that we refrain entirely from drawing conclusions regarding the specific results of any given defects. It is difficult enough to work out and prove the relationship of inheritance to anything but a specific family physical characteristic, and then only when one family line is studied. But the astonishing extent to which, in general, peculiarities in the ancestors appear in the background of delinquency can be witnessed by the following unresolved statistics. Before passing to these, some critical comment, an urgent minimum, is necessary.

We certainly have nothing like the entire story of defects and peculiarities in the immediate ancestors, and in the following enumeration we have not included any others than parents and grandparents — in order to make the findings as direct and simple as possible. We have often known similar facts about brothers and sisters or collateral lines of relatives.

As stated above, alcoholism in the parents was known to exist in 31 per cent. of Group I. We learned of many other instances of alcoholism in grandparents or uncles and aunts. In these records it is remarkable to note the incidence of insanity with alcoholism. (Of course we recognize alcoholism as the producer of a defective environment which may be a sufficient cause for alcoholism in the children.)

There is a small amount of duplication on account of some individuals coming in more than one category; for instance, one mother was epileptic, insane and immoral; and more than one case of suicide was evidently that of an insane person. The

155

great list of insane ancestors is also partly the result of alcohol-ism.   Where insanity is enumerated it means that the diagnosis was well substantiated, and nearly always the individual had been in an institution for the insane.   In our enumeration of subnormality mere ignorance is not counted as subnormality. It is certainly true that even when a parent may appear dirty, careless and brutal this is no real evidence of subnormality. It has been impossible to draw the line between feeblemineded-ness and subnormality, and when there has been a reasonable doubt we have included the individual as subnormal.   It was obviously impossible for us to apply tests even when we saw the parents themselves.   Many of the subnormals are foreigners, and the detection of real subnormality is no easy matter in such cases.   In regard to the fairness of our figures, we may say that it is no doubt true that a small percentage of our cases was brought to us because a parent was already known to be insane, and it was suspected by the remaining parent or the probation officer that the child might be affected by inheritance.   But such cases form only a small percentage and do not much affect the total findings.   In the 502 cases of Group II, making 61 per cent., in which heredity seemed to be fairly regarded in some way as a factor, we find the following important known defects.   Since the information about grandparents has often been vague we have included only what we have heard about insanity or suicide or criminality for them.

Including father, mother and grandparents there were:

82 cases of insanity.
12 cases of suicide.
79 cases of criminality.

Enumerating only father and mother we found:

39 cases of epilepsy.
10 cases of migraine.
19 cases of feeblemindedness.
60 cases of subnormality, a certain proportion of which were prob-
    ably feebleminded.
57 psychopathic cases in which there was very marked instability.
10 neuropathic cases with marked symptoms.
20 cases of marked constitutional inferiority.
112 cases in which gross immorality on the part of the father or
    mother was known — this includes many cases of maternal
    prostitution.
61 cases of desertion.

18 cases of extremely bad temper.
 6 cases of drug addiction.
16 cases of extreme cruelty.
 8 cases of extreme laziness.

In the following modification of one of Dr. Spaulding's tabulation charts a different point of view is taken. Here in the 668 cases, Group III, an endeavor was made to range the immediate causative factors of the delinquency in relationship to heredity regarded as possibly an important factor.

Group III. Summary of Direct Causative Factors as Related to Hereditary Factors in 668 Cases.

CAUSATIVE FACTORS IN HEREDITY.	DIRECT CAUSATIVE FACTORS OF DELINQUENCY.										Totals.	Percentages.
	Mental defect and epilepsy.	Aberrational and neuropathic types.	Environment partly a factor.	Abnormal development partly a factor.	Peculiar innate characteristics.	Abnormal development mental conditions.	Faulty environment.	Abnormal development mental conditions + faulty environment.	Miscellaneous factors.	Complex of factors unsolvable.		
Inheritance of mental or physical abnormality a predominating factor	125	110	.	.	.	.	.	.	.	.	235	35
Inheritance of mental or physical abnormality a lesser factor	13	.	38	7	.	.	.	.	.	.	58	9
Heredity not known to be an important factor	107	.	.	.	42	26	155	9	.	21	360	54
Suggestive of criminalistic inheritance, but other factors found to predominate	.	.	.	.	.	.	.	.	15	.	15	2
Totals	245	110	38	7	42	26	155	9	15	21	668	100

CHAPTER IX

General Conclusions — Methodology

§ 117. Methodological Conclusions.   § 118. Bearings of our Findings on Classifications.   § 119. Causal Types may be Differentiated.   § 120. Study of Mental Life Most Direct Way of Getting at the Causal Factors.   § 121. Social Predictability of the Given Case.   § 122. Intricacy of Causation.

§ 117. **Methodological Conclusions.**—Our general conclusions are concerned with methodology and therapy as sociological generalization.   First in importance, we find complete proof of the necessity for intimate study of the individual offender.   Next, our observations bear on the problems of methods of investigation, of gathering the facts for diagnosis and prognosis, of classifying individuals and facts for the purpose of treatment and generalization.   Clearly, many points of value concerning the delinquent do not appear on the surface, and will always have to be sought for by carefully developed methods of individual study. Peculiarities of mental equipment, and other sources of tendencies to misconduct cannot be investigated thoroughly by anything short of scientific inquiry.   Characterology and differential psychology rest upon deep foundations.

One might see thousands of cases, as some judges do, and develop very shrewd ideas concerning the general springs of conduct, and yet (often perforce, from press of work) continually overlook the essentials of successful treatment.   We can see that for practical purposes order must in some way be established out of a multitude of superficial observations.   Practical people of necessity become¦ theorists.   But our case material shows most clearly that *causes* are not to be widely met by any theory arising out of snap-shot diagnosis.   The roots of the recidivist's career are not uncovered by touch-and-go methods.   It is not by chance that this individual falls by the wayside and another does not.   Hence, whatever it involves, the depths and structure of causation must, for the sake of efficiency, be unearthed in the individual case.

Not only causation of past action, but the hope for the offender's future should be a matter of deep concern.   We find it necessary to make a diagnosis of special capabilities and adaptabilities

159

in order to gain the foundation for constructive and remedial work. It is socially as valuable to do this as to know the defects and negative sides. Emphasis should be placed not only on finding out what the individual cannot do, or what are the sources of his tendency to misbehavior, but also what he might successfully do, or be interested in, under different internal or external conditions. We have had plenty of evidence that unfulfilled and even creditable desires and ambitions have been factors in some cases of delinquency, and that in others unrecognized talents have been the keynote to successful therapy.

With these words we can refer to our special chapters on working methods, treatment, and statistics, and especially to our concrete case studies for further and more specific statement of the conclusions built up from practical observations. Prognosis — the outlook or predictability, under various possible conditions — is hardly to be treated under the head of general conclusions. The understanding of what may be expected to happen is only to be safely gained from the study of actual case types. From the background of the knowledge of types, it is not difficult to discern with considerable accuracy the social outlook of a case, when once all the essential facts are gathered and evaluated.

§ 118. **Bearings of our Findings on Classifications.** — Students in the field of criminology are frequently asked what classification of crimes or criminals they accept. In our practical work we have let facts gradually answer this for us, and it develops that, for the ends of diagnosis and prognosis, no classification along systematic lines is adequate. We must indulge in some explanation of this statement. Taking for example the frequent use of a general term, " the criminal," [1] in the literature of criminology — " the criminal " being an undersized man, or an atavistic phenomenon, or a product of economic conditions, as it may be — one would almost think that the offender was some species of animal, which could be accurately described by markings and habits. But any such ascribing of nature and traits in general would seem to us, after our practical work, to

---

[1] We cannot get away from the feeling, which has grown by our continuous study of cases, that this constant use of the word criminal in a generic sense is one of the most curious features of criminological literature. We might just as well speak in this way of the "hunter." All sorts of people are hunters and criminals, and they hunt many sorts of creatures and commit many sorts of crimes, and all sorts of reasons are back of their hunting and their committing of crime. We are astonished to note such a good writer as Wulffen (98) recently giving way to indiscriminating use of the word.

be absolutely theoretical and superficial. There are many kinds
of criminals, with all sorts of traits, and one would urge great
caution in speaking of them in any way as a single group.
As Goring (190) has just proclaimed from his authoritative researches, " The physical and mental constitution of both criminal
and law-abiding persons of the same age, stature, class and intelligence are identical. There is no such thing as an anthropological criminal type."

As a matter of fact, it is easily seen that there are a few well-
differentiated classes, such as the definitely feebleminded, or
the insane, or the senile dements, who readily commit crime.
One could not go as far as Quinton (149) in the statement that
there are as many classes as there are criminals, but one does
concur in his point about the danger of a theoretical classification
obstructing individual study. Human beings have many-sided
natures, and the variabilities in the proportion of this or that characteristic are immense. Even when classified on one side alone,
for instance, in regard to mentality, we find complexities arising
so that there is no fitting into single pigeon-holes. For example,
the offender who is congenitally defective may also be insane;
the epileptic may be either intellectually superior or a dement;
certain individuals may be one thing one day on the mental
side, and another to-morrow. In the legally important group of
pathological liars, some are epileptic, some hysterical, some
partially defective, some have mental conflicts, and so on. When
it comes to sizing up the individual, and classifying him with a
word, this indeed may be an impossible task.[1]

Any classification of offenders or offenses, if it is to be of practical service in treatment, must surely take account of at least the
immediate causes. And as for dealing with this conception of
causes by a cut-and-dried classification, that appears at once out
of the question. But lest we seem indifferent to the presentation
of facts, let us say that it is perfectly clear that our specifications
for an adequate study of offenders call in the end for much sharper
focusing of the findings than any systematic classification has
offered.

[1] An extremely good point is made by Saleilles (123, p. 118) when he insists
on such a distinction as that between crime and criminality. The former is
not necessarily the issue of the latter. He maintains that both scientifically
and legally the idea of the social fact, crime, should be dissociated from the
conception of criminalism, which is a psychological affair. Lombroso with
his class of "juridical criminals" had earlier developed the same idea.

161

§ 119. **Causal Types may be Differentiated.** — Out of the chaos, which some of our previous statements might seem to imply exists in the study of delinquents, we rejoice to see strongly marked causal types or classes emerging. These evidently are not to be factitiously categorized, but nevertheless represent the centering of clear-cut practical issues. Now we see mental, now social, now physical factors uppermost as each type appears, and one observes greatly mixed causes which insistently have to be interpreted for the individual case itself. Our card schedule of causative factors shows sufficient illustration of this. The main factor gives a clue to the most logical grouping. The minor and antecedent issues, may, however, have their bearing on direct treatment or on public measures of prevention. Any grouping of similar factors may be fairly denominated causal groups, standing by themselves simply because they represent answers to our formal inquiry concerning the causes of delinquency. These represent pragmatic and not theoretical groups.

We find there is much over-lapping of the types and groups, and that there is occasional difficulty in differentiation. There are border-line cases of feeblemindedness; the influence of bad companions, of mental conflicts, of physical defect, may not be separable from other influences. Different ways of looking at cases may lead to some little confusion. For example, grouping by abilities according to the psychological examination may neglect the fact that there is some psychotic tendency, especially when there are temporary and variable symptoms. Of course there is endeavor to avoid all this, but sometimes the relative importance of several factors is not discernible. We find much evidence of the truth of Galton's oft-quoted dictum, " Natural groups have nuclei, but no outlines." Luckily the main groups have central types sharply established, and for the most part the facts crystallize readily about some center.

As we have gone on with the grouping according to ascertained factors in individual cases, we have seen that many subtypes can be discriminated and related to various prognoses. This comes out distinctly in our case studies, and turns out to be the logical center for the making of case summaries. As an example, we might take the instance of an epileptic offender. Now apart from the question of the disease itself, we must take up as a subhead his environment. Let him there be tempted to alcoholism, and we have a combination that at once determines a bad prognosis in the matter of his delinquent tendencies. But if his home control is good, we can pass to another point, the form of his disease. If he has epileptic lapses with wandering, the prognosis is bad, and so on. This brings us to the conclusion that even though his epilepsy be justifiably regarded as the main antecedent, still that factor unconsidered in the light of sub-conditions is not enough to base the prognosis on, nor enough to form the unit of statistics which shall give accurate data concerning ultimate causes and remedies.

§ 120. **Study of Mental Life Most Direct Way of Getting at Causal Factors.** — Finding direct mental determination of delinquency demonstrates prime consideration of the mental life of the individual as being the straightforward way of discriminating most causal factors. Not only is this shown by the undue proportion of feeblemindedness, epilepsy and insanity among delinquents, but also by the mental disappointments, irritations and conflicts which very frequently are at the roots of offending careers. Our groupings by weight of the facts, show much more necessary allegiance to psychological than to any other classification of both offenders and causes. Not that even here we achieve consistency, since we deal now with static abilities, now with functionings, now with mechanisms, and now with content. We are forced first to the use of a differential individual psychology, and then, as best we can, later, to the formulations of group psychology, as well as to analysis of mental mechanisms and mental content.

A corollary to be drawn from the above conclusions is, that every evidence goes to show that progress in investigating, collecting and demonstrating the underlying factors of delinquency is to be made only by development of the case-study method, without prior attention to classification. Most arguments being urged for the adoption of this method in professional teaching hold here, and are doubly valid, for there is as yet no accumulation of psychological knowledge by which one can safely proceed by principles alone in the determination of the causes of misconduct.

§ 121. **Social Predictability of the Given Case.** — A fair question here is whether, after diagnosis of the causal type, our follow-up work has proved the predictability in any considerable proportion of cases. Assuredly it has. By the use of the well-rounded methods of arriving at conclusions that we have insisted upon,

163

one gets an outlook upon the whole situation that very frequently affords an entirely safe basis for prognosis. Such prognosis is not to be offered, however, until all the facts which are likely to have a practical bearing are in. There is nothing occult or difficult about this arriving at conclusions when once the case has been thoroughly studied. It is the prediction based upon half-truths which invites suspicion about methods. Naturally the closeness with which prediction can be made varies greatly, and nearly always stands in some proportion to the variation of environmental conditions. For example, of this person we may certainly say: With his innate defect there will not be normal resistance to anti-social impulses and suggestions, consequently the strictest guardianship, impossible for his hard-working parents to give, is necessary. Of another: In this case there are good working powers of mind and body, but healthy interests are all undeveloped, and unless some environment furnishes them, the past with its transgressions most likely will be repeated. Of another: There is a mental conflict present, a grudge-forming process, which must be unearthed, or it will probably crystallize and permanently warp the subject's character; — mere punishment will add strength to the process. These and many other general prognostications, sharp enough in their statement of practical issues, and closely leading up to the details of treatment, can be safely asserted after careful study of the case as a whole.

§ 122. **Intricacy of Causation.** — The discovery of great intricacy in causations appears so momentous for the treatment of the individual, for those who are concerned in any way with general causes, and for the projection or interpretation of any statistics, that we have diagramed group connections of some simple findings to bring out sharply their vital interrelationships. We show in this at three levels the delinquency, the offender as a member of some general class, and the causal antecedents back of his tendency to delinquency. The combinations are made from only a few of the ascertained facts and types and could, of course, by the addition of facts, be made infinitely more complex. The combining lines represent either sequence or conjunction of the portrayed elements.

We observe from the diagram that classification on any level tells very little of what is of practical importance on other levels. For example, petty thieving may be committed by any one of the types of offenders on our diagram, who may in turn have

been influenced by any of a number of different remotely antecedent or immediately inciting factors. As an instance, the
feebleminded individual, the least difficult of all to group, may be
with his deficiency the result of several possible causes, may be
directly incited towards crime by inward or outward influences
apart from his defect, and may commit any of the diagramed
offenses.

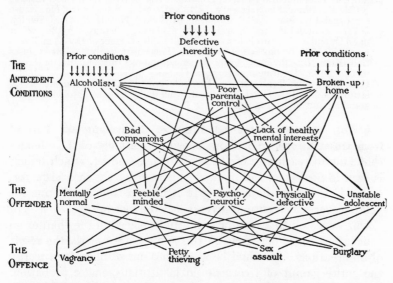

DIAGRAM OF SEQUENCE OR CONJUNCTION OF SOME SIMPLE ANTECEDENTS AND
CONSEQUENTS

The criminal is not in himself to be grouped according to any
logical system, and mere classification of either the antecedent
or the consequent of his tendency leads only a short distance
along the path of scientific and practical aims. This is the first
lesson to be learned from the diagram. The second is, that
each nucleus of fact cannot, in any fair-minded way, be interpreted as being or having a sole antecedent or a sole consequent.
The diagram is worth pondering over with this in mind, before
spending time on the estimation of the responsibility of alleged
main causes, or the values of even partial panaceas.

On the other hand, when it comes to the particular case, we
find the greatest help from this articulating and viewing the facts.
It leads to evaluation of causes by which adjustments become
actually possible that otherwise would be blunderingly missed.

CHAPTER X

GENERAL CONCLUSIONS — TREATMENT

§ 123. Our Fundamental Ideas of Treatment Are Derived from Observations. § 124. Punishment is Necessary. § 125. Defective Self-Control No Excuse for Legal Freedom. § 126. Punishment Should Not Harm the Offender. § 127. Mental Life and Moral Dangers During Custody. § 128. Effect upon Offender of Attitude towards Him. § 129. Danger of Deceit in Treatment. § 130. Advantage of Beginning Treatment Early. § 131. Causation Often Not Obvious. § 132. Organization of Courts for Better Treatment. § 133. Treatment of Physical Causes. § 134. Treatment of Mental Causes. § 135. Treatment of Environment. § 136. Treatment in Institutions. § 137. Good Treatment Can Only Come Through Understanding and Following Up.

§ 123. **Our Fundamental Ideas of Treatment are Derived from Observations.** — Shallow indeed is treatment of the offender that fails to reach any of the roots of misconduct. Such failure is seen in neglect of the therapy indicated by the mental factor, which is the immediate root. It is like the old quarantine for yellow fever which entirely overlooked the mosquito.

Our words on treatment are rightfully placed in the chapter on conclusions, since our ideas on this subject are exactly the result of observations. It would be altogether out of place here to run the entire gamut of treatment in institutions, under probation, and so on — most of these details must be coördinated with the exigencies of the given situation. We shall, however, deal with general measures and general opportunities, insisting on the great importance of knowledge of specific needs for the success of any treatment. Some indication of the varieties of these specific needs, shown as essential by individual studies, may be seen in the case histories in Book II.

§ 124. **Punishment is Necessary.** — First of all, let us deny that our studies tend to show any desirability of eliminating punishment as such, or that they prove in any way that punishment of offenders is not a deterrent to some who might otherwise commit crime.[1] It may be positively affirmed that there is much evidence

---

[1] We have been rather disappointed not to find in our case studies any facts from which one could form an opinion on the desirability of capital punishment. We have become, moreover, skeptical as to whether the forfeiture of life can fairly be regarded as the worst retribution society offers. Certainly there are other issues, however, in the question of dealing the death penalty than observation of the effects of such a legal provision upon offenders.

that the thought of penal consequences, in persons of normal self-control, often makes for self-restraint. It certainly is the sincere opinion of many offenders that if punishment were more swiftly and surely carried out, its deterrent effect would be commensurably greater. Who can doubt that to hold up the picture of future suffering and painful retribution which would far outweigh the pleasure accruing from the deed, is an effective argument to any one who can keep the idea in mind. (Observation of the effects of simple rewards and disciplines in modifying the conduct of many of the actually insane or feebleminded leaves no room for doubt that even in these cases the apprehension of future discomfort is often a deterrent of misbehavior. But, of course, here the conception must be unusually well established and the possibility of consequences easily perceivable.) We are altogether inclined to agree with Conti (285), who, after looking over our American institutions, still feels that reformation as the sole basis of a penal system is an untenable principle.

§ 125. **Defective Self-Control No Excuse for Legal Freedom.** — Any idea that the state ought to lessen its hold upon offenders because of the fact of their diminished or partial moral responsibility cannot be logically substantiated by our findings. In this matter again there is the greatest need for individualization. To put a concrete case: the authorities who freed the epileptic inmate of a reformatory because he was epileptic (Case 78), acted most unwarrantably. The individual who is liable often to be only partially responsible, and who has developed criminalistic impulses is the most dangerous of citizens. To adjudge the law to have no hold upon him because he is not always entirely responsible, and then to set him at large because he cannot be proven out-and-out insane, is to perpetrate a grievous fault against society. There is all the more reason for retaining control of this individual because he cannot exercise normal inhibitory powers.

Then we also perceive other important points in this matter. It is certainly true that the offender may exercise considerable effort to bolster up the powers of self-control, if he is properly kept under surveillance and the idea of legal retribution still prevails. I mean that, with full appreciation of the offender's personal background and with attempt at all needed therapy, there may well go hand-in-hand the deliberate idea of building up inhibitory powers by maintaining the conception of possible future

167

penalty. Even in the cases of short periodic relaxation of will power (*vide* § 310) there is no reason why the idea of retribution should not be invoked to aid in moral reformation, though the conduct has a definite physical basis which demands consideration. To excuse an offender of this sort and do nothing further about the case, is not exercising full powers that make for social welfare. It is just here that probation, parole, suspension of fine or of other sentence, together with the development of constructive measures, should be brought into play.[1]

§ 126. **Punishment Should not Harm the Offender.** — But following these disclaimers, we should like to make one of the strongest pleas of our chapter against carrying out the idea of punishment in such ways that the mind or spirit of the offender suffers harm. There is no doubt that from the moment the policeman claps his hand on the offender, the notion of punishment does rule, and it is because this idea is so immediate and so prevailing that fartherseeing modes of treatment are not even considered. One of the most appalling discoveries made in the study of offenders is that in attempting to protect itself, society so frequently ends by making matters worse. Yet nothing should be easier to perceive than that all sorts of punishment must be carefully safeguarded if they are to leave no ill effects. The possibility of breeding evil by punishment is seen in several ways.

§ 127. **Mental Life and Moral Dangers During Custody.** — The danger begins with the moment of arrest. One has traced only too often the boldly formed anti-social grudge that dated from the moment of ill-treatment by an officer of the law. The danger continues through all jailings and court procedures, and is much more an affair of the mental and moral than of the physical life. After learning some of the genetics of criminalistic tendencies, sanitation and physical features of the building where offenders are detained appear quite secondary in importance to the moral possibilities of the place. (Note our observations, § 226, on experiences during custody as causing delinquency.) Fortunately the equipment that maintains physical health conserves to a certain extent the moral well-being of prisoners, although they are by

---

[1] The disadvantages of any system where hard and fast measures of procedure are outlined, may be seen in the difficulties lately experienced in the attempt to adjust the German criminal code to scientific knowledge. The application of scientific study to the individual involves many matters upon which it is difficult to generalize, and room must always be left for the development of scientific knowledge.

no means identical. Lest there be any mistake as to how the ill results originate, even in the case of grudge formation on the part of offenders, it may be said that one has never heard that any mere experience with walls and bars set the offender's face against society; the morbid influence has always been engendered from human associations.

It is no lack of wisdom that leads the shrewd policeman to say to the young offender, " You 'd better keep out of jail, because if you 're not a crook when you go in, you will be when you come out." What a very strange anomaly it is, that society should take the person from whom it desires better actions, and place him under conditions which offer every chance for the creation of worse tendencies. One cannot conceive of a more foolish, uneconomical piece of work. Just what is it that creates the bad effect? In scores of cases, now, we have heard the calm statement that the offender's real career began with what he learned from others in the police station, or county jail, or even in the detention home for juveniles. There is no local setting for this, we have heard it everywhere; and it simply means that, as in any idle crowd, what the worst knows will soon be the property of all.

The problem of moral contagion is undoubtedly the most important one to be reckoned with in handling offenders. Efforts to prevent further immoral or criminalistic experiences and communications should preface all other phases of treatment. Placing any but the most hardened under typical jail conditions, where evil intercourse is rampant, whether before or after sentence, can be safely proved to be one of society's insanest extravagances. One sees difficulties in individualization here; the usual application of an age limit helps but little, for with the liberal interpretation of juvenility by the American law many a dissolute criminal with untold potentiality for harm is deliberately placed among genuine children. Unfortunately, some offenders of 15 or 17 years are already men and women in physical development and knowledge of the underworld. However, the difficulties of moral diagnosis are not practically insurmountable in the vast majority of instances, and isolation from even probable bad influences under detention could and should be made a part of the offender's régime from the first.

The throwing of unknown personal quantities together in any form of jail life is pernicious in its possibilities at any time, as we know from much tracing of cause and effect, and is unutterably wretched in the more formative years of life. The development of a community of interest among offenders as such, is unfortunate both inside and outside penal jurisdiction. It is worth much endeavor to prevent delinquents leaguing in any way together against society, because the strength of their offensive and defensive union more than equals the force of their totality as separate individuals. The helpful ties that are formed from acquaintance and friendship in the business world are similarly operative here. Many a secret plot solaces the hours of confinement, and confederacy outside prison walls keeps plenty of criminal careers going which would otherwise spontaneously terminate. It is obvious that officialism, ill-treatment, and unfavorable chances are likely to cause banding together of offenders. It is less understood that group classification, uniformity of institutional conditions, and non-understanding of individual needs may also produce undesirable gregariousness.

The highest exponent of treatment *en masse*, is the prison building where, even if the aim be not to depress all consciousness to a bare vacuous level, such largely is the effect. No better illustration of the childishness of our efforts to ameliorate criminalistic conditions can be found than the planning of buildings which does not first and foremost take into account the conditions and possibilities of mental life. Especially does this appear absurd when we consider the fact that future actions depend directly upon the conditions of mentality. The immediate surroundings that may be necessary to make one man better may be very different from what is desirable in another's man treatment. May we see the day when carefully worked up studies shall be available on this subject!

Another general condition to be vastly deplored while society is detaining the offender may be simply named mental vacuity. What can any one conceive to be the mental content of prisoners when they are unoccupied? " What the h— do you suppose we think of," was the laconic answer of an intelligent old-timer. We have much evidence of what detained girls think about — and talk about when they get a chance. And as for the males, no greater proof can be conceived of the truth of the empty mind being the devil's workshop, than what we have learned to be the thoughts brewed during the unoccupied moments of prison life. To take the simplest case: it seems clear that the result of throwing a group of arrested young boys together without the most effective occupational control, is similar to the idle gatherings of criminalistic gangs which inhabit a deserted barn for some days. Even when school or vocational treatment is instituted for offenders, the idleness of Saturday and Sunday, with or without congregation, is a highly dangerous moral period.

One might well have prefaced the above short recital of conditions to be prevented, by a statement which more than one keen observer has offered, namely, that general principles for the treatment of the offender will have to be vastly more developed before society through its own efforts will cease to be pushing itself in this matter continually further in the hole.

§ 128. **Effect Upon Offender of Attitude towards Him.** — To come now to more positive considerations we may, even at the risk of reiteration, emphasize once more the importance of attitude towards the offender. Here, however, attitude is to be spoken of only in its general relationships. Eschewing for the moment the question of personal contact, let us think of the effect of legal formalities, as such, upon the offender. It is most interesting to note that even young delinquents assume towards the law that sporting attitude which they conceive to be its own towards them. Even a little lad says, "I'll take my medicine when the judge hands it out," and an older fellow blurts out, "It's one to ten (years) for assault with a deadly weapon and that's all there is to it. I took my chance and lost." Set rules induce just this give-and-take attitude, not only on the part of the offender, but also on the part of officers of the law. A game of penalties is played — a gambling chance is taken on the avoiding of specified results. The theory of set punishments in the law [1] is altogether easy for the criminal to comprehend, and this gives him a sense of playing a game where he is pitted against obstacles which his skill may or may not be able to avoid.

The folly of short-term punishments without any constructive measures being undertaken in any way is too obvious and has too often been deplored by good authorities, to need reiteration. In the case of older adolescents it particularly serves to famil-

---

[1] The building up of the criminal law upon theories which are not based upon thorough-going ascertainment of the facts, either statistical or personal, is simply evidence of the immaturity of our knowledge of the whole subject. The contrasted opinions of learned men, such as Saleilles (**123**), who believes in the individualization of punishment, as set over against Koehler (**157**) and Allfeld (**158**), who stand for firm adherence to definite penalties for definite crimes, may also be explained by the lack of thorough research on the outcomes and possibilities of various forms of treatment.

iarize in an unfortunate way with prison life. The result of this treatment on them is one of the best arguments for extension to 20 or 21 years of the juvenile court methods.

Quite another feeling on the part of the offender, *vide* § 36, may without any doubt very often be engendered by an honest and studious attempt at interpretation of his delinquency. We have endeavored to set forth these possibilities in other places. Here it will suffice to say that efficiency in handling these grave human problems will ever depend largely upon the emotional and intellectual reactions which are aroused in the offender during the whole course of his treatment under the law.

§ 129. **Danger of Deceit in Treatment.** — We cannot decry too strongly the use of any kind of deceit in dealing with offenders. We have many observations to show that lying on the part of those in authority creates in the offender a unique feeling of distrust towards the world that stands greatly in the way of his moral recovery. The stronger the natural expectancy of truth from any given source the greater is the emotional upset and reaction in behavior to prevarication. Parents, teachers, court officials, all ought to scrupulously avoid misstatements. Every one ought to recognize that the first step towards getting the right kind of influence over a person is to treat him with the utmost squareness and openness. Young and old, all detest being met by a falsehood. We have seen cases of mental conflict and serious delinquency (§ 240) that have arisen largely from a basis of deceit, even well intentioned. It may be just the best type of person who has the most sensitive temperament and who reacts socially most strongly to falsehoods. As a preventive measure this is a matter for serious consideration in the case of the adopted child, who notoriously resents year-long deception about parentage.

§ 130. **Advantage of Beginning Treatment Early.** — The overwhelming importance of beginning treatment of the offender as early as possible in his career has been carefully elaborated in our opening chapters. This, together with the employment of persons with the right type of understanding, are two of the most fundamental considerations. Eventually, it seems clear to me, the way will be opened for the work of efficiency students who will have a scientific background for safely estimating results of treatment as offered under the auspices of various courts and institutions. It would be trite to say that here in America our officials who have to do with this most business-like affair must be taken away from political influence. We might better state that the first step must be educational, with the establishment of such institutes as may train all who handle delinquents for their grave professional duties.[1] How grave these duties are we realize when we remember that mistakes of treatment are tremendously reactive upon society. The offender who is harmed or who develops a grudge wreaks vengeance in return.

§ 131. **Causation Often Not Obvious.** — In many cases of delinquency, features are discovered that at first sight are not obvious. Only through appreciation of these features is there any straight path to understanding and developing possibilities of treatment that offer high chances of success. Much of what there is to be discovered that is useful can be discerned in our chapters on causal types. The newer ideas, such as represented by the Hungarian Law and the recent Ohio provision, which contemplate careful study of minor offenders after trial and before sentence, are steps towards better things. But unless the spirit of scientific inquiry is caught in observational institutions, these new legal provisions will still be ineffectual.

§ 132. **Organization of Courts for Better Treatment.** — The organization of courts that shall enable the most efficient treatment of delinquency must include two fundamentals which are wanting now: One is extension of the juvenile court method and juvenile jurisdiction to offenders up to the age of 20 or 21 years, with powers of committing proper cases (perhaps through the adult criminal courts) to penal institutions. My years of daily work in courts have served to enforce upon me, what everybody knows, that most boys and girls do not cease to be boys and girls at 17 or 18. As we shall say in our discussion of adolescence, § 336, the formative period of life is variable in different individuals, but is almost never ended at the limit fixed now as the juvenile court age. Practical workers, as well as scientific students of adolescence, perceive remarkable changes of character taking place between 18 and 20. Every safeguard that society can throw

---

[1] In Germany courses on forensic and penological medicine have long been offered. In Paris the "Institut de medicine légale et de psychiatrie" was established a decade ago. This type of instruction deals for the most part with questions of responsibility under the law. The Imperial Criminalistic Institute at the University of Graz, Austria, offers instruction in all branches of criminology. The course offered at Harvard by the psychological department in the summer school, and given by the author, has been, so far, the only systematic instruction in this country on the clinical study of delinquents as such.

about these important years by virtue of the parental method of the juvenile court, with its properly gathered knowledge of causations and results of previous efforts, should be continued.

The other fundamental is that any court handling an offender should have direct jurisdiction over the contributing agencies to his offense. The greatest travesties in justice occur through this omission, found almost everywhere. The failure to do justice to the total situation involved in the case betokens the utter weakness of this branch of social effort. The conveying of a complaint and of evidence to another court, to be tried perhaps weeks hence, without the intimate knowledge of the facts concerning the primary offender and his case, is psychologically and practically a very weak proceeding.

There are many other fundamental needs in criminal procedure, which members of the legal profession see, but the above two are matters of organization where decisive human factors are not taken into account.

§ 133. **Treatment of Physical Causes.**—The actual therapy may be discussed under several heads — physical, psychological, educational, religious, and so on. Treatment of the physical ailments and incapacities of the offender is often an absolutely indispensable condition for his moral success. A physical irritation may be immensely formative of character (*vide* § 174). More often there is some disability which tends to prevent giving or receiving satisfaction in employment and education. A good example is that of a young man who had been committed by courts some five or six times, and had been sent out as many times from institutions, without anybody ever paying attention to his vision, which only equalled about one-fifth of normal, to say nothing of his general physical make-up, which was such as to preclude his success at most kinds of labor. When he failed again and again in his utterly poor environment, society passed him along with the offenders of the day through the mill of the law, and that's all there was to it. It is clear that whether physical conditions stand directly or indirectly as causative factors of delinquency, they should never be neglected.[1]

---

[1] Much is to be learned about the medical correlatives of delinquency from the extended reports of the Chicago House of Correction where Mr. Whitman (156) and Dr. Sceleth organized some years ago an unsurpassed medical department. Survey of the wide range of defects and ailments observable from a routine medical standpoint, to say nothing of all the psychological and social factors in the background of criminal tendencies, leaves no room

§ 134. **Treatment of Mental Causes.** — Specific possibilities of psychological treatment arising from ascertainment of the mental background of delinquency are suggested elsewhere in this work. General *educational* features of treatment are better mentioned here. There can be no doubt that educational treatment is essential for many delinquents, even though they be adults. Leaving out the mental defectives, there is still a great deal of intellectual retardation among offenders. The keynote to success in educational effort is the offering of such material as will arouse healthy mental interests, and add to healthy mental content. The mere giving of formal education, as such, affords hardly any part of the solution. The school-room, for the delinquent, should be the avenue to higher vocational possibilities, to better recreational resources, to appreciation of right methods of thinking. Ethical comprehensions may often be skilfully developed in connection with the learning of other material. All through there must be individualization, and understanding on the part of the teacher of the genetic issues which may be met.

We are chary of discussing *religious* education or religious treatment in any form, on account of the strange controversial aspects immediately arising. In any case, however, one finds no sound argument against the application of efficiency studies to this form of treatment — that is, if such studies can be fairmindedly carried out. Religious teachers of many faiths are undoubtedly accomplishing results, and many people who receive their impulses to service from religious faith are, in various situations, dealing wonderfully well with the special problem of individual delinquents.[1] But whatever is already done in this field could be vastly increased if the ground for such work could be cleared of impediments. Religious workers themselves frequently do not see what stands in their way. They should ask that their failures be analyzed for them, and out of the analysis might come to them more instead of less hope. They would be able to build up better constructive measures if they understood various fundamental

for belief in anything in any field even remotely suggesting a panacea. We say this because every now and again there is recrudescence of the notion of some wonder-working reformative medical treatment of the offender. Sometimes it is special surgery (usually, of course, of the head or brain), and sometimes it may be hypnosis of the delinquent that is proposed.

[1] I fail to find any accurate studies of the result of prior religious education of offenders. Perhaps they are not feasible. The biographical studies of Begbie (**159**) contain striking information about the possibility of treating certain cases which otherwise must inevitably fail.

needs. Here, as in the case of school education, the formal training is not sufficient in many cases; an understanding of perplexities and·disabilities must be obtained and met.

§ 135. **Treatment of Environment.** — Environment is a fit object for treatment in very many instances of delinquency. There
are a thousand and one ways in which it may be defective, and a
thousand and one ways in which it may be altered. We would
refer to our chapters on environment for concrete observations
on the subject. It has always to be taken into account as a formative influence, at least until the individual is thoroughly crystallized
in his habits. The point here again is, first to start out from the
standpoint of what the individual really needs, and sometimes of
what he definitely wants. Merely to blame the environment without constructively altering it is, of course, thoroughly weak.
Many times have I seen parents and officers and school people
complaining bitterly about an offender, when not one single measure that could be of constructive benefit had been developed in
his environment. The tremendously important correlations between alcoholism and delinquency which we, as well as many others,
find, show an example of neglect by society of environmental conditions which fairly eat at the heart of civilization.

§ 136. **Treatment in Institutions.** — Institutions have a great,
fundamental opportunity, inasmuch as they offer a controlled
environment. Of course the reformatory is built up on this idea.
The difficulty is, that, following the establishment of a plant there
has been too much complacence. It is one thing to develop an environment, and another thing to know that it fits the individual. As
a matter of fact, there is a great deal of evidence that institutions
do not fulfill the needs of a goodly number of inmates. Where
effective results are achieved they are due largely to the fact that
offenders are steadied through certain unstable age periods. The
efficiency of institutions could be greatly increased if they were
divided into smaller units, where offenders could be classed much
more nearly according to the possibilities of their treatment. This
classification should be studiously developed·upon a psychological basis for the most part, for the many reasons which are established throughout this volume. It should begin with segregation
of mental defectives, to whom standard treatment is not fitted.

In any reformatory type of institution it seems perfectly clear
that great practical benefit might accrue from much more individualization of understanding and treatment than obtains even

in any ordinary school system. The results obtained in these institutions, we can safely predict, are nothing like what they might be if measures more appropriate to the needs and possibilities of different offenders were skillfully reckoned with. A general professional understanding of this whole topic must be developed for the sake of improvement of efficiency. There is the greatest need, as our observations show, for teachers understanding the special problems of offenders, who, as a class, present an unusual number of special problems. The individuals who are the victims of various mental and nervous habits, who have speech defects, who belong to the class of specialized mental defectives, and so on, all are going to receive large benefit only through highly individualized methods of training. One might pick out certain other points; for instance, the phenomena of puberty and adolescence, as we have sketched them elsewhere in this volume. The necessities of the adolescent period are far from being obvious, but they are vital for society. All these should be understood enough so that they may be reckoned with by those in control of young offenders. Altogether, we might rationally demand for delinquents in charge of the state the same sort of careful scientific study and treatment, even if more difficult and complicated, that is accorded to plants and animals under governmental auspices.

§ 137. **Good Treatment Can Only Come Through Understanding and Following Up.** — In this country we have established several notable systems for the treatment of offenders; the reformatory, the juvenile court, the junior republic, and the big brother movement.[1] But all of these will remain just bits of machinery, and will never do thorough work in the treatment of offenders unless they develop something more than the mechanics of procedure. The juvenile court as an institution, without intelligent personalities and methods, can do nothing, although at times it seems almost a word to conjure with. As a matter of fact, recidivism is rampant there as elsewhere. The junior republic, with its splendid ideal of personal development, may be absolutely unfitted to certain types of offenders. As one highly intel-

---

[1] In this connection, although it undertakes for the most part social study and prevention of delinquency, rather than primarily the treatment of the offender, should be mentioned the work of the Juvenile Protective Association, one of the best balanced efforts now being carried on anywhere in this field. As established in Chicago, the organization at present is doing its work by notable, scientifically efficient methods, and this partly because the need of thorough understanding is recognized when it comes to any question of handling the individual case.

ligent lad said to me of it, " Did n't you know that was the worst place in the world you could send me to? " The reformatory, which it has been the pride of America to establish, is often very far from accomplishing its projected aims, because a system has been built up as if there was a universally applicable scheme of treatment. Even the big brother movement, which represents, both here and abroad, the high-water mark of effort to reduce delinquency, is as a movement only a little better than other things. Merely the idea of one man to one boy, or one woman to one girl, will never solve the problem, if the man or woman has not a deep appreciation of all the needs and perplexities of the offender, and does not attempt to adapt treatment to these things.

As one makes more and more studies of the formative period of life, and watches cases go on to success or failure, one sees clearly that a great feature of treatment is the careful carrying over of offenders through the period of adolescent instability. A little touch here and a little touch there to the young individual is not sufficient; there must be that prolonged studying of the case that offers the best chance of forfending the growth of delinquent tendencies. Natural development involves a period of impressionability and instability during those years when many important social facts are first met. To tide safely over these times of stress is to do more than later can be accomplished in decades.

A very weak point in practically all social and moral therapy is the lack of follow-up work. Criticism may be extended to parents who have no patience to deal systematically with a problem child, to court admonitions which imply the ability of human nature to change itself in a trice, to public administration which sends back old offenders from institutions to an environment where they are almost sure to fail again. (The wastefulness of the latter, after spending so much for punishment or reformation of the individual, I call attention to elsewhere, § 203.)

All through safe and sane consideration of the various aspects of the treatment of the offender should run the idea of the human family, with full sensing of interdependence. Complete vision of community of interests is not easy to attain, but once clearly arrived at, the application by society of wholesome paternal and fraternal control of treatment of offenders will win approval. The honest inquiry which precedes good parental reaction to filial misconduct will then be comprehended as imperative for the best interests of society. Offenders can never be treated properly unless their problems are understood. No machinery of court or institution, however well organized, can ever take the place of deep humanistic understanding. The girl put it well who blurted out to a certain judge, " You and your officers are here to do your duty, and I suppose you are going to send me away, but before I go I want to tell you one thing; you don't at all understand me."

BOOK TWO

CASES, TYPES, CAUSATIVE FACTORS

FOREWORD

§ 138. Cases and Causes Treated in Book II. Complexities. § 139. Our
Concrete Data Available for All Concerned. § 140. Plan of Presentation
of Cases and Causal Studies.

§ 138. **Cases and Causes Treated in Book II. Complexities.** — This second division of our work presents the concrete
outcome of our eminently practical attempts to understand the
offender and the forces which work through him to produce delinquency. Here we deal with both individuals and causes. As
before stated, it disturbs us little to find the array of facts too rich
to permit the use of hard-and-fast lines of classification. Nor are
we nonplused by discovering the complexities of causative factors in the individual case. Indeed, it is often by perception of the
issues which emerge from the interweaving of factors that the
greatest hope for the whole situation in handling the offender
arises. For example, we may discover that some individual (§ 271)
who is subnormal according to formal educational tests, has very
special abilities which may prove to be his social salvation if he
is properly handled. Or by delving deep below the surface, we
may ascertain that a second offender (§ 235) is burdened in his
inner consciousness by mental conflicts or problems, the solution
of which offers the direct remedy for his conduct. Or in another
case (§ 188 ff.), one finds certain conditions of physical development, unalterable in themselves, which have to be unhesitatingly
met as important facts if delinquent tendencies are to be thwarted.
In other words, there is generally much more to the case, especially for remedial purposes, than can be learned by superficial
observation of the individual, or by enumeration of the apparent
conditions of his environment.

It is also true that for other phases of dealing with the offender,
segregation in particular, there are deeper facts which will help
to more accurate determination of the outlook, and consequently
to scientifically based decisions concerning treatment. In developmental or family history, for instance, we may find a background of conditions which permanently burden the delinquent,
and which could not be detected by a simple examination. Our
case histories abound in particulars of this kind, many of which

are definitely applicable to our knowledge of possible outcomes. One might observe a big young vagrant (§§ 256, 350), and never understand in the least what to do about the case, if knowledge was not forthcoming of the antecedent early years of convulsive attacks. And concerning the victim of border-line aberrational tendencies: it should make a vast difference to prognostic opinion whether this individual (§ 343) came from a defective line of ancestors or not. Thus, for their bearing on questions of permanent segregation or prolonged treatment, we need even this more pessimistic type of facts.

§ 139. **Our Concrete Data Available for all Concerned.** — We present our concrete data for the use of judges, officials of probation, parole or pardon departments, for institutional officers, professional people, and all others who should have close scientific understanding of what makes for criminalistic proclivities. All concerned should have at heart the two aims on which the concrete facts bear, namely, the protection of society and the improvement of the criminal himself. One may venture to insist that all workers anywhere in this field should have at least an acquaintance with all the types of individuals and causes which find place in this practical study of delinquency. Theories may be dispensed with, but not the scientifically grouped facts which throw light on handling individual offenders. There is a good deal of broad human interest in the material we have to offer, and special phases of it bear on many a particular human situation. As a single illustration, we might point out that legal people all should have definite understanding of the existence of certain types which play an unduly large part in court work — (a) the mental defectives in general, and especially those with particular abilities, such as (α) industrial capacity (§ 272) which can be utilized to keep them out of social difficulties, or (β) unusual verbal capacity (§§ 273, 276), which may cause them to be great trouble-makers; (b) the several types of border-line psychoses in individuals who consequently are morally only partially responsible; (c) the highly interesting cases having the hidden mental conflicts often in the background of definite anti-social careers; and (d) the strange class of pathological liars and accusers.

This does not mean that judges and other officials are to spend time qualifying to make diagnoses themselves. Their prime need is to cultivate appreciation of the facts and of essential values. The movement is already well on foot, particularly in Germany and

America and with indications of it elsewhere, to have indispensable studies of offenders carefully made and reported on. The coming years are bound to see much growth in this feature of court and institutional life. It is to be hoped that with the advent of even greater foresight such studies may be commenced in still earlier formative years, preceding any appearance of the individual in court.

§ 140. **Plan of Presentation of Cases and Causal Studies.** — All chapter and section headings in this division represent the various groupings of causative factors as observationally ascertained. We have not followed classification lines according to individuals, offenses, or anything else — we have previously shown (§ 122) the inadequacy of this plan. And particularly have we avoided dwelling on data of mere general interest, such as climatic and racial correlations, about which nothing can be done. Again it must be remembered that our causes are always the *causes of delinquency.* If we were regarding the individual simply in his mental qualities, our schedule of related causations would show very differently. For comprehending the causative factor cards, which we frequently append by way of graphic illustration to a case study, this practical limitation should be kept in mind. Our presentation of cases and causal types follows no preconceived logical order; the subdivisions correspond to nothing but practical issues.

We again would emphasize that living material shows much overlapping of types and causes, and that it is exactly this admixture of facts which must be comprehended in order that justice may be done to the whole situation. It has been frequently pointed out by many authorities that there is no wall of division between the normal and abnormal, either in defect, aberration or development; in our material this fact is always patent. But nevertheless most cases have outstanding characteristics that are clearly marked.

Despite the difficulty which we seem to be bringing down upon our heads by introducing all this idea of complexity, we really are opening the way for clarification of decisions concerning practical measures. We ask for studious consideration of the cases that this point may be clear. The true picture of the whole case, we insist, is the only one scientifically desirable, and the only way of getting a true picture is through shedding on the subject the light of keen analysis.

The logical method of dwelling proportionately longer on numerically more important types has been only partially followed by us. We have merely outlined, for example, characteristics of the obviously feebleminded and insane offenders, and have only in summary dealt with well-known environmental factors. This has left us more room for discussing the less generally understood features of causation, features that frequently present the greatest constructive possibilities.

Our portrayal of facts is based, as may be seen, on prolonged studies of cases. We realize that many types of individuals and causes need, at least for specialists, more elaborate study records than we can afford space for here. Publication of such detailed observations will form part of the future development of the science of clinical criminology. We have stopped short of the anecdotal method, that is, we have not related many an interesting study of some single striking case because it was too unusual. And nearly always we have purposely avoided presenting the most exaggerated types of offenders, and of extreme delinquencies, for instance, murder. We are in this work primarily dealing with genetics, and the commission of desperate offenses usually comes after many years of delinquency have added the force of mental habit and accumulated environmental stress to the original source of misconduct. The individual thus far along in his career is like the case of chronic disease in which many secondary conditions have arisen that obscure knowledge of the onset and " materies morbi." But even within our set limits, if we had talent and space, our case studies might ring true to the requirements of that best type of biography which focuses upon the beginnings of careers.[1]

For professional people it need hardly be said that the personalities of all our cases are fictitious and that facts of time and place are effectively disguised. The fictitious details, however, have been carefully selected with a view to not damaging the record of causation. Measurement of height is net, but weight is subject to deduction of about 5 lbs. for clothes. In the case of

---

[1] We do not deny that occasionally it is quite possible to have biographical material of considerable interest in criminology, even as related to treatment, without attempts at well-rounded estimation of the individual and his driving forces. All studies, however, would be immensely strengthened by more complete data on many points. One finds himself unable, for instance, on account of such omission, satisfactorily to diagnose certain types of apparently recoverable chronic cases in Begbie's (159) interesting work on moral regeneration.

the youngest offenders, subtracting 4 lbs. is more nearly correct. The record of the physical examination which showed normal conditions is, for the most part, omitted.

For those with special interest in the psychological phases of our work, we have, in many case studies, inserted in smaller type the results on tests, which may be interpreted by reference to § 82 in our chapter on methods. Why there has been great variation in the tests given is easy to see. We have had to deal with many ages, and all classes of mental ability. We needed to have one sort of information in one case, perhaps about vocational aptitude, and another sort, perhaps concerning the general level of intelligence, in a second case. The wide range of knowledge desirable is discussed under the heading of mental tests (§ 54; *vide* also § 34). The undesirability of any cut-and-dried system is clearly demonstrated by a survey of our material.

Not so much has been said about treatment as would be justifiable if this book were written for any single class of those who have to do medically, educationally or disciplinarily with offenders. Our task is mainly to present the essentials of diagnosis and prognosis, but since many points of prognosis are only to be decided in the light of possible treatment, general considerations of therapy have been treated. The time will come, we feel sure, when on the basis of carefully rendered diagnosis, really scientific work will be devoted to studying the possibilities of individualized treatment under the various conditions in which offenders may be found. While treatment in reformatory institutions has been more considered in the light of observed results than has any kind of court work, still institutional efforts in general are very far from having been developed with the scientific impetus that their importance would justify. Here, too, is a field that lies fallow for the cultivation of better discriminations and better methods.

The bibliographic references, as in Book I, have been selected with much care from extensive reading. Students of special problems are offered here and there an introduction to the most important material on the given subject, whether as gauged by its recency, its originality of research, or the fact that it valuably summarizes previous work in the field.

CHAPTER I

HEREDITY

§ 141. Studies of Heredity Need Critical Methods.   § 142. Inheritance of Excess of Energy.   § 143. Inheritance of Irritable Temper.   § 144. Inheritance of Hypersexual Tendencies. § 145. Inheritance of Physical Traits. § 146. Familial Biological Defect.

§ 141. **Studies of Heredity Need Critical Methods.** — In the light of the enormous literature on heredity, and especially of the recent excess of writing on this subject, we have been, during the years of our research, carefully on the lookout for data that shall stand scientific scrutiny.[1] The whole problem of human conduct is so complicated by environment and other genetic factors, that only now and then do we get satisfactory positive evidence of the part that heredity plays in the background. We have dealt with our general findings, § 116, in the chapter on Statistics — it remains to give instances of some of the definitely inherited subfoundations of criminalism. Inheritance of certain types of feeblemindedness, epilepsy and insanity is such a well-established fact, and is covered so well by many published researches, that nothing need be said here about all this, in spite of the close relationship of these abnormalities to criminalism. There are less well-known inherited conditions also in the background of anti-social conduct.

From our experience we would warn at this place once more against the danger of drawing easy conclusions about heredity being the main factor back of misdeeds simply because some progenitors or other members of the family were guilty of delin-

---

[1] We have also searched the literature for recent careful studies on the inheritance of criminalistic tendencies. Apart from the researches on the inheritance of various mental and nervous defects or aberrations that are so frequently correlated with delinquency, we find nothing in the least convincing — nothing to add to Aschaffenburg's summary (1, Eng. ed. p. 129) of work done on the subject, or to his words, "This makes it possible to dispense with the hypothesis that criminal tendencies, like artistic talents, for instance, are transmitted from parents to children. I expressly say that we can dispense with it for it cannot be refuted or proved." Our statement on heredity, under Statistics, § 116, and the results of a special research (Spaulding and Healy, **162**) on cases seen in the Juvenile Psychopathic Institute should here be consulted.

quency. Both mother and child may be prostitutes, and both be victims of environment. Grandparents and parents and children may be liars, or thieves, or misdoers in other ways, and very little cause of their conduct be protoplasmic carrying over of special traits. Some changes or reformations that may be witnessed through alteration of environment, make one very skeptical about deciding the rôle of inheritance in criminalism, unless other proof than that of similar misconduct in successive generations is brought forth. We feel certain that absolutely the only fair way to study inheritance in criminalistic families is to ascertain the various causes of misbehavior in individual cases, and then to reckon up these with known heritable conditions.

Nothing is more unfair than to offer family charts alone in proof of inheritance of criminality. Without detailed environmental and developmental history they prove nothing, no matter how many criminal histories they may indicate. Studying the significance of delinquent tendencies, which may arise through any of a large number of possible biological, mental, or social factors, is altogether different from studying the heritage of a Hapsburg lip or the heredity of feeblemindedness. Facial features are altogether simply derived, and even feeblemindedness arises from merely a few general biological causes. The unsafeness of interpreting from graphic representation and isolated facts is obvious from the above considerations.

§ 142. **Inheritance of Excess of Energy.** — We may have overlooked much in our individual studies, but at least the things we are about to tell of are typical of what may be seen, and the details speak for themselves. Inherited excess of physical development, strength and energy, with accompanying self-will and self-assertion, as it leads to delinquency, may first be dealt with.

Case 1. — A bright girl of 16 years. English parentage. Father is dead. The girl has been guilty of much misbehavior. She has stayed away from home on numerous occasions, going to work when and where she pleased, unbeknown to her mother, threatened physical violence, showed extreme temper, and indulged in sex delinquency.

Physically, we found her in tremendously good condition — very well; symmetrically developed. Very strong. Weight, 152 pounds. Height, 5 feet, 1 inch. Notable is her mature type of face, with its decidedly good features and firm chin. She has defective vision, and headaches, perhaps from eye strain.

Although she refused to do the tests for us, we could fairly judge her to have ordinary mental ability. We learned of her accomplishments in other directions, and she showed signs of the possession of quick intelligence. Her school work is fairly well done. She showed under observation a great many indications of mental energy and will, she formed quick opinions of persons — perhaps taking a sudden grudge against them. She said that she would purposely do the tests wrong if she did them at all. She cares much for her physical well-being, and is said in some ways to be decidedly lazy, but not at all so on the mental side.

The family history is said to be remarkably free from taint, even of alcoholism, on both sides. The father was a good man. This child was fourth in fifteen pregnancies, eight children being alive, several of them sickly. Her development was normal except for two very severe illnesses, once with some gastrointestinal disorder, and again with scarlet fever during childhood. She menstruated at 13 1-2 years.

Interest in the hereditary aspects of this case was immediately awakened by viewing the mother. She and the daughter were cast from exactly the same mold. This woman of a little more than 40 years, with her fifteen pregnancies, and much trouble on account of poverty, the death of her husband, and other family troubles, is still enormously strong, healthy, fiery and emphatic. The powerful physiognomy of the girl was inherited straight from this vigorous personage. The mother freely told of beating the daughter, and displayed much temper in recounting the girl's delinquencies. In fact, she stated that on account of certain things her daughter had said about her she really feared she would choke her to death if she got hold of her again.

The girl met us in the same straightforward way as the mother. " I can't see why mother thinks I 'm so bad, since she 's just like me." She went on to tell us that she did what she did just because she wanted to. She knew all about what she was doing, even about sex things. Her mother had told her much. " I 'm not weak — I just do as I want to."

After careful warning and obtaining for her another position, this girl kept exactly on the path she had previously pursued, and there was nothing to do but send her to an institution. Ordi-

190

nary treatment could hardly be expected to succeed in this type of individual, when even fifteen pregnancies and much hard work had not worn out just the same sort of vigor in the mother. Of course, as the card of causative factors shows, there were other elements in the case, but the background of the trouble was certainly the inheritance of a remarkable physical organization, the substratum of her mental qualities and her delinquency.

Mental peculiarities:
    Very strong type.   Self-will, self-assertion
    excessive.   Reckless.

    Physical conditions: Over-development
                    and prematurity.

        Heredity: M. same type.

          Adolescent instability?
             perhaps a factor.

Delinquencies:
Leaving home.
Threatening violence.
Sex.

Case 1.
Girl, age 16.

Mental:
Fair ability.

---

§ 143. **Inheritance of Irritable Temper.** — As throwing light on the question of inheritance of such traits as bad temper and irritability, one finds many evidences of inheritance of physical characteristics, some of them plain inferiorities and some only vaguely definable, which may underlie the irritability and " nervousness." (A point to keep in mind in this connection is that outbreaks of temper may be an epileptic equivalent, § 250.) However, where one hears about bad temper both in parents and children, there is always the possibility of parental reactions in the household having been partially responsible for the character of the child. In one instance this could well be ruled out.

Case 2. — We studied a very attractive Irish-American boy at the request of his mother, who had had much trouble with him on account of exhibition of bad temper combined with violence. We found a nervous, active, strong-featured boy with no defects whatever discernible, except enuresis, which still persisted at 13. On the mental side there was not the slightest difficulty in classifying him as normal in ability, with a good range of information. There were varying reports from teachers, one of them stating he could do only second-grade work. But this we were able to prove was due to his reaction toward her. So far as we could ascertain, everything about development and heredity was negative, except that the boy is the image of his father, who was a very active, good-hearted, and remarkably quick-tempered man. He has been dead six or seven years. The other children do not physically resemble the father, and are more quiet and stable. Our youngster had got into very serious trouble through fighting with weapons. In spite of all this we felt that the prognosis was distinctly good. At present, in the beginning of adolescence, there is undoubtedly lack of developed inhibitory powers to overcome the traits which he had derived in such full measure from his father.

Mental peculiarity: Terrific temper. Active,   Case 2.
fiery type. Lack of   Boy, age 13.
self-control. (Enuresis).

Heredity: F. same type.

Adolescent lack of self-control.

Fighting.   Mental:
Violence +.   Fair ability.

---

§ 144. **Inheritance of Hypersexual Tendencies. Case 3.** — A short summary of this case will show the significant facts of heredity which have to do very definitely not only with physical structure, but also with sex impulses. A girl of 16 years, in splendid physical condition, very strong, weight 121 lbs., height 5 ft. 1 in., over-development of structural sex characteristics for her age, had already been delinquent enough to have had two miscarriages. With the exception that she bit her nails excessively, there were no findings of physical abnormality. On the mental side we diagnosed her mental ability as rather poor and educational advantages poor. She showed no aberrational tendency whatever, and very willingly coöperated in tests.

The heredity in this American family is decidedly interesting. The mother's father was a saloon keeper. The mother herself was notoriously gay when young, so much so that she had to leave the small town in which she was brought up. She then met and married an alcoholic reprobate, by whom she had no less than fifteen children, six of whom are living. Several of the children are said to have had convulsions when very young, and four of them are said to have died from this cause. No other tendency to convulsions is known in either family. In spite of the father's alcoholism, he had fairly good health, but he failed to support his family, and his wife worked out a great deal. From reliable sources we learn that this woman is a very fine worker and is well liked. She is tremendously active, full of life, rather witty, and much given to smutty talk. Recently she has parted from her husband. This woman, now about 45 years old, having had children part of the time at the rate of about one a year, shows herself to be fairly intelligent, hard-working, still very strong, and inclined to the erotic.

It is important for treatment in such cases to note that our girl, who had early shown such an excessive desire for the opposite sex, in spite of much warning and many good advantages offered, finally showed that she never had done so well morally as when she had to do very hard work. The miscarriages left no bad physical effects, and when she was working out in a place where she had to do big washings she controlled her sex tendencies much better than previously.

Physical over-development: general and sex   Case 3.
                             characteristics.   Girl, age 16.
    Heredity: M. early sex delinquent,
               fine physique.
           F. alc.

    Home conditions: M. careless morally.
                   Poverty.

     Lack healthy interests.

Delinquencies: **Mental:**
Sex +   Poor in ability.

Still better evidence of the same type of inheritance in early development of certain physical characteristics is shown in the following instance.

Case 4. — This is a boy of 15 years, German parentage, who has caused his hard-working mother an excessive amount of trouble. Physically we find him to be well nourished and developed, with remarkable sexual over-development for his age. Weight 120 lbs. Height 5 ft., 4. He has a well-shaped chest. The boy is to some extent a mouth breather on account of partial occlusion of the nose. Dull-looking eyes, dark underneath. We note his general dull, sheepish expression, thick lips and sensuous face. Slouchy in attitude. No sensory defect.

Mentally, we classify him as having fair ability and fair advantages, although showing an element of mental dullness, perhaps from debility caused by his bad sex habits. Although his record on some things was good, his work was irregular and unequal.

Results on Tests: (As stated previously, records on our own tests throughout Book II may be largely interpreted by reference to § 82.)

I. 3'. Repeated trial and error on the triangles — a very stupid attitude at the beginning of his tests.

III. 5' 17". 25 trial of impossibilities. Only 3 retrial of obvious impossibilities. This curious result was brought about by his not taking in our original statement that the pieces must exactly fill up the frame. He did the test immediately again without error.

IV. 1' 20". 11 moves — the smallest possible number. Contrast this splendid performance with the above.

V. 3' 43". Between step 1 and step 2 he interspersed 3 errors.

VIII. All correct.

IX. Correct at 2d trial.

X. Correct at 1st trial.

XI. He got the idea very quickly but was very inaccurate in his work, making 7 out of 11 possible errors. Strangely, some of the more difficult parts of the code were correctly done. His mental control seemed quite inadequate to the performance.

XII. 13 out of the 20 items given with a fair amount of accuracy and understanding.

XIII. 11 out of the 12 items given correctly and without attempt at verbal accuracy.

XV. 1 failure. Average time 1.8".

XVI, XVII, XVIII. In school work equals 7th grade.

XXII. Simple history items and contemporary items given correctly. Is a reader of books and mechanical magazines, and desires to be an electrician.

XXIII. Pictorial Completion Test. 3' 17" and no final errors.

This boy is said to come from very good stock indeed on both sides, with the exception of the father, who was the only black sheep in his good family. No insanity, epilepsy, feeblemindedness or familial disease is known on either side. Our boy was first-born of four children, the two middle ones having died in infancy. A younger brother of eight is showing none of this boy's peculiar traits. The pregnancy occurred during a very unhappy time on account of the father's misbehavior. The birth was normal and the development was quite healthy. Enuresis persisted until a few years ago. From perhaps one to four years the boy showed excessive bad temper, throwing himself upon the floor in rage. The father and mother married when very young. He proved at once to be a drinking man, and although well able to do so, has failed a great deal of the time to support her. Even during this pregnancy she had largely to support herself, evidently out of pride, being unwilling to apply to her family. But his drinking, however, was not so bad as his excessive sex delinquency continued over many years. At present he is serving a long term for engaging in immoral practices with two young girls.

This boy already has a record of many delinquencies. He has been a runaway from home, previously showed a boyish tendency for the possession of guns, and engaged in Indian warfare and the like, which got him into trouble. Recently he has been loafing on the streets much, and often stealing. Already he has been committed four times. The worse feature about his case is his sex delinquency. This has been engaged in to such an extent in schools and institutions that he is everywhere regarded as a most serious menace. Again and again he has deliberately taught smaller boys the worst kinds of sex practices. His mother, thoroughly aroused about the whole matter, is at her wit's end to know what to do to check his tendency. Many others who have had him in charge also have failed utterly with him. These tendencies were shown many years ago. The mother states that already at 3 or 4 years of age, long before he had engaged in any bad habit, he was showing extraordinary physical signs of sexual activity.

Now in adolescence the boy is much inclined to lie in bed, and although because of his ability he has had many good positions offered him, he does not seem to be able to keep at them. It is comparatively recently that his more shameless teaching of others has taken place. At one time when he ran away he is said to have lived in a hut with a man who was thoroughly bad, but the association was quite voluntary on the part of the boy. It was interesting to note that the mother realized that this boy was as desperate a problem in general life as he was in the family. She was most earnest in her desires for something thorough to be done to prevent his injuring others.

```
┌─────────────────────────────────────────────────────────────┐
│ Physical: Sex over-development +.              Case 4.        │
│    Developmental: Abnormal early            Boy, age 15.      │
│                   development of sex.                         │
│       Heredity: F. great sex offender.                        │
│          Mentality — dull and lethargic,                      │
│                      probably from bad habits.                │
│              (?) Prison type of repression.                   │
│  Stealing.                                                    │
│  Runaway.                                                     │
│  Sex offenses +, including                      Mental:       │
│     homosexual.                               Fair ability.   │
└─────────────────────────────────────────────────────────────┘
```

Case 5. — Another case of a little boy of eight years, Austrian father, Scotch mother, already notorious on account of sex-pervert tendencies, might be used as complete evidence of remarkable heredity of sex traits if it were not for the fact that environment, as commonly found in these cases, cannot be ruled out. Most frequently one finds on the part of the parents defects which produce bad environment, and thus complicate the problem. This little lad was physically and mentally normal, but a very impudent and turbulent specimen. He had already associated with some of the vilest human characters. He had shown very marked sex tendencies, himself being already a seeker of the bad. The mother, despite one's sympathy for her, must be regarded as a careless individual. The father was an exceedingly bright man, known to possess much ability, very large and strong. He had been married several times. Besides this he was frequently immoral with other women. He has already served two terms in different states on account of bigamy. The mother desired the boy placed under better circumstances, and a remarkable result was obtained after a few months of treatment in a better home. The boy seemed to lose his bad tendencies.

In another instance we had most remarkable testimony from several reliable sources concerning excessive sex tendencies on the part of a whole family — father, mother, at least one grandparent, and others in the generation of the boy whom we saw. Mentally he was a normal lad, a great deal of a reader, and at 15 1-2 years had already the stature of a big man, with complete adult sex development.

We have seen indication that the trait, evidently sometimes

196

inherited, of hypersexualism may be passed over from a parent to a child of the opposite sex. The following case seems to prove the point clearly.

Case 6. — This is a girl of American parentage, 14 years old, very strong, good nutrition, strong type of face, rather prominent chin, no sensory defects. No signs of over-development. Menstruated at 13; complains much of headache and dizzy spells at these times.

On the mental side we had no difficulty in diagnosing this girl as well up to the ordinary in ability and information, although in her early life her school advantages had been poor. More recently she had taken a course in a business college. No aberrational tendencies whatever were discoverable. Our series of tests were done rapidly and uniformly well.

The developmental history is not completely ascertainable, but there is fairly good evidence that there was no serious trouble, or the relatives whom we saw would have known about it. The mother has been dead since the girl was four years old, and later there was a step-mother who was deserted by the father. The relatives of the girl's own mother are of a distinctly refined type, not at all like this child in ruggedness. There is an older sister who is much more delicate. We have a definite statement that no insanity, feeblemindedness or epilepsy is known to exist in either family. The general character of the father is, simply, that he has been crazy after women all his grown life. As a married man he eloped with one of the girls he later married. All his family know full well his traits.

The girl who is the subject of our study has already had many sex experiences, and when boys have not been available she has indulged in homosexual affairs, even to the extent of attacking a little girl in her bed. Her relatives state that she will at times grip them in a tense, peculiar manner for a moment and set her teeth. It is interesting to hear from other sources that the girl seems to have no inclination whatever to associate with bad girls. This is indication that her sex tendencies are primarily autogenetic. The girl spoke freely of her own traits, of her desire to kiss other girls, and of her earlier affairs with boys. She says that since she learned of the danger of having a baby she has never been with boys. Before that time, and in a general way, she thought, she says, it was not a right thing to do, but did not realize much of what she was doing.

197

Mental or physical peculiarity:	Case 6.
Sex tendencies excessive.	Girl, age 14.
Heredity: F. sex offender.	
Home conditions: through these early acquaintance with sex immorality.	
Sex delinquencies + including homosexual.	Mental: Good ability.

§ 145. **Inheritance of Physical Traits.** — The inheritance of other physical traits and characteristics, especially of the nervous system, which may have much to do with the production of crime, is so well substantiated that it hardly needs to be mentioned. We know, for instance, that an early onset of puberty, morally a dangerous event under certain environmental conditions, may be a family characteristic. Then, we have seen some very convincing examples of the inheritance of a lazy disposition in physically well-endowed people. In the case of one girl, unusually strong and capable, and for whom a great deal was done in an effort to save her from going to the bad, there seemed always to stand in the way a very definite temperament, showing itself as an innate tendency to take the easiest path. Although this girl lived far away from her father, in a different climate and among totally different people, she was said by those who knew both to be exceedingly like him in practical attitude toward life. The physical substratum of this physical and moral inertia, in the face of abundant good health, is hardly to be surmised.

The inheritance of inferiorities of mind or body, even outside the realm of feeblemindedness or insanity, is so well known that we need not give examples. Those of our cases of constitutional inferiority which have developed on the basis of inheritance may be studied. The many other points which our various individual studies suggest concerning the problem of inheritance, can receive such elucidation as our present knowledge affords, through reference to the many technical works upon the subject. The effect of alcoholism of parents upon the offspring is discussed under the head of alcoholism, § 194, and in our chapter on statistics, § 115.

§ 146. **Familial Biological Defect.** — At this place we should call attention to a possible misinterpretation of causative factors.

If several of a family fraternity are found mentally defective it is generally inferred that their characteristics are derived from ancestral strains where such defect must have been potent. But this is not always the case, for the results of the union of two elements, growing under definite conditions, may be regularly the production of characteristics which are not somatically innate in either one of the ancestors who carried these elements. The following family history is illustrative of this point.

Case 7. — We have studied four members of a fraternity of nine, five of whom are defective. The father and mother are both honest, fairly intelligent and reliable people. They utterly deny the existence of mental defect on either side. In neither family has any one been in an institution. All brothers and sisters of the father and mother are self-supporting and their few children are all said to be normal. We can imagine no reason why, in the face of other frank revelations they have made, the parents should conceal family facts, and they corroborate each other. Certainly if one were to go by Mendelian proportions, one would expect a trait which shows itself in five out of nine children to be prepotent in the ancestral history, and therefore to be well known as family characteristics.

The father and mother were married at 23 and 21 respectively. The mother is a healthy, strong woman, and the father has held a federal position for some 20 years. Since our acquaintance with him he has been incapacitated for 2 years with tuberculosis. When we first knew him, 3 years previously, he was recognized, although quite able to work steadily, as having the disease in an incipient stage. How long he had it prior to that time is not known. He has been non-alcoholic. There are no signs of syphilis or of any other constitutional disease in the family. No children dead. The children's characteristics run as follows: I. Girl, 19, reached 8th grade. Supports herself. Comparatively healthy. II. Girl, 5th grade at 14 years. Never seriously ill. No convulsions. Decidedly good-looking. Became a tremendous sex delinquent. When studied by us she graded only as a moron, but it is possible, since she had a record of 5th grade, that she was in a temporarily poor condition. She later was reported as doing well morally and being a good worker, but undoubtedly is subnormal mentally. III. Boy of 16, imbecile. When outside of an institution is much of a menace on account of bad sex habits. Severely ill with spinal meningitis at 2 1-2

199

years, but before then seemed to be defective. IV. Boy of 12. 1st grade. Cannot write; speech defect. V. Boy of 9. 3d grade; seems normal. VI. Girl of 7 years. 1st grade and seems normal. VII. Boy of 5 years. Had spasms three times during infancy. Does not talk plainly. Evidently defective. VIII. Boy of 4 years. Only just commenced to talk. Did not walk until he was 2 1-2 years. Once had convulsions. IX. Girl of 15 months. Walks and runs about very well. Seems normal. In this family history of defect the possible influence of the father's chronic disease, tuberculosis, must remain for us merely a matter of conjecture.

CHAPTER II

FACTORS IN DEVELOPMENTAL CONDITIONS

§ 147. **General Statement.** — As may be seen by our analysis (§ 99) of defective developmental conditions which, in our young offenders, could be regarded in any way as causes, we divided the developmental period into antenatal, natal and postnatal, including in the latter the usual developmental period of childhood. Some general discussion of this whole matter is needed. All these causes in early development are merely antecedents of present conditions which are to be found in mind and body. They are to be regarded as causes only inasmuch as they do produce discoverable effects or peculiarities; they can never be in any way regarded as directly responsible for delinquency. From this it may be easily seen why, although we would not in any way undervalue this group of causes, in our classification such antecedents never emerge as major factors. To make it clearer we may state, for instance, that old age of the father at the time of conception could not be scientifically considered as having any relationship to delinquency unless the individual produced from this conception was mentally or physically inferior. Or some head injury in childhood, which is often alleged to stand in relationship to delinquent tendencies, cannot be recognized as a cause unless one finds evidence of possible resultant physical trouble or mental instability. But the obviously varying import of the factors as they are discussed will make this whole matter much clearer, and will show the need for individual interpretation of earlier conditions.

201

A. Antenatal.

§ 148. **Physical Conditions During Pregnancy.** — It will be noted (§ 99) that in 40 instances, or 5 per cent., of our analyzed cases we learned of ailments during pregnancy which were severe enough to lead us to consider them probable antecedent causes. What we discovered abnormal in the offspring — anything from mental defect to the various signs of physical inferiority — was very likely, and in some cases without doubt, due to the antenatal conditions. Sometimes our evidence was made strong by the fact that this given individual differed from the others of the same fraternity, all of whom had been born after a normal pregnancy.

It is hardly necessary to give each specific condition of the mother which may cause trouble. It is obvious that a wasting chronic disease, or a severe acute ailment, might be sufficient. Among our cases are instances of a child being born of a mother suffering either from cancer, tuberculosis, extreme debility from a recent illness, and so on. We have seen two cases where children were born when the mother had puerperal eclampsia. Both came from highly intelligent families, and were the only members of the fraternity or family who showed mental abnormality. One has specialized mental defects, and the other is a subnormal, unbalanced individual. In both, tendencies to antisocial conduct have developed. One showed defects of the teeth which are ordinarily accredited to the effects of syphilis. The latter could without much doubt be ruled out — a fact especially interesting to syphilographers. A similar dental condition was found in an individual born of a cancerous mother. Other severe illnesses, such as typhoid fever during pregnancy, without any doubt leave influences, as we have observed, upon the offspring, which may result in mental abnormality later connected with delinquency.

§ 149. **Abuse During Pregnancy.** — This is a factor that is much more difficult to evaluate, and we have only included it when the history showed it to be an exaggerated case. If a woman is half starved and brow-beaten, or actually beaten, as women are sometimes by brutal and drunken husbands, she is likely to become herself a poorly-nourished individual, and to poorly nourish her infant. We have known of a number of extreme cases of this kind: a woman lying in bed perhaps for days as the result of mistreatment and lack of food.

§ 150. **Mother Mentally Troubled.** — It is still harder to gauge this, and in the vast majority of cases we have not included it at all as a cause, but when one hears of worry to the extent of causing malnutrition and much physical disturbance it can be fairly considered that the unborn child is a probable sufferer. An extreme case of this kind which very likely resulted in the mental defect of a child, who is a tremendous delinquent, runs as follows: An immigrant woman of good physical strength, who, according to her account, comes of a healthy and mentally normal family, had a terrible trouble in the 6th or 7th month of pregnancy. She came home one day to find her home destroyed and her husband and four children burned to death as the result of an explosion. But the difficulty of proof of cause, even in this case, is great, since we cannot trace the family history. This mother at first seemed reliable, but as the years have gone on she has become very unreasonable, perhaps simply as the result of her very great and continued troubles. She has always insisted that her other children were normal, and that there was no feeblemindedness in either family. The mental shock caused, of course, physical debilitation. Clearly, we should put down this as the probable main factor of the feeblemindedness which is the more direct cause of the delinquency.

Excessive worry, such as that connected with a husband's illness and death during pregnancy, may very rationally be supposed to so interfere with the mother's physical conditions as to affect the child. It would be more difficult to prove the connection between such a shock, *vide* § 159, as the mother being in a big train robbery. In one case like this we were unable to find that the child really was left with any definite physical or mental signs which would make the claim of causation clear.

§ 151. **Insanity and Epilepsy of the Pregnant Mother.** — It is often impossible to know in what proportion the abnormalities of the offspring of a mother who is pregnant when insane are due to heredity or to antenatal condition. In all but one case we have ruled out the latter, but there we learned of the mother being terribly negligent of herself, and very likely this negligence helped to produce the child that was not up to normal. The child of an epileptic mother who is having attacks during pregnancy is much more likely to suffer from defective antenatal conditions. It is well known that there is toxemia at the time of convulsions and, of course, the unborn child must directly suffer from the poisons which are circulating in the mother's blood.

§ 152. **Alcoholism During Pregnancy.** — Difficulty that there is in understanding the bad effect of alcohol upon germ cells is not paralleled by its obviously easy influence upon the growing fetus. Alcohol circulates with great ease through such membranes as separate the mother's blood from the embryonic circulation, and thus the growing brain cells are bathed in it in proportion as the mother takes it into her system. There is much to prove that cells in the younger stages of growth are more plastic and more readily affected by alcoholic poison. So the drinking mother stands a very good chance, by all accounts, of bringing forth children with defective or unstable nervous systems. We know the relation, in turn, of these abnormalities to human inefficiency and to criminalism.

Proofs of the above as a cause are, very naturally, vitiated by the fact that a later defective environment practically always is also a factor. Indeed, in cases where we heard of the mother's alcoholism during pregnancy, we found that there was so much else that might account for the child's bad conduct that we have been obliged to refrain from ever including this as a main factor. As in the case of probable alcoholic deterioration of germ cells (*vide* § 194) proofs of actual deterioration will have to come through direct physiological, rather than through social and psychological studies.

§ 153. **Morphinism During Pregnancy.** — It is certain that morphine taken by the pregnant mother affects the unborn child. The infant sometimes will not survive unless it is given some allowance of the morphine which it has been previously receiving. In a couple of our case histories of constitutional inferiors, morphinism of the mother appears in the background, but, of course, there is difficulty in knowing how fairly to interpret the inferiority which we find. The mother herself may have been a morphinist because she was already an abnormal individual.

§ 154. **Congenital Syphilis.** — The germ of syphilis is now known to infect the embryo and to cause its results in this way, rather than by deteriorating the germ cells of the parent, as was formerly supposed. The after-effects in the further developed individual may be seen in numerous organs of the body and in

the central nervous system. The diagnosis must be left to the
physician who nowadays is not satisfied with the old pathog-
nomonic signs, but requires tests made from the blood. The
length of time the disease is active in an individual who is born
with it varies greatly, both with and without treatment.

It is clear that when the central nervous system is much affected, or when there is a sensory defect as the result of congenital syphilis, the relationship of the disease to delinquency
may be close. Feeblemindedness or epilepsy or some forms of
insanity may follow from this congenital disease; the relationship of these mental troubles to crime is elsewhere shown. There
is a tremendous variation in the possible effects upon the nervous system which runs all the way from idiocy or juvenile
paresis to mere headaches or nervous instability. One case
(§ 300) we studied was that of a boy who had long unsuccessfully
been tried under probation and who was readily found to be
suffering from juvenile paresis with the usual physical signs.

We expect sometime to see these harmless blood tests for
inherited syphilis done on all children who come under public
care, in order that any who are infected may receive appropriate
treatment as early as possible. Such protective measures will
yet come to be regarded as a sacred duty. If only one case out
of 50 among dependents and young delinquents was found suffering from the disease, the possible outcome of treatment might
readily pay for the effort. The fact is that when numbers have
been tested, as in a few European centers, a very considerable
percentage has been found infected. For our American population it would be unwise to predict at all what would be found
among the young people who come under public care.

It is a matter of much public interest to know what is the after-
history of children with inherited syphilis, as gauged by the
study of large numbers. Study of this kind involves much effort
and only recently have results been obtainable. The findings [1]

---

[1] Several researches involving arduous labor in following up cases of congenital syphilis have recently appeared and are worthy of careful attention.
Peiser (269) reports on conditions of general health in cases of congenital
syphilis which have been treated. He maintains that general physical conditions are by no means so unfavorable as frequently assumed, if the individual
survives infancy, and most of them do. Among those treated at the Breslau
clinic during a 10-year period, 39 per cent. were later found in excellent general condition and 37 per cent. in fair condition. Hochsinger (270) traced
263 children whom he has had under his charge for many years. He found that
14 per cent. died during the first year, and 25 per cent. grew up to be healthy
adults. If puberty is passed without manifestations, there is every probability

lead us inevitably to the conclusion that syphilis in the parents which is passed along to the offspring has a more injurious influence upon the physical and mental development of children than is observed in any other disease. Several writers who have followed up cases state that even when there are no ordinary physical manifestations of the disease itself, the children are found physically and morally inferior. Vas (**271**) reports that even when the mental development was satisfactory many parents complained that the children were extraordinarily nervous and naughty. Hochsinger (**270**) notes a great deal of trouble with moral development in these cases.

The exact relationship of syphilis to epilepsy and feeblemindedness has been worked up by modern methods in some places. The result has been unexpectedly small, but, of course, varies greatly according to the community from which the patients are drawn. In Denmark, *vide* Thomsen (**272**), it is clear that in less than 2 per cent. of 2000 cases of mental deficiency was congenital syphilis of etiological moment. Such a small finding as this is of great interest to us, but it involves only a very small part of the whole problem of the possible connection between the disease and future delinquency.

§ 155. **Old Age of Parents.** — There seems to be good evidence that a child born of a mother long after she has had other children, and after she has begun her involutional period may be physically or mentally defective. We have seen several such cases. Old age on the part of the father has only seemed to figure in one case, if we compared the individual with his fraternity.

§ 156. **Attempted Abortion.** — It is extremely difficult to know to what extent attempted abortion may be a cause of deficiency on the part of the child. Certainly in many cases we have heard of it without there being any defect, and yet in others the case seemed clear, but mostly when there was a hemorrhage. Again, one would have to be very careful in evaluating this as a cause.

§ 157. **Twins.** — It sometimes happens that one of twins is

---

that the individual will permanently escape them. But he found only 51 individuals absolutely normal out of 208 cases who had been years under observation. None of the children with pronounced symptoms soon after birth grew up to be healthy. There are many cases of defective mental and moral development as well as physical. Vas (**271**) reports on a large number of children as observed a few years after passing through the policlinic. One-tenth of these had convulsions; one-third suffered from habitual headache; enuresis was comparatively common, and there was much complaint from parents of bad behavior.

smaller than the other, and seems to have suffered the result of nutritional "crowding," leaving it very defective in comparison to the other.

§ 158. **Mother Working During Pregnancy.** — The effect of hard work must be interpreted according to the conditions. The unborn child of many a peasant woman seems to thrive while its mother labors, but we have heard many times of what was undoubtedly over-work, which may very largely have affected the infant.

§ 159. **Maternal Impressions.** — The effect of so-called prenatal influences or maternal impressions (namely, some condition or activity of the mother's mind) in molding in any way the mind or body of the unborn child has yet to be proven.[1] This is in nowise controverting the well-known serious effects of disease, sorrow, or worry shown in nutritional disturbance, or the effects of lack of food, poisoning, etc., during pregnancy.

Very many times we have heard mothers or even fathers, harking back from the fact of their offspring's delinquency, state that the cause was to be found in some of the mother's mental experiences during her pregnancy. But in every such case we have also heard of, or found, other more direct influences (quite sufficient in hundreds of instances to produce delinquency when such maternal impressions were lacking). So there was neither the logical necessity nor the scientific right to seize upon this supposed cause. An example of the type of explanation we hear offered would be the case of a thieving and runaway constitutional inferior of 16 years whose father insisted that the boy's disposition came as the result of the mother handling money in covetous spirit during this pregnancy. As a matter of fact the boy struggled with very irritating physical conditions during his childhood and then later was taken in hand by the worst sort of rascals and instructed in pernicious habits. But of course the father did not realize either of these other points. And so it has gone in all cases where we have heard of prenatal influences in explanation of criminality.

Superficially it suggests direct causation to argue, for instance, from the child's thieving back to the fact that the pregnant mother

---

[1] I particularly like the scholarly and temperate summary of Thompson (**224**), one of the foremost students of heredity, on this subject. Perhaps in the present stage of our scientific knowledge it is better to be a little less sure than recent, widely distributed statements, *vide* West (**225**). However, these much more nearly approach known truth than fulsome injunctions to mothers about mentally influencing their embryonic children.

was forced to harbor a thief in her home. But never have we found
such an explanation standing alone as a probable or possible cause.
For the same reason we are logically forced to neglect the statement, often heard, that some given child at conception was not
wanted, and therefore shows anti-social traits.

B. Natal.

§ 160. **Premature Birth.** — The prematurely born child has a
poor start in the world, but it is not necessarily permanently handi-
capped by it. In our type of studies premature birth could not be
included as any possible cause of delinquency unless there were
physical or mental evidences of defect which may have been in
turn the result of premature birth.

§ 161. **Difficult Labor.** — In this, again, the results are not
easy to interpret. We have as a matter of enumeration put down
the cases where we had history of extremely difficult labor, which
may possibly have caused intracranial conditions that later tended
to produce delinquency. But altogether the interpretation is
most unsatisfactory. Certainly there is no reason to suppose that
instrumental delivery in itself results in mental defect, any more
than merely prolonged labor where the head is for a long time
compressed. We have the same difficulty about evaluating
asphyxia in the new-born. This, together with prolonged labor
and the use of forceps, has been blamed by several authors for the
subsequent appearance of nervous disorders and mental defects.
The only comparative study which I have been able to find is
that of Hannes (250), who investigated the after-records of three
series from the same maternity hospital, cases of asphyxia, artificial delivery, and normal spontaneous birth, 150 of each. He
found no significant difference whatever between the outcome of
these three series. He concludes there is no ground for the belief
that forceps have any permanent injurious effect. He also sees
every reason to believe that if an asphyxiated child is resuscitated,
and has no complication during the first week, it will not subse-
quently suffer from this cause.

Of course there are exceptional cases where the effect of accidents at birth is very plain, or where the individual has permanently suffered from intracranial hemorrhage within a few days
after birth, but Hannes seems to show clearly that in general
one cannot fairly place much stress upon untoward birth conditions as such, if they are properly handled.

C. Postnatal.

§ 162. **General Statement.** — All the conditions enumerated in § 99 as defective features of early development can be directly interpreted without further discussion. The bearings of cranial injury, chorea, epilepsy, etc., are discussed under their appropriate headings. They are effective in the production of delinquency only as they cause some form of mental abnormality. In an undue number of cases we have learned of convulsions during childhood, quite apart from the positive demonstrations of epilepsy. Then brain fever and meningitis have figured in our cases to a much larger proportion than would be found in the ordinary population. The relationship of both of these to possible brain-cell injury is clear. In numerous other cases we have heard of extremely defective conditions of nourishment and general health during infancy. It is hard to interpret these for our purposes. Neither is any connection of rickets with mental conditions certain. When we have heard of illnesses, such as cholera infantum, with evidence of accompanying involvement of the central nervous system, for instance, coma or convulsions, it is to be fairly thought that there may have been some damage to brain cells.

It is easy to appreciate that illness during the normal period of school life may have social as well as direct physical significance. If the individual's schooling is ended at 14 years, whatever the acquirements or non-acquirements, as it is in many we have studied, then previous periods away from the school-room may prove a distinct disadvantage, which can, in turn, cause tendency towards delinquency.

The effects of stimulants and narcotics in early development are mentioned in Chapter V, Book II.

D. Senility.

§ 163. **Nature and Causes of Offenses of Old Age.** — In dealing with the offenses of old age we may see for the first time a practically valuable correlation between age and the type of offense. Although directly due to mental aberration, the delinquency is properly chargeable to unfortunate features of physical involution of the individual. We ourselves, as students of genetics, have particularly easy sailing here because so many of the senile delinquents are first offenders, as will be shown later, and therefore the causative factors are immediately at hand.

Comparatively few of the offenses of old age are committed by individuals previously considered demented. With far-gone senile dementia there often comes much bodily weakness. Or even if not, there is excuse in an obviously childish person for childish type of misconduct. In instance, we might cite the case of a man, cultured and of previously good reputation, who purloined flowers at intervals from a public park when he was about 80 years of age. His general dementia was so evident that no policeman ever felt justified in taking him even to the station house. But yet, though delinquency in old age be the only expression of senile dementia, it evidences just this. It is a phenomenon unquestionably dependent upon the defective physiological conditions of blood vessels and brain cells which lead to a break-down in the efficiency of the mental processes. Study of such cases shows that the trouble comes from defect in force of will power and ethical discrimination.

The several main considerations concerning this whole subject can best be dealt with categorically as follows:

(a) *Type of offenses peculiar to old age.* Beyond 60 years of age, when the general tendency towards anti-social behavior is markedly diminished,[1] we find certain types of misconduct springing up in unexpected places. Comparatively few women at this period of life engage in offenses, and these usually for petty stealing. Most of the offenders are old men, and their delinquencies are nearly always sexual. Bresler (266), who has contributed the only extended writing upon this subject, makes many points clear to us. He strikingly shows that while the proportion of general crime after 70 years is only $\frac{1}{4}$ to $\frac{1}{8}$ as much as in the previous decade, sexual offenses are $\frac{1}{2}$ as many. Aschaffenburg (1, Eng. trans., p. 154) puts it differently. He says that grand larceny after the 70th year is only $\frac{1}{150}$ part of what it is between 18 and 21, relating the delinquency to an equal number of persons of the given ages. But convictions for indecency and rape are almost $\frac{1}{4}$ as many, proportionately to the same number of persons.

---

[1] On this point the convincing figures of the "Statistik des Deutschen Reiches" N. F. LXXXIII, II, (concerning the proportion of crime by ages and number of inhabitants) may be consulted. Aschaffenburg (1, Eng. trans., p. 155) gives the figures in detail.

Now this peculiarity of old age finds other social expression, which Bresler has delved out of national statistics. He shows that in the 5 years from 1900–1904 the marriages of girls of 20 years and under run as follows: 401 married men between 40 and 50; 1521 married men between 50 and 60; 1762 married men over 70. These figures must have increased significance in the light of the fact that there are considerably fewer men living over 70. But, of course, there are somewhat modifying circumstances, such as an increased number of widowers, and so on. Still, even so, Bresler's figures are very interesting.

(b) *Many senile delinquents are first offenders.* It has been generally noted by all who have had much experience that many old men who commit sexual offenses have never before been in collision with the law. Indeed, some of them are people of high previous reputation, professional men, and men of distinctly religious proclivities. This point is also much more convincingly dealt with statistically. Notwithstanding the greater chances which a long life offers any one for at some time becoming an offender, Bresler shows that the proportion of first offenders increases from 50 years onward. The maximum number of first offenders are punished from 18 to 21 years. Of the offenders between 40 and 50 years of age, 49 per cent. are punished for the first time. Those between 60 and 70, 60 per cent.; those over 70 years, 67 per cent. Beginning with 60 years a greater percentage of first offenders among convicted criminals are found than at any other period save between 18 and 21. Pathetic instances are known to all of us of men who have fallen from a previously high estate by indulging in uncannily morbid sex offenses. It is unnecessary for us to take space to relate the details.

(c) *The mental condition of aged offenders.* There can be little doubt that in every one of these aged offenders some mental changes have taken place. The alterations are mostly in the field of will and of the ethical sense. Every one has recognized the lowering of emotional tone in old age. Whether these changes should come under the category of legal insanity is not a matter for us now to discuss. As we have frequently stated, such problems are only solved according to general social (legal) plans and principles. Aschaffenburg (263) maintains that every case which he has ever seen has shown senile mental decay. Kinberg (52), as the result of his prolonged experience with prison cases, demands that there shall be obligatory psychiatric examination for every offender over 60. Krafft-Ebing (267) long ago in his work on forensic psychology maintained that the main trouble in these cases is involutional degeneration of the brain. Anatomical changes bring about both weakened ethics and decreased resistance to sex feeling.

(d) *Local physical irritation and treatment.* A significant feature of these sexual offenses is that they mostly occur after 60 years of age, when sexual powers normally have waned or practically disappeared. The explanation that senile brain degeneration causes lowered ethical discrimination does not to some satisfactorily explain the great increase in sex stimulation, which only can account for the nature of the delinquencies. There are several points which here have to be considered.

The fact is that there is a marked tendency towards the selection of children for these offenses. More occasionally abnormal acts are indulged in, including exhibitionism, the latter representing the most impotent procedure. Krafft-Ebing suggests that the peculiar sex objects selected are indication of weakened potency. Another general tendency of the same period of life is toward the use of obscene language. This has been specially noted as a phenomenon of advancing age. But none of this tells perhaps the whole story.

It is undoubtedly true that in some cases there is much actual sex stimulation and apparent sex power. It has been more recently suggested that a considerable share of these unfortunate tendencies of old age are immediately due to local irritative conditions in the pelvis, particularly as brought about by the characteristic senile enlargement of the prostate gland. Percy (268) makes a special point of this. While he, and other surgeons perhaps, take into account too little the well-known brain degeneration of old age, still one sees no reason why local irritation may not be all the more productive of offensive tendencies because of lowered inhibitions. The reported cases of complete alteration in this respect after operation must be regarded cautiously as proving the original factor, because of the great moral influence that an important operation might have. Elsewhere we have had to insist on this point in connection with surgical measures. There is the possible element of suggestion, and there is the shock which might very well stimulate will power. When a man's conduct is sufficiently anti-social to demand a serious operation, there is pretty likely to be contrition and constructive apperception following the operation, even in cases of mild dementia. We eagerly await the accumulation of more proof on these points.

In regard to treatment we can but see every reason for carrying out surgical measures whenever indicated. With the physical benefit, we may hope for commensurate moral improvement.

CHAPTER III

PHYSICAL CONDITIONS: PECULIARITIES AND AILMENTS

§ 164. **General Considerations.** — It is far from my purpose to go at length into the question of bodily characteristics of criminals taken as a class, or even of alleged special physical types. Much discussion has arisen over various data collected on this separate point, but it is almost valueless for any one who sees the practical, scientific necessity of reviewing *all* probable causes before arriving at conclusions. Again we might remind the reader that studies, even of the brain and skull, such as Sernoff's (**195**), leading to supposed discrimination of types, are fatally weak if complete differentiation is not made, for instance, between mentally defective and mentally normal criminals. Of course we should expect the former frequently to show anomalies of brain and skull, and we well know from recent studies by psychological tests what a considerable proportion of prison populations these mental underlings form. The large, well-substantiated correlations that should at once be grasped by the student of criminalistic genetics are, first, that the mentally weak readily become members of the chronic offender class, and, second, that innate mental weakness is very often accompanied by signs of physical defect or anomaly. Nowhere in the extensive literature do we find any evidence whatever that mentally normal delinquents have typically peculiar bodily characteristics.

As we stated in our chapter on statistics, where our specific findings on bodily conditions may be reviewed, statements about the physique of American prisoners or other delinquents must be compared with American norms. More than that, for the fair deduction of conclusions they must be compared with norms for the classes of the population from which the given criminals come. The oft-quoted findings of Elmira Reformatory, where

214

so many thousands have been physically examined and found exceedingly wanting, unless these delinquents were to be compared with others of the same family, nation, or environment, have no value for proving that the physical conditions were responsible for the criminality — and that is one point at issue. From different parts of the country we get differing facts, as we might well expect. Sleyster (**196**) recently reports from Wisconsin that 1521 adult criminals studied by him there at the penitentiary, as a class are well nourished, that they are only 1.8 inches below the average American height, that they weigh about the same as the average American for their height, that their chest measurement is quite fair, and so on. Can any one doubt the good physique and keen senses that go largely to the making of a desperado in our western states? The gist of this situation is undoubtedly best stated by Goring (**160**, p. 370) from his most careful researches: " The physical and mental constitution of both criminal and law-abiding persons, of the same age, stature, class and intelligence, are identical." In many places the prisoner is, on the average, markedly differentiated from the normal population by defective physique — and so is the general social class he is drawn from. Then, of course, the possession of a certain type of physique, as in Fagin's gang, may be an asset for engaging in a certain type of offense.

In any study and discussion of the general criminal physique, it must never be forgotten that calculation of average types is probably largely spoiled by the fact that it is the criminal weakest in mind and body who is most frequently arrested and rearrested, entirely out of proportion to the total number of persons committing crime.

The good to be derived from deciding on what are the physical characteristics of whole groups of delinquents — and only by grouping them rationally can any good at all come — is in the establishment of accurate bases for social action, either in providing for treatment, legal or otherwise, of the person, or in treatment of living conditions, such as poverty and slum life. Even then the facts will always have to be locally surveyed — witness the difference there must be between need for medical treatment of prisoners in the just-mentioned Wisconsin prison and at Elmira.

With the above comment on generalities, and with reference to our chapter on Orientation for some statement of our relation to anthropological criminology, and to our chapter on Treatment

215

for other matters connected with physical conditions of delinquents, we may return to our particular business—the individual, and the gaining of knowledge concerning the causation of his tendencies. At once we may restate the fact, concurred in by all careful students of criminalism, that no one single measure of relief or alteration of physical conditions, whether it be correction of eye strain, circumcision, operation on the head, or what not, offers the chance of any considerable amount of total reconstruction in the crime situation.

On the other hand, it ought to be generally realized, in all common sense, that any physical peculiarities, defects, or diseases of the offender which stand in the way of social success should be as efficiently treated as possible. It is of the utmost benefit to society to equip its members who are costly failures with the foundations that are necessary for betterment of conduct. The treatment may require any of a large number of measures; perhaps removal to a more suited environment, perhaps a surgical operation, perhaps segregation in a special colony. One of the best things that we can do in this chapter is to state most of the defective physical conditions (this does not include the stigmata of inferiority or degeneracy elsewhere touched upon, § 106, § 295) which appear to be in any way causative of delinquency. The handicap which many of these are to the individual's well-doing is so obvious that, for the most part, case histories need not be given. The importance of certain physical conditions is altogether so clear that giving small space to their consideration will not be charged to indifferent concern about their treatment.

In thinking of the possible effects of treatment we must always remember, even when physical conditions are diagnosable as probable causative or contributory factors, that mental habits may have been formed. These will leave sufficient cause for continuance of the effect, namely, delinquency, even when some original causes may be removed.

Physical conditions concerned at all with the causation of delinquent tendencies could rather readily be divided into those which cause weakness and those which cause irritation. In thinking of how the bodily condition acts in a causative way, both possibilities should be kept in mind. Of course plenty of inimical bodily conditions, such as large tonsils, may be found in delinquents, and, while offenders should receive treatment as well as anybody else, many of such troubles cannot be said to

216

have any traceable relationship to the misconduct. Several physical findings of great importance for understanding the causative development of criminal careers belong properly among developmental abnormalities (§ 182 ff.), where we shall discuss them.

§ 165. **Ocular Ailments.** — In our estimation of causes of delinquency it appeared that defective vision could be regarded as either a major or minor factor in over 10 per cent. of the cases. Vision, to be sure, was not perfect in many other instances, but in these it was hardly to be regarded as any cause of the delinquency. There are several sides to the resultant effects of bad eyesight, so far as delinquency is concerned.

Eye strain notoriously leads to irritability, discontent, headache, various feelings of bodily discomfort — all of which may be contributory to the individual's delinquency. Now eye strain, it should be remembered, is not always to be readily measured by what the individual can see on a test chart. Defective vision may exist without strain, and strain may result from not readily discerned defects, such as astigmatism. This latter may be provocative of such unconscious irritations as we are interested in. These irritations are just such feelings as are likely, especially during the adolescent period, to cause a reaction in anti-social acts.

Another important side of this question concerning eye trouble should be thoughtfully considered by those who work for the prevention of delinquency. This consists in the relation which defective vision bears to the acquirement of education and interests. We all acknowledge that we must considerably rely for the prevention of the development of delinquent impulses upon not only giving the individual the foundations for earning a livelihood, but also upon developing desire for wholesome recreations and pursuits. With poor eyesight the carrying out of both these desiderata is seriously impeded, and the pathway to undesirable tendencies is left abnormally easy of passage.

Engaging in satisfactory occupations may be interfered with to various extent by defective vision. We remember the exaggerated instance of one lad placed out on a farm, who was returned by the farmer as of no account because of his carelessness. This boy was then found to be so nearsighted that he was not able to clearly see the holes in which to drop the seed corn. In vocationally training individuals in reformatories this factor of vision should ever be kept in mind. I have noted the instance of a

217

young fellow with exceedingly bad eyesight, partially corrected by glasses, being taught in a reformatory the craft of engraving.

It must not be forgotten that children who have never known what it was to see any better may not understand the basis of their own troubles. They may never complain to the teacher or parent. They merely react with disgust or recalcitrancy, whether in school or at work, if the demand upon their vision is beyond easy fulfillment.

Strabismus is one of the ocular troubles which may cause a tendency towards delinquency. There may be annoyance through eye strain and also through the jeering of comrades. We have seen some distinctly good moral results from the straightening of eyes by operation.

In less measure, one might offer the same statement about ailments of the eyelids, when vision is somewhat attended with discomfort. At the risk of being anecdotal we may speak of a curious case where capital was made of such a physical ailment.

Case 8. — A boy of 14 had chronic inflammation of the eyelids, and a consequent stoppage of the tear ducts. As a result of this, the little fellow by squeezing his eyes could cause tears to run down his cheeks. He and his family found this a source of considerable income. The boy haunted the down-town districts at an hour when people were in sympathetic mood, coming from restaurant dinners and the theatres, and, offering chewing gum for sale, he would be seen profusely weeping. This often brought to his pocket quarters or even half-dollars in place of the usual nickel, and the boy was thus able to enjoy a right royal income. When sent to the eye infirmary his parents at once objected to his receiving any treatment. It is quite fitting to relate that these parents themselves more recently have had to bring this boy to court for delinquency. He is somewhat subnormal mentally, and after his prolonged experience of earning money easily has been quite unwilling to work at any honest occupation. This type of a cause of delinquency belongs in the same category as some mentioned in our chapter on abnormalities of development, where capital has been made of the possession of exceptionally small physical stature, *vide* § 185.

§ 166. **Ear Troubles.** — Markedly defective hearing is not nearly so frequently found among delinquents as defective vision. Even then we cannot regard it as of any importance, except when it has interfered with education, or with the development of

218

wholesome interests, or with occupational success. The peculiar characteristics, often recalcitrant, of the deaf person, are well known. The varying conditions of hearing which arise from middle-ear infection and otorrhea are notoriously irritating. This having good hearing one day and poor the next, causes both sufferer and teacher, or any one else associated, readily to become provoked. Tinnitus aurium, ringing in the ears, in several instances of delinquency we have found to be a great source of irritation, as might naturally be expected. It has been more than once pointed out that such annoyances may lead towards the establishment of chronic mental troubles. Inflammations of the mastoid cells, those which lie in close contiguity to the ear, with the continual throwing off of poisons into the system may be of importance in our studies. Frequently such inflammation arises from middle-ear infection and sometimes is accompanied by the annoying subjective noises of which we have just spoken. Low-grade inflammations that reach up through the mastoid bone to the meninges may occasionally cause even disturbances in brain function.

§ 167. **Nose and Throat Obstructions.** — Occluded pharynx or nostrils, adenoids, and excessively large tonsils may readily be sources of physical weakness and general malaise. The results are so obvious and have been dwelled on in so many works on hygiene that we need not discuss them here, except to say that one can be very certain that these conditions may occasionally be at the basis of such delinquent tendencies as grow from weakness and discomfort. The trouble may begin with a distaste for school work. While, of course, adults suffer much less from these conditions, yet there may be interference with success at employment. No doubt there has been much exaggeration in general of the effect of the above conditions. We are much inclined to agree with Gulick and Ayres (**201**) who, after having made a most extensive survey of the conditions among large numbers of school children, become very conservative in a general statement about the matter of the final results of such physical defects as large tonsils and adenoids. They show clearly that these troubles tend to disappear with increasing age. But, of course, no one doubts the value of removing actual obstructions to proper breathing, or tissue which is definitely engendering disease.

Mouth breathing is usually caused by the above conditions, but may in other cases only be a habit. In either instance the

219

expression of the mouth breather gives him a distinct disadvantage, inasmuch as the first impression the employer or other observer gains is one of inefficiency.

§ 168. **Teeth.** — It should go without saying that extremely carious teeth are not only a menace to the general good health of their possessor, but also stand in the way of normal social achievement. It is to be emphasized that it is not the local discomfort, or the inability to properly masticate, so much as it is the constant absorption into the system of poisons generated by decay, which does damage. It might be difficult to estimate the social results of taking care properly of the teeth, although some have attempted this task,[1] but there can be no gainsaying the common sense that should lead to proper dental treatment of a delinquent whose mouth conditions are thoroughly bad.

Within a few years some little stir has been made concerning the relationship of dental impaction to the production not only of nervous troubles, but, it has been suggested, also of delinquency. There have been only a few contributors to this subject.[2] Dental impaction, it must be understood, means the crowding of teeth in the jaws before eruption. The diagnosis in many cases is only to be made by use of the skiagraph. The gist of the whole subject is that while no doubt there may be considerable peripheral nerve irritation as the result of impacted teeth, and this may result in unfortunate reflex conditions which are not consciously perceived, still the proof is quite wanting that there is any marked connection between this and bad behavior. All the dental surgeons we have consulted are extremely skeptical of the alleged facts. The skiagraph also may show chronic abscesses about the roots of the teeth, and these may be the cause, in turn, of chronic systemic poisoning of mild degree.

§ 169. **Speech Defects.**[3] — From time to time we have been tremendously impressed in the study of certain cases with the influence which a speech defect has had upon the personality of the offender. We agree entirely with several authorities

---

[1] The interested student should consult the attempt of Wallin (**212**) to estimate psychologically the effect of dental treatment.

[2] The principal writer has been H. S. Upson (**213**) who has proceeded in an investigation by careful methods. The only instance known to me of delinquency treated and "cured" by the relief of dental impaction is reported by Holmes (**214**).

[3] A speech defect is a totally different affair from a language defect. The former is a trouble with the articulation of words. The latter is a mental defect; it is treated by us in § 278.

who state that the tendency of stuttering is to make the individual highly anti-social. The victim of this annoying disorder looks upon himself as very different from others of his kind, and is easily won by suggestions of anti-social behavior. It seems to be not always that the individual wishes to wander off by himself, although that is sometimes the case, but he finds comfort in the society of those who will readily put up with his disorder without comment, and who make little demand upon him. We have seen just this tendency result in miserably inferior associations on the part of otherwise normal young fellows. Thieving, vagrancy and homosexual practices have in consequence been indulged in.

Character deterioration has been made much of by specialists in speech defects. These maintain that the emotional disturbances and discouragements lead all the way to a definite psychosis and marked suicidal tendency.[1] From our own vivid experiences, for which we cannot afford space, as well as from the emphasis placed on the subject by others, we are convinced that a stuttering offender needs, above anything, encouragement and special treatment. We grant the difficulty in the way of the latter, accentuated by the double fact that treatment must be prolonged and that it requires the exertion of much will power, in which, of course, many of our offenders are lax. The whole matter is another argument for teachers with special knowledge to do imperatively needed work in reformatory institutions.

We grant at once that both stuttering and other speech defects may be one of the signs of essentially degenerate or defective traits. For adequate diagnosis and prognosis much more must be known of the individual than that he stutters or lisps. But by no means all people with speech defect are defectives in other abilities. We can all point out examples of the complete or partial overcoming of this disorder, and indeed the attainment of social success without entirely overcoming it. No doubt in such

---

[1] From the extensive literature on this subject we may select the following as specially bearing on the relation between speech defects, particularly stuttering, and character defect. Conradi (**215**) in a striking, short article calls attention to the relation between stuttering and mental retardation, with its consequent feeling of inferiority. Hoepfner (**216**) specifically deals with the peculiar character of the stutterer and his tendency to anti-social development, both on account of inner and outer conditions. Scripture (**217**) in his recent, most practical work on this subject also strongly emphasizes the peculiar mental disposition and conduct of the person suffering from speech defect. Many sides of the whole subject are dealt with in Gutzmann's (**218**) monograph.

cases the encouragements and mental training of a good early environment have had much to do with the outcome. In some of our delinquent stutterers we know there has been nothing but jibes and discouragements.

Aside from treatment of this trouble itself, one of the main points in handling a delinquent stutterer is to find for him a suitable occupation where a daily stint of work can be done without it being continually borne in upon the sufferer's consciousness that he is a defective individual. Work that requires as little association with fellow beings as possible, such as farming, may in consequence be most desirable.

§ 170. **Deaf-mutism.** — It should be easy for any one to believe that such an affliction as deaf-mutism might lead to extreme recalcitrancy, because of the dissatisfactions and irritation which follow attempts at social intercourse. Perhaps it is fortunate on this account that so many thus afflicted are taken care of in institutions. In some cases the inherited or acquired cause of the affection, generally one of the nervous system itself, has also left in its train a thoroughly unstable nervous make-up. The individual then is, of course, a constitutional inferior, presenting the typical signs, and should be treated as one. Such offenders may be terrible trouble-makers, as have been some cases studied by us.

The peculiarities of two of these cases, though deaf-mutism be comparatively rare, illustrate so well various features met with in the study of personalities of offenders that they are worth recounting. This can be done in short.

Case 9. — This was a boy of 15 who had been creating a great deal of trouble for years. His delinquencies may be summarized as; deliberately associating with extremely bad companions, quarrelsomeness, violence, great disobedience in school, running away from home and institutions, vagrancy, stealing. Besides the deaf-mutism we found physically a great contrast between general poor development and premature sex development. This was a marked anomaly.

In tests for mental ability he showed himself very keen and dexterous. We otherwise noted him as excitable, nervous, irritable, obstinate, changeable, and lacking in self-control. He was all this in spite of prolonged care in a model institution. He was born with the defects in his nervous system which prevented hearing. Altogether, he might be classed as a constitutional inferior. Outside of the fact that both his parents were deaf-mutes, his family history is unknown to us. The poor moral and social prognosis in such a case of extreme instability was quite evident; of course probation would fail. The last heard of this case was that he was again under arrest in another city for obtaining money under misrepresentation.

The other case involved malingering.

Case 10. — This was a boy of 15 who, after getting into various difficulties, engaged in a street robbery. At this time he was found in fair physical condition. He had been taught to speak in an institution. As a result of early illness he had very defective hearing, but his speech when he chose to use it was quite understandable. We graded him as being perhaps somewhat mentally dull on account of his auditory trouble, but even by the little work he was willing to do under observation he was found to be not feebleminded.

Our decision in this case was important, because one feature of the boy's malingering concerned itself with his pretending to be mentally defective. He had conceived the idea that if he were considered irresponsible he would be sent to an institution desirable from his standpoint. Our opinion was partially framed on the report from his old school, which told of the boy's ability and cunning. One difficulty in this case arose from the home surroundings which were atrociously bad and poverty-stricken. It was easy to see in this case that prolonged treatment in a reformatory institution was necessary, unless some one would be willing to try him by giving him a chance in a better home.

§ 171. **Minor Nervous Disorders.** — Most of the external signs of mild nervous disorders in offenders, whether they be habit spasms, great restlessness or what not, are accompanying phenomena, and not really any causes of delinquent tendencies. (It is in line with many professional observations to state the fact that neuropathic disorders are often found, entirely out of numerical proportion, among Jewish offenders.) The underlying nervous trouble must be sought out if moral betterment is to be expected. No doubt many of the observed symptoms grow from a neuropathic basis that not infrequently also engenders criminalism. Even for moral success the cases of offenders showing nervous signs should be placed in competent professional hands and a sufficiently prolonged adjustment with proper environmental conditions be undertaken. There is little room for doubt that many a criminal career would be prevented if neuropathic children were properly recognized as such and adequately treated early in life. Arguing to this point we may offer in bare summary two cases, the contrast between the outcomes of which has high significance.

Case 11. — A little boy of 10 years, already remarkable for his unreliability and his repeated running away from home (during which times he had gotten into sex-pervert practices) was found to be a highly nervous individual. He had previously suffered from rheumatism and, judging from the history, mild chorea. We also found traces of an old endocarditis. The main signs of disorder at present are what might best be termed general nervousness. By tests his mental ability was found fair: his advantages had been poor. So erratic was he, however, that the temporary diagnosis was neuropsychosis. The environmental conditions included poor parental oversight and poverty. Any one could see the type of treatment this boy needed. This was not carried out, and four years later, after a varying career of unreliability and petty stealing, committed more serious faults and had to be committed to an institution by the court.

Case 12. — The contrasting case is that of a boy of 13 who was rapidly becoming an out-and-out delinquent. The general charges were extreme disobedience, incorrigibility and stealing. This boy was found to be definitely a psychoneurotic. He showed various habit spasms and other nervous conditions at the time we saw him, and previously had been a very marked sufferer from morbid impulsions which had led him to extraordinary behavior, such as kicking himself while he walked, retracing his steps to touch posts, etc. General physical conditions were not extremely poor. Mentally he was found by tests to be a supernormal in ability. In the background there was defective heredity. The father, a gambler, was accustomed to gross sex immoralities. During the pregnancy the mother was much abused and had insufficient food. Home control and general advantages, particularly on account of poverty, were decidedly poor. This was a case which was promptly taken in hand, with the result that some months of life in a good environment in the country lowered his tendency to nervousness and gave the needed basis for the cessation of delinquent tendencies. With a small amount of attention from time to time this case, which easily might have developed seriously, has been carried along fairly satisfactorily.

Chorea (St. Vitus dance) is frequently accompanied by mental

symptoms and is discussed by us under the head of minor psychoses (§ 308).

§ 172. **Phimosis.** — As the result of assertions concerning the
relation of phimosis to disorders of character, we have been
constantly on the look-out for proof. It is quite proper for surgeons
and others to be always seeking possible causes for the genesis of
criminalistic tendencies, but on this point only a slight amount
of corroborative evidence is to be adduced. (We must caution
the reader that the word phimosis means a very definite condition, namely, imperfectly retractable prepuce.) The number of
times phimosis was found may be seen in our statistics (§ 97), and
it should be stated that never was it found as the sole physical
trouble. Under these circumstances it would not be safe to interpret any correlation with a given delinquent tendency, or
with the results of treatment directed simultaneously to several
conditions. The difficulties in the way of honest conclusions
about any single factor are demonstrated by the following case,
which, however, well shows the value of constructive measures.

Case 13. — This is a case of a boy, which for our immediate
purposes, may be summarized on a causative factor card —
with the additional statement that he has been in no more trouble
with the authorities since he had the benefit of surgical treatment
during a short stay in an institution. This treatment, however, was not circumcision alone; his nose conditions also were
looked after. Unfortunately, we cannot rule out of the result
the effect of the idea of punishment, which sometimes, even in
such cases, constrains to better behavior.

Physical conditions: Case 13.
    Teeth very crowded (earlier impaction?).   Boy, age 14.
    Very nervous.
    Deflected nasal septum — entire occlusion.
    Phimosis in excess.
    Poor development and nutrition.

  Heredity: Father terribly alcoholic.

    Antenatal: Mother much troubled.

      Masturbation as a very young child.
        Smoking.
Stealing.
Assault with weapon.   Mentality:
Sex, with girls.   Ability fair.

225

We have no doubt that phimosis in young children does cause irritability and nervousness, and the reaction may be bad behavior. But by the time the individual gets under the auspices of court people, either this phimosis, as such, has disappeared, or bad impulses and habits of thought, quite beyond the reach of a surgeon's knife, have been established. This may be so with any physical condition which was originally a cause, and certainly is true in the considerable number of cases where we have noted that circumcision has been followed by no change of character. Then we must not leave out of count our Jewish offenders; they display just the same types of conduct. Now all this is not denying that in very rare instances we have felt sure that the operation in young boys did result in a very considerable change of behavior. Nor do we assert it should not be done whenever there is any fair chance of it doing good. Where the trouble exists, however, it should be surgically met early in childhood. One is astonished to find so little reference to it in professional works on examination and hygiene of school children. These books ought to insist that all physical, as well as environmental causes, should be met, by way of prevention, in early childhood.

I have to confess only a very moderate amount of faith in this operation done for the cure of the habit of masturbation in adolescents. Usually this treatment then either fails to strike the cause, or is too late; the grooves of habit in the central nervous system have generally been already worn deep.

In females there is an analogous phimosis recognized as provocative of nervous symptoms — and hence of bad behavior. Even conservative gynecologists have advocated a slight operation, somewhat similar to that in the male, for suitable cases. But, as in Dudley's (220) statement about masturbation in girls, often what is called 'a guarded prognosis' is to be offered; — the operation *may* be followed by a cure, if supplemented by positive and proper moral instruction and judicious hygiene.

§ 173. **Enuresis.** — Lack of control of the functions of the bladder is found with astonishing frequency in delinquents, taken as a class. This is, of course, due in part to the considerable proportion of mental defectives among offenders. (Many of the feebleminded have trouble controlling themselves in this way.) It is also partly due to the characteristic lack of self-control found in the constitutional inferiors, neuropaths, those who have a special defect for self-control, and other types of offenders.

Sometimes it accompanies bad sex practices, or the weak will which leads to these. Then there are the few who suffer from the local causes of enuresis. In nearly all cases the trouble tends to become less with the beginning years of adult life.

Ordinarily this trouble can be said to be rather the accompaniment of delinquent tendencies than any cause. But yet in a few instances the shame and discomfort connected with this disorder has stood very clearly in relationship to anti-social behavior. In one plain case we studied, the nature of the trouble, which had resulted in a good deal of mental conflict, had not dawned on the family nor the school people. They noted the growing delinquent tendencies, truancy and its accompaniments, and they knew of the difficulty, but had not appreciated the psychological lines of causal connection.

Lack of control of functions of the rectum belongs, of course, in the same category, and we have seen the same results, but this trouble is much rarer.

Physicians have loud demands made upon them for the cure of such disorders, particularly because of the household discomfort. The cure is sometimes difficult and even impossible, unless the morale of the individual can be built up. In medical literature much has been written on the subject of enuresis.

§ 174. **Other Physical Irritations.** — It should be clear enough from the standpoint of common sense that in the study of the genesis of tendencies to bad behavior and to bad habits of thought, to say nothing about the beginning of bad physical habits, we should hark back to any physical conditions which may appear to be the first roots of the trouble. Practically, as a matter of fact, over and over again parents or guardians have called our attention to the former existence of these antecedent conditions. Most important for us, after the abnormal conditions of eyes and ears, is *irritation of sex organs*. In a word it may be said that this irritation and undue stimulation may be caused by local uncleanliness, or inflammation, acidity of urine, local enlargements, and chafing of clothes. It is quite unnecessary here to give cases; for details we may refer to standard works on children's diseases and gynecology (unfortunately one has rarely seen any mention of these things in works on child hygiene). It will suffice to say that I see no reason to discredit the opinion of observers who tell me that they have witnessed definite character tendencies develop upon a basis of local irritation, though I would insist that

227

in most cases there must have been also in the individual a foregoing neurotic or psychopathic tendency.

Local irritation in any sensitive parts of the body from *rupture, tight sphincter, chronic inflammations,* etc., even in adults notoriously leads to chronic bad temper and anti-social behavior, which may undoubtedly at times assume criminalistic proportions. Many medical authorities have noted cases of the kind, and accounts of the various ailments may readily be found in medical works.

My appreciation of the effect of physical irritation upon character dates from the life story of a patient told to me long ago. A certain man revealed to me his appreciation of his own character, which was notorious for meanness and misconduct bordering on criminalism, and asked how it could have been otherwise. For years he had been suffering from an excruciating irritation which was always in the background of his consciousness. It seemed highly probable that he was right in believing that a long-standing fissure with pruritus [1] was responsible for his anti-social conduct.

In chronic offenders or in any problem cases there should be thorough questioning and examination for any physical causative influence. Many a person shows a mean disposition, or anti-social conduct, without hardly knowing why, and in occasional cases there is physical cause unrecognized as such.

The theory of so-called reflex irritation from bodily abnormalities, causing mental tendencies as well as physical reactions, gains full expression in the idea that the *enlarged prostate* of old men is an inciting cause of sexual offenses. Trouble in establishing the fact, here again, is met by the coincidence of the local condition with failing mental powers. We discuss this latter point under senility (§ 163). Even the asserted cures of cases do not prove the theory, for such a severe operation as the removal of this gland is quite likely to give a shock or to arouse apperceptions that may themselves result in better moral tendencies — quite without any specific action. However, it may be, as suggested, just exactly the concatenation of the constant and subconscious irritation of this abnormal condition with the lowered inhibitory powers of old age that brings about the bad behavior. The argument then is that there is only one of the two ailments which can be altered, and all that can be done should be done to prevent further social damage and personal disgrace.

---

[1] Gant (155) and other medical writers state frequent observance of the disturbing influences upon conduct which this class of ailments causes.

§ 175. **Syphilis.** — The effects of syphilis, either congenital or acquired, have relation to the production of delinquency only as there is some disability or irritation produced. The individual in general may be rendered more inefficient through weakness, general or local, or some sensory function may be impaired, or the central nervous system may be affected. The result of the latter can be feeblemindedness, as in some cases of congenital syphilis, or can be any of the well-known psychoses or minor aberrations which in some follow acquirement of syphilis. However, the resistance of the individual to the disease and the effects of treatment must never be lost sight of, for it is certainly a fact that many a case of congenital lues develops fairly normally, and that only a few of those who have acquired the disease become mentally affected. Paresis (*dementia paralytica*), everywhere recognized as a form of insanity which gives rise to criminalistic behavior (§ 299), is caused by syphilis. Certain forms of epilepsy develop on a syphilitic basis.

In the above ways the relation of syphilis to criminalism is frequently masked, because the individual is primarily classed as mentally defective, insane, epileptic, and so on. This is true also of our cases. However, it would not be fair to take the figures gained by tests for this disease among offenders [1] as indication of its extent as a cause of delinquency. Very frequently, as among prostitutes, syphilis comes in the wake of the delinquency. But taking the question altogether, and including the congenital aspects, there is no gainsaying that the annals of criminalism would have far fewer black pages if this important disease were stamped out.

§ 176. **Under-nourishment.** — A problem somewhat distinct from that of underdevelopment in relation to criminality (*vide* § 185) is that of undernourishment and debilitated physical conditions. Disgust with school work or with steady employment follows naturally from the bodily weakness, — the accompaniments and

---

[1] The many-sided importance for society of investigating properly this question of syphilis among offenders has been shown by some recent careful studies with the Wasserman test. The New York State Reformatory for Women (*vide* Kneeland **324**, p. 189) reports 48 per cent. syphilitic among 446 inmates, and the Massachusetts Reformatory for Women (*vide* Spaulding, **222**) 44 per cent. of 239 inmates. Among the definitive prostitutes at the latter place 63 per cent. were thus diseased. We look forward to similarly careful reports from institutions for men, but expect the proportion of syphilitics to be very much smaller, because so many of the women are primarily sex offenders. Reports from foreign prisons are of little use for us, and different localities in our own country may show greatly varying results.

sequels of truancy and loafing need not here be mentioned. (Possible causation of mental dullness is elsewhere discussed — § 282.) In these cases the outlook is often quite different from what it is when the difficulty is developmental and unalterable. Proper treatment should be assiduously undertaken, without considering the individual permanently limited, as if he were not always to be a weakling. There is very often great trouble in logical separation of undernourishment as a cause of delinquency from the frequently accompanying poverty and alcoholism, and the undue ingestion of stimulants and other unhygienic practices of an ignorant family. No doubt the great success of industrial schools in bettering bodily conditions is due largely to separation from actively pernicious prior methods of living, as well as through increasing nutritional values of the food taken.

The following card shows the causations in a case, of which we knew well the surrounding circumstances, and indicates complications which are practically always encountered when focusing on the question of poor nutrition.

Case 14. — This boy, age 12, weighed 63 lbs.; height 4 ft., 3½ in.; hollow-eyed, tired-looking.

Physical conditions: Case 14.
  Long under-nourished; partial nasal   Boy, age 12.
    obstruction.

Heredity: Father not bright, gambler, deserter.
  Sister feebleminded.
  Sister paralyzed.

Home conditions: Poverty. Mother works out.
    Much bickering.

Bad companions.

Temperament: Very nervous and irritable.

Truancy +.
Runaway +.
Petty stealing +.   Mentality:
Sex offense with girl.   Ability good.

At 14 years, 8 months, this boy weighed 85 lbs.; height 4 ft., 8 in. He was still tired-looking. Poor musculature. His delinquent tendencies had been growing less. He then was having much difficulty getting employment on account of his small size.

§ 177. **Excess of Physical Vigor.** — Excess of vigor is justifiably considered in rare cases as a direct cause of delinquency. There are some individuals, misplaced in an environment which does not call forth all their powers, whose very superabundance of animal spirits makes for criminalistic tendencies. This phenomenon stands out more self-evidently when we discuss it under the head of over-development, as judged by age, in our section on physical abnormalities of development (§ 188). There the main point is the lack of correlation between physical over-growth and child-like type of mental powers. But even in an adult, mentally normal, too great a surplus of general or special energy under the conditions of an ordinarily civilized environment may occasionally lead directly to anti-social conduct. The exceeding restlessness and restiveness of a tremendously vigorous man or woman may, of course, lead to misdeeds.

The excess of certain special physical vigor, best denoted by the term *hypersexualism*, is entirely another matter. This may be, of course, very hard to differentiate from the results of strong mental stimulation when there is mental over-stress in the direction of sexual things. (We discuss this subject as a whole elsewhere, § 243.) Certainly, however, in men, and more rarely in women, there is sometimes a physical foundation in organic over-development, or over-energizing of related nerve centers. The result in behavior may be excessive impulsions, perhaps paroxysmal. The relationship to the commission of offenses, ranging up to very serious ones, may readily be appreciated. Operations, self-desired, have been successfully undertaken on women to relieve this condition.[1] We are inclined to believe that society might be better off if occasional cases of the same nature in men were treated by preventive surgical measures.

When excess of energy in the direction mentioned above is combined with a defect of mentality, as it unfortunately sometimes is, particularly in epileptics, society is apt direly to suffer the consequence. The most vigorous man sexually of whom we have ever heard, was a large and strong epileptic, feebleminded

---

[1] What can be accomplished by an operation depends entirely upon the nature of the case; there are many modifying circumstances. It is only fair to say that it is the rare instance when a hypersexual woman can be benefited by anything short of an extensive operation. This is not the place to cite professional literature on the subject, but we may add that a few cases of uncontrollable erotic paroxysms have been reported as cured by a moderate surgical proceeding.

individual (*vide* § 256), who committed at least one typically degenerate murder.

§ 178. **Menstruation and Pregnancy.** — Although both of these conditions, especially the former, may have definite relationship to delinquency, it is not the condition in itself through being an irritating or weakening factor, which causes the delinquent tendencies. The individual is only influenced towards delinquency because the mental state at that time is not quite normal. Properly, then, we shall discuss these subjects under the head of minor psychoses (§ 310, § 311).

Premenstrual restlessness and sex stimulation, as we have elsewhere stated, § 310, may be correlated with sex offenses and also other delinquencies.

§ 179. **Headaches.** — Although belonging in the category of minor nervous disorders, headaches have a definite relation to delinquency because of the irritating and even disabling effects. When an offender really suffers much from them, any one who would reform his conduct should take thorough cognizance of the possible effects of this trouble upon behavior. The only thing necessary to say about treatment is to state that headaches come from a wide variety of causes and the underlying trouble must be carefully searched for.

§ 180. **Head Injuries.** — No injury to the head any more than to any other part of the body will affect character or behavior unless the brain and, through this, the mind is affected. The finding of even a considerable scar on the scalp of an offender, even with evidences of injury to the cranium, is not any proof of damage significant as a cause of delinquency. Cases where there has been resultant mental change will be properly discussed in the chapter on minor psychoses (§ 309). To seize on statistics showing the strange frequency with which a history of head injury is obtainable concerning offenders is not our method of procedure. But the bare facts as we find them (*vide* § 99) and as others, such as Sleyster (**196**) who says that 11 per cent. of 592 penitentiary prisoners have suffered injury to the head, find them, are indeed striking.

§ 181. **Other Physical Ailments.** — A glance at our statistical analysis of causative abnormal physical conditions (§ 97) will show that various other ailments may be fairly regarded as causative factors of delinquency. The boy with *ringworm*, for instance, was rejected on this account from the schools in two cities, and

232

began his criminalistic career through this expulsion. The man with *tuberculosis* was unable to work, and in his idleness, and perhaps through his prescribed over-feeding, developed lewd thoughts that led him to use the mails for sending obscene communications. The boy with *heart disease* cannot work steadily; his leisure gives him opportunity for working up the thieving schemes that have made him easily the leader of a criminalistic gang in his wild neighborhood. The young man with the *venereal disease* developed such a morbid attitude towards himself that he became willing, even in modern America, to assault a pure little girl, in compliance with the old superstition that by so doing his disease would be cured.

The general physical changes of old age, *senility*, have significance as the mind and character are changed. The subject is treated in § 163.

CHAPTER IV

DEVELOPMENTAL PHYSICAL ABNORMALITIES

§ 182. General Statement and Definition. § 183. Statistical Findings. § 184. Developmental Age Norms. § 185. (A) Very Poor General Physical Development. § 186. (B) (C) Delayed Puberty with Either Poor or Normal Development. § 187. (D) General Sex Characteristics Undeveloped, with Normal Puberty. § 188. (E) General Physical Over-development. § 189. (F) Over-development of Both General Physical and Sex Characteristics. § 190. (G) Premature Puberty with General Physical Over-development. § 191. (H) Premature Puberty without Over-development. § 192. (I) Premature Puberty with Distinctly Poor Development.

§ 182. **General Statement and Definition.** — An important feature of our practical findings is concerned with the several developmental abnormalities which clearly stand in causative relationship to delinquent tendencies.   Our specific data on this point persuade one that altogether too little attention has been given to this subject by students of the genetics of criminalism. It is true that some European criminologists have dealt with poor physical development, and several writers have suggested that the phenomena of adolescence (*vide* § 336) may include several of these anomalous developmental conditions. But nearly all this has been without careful attention to case studies.   In the light of what we afterwards found, I feel indebted to Franz Boas and W. T. Porter for the emphasis which they both placed upon this topic in discussing with us the beginning of our research.   Their insistence on the possibility that abnormal development might be one determinant of delinquency led us, already partially convinced, to lay special stress on the observation of data concerning this point.

By physical abnormalities of development we mean physical conditions which are disproportionately correlated with the age of the individual. Of course, if we observe a very large man or a very small man we do not say that, as an adult, he is suffering from a developmental anomaly, although such may have been the cause of his being an uncommon physical specimen. Moreover, with adult opportunities for self-adjustment his case is not of great practical interest for us as students of criminalism. But when a growing individual is so slight that he cannot com-

234

pete fairly with his fellows who are classified with him according to age, or when a boy or girl prematurely develops the physical basis of adult impulsions, then we have a right to speak of developmental abnormalities as involving social and moral issues. We find that these imperfect correlations lead to such defective social adjustments and moral stresses as may determine criminalism.

It should be thoroughly appreciated that the physical anomaly may be only temporary; the individual may grow larger or stronger, or, in the opposite type of case, may never develop further than the dimensions which appear excessive for the given age. A characteristically overgrown girl of 12 may be a perfectly normal woman when she is 20, and the same is true of the overgrown boy. But none of this alters the fact that during an exceedingly important period of life, when the powers of adjustment are by no means as strong as they will be later, there was a determining amount of mental and moral stress.

It should also be definitely understood that in our discussion of this subject we are not including cases in which the cause of the delinquent tendencies can be attributed to aberrational or defective mentality, even though in instances of the latter there may be causally important physical abnormalities of development. We describe elsewhere the anomalies of involutional development which play also a part, fortunately a minor part, in the production of criminalism. We deal with this subject, § 163, under the head of senility.

In our estimation of developmental anomalies we have often wanted to know, for the sake of comparison, how our findings on premature development and over-development compare with the status of young offenders elsewhere observed, but we have been able to find no adequate studies of this feature of criminalistic genetics. A large share of this whole subject, since it deals so much with youthful development, and especially the development of sex characteristics, might be thought to belong properly under the head of studies of adolescence. However, in the cases now under discussion there are certain extra physical features, which bring about a stress that is certainly no part of ordinary adolescent life. The many writers on adolescence fail to discriminate a great deal that is pathological or anomalous from what is usual in the stress and storm belonging to this period.

235

§ 183. **Statistical Findings.** — To get this important matter concretely before ourselves, we have carefully gone over our related observations. We find that of our statistical Group II (*vide* § 97) of 823 cases, 13 1-2 per cent. have some anomaly of development as one of the probable causes of their delinquency. Even these figures leave out entirely the mental defectives and the aberrational types, in which the pivotal fact, so far as criminalism is concerned, has sometimes been abnormal early development or an over-development of sex characteristics. We have scheduled our youthful offenders with these anomalies in the classes given below — enumerating them only when the anomaly was fairly to be considered a cause of delinquency. This point must be insisted on because in other instances there may have been, for instance, poor development or over-development when it seemed to have no logical relationship to the misconduct.

	Males	Females
(A) Very poor general physical development . . .	26	0
(B) Delayed puberty plus poor development . . .	7	0
(C) Delayed puberty with normal development .	2	0
(D) General sex characteristics undeveloped, with normal puberty	2	1
	37	1
(E) General physical over-development	6	0
(F) Over-development of both general physical and sex characteristics	0	17
(G) Premature puberty with general physical over-development	9	19
(H) Premature puberty without over-development	4	14
(I) Premature puberty with distinctly poor development	4	0
	23	50

Some words of explanation are necessary for understanding the above table. The figures cover only youthful developmental anomalies which are discernible as causative factors of delinquency. All cases where mental defect, epilepsy, or psychosis was the major factor have been eliminated. Our lines of demarcation of under-development, over-development, delayed and premature puberty are gauged very broadly. Over-development of general or sex characteristics is naturally most readily recognized, and is only included by us when the anomaly was very marked. Most frequently it may be said that the individual was an anomaly in his own family circle. Poor development also is readily recognized by ordinary observational standards. When the under-sized individual at all approached the normal his lack of development was not considered causative. In our given cases we had special reason to know that his poor development stood in the way of his moral and social success. What constitutes a premature or a delayed puberty is not to be so roughly adjudged. We have discriminated according to the following criteria.

§ 184. **Developmental Age Norms.** — In dealing with the problem of abnormally early or late puberty it is not scientifically accurate to consider averages. Wide time limits must be taken as representing the normal. In the case of girls, as might be supposed, the age of first menstruation is the best known of any facts connected with the onset of puberty. Englemann (**34**) in a careful study of this subject states that the average age in the United States for first menstruation is at 14 years (earlier than the average in Europe). In a vast proportion the age of first menstruation centers closely about the average, so that one may safely regard puberty beginning at 12 years or earlier as an unusual phenomenon, and likely to throw considerable stress socially upon the girl.

The age of puberty in boys is not nearly so well known, nor so readily distinguished. Until the recent research of Crampton [1] we had little that was accurate to guide us, but yet, after all, in such work as ours we have not felt the need of recording anything except extremes. In general we may say that if signs of puberty which appear normally at 14 1-2 to 15 years are already present by 13 years or earlier it is a possible danger sign. Most individuals at this earlier age are not yet mentally equipped to stand the burden of this new life.

§ 185. (*A*) **Very Poor General Physical Development.** — Of all our topics in the present chapter, under-development has been most emphasized as a cause of crime, particularly by foreign criminologists. In this country it certainly does not play the part that it does abroad. Morrison (**223**, p. 102) states that from his long experience with English offenders he judges that phys-

---

[1] To the work of Crampton (**229**) we would refer all students for definitions, criteria of growth, and positive statement of numerous observations. The work of the past has been impressionistic, but Crampton's effort has been to establish accuracy.

ical inferiority is one of the most important causes which produce criminality. As he sees it, there are several reasons for this. The inferior offender comes from a class who have to live by the labor of their hands, and who, when deficient in strength, are in a position of disadvantage. Through ordinary industrial selection the weak ones tend never to be incorporated properly in the army of labor. As a consequence they find pauper life easy, and even crime not uninviting. With our much more fluid social conditions and the greater chances of employment, this is not nearly so true. But even in this country there are still plenty of discouragements and proofs of social inefficiency forced upon the victim of physical inferiority.

Distinguishing the difference between social demands made upon the sexes, as well as their respective temptations, we can fairly say we have never seen a single instance in which poor general development seemed to be the important cause of delinquency in a female. On this point our statistical charts, § 105, should be consulted. But we would not deny the possibility of finding it as such elsewhere.

It would hardly seem necessary to mention the type of physical condition which seriously interferes with normal school life and normal employment, yet short case summaries may serve to show the various complications of antecedent and consequent amid various environmental circumstances.

Case 15. — A boy of 15 1-2 years, who earlier was a great truant and mischief maker in school, later became much of a runaway from home, stealing from his mother, not working, and living at times a most irregular life in the business districts. Physically very poorly developed. His height was 4 ft. 9 in., and he weighed only 79 lbs. Moderate hypermetropia. Slight tremor of hands. Bites finger nails much, and is distinctly a nervous type. Examination otherwise negative. Mentally we found the boy to be rather bright, as shown by his work on tests, general reactions, and range of information. He also showed some artistic ability.

In the background there were important factors. (a) At the time of this boy's conception the father was suffering from a chronic illness from which he died while the mother was in mid-pregnancy. Consequently (b) antenatal conditions were very defective on account of worry and trouble. (The older children were born when the father was well and are very different both morally and physically.) (c) Years ago this boy began the excessive use of stimulants, which he craves. He has been accustomed to taking an excess of tea and coffee and smokes a great deal. (d) Home control was bad on account of the mother having to work out every day and consequently he (e) fell in with bad companions. (f) On account of his small size he has never been able to get desirable work.

This boy has been in at least four different institutions and has run away from some of them, as well as from home. He was tried on a farm, and did not do well. He finally disappeared.

Many other cases bearing on the same point could be given. The under-developed individual frequently comes from an atrocious environment, often is the result of defective heredity or congenital conditions, early seeks the use of stimulants, and feels himself utterly unable to cope on even terms with others. Nothing is more natural than that cunning, vagrancy and low forms of enjoyment should be resorted to in the individual's endeavor to get out of life what he can by the easiest means.

Occasionally one meets a case in which under-development points the way along a profitable path in crime, as in Fagin's gang, where the small-sized fellow was of special use.

Case 16. — Boy of 11 years, a truant and a thief; already considered by the police authorities to be an expert pickpocket. We found a little boy of net weight 47 lbs., height 4 ft., 1 in. Examination brought out no defect. The boy was a humorous type, old in expression, quick in movement. He had noticeably small hands. On the mental side we graded him as having fair native ability. His motor dexterity was noteworthy. In fact, he was proud of showing his ability in this direction.

This delicate, fairly bright, and naturally dexterous little boy had had years of instruction in stealing, and on account of his success took to it with delight. He demonstrated to us very cleverly the skill with which he could insinuate his small hands unnoticed into people's pockets.

In such a case one could be quite sure that only prolonged care would reform. Of course poor home control was a large factor in the case. Even an ordinary term in a boy's industrial school would not be long enough at this boy's age to overcome the tendencies. The instabilities of adolescence in such a case must be reckoned with, and prolonged care be given accordingly. As a matter of fact, this boy proved to be a model in the institution where he was sent, but, after a year and a half, return to the old environment brought renewal of old habits, and he had to be sent back for another period.

§ 186. (*B* and *C*.) **Delayed Puberty with Either Poor or Normal Development.** — Nearly all cases which come under these headings clearly belong to the category of constitutional inferiority, discussed at length elsewhere (§ 290 ff.). We have not seen delayed puberty figure as a cause of delinquency among girls. The retarded older boys show a strange mixture of childish and adult characteristics, which is perhaps just what might be expected. The following case is a fair example.

Case 17. — A young fellow of almost 17, weight 121 lbs., height 5 ft. 6 in., is just entering puberty. He has unusually good mental ability, and a good range of information, but his emotional reactions are absurdly childish. He cries upon the slightest provocation. He is well behaved and affectionate at home, but he cannot stick at anything, and whenever he gets tired of doing the same thing for long he finds it very easy to steal and run away, making his own living elsewhere by working for a time. This boy did excellently in school, graduating from 8th grade at $12\frac{1}{2}$ years. From that time on he has grown more unstable morally, becoming lately rather bold in stealing, but never showing viciousness. One of his escapades illustrates well his traits. Working on a farm where he was much liked, he suddenly stole about $20 and ran away. He was easily caught. He stated that the deed was committed under the impulse of homesickness. A chance was given him to work at another place and pay back the money. He did this faithfully in his customary spirit of penitence. No other factors in the background stand out convincingly as causes, and the whole case seems to hinge mostly on this instability of character correlated with very backward puberty.

In such a case, where the marks of constitutional inferiority are not clear, the prognosis, judging by our experience with others, is good if the fellow can be tided over his unusually late adolescent period amid decent associations. This affords another lesson for us always to individualize cases, and not to estimate possibilities and probabilities in chronological terms, when they should be reckoned according to physiology.

§ 187. (*D*) **General Sex Characteristics Undeveloped, with Normal Puberty.** — The only bearing this phenomenon has for us is in the two types of cases where non-development of general sex characteristics brings to the individual some suggestion of a pathway in delinquency. In the case of a girl or woman with masculine contour, especially if there is unusual muscular strength, masculine type of delinquency or adventure may suggest itself. We have studied a notable case of this kind where male disguise was assumed and male employments were readily followed in adventurous spirit for weeks at a time. Old country annals of the unusual in criminalism give many such instances among brigands and other classes of offenders. Then there is the masculine type of woman who plays the male rôle in homosexual love affairs, Platonic or complete perversion.

The other type comprises the young man or adolescent youth who retains his childish general physical characteristics, and is ordinarily designated as effeminate. It does not seem to be generally recognized that there may be abnormality in the correlation of the various signs of adult masculinity. Such, however, is the case. There may be complete normal pubescence (growth of pubic hair as an indication of puberty) with retention of childish (effeminate) contour of face or torso, and even retention of childish voice tones. Most unfortunately, occasional individuals of this type, by reason of some maldevelopment of sex instinct, and sometimes by reason of their attractiveness for individuals with predilection for unnatural sex behavior, are readily recruited to the ranks of sex perversion. (*Vide* Case 114.)

In considering care of individuals of this last class, temptations, inner and outer, should be considered. Chances for developing the healthiest possible mental and physical interests should be given. The excessive stimulations, as well as direct temptations, found in city life are inimical. Students of social vices know well the astonishing amount of tendency in this direction.

Case 17 a.—As an example of the dangers we could cite the case of a boy nearly 17 years old, weight 110, height 5 ft. 4 in.; fairly nourished, but very small bones, delicate fingers, childish shoulders and torso, normal pubescence, high voice. This lad up to within a month or so, had been singing soprano parts on the stage. He had been frequently approached, even on the streets, by a certain class of men who have recognized in him a special type towards which they are attracted. This lad has apparently rejected all advances, but has gained worldly wisdom on the subject, and manufactured altogether from this experience and his own recognition of his innate peculiarities, an anti-social attitude, which bodes ill for both his mental and moral future.

Treatment of such cases, even when they have dipped into bad practices, is not necessarily hopeless. From appropriate moral and social measures, which must be highly individualized, we have seen splendid results ensue.

§ 188. (*E*) **General Physical Over-development.** — We need barely touch this subject except as applied to males, because whenever the same physical phenomenon has been observed in females there has always been corresponding over-development of sex characteristics which heavily complicated the case. Even when excess of general size and strength in girls or women has seemed to be a main factor (*vide* § 142), sex affairs always complicate, which leads us to negative conclusions about the responsibility of general over-development alone. No doubt some of the vigorous female offenders instanced by Lombroso (**230**) have been incited to criminalism through their tremendous physique, but such cases are decidedly rare in this country and need only this bare mention.

Concerning general physical over-development as a cause in youth of delinquent tendencies, which may stand at the beginning of a whole criminalistic career, we have very specific data. Here, once again, in considering the possible results of proper treatment we are confronted with the essential fact of the formation of mental habit (*vide* § 234). Specific thoughts and temptations being once aroused, avenues of action clearly opened, and unfortunate associations with other delinquents formed, even if there be offered a chance to tide over part of the adolescent period with fitting mental activities, there may not be a satisfactory outcome. What I have said elsewhere about much of the good results of industrial school training being due to carrying the individual over what is a normally unstable period of life, applies here, when an anomalous physical condition adds to the ordinary difficulties of this period. What we have ourselves seen of the effects of proper treatment in cases of this kind should be highly instructive to all students of the subject.

Case 18. — A boy of 14 years, 9 months, was studied by us after a considerable career of delinquency. He had already run away from home six times, once having been gone 3 months. On these occasions he had made his way hundreds of miles, generally towards the western plains. He had been arrested at least twice for stealing; once that we know of he had taken small things from a store, another time he had helped himself to a neighbor's horse and buggy with which he had gotten a start on one of his expeditions. His intelligent parents were in a quandary about him.

We found this young boy to be a strong, alert, bright, and enormously over-grown lad, with no ascertained physical defect. Weight 145 lbs., height 5 ft. 10 in. On the mental side he showed himself to be well up to the ordinary in ability. Naturally his school record was defective on account of his being away so much, but he had entered 6th grade. We were much interested to note that his interests strongly centered about out-door and ranch life.

The quandary of these good parents seemed to us entirely uncalled for: there was only one sensible way to look at the case. Here was their son, whom they regarded as a young boy because of his years, already towering above them. In his physical make-up he was at least five years ahead of the children he had been called upon to associate with, and the confines of the small city apartment which the family occupied were altogether too narrow for his actual requirements. The circumstances of life provided by his parents were totally unfitted for him. On our advice he was given a chance to play a man's part on a far western ranch, and this at once checked his criminalistic career. A return a couple of years later showed him with a still greater development, and, of course, still unfitted for indoor city life. The fact that this boy had a roving frontiersman for a grandfather might be considered in evidence of the inheritance of roving instincts. But as we have elsewhere (*vide* Spaulding and Healy, **162**) pointed out, what really was inherited was the physical basis of such instincts.

Physical over-development + + +.   Case 18.
    Environment: unfitted.   Boy, 14 years, 9 mos.
       Heredity: grandfather, very active
               physically, a frontiers-
               man.

Stealing.   Mentality:
Runaway + +.   Good ability.

Case 19. — A boy of 15½ years, we saw at the end of a tremendously aggressive career of delinquency, which he had begun before he was 12 years of age. His offenses consisted of much

243

truancy, staying away from home over night, petty stealing, then burglary, and running away from home. We found a boy with man's stature, and no observed defects except carious teeth and two slight physical stigmata. Weight 125 lbs., height 5 ft. 7 in., strength great, bones large, carriage slouchy. It was quite easy to decide that he had fair mental ability; he even did rather well with school work, in spite of very irregular attendance. Certain other mental characteristics were very notable. When guided by those he liked in an institutional school, he was found tractable and even helpful. Under other conditions he showed great instability and recklessness. In court he exhibited absolutely no feeling in regard to his record of bad conduct, and simply desired to be sent away to an institution by the judge, as he had been three times before, in order, as he said, that he should not have to work hard.

This boy came from a poor, but non-criminalistic family, and had been mixed up with bad companions in his neighborhood, but it seemed to be clear that physical conditions and adolescence were largely responsible for his behavior. Reckoning with these it might have been foreseen much earlier that a long period of protective disciplinary treatment would be necessary. The outcome of this case is of great interest to us, and proves as much as we could hope to have proved when observing the various admixture of conditions in any case. At about 17, with his chronological age gradually catching up to his physiological conditions, this young fellow has grown more stable, and, so far as known, gradually ceased to be an offender.

Adolescent characteristics +.	Case 19.
Physical over-development.	Boy, 15 yrs. 6 mos.
Bad companions.	
Truancy.	
Stealing.	
Burglary.	Mentality:
Runaway.	Fair ability.

§ 189. (*F*) **Over-development of Both General Physical and Sex Characteristics.** — In one sense, the subject as discussed at this point belongs to the problem of abnormal, early maturity. But since very special complications for the individual are involved in a premature appearance of puberty, as well as in over-development during adolescence, the subject of prematurity itself will be dealt with separately in the next section.

Adding to our statement above that mere general physical over-development has little connection with delinquency in young women, we may now say that when there is over-development of general sex characteristics, the relationship to delinquency is very marked. This latter over-development does not necessarily imply a very early puberty. Perhaps we should state that what we mean by general sex characteristics is marked over-development for the age of the ordinary signs of female maturity, particularly enlargement of the hips and bust, and general rounding of the figure. Again in this matter our estimations have been made on the broadest lines: we have only included cases of very marked over-development. It should be remembered that delinquent tendencies caused by this type of over-development may arise both from within and without. Well-developed young women are very prone to have an unusual amount of sex feeling and sex consciousness, and just such a person is regarded as especially attractive by the opposite sex. It would hardly seem to be necessary to illustrate by cases these obvious facts, but a couple of very short summaries may serve to clinch the point.

Case 20. — Girl 16 years, weight 160 lbs. Regular, strong features, bright eyes, decidedly good-looking, altogether large and mature type. First menstruated when 13 years old. Mentally, distinctly good native ability, but defective range of interests and information. Delinquencies, very repeated sex offenses. Now pregnant. This girl comes from a very pious and stern family where there has been attempt to utterly repress her instincts. Although apparently she has many ladylike feelings, she is hot tempered and is extremely defiant.

Case 21. — Girl of 16. Delinquencies, repeated sex affairs over two or three years. Ran away to another city. Violence even to the point of desperately engaging in a street brawl. Weight 153 lbs. Height 5 ft. 2 in. Tremendously well developed in strength as well as form. Large, well-molded, regular features. Very firm and alert expression. Menstruated first when over 13 years old. On the mental side she proves herself to have normal ability. Is a very marked type, talkative and responsive, but lies without a shade of emotion. From her own account of herself she evidently is the bold, willful, quick-tempered, headstrong, and physically

245

brave individual that her family portray her. She has been married to a very decent young man, but finding home life too tame, she leaves him whenever she wishes. Life in an institution, whether as ordered by the court earlier, or which she has been persuaded later to voluntarily seek for a couple of months, has not caused the slightest abatement of her native tendencies. Other factors in the background complicate the case. She comes of a distinctly neuropathic family, with high temper, alcoholism, hysteria, and probable epilepsy all playing a part. Previously she has never had anything but the best of health, but within the last year there have been attacks of hysteria when she would long remain rigid, with arms extended. Lately on account of flagrant sex delinquencies she had to be sent again to an institution. (In institutional life she again proved herself willful and vicious.)

There are several subtypes, some quite different from the above, which come under our present heading. One is the lazy and easy-going, over-developed girl, either frank in sex desires or perhaps indulging in glib talk about religion and personal reformation. Some of stronger character definitely battle long against their own inclinations or temptations.

Consideration of treatment for this class brings us to some vital points in social welfare. It is ostrich-like not to see the critical dangers surrounding over-developed girls, under many of the conditions of social life. It is fortunate that these untoward conditions confront only a small minority of adolescent girls, for it may be readily appreciated that this type is a menace in more than one social stratum. When a typical case is recognized what can be offered in the way of treatment?

It is perfectly clear that the large share of delinquent girls of this type cannot be safely taken care of in their old environment. Even if families wake up to the need of more efficient control, still there are constant suggestions in the presence of old associations. The main consideration here, as ever, is complete study of the needs and possibilities of the case. This is rendered all the more necessary because there is little chance for prolonged segregation of many cases; there are few institutions which can tide a girl even through 3 or 4 years of instability. Occasionally short segregation with the repression that ordinary institutional life affords will be found sufficient, but in many cases this is not enough.

Leaving out of account, for the moment, the question of very early marriage, which in our particular civilization is rarely justifiable, we can find to offer as constructive and off-setting measures just two types of treatment. One involves the using up of physical energy, the reducing of restlessness and animal spirits by physical labor. By this one does not mean ordinary enjoyment of out-door life; we have seen cases in which out-door life has built up even more physical feeling. As in the case cited in § 142, excessive labor may be the price of personal salvation, and of the protection of society.

The other point in treatment has to do with better mental and, particularly, more wholesome recreational interests. As pointed out by Jane Addams (231), it is in connection with recreation that the ordinary girl finds the most suggestion towards delinquency. Many of the modes of recreation of to-day, whatever they may have been in the past, are conducive to the development of offenses against the better social order. In natures such as these under discussion, where great outlets are needed for self-activity, vigorous pleasures of the more innocent type must be definitely offered. The attempt at substitution of religious for sex impulses may be rarely wholly successful, and often is in part, but it behooves all to know that any form of substitutive repression and inactivity is likely to result in the hypocrisy we have often seen, when there is glib talk about being good, while secret actions are the opposite.

Just what mental and recreational interests will prove most valuable depends naturally upon the capacity of the individual. It is safe to say that for any girl who has normal self-control, who is not suffering from mental defect or aberration, activities and interests sufficient to outweigh physiological sex impulses can be found by skilled and understanding people. Great difficulty is found with the indolent members of this group, and for some of these we should be quite willing to recommend, under medical supervision, a course of asceticism. We have not heard of individualization anywhere being carried to this extent, except as a very temporary matter, but it has been personally indulged in by many good people, and there is no reason why it should not be considered as a method of treatment.

The whole idea of segregation and repression for young women of this type is often scouted by those who say that this means flying in the face of nature. The chief answer to this is that these individuals under modern conditions are frequently a great menace to the welfare of society. They are tempters of the opposite sex, purveyors of disease, and spreaders of vicious knowledge among other girls. Society has a great deal at stake in protecting itself and the individual. Even if we proceed somewhat against nature, and even if some happiness of the individual is sacrificed, the effect of a proper segregation is better than the opposite.

It is many times proposed that early marriage is a proper solution of these cases. Nature has matured these individuals, and fitted them for adult sex life. Among uncivilized peoples and in simpler phases of civilization early marriage is readily enough carried out. But with us economic and many other conditions are all against this. We have many times heard from families that though they perceive the benefits of early marriage for the over-developed daughter in the family, it is impossible to be carried out, because either no one is in love with her, or the only one who would marry her was too disreputable, too youthful, financially incapable, or otherwise undesirable. The customs governing marriageable age are imperfect, when based chronologically, as are the laws concerning working age, or any formal limitation of what is a matter for individualization. Occasionally a girl of 16 may be the physical and even the mental equal of many a woman of 30, just as some boys at 14 or 15 are endowed with adult working strength. Years may add steadiness and discretion, but already there is maturity.

We can leave this problem of treatment, with the statement that the suggestions apply perhaps even more to the cases of early puberty plus physical over-development, those which will be discussed in the next section.

§ 190. (*G*) **Premature Puberty with General Physical Over-development.** — In the case of girls, the conditions implied by this heading include over-development of the sex characteristics already spoken of. With boys it usually means very early general physical development, and often includes premature post-pubertal signs, such as deep voice, appearance of hair on face, etc. At this point again a little discussion of the whole subject is in order. We may repeat that the material of this chapter differs from consideration of adolescence (§ 336 ff.) as such. Adolescence has its bearing quite apart from the added stresses of physical anomalies of growth at this important period.

Our charts of developmental conditions (§ 105) shown by weight correlated with age seem to indicate the much larger part which over-development plays in the production of delinquent tendencies in girls than in boys. These charts, it should be remembered, merely give the isolated facts, but even our analyses of causations show the importance of over-development. It is rather astonishing that so little attention has been called to this subject in the literature. However, judges of wide experience, and others who see adolescent delinquents, often make the observation that many young people, girls in particular, do go astray on account of over-development.

The excessively early maturing of an individual is a physical phenomenon to be distinguished from its mental analogue, precocity, which brings none of the special problems concerning delinquency in its wake. Indeed, it is just the lack of correlation between physical and mental qualities which causes the trouble. In other words the prematurity does not extend to the psychical sphere. It is easily seen to be antecedently probable that the effect of early development, whether of general physique or sex functions or sex characteristics, is to be considered a highly dangerous influence in the life of a young individual. Without the development of those mental qualities which give full power to social inhibitions the temptations arising from inner and outer conditions unduly stress the individual.

In the class of cases immediately under discussion we are dealing not only with prematurity, but also with over-development, which makes a double social and moral burden upon an immature individual. Here it should be stated again that both these conditions are, for our purposes, estimated as factors only when in well-marked exaggeration. In the consideration of the combination of prematurity with over-development we should remember that the onset of puberty does not necessarily bring about immediate development of other mature characteristics, either sex or general. The age of first menstruation is not the age of the development of the womanly contour which is evidence of still further maturity. It is true that Williams (35), who has made a special study of menstruation in girls, says that the early appearance of this function is generally indicative of vigor and vitality in excess of the average. (Perhaps the nutritional theory explains the much earlier average age of menstruation (§ 184) in this country than among the Europeans from whom our people have sprung.) Certainly our own experience tends to show this true in many cases, although there are exceptions, and enforces our own perceptions of the dire need which exists for the utmost parental or equivalent protection, with the developing of safe-guarding interests and occupations to suit the needs of this period of great stress. The same considerations in a different measure are applicable to the prematurity and over-development of boys. For studies of this sex we would again refer to Crampton's (229) valuable work.[1]

The question of heredity in relation to prematurity and over-development is of great interest, and satisfactory data might be extensively gathered if one were to make a special investigation. As we have stated in our chapter on Heredity (§ 144) we have often heard, where there was excessive and premature development with tendency to sex delinquency, that a parent was peculiarly disposed towards sex indulgence. And sometimes it has been stated that the parent had matured early and was unusually developed physically.

The following cases are selected to bring out several of the most significant points. The first one, which gives us a social, physical, mental, and moral comparison of twins, is of great value.

Case 22. — Maria X. This girl of 12 1-2 years was brought to us by her straightforward New England parents. They were intensely disturbed about her delinquency, and blamed themselves for not having been foresighted enough to have prevented it. They are both healthy. We obtained at that time no facts of significance in regard to heredity. The last two children were twins, and one of them was the subject of our study. The girl has been all her life in a lively manufacturing town. Her developmental history is said to have been absolutely normal and free from illness, except for the fact that she has twice had convulsions. The first attack came when she was 9 and the second when she was 10 1-2 yrs. During her recent years she has been notably larger, stronger and better developed than her twin sister. She menstruated when she was just 12. Her sister has not yet done so. There is a difference between them also on the mental side, but this is much in favor of the sister, who is a full grade higher, and seems considerably brighter. (As we observed this sister, she is a typically slim and physically unattractive girl,

[1] Recently there has been much more attempt to study accurately the highly important relationship between prematurity and mental conditions. We have noted Crampton's (232, 233) papers, Foster's article (234) on physiological age, and King's (235) study of physiological age and school standing as a basis for classification of pupils.

quite normal for her age.) The parents tell us that Maria has
been discovered to have been long engaged in sex delinquencies
with young men.

On the physical side we found an extremely well-nourished
girl of 4 ft., 11 in. In general sex characteristics she is astonishingly developed; attitude and bearing strong and upright; well-
muscled arms. We also noted that she had a pleasant face,
good features, beautiful skin, and the broad hips and prominent
bust of a well-developed young woman. One observer states that
the girl has the most beautiful neck and shoulders she had ever
seen in a young girl. Vision slightly defective. Speech rather
hesitating, with a hardly perceptible stutter at times. Tonsils
and adenoids had been removed. Other examination negative.

The summary of our psychological findings is that the girl
showed a good deal of mental irregularity and lack of control.
To be sure she was under some emotional strain, but, even so,
her ability could hardly be called better than poor. After we
heard the story of her delinquencies we were inclined to believe
that perhaps she might be dull by reason of excessive sex practices, or at least that her mental processes were under poor control for that reason. Even more noteworthy than the result on
performance tests, was her absurdly small range of information. She was not sure who was the president of the United
States, and did not know what the Fourth of July celebrated.
When telling us her story, we found her attention had to be
frequently called to the matter in hand, although we observed
nothing definitely like *petit mal*.

Of course Maria's mental condition as well as her physical
make-up was a matter of grave interest and importance for prognosis and treatment. She was reported thoroughly dutiful,
and a good worker at home. Sometimes she tells fanciful stories
for the sake of deceiving others, but is not a great liar. The
mother says the girl seems almost to wander in her mind at times,
but after we heard of her behavior we did not wonder at this. We
felt, too, that her habits might account for the fact that she had
not yet passed into 5th grade, in spite of having gone to school
between 7 and 8 years.

The freely told history of delinquency revealed to us the most
extensive amount of sex indulgence with others that we have
ever heard of from a child, except in the case of some feebleminded girl. For two years, between school and home, she has

been engaging in sex misconduct with various boys and young men. On account of her charms she has even posed for pictures of the nude. She wrote suggestive notes to boys in school.

The most remarkable social feature of this case is the fact that the twin sister had accompanied this girl back and forth from school, but had taken no interest in what was definitely going on between her sister and members of the opposite sex, and seems to have been in no moral danger at any time. She had simply waited for her in this or that place, and either did not wish to tell tales, or did not concern herself enough to inform her parents.

We never felt certain of the diagnosis in this case, especially in regard to abnormal psychological features. But the physiological aspects stand out in great prominence, especially in comparison to the make-up of her sister. The social bearings of her unusual development are obvious. It was evident that Maria needed the utmost protection and control, and her parents now realized this. Our card of causation as ascertained at this time runs as follows:

Over-development and **premature puberty.**   Case 22.
　　　　　Remarkably attractive   Girl, age 12 yrs.
　　　　　physically.

Mentality: Dull, perhaps from epilepsy, or
　　　　　sex practices.

Parental neglect — unwitting.

　　　　　　　　　　　　　　　Mentality:
Sex + + +.　　　　　　　　　　Dull as above.

The parents soon decided it was impossible for them to properly control this girl on account of the extreme tendencies she had developed. They placed her in an institution. A year or so later she returned home. Recently we have again been consulted about her. It seems that after a few months at home she again became a sex delinquent. Study of her case now shows that she has frequent attacks of *petit mal*. They are described by Maria herself, and have been observed by her parents and others. There is no longer any doubt of her being an epileptic. The family now give a history of epilepsy in a maternal great-uncle to Maria, of fainting attacks in Maria's maternal aunts; also a paternal uncle had convulsive seizures following an accident. At 16 Maria is no longer so disproportionately over-developed, and shows little of her old attractiveness. Again we find it necessary to recommend an institution.

This case illustrates two of the points we have elsewhere made in regard to over-development. Premature development and over-development are found with astonishing frequency in cases of epilepsy (§ 254). Secondly, early over-development does not always mean great size later.

The following history of a young woman whom we have known for several years brings out again the point that over-development at 12 years may mean normality at 19 or 20. Also it brings out that the young adult has the mental power to control a physical and social situation which may be overwhelming in earliest adolescence.

Case 23. — This girl when seen by us at 15 had already had a long career of sex delinquency. She willingly began her affairs at 10 years of age, and actually supported a " cadet " by prostitution when she was 12 years old. We found her to be magnificently endowed with strength, general development and good looks. She weighed 151 lbs., height 5 ft., 1 1-2 in. No physical defects of any kind noted. General development of a mature woman. She menstruated first at 11 years.

On the mental side she demonstrated herself to have decidedly good ability and an unexpected range of interests. We particularly noted her apparent mental instabilities, which we felt best able to characterize as social suggestibility. From what we were able to learn about her we had reason to believe, however, that she was suggestible for good as well as for bad.

This girl came from a family not showing, as far as we could learn, any marked mental dullness, but thoroughly immoral on both sides. Her own beginning sex tendencies were allowed full sway by a dissolute mother, and a male relative had proposed to start a house of prostitution with this girl. When we saw her she had already been in a reformatory school in one state and had belonged to the " street-walker " class in several cities. Notwithstanding all this, the girl's good mental qualities, her range of interests, her previous lack of chance in a better social circle, and even her social suggestibility led us to believe there might be a favorable prognosis.

This girl was taken by a high-minded and practical woman, entirely away from her old associations, and the outcome of the case has been wonderfully successful. Now at 19 she appears a very normal young woman. She is no larger and perhaps weighs a little less than when she was 15. Her good mental qualities have been well utilized and she has steadily been making a brilliant record in arduous studies leading towards her chosen difficult profession.

Over-development excessive: Premature puberty.   Case 23.
  Home conditions: Mother immoral, etc.   Girl, 15 yrs.
     Heredity: Father alcoholic.   Mother immoral, etc.

Delinquencies: Mentality:
Sex + + +.   Good ability.

Case 24. — A girl of 16, who is said to have been in scores of sex delinquencies. The father says she is just the mother over again. His wife left him when this child was three years old. One other child is said to be a good girl, but has convulsions " when she eats certain things." We found a strong girl, with decided over-development of sex characteristics for her age. Weight 145 lbs. Fairly good features. Bright eyes. Good color. Severe visual defect in one eye for which she has worn glasses. She had menstruated by the time she was 12.

The girl's mental powers showed her to be poor in ability, but hardly defective enough to be called even subnormal. Her use of language was good, considering her social station. She was polite, and might be considered decidedly attractive in some circles. In this case it was very difficult to say which was the major factor. The causative factor card ran as follows:

Early sex teachings: Case 24.
  Boys, *et al.*   Girl, age 16.
  Over-development, premature puberty.
    Home conditions:
       Father rules by repression.
       No healthy recreations.
         Heredity: Mother immoral.
              Sister epileptic.
Sex offenses + +.   Mentality:
Stealing.   Poor in ability.

The problem of *prematured and over-developed boys* involves, naturally, very different features. Here, for the most part, it is restiveness and desire for self-expression and for general physical activity that has to be met. In some cases there is early accentuation of sex impulse, but it is quite likely to be a minor factor as compared to the overt tendencies of girls in this direction. The two cases cited below are fair examples of the problems involved.

Case 25. — We were asked to see a boy of 15 1-2 after his arrest as an adult for a petty misdemeanor. He was then living away from home, as he had many times before. He had been more than once previously arrested. His well-to-do and unusually intelligent parents gave a very clear story of his life. They have a very attractive home in a neighboring state, but he merely visits them and lives with them as inclination dictates. His delinquencies began by his running away from home for a number of days when he was only 9 years old. Since then he has misappropriated and stolen at times, apparently as the result of the conditions of actual poverty in which he sometimes gets while away from home. He has worked at the most arduous occupations, sometimes as a stevedore, and even as a coal passer on a transatlantic liner. His affectionate parents, as we had reason to perceive, were very sympathetic in their attitude, quite commanded his love, and had done much for him. The boy had even been taken on foreign travels.

We found this boy with the physical make-up of a strong man. Height 5 ft. 10. (He was already a head taller than any other member of his family.) Large boned. Lean, and well muscled. Weight 145 lbs. Fingers broad and misshapen, probably from his early hard work. No sensory defect. Badly deflected septum. Chin small in proportion to his other large features. Sex development completely adult. On the mental side the boy presented nothing peculiar. He was a fluent reader. He did arithmetic equivalent to the 5th grade, despite excessive truancy. Normal emotions. A very frank pleasant fellow with decidedly good orientation as to his own career and place in the world. We found not the slightest evidence of anything pathological in his mental condition.

Speaking of himself, he tells us that it is just his natural cravings, " My crazy roving habits," that lead him to his delinquent running away from home, and then to occasionally taking

255

things when he is hard up. Often he is too utterly ashamed of himself on account of his unkempt condition to turn up at home even when he is near there. He wanders all over the country, and even abroad, taking care of himself by the labor of his hands. The boy believes that his innate sex inclinations are partly responsible for his restiveness, and at times has given way to gratification, but, of course, this feature has been greatly minimized by his hard labor and even semi-starvation. His excessive general development was already marked at 10 years, but no accurate data upon the beginning of pubescence could be otained. Early in his school life he hated to be with small children.

It is a matter of no small interest that this intelligent boy early took his case in his own hands, and prescribed his own treatment. He perhaps did more for his own salvation than his parents, who desired to give him luxuries and to further his career along commercial lines. The fact that he needed a place for himself in the forest, on the mountains or the plains should have been as obvious years earlier, as it became now, after our study.

Over-development extreme with premature puberty.   Case 25.
Boy, 15½ yrs.

Adolescent instability for years.

Early **school dissatisfaction** on account of above.

Love of wandering.

Delinquencies:
Running away + + +.
Petty stealing.   Mentality:
Fair ability.

---

§ 191. (*H*) **Premature Puberty without Over-development.** — In order to show that the problems of prematurity may occur without general over-development we offer the following cases. The point is important because it is generally considered that prematurity is accompanied by over-development either of general physical or of sex characteristics.

Case 26. — We studied this girl when she was 14½ years old. For more than two years she had been engaged in sex immoralities, beginning with boys and more recently continued with men. Physically we found her very strong and well, of distinctly boyish form. Weight 130 lbs., height 5 ft., 5¾ in. Regular features and thick lips. A frank bold type. The fairly intelligent father gives us a full account of the case. The mother became after marriage free in morals, and separated from him. This girl lives with him. One sister became immoral, but three older children have never caused any trouble. The girl we saw menstruated before she was 13. According to the father, the whole trouble with her is that she is naturally inclined to sex immoralities. Our study of her mentality showed her to be rather poor in ability, but we could not denominate her subnormal. She had gotten to the 5th grade, in spite of her delinquent tendencies.

This case is rather notable for the premature onset of puberty and of sex feeling without development of general physical sex characteristics. The prognosis was plainly unfavorable. She was placed in an institution for a long period and while there is said to have learned well and behaved properly. After a year she was released, being then about 16 years old. At once her old proclivities strongly showed themselves, in spite of normal advantages and probationary care. Renewed delinquencies made it necessary for her again to receive institutional protection.

Premature puberty.   Case 26.

Physical or mental peculiarity.   Girl, 14½ yrs.
    Marked sensual type although not
        over-developed.

Heredity.   Mother immoral.

Home conditions — earlier defective.

Bad companions earlier.

Delinquencies: Mentality:
    Sex + + +.   Poor ability.

Case 27. — Boy of 14 years and 3 months. Much truancy, considerable petty thieving, incorrigibility at home, out much at night.

Physically, stoop shouldered, a mouth breather, but no obstruction in nose or throat. Very defective occlusion of the teeth partially accounts for his mouth breathing. Has a peculiarly weak physiognomy, with retreating chin. No sensory defect. Poor color. Weight 119 lbs. Height 5 ft. 6 in. Complete adult type of sex development. Well-shaped head.

On the mental side we found a quiet, subjective, suggestible type. He complained of slight feelings of faintness, perhaps mostly from weakness. Has been to the 5th grade in school.

From the results on tests we decided that he showed mental dullness, probably from poor physical conditions and bad sex habits. It is difficult for him to carry through a long task of any kind.

He is said to have been a very bright young child. Other members of the family are very well endowed mentally. He had a very severe sickness at 9 years, following a heat stroke. Heredity negative. Age of first pubescence not obtainable.

In this case there was not only a marked lack of correlation between age and onset of puberty, but the boy was too much of a weakling to have this burden thrown upon him. He was led into the practice of bad sex habits early. The whole case was felt to be one for hygienic treatment. It is interesting to note that as time has gone on, and the case has been taken well in hand, that there has been great improvement in behavior.

Premature puberty — very marked.   Case 27.
    Physical conditions poor.   Boy, 14 yrs.
      Developmental.   Early severe illness.
        Bad sex habits.
          Bad companions.
Truancy.   Mentality:
Petty thieving, etc.   Dull from physical causes.

---

§ 192. (*I*) **Premature Puberty with Distinctly Poor Development.** — Cases of the kind denoted by this heading have still other points of difference, and involve other moral and social complications. The young person who is already somewhat socially incapacitated by general poor physical conditions is badly equipped for standing the extra burden of an early puberty. The peculiar significance of this unfortunate combination of circumstances varies, as may be seen from the following cases.

Case 28. — Boy, 11 years, 4 months. This boy has long been thoroughly delinquent, a great truant, and has engaged in petty stealing from home and stores on numerous occasions.

We found him defective in nutrition and general development. Weight 62 lbs., height 4 ft. 3 in. Poor strength. No sensory defect. Large tonsils. Very evasive expression. Ears poorly formed. Other physical signs negative, except considerable development of pubic hair and other signs of puberty. A most unusual case and in sharp contradistinction to general poor development.

Mentally, fair in ability.   Was in the 4th grade at school.   He is one of three children;   an older boy was delinquent.   The father deserted years ago.   Mother works out.   This boy has been hanging about a disreputable store where girls go, but he denies sex delinquency with any one.   He has been left much to his own resources.   Uses tobacco.

The outlook was, of course, poor in his old environment and after probationary oversight for a time he got into more difficulties.

Home conditions: Father deserted.   Case 28.
    Mother works out.   Boy, 11 yrs. 4 mos.
  Physical conditions: Weakly type.

    Premature puberty.   Very marked case.

      Smoking.

Delinquencies:
  Truancy.   Mentality:
  Stealing.   Fair mental ability.

Case 29. — A boy of 15 years who has been under arrest many times, was finally seen by us because a police officer was interested in doing something for him.   His delinquencies had been going on for many years, and consisted in much truancy, street loafing, sleeping away from home, and stealing.   He has long associated with some of the worst people to be found in city life.   At last he was arrested in company with a notorious seller of cocaine, and had packages of the drug on his own person.   Despite his small size he has been able, perhaps by his deep voice, to convince judges in adult courts time and again that he was over juvenile age.   He has received at least one sentence to the House of Correction.   Registration of birth was looked up, and his real age found to be as above.   (Falsehood is not only a common characteristic of this boy, but also of other members of the family, so coöperation has been difficult.)

On the physical side one finds him to be very poorly developed, but fairly nourished.   Weight 98 lbs., height 5 ft.   No sensory defect noted.   Is decidedly anemic.   Poorly developed and asymmetrical chest, with prominent sternum.   Narrow, high palate. Teeth very much crowded, showing earlier impaction.   Shifty, evasive and tired expression.   Small mouth and sharp chin. Constant fine tremor of outstretched hands.   Reflexes normal.

Completely adult type of sex development. Slight mustache. Circumcised several years ago. About a year ago he had gonorrhea and chancroid. Speech is thick and hoarse, of the nasal quality found among low street types. Head well shaped; circumference 54, length 18½, breadth 15 cm.

A summary of our mental findings is that this boy shows evidences of having fair mental ability, although results on formal educational tests equal only 2d grade work. He has, however, plenty of information about ordinary street interests, shows a certain smartness in that direction, and much acquaintance with criminalistic affairs. Of the normal interests of boyhood his information is practically *nil*, although he knows some of the ordinary facts of history and geography. He claims to have gone to school very little. We found he was an excessive liar, and his irrational behavior in the face of proffered help by interested police officers threw open the question as to whether he was not possibly aberrational in type. Whether or not he was a user of cocaine we could not at first determine, although he had it in his possession. The final mental diagnosis was held in abeyance. (Later it came out that he was a cocainist.)

There was very much more in this case than the mere fact of sex precocity with poor development. He came from an atrociously bad environment, and a degraded and alcoholic family. He has been an excessive user of stimulants, *e. g.*, coffee, before taking cocaine. For our present purposes we may regard him, however, as being largely the product of a thoroughly disorganized adolescent development. The disparity between his premature sex development and his backward physical development equalled certainly 5 years.

Home conditions atrociously bad.   Case 29.
    Mother alcoholic, etc.   Boy, 15 yrs.

    Stimulants, early use of, now cocainist.

      Physical conditions — very poor in general.

        Premature puberty, marked case.

          Heredity. Mother alcoholic. Other
              facts not known.

                     Mentality:
Delinquencies: Fair ability.
  Stealing.   Probably constitutional
  Vagrancy, etc.   inferior.

It is unnecessary to give cases of girls in whom there is premature puberty plus poor physical conditions; the two may be combined in various ways. Many debilitating conditions or ailments may evidently be correlated with prematurity.

The treatment of this whole group should include measures of hygiene and environment and nourishment which shall build up the body and strengthen the will. Definite ailments are to be taken care of medically. The sex prematurity is to be thought of in the light of its being a developmental peculiarity of an individual who probably has unusually poor resistance to temptations. Unfortunately many of these cases come from families defective in morals as well as in financial status, and much of their tendency to delinquency arises from home conditions. Over and over again we have seen attempts to handle these cases in the old environment followed by failure.

CHAPTER V

STIMULANTS AND NARCOTICS

Alcohol. § 193. General Opinions. § 194. Various Ways in which Alcohol is a Factor. § 195. Effect of Alcohol on Adolescents. § 196. Effect of Alcohol on Mental Defectives. § 197. Treatment. § 198. **Morphine.** § 199. **Cocaine.** § 200. **Tea and Coffee.** § 201. **Tobacco.**

ALCOHOL.

§ 193. **General Opinions.** — The many-sided relationship of the use of alcoholic beverages to criminalism is so completely established that we hardly need to dwell on the general question, important though it is. All court officials are well acquainted with the concrete facts, and many statisticians and others have gathered the larger data.[1] We must acknowledge at once the difficulties which lie in statistical investigation of the subject in many directions. Pearson and Elderton (**240**) have, if nothing more, shown this clearly, and also Hoegel (**241**) has dwelled with force upon the point. But impossible though it may be to accurately determine the influence of alcohol in the production of this or that especially attributed condition, still taken either *en masse* or studied in connection with the individual offender, which is our special point

---

[1] From our bibliographic studies we offer the student a short list of the most available recent important statistics on the connection between consumption of alcohol and delinquency. We concern ourselves strictly with scientific and not propaganda material. Under the auspices of the French Ministry of Justice for some years an investigation has been carried out by means of reports from judges who are compelled to state whether the convicted person committed the offense under the influence of liquor, or is a confirmed alcoholic. The *Journal officiel* (**41**) from time to time has published these reports and Yvernis (**42**) summarized them in 1912. Boas (**237**) in 1908 gave a good short summary of many researches in statistics. Macdonald (**238**) in 1909 presented an interesting summary from many countries and cities. Aschaffenburg's (**130**) fair-minded and illuminating chapter on the subject is now available for readers of English, as also is Lombroso's (**239**) more general statement of the subject. Nothing more convincing is found than the statements of the diminution of criminality in Ireland as the result of Father Matthews' abstinence campaigns. According to Baer (**256**) this wonderful man in the five-year period from 1837 to 1842 reduced the consumption of spirits in that country 50 per cent. The crimes dropped from 64,520 to 47,027, and the executions from 59 to only 1 in the year.

The most important reference work on alcohol and alcoholism is that by Abderhalden (**253**), who offers a bibliography, with descriptive notes, of the tremendous number of contributions to the subject.

of view, the facts will easily justify the cold assertion of Aschaffenburg (1, p. 228) that if we could by one blow do away with the
use of alcohol, the number of annual convictions would be reduced
one-fifth. And this does not, of course, include at all the relationship which we discern so plainly between alcoholism and future
delinquency in the family. For our purposes, the whole problem
in its general features may be left, and we can push forward to our
discussion of the relation of the use of alcohol to the case of the
individual offender.

§ 194. **Various Ways in which Alcohol is a Factor.** — In studying the individual, alcohol as a causative factor appears not only
in respect to its immediate use, but also in the home, in the environment, in the developmental history, including antenatal life,
and in heredity. These points should be taken up one by one.

(a) *Heredity.* Logically, the whole question of possible defective inheritance arising through alcoholism centers about injury
to germ cells, whether the alcoholic condition of the parent be
chronic or occur at the time of procreation. The greatest difficulty, which most authors have not reckoned with in studying
heredity and alcoholism, is the fact that many drunkards are such
because they are already defective individuals with tendency to
pass down defective traits, especially mental defects, irrespective
of alcoholism. Few, if any, of the students of the subject have
taken this point sufficiently into account.[1] And here again gross
statistics may well be misleading on account of the point which
we have had elsewhere to bring up so strongly, namely, that the
character of the parents may be reflected in the child's behavior
rather through environment and development, than through
hereditary influences. The study of the relationship between
mental defect, as such, and criminalism must be kept quite apart
from our present subject. Many points in the general problem
are still *sub judice*, but various fragmentary researches are gradually being accumulated, and the general bearing of the findings
so far unquestionably is that alcohol may be in many instances a
directly deteriorating influence upon germ cells, and so fairly be
regarded as a cause of defective inheritance.

We would submit the statement that our own findings, in spite
of their total significance, cannot be used in proof of defective

[1] A fine example of controlled experiment is that by Stockard (264) who
has most cautiously studied the effect of alcohol on the germ cells of animals.
He finds that the degeneracy caused by alcohol may be passed on by degenerate offspring.

263

inheritance from alcoholism, because of the mix-up with possible inheritance of defective characteristics, and the direct influence of alcoholism upon the environment.

(*b*) *Alcohol and Procreation.* The effect which the parent, being under the influence of alcohol at the time of procreation, may possibly have on the offspring stands on the border line between defective heredity and defective environmental conditions. The time is probably not yet ripe for a definite statement upon this subject, but certainly one may assert the probable correctness of the view of those who hold that an undue amount of alcohol in the circulation of either parent at the time of procreation may be a cause of degeneracy of the offspring.

(*c*) *Antenatal Conditions.* We have already sufficiently discussed this point in § 152. There cannot be the slightest doubt that the ingestion of alcohol by the pregnant mother may have a very deleterious effect upon the nervous system of the unborn child.

(*d*) *The Developmental Period.* Very fortunately alcoholism in children in our country is a comparatively rare phenomenon. We found (§ 101), in spite of our group of repeated offenders coming largely from alcoholic families, that only in 2.7 per cent. were the offenders themselves users of alcohol, and practically all of these were only occasional partakers. The exceedingly bad results of alcoholism in children as seen in certain special regions of Europe are well known. It is to be remembered that comparatively intense poisoning results in children, and that after-effects are manifested in the nervous system. Outside of actual ingestion of alcohol, many chances for defective development are found in the household of drinking people who afford their children a bad environment.

(*e*) *Environmental.* We would not presume to be able always to accurately distinguish between hereditary, developmental and strictly environmental effects of alcoholism or drunkenness on the part of the parents. But considering the general question of alcoholism in the environment, we have before us one of the most striking causative factors of delinquency. It will be noted (§§ 115 and 116) that we readily obtained information about drunkenness in at least one parent in 31 per cent. of our 1000 cases, and in 56 per cent. of the cases where there was other criminalism in the family. It must be understood that this means drunkenness, not merely the moderate drinking which so frequently in a household makes for irritation and bickering and hard feelings; sometimes in turn leading to delinquency on the part of a child. In these latter instances it has been quite impossible to fairly determine the part which alcohol played, but it is a matter of general knowledge that in some individuals alcohol incites a quarrelsome disposition. Illustrating a typical family history, and the complexity of conditions involved in chronic alcoholism, we may cite the following.

Case 30. — In this family we have had the opportunity of carefully studying one member, observing two more, and knowing much of the records of the others over many years. The father and mother were immigrants. They have five grown-up children, all of whom were born in this country. The father is a laborer who cannot write, but in all probability is not a mental defective. The mother can read and write. She has been accustomed to working out at times. For many years both of these parents have been hard drinkers. The father has been sentenced a number of times for drunkenness and violence and also for larceny. The mother is a person whom a little liquor is said to make crazy. She has received short sentences upwards of 50 times. According to her history, and as seen by us, she is probably a case of alcoholic paranoia. She readily develops a grudge against her neighbors, becomes violent, breaks windows, etc., and often moves her household. Home conditions have thus included poverty, lack of control, quarreling, and many changes.

This couple have had 12 children, 7 of whom died during childhood. Of the 5 who have survived, 4 have been extremely delinquent. They have been guilty of stealing, burglary, picking pockets, and one girl has been sexually immoral. The two older boys have both served long terms besides short ones. We know that some of the children are bright, and probably not one is mentally defective. They all have learned fairly well in spite of their interrupted schooling, and when willing to work have been good earners. The case history of the youngest runs as follows.

Seen at 14 this boy was poorly developed and nourished. Weight 76 lbs., height 4 ft. 7 in. Asymmetry of forehead. High Gothic palate. One tooth erupted out of alignment. Adenoids. Mouth breather. Dull eyes, and drawn expression about the mouth. Very slouchy attitude. On the mental side we found him well up to the ordinary, and much brighter than one would expect from his physical conditions and environmental chances.

265

Already this boy had been in several charitable institutions, and had been in trouble with the courts on numerous occasions for picking pockets and other stealing. After being taken care of for a while he was returned each time to his own environment with all its general bad associations. When less than 19 he was apprehended once more, and a charge of 21 recent burglaries was brought against him.

In this case it would be safe to say that alcoholism had directly caused the criminality of the father, the criminality and mental condition of the mother, the defective developmental conditions of this boy, and had created an atrocious environment which was in itself sufficient to account for delinquent tendencies. We can thus safely reason from cause to effect without interposing heredity and defective germ plasm, although the latter may have caused part of the trouble.

Many other cases of this same kind could be given, though few with so virulent criminalistic tendencies. We are glad to have observed a few cases in which alcoholism of a parent has been the cause of extreme reaction against it by a family of vigorous children. The condition of the latter gives us social proof that all germ cells may not be deteriorated by alcohol, and that the substructure of alcoholism is not necessarily prepotently inherited, and that alcoholic defects of the environment may by some be met and overcome.

It should hardly be necessary to enumerate the different features of a defective environment which may be caused by alcoholism of the parent. The main defects are poverty; lack of control; neglect of proper nourishment, clothing, or other hygienic conditions for children; crowded housing, with all its miserable physical and moral incidents; neglect of attention to schooling and mental and moral development; irrational disciplinary behavior, expressed in variations from indifference to great irritation about small things; immodest behavior and use of obscene language on the part of a parent, which we have frequently found to be one of the main causes of a girl going wrong; lowered moral inhibitions, which sometimes lead as far as attempted rape of a daughter; quarreling and bickering and development of grudge in the home. These several latter conditions are not often thought of, but for any one who studies individual offenders they stand out prominently as factors which decide careers of boys and girls. All these things and still others have to be reckoned with when there is alcoholism of a parent.

Our careful and conservative statistics are altogether comparable to findings elsewhere. Naturally in this matter, as in many others, the fact of alcoholism in parents would vary greatly in different regions and different countries. Figures gathered by Hoppe (242), Gruhle (147), and Wulffen (2) show that among criminals of all ages an astoundingly large percentage have had alcoholic parents. The collection of statistics on this point by Gruhle from different countries is particularly worth consulting.

(*f*) *Relation of Delinquency to the Use of Alcohol by the Delinquent.* This subject must be subdivided for logical consideration. We are especially concerned with it, and must take up its main phases.

It may be reiterated that only 2.7 per cent. of our analyzed cases of young repeated offenders were users of alcohol. This is significant since, as repeatedly insisted on in our earlier chapters, we are dealing with the genetic factors of criminal careers. Any finding that a larger per cent. of older criminals are alcoholic, bears very little on this question, since they may have acquired alcoholism. To be sure, later alcoholism is an added factor making for the continuance of criminalism, but the personal drinking was very unusual at first. Perhaps it is good reasoning to say that the hereditary, developmental, and environmental factors which made for early criminalism, made also for later alcoholism, but certainly the criminalism starts first in the vast majority of cases. We speak now for our own population and social conditions, realizing that these facts vary somewhat in places where drinking among children is much more frequent. As primarily students of the individual offender we should at once again plunge into the question of types of personalities and of causes, rather than discuss generalities or even types of drinking.

§ 195. **Effect of Alcohol on Adolescents.** — The effect of a little wine or beer upon an adolescent girl in breaking down her normal social and moral inhibitions is notorious. The effect is produced by premeditation of companions of both sexes who desire to lower the intended victim's levels of behavior. Many well-founded social studies of the connection between drinking in dance halls and saloons, and beginning prostitution are now available. One of the most simple and direct is to be found in the report of the Vice Commission of Chicago (**243**). In our own study of cases we have learned the facts over and over again, and they amount to just this: there was a desire for company and pleasure on the part of the girl; even in bad company there would be resistance to the many suggestive influences thrown about her, except for the directly decisive part played by a physiopsychological condition — with the use of liquor to which she was unaccustomed, a feeling of not caring possessed her, and the step was taken. In example is the following.

Case 31. — A very attractive girl of 15, over-developed in sex characteristics for her age, had found herself able to earn very much more in theatre life than she could elsewhere. She came of normal and healthy stock on both sides and was herself well endowed mentally as well as physically. Her earnings helped greatly her widowed mother, who carefully watched over her. All went well until the drinking men and women with whom she went out one night finally induced her to do likewise. She then and there started a career of sex delinquency which never has been thwarted except by her being held in some institution. In spite of much being done for her in succeeding years, this fine-looking girl has repeatedly entered the same life through the same avenue, namely, partial alcoholic intoxication.

Alcohol — social drinking.   Case 31.
  Over-development of sex characteristics.   Girl, age 15.
    Bad companions connected with stage life.
Delinquencies: Mentality:
Sex + +.   Good.

The type of trouble which adolescent boys get into from drinking varies considerably, especially according to their background of mental ability. The following case illustrates several points.

Case 32. — This is a boy whom we have known over several years. When first seen at 16 he was found small in size and considerably undeveloped so far as sex characteristics were concerned, but of good strength. 102 lbs., 4 ft. 11 in. No sensory defect. A frank, alert, responsive, intelligent, nervous type with much artistic ability. Already he had been in trouble a good many times on account of running away from home and stealing in petty ways, and he had also committed at least one burglary. He was said to be a very affectionate and pleasant boy. For years at home he had been allowed a little beer and occasionally a taste of brandy, and was accustomed to drinking tea and coffee three times a day. He showed a definite desire for stimulants. At 8 he began to smoke, later this habit became excessive, but in the last year or two there has been very little of it. The father is much the same type, a moderate drinker of alcohol, a large user of tobacco — a nervous man who loses his temper readily. No epilepsy, insanity or feeblemindedness is known to exist on either side. One elder brother is an irritable fellow who often gets into fights. A sister also is delinquent.

On account of his ability good people have attempted to help this boy. At times he has responded, but then again has been unable to hold himself long at work or at school. At one period he did succeed in keeping one place for seven months. The main feature of his case has always been his instability, which unfortunately has not passed away with the first years of adolescence. There has been constant desire for stimulants, with increasing symptoms of moral and social unreliability. The many splendid chances which have been offered him have been unavailing, and he has become a dissipated wanderer and half vagrant.

Back of the use of stimulants, which has steadily lowered the social status of this young fellow, there undoubtedly was a nervous organization which demanded their use. Whether this peculiarity of his nervous make-up was due to heredity, or to his earlier use of stimulants during a more plastic developmental period, it is hard to say. The outlook for such a case is not good, and splendid human material seems to have gone to waste. However, after years of wandering, such previous failures have been known to settle down and become more stable.

§ 196. **Effect of Alcohol on Mental Defectives.** — The problem of alcoholism, whether as viewed by medical people, institutional officials, planners of social reforms, or by courts who have to deal with drunkards as offenders, must include consideration of the various personal types of alcoholics and their potentialities. We recently have begun to hear something about the feebleminded alcoholic, and we shall hear still more, for it undoubtedly is true that many of the social outcasts who are merely denominated drunkards are basically mental defectives. It may be put down as a cardinal fact that no social treatment of the drunkard is going

269

to prove availing which does not reckon with the mental and physical conditions of the individual, and which does not offer prognosis and treatment in the light of these, as well as of social conditions. More of this question of individualization later. The mental defective, and the epileptic who suffers from psychical disabilities, are both prone to become drunkards. The alcoholic feeling of exaltation or superior strength, the illusion of the moment, appeals strongly to all inferior types. In the British public inebriate asylums it has finally been found that a considerable number of the inmates are feebleminded. Lacking such public institutions here we have not any figures to offer, yet it is a well-known fact that many drunkards are defectives. To effectively alter the situation they must be dealt with as defectives and not primarily as drunkards. The effect of alcohol upon a weakminded person can readily be discerned in some of our cases, such as the following.

Case 33. — Boy of 15, well developed and of fair strength. No sensory defect. 123 lbs. 5 ft. 3 1-2 in. Well along in pubescence. Over-development of sex organs. Mentally, feebleminded. He has already been several years in a school for the feebleminded, where they have succeeded in teaching him to write well and to add up simple numbers. Technically he is a middle grade moron with a good deal of industrial capacity. Before he went to the school for the feebleminded he was a truant. He came from a family who gave him decidedly poor control; father alcoholic, mother dead.

This boy had learned so well that he seemed capable of making his own way in the world and was released from the school. He obtained a position in a factory which he did not hold for long, and later went to work for a milk dealer. He did well there for some months, got tired of it, worked in an amusement park, and then obtained employment with another milk man. Here he did his work properly, and indeed during all this time, a matter of a year or so, he had made his own way in the world without trouble. One day he was given a half a bottle of whiskey which he consumed then and there. Within an hour or two after drinking this he violently assaulted sexually a little boy who came to the place for milk.

We could give other instances of young men who have considerable industrial capacity, even though not quite up to normal

270

in general intelligence tests, who could very probably maintain
themselves in society if it were not for the temptations and
results of alcoholic drinking.   Particularly have we frequently
noted the disastrous combination of epilepsy and drinking.   In
these cases, whether or not the alcohol incites more frequent
attacks, there is a marked lowering of mental and moral tone.
Epileptics who, but for perhaps a moderate amount of intoxicants, might maintain themselves just above the border line of
social incapacity and immoral living, become vagrants, prostitutes or other social outcasts.   This point should be so self-evi-
dent that we need take no space to cite any of the many cases of
the kind we know, but we may refer to § 256 and § 257 for some
indication of the atrocious crimes which epilepsy plus alcohol
produces.   This part of the subject may be summarized by saying
that many of the troublesome drinkers who cost society dear
are primarily inferiors, suffering from ailments or defects of
mind and body, and that alcohol just turns the balance against
their maintaining themselves as non-criminalistic citizens.

Other examples of abnormal physical and mental conditions
which offer undue chance for the break-down of moral equilibrium
through the influence of alcohol may be found in the weaknesses
of various chronic diseases, such as tuberculosis, and in the well-
known weakened inhibitory states of senility.   Some criminalistic behavior which is typically senile, such as exhibitionism,
may be directly incited through ingestion of alcohol, particularly
by old people.[1]   The aberrational mental states actually caused
by alcohol are considered under the head of Psychoses, § 320.

§ 197. **Treatment.** — Although we shall make no attempt
to give the medical treatment of inebriety and alcoholism — for
this special treatises [2] must be consulted — yet for all concerned
in handling offenders we would emphasize certain points.   In
the first place it should be thoroughly realized that any treatment planned for alcoholics, whether as such, or as criminalistic
offenders, whether undertaken in a special colony or within institutional walls, bears very little promise of fruitfulness unless
the background in personal characteristics and in environment

[1] Ladame (**244**) has an article on the relation between alcohol and exhibitionism.

[2] For instance, the recent English contribution by Cooper (**245**), the well-
considered statements of Neff (**246**) (**368**) from his long experience in Massachusetts, and the recent studies in the psychology of intemperance by Partridge (**247**).

be taken into account. Isolation, or deprivation, or agricultural labor, or any other proposed preventive and hoped-for correc-tive measure, carried over any special length of time may be quite beside the mark of cure. Nothing will be largely effective which does not allow for individualization of treatment.

Some indication of the suggestive values for treatment, and yet limited possibilities of set classification of alcoholics may be shown by the following: Williams (248) classifies inebriates into (a) suggestible individuals who drifted into drinking, and who were not really inebriates until the occurrence of tissue degeneration from prolonged use of alcohol; (b) individuals who get into drinking ways because they possess the suggesti-bility that is the result of not being ethically trained to overcome the impulsive tendencies of childhood; (c) those who have a weak nervous make-up that by way of longing turns towards the satisfaction of narcotics. Pettey (249) says chronic alcohol-ics may be subdivided as follows:

A. Regular drinkers.
    (a) Daily consumers who create their own need — the larger class.
    (b) Those of defective physique craving stimulants.
    (c) Pure dissipation by those deficient in moral fibre.
B. Periodic drinkers.
    (a) Dipsomania — periodic ¡insanity taking the form of un-controllable desire for drink (rare).
    (b) Moral cowards — these drink to drown troubles.
    (c) Unstable character with bad environment — drinkers who lose control of themselves when slightly under the influence of alcohol.
    (d) Bad environment; with ever present, but resisted appetite.

From these efforts at classification we can see some of the complexity of the subject. But when we realize what a variety of individuals, with all sorts of innate potentialities, may com-pose one of the classes, such, for instance, as Pettey's daily con-sumers or Williams' suggestible, drifting individuals, it becomes clear that general schemes of treatment prescribed by law cannot be satisfactorily carried out. Nothing short of some method of indefinite sentence, leaving the treatment and time to special-ists, will accomplish much. But what about the return to or-dinary social conditions? It must make the gods laugh to see this costly effort by police, court, and sanitarium methods followed up by public opportunity and even suggestion to repeat the of-

fense for which the arrest was made and the treatment given.
At any rate, until the large class of defectives and inferiors is
handled in some different way, or their opportunities for relapse
are suppressed, the old deep connection between alcoholism and
crime will ever obtain.

What attitude the law shall take in regard to *responsibility
for acts committed under the influence of liquor* is strictly a matter
of a given legal policy, and will vary as the fundamental conceptions of the purpose and possible efficiencies of criminal codes
may vary. The fact is that, aside from complete stupefaction,
the effect of alcohol upon separate mental functions, including
the will, is a highly individual matter. The loss of normal will
power is logically, as in the German code, the stage of intoxication in which the person becomes actually irresponsible. It is
perfectly clear to students of the subject that, even leaving out
of count the recognizable innate inferiors and defectives, merely
one or two glasses of beer will dispossess some persons of their
volitional and moral powers to an extent that a whole evening
of drinking will not affect another. So the quantity taken will
not tell the story of lost responsibility, nor will any other immediately applicable criterion, short of the physical helplessness
which prevents deeds of all kinds.

The many complicating features for treatment in a single case,
even before the advent of sottish habit formation, and without
a background of mental or physical inferiority, are worth illustrating. Here, too, let us take an early career, that we may
observe fundamental driving forces.

Case 34. — Young man, 22 years, big, strong, bright eyes,
unusually good features. Son of Slavish parents. He looks
anything but a drunkard, but is unduly restless and nervous.
Mental ability well up to the ordinary. He did well in school.
Is affectionate and kind. He holds a good position where he has
two assistants; has worked in the same place for 6 years. The
heredity is negative except that most of both families are drinkers; no bad drunkards among them. The father is very fond of
his beer at home, and the boy has had it in small quantities ever
since he was 12 or 13. He is the eldest of 9 children. The mother
is a good woman and much distressed over this fellow's delinquencies. He drinks only on Saturdays and Sundays. He began
to use whiskey a couple of years ago with companions, but before
that had been drunk.

About his own case this unusually fine-looking fellow explains that there is not the slightest reason for his drinking except that when Saturday comes he just seems to forget himself. He began frequenting saloons with others, but now goes alone. He seldom has any other place to go, and feels as if he is forced to pass the time away drinking. No real craving at any time. He just goes to the saloon to spend a few hours. He has a drink or two, and that would be all right, but always then wants more. He works only half a day on Saturdays, and he thinks it would be better if he worked all day. He went with a nice girl, but she put him aside — she was quite right in doing so, he thinks. She ought not to marry a drunkard. He has promised his parents over and over to do better, but when he goes out it always ends up by drinking. His companions all drink, but don't get drunk as he does.

He came home intoxicated 6 or 7 months ago and since that time is nearly always intoxicated on Saturday nights or Sundays. He has stopped drinking entirely for a week at a time and then gets intoxicated worse than ever. His parents think his mind must be weak because his promises are so readily broken. Nobody has done anything constructive in the case, there has merely been extensive scolding by the parents and others. The young man has been athletic at times, but has no special interests, and reads no books. He makes much of the companionship side of drinking, but acknowledges that now-a-days he seeks the intoxicant by himself.

In this case we have the following main factors: early moderate home drinking; possible inheritance of unknown defective qualities from drinking ancestors; influence of companionship; the invitation of social life in neighborhood saloons; lack of healthy mental interests; an already created need for alcohol through long indulgence; loss of will power after a glass or two is taken. All this overcomes an apparently very well endowed young man.

As to his treatment; of course there should be complete withdrawal of the intoxicant, and building up of the system so that future abstinence can be tolerated. This will have to be away from the scene of previous mental and social associations. Treatment thus means loss of position. But then the return home; there is a difficulty. The young man and his family want a specific against alcohol. Finding nothing offered they go away sorrowing, and the young man thinks he can gradually stop. The prognosis is absolutely bad. Not only personal conditions, strong fellow though he is, are against him, but also social circumstances. Society, which does not alter the latter, will have to stand the brunt of his downfall.

§ 198. Morphine.

Morphine in its relation to criminality is vastly more subtle than alcohol. (We include the use of opium with that of its derivative, morphine.) In the first place, it is often quite difficult to obtain the facts about the use of the drug, and, next, the effects are not nearly so obviously connected with misconduct. The use of morphine is comparatively infrequently an actual cause of crime, but in some cases it is a direct factor. The resultant effects of habitual use of this drug are fairly uniform, so that one may offer general statements, rather than take space for citing cases.[1]

Morphine is taken for its quieting effect, which is very different from the stimulation of alcohol or cocaine. I think it may be fairly said that the two main classes of users of morphine are neuropathic individuals of good mental endowment, who sometimes regulate so well the use of the drug that they can go many years without a vast amount of bad effect ensuing, and secondly, prostitutes and social failures who desire to deaden their sensibilities and appreciations of distressing circumstances. It is not always an easy matter to be sure that any individual in question is an habitué of morphine, even by medical examination, when the drug is being taken. Signs of physical distress show themselves, for the most part, only upon withdrawal of the drug. Occasionally before then indications of the effect of morphine may be discerned, but by no means in every case.

The contentions concerning the legal questions of sanity and responsibility of the alcoholic apply also to the habitual user of morphine. Morphinists, without question, are to be regarded as affected mentally by the drug. That the aberrational tendencies are not shown on all occasions, is no argument against the fact, any more than is the usual appearance of a normal mental state in the paranoiac. How much leeway for aberration or

---

[1] The best available literature on the connection between criminality and morphinism is in the treatise on drug addictions by Crothers (**260**), and his special article (**261**) on "Criminality and Morphinism."

irresponsibility is going to be allowed to the drug user under
the law which bases retribution upon " responsibility " is, as we
said of alcoholics, a matter to be established by general theory
or social policy.

There are certain typical psychic conditions and peculiarities
recognized as caused by morphine. In summary, we cannot
do better than enumerate these mental states: Prolonged use
of morphine causes (1) a distinct loss of energy. (2) This, as
observed in the psychical sphere, appears as a lowering of the
powers of attention, self-control and volition. The weakness
of the latter frequently is severe enough to be called paralysis
of the will. (3) Deterioration of moral judgments and general
character. (4) Tendency to morbid impulses of mind and body.
(5) Mental vagaries bordering on delusions. (6) Occasional hallucinatory and delusional states. (7) Rarely, well-defined psychoses.

So far as criminality is concerned, morphine may be effective
in several ways. Often there is development of the unexpected
in the individual. A woman of good reputation is found out to
be a thief; a previously honest man becomes a swindler. In one
case we knew a woman morphinist with quite sufficient income,
who trained her adopted daughter to be an expert shoplifter.
In general there is a growing laxity of character; the person
becomes less industrious and less particular in the general habits
of life, and in moral standards, perhaps occasionally showing
abnormally erotic symptoms. The evolution of unfortunate
traits may take years; if the morphinist is of strong will they
may not be shown at all.

Sometimes the beginning of the downfall is in some stress
which is made easier by drug indulgence. A typical situation involving a very grave social offense I had reason to know well. A
foreign-trained veterinary surgeon, who failed to succeed in this
country, became a morphinist. This man, after a period of meeting his misfortunes by morphine, gradually induced his wife and
then successively his three oldest children all to become addicted
to the drug. The descent of this family from self-respect, normal
earning capacity, and general decency of living, to poverty and
degradation was the most characteristic exhibition of the effect
of the drug that one could witness. The moral deterioration of
this intelligent father who involved his family in an unconquer-
able habit, was on par with the lowered powers of self-control

which led to gradual carelessness about the cleanliness of hypodermic needles, so that multiple abscesses developed over all their arms and legs.

Criminalism is developed only as the morbid mental conditions become more intense, or when the supply of the drug is not obtainable. Economic stress plays its part here. Petty thieving offers the best chance of obtaining a new supply, so is the most frequent delinquent result of morphine habituation. Perhaps, however, we should class the main delinquency as the lying, which is so notoriously characteristic of morphinists. The tendency to lying can well be understood in the light of the psychical deterioration we have mentioned above. It may go hand-in-hand with the development of vagaries, and include even self-accusations. The " dope-fiend self-accuser " is well known to experienced police officials.

§ 199. Cocaine.

Cocaine stimulates mentally and physically. The cocaine user who appears in court after taking his stint of the drug frequently passes muster as having unusually good mental ability. Cocaine increases the " nerve," renders the user more apt at repartee, and if he is not mentally weakened by its chronic use, or is not too much under the influence of it, his talkativeness hardly partakes of incoherency. When the cocainist is sentenced, and seen perhaps at a House of Correction after some days of deprivation, the underlying mental state of weakness and aberration is clearly perceived. The drug induces unwonted boldness on the part of weak individuals, and it is the sense of exaltation and exhilaration which makes it eagerly sought for by inferior types.

A case which we have given in short elsewhere, Case 29, was reported to us as being certainly that of a cocainist. This was a boy of distinctly inferior type, coming from a notoriously bad environment, who had cocaine in his possession. He was an excessive thief and vagrant, associating with the lowest companions. He glibly gave an account of the most miserable forms of life in the underworld. Already at 15 he had had two venereal diseases. Offered a helping hand by a manly police officer, he was so weak willed that he could not lift himself out of the mire, although he steadily maintained that he wished to do better.

His word was absolutely unreliable. In court this boy took on the toughest attitudes, and volubly insisted that he was being persecuted by the police. He had been already 4 times in the adult courts through always giving his wrong age, and, although small in size, had twice served terms in adult houses of correction.

Chiefly notable about him was his poor physical condition, his lack of will power, his excessive lying, and his attitude of boldness.

It is well recognized that some criminals, and rarely others, take this drug to give them physical steadiness and temporarily heighten their mental capacity. Occasionally a criminal will become so far influenced by it that he loses all foresight and self-control, and is ready to shoot to kill upon the slightest provocation. If we saw the case cited above a few years later we should probably find him a most dangerous fellow, carrying weapons, and willing to do anything desperate.

Many authors have noted the volubility of chronic cocainists, and many accounts are given of their literary proclivities.[1] Indeed some writers have deliberately used it to increase their fluency. The trouble with the acquired verbal ability is that it readily passes over into prolixity and incoherency; this characteristic is frequently noted in works which treat of the subject.

The cocainist's tendency to prevarication is excessive. So, too, is his general moral degradation. Nothing demonstrates the latter any more clearly than the readiness with which users of this drug unlawfully sell it to others, dragging them down too, in order to obtain funds for their own supply.

§ 200. Tea and Coffee.

It might be a difficult matter to show how even the most excessive use of tea and coffee could cause criminalism in an adult, but the relationship of anti-social tendencies in a child to the overuse of these stimulants is quite clear. They cause an amount of excitation and unsteadiness of the nervous system, and a general restlessness which makes the individual unable to comfortably maintain school life. Truancy is the natural reaction, and from this arises the usual range of temptations and undesir-

---

[1] In the work on drugs by Crothers (260) there is a good chapter on cocainism, and the same author has also published a separate article (262) on the subject, both of which treat somewhat of criminalistics.

able tendencies. The same is true of life in the home. With an excessive use of stimulants there is very apt to be irritability, disobedience, and family friction. These in turn may induce anti-social reactions. In a considerable number of cases we have noted this. For instance, in the following:

Case 35. — Boy, 10 years, 9 months. Weight 55 lbs., height 4 ft. 2 in. General and neurologic examination negative, except that right pupil is twice as large as left. Two years ago he fell from a second story, striking the back of his head, and rendering him unconscious. Bled from ears and nose. Eyes said to have crossed at that time. Was in the hospital for 3 weeks. Nowadays complains of many headaches, mostly on one side. Is a weak and irritable type.

Mentally we find him to be about fair in native ability. He is only in second grade, but has been out of school much. We regard him as perhaps being somewhat dull from physical causes. He gets into much trouble in the school-room on account of recalcitrancy.

This boy comes from a family which shows many peculiarities. The father was a hard drinker, once sentenced for disorderly conduct, later committed suicide. An older brother was earlier a delinquent, but later made good. One sister attempted suicide.

This boy has been found very difficult to handle through his stubbornness. There has been lack of home control on account of the mother being away working. He has been accustomed to get up early in the morning for his coffee, go back to bed, and get up later to make more coffee when his mother had gone away. He began it very early. She states that they could not afford to have meat, and so they had to have coffee. He has been accustomed to drinking about 7 cups of coffee and 2 of tea in a day.

Seen 4 years later, we still note his poor development. Now at almost 15 years he weighs only 53 lbs., height 4 ft. 7 1-4 in. He is a restless, repressed type, with overuse of the facial muscles. The pupils are still unequal. Vision slightly defective in one eye. Other examination negative, except that we note his club-shaped finger tips. He speaks in staccato voice, is nervous and furtive. His people at home say he is not right mentally and that they can do nothing with him. As a matter of fact they abuse him. Home conditions bad in many ways. A man in the same house has recently committed suicide.

The boy has been stealing and in a burglary. He has only reached 3d grade. In spite of his terrifically poor school record we find him to have good ability in many ways. He does a number of our difficult tests very well indeed, showing good powers of reasoning and mental representation. Evidently he has paid very little attention to reading for he does about 2d grade work in it. Is known in his neighborhood to have a good deal of mechanical ability. Has made a machine-like contrivance. This boy still uses tea and coffee at the rate of about 6 cups a day, and our impression is that much of his trouble still arises from that cause. A good proof was that when placed out in the country and deprived of these stimulants he began to improve immediately on the physical side.

The standard rule in pharmacy is that the effect of a drug is proportionate to the weight of the individual. If this is true for tea and coffee, as it probably is, one can best think of the result upon this small boy in terms of what a proportionate amount would do to an adult.

It is unnecessary to give other examples, because all cases of this kind read alike. It is perfectly clear that the unsettling of the nervous system which occurs in young people by the excessive use of these stimulants is a direct factor making in many environments for delinquency.

§ 201. Tobacco.

Much that we have said about the use of tea and coffee would apply to tobacco. Almost the only way in which tobacco makes for delinquent tendencies is by causing an unstable nervous system, and this it certainly does when indulged in excessively by young people. There have been many exaggerations of the bad effects of smoking. Only in occasional cases where tobacco was begun very early have we found the individual directly led through the use of it into anti-social behavior. An example is the following.

Case 36. — Boy of 13 years. Weight 89 lbs., height 4 ft. 10 in. Entire physical examination negative except for a very irregular pulse and a systolic heart murmur. The boy gets out of breath easily. Mentally we found him to be distinctly bright. He comes of a family where the mother works out, the father having deserted years ago. He does pretty much as he pleases.

His delinquencies consist in stealing and truancy. He is an excessive smoker, which perhaps accounts for his heart irregularity. He smokes a pipe and some cigarettes every day. This boy made so much improvement in the institution to which he was sent that he got into no further trouble.

Under the head of mental dullness from physical causes (§ 285), we have given the case of a girl in which smoking seemed to have direct effect upon her mental conditions. We have also cited (§ 328) a remarkable case of psychosis apparently induced by tobacco in the form of snuff. The typical signs of overuse of tobacco are nervousness and tremor, while mentally the individual shows inability to concentrate attention, or to engage in any prolonged task. A feeling of restlessness goes with the objective nervous symptoms. The treatment of this condition, the same as of the overuse of tea and coffee, consists in building up the individual physically, and entirely or partially stopping the habit. There can be no denying that very many individuals after having been overusers of such stimulants have been able to stop or modify their use so that there has been no permanent deleterious effect. In this there is a great difference from the effect of alcohol or of the habit-forming drugs.

The following is a point that must never be forgotten, a point that is important for treatment as well as for diagnosis of delinquents. The overuse of tobacco and of tea and coffee most frequently signifies a defective underlying condition which is the fundamental cause of their several unfortunate tendencies. To pick out tobacco as the cause of a person's moral or social inefficiency, simply because it is the most visible fault or weakness, bespeaks a very shallow method of approach to the subject. If one digs deeper one finds out why these things are craved, and that there is some feature of the background which has a stronger connection with delinquency than the more easily observed fact.

CHAPTER VI

ENVIRONMENTAL FACTORS

§ 202. **General Statement.** — Generalization about environmental factors as causes of delinquency is not our immediate business. We are students of the individual, and evaluators of causal factors in the specific case. That this does not imply neglect of the environment as a cause may be witnessed by our general statistics, § 93, where defective home conditions alone are numerically a close second to the mental conditions responsible for delinquency among our repeated offenders. In this matter, once more, we strongly counsel against reckoning up the total dynamic value of any cause apparently making for delinquency by regarding it as an isolated fact.

If we desired to pick out one topic we might go much farther in our consideration of home environment, for instance, as a causative factor of delinquency. It would be easy enough to credit the home which the delinquent comes from with being the main cause. Since he lives there of course his troubles mainly originate there. If all offenders came from institutions then we could just as well blame the institutions as we may now blame the homes. We show clearly, and others have shown, that in the majority of cases offenders are bred under bad home conditions. But it is pertinent for the scientific observer to ask what makes the homes defective. It is altogether possible that some anterior cause is directly responsible both for the poor home and the moral failure of the offspring. Such causes would be alcoholism, feeblemindedness, epilepsy, and so on. We recognize a common factor back of both defects in many of our cases.

282

We see altogether many reasons for not throwing entirely un-qualified stress upon environment, either in most individual cases, or as a general cause. The make-up of the personality is the larg-est part of the story. Many of the families in which there is a delinquent are doing as much for their children as other families of the same grade of intelligence or economic capacity, whose children are turning out well. Indeed, as may be shown by our interesting family tables, § 108, very often other individuals in the same family, and under the same environment, are doing quite well morally. Without drawing on the many concrete illus-trations which could be given, bearing positively as well as nega-tively on this point, it may at once be clearly appreciated that delinquency is the product of a personal reaction to a given envi-ronment. And the reactions of differently constituted persons to the same environment vary immensely.

It is not always easy to keep a clear-minded balance between opposing arguments on causation, for instance, those of the heredity specialists versus the environmental enthusiasts. We have attempted everywhere to be open to both sides, even in trying to show that the feebleminded individual, who may other-wise pose as a " born criminal," (vide § 371), is almost free from delinquent behavior in the right kind of an institution. Which, in his case, is to be regarded as the main cause of delinquency, as well as in many others, might be very difficult to answer if it were not for the fact, which we must always remember, that conduct is the direct outcome of mental life. Any defect or peculiarity of the latter is thus to be regarded as much more immediate in the causation of behavior than any other condition of life.

No contention on opposing points is necessary or desirable. In many cases it is the environment that can be more easily altered than anything in the individual's personality. In a fewer number of cases the opposite is possible, and an individual can learn to conform without change of surroundings. Which modification is best to aim at can only be answered by the careful survey of the facts we have everywhere urged. Among repeated offenders we have in some cases found, apparently, that environment was solely to blame. But in illustration of the complications which there are in the solution of the problem, even when environment is to be regarded as the main factor, we offer throughout this chapter various cards of causal factors. I have little doubt that offenders who do not become repeaters much more frequently have environmental conditions alone at the root of their breach of conduct.

The story of the effect of bad environment in producing delinquency is only to be told by giving an account of the psychical effects of the unfortunate conditions. Poverty, and crowded housing, and so on, by themselves alone are not productive of criminalism. It is only when these conditions in turn produce suggestions, and bad habits of mind, and mental imagery of low order, that the trouble in conduct ensues. The construction of environmental measures calculated to prevent delinquency must be looked at in the same light. A public playground is no incentive towards good conduct unless better mental activities and better mental content are fostered there. In illustration we might tell of conditions which have arisen where such a meeting place has been afforded boys and girls, which otherwise they would not readily have had, and where many ideas of delinquency were concocted and spread. All problems connected with bad environmental conditions should be carefully viewed in the light of the mental life.

We have felt so strongly that the effect of a bad environment was only to be measured in terms of possible harm done to the mental content that we have repeatedly ventured prognoses on this basis. We have said, for instance, that a girl who may have been through the depths of immorality can yet rise above all, if there has not been mental contamination. We are convinced that physical experiences do not necessarily mean permanent mental degradation. Cases well studied and evaluated by their mental aspects (*vide* Case 23), and watched over a number of years prove this point. We would sharply contrast the prognosis in an individual whose delinquencies have been merely the result of environmental conditions, and those who may not have been offenders to anything like the same extent, and yet whose mental attitude and mental content are indicative of a deeper-set tendency.

Parenthetically, by way of giving another illustration on this point of the psychical aspects of environment, we may mention the fact that a prolific source of delinquency arising from home conditions is the use of bad language on the part of parents. Many times, both from boys and girls, and particularly from children of rather finer fibre, we have heard the ingenuous statement that the main source of their delinquent tendency has been vile language heard at home.

We should always like logically to separate physical from psychical environment. Occasionally this can be successfully done, but frequently the two conditions thoroughly overlap. As we look over a long list of environmental conditions which we have found as causes, it stands out clearly that most of the defects can be classified properly only under the head of conditions which have directly had mental influence on the offender.

§ 203. **Treatment of Environmental Factors.** — The definite, highly important, struggle against environmental conditions for the prevention of further delinquency, should be based only on a knowledge of how they have affected the delinquent. Some circumstance in the environment, perhaps generally exploited as cause of delinquency, may be directly assailed when it was not in the least a factor. Much expense in time and labor can thus be wasted. The well-directed procedure first establishes the relation between cause and effect; it does not proceed from a possible cause to a perceptible fact, which may really be due to another cause. The knowledge that 60 per cent. of all repeaters come from bad homes does not prove that any particular repeater comes from a bad home, nor does it prove that the bad home in any given case produced the delinquency. There should be evaluation of the personal traits of a bad young man from a bad home, as well as a bad young man from a good home, if effective reconstructive measures are to be undertaken. Treatment of environment, as many a wise probation officer clearly perceives, turns out to be another highly individualized problem.[1]

There is not the slightest doubt in my mind that effective preventive treatment of delinquency under the law will never be carried out until there is completely adequate power over the *environmental contributors* to delinquency. A prime necessity, in

---

[1] The best philosophic conception of crime from the environmental standpoint is undoubtedly that given us in such good literary form by Tarde (**122**). Naturally, many writers on criminalistic subjects have dealt with social causes, but there have been few attempts at extensive survey of American conditions. Various corners of the field have been looked over by different students. Some larger areas have been surveyed, notably by the Vice Commission of Chicago (**243**), by Kneeland (**324**), in his study of vice conditions in New York, by Hayford (**325**) in the Immigration Commission report on immigration and crime. The study by Breckenbridge and Abbott (**318**) is the best presentation that has been offered of the problem of home conditions which surround juvenile offenders. Mary Conyngton's report on the Relation between Occupation and Criminality of Women (**370**) is a recent contribution.

turn, for carrying this out is that the same court which comes to understand and adjudicate the affairs of the offender shall have authority to remedy as much as possible the external source of the trouble. Without this the procedure, even in juvenile courts, frequently becomes nothing more than a farce.

The environmental circumstances of *released prisoners* is a topic that requires the greatest consideration, regarded merely as a causative factor of delinquency. Treatment of these conditions is as yet a very slightly appreciated need. Comparable is the new social service work done in connection with hospitals — the principle being that if the hospital has given its services as far as the convalescent stage, it is a matter of the greatest economy to carry them still further, and see that the patient is restored to social efficiency. Now the hospital patient's inefficiency is mostly a negative quantity. The ex-prisoner's failure is a positive menace. Society has undertaken to treat him for his misconduct; it desires his moral well-being and general welfare. The penal failure, which is everywhere witnessed to by recidivism, can best be prevented by after-care methods that are based on full appreciation of the offender's needs and possibilities. Perfunctory parole work is to be regarded as a weak effort. The same is true of aid to discharged prisoners by whatever agency — successful relief must be based on understanding of the individual and his relation to his environment.

§ 204. **Method of Presentation of Data.** — In presenting the main points of defective environmental conditions, case histories are unnecessary, and many details, while important, are so obvious that they hardly need mention. The use of our causative factor cards will bring most of the concrete issues to light. As we said before, since practically all offenders live with a family, in some sort of a home, very many environmental factors, whatever they may in turn be caused by, center about the home. We focus on home conditions first in our discussion.

§ 205. **Parent Alcoholic.** — The influence of an alcoholic parent on home conditions that produce delinquency is one of the plainest facts observed in the study of criminalistics. It should be necessary but to enumerate the physical and the psychical environment which emanates from alcoholism of the parent to show the relationship. Alcoholism of the mother is undoubtedly worse than that of the father in this matter. A child of an alcoholic parent is prone to be confronted in the home by any of the following: — poverty; lack of parental control; cruelty; immodesty and obscenity; sex immorality, amounting sometimes to rape and incest; familiarity with social disorder and crime. From what might be thought to be minor conditions resulting from alcoholism, such as quarreling and home irritation, and the use of such language as many a drinking man indulges in, we have seen delinquent careers straightway arise. From our scores of cases the following cards illustrate a few of the conditions.

Home conditions: Mother alcoholic.   Case 37.
    Early puberty.   Girl, 16 yrs.

        Physical conditions — over-development +
                                   extremely defective vision.
            Heredity: Mother very weak willed.

                                                    Mental:
Runaway.   (Unsuccessful under probation   Ordinary in
Sex.   and sent to institution.)   ability; B.

Home conditions: Much poverty, irritation.   Case 38.
                     One brother epileptic.   Boy, 17 yrs.
                     One brother thief.
                     Father as below.
    Heredity: Father alcoholic, wife beater,
                  deserter and epileptic.

                                                    Mental:
Forging.   (Much help on probation,   Fair ability, poor
Stealing.   but never successful.)   advantages.

Home conditions: Mother dead.   Case 39.
                     Father alcoholic + +.   Boy, 15 yrs.
                     Step-mother shiftless.
    Bad companions with street life.

Early truancy.
Stealing.   Mental:
Later, burglary.   Ordinary in ability, B.

287

§ 206. **Immoral Home Environment.** — Whether or not the parents show active criminalism or immorality, the moral conditions surrounding the home may naturally be a vital point in the production of delinquency. Thus a home in association with a saloon, or in contiguity to a vice district is likely to develop delinquents. Women who support themselves keep rooming or boarding houses sometimes where rather questionable people congregate; it may be difficult to avoid secretly bad characters. We have known such homes to be absolutely disastrous to a young man or woman.

§ 207. **Irritation at Home.** — One hears extensively of the effect of quarreling and nagging and teasing as causes of delinquency, both from offenders and their relatives. A young man's reaction to a father's quarrelsomeness, which perhaps the mother endures, may be delinquency. Sometimes there is a mental conflict set up from this cause, as when a child suppresses the tendency to direct reaction. The irritation may come from home quarreling with others than parents. A very frequent irritation is the abnormal social reaction which obtains between a stepparent and child. It is a matter of interest to know that sometimes an insane person being kept at home proves irritative enough to create a tendency towards delinquency.

Home conditions: Father earlier alcoholic and deserter.   Case 40.
Boy, 15 yrs.
Now very abusive.
Another boy ran away on account of the father.
Mother works out. (Another brother under sentence.)

  Heredity: Father as above.

Truancy.
Stealing.
Runaway.   (Several times in   Mental:
Burglary.   institutions.)   Ordinary in ability; B.

---

§ 208. **Members of Family Immoral or Criminalistic.** — The only way in which it is necessary to illustrate this point is in showing the relationship there may be between criminalistic home conditions and mental abnormality.

Home conditions: Father and mother fla-   Case 41.
             grantly immoral.   Girl, 14 yrs.
             Lack of parental control.

  Heredity: Mother epileptic, probably insane.
             Maternal grandfather mentally peculiar.
             Father immoral, mean and vicious.

    Bad companions.

            (Unsuccessful on probation   Mental:
Sex + +.   and sent to institution.)   Fair in ability.

Home conditions: Father saloon keeper and   Case 42.
             alcoholic.   Boy, 17 yrs.
             Three brothers criminalistic.

  Heredity: Much mental dullness among children of
             3 sisters, ten delinquents among them.
             One brother of this boy epileptic, one con-
             genitally blind and one a dwarf.

    Bad companions — at home and elsewhere.

Stealing +.   Mental:
Away nights.   (Often under arrest.)   Fair ability.

---

§ 209. **Severity and Harshness of Parent.** — The effect of severity on the part of a parent may have a direct reaction in delinquency. As we have had to reckon with such behavior, it runs all the way from mere repression to putting the child out of doors, or actual fighting. The immediate reaction of one boy to a father who kicked him was a stabbing affray. Excessive strictness on the part of a parent when no normal outlets are provided for the boy's or girl's activity may, of course, directly lead to misconduct.

§ 210. **Incompetent Parental Control.** — Poor parental control arises from weak will on the part of parents, or through their actual irresponsibility or semi-responsibility, or through their having some sensory defect, even such as deafness, or on account of family illness. Then, too, it frequently occurs as the result of there being many children in the family. Both ignorance and poverty may cause lack of proper control. The number of cases in our series in which the mother was working out may be seen by reference to analysis of home conditions (§ 93).

The children who are obliged to shift for themselves because the mother is out working during the day, or who live in a boarding house with a father who works all day are apt to be living under very dangerous conditions.

§ 211. **Home Uncongeniality.** — One of the most peculiar phases of family life that has come to our notice as a cause of delinquency is the uncongeniality that arises through a young individual desiring to better himself. This ought not to lead to delinquency, but sometimes the irritation caused by the thwarted desire creates such reactive tendencies that the ambitious one gets into court. We have seen now several such instances. The elders in a family are perhaps of a peasant type, immigrants without education, not caring for social advancement. A son, or even a daughter, becoming in this country educated and ambitious, finds old country customs and ignorance irritable to the highest degree. Family quarrels, even violence may ensue.

This factor of irritation because of ambition rarely appears alone, nearly always it is in connection with the hypersusceptibility and instability of adolescence. We have known well-endowed boys to show the irrational reaction of becoming violent and otherwise intolerant in their own homes from very slight uncongeniality. There may be repeated attacks of temper which finally lead to arrest. Such a case is not to be readily understood by mere court-room procedure. Wise probation officers have over and again, however, been able to size up the situation and help towards readjustment. Mere punishment without appreciation in the case of such sensitive adolescents is likely to prove disastrous for them and, of course, is in turn inimical to society at large.

§ 212. **Parents Separated.** — A very fruitful source of delinquency is found in the separation of parents, either with or without divorce. One cannot deny that in some cases the character of one parent is such that the child would better not be with that one. And then one would not argue from our large findings, § 93, on families of offenders being broken up from cause other than death, that it was the mere breaking up which created the delinquent tendency. Equally back of both delinquency of the child and the separation of the parents there may have been an anterior factor, such as alcoholism or immorality. The fact stands out very clearly, however, that the child who is not controlled under the united efforts of both father and mother is at great disadvantage, and readily acquires anti-social tendencies. The breaking up of a family is in itself an act of anti-social portent, and seems the blackest from the standpoint of the child's moral welfare. Where a child goes from one parent to another, and thus feels in an entirely different social situation from that of children in happier families, the reaction is very likely to be dangerous to society. So not only in their personal habits, but also in their attitude towards the marriage relation, parents influence their offsprings' behavior.

It is altogether insufficiently comprehended that children are immensely susceptible to the influence of the conduct of their parents. It is not that they often copy the type of action of the elders, but there may be sorenesses of spirit and hidden mental conflicts about parents' misconduct which unconsciously seek relief in other kinds of misbehavior.

§ 213. **Crowded Housing Conditions.** — The material foundations of social life deeply influence morality. In the matter of the many decencies that depend upon housing conditions this stands out very clearly. A considerable cause of sexual vice is to be found in the spacial circumstances of home life. The mere huddling of people together would do little harm if it were not for the mental results of such conditions. I mean by this that it is asking too much to expect people who are brought up under conditions which necessitate bodily exposure and premature acquaintance with sex affairs to respect related types of conduct which make for the welfare of society. Again, in this matter, we speak from experience. We find that children who have seen cohabitation between parents, for instance, are deeply influenced by it, and that exposure of the body under our modern civilized conditions, where such exposure is not common, creates mental imagery that may be all against sex morality. We say nothing of the actual sex practices which unfortunately tend to occur between members of the same family under crowded conditions, these are obviously and hideously bad; there are other more subtle features to consider.

After all, respect for parents, and for the integrity of family relationships, and for the human body itself, is largely the basis of the morality of our civilization, and nothing so easily militates against this respect as crowded living conditions. It is hardly necessary to enlarge upon this, hardly necessary to show the relationship of tenement house life, and of crowded shanties, and of irresponsible boarders in the home, to the development of perverted sex instincts among children. This is another subject we cannot take space to do justice to, but we may be allowed to say that until communities realize the dangers from crowded housing there is simply bound to be a considerable quota of prostitutes and other loose-living people emerge from these conditions.

§ 214. **Poverty.** — The general relation of poverty to criminalism it is not necessary to expatiate on. We have endeavored in different places to point out the particulars. There can be no doubt in the mind of anyone who has compared by observation conditions of European cities with ours that poverty here is vastly less a factor in delinquency. Frequently we have had to call attention in a given case to the fact that one could throw the blame on family ignorance, fully as much or more than on the family poverty which was present. But perhaps a counter argument might be made that against the existence of ignorance itself there are no active influences possible under the conditions of poverty. However that may be, the fact is that frequently conditions of poverty must be alleviated in order that delinquent tendencies may be checked. This is seen and amelioration, if very partially, accomplished through the modern socialization of courts, those which have operating in connection with them various helping agencies.

§ 215. **No Home.** — An adolescent without a home is under the most favorable circumstances for the establishment of criminalistic behavior. Studies we have made of youthful itinerancy when the wandering has been even in company with one parent, have led us to see that there is very little hope for the development of moral life under such conditions. The homeless child that for any reason is changed about from place to place, or from institution to institution, gets in much the same unsettled mental state as the wanderer and gains the same feeling of the instability of his social milieu, which is not comportable with the establishment of good conduct.

§ 216. **Parental Neglect.** — The subject of the effect of parental neglect as productive of delinquency is altogether too trite to be dwelled on in detail. The one point in this subject to which we would draw intimate attention is the factor of non-understanding as a feature of parental neglect. So very frequently have we become acquainted with cases in which the source of delinquency was not in the least comprehended by parents, that we feel strongly on this point. Even when parents have attempted discipline and have warned, there may not have been the least understanding which was necessary for the application of adequate therapy. In fact, very frequently there does not seem to be the glimmer of appreciation that any understanding was necessary. The adults, forgetting their own formative period, have projected their adult point of view absolutely. The unfortunate feature here is that very frequently the situation in this respect is irrevocable. The parents *will* not understand. Their usual response is that they have put up with the situation as long as they can, and have become so provoked, or so nervous about it that they can do nothing more. If the environment in this way is unalterable, then there is nothing further to do about it except to attempt to get the delinquent to take himself in hand with understanding of the causes of his own trouble, or to obtain for him better understanding in another environment. The better understanding is quite possibly gained for him in good institutional life, as we have had reason to know. The above feature of parental neglect is beyond the power of any court proceeding to alter.

§ 217. **Bad Companions.** — As observed in any phase of court life, bad companions play an immense part in the production of criminalism. To be sure there are quite solitary individuals who have developed an anti-social grudge, or who have deliberately entered upon a professional criminalistic career, but the majority work up their impulses gregariously. Bad companions may be considered as part of the psychical environment, and may exert influence under many varying conditions. We have as a matter of interest enumerated the following types of bad companions: (*a*) As found in the home. This may be either the father or mother, but far more often is either brother or sister. All sorts of criminalistic and vicious behavior may thus receive its first incentive in what should be the most protected environment; (*b*) School companions; (*c*) Street companions. There are various types of these — loafers, occasional thieves, gangs of thieves, and gangs in general; (*d*) Companions found in institutions, where some of the worst of moral contagion takes place. We have spoken of this elsewhere; (*e*) Influence of one criminalistic companion, particularly an older person; (*f*) Influence of a person of the opposite sex. There are all sorts of possible variations here on the sex impulse; (*g*) Influence of stage people; (*h*) Influence of a feebleminded companion. This is rather striking because the influence is usually supposed to be the other way, but, as a matter of fact, a feebleminded individual who has learned vicious ways, may be a tremendous teacher of bad conduct.

We have shown in our statistical summary, § 96, the part which we found bad companions actually play as a causative factor. Neither there nor here does the subject seem to call for further analysis or case studies. The effect of a bad companion is altogether too clear to need illustration, but we should state that almost never have we found the effect of bad companions to stand alone. Weakness in the situation has appeared elsewhere, either in the individual's own personality or in some neglect which centers about home life. Any overwhelming influence of a bad companion, as a peculiar phenomenon, itself needs explanation. The following cards give some inkling of adventitious facts.

Bad companions. Influence of one young thief.	Case 43. Boy, age 14 yrs.
Poor parental control. Large family. Poverty.	
Delinquencies: Stealing. Sneak thief.	Mentality: Fair ability.

Bad companions.	Case 44. Boy, age 13 yrs.
Defective vision. Headaches.	
Delinquencies: Stealing. Gambling.	Mentality: Good ability.

§ 218. **Theatres.** — Possible effects of theatrical presentations in producing criminalism is obvious when it occurs at all. High-priced plays are as a rule not seen by adolescents, and it is doubtful if theatres ever influence towards criminalistic conduct except at this impressionable age. Melodramas urge to action much as moving pictures do. We were interested at one time to know that the most popular play ever seen by a series of

young offenders was one that had to do with convict life, but
there was never any evidence that the play had induced bad
conduct. There cannot be the slightest doubt that the stimulation of certain shows is towards misconduct in sex affairs; the
influence is direct.

The main point of contact between theatres and delinquency
is in connection with the life of the stage itself. The attraction
which it has for immature young women and young men, and
the freedom of intercourse which it brings about, and the perverted notions of sex morality which center about this life are
frequently disastrous. But except in the case of young men who
steal or young women who run away in order to enjoy some
phases of this exciting life, the delinquencies are nearly all confined to sex affairs.

§ 219. **Social Allurements.** — The various allurements of
social life which stand out in the causation of delinquency form
a great variety which are too long to recount. We find, for instance, a defective boy who is a great runaway always going to
the *shops* down town. We note a strong young man, who is
turning alcoholic, finding the *social life of the saloon* his chief
source of downfall. *Dance halls* nowadays are notoriously great
factors in breaking down morality. In the study of the individual each of these must be estimated for just what it is worth.

The allurements of *fine clothes* as worn by others or as seen in
shop windows is, to those who have a native desire for finery,
an undoubted temptation which may result in some form of
dishonest acquirement.

§ 220. **School Irritation.** — As part of the psychical environment we must very properly reckon with this factor, although
in the study of the individual the prime cause would undoubtedly
be the personal peculiarity which leads to the irritation. We
find the specialized defective (§ 277 ff.), for instance, developing
anti-social tendencies because he was kept with small children,
although in many respects he had mental powers corresponding
to his age. Others on account of nervous trouble or physical
ailments, including uncorrected sensory defects, are irritated
by the confinement of the school-room. Conditions of hearing,
which are more difficult to correct than vision, may cause great
irritability and recalcitrancy. Then we might cite the case of
the boy who, as educationalists say, was not book-minded. His
traits required that he do things with his hands; his delinquency

was the result of impulsions which arose in this way. Attendance at a school where there was poor teaching and poor discipline, or where language was taught that was not the general language of the community — have all figured as causes.

§ 221. **Unsatisfactory Vocation.** — On some occasions we have found hypersensitive adolescents to whom the vocations they were following were highly irritative, and who showed delinquent tendencies as a result. In others there has been fancied possession of some special talent, with constant complaint, accompanied by recalcitrant behavior because they had no chance to use this special talent. In reckoning with adolescents, matters which in older years would be less productive of irritation, are properly taken into account. Adolescence is the age of hypersusceptibility as well as the age of high development of criminalistic tendencies. So the adult point of view in regard to affairs which later would not be irritative, is not a safe guide for the student of causations.

CHAPTER VII

ENVIRONMENTAL FACTORS — *Concluded*

§ 222. Lack of Healthy Mental Interests.   § 223. Influence of Newspapers.
  § 224. Influence of Pernicious Stories.   § 225. Influence of Pictures,
Especially Moving Pictures.   § 226. Experiences During Custody.

§ 222. Lack of Healthy Mental Interests.

We have been exceedingly impressed by what we have learned
concerning the paucity of mental interests of individuals who
start criminalistic careers. If we were believers in statistics, as
such, we could offer extensive findings on this point. In our
routine inquiry into not only actual activities of adolescent offenders, but even through evidences of their lack of knowledge
of what should be every young person's birthright in the way
of wholesome interests, we have found the most astonishing
deficiencies. These unfortunate individuals are generally unaccustomed to playing games that have interesting mental content, they rarely are found to read the type of books which lead
them into constructive activities. They have, almost universally, very slight knowledge of the modern scientific interests,
such as electricity, which fairly possess the minds of more fortunate young people. Such normal activities as that of collecting
objects of interest [1] are rarely met with.

Impressive though these findings have been, and though they
clearly bear in the individual case upon the production of anti-
social tendencies, yet one would be careful in drawing large
conclusions concerning the lack of these activities in offenders
as compared with what we might find in other members of the
same family or the same social group. It is true that in certain

[1] Norms for the collecting activity have been more or less gathered, but
not, of course, for the non-delinquent members of the same social groups that
our offenders come from. Stanley Hall (**320**), Earl Barnes (**321**), and Caroline
Burk (**322**) have all made studies on the collecting instinct in children. They
show that it is very common. Elizabeth Howe (**323**) also has an interesting
short paper in which she raises the practical question of the utilization of
this activity. We do not intend over-emphasis of "collecting"; we merely use
it by way of concrete illustration of the lack of healthy mental interests in
offenders' early lives.

instances we have known the offender's healthy young activities to have been suppressed beyond the normal of others in his sphere, but no general theories therefrom can be safely adduced. But certainly if one were to think of very many of these cases in terms of what could be done to prevent the growth of anti-social tendencies, the consideration of the development of healthy mental interests should be uppermost.

The emptiness of home life in the above matters is partly due to poverty, but undoubtedly ignorance, again, is more directly responsible. Many families who have no greater means look after the mental content and the general activities of their children with at least some conception of the fundamental principle that mental vacuity is pernicious. Then, too, we have on numerous occasions become acquainted with family life where the funds were ample and yet the young people's activities had never been developed along wholesome lines.

Even in this matter, where we feel convinced there is one of the greatest origins of delinquent tendencies, personality must once more be taken into account. What would offer sufficient satisfaction for one type of mind, might be quite inadequate to supply activities to another. The fact of this variability, as well as proof of our main theme by results obtained by treatment, lead us to offer some short sketches taken from among hundreds of cases which we could cite.

Case 45. — A boy of 15, of foreign parentage, small in stature, but otherwise normal physically, and of fair mentality, was out much on the streets with bad companions. He had repeatedly been stealing and was connected with several burglaries. He comes from a family of ten children. Father a laborer. At least two older brothers were delinquents. This boy had been mostly to a foreign-speaking school. He reads the sporting pages of the newspaper and some cheap novels, but nothing else. The only books at home were his school books. He played ordinary athletic games with the other boys. His knowledge of scientific items was practically *nil*. His parents were deceitful and untrustworthy, characteristics which this boy strongly resented. He begged for a chance to get away from the city, where, as he said, there was nothing for him to do but to get into trouble, and where all activities centered about the street life. Given a chance elsewhere, he took hold of his new interests with a vim, and as observed over a period of years has done absolutely well.

Home conditions. Parents severe, unsympathetic, and untruthful. Large family.	Case 45. Boy, 15 yrs.
Lack of healthy mental interests, either recreational or occupational.	
Bad companions.	
Stealing. Burglary.	Mental: Fair ability.

Case 46. — Another very different type of case was that of a very strong, well-developed boy, of more than ordinary ability, who was the only member of his family that had become delinquent. He was one of 9 children. The father and mother are thoroughly good people, but have had a hard struggle financially, and feel keenly their inability to give this boy what he really needs. The home life has satisfied the others, but not this lad who has always been very active in mind and body. When sent away to a model public institution on account of a minor delinquency, he was a great favorite and grasped greedily all the opportunities which were there afforded him. His intelligent mother was bitter on that point, for he came home more spoiled than ever. At 15 he was quick and bright and self-assertive, but not shrewd enough to keep out of mischief. At last he stole several hundred dollars, which he was about to use for the purposes of travel, when he was caught.

From this case we learned an important fact for the treatment of similar individuals. It appeared that a gentleman in business knew of this lad's home circumstances, and his ability, and had given him in an office a position which was created for the purpose. There was almost nothing to do all day. The boy stayed a couple of months resisting temptation before he finally succumbed.

A few words from his own story show the need for supplying such minds with activities. " I 'd like to be an electrician if I could. I don't care for office work. I 'd like to know about machines. When I was younger I used to go with a bunch of bad kids, but since I was out at that place I know enough to keep away from them. Mr. Y. did not have work for me. I was just sitting around there nearly all day. I would do about a half-hour's work all day. I got tired of reading the papers. I was thinking I would rather be working hard and doing more. I can't stand sitting around. I'd rather be blacksmithing or anything. I was just crazy enough to think I could get away with that money. I was thinking of going somewhere west of here, anywhere, and was buying those things ready to start."

Lack of sufficient mental interests at home,   Case 46.
and where employed.   Boy, 15 yrs.

Home conditions — large family and poverty.

Adolescent instability
Lack of foresight.

Truancy.   Mental:
Stealing.   Ability above ordinary.

Neglect of education may well be considered under the head of not providing an individual with sufficient mental interests. If, as a simple instance, the ability to read easily is not acquired there cannot be the opportunity there otherwise would be for the gaining of healthy ideas. To some extent the same is true of the gaining of dexterity in other activities. But it is not only in the matter of teaching the ability to handle mental tools, so to speak, that the schools can do good in this respect. It would be well if there were a more definite attempt to increase in early school life the acquirement of such mental interests as might save many from delinquency. This could include recreational as well as occupational interests.

If one were to go into a household where the children had sufficient in the way of interest to keep them healthily occupied, one might make a long list of very simple and inexpensive articles which serve the purpose. The question of getting the right things is more one of intelligence than of amount of money spent.

This question of supplying healthy mental interests has important bearings for those who are shut out in any way from normal participation in what is ordinarily offered by way of occupation or recreation. I am not sure but that a goodly share of the reason for the feebleminded falling into evil ways is because they in an ordinary environment are not afforded suitable mental interests. We have had the good fortune to witness some striking examples of the effect of suitable mental interests given to individuals who

had been largely deprived of them. One boy, who was notorious
for indulgence in vicious misdeeds, was found to have a harassing
ear trouble. This had largely precluded him from being interested in ordinary school life, or from enjoying other social advantages. Then it was discovered that he had a talent for drawing.
He was so thoroughly delighted with his new-found abilities and
with the opportunities given him, that, although he has not
been a startling success, he ceased to be a delinquent from the
very day of the discovery. The career of this young man, over
the years we have known him, is the sharpest possible contrast to
his previous life, as far as conduct is concerned. The main change
has been through finding for him an interest and outlet in self-
expression which was utterly denied before.

We can afford no further space for study of this subject because
its bearings and details should be clear enough to the student. We
are inclined to think that herein lies a most important consideration for the treatment of offenders in any situation, especially
if they are taken early. A deep psychological fact is involved
when we consider the possibility of introducing mental activities which may win the day against less desirable ones.   Difficult though this may be in handling offenders in a poor environment, as many probation officers know, yet the ideal is always
worth striving for. The good mental activity, if suitable to the
needs of the person, can frequently be calculated to drive out the
bad which is not, by comparison, always of commanding interest.
This should be a fruitful matter for consideration in all industrial
schools and other institutions. The best possible way to prevent
the growth of delinquent tendencies is to give the individual an
equipment of better interests which may command his thoughts.
The same principle works even in the treatment of defectives.
In the best institutions for these unfortunates it is most noticeable that the development of satisfactory interests for them so
commands their attention that they are not at all the criminalistic persons which they would be outside. The above few considerations do scant justice to this most important topic.

§ 223. Influence of Newspapers.

Consideration of the question of the influence of newspapers
in producing anti-social conduct has brought forth results surprising to ourselves. It would seem, *a priori*, that the great

amount of material which the newspapers publish relating to delinquency must certainly very definitely harm the readers. Fenton (295) in his highly interesting study of this matter proceeds from this standpoint. He shows that a very considerable proportion of the news space of the ordinary daily paper is taken up by accounts of criminalistic and other anti-social affairs. But when it comes to anything like the proof of this supposed effect in a given case it appears singularly hard to obtain. General impressions from many sources are readily forthcoming, but no satisfactory exact data, and yet, of course, this does not deny certain eminently bad influences which such literature may have.

From our own studies we get the following results. In no one single case can we in the least show that the reading of newspapers was a strong cause of criminality. We have inquired about mental influences in many hundreds of cases, and, while other factors stand out clearly as affecting mental processes, this one does not. Nor do our results contradict anything that other authors have actually been able to show. Hellwig (296) in his well-balanced consideration of the subject comes to just the same conclusion.[1]

Before passing on to a word about the bad influence newspapers can be shown to have, it may be worth while theorizing a little about why they do not appear as any great cause of criminalism. We know in the first place that most criminal careers are begun before there is extensive reading of the newspapers. Young offenders as a rule, we find, care for little but the comic portions. They are just as much interested in accidents as in criminalistic material, and only rarely have we met the slightest indication that a newspaper story of a criminal has developed hero worship.

We should be inclined to believe that there are good psychological reasons why newspapers do not have anything like the same bad effect as literature of the dime novel order, or as pernicious moving and other pictures. There is ordinarily no glamour whatever about the story of a criminal as told in the papers. He is nearly always a sufferer, being either hunted for or under duress. He is often shown with a haggard face, and his suffer-

---

[1] Fenton, despite liberal quotation of impressions, was unable to give a single carefully studied case where newspapers had been found to be the main source of a tendency towards a delinquent career. It seems strange that none of his correspondents was able to give satisfactory data. We are genuinely surprised at this as well as at the results of our own inquiry. The student will find in the thesis of Fenton (295) and in the article by Hellwig (296) the best sources of information, and many references to the other literature.

ings are recounted. This is altogether different from the history of a bandit as told in cheap novel form. Then the constant crowding of the newspapers with all sorts of ideas can but tend to militate against the influence of any single story. There is no chance for following up and living in a life story as there is in a novel, or in a story as told by moving pictures. We should also remember that many newspapers have the best sort of personal counsel in large type in the very same edition where the gruesome is carefully depicted. Perhaps these facts account for the unexpectedly slight proof of bad influence.

Now in regard to what bad influence newspaper presentation of pernicious subjects really does have we may consider the following. No one can possibly doubt the general lowering of good taste and, perhaps, of moral tone, that must come from daily education in the more notorious and less decent aspects of life. Beyond this we must look to specific cases for proof. Perhaps newspaper stories of expert criminal methods may be, as Fenton suggests, somewhat educative — but, of course, only to those with a predilection for criminality. And even here one must remember that through individual enterprise and the teaching of " schools of criminals " the development of methods is far greater than represented by the meagre details given in the newspapers. Information and news of all kinds peculiar to their pursuits spread among the denizens of the underworld in ways quite apart from newspaper activities.

The effect of suggestion may occasionally be seen, but we have never observed it except in unbalanced persons. An abnormal young man becomes a self-accuser as the result of reading about a robbery and murder. People on the verge of suicide may suddenly carry out the idea as the result of reading of the self-destruction of some one else. We have no doubt of this, although even here, we have had no proof of a single case. The suggestion has always come in our cases from other sources. We have several times known a newspaper account of a girl adventuress to cause unstable adolescent girls to seek like notoriety, but never was out-and-out criminalism induced. Weakminded people, in general, are very prone to accept suggestion. One source of suggestion inevitably must be the newspaper, but we are thoroughly convinced by our own inquiry on this point, as well as by the failure of others to definitely prove it, that, as compared with other possible sources of pernicious influence, the newspaper plays

303

a comparatively small part. If it were otherwise, the enormous amount of reading of newspapers that goes on would result in an obvious connection with the production of delinquency.

Of course we have frequently met with a show of personal pride in an offender at being written up in the newspaper. However, this was always after the deed and we have never actually known that the desire to be written up had anything to do with the production of an offense. "Getting into the newspapers" probably figures in sensational impulses to which many young people as well as some older ones are prone. We have never seen suggestion from newspaper reading so clearly manifested as in "black hand" schemes. But where these were imitatively attempted it is likely that the desire for the sensational "write-up" was the main motive. Of course, deep-laid plots of blackmail have their instigation in other things than newspaper suggestion.

§ 224. Influence of Pernicious Stories.

One of the most exploited causes nowadays of criminal behavior is the pernicious printed story. Quite in contradistinction to the supposed effect of newspapers, we can prove this fact by numerous cases. The subject is dealt with by us partly under the head of mental imagery (§ 233), and there, in its psychological aspects, it properly belongs. The influence of bad literature is established only through definite mental processes; specifically, by virtue of arousing certain imagery which spurs to action. The hold that such imagery has on the individual, following unfortunate acquaintance with harmful literature, may be most powerful and frequently recurrent. (We should at once state that some of the most striking cases of the unfortunate development of recurrent criminalistic mental pictures originated in viewing actual cuts or photographs in a text, and are properly to be considered partly under the head of the influence of pictures.) We have come to learn that the perusal of a connected story of an exploit, or a career, may strongly impress itself upon the mind — so strongly as to incite to like activities.

As in all cases where comparisons of influences can be made, we find that the greatest possible effect is *via* the several aspects of sex life. The elements of universality of experience, emotional context, and sensory stimulus account, of course, for this. Erotic stories read in youth are universally recognized as forming ineradicable mental content. All who have inquired widely have heard from men and women that they have always regretted reading or hearing such-and-such stories. There can be no doubt of the exciting influence of the erotic narrative and, indeed, this fact is widely made use of for a definite purpose. The relationship of such literature to the moral break-down of young men and women in sex affairs is so well recognized that it would be superfluous to offer cases. It is ground already covered by Havelock Ellis (186) and others.

The influence of blood-and-thunder literature is still another matter. It has been suggested that there is quite a proper use for such writings of the better sort in vicariously disposing of anti-social instincts for adventure. Very likely this is true, for who has not been pleasantly satisfied by the reading of " Treasure Island." The influence of particular criminalistic characters in fiction has been studied by Sighele (297), who is apparently able to prove that the depiction of these characters has, at least, had considerable influence upon the behavior of rather unbalanced individuals.

The type of influence, however, which is most prevalent in American life unquestionably arises from perusal of those cheap novels which deal with bandit and detective life. Judges in juvenile courts learn frequently of the effect of such reading upon even quite normal lads. Fenton (295), in his thesis on newspapers brings out the influence of cheap novels with considerable force. It is easy enough to learn from many young and old offenders that one of the chief formative influences of their careers was this reading matter. We can get at the facts in several ways. It is a very common occurrence in any place where adolescent offenders are searched to find these stories in their pockets, well thumbed over. The fires of the spirit of adventure are not only kindled, but are kept going by this fuel. A definite habit and craving for this type of reading is developed just as the individual develops a habit for alcoholic stimulants. The force of the effect can best be studied in our § 233 on mental imagery.

In our classification of causative factors it was nearly always found difficult to say whether the principal reason for the influence of such literature was not negative rather than positive — was not rather through the absence of opportunities for wholesome activity and adventure, than through the effect solely of this literature which came in to fill a vacuum. This was not always the case, but certainly it was true in the vast majority. However we have seen instances (Case 171) where an innately adventuresome spirit was fed by exciting literature and grew beyond any ordinary means of satisfaction.

In this matter, as in the question of any kind of influence or suggestion upon the individual, personal peculiarities form part of the reason for the effect. It is certainly true that a very small minority of all who have read blood-and-thunder stories have been moved to act in similar fashion. Then, too, such stories are not dynamic for adults. This literature stirs to action young individuals who have peculiar plasticity in a given direction. Affected, however, may be those of distinctly good mental parts.

Except in the instances where there is definite obsessional mental imagery involved, the reading of blood-and-thunder literature is rarely found to be the main factor. At least in all our cases there have been other negative and even other positive causal conditions implicated in the results. The following is an illustration:

Poor home control.	Mother works out.	Case 47.
	Father careless type.	Boy, 14 yrs.
	Lack of home discipline.	
	One brother delinquent.	
Lack of healthy mental interests,		
	except in reading.	
Pernicious literature.	Boy is a great reader, but	
	takes mostly to bandit	
	and detective stories.	
Picture shows, where boy sees same things.		
Poverty.		
Truancy.		
Stealing + +.		Mental:
Burglary.		Good ability.

This boy gradually became more stable after being sent to a corrective school a short time.

§ 225. Influence of Pictures, Especially Moving Pictures.

There is an entirely sufficient psychological reason why, of all forms of presentation, pictures should have the strongest influence. In nearly all people visual memory and visual imagery play the most dynamic part in mental life. It is the thing seen which is represented again in consciousness with the greatest force and with probably the greatest frequency. The strength of the powers of visualization is to be deeply reckoned with when considering the springs of criminality. When we inquire from the offender, young or old, concerning that portion of his mental content which seems to urge him on in his career, we always get more or less clearly framed, the answer that it is stimulation from a visual type of imagery. (We need not here go into a discussion of the more technical considerations about visual imagery being frequently mixed with motor imagery and so on.) It is the mental representation of some sort of pictures of himself or others in the criminal act that leads the delinquent onward in his path. The vacuities of prison life, as we have elsewhere insisted, § 127, § 226, leave room for entrance into the mind of just such pictures.

Some of the most graphic accounts of the influence of pictures have come from personal interviews with offenders, where in detail the vivid nature of the mental process is exposed. Nor do we have to turn to offenders merely to prove this point. Most of us have had like experiences. A prominent educator, a man of active mind and purity of thought, tells me that one of his main regrets is that he once saw a certain pornographic sketch. It was indelibly impressed. Offenders we find, *vide* § 233, have been sometimes fairly obsessed and impelled by the character of pictures seen. In this matter, too, the pervasion of the sex element makes the chance of future representation all the stronger on account of natural impulses in that direction. The combination of sex offenses with other criminality forms an unusually virulent admixture for later mental depiction.

When it comes to motion pictures we have added elements of force for the production of either good or bad. Not only a single event, but chapters from life histories are depicted. Not alone is one action or posture depicted, but there is added all of the motor phenomena active through a period of time. The act is not suggested; every detail of it is made clear. The breaking open of a safe, the holding up of a train, the effort at suicide are all presented in such fashion that it is bound to recur as a memory picture of detailed events, if there is any tendency or opportunity for its mental reproduction. Added force comes from the concrete issues which are represented.

We have had much evidence, sometimes in remarkable ways, that moving pictures may be stimulating to the sex instinct. We should expect pictures of love-making and similar scenes to have this effect on young adults or older adolescents, but we have very strikingly heard of it in children. The effect is not only felt at the moment, but also there is the establishment of memory pictures which come up at other quiet times, such as when the individual is in bed. We have found that bad sex habits sometimes center around these pictures. In some instances a very definite mental conflict ensues, with production of delinquency along other lines.

(No one considering the effect of moving pictures can neglect the possibilities for bad behavior which occur through the darkness of the hall in which the pictures are shown. Under cover of dimness evil communications readily pass and bad habits are taught. Moving picture theatres are favorite places for the teaching of homosexual practices.)

There can be no fair consideration of the whole subject of moving pictures unless we remember that, after all, the amount of delinquency produced by them corresponds but slightly to the immense number of pictures which are constantly shown. This partly tends to show the innocuousness of the greater number of these pictures, but it also brings us back to our old question of personal equation. Some individuals are susceptible to pictorial suggestions and others are not. However, there is no excuse for showing pictures which damage the morals of any one.

The main hope for the prevention of these undesirable effects will be found in rigorous censorship of perverting pictures, and in radical prosecution of those who produce and deal in obscene and other demoralizing pictorial representations. Never have we heard one word indicating that bad effects have arisen from representations that could in any way be interpreted as productions of art. The type of thing we mean is altogether unsavory, and obviously manufactured for its appeal to the passions, or to other unhealthy interests.

It seems unnecessary to add specific examples of the influence of pernicious pictures to those given under Criminalistic Mental Imagery, § 233. Scores of cases could be detailed in which the same type of causation is clearly apparent. It is not unimportant to note that we have heard much condemnation of pictures from offenders themselves who have been thus influenced.

The effect of moving pictures in starting criminalistic tendencies in children is almost always along such conspicuous lines that it is not necessary to cite cases. It is nearly always a boy who is affected, and the impulse started is an imitative one. He proceeds to get weapons and cowboy clothes, and wants to make off for the plains. Or else he desires to become a soldier and get into warfare. The stealing suggestion is much more rarely taken up with.

In considering the total social results of the introduction of moving pictures one must not forget the astonishing appetite which is created for the particular mental pabulum which they supply. In many instances the stealing has taken place in order that the individual shall have his fill of going to such shows. Often we have heard of a perfect orgy in this direction — the delinquent staying away from home and going from one show to another during the entire day and evening. Several possible features of the whole situation are brought out in the following instances.

Case 48. — William J. This is the interesting case of a very charming little boy, not yet 11 years old, who is in good physical condition and of supernormal mental ability. He belongs to an exceptionally nice family of immigrants. His father and mother are decidedly rational people who have been willing to do much for him, but he has caused them an excessive amount of trouble for about a year. He has very repeatedly stolen, and very curiously, in the light of his physical delicacy and mental ability, often stayed away from home all night. He sleeps in boxes or under porches even in cold weather. Punishment has done no good, and even when he has been promised money to stay at home, he has jumped out of the window. When he is away from home he begs for his meals. At home he is very reticent. The only causes for his misconduct which his mother can think of are that he was taught bad sex things by a girl when he was four years of age, and that later on he was caught at the same thing with other boys, but there has been frankness in the family and his parents are sure he is not given to an excess of sex habits. He does go with bad companions, first one and then another, but when he is out all night he is always by himself. He wants to go to nickel shows every day. Neither in hereditary nor in developmental history do we hear of items of great importance.

We had reason to see this little boy on a number of occasions, and we and others found him a very open-hearted and charming boy. One can hardly believe that he carries on the life that he does. He frankly acknowledges his stealing, and his perfect craze for moving pictures. He goes practically every night to them and stays all evening in one show. In the winter he stays out until 11 or 12 o'clock, and in the summer until 2 or 3 in the morning. Sometimes he sleeps in a box, or under a porch, before going home. Sometimes he does not go home at all during the night. He is fondest of cowboys and Indians, and with a poor show of talent he draws many pictures of Indians for us. He runs away because his mother does not want him to go to the shows. He says he does not want to be a cowboy. He would rather be a soldier or an engineer. When he steals he spends it for shows, and perhaps treats other boys. Some of these boys are pretty bad and have initiated him into sex affairs, but his father has counselled with him about it. He finds sex stimulation in the nickel shows when he sees lovers' pictures, "when they kiss theirselves," but he likes cowboys better. He thinks about sex affairs and sometimes practices masturbation afterwards. Often he does not get his supper, eating nothing between noon and breakfast the next morning. He stays away from home at supper time so that he may go to shows.

After a long trial in his old environment it was finally found impossible for him to succeed there. Old associations connected with the shows had too strong a hold upon him. He repeatedly stole several dollars at a time, and finally had to be put in an institution.

§ 226. Experiences During Custody.

Among all environmental conditions which tend to create anti-social conduct none is better known than those which surround the offender during custody. The very individual whom society would turn into the paths of rectitude is often made much worse by experiences forced upon him. The neglect of this thoroughly substantiated fact is a plain token of our colossal failure to appreciate and meet the springs and sources of misconduct. Let there be no misunderstanding; the question of how prisoners become worse through imprisonment does not even involve consideration of the well-accredited general social values of punitive measures.

If one might hazard an opinion concerning the general disre-

Plate IX

A group of faces illustrating "der Gefängnissblick"—the prison look.
Taken from Kauffmann's "Psychologie des Verbrechers."

gard of custodial injuries, it probably could be accounted for by the superficial mixing of ideas that often occurs in practical life. The feelings that obtain during handling of the delinquent are that he is a punishable individual, that no special pains ought to be taken for his comfort, that he ought to reform. As ordinarily carried out, the whole custodial procedure has little sanity in it. It is forgotten that society as a result of incarceration is likely to have a deteriorated individual free again in its midst.

Authoritative testimony on the frequently baneful influence of experiences under detention is abundant. All criminologists acknowledge the evil. We cannot afford space to more than summarize the trend of their observations. In his chapter on the etiology of crime Lombroso (**239**) devotes a section to prisons. " One of the greatest factors in crime is the prison." This author (**239**, p. 114) went so far as to say that the introduction of schools into prisons, developing the intelligence and power of bad men in contact with each other, would increase the number of recidivists. He certainly is right when he states that the pickpocket and the cutthroat often have learned in prison, at the expense of the state, skilled methods of committing misdeeds. Tarde (**120**, p. 256) says, " The criminal is partly the result of his own crime and partly of criminal justice." Kauffmann (**81**) finds a large place among the causes of crime for the conditions under which punishment is carried out. Ellis (**124**, p. 305 ff.) has gathered a considerable number of important practical observations on this point. From among the writings of men of the widest personal experience with offenders we shall merely cite Devon (**73**, p. 271), " In my opinion it is beyond dispute that our methods result in the making of criminals: that in the majority of cases imprisonment not only does no good, but does positive and serious harm." And Holmes (**66**, p. 244 ff.) says, " Why is it that a man's facial expression changes during a long detention? Why is it that his voice becomes hard and unnatural? Why is it that his eyes become shifty, cunning and wild? . . . It is not because of hard work, . . . it is the system that does it, the long-continued soul-and-mind-destroying monotony. . . ."

The change of physiognomy indicative of a change of personality, resultant upon incarceration, has been a subject of thoughtful comment. Gautier (**326**) noted keenly the psychological changes which take place during imprisonment, and the manufacture under these conditions of a changed and special type

of individual. He long ago spoke of "*l'air des detenus.*" Kauffmann (**81**, p. 70), following up an observation by Flynt (**310**, p. 9)
devotes much consideration to what he calls the "prison look,"
(*der Gefängnisblick*). This peculiar type of physiognomy he
finds every reason to believe is simply the product of the set life
of incarceration. Flynt thinks that "prison life," if taken in
large doses and often enough will give the most moral man in
the world prison features.[1]

The most untoward effects of incarceration, those which have
always impressed us greatly in our study of causes, are in the
realm of psychic contagion. As we have said elsewhere, it has
hardly ever proved to be the physical surroundings which have
done the offender most harm. We have heard the testimony
many times, and received ample corroboration on several occasions, that when offenders are thrown together the worst of
knowledge has been spread and powerful stimulus has been dis-
seminated towards anti-social conduct. The experiences are
often the worst in the delinquent's whole life. These distressing
results are so contradictory to the intended effect of legal treatment that the situation is nothing short of tragically anomalous.

We may note the several classes of undesirable mental effects
entailed by incarceration: (*a*) Under any short term method
of punishment, for young or old, there often is developed the
conception that imprisonment itself is not such a bad thing after
all. It is medicine, the bitterness of which is found to be much
exaggerated. Statistics everywhere, as well as personal observations, bear out this fact. Garofalo, from the lawyer's standpoint
one of the keenest observers of penal methods, lays much stress
on this weakness of short incarcerations; "for it is evident that
imprisonment for such short terms is wholly devoid of intimi-
datory effect. As for its reformatory effect, it is not worth wasting words on " (**328**, p. 424).

---

[1] The striking assertion by Ruggles-Brise in his introduction to Goring's
work (**160**), that the statistical method demonstrates "that imprisonment
does not have the adverse physical and mental results which are often alleged," we do not find corroborated by Goring's own statement. The latter
says (p. 371), "We find that imprisonment, on the whole, has no apparent
effect upon physique, as measured by body weight, or upon mentality, as
measured by intelligence." Now this latter is a very limited statement, and
not at all contradictory to the contention of all the other observers who have
set forth the opposite. Body weight is notoriously a poor criterion of physical efficiency, and there are many mental conditions and effects, particularly
such as may be correlated with immoral tendencies, which are not discovered by simple intelligence tests.

PLATE X

Two family portraits illustrating the acquirement of the prison expression in a normal person. Above is the boy of 15 who has committed some minor offense, and below is the same individual at 20 after serving two years for petty stealing. Note the unfortunate change of expression about the mouth. Even these portraits fail to do justice to the marks which have been set on this face from long repression.

(b) Often during custody there is a spread of pernicious ideas about sexual affairs, and the acquirement of bad personal habits, both through verbal communication and actual experience with others. This is a subject of great import. We have learned so much, witness our case histories, which proves that undermining of moral regard for the natural and social laws concerning sex affairs is provocative of other criminalism that we must be convinced of the seriousness of this matter. There is much more significance to the fact than the mere learning of sex knowledge would seem to imply. A wide range of new anti-social impulses often follows. That contagion of this sort takes place with great frequency in all sorts of custodial institutions is acknowledged on every hand. Church reformatory schools form no exception. Where old offenders are mixed with young ones, as in many jails, the results are intolerably bad. It is probably merely the nature of the subject that has not caused its more frequent discussion in open conferences. If there were more appreciation of the psychological ramifications of this psychic infection more justice would be done the importance of the matter. A student of prison conditions, Widen (327), in one of our younger states where degenerate practices are supposed to be less frequent, finds that these form the greatest danger of prison life. Sixty per cent. of the young men he consulted in the penitentiary asserted that they thought there was a great deal of sexual vice practiced there. What goes on in other institutions has either been hinted at or specifically stated by many observers.

A characteristic phase of this whole matter is that communications between adolescent girls under custody are much more pernicious than between boys of the same age. Many a girl has testified to us that she learned more in the first twenty-four hours under custody than she knew in all her life before. Attendants among female offenders all bear witness to the peculiarly vicious type of conversation ordinarily carried on by these women and girls.

(c) Development of prison friendships. Human affection, however perverted its forms may seem, plays its part within prison walls. Indications of this fact can be found in literary productions as well as in the miserable annals of recidivism. Our experiences have taught us that many times when a young offender, especially if he has not strong home ties, is committed for a few months he is apt to form friendships which are productive of

313

misconduct later. Dozens of times we have known two young men, who were not acquainted with each other before incarceration, to meet after they had gained their freedom, and indulge together in further misdemeanors. The main suggestion of companionship thus acquired is naturally towards anti-social conduct. We have never heard of a single case of a prison friendship being active upon the basis of mutual help towards better conduct.

(d) Development of criminalistic knowledge and technique. Ellis (**124**, p. 230 ff.), quotes from an interesting autobiography of a noted Australian criminal. In his teens he was imprisoned where he had a chance to meet older men, under conditions such as exist in many of our American county jails and elsewhere in the world. He later wrote, "The instruction I received during these three months considerably improved me in my profession. The Government had placed me in the position to learn a trade, and having learnt it, I was determined to work at it."

The most acute observations on this point to which I have ever listened came from the lips of a free professional, *vide* Case 49, who had reason to be frank and friendly. He sees a great causative factor of criminality in the enforced congregating of offenders. During imprisonment the older man is on the lookout for future partners, and tries to enlist those who have intelligence and nerve. Perhaps the actual teaching of new recruits may not go on in custody, but the opening wedge is placed, and when acquaintances meet on the outside definite plans are formed. Communications, even in penitentiaries, cannot be stopped between shrewd men. They learn to talk without moving their lips, and to communicate in other ways, and so readily form acquaintances. "It is quite taken for granted," said this man, "that if a fellow once gets in the toils he will be ready for further crimes, even if his earlier deeds have been only minor offenses. It is assumed to be a certainty that the 'nervy' and intelligent fellows will commit crimes again; they will naturally be against society." Friendships formed in prisons, however, are a big factor in this result.

(e) Development of mental content which drives towards criminalism. Here we need barely mention the various undesirable forms of imagery which are likely to rush in to fill the prolonged vacuities of mental life during custody. It should require only common sense to appreciate that the thinking which is done under

314

these circumstances partakes often of the nature of evil. There is the constant suggestion towards misconduct which comes from thinking of one's self as an offender. There is the definite picturing of profitable depredations. There are all the sex imageries which come from deprivation. There is the inner restlessness resulting from lack of physical activity.

When it comes to giving cases to prove the baneful effect of experiences under custody there is an inevitable difficulty, except about certain details. Offenses had already started before arrest, so at no time can one fairly assert that custodial experiences formed the major cause of a career. But this thing is plain; if absolutely innocent individuals were put under prison conditions they would tend to develop anti-social conceptions of conduct. The details which we have heard from offenders themselves, and have had corroborated in various ways, form the basis of the enumeration of the unfortunate mental effects of custodial life given above.

Remedies for all this are matters of the deepest concern. It must be the part of our new science, as this develops, that there shall be understanding of all the influences which custodial conditions may have upon the human being. The effects of various treatments will have to be evaluated in the light of thoroughgoing studies of outcomes, such as yet have never been undertaken in this field. Some part of institutional considerations will always have to do with bricks and mortar, but the core of the whole matter is the influence of man on man, — the influence of officials on prisoners, the influence of prisoners on each other. And some day will be found out the economy of paying salaries sufficient to get better people officially to influence towards the good. There are many ways in which the incarcerated may be turned towards good or towards bad. To this end we must, with a gradual accumulation of scientific, and particularly of psychological knowledge, build upon the foundation started by John Howard (329).

CHAPTER VIII

PROFESSIONAL CRIMINALISM.   DELIBERATE CHOICE

Professional Criminalism. § 227. Definition of Terms. § 228. Frequency of This Type. § 229. Genetics and Characteristics of Professionalism. § 230. Presentation of Cases. § 231. Treatment of Professionalism. § 232. **Deliberate Choice of Criminalism.**

PROFESSIONAL CRIMINALISM.

§ 227. Definition of Terms. — The term "professional," which is applied by certain criminals to themselves, and which is used extensively by those who have to deal with offenders, serves well to discriminate for practical diagnosis and treatment a most important group. The adoption by some individuals of crime as a trade, or calling, or profession is as much an actuality in our civilization as was the development of the gentle art of brigandage by the Thugs of Tartary. Many authors have insisted on the necessity for distinguishing the professional group, which seems to stand out sharply by itself, at least for practical treatment. The exact significance of the term and the striking characteristics of professionalism should be made clear.[1]

Under the head of habitual offenders we may discriminate the professional and non-professional classes. An example of the latter would be the subnormal individual who habitually transgressed, merely in obedience to uninhibited impulses. Professionals belong to the group of premeditated offenders, but not all of the latter belong to the former class. Wulffen (**2**, vol. 2, p. 282) and Mercier (**3**, p. 50) bring this out clearly from both the practical and theoretical standpoints. It is a fact, of course, that a single offense in a person's whole career might be premeditated. In general the criterion for discrimination of this professional class is that their criminalism is deliberate, premeditated and repeated, as compared to the type of action which is the result of the impulse of the moment.

It is well recognized that the so-called occasional criminal,

---

[1] The use of the term "professional criminal" coincides with *Berufsverbrecher* and *Gewerbsverbrecher* as used by German authors. The habitual criminal, the *Gewohnheitsverbrecher*, may not be a professional.

that is the individual who becomes an offender only as opportunity is clearly offered to him, and delinquents of other classes to whom avenues of honest livelihood become more and more difficult on account of their offenses, may ultimately develop professionalism. This should be thoroughly taken into account in considering measures of treatment and prevention.

The " professional " has received literary portrayal to a much greater extent than other classes of offenders. He is shown to be the one who engages in criminal undertakings as a matter of business, with the deliberate choice and calculations of chances and profits, of personal adaptabilities, and of methods of efficiency that are given ordinarily to the successful carrying on of other pursuits. To be sure, the environment limits opportunities, but so it does in other affairs. In different communities different types of crime are in vogue. In the small towns there are no pickpockets, but in them, and even in country districts, the professional swindler finds a fair field. The remarkable competency of the professional criminal, or the detective for that matter, portrayed by romancers on this theme, is rarely met with in real life, but still all those who have had much experience must acknowledge great respect for the ability and dexterity frequently shown by professional offenders.

§ 228. **Frequency of This Type.** — A word of comment about the statistical frequency of this type of offender is in order. It is well understood that in the records of courts or institutions the professional is in small proportion to the total number of criminals. Even a superficial observation of the population in reformatories or houses of correction where petty and habitual offenders are sent, will show the small representation of the professional. In penitentiaries the latter shows in larger proportion, but even there the percentages are surprisingly small. A salient reason for the above fact is that the chief requisite for a successful career in crime is ability to escape detection.

In our study of beginners we have all along noted the comparative infrequency of appearance in juvenile courts of the delinquent who is verging on professionalism. It is the stupid types who predominate in the records as repeaters, but this by no means proves that they carry out the largest number of crimes. The situation is quite analogous to that of the girls and women: the ones who get caught are those who are not shrewd enough to conceal their delinquencies. As careers develop, even greater

317

skill is acquired in avoiding detection, and fewer professionals in proportion are apprehended during the years of their greatest vigor than at an earlier stage. It has been frequently estimated by police officials that there are from five to ten times as many criminals at large as in custody. A considerable proportion, how great I doubt if any one can judge safely, of those at large belongs to the professional class.

Advance in our practical knowledge of the professional criminal must come almost entirely through investigation of two main questions: What are the foundations of the professional criminal's start? What holds him to his career? These are the points most valuable for developing the conception of adequate treatment. From the standpoint of ordinary penology the professionals are generally regarded as incorrigible. They are included in the classification of the International Criminalistic Union (346) as "criminals whose rehabilitation in regulated social life can no longer be expected." If this be quite true — I am not sure of it myself — then the only study that can be worth much, is of the two questions we mention. That brings us back once more to the genetics of criminalism.

§ 229. **Genetics and Characteristics of Professionalism.** — It is easy to see that a number of innate personal characteristics may induce an early trend towards criminalism. Following our studies of personalities, as offered elsewhere in this volume, we may note such widely divergent characteristics as laziness, motor dexterity, smallness of size, mechanical ability, abnormal social suggestibility, and many others which have very evidently made for criminalistic pursuits. No doubt in some chronic offenders there are peculiar mental incapacities and feelings of social irritability, but such cannot be alleged to be general traits of the professional. An interesting suggestion is that of Wulffen (2, vol. 2, p. 285) who thinks that fundamental craving for adventure may be at the root of many professional careers.

As an example of a frequently cited characteristic of professionals we might take egoism and vanity. To these people their very notoriety, as well as their shrewdness in evading detection and their operative dexterity, appear as matters for self-congratulation. They do not refrain from boasting of their prowess to their friends, or even to the authorities when under arrest. Many striking anecdotes have been recorded bearing on this point. But there is no reason why this should not be so.

A real or an assumed self-satisfaction in any line of conduct is a prime requisite for its deliberate selection. The usual springs of satisfaction in activity and achievement are available for the professional criminal as well as for the honest workman. Even in such a gentlemanly and quiet type as the one quoted below, Case 49, it was quite plain that there was ample felicity in the fact of his own skill and fame. Certainly, however, in many instances this egoism has not at all killed out the power of experiencing normal feelings of affection and friendship, although the irregular life and breaking of home ties which ensue from criminal operations and occasional incarcerations interfere considerably with normal enjoyment of human relationships. The constant taking of big chances and the facing of danger with one's hand against his fellows must inevitably lead to a hardening of spirit which therefore is to be regarded as the result of the occupation rather than the cause of it.

That professionals or recidivists in general are devoid of feelings of remorse, as maintained by Pollitz (8, p. 131), we cannot agree to. The fact that they show no sorrow for having engaged in a certain class of deeds may be the result of general environmental conditions or of early teachings. We know very well how ethical feelings and conceptions are built up as the result of social experiences. As we show later, the very delinquent who has no hesitation whatever about committing certain types of crimes will show great honesty in other affairs. This same author should see reason to think differently, since he himself brings out that repetition of crime does not necessarily mean innate criminal tendencies. For instance, we might cite the class of offenders who transgress only when they are out of work during certain seasons of the year. The category of offenders proposed by Garofalo (10) which includes one large class with many subdivisions, said to be composed of criminals devoid of a sense of honesty, must fairly receive the same criticism. (If the question of innate lack of moral sense is involved here we must refer to our discussion of " moral imbecility," § 372.) There is a proverbial honor among thieves, and honesty may be found in one sphere of action when it is entirely lacking in another. The sense of honesty may not be at all lost, even in the most confirmed offenders.

The older conception that professional criminals belong to a natural class because they show marked characteristics of physique or expression is exploded. Inscrutability, shiftiness, the occasional keen furtive glance, and other peculiarities of physiognomy are of no more fundamental significance than is the fact that various occupations develop peculiar characteristics. We can at once think of the clear gaze of the seaman, the kindly expression of the family physician, the vivacity of the society woman, the bland joviality of the politician. As Devon (6, p. 11) from his long practical experience puts it, "The criminal is born and made just as the policeman is born and made. To see him early in his career it is impossible to tell what he is, but when he has undergone his training it may be expected to leave its mark on him, which those who know may read with more or less success." More on this point comes out in our discussion of the results of prison experience, § 226. If innate traits at all determine professionalism they should be discernible at the early age which we insist on is the proper time for studying criminalistic genetics.

Many economic and environmental conditions have been cited as cause for the establishment of professional criminal careers. It is quite unnecessary to go over these conditions, most of which have been enumerated in our chapter on environmental causes. They are both negative and positive, and involve neglect, poverty, lack of opportunity, criminalistic teachings, and many other factors. Tarde well lays great stress on the social aspects of criminology, and emphasizes (5, p. 252) that the criminal career is one into which the individual has been thrust usually from an early age, and that the influence of pillaging comrades, lack of education, and other living conditions are often responsible. Institutions for criminals, as we elsewhere (§ 226) show, are themselves to be regarded as great breeders of professionalism.

The class of criminals who develop their careers in a business-like way are given opportunities by delays in the law and sinister protection of many kinds. Certain economic laws also are in force here; professional criminalism would not be pursued were it not profitable. It is hardly necessary here to enlarge on the possibilities of graft and protection which involve those who are concerned with carrying out legal and police measures. Some intimation of what really goes on may be seen below, in Case 49, our professional's story.

Teaching the tricks of different branches of professional criminalism goes on regularly. Tiny little fellows are instructed in the art of inserting their slender hands in people's pockets, they practice purse-snatching until skill is acquired, the use of burglar's tools and of explosives are studied in the same way that the employment of implements in any trade is learned. There are even nowadays occasionally to be found " schools of crime."

In our own studies we have been much impressed by the experiences and mental reactions which set an individual definitely in the direction of anti-social actions, such as find expression in professional criminalism. Several of our chapters are devoted to these phenomena. The opportunities for learning the arts of criminalism are sometimes sought out by the individual, rather than thrust upon him. Just as in the case which we cite later, Case 50, frequently there are features of the environment which create a mental attitude that is a favorable soil for criminalistic impulses, determined though the latter may be in this or that direction by special aptitudes or abilities.

§ 230. **Presentation of Cases.** — In our study of individual cases we go farther in discriminating the factors which make for professionalism than do those who have observed merely the full-grown professional as such. This has led us to see how careers which might rapidly become professional in tendencies may be entirely checked by changes of environment, the offering of suitable educational and vocational inducements, the modification of mental conflicts, the satisfaction of legitimate but o'erweening desires. We could not offer cases which represent the range of personality types that develop into professional criminalism. Many types are represented, all the way from absolutely normal individuals to the constitutional inferiors, or those with slight mental defects. But we can offer a few studies which present live issues pertaining to the subject. Any practical consideration of this matter will always take in both peculiarities of personality and other causative factors.

Case 49. — No more striking evidence of the concrete issues of professional criminalism can be gained than from the words of one of America's most intelligent and successful criminals, whom I have had the opportunity of knowing, as Devon says every offender must be known if one is to be really acquainted with him, entirely outside of institutional life, or of police surveillance. Inasmuch as the hereditary, developmental and early environmental history of this man is unknown to us, he represents only a

321

partial case study. But from his personality, his social philosophy, and good apperceptions we may learn lessons of great import.

This man is possessed of unusually fine presence, keen sensibilities, and good speech, and is educated far above the ordinary offender met with in court work. He is unquestionably a man who might have filled some important position in commercial life. The experienced observer would detect about the set of his mouth and other facial expression some indication of the months of silence that he has been through during his incarcerations, but perhaps a thoroughly taciturn individual might show the same type of physiognomy. This man speaks of his " work "; with conscious pride he calls himself a professional. To him expert safe opening is a science, involving knowledge of mechanics and chemistry. He belongs to what has been denominated the " aristocracy of criminality." He has served several short terms, but never has there been fastened upon him any major deed. In the meantime, when in funds, he may live like a millionaire at a first-class hotel, or enjoy the home where his wife and child abide.

His sentences have been given him on general suspicion, or when he has plead guilty to some minor charge in order to save himself from the graver one of being an habitual offender. This is one of the tricks of his trade — one that is particularly made possible by the methods of states attorneys who will sometimes give him the choice of so pleading guilty, or of taking his chances on being tried for a major offense, which perhaps he has committed, but which they cannot well prove. His last sentence was received in just such a way as this, and he remarks to us that at about the same time he noted by the papers that another criminal in another state was sentenced for an offense which he (our friend) had committed. By pleading guilty to lesser crimes, he says, one may thus keep out of worse indictments, and then the police will get credit for having captured the right man.

" If you good people want me to stop my career you must make it worth my while to stop. I 'm just like the rest of professionals. I love good living. The only way to stop us is to find out who and what we are and what we are good for. Then you 've got to make punishment severe enough or opportunities good enough for us. Society does not do either one of these now. I 've got to have a good living when I get out. I can stay at the Waldorf or the LaSalle when I 'm in funds, but I would rather have less and a steadier job. I 'm not a cheap-looking fellow, and yet all I could hope to do, if anybody takes me in, is to get perhaps $15 a week for doing work that would be worth twice as much. If I am recommended nowadays anybody thinks he is doing a great charity to hire me at any price. There's no trade I can easily get into, and when I get out of the 'pen,' all I have is a few dollars and the suit they give me, which would tell anybody where I had come from. Now what do you think a fellow is likely to do and what will be his natural temptation? Why can't they give a fellow work in the penitentiary, and wages that can be saved up for him so that when he comes out he can have some kind of a start? Either you have got to make it so hard for me that I would rather work at laborer's wages than take a chance, or else you have got to give me a decent job — neither of these things has come about yet. Certainly very few of even the best professionals make a success of it in the long run, but there is always a chance.

" Your first step towards stopping me would be to have a central bureau of identification in Washington. Then you could check me up and know who I am, and the parole system could be extended with perfect safety. As it is, I am one person in one state and another in another, and there is no following me up in any way. As a matter of fact, society does not know yet the first steps about effective ways in which it might treat its criminals."

We tried to get this man's point of view in regard to the genetics of professionalism. Of course he knew little about beginnings in youth, nor did we ever learn of his own early life. (It is only fair to say that about some details given by this man we were able to get corroboration.) " Well, what the hell do you think we have to think about when we are in prison? Even in well-ordered penitentiaries we find means of getting into communication with the other fellows, and soon learn to speak without perceptibly moving our lips. We are always on the look-out for shrewd and teachable young chaps. You take a fellow who has not done much but just fall in line with the temptations that have been offered him and who has been sentenced for it; of course he is feeling sore. And when he realizes he is going to be called a gaolbird for all his life he is willing to learn more about the game. Even if we don't have much to say to him on the inside we can find out where to meet him later on. That's how the best pals are made."

This man made much of the difficulty of leaving the path of professionalism after once started on it. He, for instance, (we had corroboration of this) had been run out of a certain city when he had started in business with a capital obtained from family friends — run out by the police on general principles. They said he was too dangerous to have around — " he might be pulling off some deal sometime." He also made much of certain other persecutory features of police life, which for obvious reasons one is unable to corroborate. He asked what is easier than for a shrewd detective to recognize a man by his picture, then to look up his record and confront him with immediate arrest, alleging the possibility of his having committed some recent local crime of the kind which his past record would suggest. Nothing offers an easier way out of this than to hand the detective a matter of $25 or so, and there is no possibility of any charge of " graft " being made, because in the course of such a charge the criminal's whole career would be brought to light — a most undesirable occurrence, whether he be going on in a professional way, or trying to live an honest life.

This man through his moving about from state to state belongs to what in Europe is called the highest type of his profession, namely, the traveling or international criminal. Through the lack of coöperation between the police, the courts, and institutions of our different states, this man's situation is almost as if he were in another country when he goes from one state to another. Indeed it is quite doubtful whether there is in America as good a chance to obtain information about the career of a criminal in another state as the chief of police in Paris has for getting knowledge from Scotland Yard.

Case 50. — Boy of 16 years. Arrested for having calmly walked into a place where a public reception was going on and appropriated some watches. He was found to have a number of other charges against him. Interested officers attempted to get family coöperation, but this was only partially obtainable, because of the hopeless attitude of the mother toward her whole family situation, and because of the low character of the boy's father. With us the boy was so frank in exploring his career as an expert thief that one got a very full picture of some beginnings of professionalism. His statements, which were checked up as far as possible, were found reliable in many details, even as pertaining to different localities.

His mother gives him the reputation of being a terrible thief. She is inclined to attribute his deeds to some mental injury which she thinks he must have received when he fell from a second-story window a couple of years previously. (As a matter of fact we found no signs of head injury of any kind, and his own story of misdoing goes back many years prior to the fall.) Although we did not get a detailed developmental history, it is stated that he has never been very ill. He is the oldest of three children. His father is an excessive alcoholic who has been arrested many times for fighting and drinking. He has been known to wear a gold watch his boy had stolen, but is said not to be a thief himself. The family is largely supported by the mother doing washing. The boy's sister at 13 is in 7th grade. The third child died in infancy. The mother shows signs of having had some education and ambition.

Physical examination: the boy is fat, slouchy and very short: bright and responsive expression; pleasant features. Notwithstanding the boy's waddling gait and apparent lack of muscular tone, he is very quick and active; weighs 115 lbs. and is 4 ft. 9¼ in. in height; long narrow head; circumference 53.3, length 18.3, and width 14.3 cm.; teeth crowded; right upper lateral incisor missing — said not to be erupted; as yet no external signs of puberty; nystagmoid movements of eyes on lateral deviation.

Mental tests: our own series.

I. 59″. Practically no trial and error.

II. 46″. No error.

III. 41″. 14 moves.

V. Much interested in this test. After several quick trials and errors, steps done rapidly in correct order. 1′ 37″. It is remarkable that this was done entirely by the use of the fingers instead of the hook — the only time we have ever seen the box opened in this way. Great adeptness shown.

VI. "Aussage." Fairly full enumerative account with no suggestibility.

VII. Both well done at the first trial.

VIII. Four errors with a curious reduplication of numbers. Carelessness, as elsewhere, is the only explanation of this.

IX. Correct at first trial.

X. Correct only at the third trial.

XII. Only 7 items out of 20 given correctly. Very childish and careless result.

XIII. 7 out of 12 items given correctly in logical sequence.

XIV. Fails on the first trial to open the box by reason of a small final error. Opens it in 55″ at the 2d trial.

XV. Average time 3″. No error, 2 failures.

XVI. 102 squares tapped at first trial with 4 errors. 106 squares tapped the 2d time with 3 errors. An unusually rapid performance.

XVII. Writing is rapid and normal for his age.

XVIII. Through an oversight no record of his arithmetical ability was made.

XIX. Fluent reader.

XXI. The reaction to the 2d moral question was that he would rather give the man up than get killed. He was pretty sure on this point.

XXII. Fair amount of information obtained from considerable reading of newspapers and books. Has merely a common-sense view of scientific things. Never been interested in them. Has read stories of New England and of olden days, about King Arthur, Benjamin Franklin and "all them books." Is fond of magician tricks, plays cards, is fond of bicycling, swimming, and baseball. Plays with some skill the violin, piano, and cornet. Has taken music lessons for years. When under custody, on account of his ability to entertain, he is a great favorite. He will sit at the piano and perform for long periods in music hall fashion.

His method in work with tests showed definite characteristics. He was interested, quick, but utterly careless. Without waiting for full instructions he plunges ahead. He is quite devoid of quiet thoughtfulness or of deliberate foresight. Relies entirely on quick perceptions. Emotions normal. Is much worried about the prospect of being sent to an institution.

In spite of much changing of schools and truancy, this boy reached 7th grade when he stopped at 14 years. Since then he has held many positions for short periods each, and there is no doubt of his ability to earn well if he were only more stable. One could readily classify him as having fair mental ability, and also as possessing certain special aptitudes, as indicated above.

His delinquency consists of an excessive amount of stealing continued over many years. He has already been in court in different cities a number of times. On all except one occasion he has been placed on probation, but he found this no bar to his traveling about the country whenever he felt like it. On a number of occasions of which we learned from other sources, he has boldly executed shrewdly planned escapes from places where he was detained. On two occasions he has with the utmost effrontery simply walked away in full view. Many tributes to his shrewdness and motor dexterity are rendered. One experienced person says, "He is as quick as greased lightning." No efforts were ever seriously put into effect for this boy's reformation, because he never gave any one the chance.

In describing his own career this boy was very frank and helpful. He seemed distinctly to have the idea that he would like to do

326

differently. In fact, he made direct appeal to us to help him get into some life away from temptation. But before anything could be done for him he had escaped again. He made the same impression on us as on others, namely, that he was frank, intelligent, well-mannered and pleasant.

" Well, I don't remember exactly what I stole first, but know I stole a cornet when I was in S., when I was 5 years old. I took it out of a trunk. I guess I was a pretty bad kid. I drowned some cats. Can't tell exactly how it was I began stealing. I never did run with any bad boys. I was in court last year; stole forty dollars' worth of pocket knives from B's, down there at their main store. It was about 6 o'clock at night. I was alone. The judge let me go on probation. I took the knives because I wanted some money. I sold them to some man for about 50 cents apiece. They got most of the knives back. I took a detective up and got the knives from the man. It was around in the M. building that I went and peddled them. Well, maybe it was not in the last year I took those knives. They really caught me about the sixth time I was stealing there. A thief always goes back for more. I used to keep the things under the sidewalk.

" After that when I was on probation I was supposed to come to court, but I ran away the night before. I went to L. Stayed in a lady's house there. Then I stole a watch and got arrested. I was trying to sell it and a boy went up and told the copper about it. I wrote home from there, and my mother sent me railroad fare, and the judge let me go and I came back here. I did not work then, and I stole a bicycle.

" There was a woman kept a little store up near where we lived. She told me anything I would steal she would buy it off me. The first thing she bought of me was a pair of opera glasses. They were my mother's. Then she bought a diamond ring off of me. I got that at the bathing beach. A lady had it on and she was sitting on the sand cleaning it. I came up quietly behind her and reached over her shoulder and grabbed it and then walked off in the crowd. She could never tell who it was. After I worked at R.'s about a week I took a $5 bill. It was lying on the counter. When I saw the cashier lady coming I threw it back. I did not steal any watch from a store that I can remember of. Oh, yes, I do remember that, too. It was from a jewelry auction store. She paid me $2 for that. She's never been arrested.

" Nobody ever started me. Maybe it was on account of my

mother telling me to go through my father's pants. That was when he was drunk. I guess it was so he would not get drunk so much. I was about 7 years old when I did that. He's been drinking all the years. I'll bet he is drunk to-day. When I went into that place the other day I did not go in to steal. If I'd get a chance I'd take things, but I did not go in to steal there. When my father is drunk he tells me to go and steal, and when he is sober, too. When I worked I always took my wages home. My mother never got cheated out of a single week's wages. She can tell you that herself. Father never stole as I know of.

"That woman that runs that store she's about 45. There's always men there. Everybody says she goes with men. She always has a gun with her. One day she pointed the gun right at me if I would not get out of the store. She has a man there who will strike a man down all right if he comes in drunk or anything. I told the officer all about her. I would not like to go out to the reform school. I want to go out on a farm. I want to keep away from trouble."

In a letter the boy says, "I had a fight with my sister and she threw the broom at me and I threw it back at her and hit her in the face. My mother got mad and tried to hit me with the poker. Then last night she told me not to come home as she had told the police on me. I forgot and they got me last night. I just escaped from this place about a year ago."

About the time that we last saw this boy he made confession to the police that cleared up a number of cases of stealing which had baffled them. The woman who conducted the "fence" was convicted largely on information obtained from him. Some time after his last escape he was arrested in another state for stealing, and for the first time was placed in a reformatory for a long term.

In the background of this boy's personality and delinquency there are some abnormal physical and social conditions which no doubt have had a partly determining influence. But it is certainly most reasonable to conclude that his career directly centers about certain special abilities, particularly motor dexterity. With the exercise of these and his cool shrewdness he is well equipped to be an expert sneak thief. Bad though his home is, his mother is a good woman, and he has been given some special attention, such as receiving music lessons. He is capable of earning a very good living, but deliberately chooses to exercise his ability in dishonest ways; he has definitely begun following crime as a trade

328

or profession. There may have been other causal elements, particularly in the field of inner mental life, which we never ascertained, but we did learn a great deal in this case of how beginnings of professional criminalism may develop.

Special abilities: Early discovered motor   Case 50.
     adeptness and satisfaction in it.   Boy, age 16.

Home conditions: Father alcoholic and bad man.

     Heredity: As above. (Otherwise not known.)
        Stigmata: Delayed puberty.
        Irregular physical development
         and dentition.
        Nystagmoid movements.

                            Mentality:
Stealing + +.   Fair intelligence with
Sneak thief — professional type.   special ability.

---

§ 231. **Treatment of Professionalism.** — In any practical scheme
of treatment of professionalism in crime one would insist upon
the necessity of thorough diagnosis. We should be much inclined
to lay stress upon the above views expressed by the thoughtful
professional. This is a field for deterrent possibilities. We should
hesitate much to discuss punishment as set forth in any schedule,
such as that of Garofalo (**10**), because our stand is primarily for
diagnostic study. It seems perfectly evident that many features
of even penal treatment should be based upon facts which can
only be learned through careful study of causative factors. There
are individual needs, and individual differences in response to deterrent laws, which can be more or less estimated by careful diagnostic methods. Professionals differ widely in personal characteristics and in the other background for their offenses. But if
one will consider merely the readily available American literature
on the subject of professional criminals, for instance, the work by
Inspector Byrne (**53**), the autobiographies of Moore (**347**), and
White (**348**), there will be little question about the value of more
efficient police methods, and of the application of swifter, surer
and longer penalties for this type of crime. Thoughtful students
must necessarily agree with Garofalo (**328**, p. 211), who says,
" Short punishments invite the criminal, monstrous as it may
seem, to mock the law, to snap his fingers at justice." Prevention

is the watchword in the treatment of professional criminalism. In this there is a great opportunity for work with the young, which will prove satisfactory only through study of the determining forces of their careers. We have observed a number of instances in which an impending career of professional criminality has been thwarted by constructive measures. The following is a splendid example, inasmuch as there was considerable likeness of environmental and family background to the case given in detail above.

Case 51. — This was the instance of a boy, who at 13 was already the leader of a gang of youthful burglars, who planned and executed skillful and lucrative depredations. Apparently the boy had discovered what he was suited for, and the future seemed to offer many chances for him in this line. He was physically and mentally alert and active. He was courageous and aggressive. There was nothing hopeful in his environment. Here, too, was an ignorant and excessively alcoholic father, and a step-mother who kept a slatternly home. Thieving and burglary offered to this young adept the pleasures of adventure, occupation, easy acquirement of possessions, and money to spend — altogether a lively set of interests and satisfactions.

With this boy's good mentality was a forceful personality and freedom from vice. A study of his case after a " big haul " led to the introduction of live interests in another environment. This boy soon realized that satisfaction accrues along other than criminalistic lines. Opportunities for normal boyish possessions and interests and adventures in a very ordinary country home were all that were necessary to change him into a self-sustaining and useful member of society. He has been a continued success over the number of years that we have known him, even when occasionally returning to the formerly tempting, home environment.

Many of the points which are important in considering treatment of the professional criminal, either as a fully developed character or in the formative state, are dealt with elsewhere in our work. We have spoken of the definitive field of the reformatory institutions, and the need for individualization there, of the weaknesses of penal institutions, of the absurdly expensive procedure of sending adolescents back into old environments before they are able to stand on their feet, either morally or financially. We have discussed mental habits and mental imageries which make for the establishment of behavior characteristics, and we have insisted on the necessity for after-care when a prisoner is discharged from the custody of the institution. There is much value in the Hungarian and the Ohio laws which provide for the study of all young offenders before they are sentenced, in the work of prisoners' aid associations, in the recent, shrewd, common-sense efforts of several of our penitentiary superintendents who have started practical measures for making better human beings out of their prisoners. The further need is for the scientific unification of all these and still other profitable measures of treatment.

§ 232. Deliberate Choice of Criminalism.

Justification for any consideration of deliberate choice as a causative factor of criminalism, especially apart from the caption "professionalism," is found in the following facts: Antisocial deeds may be committed with premeditation, but with no notion of making criminalism a trade or profession. It is an opinion held, sometimes by those who do not proclaim themselves against determinism, that deliberate choice of criminalistic conduct is quite a common phenomenon even among young delinquents. We have several times in individual cases ascribed to deliberate choice the main part in causation, but, on more thorough study of discovered factors, we have been inclined to discount our earlier view. We below illustrate the complexities. It finally has seemed patent to us that both for prognosis and treatment this difficult element of diagnosis might nearly always be left out of account.

Perhaps a definition of the term deliberate choice is necessary. I mean a choice made by those who possess mental powers sufficient for self-determination of the direction of their careers, in whom there are not — perforce of overpowering physical and mental characteristics — such internal tendencies as well might be calculated to develop criminalism, and in whom there is no overwhelming push from environmental sources. I should insist that if deliberate choice is to be invoked by way of explanation of an anti-social career, there must have been plenty of opportunity, and even invitation, to take advantage of occupational or recreational interests which would have proved enticing enough to cause others to choose refraining from misdeeds. Here, as elsewhere in our work, we must carefully avoid the unfruitful theoretical discussion of determinism *versus* free will.

No doubt if one were to take a mentally normal offender who

has passed the more formative period of life, and were to judge him by the immediate and obvious causes of his action, one would frequently ascribe much to deliberate choice. But as we stated early in our book, the cases we have put into our series are those in which the background of causation was largely known. Perhaps this is why we find so much else than deliberate choice at the roots of misconduct. If I were asked to pick out the most egregious examples of criminalistic conduct that betokens deliberate choice, I am inclined to think I should select panderers and "cadets." And yet of this most despicable class those members of which I have knowledge have come from such family circumstances that to know the latter would be to say that from such influences nothing good could be expected.

Professional criminals of other types have, many of them, started their careers under decidedly determining conditions. Some themselves maintain that, once started, society itself continues to prevent them from exerting deliberate choice of conduct. Making up our minds at many different times, and often in consultation with experienced people, and with the great amount of material which often has been collected on a case, it is significant that we find justification for applying the phrase " deliberate choice " as a cause in less than half a dozen instances in more than 1000 cases of repeated offenders. Let the casual onlooker, who sees only the deed and the apparent choice of action, follow up the data and see how many other factors loom up as determining forces. The first case given below seemed to present to us as marked evidence of deliberate choice as we have ever seen, and yet note the many other factors.

Case 52. — A mother brought her problem to us considerably in advance of the time we were able to see her boy. Although only 15, he had for years been getting into an excessive amount of trouble on account of misconduct. Recently his delinquencies had culminated in a well-planned theft of a considerable sum of money which he divided with a bad woman with whom he had lately become acquainted, and who had partly instigated the plot. The theft and burglary might have involved the murder of a certain old relative, and it had been planned to carry that out if necessary. These facts will give some indication of the boy's recklessness. His delinquencies had begun before he was 10. He was a great truant, sometimes managing to evade school for months at a time, although he had been sent to more than one institution on account of truancy. By the time we saw him he had already engaged in various sorts of thieving, several burglaries, the forging of checks, and had indulged in sex dissipation of several kinds.

The mother, much broken down by her family troubles, felt that her son was quite beyond her. He is her only child. The father has been dead since the boy was 10. He was an alcoholic, but never criminalistic. No features of any significance about the boy's heredity were available. The mother's side was said to be clear of defects, but on account of the absence of specific information concerning the father's side, who was an immigrant, we cannot fairly state that heredity was all negative. The pregnancy and birth were normal. The boy is said never to have been seriously ill. No injuries or convulsions. At one time he had tubercular cervical glands, but those are now well.

The boy has lived at home only intermittently. He has been taken to their homes by various members of the mother's family, and has already been five times in different institutions on account of delinquency. From each place he has run away, or has created so much disturbance that all have been glad to get rid of him. A notably good institution for boys could not offer anything that he regarded as worth while, and they relinquished their guardianship. He has never been committed to a reformatory from which he could not readily escape. He has never worked steadily, but has taken odd jobs for a time. There has always been money enough at home for ordinary needs, and his family have been very ambitious for him, particularly because he has always shown such good mental ability. A very good and strong man, who is the guardian of his financial inheritance, has been unable to influence the lad in the least.

Physical examination; fairly good general development; slender type; strength good for age; no sensory defect noted; tonsils very large; gonorrhea; marked tremor of the hands; pleasant, regular features; intelligent face and vivacious expression; many evidences of good physical care in the past; dome-like forehead with prominent frontal bosses. Head; circumference 54.2, length 19, breadth 15 cm.

Mental examination. Tests not completely carried out because of his obvious great ability in many directions and his dislike to do what he called the childish type of tests.

III. Construction Test A. 10″. 5 moves. Our fastest record.

IV. Construction Test B. 27″. 11 moves. Also record time.

V. Puzzle Box. 30″. Step one accomplished in 10″, and the others done with simply marvelous rapidity. Nothing like this ever seen by us previously.

VI. "Aussage." Gave one of the fullest accounts ever given of this picture, with much slangy and humorous interpretation, altogether, however, directly to the point. Not the slightest suggestibility shown.

VIII. Learning Arbitrary Symbol Associations. Done rapidly and altogether correctly.

IX. Cross Line Test A. Correct at first trial.

X. Cross Line Test B. Correct at the second trial after drawing the figure once himself. Rather curious to note that he did not see his own error in the first attempt where he had duplicated number 7 in different compartments.

XI. Code Test. Two errors in final result. Considerable difficulty with this on account of his nervousness and trouble in concentration.

XXII. Information. All ordinary items of geography and history correct. Reads books — reads anything. Likes good plays. Is remarkably ignorant of scientific information in which boys are usually interested. His verbal reactions to the tests were most instructive.

"Well, do I do these things fast enough for you? There is no kind of a lock or a box that I can't open. I'm a locksmith, I am. Collections of anything? I should say not. It's nothing but foolish people who harbor a lot of trash. It's the theatres all the time — that 's me. I like the drama — Chauncey Olcott and the rest of them. I took lessons on the piano for three years, but forgot it all. I was never round machinery. I never studied any steam or electricity, don't know anything about them. I'll tell you the kind of a fellow I am, if you want to know how I can play checkers. I'll play well enough so I can cheat you if I get an opportunity, and prevent you from cheating me. I'm a fellow who is not going to let anybody get ahead of me. I shot a couple of kids once. One of them was trying to steal one of my chickens. The other was entering our barn. I'd knife or stab anybody before I 'd let them get ahead of me. A sporting life is the life for me. You can only live once, and you might as well die now."

In this case we saw exhibited some of the quickest perceptions ever observed by us. Great accuracy and promptness were displayed where any task could be done with rapidity. The powers of attention and concentration were somewhat faulty. It was quite clear that we had to do with an individual of supernormal ability.

In conversation he always showed himself extremely bright and apt, but he was almost always flippant and showed a very perverted philosophy of life. His self-orientation was perfect.

He did not hesitate to talk of his whole career. Indeed, he seemed to be rather glad to have a chance to do so. He vowed vengeance on everybody, and threatened murder and disaster everywhere. He told about his association with bad women, both in the red light district and in private homes, but evidently his delinquencies began long before then. It is only fair to state that the boy did voluntarily tell us that he wished to be somewhat different, and that although he had such a bad record he did not desire to be a criminal.

" Did I go with a bad bunch when I was a kid? Well, I should say. Why, they are all in states prison or the reformatory now. One got three years in the band house. Say, did you ever hear of the X Street bunch, or maybe of the L Street gang? What else could a feller do? I did n't have no father. My mother always used to say, ' First it 's bumming and then it 's stealing.' Did I bum? Well, I should say so. When I did start truancy, I tell you I did. One four months I did not go a single day. When I see any kids get into trouble I can give them good advice — don't start bumming and keep away from a bad bunch. Oh, I smoke cigars and tobacco all right. I never smoked 50 cigarettes in my whole life. I did not go out at nights much. She would not let me, but I was up to devilment in the daytime."

" I was sent away to that school. I suppose my guardian thought it was a good school because he had to pay well there, but I tell you that 's the rottenest place you ever heard of. I have never been in any reformatory. Got pinched now because of some trouble with some money."

This boy in his appearance and general attitude seemed to be anything but the vicious fellow which he has been, and which he frankly states himself to be. It is perfectly evident from much that he told us, and from the accounts of his mother and guardian that the boy has really had exceptionally good chances in life. They would at all times have furthered his vocational inclinations, and they always desired the best of recreations for him. In an ordinary environment it was found impossible to control him. The only check to his actions has been when he was sent to an institution by order of court. Everywhere and under all conditions, and even according to his own story, he has deliberately sought out the worst in life. Early bad companionship partially determined his career, but yet there was always the chance for other friends.

Deliberate choice??

Case 52.
Boy, age 15.

Bad companions — early in life and later.
Much dissipation.

Home conditions: Lack of control when
boy most in need of
help.

Sex experiences: Early and excessive.

Heredity: Father unstable alcoholic.

Running away.
Stealing.
Burglary.
Sex +.
Forgery.

Mentality:
Supernormal ability.

Case 53. — Another case of which we have the most intimate details and have known for a long period is that of a man who has shown many criminalistic tendencies in spite of unusual opportunities. The first study of this case brought out points quite unsuspected even by the relatives.

Deliberate choice??

Case 53.
Man, 33 yrs.

Mentality: Slightly defective as shown
by lack of self-control and
by tests.

Home conditions: Defective discipline.
Much leniency early.

Bad companions — richer young men.

Stealing.
Lying.
Gambling.
Fraud. All excessive.

Mentality:
Poor in ability;
really subnormal
for his own social
group.

Case 54. — A girl of 19 whom we have long known has exceptionally good mental powers and developed normally. Her firm strong carriage and frank expression made her notable among offenders. This girl, after some little period of mischief making, began stealing and entered into sex delinquencies. Then she was given chance after chance under good conditions, sometimes in the very environment she said she had craved, but everywhere she threw away these chances, and finally, in the course of two or three years, and after thus being helped out of one scrape after another, she deliberately became a prostitute, and proceeded to make the considerable amount of money which was possible on account of her attractiveness. She was rescued from this and asserted she had simply used her own choice in the matter. She said she deliberately chose to do these things because they were the easiest, and she preferred them rather than work. She, too, had supernormal ability. From our long acquaintance with the case we know that the following factors were in the background:

Deliberate choice??   Case 54.

  Mental peculiarity: frankly lazy and   Girl, 19.
                  sensuous type.

      Heredity: father notoriously lazy and
             shiftless, although mentally
             bright.

        Masturbation — begun early and
               continued long.

          Home conditions: Mother died early.
                Girl much shifted about.

                          Mentality:
Mischief making.   Supernormal abil-
Stealing.   ity when first
Sex + +.   studied.

Other cases which we have studied and which, even by their own confessions, seemed to be based on deliberate choice have turned out to present many other factors. One of our most marked instances of apparent deliberate choice was that of a girl who, we came to learn, had unfortunately early and without volition, developed excessive phases of the sex instinct. Another was a young pickpocket who only occasionally plied his craft. In this case we found his older brothers had taught him, and that his home conditions were miserable on account of lack of care by an unintelligent mother and the presence of an insane father. Then perhaps nowhere are the superficial evidences that lead to interpretation of deliberate choice as a cause, more prominent than among the cases where anti-social behavior is based on mental conflict (*vide* § 237).

Consideration of deliberate choice leads directly to at least one practical conclusion: The opportunity for doing right should, in ordinary measure, be furnished to every one. In other words, even though one cannot say whether or not a given offender of normal mental ability did exert deliberate choice in past conduct, the student of the causation of his offenses should endeavor to point a way so that those in authority may give him opportunity to make deliberate selection of good conduct in the future. This often involves attempt at alteration both of environment and mental content. What there may be in the background of failures, even under apparently bettered conditions, is indicated in the few cases given above. The many successes need not be cited because they merely represent the natural outcome when environment and personal tendencies are more normal.

CHAPTER IX

Mental Imagery.   Mental Habit

§ 233. Criminalistic Mental Imagery.   § 234. Criminalistic Mental Habit.

§ 233. Criminalistic Mental Imagery.

The general relation of mental imagery to conduct is a subject still open to inquiry which may prove vastly interesting and important. By imagery we mean mental copies of former sensory perceptions which arise in the absence of stimulation of an organ of sense. For some psychologists imagery and imagination seem to be much the same process, but others have discriminated clearly between the two. At this place we do not care to go into this discussion, nor to take up the rather intricate problem of the sensory types of imagery. In the examples which we have to offer, the diagnosis of the actual memory or imagery type, a point of interest to psychologists, would hardly be possible. Indeed, we have rarely asked for careful introspection on this by the offender; conceding most value to more direct issues and to spontaneous utterances. Our interest in this matter was aroused by naïve and non-suggested statements, and has been continued simply along the lines of noting the driving force towards misconduct which mental imagery often seems to be. We acknowledge that this factor is most inadequately treated here by us; we hope that some day thorough study may yield the values which the subject promises.

The connection between earlier human experiences which lead in the direction of criminalism and the criminalistic deed itself is certainly very largely *via* the path of mental imagery. The mental reproduction in some way causes the tendency to misconduct. Just how the anti-social impulse is aroused we cannot always be sure. Some indication of the part which imagery plays in some mental conflict which leads to criminalism may be seen in our chapter on that subject, § 235. Why there should be an outcome in bad impulse, as well as the fact of the vitality of the specific imagery, is a fitting subject for future students of dynamic psychology. The people who have told us of their

339

imagery and the part it has played in producing their conduct of course have no explanation to offer of the process. All they know is that this is the thing that seems to be a paramount influence. We have no reason to doubt their testimony on this point. Psychologists recognize what Angell (**335**, p. 152) calls the motor consequences of imagery. He points out that certain persons may have imagery that takes on almost perceptual vividness and, as in the case of the thought of a wound, may result in even such marked phenomenon as nausea and vomiting. It is a long step further to proceed from such reflex disturbances to the complexities of conduct, but no longer than is justified by many features of the psychological elements in the causation of behavior.

Many of the facts of imagery which we have heard from offenders show extraordinary vividness. Occasionally it has been difficult to discriminate the more normal processes from actual hallucinations. One young fellow tells of the walls opening up in the dark at night, and blood-and-thunder scenes being enacted there. The material was drawn from melodrama, moving pictures, and wild west narratives. The responses have followed our very simple questions; invariably little more than, " How did you happen to think of these things you have been doing? What comes up in your mind to make you do them? What do you think of usually in connection with the wrong things you do? " In some cases we have directly asked if pictures of any kind come up in the mind which have anything to do with the misconduct. We have ever felt it unsafe to urge introspection to the point of suggesting mental pictures as causes. Perhaps in the latter way we should have heard many more details, but undoubtedly they would have been much less reliable. There is never any reason for falsification by offenders on this point because their inner mental processes obviously have nothing to do with the outcome of their case as handled by the authorities.

The urgency and power of imagery impelling to misconduct has been witnessed to by the fact that some individuals have maintained that their whole welfare depends on preventing this imagery from dominating their activities. One intelligent boy of 14 himself urged the necessity of his going to a reform school in order that he might be freed from the environmental suggestions which caused mental reproduction of impelling pictures. He had once seen them and they viciously reproduced themselves. More of the significance of this whole matter may be realized by our consideration of the influence of pictures, § 225.

I see every reason for believing that there are negative as well as positive considerations concerned in the development of mental imagery that is provocative of misconduct. The individual with paucity of healthy mental interests is much more likely to be obsessed by the recurrence of imagery of some experience, which in a more healthfully occupied mind would be almost a negligible influence for the bad. We have dealt with this from other standpoints, § 222, and we have elsewhere, § 127, attempted to emphasize the importance of this psychological consideration in penal treatment. The old saw that "the empty mind is the devil's workshop," means that mental vacuity permits the growth of pernicious imagery. I am inclined to think that here is one of the greatest psychological principles that can be used in the effective treatment of the offender.

The most effective imagery in leading directly or indirectly to misconduct consists mainly of the visual type, but other elements are added, as may be seen by our examples. Of course mental peculiarities play a large part. In this we get explanation of the fact that some have been deeply affected by experiences innocuous to others. Imagery, such as of sex subjects, which is potent to stimulate physical powers, and imageries that create feelings of restlessness and other desires are the most forceful. Mental conflict plays its part here too. Imagination, with its production of new situations, is effective in various ways. It must not be presumed from all of the above that imagery, even visual imagery, in its forms potent for misconduct, always arises from the seeing of pictures themselves. A story read or heard may be translated into visual terms; an incident witnessed may be reproduced. And there is the possibility of all sorts of imaginative representations, made up of separate bits of remembered experience, becoming obsessive mental imagery. We might go on at great length in considering this whole topic, but it is worth most to relate what we have actually heard of the influence of mental imagery in producing misconduct.

Case 55. — Ellen B. A girl of 12, normal in development, good nutrition, without sensory defect, easily found to be quite fair in mental ability. She is somewhat backward in school on account of being changed about so much, but does well on mental tests. By getting detailed descriptions from her of moving pictures and other things, much beyond what is ordinarily obtainable from young people, as well as by listening to her story, we gained evidence that imagery played a large part in her mental processes.

Heredity is decidedly defective. The father was alcoholic, and criminalistic, a very bad man. Home conditions on account of the father have been deplorable. The mother works out, and the girl has been left much to herself, being the only child in the family. A man once started to attack her, and on account of this and certain other sex experiences there has been considerable mental conflict of which her mother has been quite unaware.

Stealing has been carried on by this little girl a number of times by gaining entrance to neighbors' houses. She has taken moderately large sums of money and other valuables. On one occasion when the robbed people were telling their neighbors, this little girl gave a very vivid description of a man whom she had seen go into the house. On another occasion she came home late at night and said she had been kidnapped by a man who locked her in his room. In general she is good and a very helpful child. After her stealing was discovered Ellen was handled very kindly by her mother and friends.

Ellen became frank with us after we had learned the circumstances of her life. She blamed no one else in any way, but when she was asked where she learned about stealing she said, " I was to a show. It was long ago. I saw about burglars. That was before I stole anything at all — not even that 25 cents from my mama. One went in the window and took money out of the drawer. He went out again and was not caught." Do you think about that? " No, I don't. It comes up in my mind when I 'm at home. It comes up when I was thinking about other things. It comes up lots of times. When it comes up in my mind I thought I 'd steal. I never stole with anybody else. I was alone when I saw the burglar picture. I was thinking about getting in that last place long before I did. I was playing with the little girl at that house and I found a key on the floor. I kept it. I saw them going out and then I went and tried the door." Why did you think about using the key? " One of the burglars had a key. He had keys on a chain. He tried one and it would not fit and then the next one did. It was the other one who got in through the window. It was in two parts — that show was." On another day Ellen reiterated to my assistant that the only notion she ever had of stealing was from that picture which was reproduced in her mind, but she was also much disturbed about some words which she said boys had told her and which she said scared her very much. These words, or at least one of them, came up in her mind very often and she had never told her mother. She tried hard not to think of this, but it would come up in her mind.

Ellen was a well-behaved and most reasonable child and her mother was apparently a thoroughly good woman. After these matters were cleared up there was no further trouble about the stealing which had beeen carried on previously for several months.

Case 56. — Albert R. This is the case of a bright boy of 10 years, who has very defective eyesight and suffers from headaches. Earlier he had many children's diseases severely. Home control had been distinctly deficient because of much illness in the family, and there had been a great deal of bad companionship. His delinquencies have consisted in staying away from home at night and then romancing about his adventures. Besides this he has been stealing, what for him were large sums. We found him to bear out the general reputation he has of being a very pleasant little chap. He proved to be frank and a rather talkative little boy, with decidedly nice feelings towards the world, and good perceptions of ethical differences. It seems he was once with another boy who skillfully picked the pocket of a coat when the owner was in the same room. Later this older boy was put in jail. Now this thief used to tell the little boy what he calls " dirty stuff," things that the little boy maintains he did not like to hear. " He is not there. His family moved away. All of the boys are glad he went. He 's the first ever said such bad words I heard. He would tell bad stories. Sure, I think of these. That 's why it spoils me. I used to tell bad words, but not no more. You can't help it. When a kid gets to know these things he feels like saying them out. It makes me sick. I see sometimes I feel like saying them and that makes me feel bad. When I come right up to it and get ready to say them I stop." (Questions: Do you mean it 's a temptation? Do you know what temptation is?) " Yes, I know what that is. It 's when you start to say a thing and then you don't. I think of things. It sounds it — it sounds it. It would be words — what he said, those bad words — words I would not like to tell you, I 'm ashamed. It does bother me. It makes me think. Nobody ever said that

343

before. I see a lady with a baby and I don't like to see her, and I think maybe she has no husband. It makes me think like anything about bad, that does. It's the bad words he said, and what he says about ladies."

Nothing in the tests we did with this boy showed indication of any peculiarity in his imagery. His defective eyesight caused him a good deal of trouble, but in spite of it he was able to do well in many things, and was only slightly backward in school work.

Case 57. — This is an instance in which a young woman of 18 had been stealing from places where she worked during a considerable period. She had taken many things for which she had no use and merely kept them locked up. It was unquestionably an exaggerated case of pathological stealing. The list of articles recovered, as an attorney said, sounded like a stock list. There was a great deal of mental conflict in this case as the result of several unfortunate experiences. There was also defective heredity, and some years earlier this girl had herself shown signs of major hysteria. At present she is extremely strong and of good carriage. Dresses well. Bites finger nails much. Has demonstrated in various ways, besides on our tests, the possession of good mental ability.

With us she is absolutely frank and tells at length of her escapades and troubles. Her family corroborate much that she told us. In spite of the usual school training she never reads at all. " I never could get interested in reading." In the last couple of years she has been going excessively to picture shows. During one winter, living in contiguity to one of them, she went every night. She has seen so many that no particular one has taken any hold upon her. But when she has been at work pictures have come up in her mind. " When I was at work lots of times I would forget what I was doing when these things would come up in my mind. I would think about what I was going to be and dress pretty." " I saw lots of pictures about stealing — men would take things and get away to different cities, but I can't tell anything special. Saw lots of pictures about lovers and about people being dressed nice. I would think that when I was older I would like to be the same. At other times used to think about these things. I would dream a good deal about boys and about their doing bad things. Sometimes it would worry me for a couple of days. I would think of that dream when there were boys around. I did not want to run around with the boys. Yes, I think it is worse than stealing. Pictures about the west would make me think I wanted to go out there. Pictures about lovers I thought I ought to forget, but it would sometimes come up in my head. It has lots of times. I 'd sort of dream when I was at work about getting married and about having a home and being dressed pretty, and then about these affairs with boys. Lots of times in the daytime these things would come up right before me, mostly about lovers, I guess."

This girl seemed to be rather a stolid type and not at all given to introspection. However, she made much of her mental content. Without going into details it may be said that her imagery was almost obsessional. The family had noted that frequently she would stand as if she did not know what was going on about her. She told us that at these times her mental representations had possession of her. The component parts of the imaginative scenes and actions were made up of what she had seen in moving pictures, what had been suggested to her by companions, and what she had actually dreamed. She was quite sure this was the main cause of her bad conduct.

Case 58. — John H. This was a particularly interesting boy of 13 years who lived in a suburban town. He had been truant, had run away from home, often stolen in petty ways, and had even broken into a store. These things had been going on for a couple of years. One police official was convinced that the boy was not right mentally because long ago the little fellow had told him there was something inside himself that said, " Go, go, go," and he had no power to control himself. The school people said that he was mischievous and restless, but felt that there was nothing the matter with him mentally. His father, a rather intelligent laborer, tells us that the boy is a tremendous problem. There had been a normal developmental history. Important defects in the family line were all denied. The boy had been going with bad companions for longer than he had been a delinquent himself. His depredations and excursions had been extensive. At one time he was found out in the country hunting, another time he had rented a room in a hotel in the city and was living there. Officers who know the boy say that he is quick and shrewd.

Our study revealed a boy without any noticeable physical defect. Tests show him to have fair ability, as the school people said. Except for his excitability and easily aroused temper no peculiarities were found. Our tests revealed no extraordinary powers of visual imagery. According to the boy's story he began to go with bad companions soon after the arrival of the family in this country, four years previously. He thinks his family are good to him, even though he does get whipped. " You see I do lots of times bad things. I think about stealing. Sometimes I dream about it. It 's nickel shows — that 's what made me — seeing about robbers. Nearly every show when I used to go with them fellows was about robbers. The funny part of the newspapers was about robbers. Some pictures come up in my mind about them. I can't remember them good though. One I remember was where three guys held together." The boy then went on and told a long story about a burglar who saw a little girl in bed when he had broken into the house, and the sight of her reformed him. That picture did not make him feel like stealing, but others do. " One was in a funny paper. I was just thinking about it that time when I was going in that store myself."

This boy in his broken English then told very dramatically a long rigmarole of the details in a series of pictures seen in the newspaper. Under observation he proved to be a great reader.

Case 59. — In this instance we had to do with a little boy of 12 who suffered from various pathological conditions. Poorly nourished. Mouth breather on account of some nasal obstruction. Defect in skull from a severe head injury — pulse visible where bone absent. In spite of his disadvantages we found him to be a decidedly bright boy who tells a charmingly naïve story of his own troubles. His delinquencies consist in stealing considerable sums, principally from relatives, and in running away from home. One would hardly believe such a small boy to be so planful and venturesome. Asking him why he did all this, we obtained a long story, many points in which were easily corroborated.

" When I wake up at night something bothers me. Something won't let me sleep. When I wake up this stops beating in my head and something starts back here (the boy points to the opposite pole of the cranium) that tells me to do something." The little lad says he has never stolen with other boys and never knew one that stole, and no one told him about these things. He has seen about cowboys and robberies in shows, and in the newspapers he has read about boys who· run away and steal, and he has bought and read some cheap literature on that order. " The trouble is something works in my head. Sometimes it is like somebody right in front of me making me take things. It makes me get up at night and take things." It is true that this boy used to wake up in the middle of the night, dress himself, steal, and run away. "The other night I could see pictures of shows, wicked pictures — fellows upsetting trains and like that. And then one dream comes nearly every night. Somebody falls out of a balloon and I always rescue them. They fall way out in the water. Sometimes I get money from them and maybe I run away with it and don't come back. When it is all spent I dream I come around the house again. I heard about robbing when my pa would come home and tell about robbers and thieves. He had seen it in the newspaper. I would listen to that and sometimes I would do the same thing."

Notwithstanding the obsessions, we did not obtain by our simple methods any evidence of the existence of clear and definite mental imagery. The boy maintained that he remembered some robber scenes which he had witnessed years before, but of course we could not corroborate. In testing later his memory of a picture reported on during our regular tests, he showed himself voluble, but quite inaccurate, and he accepted many suggestions.

Case 60. — A little boy of 8 years, physically quite normal and mentally precocious, a wistful and dramatic little chap, was discovered with a rope about his neck, just as he was going to jump off a porch. He had only been a year in this country. He was tired of living. He said that a little while before with another boy he had once planned to kill himself. The mother was dead, and the father having a hard time making a living for the children. The immediate cause of his present suicidal impulse was that he was lying on the floor when another boy jumped over him back and forth. In the old country there is a superstition that if this is done the person jumped over will never grow any more.

"I was tired for my life. That boy he did not think. I said myself what have I done. God, He don't like me. I never grow any more." "I started to hang myself. I saw it in moving pictures, in a show, in New York a year ago."

It seems that at this impressionable period, just after landing, this boy was taken to moving picture shows in New York. We asked for a description of just what he had seen there and in response obtained a most dramatic story of a suicide by hanging.

347

Accompanied by gestures, this little lad, who used good English considering his age and his short time in this country, gave an extraordinarily vivid account of those pictures seen long ago. They had been in his mind frequently ever since. He remembered them (he says he saw them) every night. The story was that of a poor fellow who killed a rich man for his money, and who then felt remorse, which grew upon him from day to day, until finally as he was walking along he saw a rope dangling from a tree. In this he made a noose and hanged himself. The appreciation of the feeling of remorse and of disgust with life on the part of our little boy was extraordinary. The climax was reached when he walked out on the porch of his house in a depressed mood, and saw a rope, which was used to haul up things with, swinging just as it had swung in the moving pictures.

Mental Imagery obsessive.	Case 60.
Pernicious Moving Pictures.	Boy, age 8.
Family conditions: Mother dead.	
Poverty.	
Recent immigration.	
Superstition: folk lore.	
Attempted suicide.	Mental ability: Supernormal.

Another boy who is much of a thief tells us that when he wants anything he has seen he keeps thinking about it, and "lays for it" until he gets a chance to steal it. This is also a boy with very defective vision. To what extent such mental content partakes of ideation rather than imagery we are unable to say.

The mental imagery developed during the mental idlenesses of prison life we may barely mention. An expert professional maintains that a great deal of the criminal's time is taken up with such mental processes. In numerous cases we have had intimation that one of the chief results of incarceration was the development of this side of mental life. One bright young man who came from an atrocious environment, and who had been already as a boy committed several times, maintains, "Whenever you have a chance to talk with the fellows in such places, it is always about what you 'll do when you get a chance on the outside." Evidently the reaction is that many a fellow feels himself delinquent among delinquents, and so proceeds to boast about his misdeeds, and build up more imagery and imagination centered on the same subject. We have little doubt but that psychologists might discover in this field facts which would prove of the greatest value for the development of a real science of penal treatment.

The necessities and possibilities of treatment of cases where mental imagery is obsessional or perniciously active we have attempted to connote all through this discussion. The need for understanding the facts and individualizing the treatment should be manifest.

§ 234. Criminalistic Mental Habit.

Quite in contradistinction to the many psychologists who have written on the ethical import of habit, students of criminalistic etiology strangely have paid little attention to mental habit as a driving force. Rarely one sees hints, as in Tarde's work (122, p. 266), that criminals may remain such because of habit formation, but we have found no elaboration of the subject. In police circles nothing is better recognized than the force of criminalistic habit, because of its intensely practical bearings. The well-known return of the offender to the old scene, to the old type of misdeed, to renewal of life with former companions; the engaging in prior occupations, the succumbing to temptations which previously won the day, are all evidences of deep-seated psychological laws.

Possibly the usual conception of the etiology of delinquency takes the fact of habit for granted and sees no need for specifically discussing it. If so, this suggests the old saying about not being able to see the forest for the trees. In reality criminalistic habit is so important that it should form a subject for prime consideration. In rendering a prognosis, logically based, as it should be, upon etiology, the possession and the susceptibility to anti-social mental and physical habits should be, whenever possible, taken into account. In our own case studies we, too, have often committed the sin of omission, and probably have undervalued estimation of habit by not enumerating it as a main causative factor. However, the subtle difficulties of getting at the mental insides of an individual, and knowing what part mental habit plays, preclude the matter from being proportionately or statistically treated. Of course, back of habit formation stand prior experiences; it is directly these, as well as personal peculiarities which may render formation of habits easy, that we have specially studied. In the result known as bad conduct, what proportion is the effect of the causative factors we enumerate, and what part is the effect of habit, it would always be difficult to say.

Other practical workers besides the police have a clear understanding of the power of habit in offenders. Perception of this psychological law is one of the foundations of real reformatory treatment. No one has seen this any better than Brockway (**333**, p. 27), who laid great stress on the effect of habit in producing crime and on the value of the formation of new habits for altering behavior tendencies.

Every one active in the field of criminalistics should be familiar with James' (**334**) famous chapter on habit. The bearings upon conduct are also forcefully elaborated by Angell (**335**): " The man who has been vicious all his life is hardly free to become virtuous, and the virtuous man is in a kind of bondage to righteousness. . . . No one can overestimate the ethical importance of habit." When it comes to evaluating the part which habit plays in conduct, as we have said, it depends on many personal and environmental conditions. Thorndyke (**336**, p. 205) says, " The likelihood that any mental state or act will occur in response to any situation is in proportion to the closeness of its inborn (instinct) connection therewith, to the frequency of the connection therewith, and to the amount of satisfaction resulting." In a broad generalization, for the sake of emphasizing the importance of habit formation, Yerkes (**284**, p. 401) states, " Something like one-third of our lives is instinct, as much is habit, and the remainder is in process of becoming the one or the other." All summed up, we may be sure that what James calls the habit-worn paths of association forms a very deep consideration for students of criminalistics.[1]

The phases of our investigation which seem to show most clearly the preponderating effect of mental habit, have been

[1] Knowledge of the fact and laws of habit-formation rests partly upon discoveries of the mechanisms of the nervous system, as well as on evidence drawn directly from the content and result of mental life. One can with correctness speak literally of paths worn in the nervous system so that the travel of impulses is easier than *via* other routes. The interesting attempt of Max Meyer (**337**) to formulate the principles of social science upon the laws of the functioning of the central nervous system brings in at many turns the result of groove-wearing or habit formation.

those concerned with the following phenomena, all of which are discussed elsewhere in this volume: Mental imagery; association with bad companions; the use of stimulants; the cultivated craving for exciting literature, for shows and adventure; the indulgence in sex habits; the development of certain definite attitudes of mind, such as that of grudge formation. But everywhere we see danger in generalization. Unquestionably certain types of individuals are much more prone to develop automatisms of conduct than are others. How to evaluate this fact for purposes of treatment is almost beyond us at present. One could conceive of vitally important studies along this line being carried out in reformatories for young individuals. All psychologists insist on the great advantages of dealing early with the habit formations. The general point for us to remember is that acts once done are, other things being equal, prone to be repeated.

If we were writing a work on treatment, all the considerations which center about habit formation perhaps would form one of our main theses. A vital question in handling offenders is how to induce such a new set of habitual reactions towards environmental conditions that the tendency shall not be towards misbehavior. Any one who is undertaking this should be acquainted with what psychological students of the subject have had to say about the most effective methods of procedure.

There is hardly necessity at this point for presenting from the case histories the isolated facts which have to do with mental habit. Certainly nearly all show the phenomenon in some way. The objective evidences of the influence of habit are multitudinous. The offender is sailing along smoothly until he meets a former companion in offense, and instantly both revert to contemplation of misdeeds — by force of quick renewal of old associations, mental habits. Another says, " I can't keep out of that place. Whenever I go down the street I just have to go in." One young man tells us, " All this is just a crazy habit of mine." A girl states that she simply can't keep away from such and such thoughts. And so it goes. Many illustrations of the effects of habit formation are either stated or intimated in our case histories.

351

CHAPTER X

MENTAL CONFLICTS AND REPRESSIONS

§ 235. General Statement.   § 236. Nature of Mental Conflicts.   § 237. Types of Delinquency which Ensue.   § 238. Success or Failure in Treatment. § 239. Our Material.   § 240. Causes of Mental Conflicts.   § 241. Illustrative Cases.

§ 235. **General Statement.** — The greatest interest and importance are to be attached to certain sharply out-standing facts in the realm of criminalistic genetics which are best discussed under the head of mental conflicts and repressions. That considerable subtlety of mental processes is uncovered by the concrete findings should not deter either students or practical workers; it is to be always remembered that when we deal with conduct we have in hand direct expression of mental life, and the recesses and mechanics of mental activity are more complex, subtle and profound than has ever been measured. In this chapter we are not indicating the necessity for examination of anything like the mental depths which professionally have been drawn upon for the relief of mental and nervous symptoms. Our subtleties are, after all, comparatively shallow, but the tremendous force and effect upon conduct of some of even these less deeply hidden mental states have only once to be witnessed to be unforgettably appreciated. We have gone very slowly, and waited for much demonstration in our own work, despite some apparently extraordinary assertions from European sources, before definitely reaching conclusions for ourselves, and as yet are only willing to state what concrete facts and practical outcomes have taught us. But this is enough to show that under the shadow of conflict in hidden mental life many a criminalistic tendency is born.

To assert that the sole cause of development of delinquent tendencies in the cases under the present category has always been the mental conflict, is beyond our intention. Undoubtedly the hypersensitive temperament, or the slight tendency to mental instability — adolescent or constitutional — or the minor defect in the realm of will or apperception, or a weakness in heredity, all

352

of which factors we have discovered in various cases, may be a predisposing cause. And yet most of the cases have shown an effect and a reaction which might well, "but for the grace of God," have been duplicated in many a one of us. Certain it is that some of the delinquents whom we have observed to be victims of this type of cause, have been those who in other ways have shown high characteristics, and that they have often struggled against what, to their inner view, was a worse form of delinquency than the one to which they gave way.

§ 236. **Nature of Mental Conflicts.** — A mental conflict presupposes, of course, some emotional disturbance, or else there would be no opposition between different elements of mental content or activity. Since nothing, by the innermost nature of animate beings, so stirs emotion as the affairs of sex life, taking this term in its broadest sense, it is to be presupposed that we should find most cases of mental conflict to be about hidden sex thoughts or imageries, and inner or environmental sex experiences. And so we have found it, but by no means all of our cases have had sex experiences themselves as an immediate basis of conflict. For the specialist I may say that the sufficiency of going only as far as this immediate basis, at least in many cases, is witnessed by successful outcomes. Our conscious limitations, as well as other important considerations for study of this type of case, we have discussed under Psychoanalysis, § 85, in our chapter on methods.

It is true that nearly all of the mental conflicts which have been brought to our attention in girls and young women have centered on unfortunate aspects of the sex problem, sometimes, to be sure, existing only as matters of conceptual mental activity. Considering the usual suppressed attitude in these matters, following what society, and perhaps nature, would seem to regard as the part of womankind, this is not to be wondered at. In the opposite sex, it may be oftenest this theme, but there are, nevertheless, many other immediate causes of mental conflict. There are questionings of parentage, and of position in the world, and experiences of treatment by those who are bound by family ties — all of which may cause unfortunate shock, and unconscious inner strife and reaction.

The obsessional mental imageries that sometimes overpower the will to do right, often cause much mental perturbation and conflict, as do certain other objective forms of human experience, but on account of their peculiar social bearings these causes are dwelt on elsewhere. Of course many of the points brought out in this section have social significance, for instance, the widespread and often morally fatal neglect of precautionary mental sanitation on the part of parents, who often leave children to struggle alone or amid bad companionship with vilest introductions to the most wonderful, vital, and emotion-producing phenomena of life. The concealment of family relationship, such as the child's actual parentage, and the temporary misrepresentative withholding of deep-striking facts from young individuals who eventually will learn the truth, we perceive also to be matters of great concern.

§ 237. **Types of Delinquency which Ensue.** — Many types of delinquencies, it will be noted, are committed by sufferers from these conflicts under consideration. The conflict about sex does not always lead to sex transgressions; indeed, one of our main theses concerning this whole subject is that there are substitution delinquencies. The individual gets relief, as it were, perhaps quite subconsciously, by entering into misdeeds which may seem altogether less reprehensible than gaining experience in the manner dwelt on inwardly. This fact comes out again and again in our case studies. A directly meaningful relationship has been suggested between the kind of delinquency, even of the given objects figuring in the delinquent act, and the content of the mental conflict, but we have found little in this for us scientifically, and for practical treatment of the cases nothing at all. Mental conflict as seen in our numerous cases may find expression in truancy, all sorts of stealing — the most exaggerated cases we have ever seen, sleeping out nights, running away from home entirely, display of great temper and insubordination, setting fires, and so on. To note the wide range of substitution or relief possibilities is of practical importance for interpretation and understanding. A curious feature of much of this conduct is the readiness with which trouble from it may be expected — actual suffering encountered by the offender is sometimes great, and yet delinquencies are repeated. Every case of delinquency showing repetition of such readily foreseeable suffering should be regarded as a proper subject for the most careful study.

The importance of mental conflict as a factor, often effective in individuals and careers otherwise normal, is easily seen from our case histories. This importance is simply that of any factor which gradually creates a criminalistic habit of mind; in the train of continued misdeeds come all the usual evils of pernicious habit formation, and also many of the social disadvantages which accrue through disapprobation expressed by other people. We can easily picture the steady growth from these beginnings of a whole long career of criminalism. The growth of a criminalistic tendency from mental conflict as a first nucleus seems especially prone to carry with it development of that peculiarly stubborn obstruction to reform which we have elsewhere mentioned, an anti-social, grudge-like attitude.

§ 238. **Success or Failure in Treatment.** — The success or failure of treatment in any one of these cases depends on several important considerations. No doubt the exploration, or bringing clearly to the offender's mind the innermost cause of his mistendencies, is the greatest single step towards a cure, but most often that is not enough. We know of failures — thoroughly predictable, however — after this exploration, as well as successes. Conditions must be right for the reconstruction of mental habits, and the path must be cleared as much as possible of material which awakens old associations. In young people, who cannot command their own environment, a vast deal depends on the intelligent coöperation of relatives. Unfortunately the matter is sometimes too deep for their poor understanding, and even after they learn the facts, little can be accomplished in the old environment. The joy of success, however, has resulted from sincere efforts of relatives in other cases.

§ 239. **Our Material.** — Out of the wealth of material from which we have learned our facts it is necessary to give space only to a few typical cases, but these are chosen as representative of the relationship of mental conflict to criminalism. There are many details in some of the cases which we are glad to spare as properly belonging only to technical medico-psychological discussion— the omissions will not dim the significance of the main facts. Some of our conflict cases have shown distinct hysterical phenomena — these types are treated under another head. The relationship of the childhood experience to the possible adult career may be readily appreciated in our case studies; some of our instances are, indeed, young adults, but the freshness and comparative ease of the findings in younger individuals leads us to dwell mostly on the latter.

§ 240. **Causes of Mental Conflicts.** — Hidden mental conflicts may rise, obviously, from any strong emotion-producing experience or thought which is repressed. We have previously dwelt, under the head of Psychoanalysis (§ 85), on the cardinal features of mental conflicts. Leaving out of account, as we have attempted everywhere to do, mere theoretical considerations, we find certain types of experience and of mental content to be of vast importance in the development of mental conflicts which lead to anti-social acts and attitudes.[1] Without in any way believing ourselves to exhaust the field by so doing, we may name the following main causes of mental conflict and repression as we have found them in the background of certain cases of criminality. Most of these causes are sufficiently illustrated by the cases we cite.

(a) Uncertainty, on the part of the child, concerning parentage, is a prolific source of deep-seated emotional disturbance, and, as we find the facts, the reaction may be towards a career of misdoing. The various forms of jealousy centered about a step-parent may also lead in the same direction.

(b) Deceit and lies on the part of those presumably most to be trusted, is another cause of deep emotional and moral upset.

(c) The various features of sex life, themselves the most emotion-provoking of all human experiences or aspects of mental life, naturally prove to be the most frequent cause of conflict. It is most important to note that very often it is not at all the early awakening of sex instincts themselves, or any physical sensation or activity that causes the trouble in childhood. It may be, rather, merely the mental representation of subjects shrouded in mystery, revelations of which have been gained from things seen or things heard. There may be a strong struggle against invitation from within or from without to express one's self in language or action as others do in these affairs. In such cases it is a universal rule that there has not been wholesome freedom of speech with those who ought to be confided in about these matters. The young individual has been left to gain its understanding and fight its battles alone, amid the silence of the world of authority on this most vital topic, which involves

[1] The rapidly growing literature on the subject of mental conflicts shows many indications of the relationship of the phenomena to criminalistic conduct. We have already noted, § 85, the main contributions; very little that has been written so far is specifically devoted to the origins of criminalism.

even the beginnings of life itself. The mysterious has great power to create strong impressions and strong reactions.

It seems from our findings as if normal curiosity on these vital topics once aroused is not to be thwarted except by unfortunate mental repressions that may loom large as causes of misbehavior. The peculiar attitude of modern civilization in covering up these things, on the one hand, and, through many aspects of our gregarious life, on the other hand, stimulating the curiosity as well as the instincts, constantly tends to incite this cause of conflict. Full appreciation of the varieties of these causes, and the manifold effects of such mental conflict, can only be obtained by careful study of pertinent case histories.

(d) Sensitive and fine natures may be thrown into much mental and moral perturbation by harsh treatment and false accusations on the part of those from whom affection and protection and guardianship is naturally expected. We have seen several cases of this kind.

(e) Deeply hidden emotions may be stirred to the point of unconsciously seeking reaction in misconduct through still other and less common causes. As instances we might give homesickness; [1] teasing on account of speech defect or lack of control of the bladder, with the consequent shame of being in company, whether at school or elsewhere; and so on. Sometimes the results are very serious, inasmuch as an extremely vindictive social attitude may be assumed.

§ 241. **Illustrative Cases. — Case 61.** — The beginnings of delinquency are most plainly laid bare in the instance of a 10-year-old boy, coming from unusually fine parents, both of them strong people both mentally and physically. This boy was brought up in an Eastern college town, and already, at his tender age, displayed most remarkable delinquent tendencies in the face of excellent opportunities for wholesome mental occupation and recreation at home and elsewhere.

Physically we found a strong healthy lad with no defect, and free from any observed abnormalities, including over-development. He was considered a strong and fearless leader in out-door

---

[1] For some reason, homesickness, with its vaguely defined, but upsetting symptomatology, appears to be a much more frequent cause of mental conflict in Europe than with us. An important contribution in German is by Jasper (**169**) on Homesickness and Criminality. Articles on the setting of fires, Martin (**170**) and Reichel (**171**), and on a case of poisoning, Feisenberger (**172**), as the result of homesickness, bring out special points. Wilmanns (**173**) has a paper on the relation of homesickness to impulsive insanity.

sports. He had a firm type of face, large under jaw, an unusual compression at times of lips that normally tended to protrude.

On the mental side he gave the good account of himself in our tests that we expected from his school record — readily doing with us what might be expected of a bright boy of his age, but hardly showing good scholarship for the 5th grade, in which he was. His achievements were not very rapid, but he did go smoothly through the tests, and by responses to our information questionnaire he gave evidence of a full range of healthy interests.

His development has been absolutely normal, indeed, unusually healthy. His ancestry is excellent, with one great-grandfather who showed a great love for frontier life, and one uncle much inclined to roving. The siblings of the boy himself were all most normal, physically and mentally, and there has been not the slightest moral difficulty with them.

The intelligent parents gave a detailed account of the delinquencies of their son, whom they felt to have the best kind of stuff in him, but whom they could not understand. There had been more or less trouble with him for a couple of years on account of various misdeeds, but for 6 months prior to our seeing him the difficulties had greatly increased. It was known that he steadily went with companions much older than himself. This was largely attributed to his physical prowess and mental advancement. He is a restless, active type; always affectionate and obedient when with his father or mother, but a few minutes after being scolded he would get into trouble again. Recently there had been a moderate amount of truancy. There was some lying about this and about other delinquencies, but the parents felt they generally were told the truth. They knew he occasionally indulged in profanity, that he engaged in quite a bit of stealing at home, where he took money out of pockets and purses and stole other things, and that he had also purloined various articles from stores. Worse than all to these affectionate parents was his running away. On one occasion he was out for two days and nights, sleeping in a railroad yard with other boys. It seemed very strange their boy should desire to undergo the hardships of tramp life, when his own home surroundings offered him many advantages for boyish pleasure and even for adventure.

As seen by us the boy proved to be quite cheerful, polite, and soon responsive, showing definite desire to coöperate with us in getting at the sources of his own troubles. This was notable in his quickly expressed desire that he might get out of his home town, even though in so doing he would have to break with his boon companions. We struck in at this point, and, after a little, elicited information altogether beyond his parents' ken. It seems the badness which they knew as characteristic of his companions was not the badness which he dwelt on. It was not at all the comradeship in adventure which drew him like a magnet, but was altogether a much deeper affair. A couple of years before this, these older boys had introduced him to the secrets of sex life, teaching him to do things to himself, which he has largely resisted, and engaging in bad sex affairs with him. Then, too, a number of older girls — the parents had spoken of there being a remarkably dissolute crowd of both sexes in the town — he had seen go with older boys into the woods, and he had followed and watched them. After very quietly unfolding the facts with us, he, evidently with a burst of bottled-up apperception, said this was the real trouble, and he had never told anybody. The secret affairs he had with these young toughs had led him to stealing money, tobacco, and supplies from stores for the company life they had maintained. He had played truant to join them. When he ran away he lived in a box car with them.

This boy's intelligent attitude led to the setting forth of mental conflict as a cause more quickly than in any other case we have seen. He explained to us how he dwelt on these affairs, how he revolved over in his mind by day or by night what the fellows had told him and what he had seen going on. He blushed and even cried a little in telling what inroads it had made upon the activities of his mind. The importance, the wonder, the culpable secrecy of it all had deeply impressed him.

It seemed easy enough for us to set down the prognosis and treatment. We stated that if this very convincing exploration of the trouble was completely followed up by these vigorous and intelligent parents there might well be success, and the definite psychic trauma which this boy had experienced might largely be obliterated. The parents should get completely into the confidence of the boy to a much fuller extent than I had attempted. They should remove him from the neighborhood and make every effort to fill his mind with the healthiest occupations and thoughts. This was what we set down.

The outcome, now after some years, can be told in a word. The advised measures were carried out, and the well-marked

criminal tendencies were so completely checked that the statement, made to us by the original complainants, was that the
boy had never again been delinquent.

One can feel pretty sure what would have been the outcome
of a case like the above without the discovery of the underlying
facts. With the growth of years, the sex practices, even with the
fight against them, and the tendency to repress the facts might
have grown much stronger, definite mental and physical habits
being formed about the old nucleus, and on top of all this a
criminal career might easily have been established.

Mental Conflict.	Case 61.
Early sex experiences.	Boy, 10 years.
Bad companions.	
Truancy.	
Runaway.	Mental:
Stealing.	Good ability.

In our citation of case histories we have largely refrained from
dealing with careers of long standing because we have desired to
keep close to beginnings, and to show what may be done by the
discovery of beginnings. The result of treatment of causes is
only fairly to be evaluated when the auxiliary results of habit
formation and social discouragement do not block the way.
The following summary of a very long case history may be offered, if there be any doubt that just such beginnings as are related
in the foregoing case often form the background of confirmed
criminal careers.

Case 62. — This story, much too long to detail here, concerns
a young man now serving a long term, whom we have known for
years, and in whose case we succeeded after long effort in analyzing
beginnings and causes of repetition of offenses. From our full
records we see that, except for defective vision, he could always
have been regarded as normal physically. We note, however,
that at the end of a previous two-year sentence he was in rather
poor condition, being anemic and flabby. At times his vision has
been corrected by glasses. In attitude and expression he has
become most unfortunately institutionalized.

Mentally, from our studies of him at various times, we have
never seen any reason to change our first opinion of him, namely,

that he was up to the ordinary for his social grade in ability and information, and showed no aberrational tendencies.

We have what is probably fairly accurate information about heredity. The father, a bright man mentally, was a hard drinker and sexually immoral. He caused the mother much sorrow. The paternal grandfather was alcoholic, as was also a paternal uncle. One maternal uncle drank rather hard. Other facts of heredity are apparently negative. Sisters and a brother of the offender are stable, hard-working people. The mother was much worried during this pregnancy on account of the father's drinking and immoral habits.

As an infant this boy had many childish diseases, and once was very low with cholera infantum. He had a fall and burn at 6 months which deeply affected the scalp, but there was never the slightest evidence there was concussion or other brain injury. After infancy his development was normal. At the present time he is a fairly well-developed man.

As a child of seven he was sent to a half-orphan asylum. He was taken home at nine years and then soon became delinquent. Since then he has been sent to reformatory institutions eight times. The trouble began with truancy and petty stealing. He has never been known to harm anybody, and the largest amount he ever obtained by stealing was probably $35. He has stolen money and many other articles. Sometimes the articles taken were of little or no use to him, and recently on parole he jeopardized his career by purloining the merest trifles. An account of all these thefts would be in itself a long story.

On analysis, we find his whole delinquent career began at the time he, green from the orphanage, was taken in hand by boys who proceeded to enlighten him in vicious sex matters, and teach him about stealing. Most remarkable it is that the life of this fellow gives every evidence that he has preserved a large share of his native modesty, and has never turned to sex immoralities. As, of course, most common in institutional life, he has fallen into self-abuse, which he so early learned about, but it is very remarkable that he has rejected opportunities for sex affairs with girls or women because, he says, he thought that doing such things was not right. He feels a strong respect for womankind.

The analysis of his frequent attacks, as it were, of stealing forms a most interesting study. Taking it, event by event, one finds there has always been at the center of each delinquent period or series of acts a subconscious mental conflict involving the young man's attitude towards sex questions. There has been, as he expresses it, a certain mental mix-up or confusion, and the facts show that some sort of relief or off-set has been unconsciously sought in the recourse to these minor delinquencies.

This marked reaction embodies as features: a feeling of recklessness, perhaps suddenly aroused; general bodily discomfort; on some occasions, local sex excitement; vague, but inhibitory perceptions of wrongfulness of illicit sex relationship; and a desire to rush out of the ordinary rules and conditions of life. The transferrence of feeling into impulse has never been thought of, as such. Thinking back into each eventful period, the young man digs out of memory his mental associations most clearly for us. The relationship of the two forms of delinquency emerges very sharply, and dates back to his earliest experiences with both, involving a well-forged set of mental mechanisms.

One illustration must suffice of how with him delinquency typically develops from a specific situation. One day as a wagon boy he is delivering goods. He drives past a restaurant where he sees in the window a young woman he knows. Ideas of her flood his mind, he grows terrifically restless and uncomfortable. He remembers that he thought he ought not to be thinking of her in this way. Confusion grows with him, and after a little he drives his horse into a byway, jumps down, ties it, and makes off down town. He spends that day and the next most of the $35 which he had collected for his employer. He goes to restaurants and theatres and a cheap hotel, but does not consort with women. Indeed, he assures us he has never done the latter in all his life. After a couple of days he returns to his mother very much ashamed. They together go to the employer who forgives him, and the fellow works faithfully for 3 months, paying back all but a couple of dollars, when another stealing affair, developing from the same sort of episode, lands him in jail.

Psychological interest centers around the girl in the affair. This young man, whom we can vouch for as being rather attractive, modest, clean, quiet and not dissipated, had known her for only a short time. She had evidently taken a fancy to him, and the night before when he had taken her home, had made up to him with kisses in the hall way. The sight of her set him all in conflict and confusion.

It does not take any deep discernment to realize the inadequacies of court and penal treatment in such a case. Their failure speaks for itself. The punishment doled out is most curiously out of all proportion to any harm done by the man, who lives a life of decency quite above the average of city toughs who do not get into jails. It is curious, too, to realize that if he followed his instincts, as many do, he might do a thousand times more harm to society than he has done, and yet probably little or no cognizance would be taken of his deeds. Scientifically, the origins of his whole career, and of the impulse to each discrete delinquency are of the utmost interest. They bespeak the possibility of practical treatment, at this late date, however, made more difficult by habit formation and the several untoward results of his being mishandled by society.

Mental Conflict.   Case 62.

    Developmental Conditions: Male, age 21.
        Many illnesses.

      Heredity: Father, alcoholic, immoral.
              Paternal grandfather, alcoholic.
              Paternal uncle, alcoholic.
              Maternal uncle, alcoholic.

        Injury: Head burn at 6 months.

      Physical: Very defective vision.

Stealing +.   Mental:
Earlier runaway.   Ability fair.

Case 63. — This is a case of most extravagant stealing on the part of a girl of 14, indulged in for three or four years. The stealing seemed to be almost a passion with her. We have observed this case over a number of years, and would at once freely confess it took us a year and a half to find out the nature of the trouble, in spite of much study in a considerable number of interviews. The girl lived in a suburban town, and was repeatedly brought to us by her parents before it was thought desirable to remove her from her environment. Her people were fairly well educated French Canadians, and kept a small shop. They were moderately prosperous, so that the girl was always well enough dressed, had ordinary educational advantages, and had no real need for the things which she purloined. Some significant incident in her family life led to her experiencing a distinct mental shock, as will be related below.

Physically we found a normally developed, well-nourished girl with pleasant features and good color. We noted her frank smile. Good strength. Some little complaint of headaches. Dental conditions: enamel defective on all incisors and cuspids, extending from a transverse line midway on the tooth to near the cutting edge. But the enamel for the most part is preserved on the cutting edge and no crescentic erosion is present. No evidence of nervousness, except excessive biting of the finger nails. No sensory defect detected.

On the mental side we soon found we had to deal with a normal child. She did some of the more difficult tests quickly and with slight errors. Not at all suggestible. Information on school topics quite normal. The record on tests seems unnecessary to give, because of the uniformly good performance. She was accustomed to playing children's games and seemed to have plenty of healthy mental interests. (In the succeeding years she has made her way through school in quite the usual manner and has developed very well physically.)

We have never learned of defective heredity in this case. The family are neat and clean, and of a good French type. Our information comes partly from the father and partly from the step-mother, who knew the own mother's family when they all lived in Montreal. There were two children by the first wife. The father is rather an easy-going type, somewhat complained of by the step-mother because he does not back her up in discipline and does not always stick to the hard facts in the case. The own mother died shortly after this child was born, suffering from a chronic illness, perhaps cancer. In fact, at the time of the birth the mother was in Paris undergoing treatment. The other child, a brother, is about three years older and has been the source of considerable trouble himself, and had to be sent away to an institution on account of delinquency. He later did better, and during the time we have known the family has shown himself to be an entirely reformed character.

Home conditions have been good, except for little bickerings about this girl's conduct, and except for certain unfortunate hidden influences which the brother and step-mother have had upon the girl. When first seen by us, the step-mother was still keeping up the farce of pretending to be the girl's own mother.

She had never told her anything to the contrary, and did not know whether the girl knew or not. Another fact that had complicated the situation, was that the brother had been left in Montreal with the grandparents, and this girl had never even been told she had a brother, until he suddenly appeared on the scene when she was about seven years of age. All this was done purposely so the girl might grow up in full affection for her supposed mother.

To give a catalog of the things stolen by this girl in these several years between ten and fourteen, would require considerable space. She had taken many things from home and from other relatives. She had taken books from the school and tried to sell them. She had stolen money and bought presents for other girls with it. She had stolen money from playmates, as well as skates, ribbons and many small things. She took from a store expensive jewelry which was later found on her person. On a number of occasions she spent money freely on her playmates, and nobody could find out whence it came. Her predilection in this direction can be well illustrated by something that took place when she was indirectly under our observation. She was placed in a certain home for trial, and purloined articles from here to take to her own home when she made a visit, and then took articles from her own home back to the other place. For a man of moderate means, her father had had to spend a considerable sum in making good the articles she had stolen, but often she had been so clever that no one knew from whom she had gotten her money.

At times with us the girl would say she was extremely sorry she had taken various things and would freely acknowledge the fact, and again, although all were just as certain of other things taken, she would indignantly deny the accusation, looking one straight in the face with tears in her eyes. At other interviews these perhaps earlier denied delinquencies would be acknowledged. Suspecting from the first that there was something peculiar in the case, we tried over and over again to get at the facts. Since the brother had been in the habit of stealing, it seemed to be clear to the step-mother's mind that it was a case of heredity, and it was alleged that the girl's own mother had been accused of taking things, but we found the step-mother really knew very little about this and the father nothing at all. Therefore we were never willing to put this down as a causative

365

factor. We readily found there had been considerable mental repression on the part of the girl because she had years ago heard from a cousin that her own mother was dead. The step-mother when approached on the subject foolishly denied it to her over and over. Then the brother substantiated the girl's belief, and she grew up to believe it as a sort of harmless lie, acknowledging the step-mother, on the whole, to be very good to her.

The girl always indignantly refused to admit to anybody that she had ever had anything more than the barest inkling of sex affairs, and so one never felt justified in attempting to get anything more than this information. The case from a scientific standpoint quite lapsed until the girl was placed in a certain unusually good environment and stopped her stealing. Then she was asked by us why she had stopped stealing, and to our astonishment she at once began to explore for us the true causative factors in her case.

Her naïve and unexpected first statement on this occasion was that she had stopped stealing because she did not hear any of the bad words in her new place that she did in her home neighborhood among the children. Then it gradually came out that she had never had an honest interview before with us. She definitely stated this, saying, " I did not know you wanted to know about these things." Just before this when asked if she yet understood what made her steal so excessively she reiterated the statement made to us many times previously, namely, she supposed she stole because her own mother stole. (Of course this was what she had heard by way of explanation from her stepmother.) As this girl's story unfolded we learned that her first knowledge of stealing came with a shock. One day her father said he was going to take her to the station to meet her brother, and she did not even know she had one. She wondered a great deal about him, and in some sort of way it made her feel very queer. They apparently became companions at once and she was with him one day when he stole doughnuts in a bakery, also when he stole other things, and was also with him one day when a policeman took him. She remembers he was very sneaking in these ways, that he used to run away from home, and she used to feel she could shame him, but now " it 's strange that he is the good one and can shame me."

She remarks that she is a girl who thinks before she speaks, that she has always " been to herself," and has never liked to talk about her own feelings and thoughts. It was about the time the brother was stealing that she first began to hear about sex things, and she says she was very inquisitive about these things, and asked many questions, and these ideas came up in her mind a great deal. But she repressed them, only once going to her mother about them. She heard more of these things day by day until she went to her present surroundings. She has heard so much about it that a great many " thoughts about boys and like that " came up in her mind. She has tried very hard not to think of these things, but they have come up quite often, perhaps not every day, and she always had to contend against it. It grew on her until she became quite nervous about it.

There can be but little doubt from her physical condition, her demeanor and her general reputation in the various homes in which we have known her, that she has kept her sex inclinations to herself, and that in all probability she has not engaged in bad habits to any extent, if at all. She explicitly denies it. The great interest in the case lies in the fact that she had her introduction to two delinquencies at the same time in her life. She has always felt herself to be at heart a nice girl, and says she has fought so hard against the one delinquency. She extravagantly gave way to the other, but now has been able to conquer her tendency to stealing in an environment which decreased unwholesome sex suggestions. It is of the utmost interest to know that in spite of our long failure to learn causes this girl finally did introspect for us, showing an example of self-exploration and self-understanding. The result of breaking up old mental association processes has been a complete cessation, now for two years, of her most extraordinary indulgence in stealing.

Mental conflict.	Case 63.
Parental mismanagement.	Girl, 14 years.
Developmental conditions: During antenatal period mother chronic mortal illness.	
Stealing + +.	Mental: Fair ability.

Case 64. — This case in its naïve expression of substitution phenomena is highly instructive. It concerns a boy 13 years old.

367

On the physical side we find him to be rather poorly developed and nourished. Weight 90 lbs. Height, 4 ft. 11 in. Nice-looking boy with regular pleasant features and responsive normal expression. Has decidedly defective vision in one eye, but in the other vision is normal. No other findings of importance.

On the mental side it was easy to find he was well up to the ordinary in ability, and that his talents were considerably ahead of his social advantages. From the tests and his own account it was plain there had been little adaption of his school work to the needs of a bright boy. On account of changing from country to city schools, he was still only in 5th grade. No aberrant tendencies were noted in any way. The tests were done uniformly well, although not with great brilliancy. His conversation was thoroughly coherent.

Both father and mother are dead. The history obtained from relatives is, that there was a very alcoholic father, a man who never seemed to realize the seriousness of his own actions. These intelligent people are sure there has been no insanity, epilepsy, or feeblemindedness on either side. During pregnancy the mother is said to have been much worried because of the drinking of the husband, and is said to have been actually in want. The relatives make a good deal of the fact that at different times she used to take little things for herself from their house — a very natural proceeding, it would seem, after all, considering her straits. The developmental history, as far as known, is absolutely negative. These people, who have always been in more or less intimate connection with the family, have never heard of any severe illness, injury or convulsions. There is a normal sister who has given no trouble.

The delinquencies have been centered about excessive stealing, most of which has been done in his own home. There was some complaint in school, but only on account of mischief and poor attention. Lying has only been in regard to stealing. At times he is very penitent for what he has done.

We found a very frank and pleasant boy, who seemed in a normal boyish fashion not to be given at all to introspection, and not at all conscious of the connecting links of his career. On inquiry it seems that practically all his stealing is connected with the idea of bartering and trading. (His relatives told of his taking articles of jewelry and all sorts of things which he gives away or sells for small sums of money, sometimes receiving

only a small amount of candy for them. He has never taken money
except in small sums.)   He at once says, " It 's that crazy idea of
trading that I 've got."

Attempting to trace back this idea of trading leads us to important discoveries. It appears that some 3 or 4 years ago when
they lived in a rural community, and he was of course a very
young boy, the older fellows engaged very extensively in bartering and selling among themselves, but he was too young to engage much in this. On one occasion he had an old watch which
he bartered, but that was practically the only thing. However,
these boys out there were accustomed to engage in pernicious
practices and initiated the little boys, as they called it. " Nobody ever told me bad things before, and there everybody did.
They were big boys. Most every other word they said was bad.
They did it once to me. Sure, I wondered, and I said bad words,
too, when I got mad. They would tell stories about bad things.
It comes up in my mind. I never saw any bad pictures, and
never read anything bad, and there were no bad girls. When I
first came here to Chicago, I was thinking about the boys out
there. Yes, they got me to do bad things, but I quit when I
came to Chicago. I did not take things at the farm — no money
or jewelry — nothing except the old watch."

" Now it 's temptation or something. I just think about it.
Afterwards I feel sorry. If I see it, and it looks as if I could get
hold of it, I just take it. Give it to the other boys sometimes.
Took money, the most at one time was 25 cents. Took jewelry
and gave it to a boy. Would ask him what he would give for it.
Maybe he would give a dime or so. Would spend it on candy.
Went to nickel shows hardly at all."

" I hardly ever think about these bad things any more. Never
think about them when I take things. I guess it has got to be a
habit. Took little things at first. Thought it was no harm —
took apples maybe. Felt as if I wanted to steal, and when I
got the opportunity would take things if I could. I 've most
stopped doing these things the kids showed me out in the country.
I think I just about have stopped."

" I think it 's all because I got that trading idea out there. The
kids would bring things and say, ' What 'll you give me for it? '
They would bring a watch chain and a few other things. It was
the same kids that taught me other things. I think that 's what 's
the trouble. It 's like trading. The kids here talk bad stories

369

like the other kids did. I never did anything bad with them. Have no temptation to do it except when one crazy boy comes jumping around."

When seen again the boy gave still clearer evidence of the strange connection of this stealing with trading and sex practices. The boys who first taught him bad sex things and practiced bad sex things with him were the boys who had the trading habit, and bartered or sold small articles. Now he takes things from home and, in the same manner as these older boys used to do, trades with the fellows in the neighborhood who do talk about bad sex things, but have not done them with him. In the meantime he is conquering these bad habits. The situation used to be; sex affairs with boys who bartered and traded; now it involves his bartering and trading with boys who merely suggest sex affairs.

It was later learned that no interest had ever been taken by these distant relatives in the inner thoughts of this boy, and that they were not in the least aware of his sex troubles — they merely saw the obvious thing, namely, the stealing. Even now, with a better outlook predictable, they refused to keep him longer. For about a year the boy has been getting along all right in a new home.

Mental conflict.	Case 64.
Early sex teaching.	Boy, 13 years.
Bad companions.	
Educational disadvantages.	
Physical conditions:	
Defective vision in one eye.	
Development:	
Antenatal conditions bad.	
Incorrigible in school.	Mental:
Stealing +.	Fair ability.

Case 65. — A girl of German parentage, who when first seen was a little over 10, for two years had been engaged in much petty stealing. She had taken money and other things, not only from her parents on repeated occasions, but also money and jewelry from neighbors, and various things from school. She had already stolen in two schools, and been expelled. In spite of much threatening of police, and reform school, and some whipping, and having been given money regularly to spend, there had been no improvement. She was said to be strong-willed, but not quick-tempered, and to lie only in the matter of stealing. Her parents, who are typical, honest Germans of the artizan class, were at their wit's end.

On the physical side we find her to be in good general condition. There is nothing special to be noted except slight asymmetry of chest.

On the mental side the girl is well up to the ordinary in ability and information. The tests were all well done for her age, and her information was much more extended than we expected, until we learned it was a family accustomed to good reading and good conversation. The result on school work was normal, indeed her reputation for scholarship was good.

There was nothing significant about the ancestry. The father is a quiet, religious man, and the mother is somewhat high-tempered, but there was nothing else of significance learned. During her infancy this child was very sickly, and long in a hospital with pneumonia, measles, whooping cough and other children's diseases. On account of these she was two years old before she walked, but she began to talk well before that time. No enuresis or evidence of any other physical trouble when we saw her.

Nothing in any way explanatory of this girl's persistent stealing at first could be obtained. She is cleanly and extremely modest, avoids vulgarity most carefully, is not quick-tempered, likes picture shows in a normal way. She has a good voice, and enjoys singing. She is very affectionate to parents. She learns games quickly and enjoys them — in all ways seems to be a normal, and very bright little girl.

In an attempt, after a couple of first interviews which brought forth nothing, to get at the genesis of her stealing, very interesting situations came to light. It seems that where the family lived two years previously she had for a playmate a little boy. She spoke of him with some vehemence, and after considerable inquiry said that this boy long ago told her a lot of sex things which she has never well understood, but which have been excessively in her mind ever since. "That was a boy across the street in X, who was not a good boy, but when a fellow comes over you have to treat him nice. He swore before me and said awful ugly

371

words. Papa threw a stick at him once. He started me on the road to saying bad words." (The latter statement was especially interesting since the parents had previously asserted she was very modest and would never say even such words of slang as were commonly indulged in by little girls.)

" He never did anything bad to me. He 's awful vulgar and says bad things. I 've never said bad words to other people, but I can't help thinking the words he said. He got me all mixed up. I told mama about it once, that he was not a nice boy, but that 's about all I ever said. His father did not support the family, and used to just lie around. He told me bad things, or hinted them to me, and mama told me never to listen to bad things."

When asked whom she first knew that stole things she says, " He 's taken many things of mine. I think that 's what started me. And then up here I know a girl, and a boy goes with her, and he told her a lot of bad things and she came and told me about them right along. Oh, they are things I would not say. These things come up in my mind often. Well, when I 'm in school and have that headache I told you about, and sometimes at night, and then I get all mixed up. They told me many bad things like that, but when I think of them I just start away and go away and that 's the only way I can get away from them. When these things come up I forget all I 'm doing and get upset and then sometimes I take things."

She assures us her papa and mama are good to her, and then tells us how she would like a chain for her neck, even if it were not a silver one, but would like one that looked like silver. She then goes on with her story, and says nobody ever actually taught her to do really bad sex things, and she does not do them, but it is just the idea of these things that worries her. She repeats a little piece of obscene poetry that she says comes up in her mind. The rest of the story all hinges on the same point. " These things come up to me when I am in school, and I can't study well. I got all mixed up at P. school, too." (This was the school where she stole.)

Corroboration was readily obtained from the parents in regard to her boy friend and the character of his family, and also that it was just when they came away from there that she began to steal. It was very hard for these intelligent parents to believe their little girl could be thinking of sex things when her demeanor was so exceptionally calculated to make them believe she was entirely innocent, as they thought. They knew she was modest even to the extent of her not wishing any one to see her take her bath. However, they fell quite in line and agreed to explore the whole situation still farther.

The outcome of this case has proved the point, for from the time of this first exploration of the trouble there has been in the following three years a complete cessation of her old stealing. The good mother took up the question of sex teaching with her child, and found all the story to be true. Then with exploration and much reconstructive work, keeping the girl's mind active in school and at home, there has been full measure of success. The child has developed well mentally, morally and physically.

No better example of mental conflict causing delinquency could be found. There was the substitution of one form of misconduct for another; the repressed type being the one really dwelled on and obsessional, but considered as altogether too bad to be engaged in.

Mental conflict.	Case 65.
Bad companions.	Girl, 10 years.
	Mental:
Stealing + +.	Good ability.

Case 66. — In another case, strikingly similar to the above, with the exception that the girl was brought up by misguided relatives who denied her help when she asked for it, remarkable evidence of the association of ideas was obtained. The dynamic quality of the associations centering about the companion who taught both stealing and the strange, new facts of sex life, is obvious in the following excerpt from the offender's statement given when an analysis was attempted of what led up to the most recent occasion of stealing.

" I was thinking about those words when I took the money from my teacher. My teacher was putting on her hat, school was over. There was just three girls with me. I had been thinking those words. Sometimes when I 'm eating I think about Sam and I think I hear him saying those words. It was in the afternoon — we was having reading at 3 o'clock — we was reading about a little boy and it said Sam, and it came up in my mind about Sam S. and the words he said."

373

Mental conflict.	Case 66.
Bad companions.	Girl, 12 years.
Lack parental understanding.	
Mother dead, ignorant grandmother.	
	Mental:
Stealing + +.	Good ability.

These histories should conclusively demonstrate a certain type of beginnings. If desirable we could add many data about longer careers of *pathological stealing*, so-called *kleptomania;*[1] perhaps one short summary, however, of a study of an older person will be sufficient here.

Case 67. — A young woman discovered in a series of thefts was considered to be a case fit for study, rather than for handling through the courts. After consulting with the family physician, a considerable analysis was made of her career. On account of her brilliant mental attainments, her present frank regard of herself as a problem to be solved, and a curious autobiographical caprice, which had long possessed her, the case was most satisfactory and interesting to study. It turned out that the thieving just then under consideration was a mere incident in a long career of stealing. Perhaps hundreds of articles and many small sums of money had been taken from home, shops, school and other places. Some of the things were desired and were used, other things were taken without thought of any possible value.

On one occasion she had taken, she told us, a mathematical text book for which she had no conceivable use, and after walking around the block she replaced it in the large book store from whence it came. At times perfect orgies of stealing were engaged in, and the articles taken were recorded carefully. It is a tribute to this woman's powers that she always managed to evade detection.

The long-kept diaries, partly in cryptogram, we were fortunate enough to be allowed to read. They were replete with self-denunciation and vows for the future. Stolen articles were sometimes enumerated with the idea of paying back the values, and indeed we learned that this young woman had on occasions worked

---

[1] The form of excessive stealing which is loosely termed kleptomania is discussed properly in another place, § 366. Many, but by no means all, among those who have a passion or special impulse to steal are the subjects of hidden mental conflict, as dealt with in the present chapter.

hard for months at a time to get funds, which she sent anonymously to various business firms as conscience money. We
learned that after a quiescent period of months there might occur
outbursts of stealing. These were accompanied at least once or
twice with a short running away from home — under pretense
of going to friends, she would sleep somewhere out of doors. All
of this was evidently, at least sometimes, followed by a keen
sense of relief or even of peace, and later by attempts to repair the
damage done.

There had been markedly good health all through her life,
with considerable over-development earlier in adolescence.
Much was made of the relation of the impetuous outbreaks to
menstrual or pre-menstrual periods, but on closer observation
it was found that the two were not always synchronous. Development during infancy and childhood was probably quite
normal. The only fault we know of in heredity is the father's
sex immorality, a fact our patient has been acquainted with
from early years. Her brothers and sisters have turned out
well, both mentally and physically.

There were many indications in this case of deep-rooted mental
conflict, strongest proof of all being in the year-long records
kept by herself of her own struggles. An early awakening of
sex impulses was accompanied by early experiences with stealing
as a hazardous and not unpleasant adventure. Later there was
sublimation of sex feelings into Platonic friendships, with only
occasional thieving. Still later there had been a reawakening of
vigorous sex instincts, a definite straightforward fight against
them, and the extraordinary outbreaks of stealing which we have
mentioned. Such is the shortest possible summary of this case.
With the establishment of the marriage relationship the impulse
to steal has been quite overcome now for a considerable period.

Mental conflict.

    Physical conditions:
        early over-development,
        early awakening sex impulses.

      Poor home control: an orphan.

        Heredity: Father immoral.

Stealing excessive.
Runaway.

Case 67.
Woman, age 20.

Mental:
High abilities.

375

Possibility of the development of an extreme anti-social attitude and a most peculiar frame of mind as the result of a hidden mental conflict is remarkably witnessed to by the following two cases.

Case 68. — Some three years ago I was asked to study a case by the judge of one of the smaller juvenile courts, a case which had proved remarkably recalcitrant, and baffling to understand. Coming and going through their city I had ample opportunity to see this boy of 12 years many times and to get well acquainted with his unusually pleasant mother, who regarded her boy as a desperate problem. That the case so far has been a failure has its lesson for us, equally with those in which there has been more success. As an example of extensive grudge formation and development of anti-social feeling at an early age, the study of this case is most illuminating. We have studied the same phenomena in older individuals, but nowhere have we found such direct proof of the peculiar and largely preventable beginnings which there may be in the background.

We saw at once that the opinion of the judge was correct — here was a most peculiar lad, so far as his attitude towards the world was concerned. According to his notion, nobody was his friend, and the very kindliest advances were repulsed by him. This judge is a man who can reach a boy if anybody can, and his court admits of much personal touch with offenders, but he acknowledged himself an utter failure. We, too, had the same opinion of our efforts even after several interviews, and no real understanding of the case was had, in spite of voluminous records of facts, until several months afterwards when we visited him in a certain reformatory institution, and we were able for the first time to get at the foundations of his attitude.

This boy was born in Germany and we found him to be a typical blond Teuton. Complete examination showed only the following peculiarities. Poorly developed for his age. Weight 75 lbs. Height 4 ft. 7 in. One tonsil much enlarged. No sensory defect. Slight phimosis which was soon afterward relieved by circumcision. Well-shaped head. Teeth crowded, with little room for those yet to be erupted. Eyes bright. Moderate biting of finger nails. Strength fair and good expansion of chest. His expression was remarkable; not exactly stubborn and defiant, with the attitude of the bad boy of the street, but rather blasé, and altogether firm. With his small features, pug nose,

376

and firmly compressed straight mouth, he made a marked picture.

Our study of the character of this boy has continued at intervals over a long period. At the time when first asked to give an opinion we had not succeeded in getting him to do the tests — his being the only case in which they have not invoked interest. He assumed a listless attitude, indifferently worked at this or that, and finally said he could not do it. When later he was asked why he failed, he said he had not tried hard enough. This attitude was characteristic. He had only advanced to the 4th grade, and yet the feeling of his teachers was that this was due to perversity rather than lack of ability.

From his mother and teachers we heard accounts of his school life which, as his mother suggested, made one very sorry for his teachers. He had been unwilling to make effort to learn, and had interfered much with the teaching of others. He had even struck some of his teachers. There had been much changing about from school to school. A teacher experienced in the treatment of offenders, who had him in charge when we first saw him, gave me an enlightening account of his attitude. She gave him a simple problem in arithmetic and he said he could not do it. She told him to try. He did it wrong and she told him so, and then he went over it some four times, showing it to her each time. On each occasion he purposely copied it wrong, so as never to do correctly her original example. At the same time when I asked him his age he said he was 13, then later said he was born in 1900. When I called his attention to the discrepancy, he shrugged his shoulders and showed sullenness. When I again kindly inquired he said, " I 'm 12. I 'm 11. I 'm 6." It was at this time that two other experienced observers of boys informed me that they felt very certain the boy was not right in his mind. They gave as reasons his persistent anti-social attitude, his lying, bad behavior, and particularly the amount of trouble he got himself into as the result of his assumed point of view.

The woman officer of the court, a most kindly personage, told us this was the only case in which she, as well as the judge, had utterly failed, and that the boy's whole attitude and behavior were the most remarkable thing she had ever heard of. My impression from the start was that his frame of mind with its stubborn recalcitrancy, instead of boyish defiance, was a very similar attitude to what one has frequently observed in adult confirmed offenders. Although the general opinion was that the boy was insane, we could not find any typical symptoms of psychosis.

In the endeavor to break through his marked attitude in the several interviews which we had in this first period, we noted it was almost impossible to get him to drop for even a few minutes his pose of perversity. The teacher at our request talked to him about his very sweet little mother, and how she felt he was almost sending her crazy by his actions. He merely tossed his head with indifference. Never were we able to get out of him the slightest show of sorrow. He grew neither angry nor sad. Let alone in the school-room directly after a demonstration of bad behavior, he took to reading a book and became thoroughly absorbed, and later in industrial work he made a very pretty cardboard house.

Before we stopped our first efforts we had ascertained from him that he conceived the whole world to be doing him an injustice. He was being railroaded through court, his mother did not treat him right, the judge was a good enough man, but nevertheless the court simply sent boys away without caring for them in the least. It was true he had stolen on numerous occasions and run away and so on, but he had good reason to — he was so badly treated. His mother wants to put him away for his life-time. He wants to live with his grandmother. We knew that he had previously told a lot of lies to the authorities, some of which had given considerable trouble, particularly when he said he had just come from relatives where they had scarlet fever, and that he himself felt sick with sore throat and so on. He insisted on the truth of this to me, although it had been found to be absolutely untrue. He said there was no use talking to him, because the court had made up its mind to put him away, and had done so from the start — the only thing anybody could do for him was to let him go free, that's all he wanted. He willingly acknowledged he had stolen from these very relatives to whom he said he wanted to go. He seemed to think no one should have any idea of disciplining or chiding him for anything he had ever done.

At this time and later he wrote elaborate letters, telling of many delinquencies which were not known to the authorities, although most of them his mother said were true enough, and endeavoring evidently to make himself out as bad a boy as he really was. Sometimes in his letters he said he hoped to go home and have a chance to be a better boy, but in general there was very slight indication of any intention or promise to change in any way his career.

The story of the very intelligent mother was told at great length at this time. She had conjectured all sorts of possibilities in explanation of his remarkable behavior, which had grieved her so terribly. She is a fairly well-educated, self-supporting, German woman. Her husband died two years previously, leaving her with three children. She knew her husband's family well. She is absolutely positive there is no insanity, feeblemindedness, or epilepsy on either side. Her husband was a perfectly healthy man. He was a moderate user of beer, but he was never intoxicated. He was employed for nine years in a responsible position as an engineer up to the time of his death, they having just previously immigrated. He died of pneumonia. The two eldest childen alive were born in the old country. The mother is 40 years of age, and had eight children and one miscarriage. The eldest is alive — a very bright boy who graduated from grammar school before he was 12 years of age. Later he went to high school, and always did well. He is a stable character. Then came a still-birth, then a premature child, then our boy, Victor, then three children who lived only a few minutes, then a miscarriage, and then the third living child, now four years of age, who is healthy. All the seven children born at full term were taken with instruments. The eldest boy had convulsions when teething, the youngest when he had bowel trouble, but Victor never had any. During the pregnancy with Victor the mother was healthy, but much worried because the paternal grandfather had been involved in some trouble in the old country, having done something dishonest, and had come over to them. He was not in the least a regular criminal, but she was much worried and has often wondered if this did not affect her boy. The birth was particularly severe. The head was badly marked from pressure but soon got over it. He walked at nine months. He began baby talk at that time, but did not speak so that people outside the family could understand him until he was six years old. When first started at school he was sent home on this account, but by seven he had become a fluent talker. He has never had any illness at all except through accidents. He once fell off a wagon and broke his arm in a couple of places, and hurt his foot. He recovered without trouble. At another time he fell

379

off the porch and remained practically unconscious all day long from concussion — there were no bruises or cuts or any sign of permanent injury.

They never had much trouble with Victor until he was about 10 years old, about the time his father died. Since then he is like a wild and reckless animal. Previously he had made one grade a year. The family have shown the utmost patience with him, but his misdeeds have been a terrible list. He has stolen the prized belongings of his dead father and sold them. He has been a great truant in spite of much effort to prevent this. He goes away some distance on the street cars, and sometimes is gone as many as three nights at a time. Many times he has gotten money in small amounts by misrepresentation. He has gone to the neighbors and borrowed money to get medicine for an alleged sick baby. There is no end of the stories he has told—they often contain terrible details and have injured the mother's reputation. He has recently taken to smoking. He is perfectly wild for coffee — wants three or four cups for breakfast. He sits and sips it, and when his mother is away he will make it for himself. He has a most peculiar appetite. For instance, he will buy a quantity of biscuits or cake, and sit out of doors, eat what he wants and throw the rest away. The mother has been at much expense for goods he has obtained at stores by misrepresentation. She had him at one institution, but they did not want to keep him and would not do so unless she would pay more than she could afford. The boy is rather boastful about wrong things he has done. The mother has never observed any bad sex habits although she has had these in mind. As far as known, there are no bad girls in the neighborhood, but there is one family of bad boys with whom Victor has associated in the past. Mother observes that pitying him, the thing she is inclined to do, is the worst thing for him, yet she has not succeeded by disciplining him, nor has the eldest brother. Victor has done the most heartless things. For instance, he has stolen the dearest belongings of an orphan girl, relics of her parents, and buried them in a pile of sand. Some of his stealing shows tremendous recklessness. He took a valuable bicycle and in a short time sold it for thirty-five cents.

He does not seem, whether at home or in the school-room, at all like other children. All he seems to care for is a place to eat and sleep. He never plays a game at home, although there are many. He never touches any of the family books. Never looks at pictures. When other boys and girls sing he never joins in with them. Does not even read the funny pictures in the news-papers. No one ever succeeded in making a friend or confidant of him. They have a very kindly family physician who has taken the boy on rides, given him money, and tried to win him, but when his back is turned Victor scornfully laughs at the overtures. In one of his letters he boasted of having kicked a teacher in the stomach and made her faint. He never wants to go to a matinée or a picnic when invited with other children. Has rejected many offers for normal fun.

After going as far as this we said we could not give a fair diagnosis nor prognosis. Although the biological and possible causative factors seem to stand out so clearly, we felt there might be much else that could account for his mental bias, and we still felt we did not thoroughly understand the case and could give no opinion either in regard to native ability or aberrational tendencies.

In the succeeding months other opportunities came for gaining further information. He was placed in a reformatory institution where we later saw him. After he had been there several months a special trip was made to study this important case. We im-pressed this fact on the boy and it rather seemed to be an opening wedge into his good will. His behavior there had been quite indifferent and he had had many demerits for various sorts of recalcitrancy. He was now more or less willing to coöperate with us on tests, although we felt at times that curious inhibitions were at work preventing him from doing his best. The findings were as follows:

Our own series:
On the Binet 12-year-old test the only failure is that he cannot give a definition of the word charity nor of justice, although he has some inkling of what they mean.
III. Done in 30″ with 9 moves.
IV. Done in 35″ with 11 moves — the minimum number of moves.
V. Worked entirely by trial and error method, pulling a little at this and a little at that, and not following up any step even when he had done it. He made no study of the problem, although he was told to do so, but even by his blundering method he succeeded in 3′.
VI. 10 items on free recital with a moderately good record on cross-examination. Only one, unimportant, suggestion out of 6 was accepted.
VII. Correct.

VIII. Only one error on reproduction and this he recognized as an error, but strangely enough did not work by the process of elimination to get the only left over number in its place.

IX. Correct at first trial. (It is instructive to note that this simple test was entirely failed on at a previous séance, the boy maintained he could not understand it.)

X. Correct at first trial.

XI. This rather difficult test he did as far as writing the first word in symbols, with only one error, and then insisted on giving up because it was too hard — a strange performance, showing still some disinclination to fall in with what was requested of him.

XII. The standard test in this case was not used on account of his poor reading ability. A test with simpler words was done very well with a correct sequence of ideas remembered.

XIII. Only 6 items out of the 12 given correctly and with some little variation in the meaning. One felt very distinctly by the result the boy was not trying.

XIV. Done correctly only at the fourth trial. Very poor performance and even then, on account of the difficulties with the fine work, he required much encouragement.

XVII. Writes a very immature hand even for his age. Spells most words correctly. He has been a good deal of a letter writer, and his composition, while childlike, is not altogether bad.

XVIII. Never even learned the multiplication tables. Is very careless in his addition.

XIX. Reads simple passages all right, but his knowledge of the longer words is very poor.

XXII. Reads neither books nor newspapers. Knows almost nothing in history. Knows the ordinary sporting events of the day. Knows the simplest of ideas about scientific things, but not much else.

The boy seemed much pleased when he did tests quickly and correctly, but showed himself to have little continuity of purpose. When he was seen this time, he was showing much more cheerfulness than he had manifested before, and was even willing to smile a little. We diagnosed his ability as fair, although even then he was not doing well at the school in the institution. We felt, however, there was an element of mental dullness from possibly other causes than his excessive coffee drinking and recent smoking, and his story later showed this to be the fact.

When we saw him at the institution he was willing for the first time to give us some account of his own feelings towards the world and how he happened to have them. He told of his own bad behavior and demerits in the institution. He spoke in a very low voice, but showed willing and pleasant responsiveness. Was biting his finger nails a great deal. Asked about the beginnings of his stealing, he gave us a story about neighbor boys whom he used to know when he was seven or eight years old. They told him much about thieving, and got him definitely into the way of stealing. I said to him that although he had proved such a difficult problem people really were interested in him and in evidence of this I had come a long distance to see him. He at once plunged into the sex question. He said the boys who first taught him stealing were the ones who told him the other things that had been coming up in his mind ever since. He gave a very vivid account of how by night and day their teachings had been with him, and how he had never given way to doing the worst things they had taught him, but had been engaged in sex habits by himself. He insists his sex troubles bothered him every night before he went to sleep or when he waked up. He was particularly bitter about the case of a little girl, which he told to us. She had never said anything bad to him, nor had he ever seen her do anything bad, and he always supposed she was a nice girl. Later he came to know she did bad things with other boys. He has thought a good deal about this ever since. Sometimes he wakes up and thinks about it, sometimes he dreams about it, and dreams he was the one doing bad with her. States that in school hours it frequently came to his mind what these boys told him. Finally got around to telling us he had really been indulging in sex practices frequently for a long time and doing it sometimes quite excessively. His mother never said anything to him about it. He seemed to think very definitely that this is the entire trouble with him, and when seen at a second interview, he again reiterated the whole point.

It is interesting to note the boy's appearance did not particularly suggest his habits, and that no one had suspected them heretofore. The boy gave some account of how secretive he had been in the matter. As seen at the institution for the first time tears came to his eyes and as I left he gave me a good clasp of the hand, the first bit of friendly feeling I had ever heard of his exhibiting toward any one. At this time it seemed the boy really wanted to change, and felt he had expressed the real nature of his trouble. It seemed without any question to be a case of mental conflict in which the temptation to the worst type of delinquency, namely, sex perversion and indulgence with girls, had been steadily resisted, and that lesser misdeeds learned at the same time, namely, self abuse and stealing had been freely indulged in. He emphasized the point of how the boys had tried to lead him into sex perversion, but he always fought them off.

383

We have every reason to believe this is true because his record at the institution, both at this time and later, does not contain the slightest evidence of any tendency in this direction.

There is little more that needs to be said in this case. As elsewhere stated, reconstructive measures in such an instance is necessary. The mother has never taken hold of the matter in spite of our request for her to do so — she has never been willing to take the trip to find out in detail what is necessary for understanding and treatment of such a case. In the interval since we first saw him the boy has been in and out of institutions. Since then he has had an admirable record in them. He is well liked by others and works up to positions of responsibility. But when tried at home the effect of old associations has been altogether too much for him, especially since no parental aid to self-restraint has been given. At each trial he has resumed stealing and other delinquencies, then has been sent back to institutional life, and at present is in an industrial school for boys.

Mental conflict.   Case 68.
   Early sex experiences.   Boy, age 12.
      Bad companions.
         Bad sex habits and fight against them.
            Developmental:
               Antenatal? Mother much worrying.
               Natal: difficult birth.
            Physical: Impacted teeth? Phimosis.
               Poor development.
Truancy.   **Stimulants** + Coffee. Tobacco.
Runaway.
Stealing +.   Mental:
Misrepresentations.   Fair ability.

Case 69. — This is the case of a little girl of 10 who repeatedly both stole and set fires. She was regarded by even her poor and extremely ignorant parents as nothing short of a mystery and a terrific problem. Poverty and delinquency have accompanied her family life, her brothers have been delinquent, but the viciousness of this little girl's behavior seemed to mark her as well beyond the bounds of what the family was acquainted with.

We found a poorly-dressed, heavy-featured little Slavic girl.

Except for rather poor color and being tired looking, she was in decidedly good general physical condition. No sensory defect. We note she readily takes on a very worried look for such a little girl, and in presence of her family her demeanor was seen to be most stubborn. An elder sister who brought her exercised the most motherly authority and seemed to be far the brightest of the family. The parents are densely ignorant and do the most menial work.

The mental examination of this girl proved to be altogether interesting and important. She was only in the 2d grade, but on account of frequent absence this perhaps meant little.

Mental tests: our own series:

I. 1' 45". At this first trial it was evident the girl was under the spell of some inhibitions, for she persistently attempted impossible placing of pieces.

III. 5' 38". 34 total moves. 12 impossibilities attempted and 12 repetitions of impossibilities. We gave this same test again after a few minutes and she did it with no errors in 12".

IV. 5' 57". 67 moves.

V. Although naturally we should expect this test to be beyond the child, she was given it in order to study her method. She made a complete failure, and did not work on anything but the lock, except when urged, and then returned immediately to it.

VII. Done with almost complete accuracy.

VIII. Done promptly and correctly.

IX. Correct at 1st trial.

X. Correct at 3d trial.

XI. Although this test was far beyond her it was given to see what she would do. Had great difficulty in getting the idea, but could analyze out a few of the symbols. Finally placed a good many more symbols than there were in the code passage.

XVII. Writes a fair hand for her age and was able to spell correctly, "The cat ran away."

XVIII. Makes most of the simple number combinations correctly. Often counted on her fingers.

XIX. In reading a 2d grade passage gets a number of the smaller words incorrectly.

Results on Binet: all of 8-year tests correct. 9 years — 1, failure; 2 and 3, correct; 4, failure; 5, failure. 10 years — 2, correct; 3, failure; 4, failure; 5, correct.

The record of tests on this case must not be taken at face value, for all the way through, many curious mental inhibitions were evidently at work interfering with results. The girl would stop during the progress of some test, and sit and run her thumb in and out of her mouth, a habit she was much addicted to. In some of the Binet questions her answers would be simply nothing, or " I don't know." Study of her ability showed she was not far subnormal, but there was evidence of aberrant conditions, and until we heard more of the story finally from her own lips, we had to regard her as a border-line mental case, showing possible symptoms of a psychosis. Our own judgment, rendered after considerable study, that there was no proof of mental defect, was apparently correct, for in the next year under better conditions she advanced to 4th grade, now being 11 years old.

Account of ancestry, as far as obtainable, seems to show that the girl comes of peculiarly long-lived families. There is said to be no insanity or feeblemindedness or epilepsy on either side. This girl was born when the father was decrepit, and about 65 years old. The mother is a hard-working woman. They are not alcoholic, but are intensely ignorant. They have lived in a crowded and vicious neighborhood, under poor housing conditions. Perhaps this has accounted for the older delinquents in the family, and perhaps for some school retardation in the others. No evidence that any of the others are insane or feebleminded. The developmental history of this girl seems to have been very normal. She talked early and walked at 1 1-2 years. Went to school first at 6, but has been out of school in intervals. No injury. Said to have had convulsions once when she was a baby.

The delinquencies of this child, even as judged by her surroundings, are great. They have had trouble with her at home for about 3 years. She has stolen repeatedly from home, from the school-room, from the teacher and others. Stayed out late in the evenings, often not coming home from school. The family have to search for her. Recently there has been much trouble with her on account of setting fires. At least three times she has set fire to things in the house. Once she gathered up papers in the middle of the floor and set fire to them; at another time she burned in a baby buggy in the house a lot of clothes her mother had washed. She has gone to neighbors and borrowed money, ostensibly for her mother. Told various people her mother was dead.

Her family believed in severe punishment, and whipped her and tied her hands. On one occasion she ran out of doors unclad, at another time with her hands tied. When she is punished she

386

merely stands and stares, the family say you might think she is a statue. Will not speak at all then to her family. If whipped will not utter a word, except, perhaps, "You hurt me." The older sister feels sure she goes with bad girls, but does not know who they are. The family are very much concerned about the case.

It was some time before we broke down this girl's inhibitions and could gain her friendship. We found her to be no prevaricator. If she did not want to say things she would not say them, and her imagination was not called into play. When we first knew her she would only speak in monosyllables, but later talked with us most fluently. It really seemed then as if she wanted to relieve her mind of all troubles and as if nobody had ever spoken to her about them. She told about a little boy who taught her to steal, and continually asked her to do bad things with him. "Lots of times I think about them — sometimes at night, and sometimes I have dreams, dream about when mother is scolding my brother, and Alex is right near my brother, and she is telling him not to play with him any more. That was because Alex was saying bad things. He said all sorts of bad things. He called me those words. They come up in my mind at school, and when I am at the board, and when I am thinking about the words I think all the time about him. It's when I'm writing a word, when I miss the word, and I don't know the word, and the teacher has us go to the board and write, and so I think about them words he said. There is a wooden gate near the school, and they take chalk, and write bad words on there — the same words he told me. It makes me feel as if somebody was talking about me, and I all the time feel as if they done these things to me. He all the times comes in our yard, even now — the boys upstairs call him in. Sometimes when I'm eating, and my brother talks about him, I begin to think what he tries to do. I feel sorry about things then — about what he does to me, and when he does bad to me."

Apropos of her setting fire, she acknowledged it and said she wanted to see the things burn. She did know the little sister and the baby were in the house when she made the fire in the baby buggy. A barn near their house had a fire — some boys lighted a lot of paper and burned the barn up. She would like to see the engines come.

"Alex sometimes comes in the yard and steals out things.

Long ago he used to come in the yard and steal. I had a little bank of money and he stole it off of us." There is much more to this little girl's story as told on successive days when her family brought her in. The child had continually in her mind the thoughts of this boy. It seems probable that she rejected all of his advances. Later she said another little girl had told her bad habits which she had practiced occasionally. The sister confirmed the story of this other girl being bad. It was very plain our offender needed a great deal of individual attention, but how to get it was altogether a difficult matter. Some people raised money and placed her in a home where a very good woman looked after her, and she made much improvement, but later when she returned home the parents were too ignorant to understand the needs of the case, and the girl fell into her old ways of stealing and staying out late at night. It was reported previously that she had made a vast improvement morally, and we felt sure of this from her physical appearance and her advancement in school. A slight operation was done, but there was no evidence to show that the effect of being placed in better surroundings was not the main cause of her improvement.

Seen after going home, and again becoming delinquent, she gave a very vivid account of her own mental struggles. " I say to myself, 'I took my communion, and I won't say these.' I want to say them when the boys say them to me, but I don't say them. If anybody hits me, I hit them. I try to say these words sometimes and it comes in my mind — it says, don't you say them words." She tells a story of much temptation, and bad home conditions, and being whipped for staying out late to go to shows. She is a strong child, and apparently has developed into a good deal of a fighter. On account of such deplorable environmental conditions, she had again to be removed from home.

Mental conflict.   Case 69.
   Sex repressions.   Girl, 10 years.
  Lack of parental supervision and understanding.

    Bad companions.

      Poverty? doubtful as a cause.

Stealing.   Mental:
Setting fires.   Fair ability.

We have had reason to study with care a number of cases in which mental conflict, leading to delinquencies, arose through the discovery from outside sources that a previously supposed parent was not really such. The following three instances illustrate this point.

Case 70. — There are many points of interest about this case which can be perceived from the following synopsis of it. Particularly should it be noted that we can find no record of delinquency against this boy until he was 14 years of age. There was not even truancy charged against him. It may be he was showing bad temper previously, but no complaint was made of it. We obtained a striking story, first from the mother, later corroborated by the boy. When seen by us he was 16 years of age. We were able to keep track of him about a year. The family were German immigrants, the boy's mother having been brought to this country when she was a child. She grew up amid surroundings of comparative poverty, but neither on her side nor the father's was there any showing of criminality or notable immorality.

On the physical side we found a particularly manly boy — broad-shouldered and well-shaped chest. Weighs 131 lbs. Height 5 ft. 3 1-2 in. His expression is responsive. Boyishly frank. Strong, broad face. Bright eyes. Speech very husky. Chronic atrophic rhinitis very severe, with pharyngitis. (Diagnosis was given by a specialist.) Many teeth badly carious. Tongue coated and offensive breath. Suffers from headaches. Poor sleep at night and dull feeling in the morning because of obstruction to breathing. These chronic catarrhal conditions excessive for years, and have been a great drawback to his school life on account of feeling dull, and because his presence was offensive to other children in the room. He never previously had treatment by a specialist. Well-shaped, large head. No sensory defect. Slight nystagmoid movements of eyes. Fine constant tremor of outstretched hands. Pubertal signs just beginning. Color good. Other examination all negative.

The findings on the mental side are very instructive because we found quite fair ability to set over against marked school retardation. Although never a truant, he only reached 4th grade at 14 years of age. His mother attributes this to his undesirability in the school-room. She maintains he was held back on account of this as well as being much complained of.

Mental tests: our own series:

I. 1′ 35″. Trial and error method in working with triangles.

II. 1′ 17″. Only 2 errors.

III. 5′. 44 total moves, but only 7 trials of impossibilities and 4 repetitions of impossibilities.

IV. 2′ 39″. 36 moves.

V. 2′ 9″. Step number 1 done almost immediately and then 5 errors before step number 2 is perceived. At this point he suddenly said, "Now I've got it," and rapidly proceeded to complete the test.

VI. 19 items given on free recital. 15 items on cross-examination and no suggestions received. A very good result.

VII. Done rapidly and very well.

VIII. Done very rapidly and all correctly.

IX. Correct at 1st trial.

X. Correct at 1st trial.

XII. 11 out of the 12 items given correctly and in correct sequence.

XIII. 13 out of the 20 items given correctly in proper sequence.

XIV. Done rapidly at the 2d trial. At 1st trial did not understand method of opening the dial.

XV. 3 errors. Average time 1.8″.

XVI. 69 squares tapped at 1st trial with no errors. 78 squares tapped at 2d trial with one error.

XVII. Writes a mature hand rapidly. Spells correctly all words.

XIX. Reads a 4th grade passage correctly and fluently.

XXII. Very poor range of information. Reads hardly any books, but does read the newspapers. Knows contemporary items of information fairly well.

At the time we saw him the boy had been guilty of extremely violent behavior at home. He had indulged in a lot of quarreling, had threatened to "fix" the family, had attempted to attack a boarder with a knife after some previous quarreling, and had been showing much evidence of a very bad temper for a long time now. Five months previously he had stolen a motorcycle, had spent some family money on little things for himself, and had run up a considerable bill against them in the same way. Other minor delinquencies were also charged against him. Altogether it seemed that the boy was making straight for a criminal career.

In this case we got an excellent account of heredity, for although the boy was illegitimate his mother knew the father's family well. Except that the boy's paternal grandmother was a quick-tempered person we could learn of no peculiarities whatever. There were but few children in either family, and the grandparents on both sides were long-lived. Despite the father's rejection of parental responsibility, he was said not to be a bad man. The mother suffered exceedingly from chorea in childhood.

The boy's developmental conditions have been normal, except possibly during antenatal life, at which time his mother was naturally much worried, she being only 16 and unmarried. The boy was never much of a smoker, nor, as far as known, engaged in other detrimental habits. It was evident that although there was so much school retardation, we had to do with a boy of good native ability, showing no distinct aberrational tendencies. His success at a place of employment also proved his fair mental endowment.

Our notes state that a woman came in to see us who announced herself as this boy's mother, although not being so according to records previously given. She seemed to be a pleasant, well-meaning woman; not dull, although poorly educated. She seemed to care a good deal for this boy, but on the whole took the attitude of an outsider. She was altogether reasonable, both at this and future interviews. She told us of his delinquencies as well as good qualities, and wound up by explaining to us her remarkable relationship to him. It seems that when the boy was just about 14 years of age, and before he had turned delinquent, she told him, on the occasion of some little household turmoil, that she, whom he supposed was his married sister, was really his mother. He did not believe it and she later, in an endeavor to exercise authority, insisted on the point.

This child was born when she was very young; the father was a fairly good man. He was persuaded by his family for financial reasons not to marry his sweetheart. They gave her a small sum of money for the boy. He was then brought up by his maternal grandparents, and taught to consider them as his parents. His mother later married, and now has a number of other children. The boy laughed at her first statement about his parentage, and continued to say he did not believe it.

His mother says the main trouble is temper, which has grown worse of late, and the boy does not stop to consider what he is doing or saying. His grandparents are getting old, and he knows he can pull the wool over their eyes. The grandmother wants him to pay back what he has cost her, especially in the way of having goods charged. In a vague way the mother feels the family situation may have much to do with the trouble, and asks us to see the boy and explain it to him. She states she does not know where the father is.

We had previously seen the boy, and gotten a naïve statement of his bad temper, in addition to some small falsifications about delinquencies. Later when asked about home conditions he said, "That sister of mine has been causing more trouble than any one. She comes over to our house and says, 'There's the loafer and bum.' If there's any one tries to work more than I do, I'd like to know who it is. There's no one stayed at home more to help out when she was sick than I did. She tells me she's my mother. I think she's a liar when she says that. She ain't been married 13 years yet. She tells me about it every time she comes over. I ain't been in her house for 2 months. She says I ain't been working enough to pay for my board. My father says about that way, too. That all has been bothering me some. The fact is I don't know which is my mother. I always thought the mother I'm living with now was my real mother. No neighbors or anybody ever told me any different. I sometimes think about it at nights." (Tears well up in his eyes.) "I certainly do feel sore about that business about my mother. I heard them talk together about adopting me. There ain't no property," etc., etc.

I had a more extended talk with the boy, as the mother requested, and this manly lad burst into tears and explained how he had been feeling that on all sides he had not been treated squarely — how not only his physical ailments made him feel badly, but also this other worry, which he had now had for a couple of years, had been a big influence leading him towards delinquency. The boy gave a very graphic account of his own feeling that developed in response to this astonishing statement by his sister, and how upset he was by it, and how it led to his misconduct. It was clear there were also nagging influences at home, over and beyond what was caused by this queer mix-up in relationship. His boyish activities were too much for the old grandparents, and the natural sympathy he looked for from them was not forthcoming.

We put it down that this boy's manly attitude, his neatness in dress, and rational reaction to the whole situation spoke much in his favor. It was clear that his miserable nose and throat conditions should be cured if possible, and his bad teeth removed. There should be a straightening out of the whole family relationship. The boy had been going through a stormy adolescent period with much stress on account of the above conflict, and had met the situation, it seemed to us, fairly normally.

The boy was in court a little later on account of stealing packages from a place where he was employed. At that time, through neglect, the constructive measures had not been carried out. The judge then took it in hand and insisted it be part of his conditions of parole that he go regularly for nose and throat treatment. The reports then varied from time to time, but his employers were satisfied with his work. Still later he was very evidently endeavoring to straighten himself up, and when last heard from he had been released from parole with a satisfactory record.

Mental conflict — about parentage.   Case 70.
    Home control irrational.   Boy, 16 years.
        Physical conditions: Severe chronic catarrh,
                               nose and throat.

Violence.
Lying.   Mental:
Stealing.   Fair in ability.

Case 71. — We studied the case of a 12-year-old boy who quite deliberately set out on a criminal career after a number of months of secretly harboring the knowledge, given to him by a meddlesome neighbor, that his own mother was long since dead, and not at all the person he supposed she was. Being a normal and sensitive boy, this hurt him to the quick, and he immediately saw many reasons for believing himself discriminated against, and for believing this was a world of lies. We had reason to think it probable that the reading he did at this time, about robbers and the like, was deliberately undertaken. After stealing a considerable sum and running away from home, he definitely made the statement he was going to become a criminal. This case when explored immediately took on new aspects, and while there have been backslidings, up to the present the outcome is very satisfactory.

Case 72. — A cause similar to the above occurred in the case of a young boy, light octoroon type, who lived with his supposed mulatto parents. He is a bright and sensitive child, who when

a neighbor told him that he surely could not be the son of these
people, dwelt on the problem of his parentage at great length.
The embitterment which the secret of his birth has engendered
in the boy's breast easily accounts for his recalcitrancy, even
in face of great kindness by his foster-father. He runs away and
steals and associates with bad boys and bad men, and has developed a very marked anti-social attitude, in spite of good opportunities at his home, which is unusually well kept in comparison
with the homes of most colored people. The boy has mental
abilities far above those of his foster-parents, inheriting these,
as well as his white skin, from a southern man of good family.
The foster-parents took the boy as an infant, and have bestowed
much affection on him, but all to little purpose when the boy
began to suspect the irregularities of his own parentage. The
case proved too difficult for solution in the old environment, and
the best treatment appeared to be placing the boy for a long
period in an institution.

The origin of mental conflict in a hypersensitive person from
what would offhand seem to be slight grounds, and the delinquencies that may thereby be engendered are illustrated in the following case.

Case 73. — This boy of 16 we had occasion to become acquainted with on account of his running away from Pittsburg,
and the father coming on and wishing to go thoroughly into the
case with us. The father is a good type of Irish American,
a clerk in public service, and a man of highly sensitive temperament.

Physically we found a very tall, slim lad, height 5 ft. 9 in. and
weighing 119 lbs. (The father said of himself that he grew in
exactly the same way.) The boy has pleasant irregular features
and good color. No sensory defects. Very pleasant, sensitive,
responsive boy.

On the mental side there is nothing much to record because
he showed himself well up to the ordinary in ability. On account,
probably, of nervousness when first seen, he did hardly as well
as we expected on a few of the tests, but he had graduated from
the grammar school before he was 14 years of age, and, being a great reader, gave us indication of a very good range of information. He is slow and deliberate in his work, but works
steadily and understandingly. He was as successful in business

for one year as he was in school, and everybody gave him credit
for being a very bright boy.

In heredity we can learn of no defect. But it stands out sharply
that father and son are of the same temperament. All through,
the boy comes from an unusually healthy family, and on the mental and moral sides there has been no trouble. Developmentally
the boy progressed without a set-back. He never had a serious
illness. The pregnancy and birth were quite all right. Unfortunately, the mother died two years ago, leaving the father with
six boys to take care of, this one being the oldest. He has never
succeeded in getting the right kind of housekeeper since the
mother's death, and he is finding it very difficult to keep
up the house on his salary. This father occasionally has felt
terribly discouraged, taken a drink or two of whiskey, and come
home in a cross and scolding mood. He acknowledges as much;
the world is a hard struggle.

Up to one year ago this boy was a model lad. This stands
out very definitely. He worked steadily after his graduation
and gave all his earnings to the family. Since that time there
has been a succession of troubles with him. He has run away
from home three times, on one occasion staying in the neighborhood of Pittsburg four months, sometimes working on farms,
and occasionally visiting the home when his father was absent.
Although he had a perfect record for a year in an office where
he worked, he has never since held a job for longer than two or
three weeks. His character seems to be utterly changed. On
one occasion he attempted to get money by forging his father's
name, and at another time when away from home obtained
supplies on his father's credit. However, he has never really
stolen. The father feels utterly discouraged about the situation
and blames it to cigarettes, believing his son to be a nervous
wreck from smoking them. The boy also suffers from frequent
enuresis, and this the father also cites as proving the nervous
condition.

We had ample opportunity to study this case while the father
waited to take his boy home, and fortunately we were able to
bring the two closer together in understanding. Our first information from the father showed that there was a very definite
period when the boy started to go wrong. We undertook then to
search for beginnings. The history obtained received satisfactory
corroboration on both sides. In regard to the cigarettes it turned

out that the father merely judged the boy was smoking excessively; as a matter of fact he probably never did smoke more
than three or four in one day. Concerning the enuresis; as
observed in Chicago our lad did not suffer from it, and he
stated that out in the country he had no trouble from it. On
inquiry, we found his habit at home was to drink strong coffee
at supper and also just before he went to bed, making it himself, while at these other places he had none after breakfast
time.

In regard to beginnings; it seems this father came home in a
petulant humor one night, and found the boy had missed a couple
of days at work. The father always left early in the morning,
and had not heard of any complaint of sickness. Although this
was the only occasion on which time was missed, he said to a
younger son, who reported the staying at home, " It 's a lie, he 's
no sicker than I am." This speech was repeated to our young
friend, and as he said to us, " Since then things seems to be going
backward with me all the time."

In every way we saw we had to deal with a hypersensitive lad
who, in this very trait, was strangely like his father, as the latter
acknowledged. The boy told us that up to the time of the un-
deserved reproach, so far as he can remember, he had never told
a lie in his whole life. He had resolved, especially after his mother
died, to merit the very best that could be said of him. " I always
had lots of friends and everybody spoke well of me." He worked
hard and gave his father all his earnings. To have his father
say what he did discouraged him terribly. " It seems to me
now that was what was hurting me." He never even smoked
before that time, but after that it seemed as if nothing mattered.
He would just let things take their own way. He would even
just as soon get arrested and sent away.

After two or three weeks of nursing his injured feelings he
deliberately left his good position. During the next year the
boy's record is a constant succession of delinquencies, especially
in the light of the family needing his help. He worked only
for a week or two at the time, and at irregular intervals. Sometimes when he pretended to be at work he really spent all day at
the Carnegie Institute, or the library. He never did go with bad
companions, and never cared in the least for them — the father
made this point clear. He avoided his father, who continually
scolded him, often sleeping away from home. He tried evening

school and learning shorthand, but soon gave it up. He continually lied and got into money difficulties and ran away three times, as mentioned above. After his forging, his father twice took the lad to the police station and left him there over night.

The boy's story fitted in with the father's, and he said, "It seems to me now as if I don't care who calls me a liar — I am one." Speaking of his experience with the police, who urged him to behave himself, he stated, "When I said anything, they said, 'It is n't that way at all, you know you are lying,' and so I kept still. There was no use saying anything." This was very interesting, because the father had reported that the boy at times was absolutely silent, refusing to say a word about himself, to either his father or the police, of whom assistance had been asked. Several other striking points also came out. It seems, as in many another case of youthful delinquency, the offender suffered from discomforts all out of proportion to the realization of pleasures. When he was away from home he slept in a haystack part of the time, and meals were altogether uncertain. The boy says he had no good times then.

For purposes of scientific elimination other possible causes were inquired into with negative results. Asked where light for the future seemed to shine, the lad tells us he could get straightened out if he did not brood over what people said to him or said behind his back. "I simply can't stand to have my father say harsh things." "You bet I like him." (Later this father told me that he himself felt this way, and when unpleasant things were said in the office, worried about them all day long.)

In this case a definite tendency to delinquency was under consideration, a tendency that had not been modified by admonitions or threats. The outlook now, with understanding of beginnings, was altogether different. The coffee and smoking should be stopped, the evening reading, which had been somewhat opposed, should be allowed at home, but above all there must be modification of parental behavior. The scolding, even though justified, and especially the speaking of the boy behind his back, should be abandoned. The mediation which our discoveries led us to offer, was well received, and the father's negotiations for placing the boy in a reformatory institution were broken off. For the six months elapsed since we saw this case, the report is that there has been an entire change of conduct.

Mental conflict.	Case 73.
Mental peculiarity: hypersensitiveness.	Boy, 16 years.
Heredity: father same temperament.	
Home conditions: mother dead.	
Runaway +.	
Not working.	Mental:
False representations.	Good ability.

People who handle children out of the natural family environment should be acquainted with the type of fact which the following case exhibits, although, as we said above, homesickness seems to figure much less as a cause of delinquency in this country than abroad.

Case 74. — This was a little girl of 12 who had been given a very black name by certain institutional people and others on account of alleged exceedingly bad behavior; in fact, reformatory treatment was demanded for her. Not only was it said that she was a delinquent, but that she was also a mental defective, on account of apparently proved inability to grasp school work.

We found a rather poorly nourished little girl who was suffering frequently of late from headaches. These, she told us, sometimes lasted for hours and were accompanied by curious sensations of lights in her eyes. Different colors appear, and the lights seem like snakes coming from all directions, while perhaps she cannot see anything at all for a time. She bites her nails much. Both vision and hearing were slightly defective, the latter on account of a previous middle-ear infection. On the mental side it was a matter of only a few minutes to prove that she was anything but a mental defective, indeed we graded her as being well up to the ordinary in ability and information.

We could learn from the father nothing of significance in the family or developmental history. None in the family of either parent is known to be epileptic or insane, nor can we hear of any migraine. The mother died of cancer four years previously, and the father was previously alcoholic, although for some time now he has not been drinking hard. The whole story centers about the fact that this child's older sisters, after the mother's death, considered the father as unworthy, and some six months prior to the time we saw her, practically kidnapped the girl from home.

There was no statement that he had ever mistreated the child in any way. She was not said to be delinquent before then, and she had been doing well in the 5th grade at school. Up to that time she says she had suffered from headache perhaps only a couple of times.

The little girl readily acknowledged her misbehavior, which consisted, according to the institutional people with whom she was placed, in running away (it seems she once got as far as the railroad station in an endeavor to get back to her father), in clandestine correspondence, lying, and refractoriness in the school-room. Besides this she was found "mentally queer, dazed and stupid-looking at times. She once threatened to kill herself."

From the girl herself we get an account of terrific loneliness, with whole days of distress, although she has been away months from her father. "I'm not happy. He was always good to me. I've written for him to come, but they got the letters first. I'll sit there and not know what I'm doing, I'll be biting my finger nails and everything. My sisters think my father is mean, but he treats me nice. I never ran away except from this here Home. They treat me all right. My heart hurts me. Only one thing, I didn't want to go to a Home."

The father's sympathy and love were really proved in this case by his quick response when he knew that the child wanted him.

Here was an aspect of child life totally overlooked and misunderstood by people dealing constantly with children, as well as by some court authorities. For us the point is not only this, but also the details of the physical and mental conditions and the delinquent reactions which have arisen psychogenetically, namely, from the repression and ferment in the mind. Even the first analysis of the case brought out the fact that she thought homesickness was all that was the matter, although she had never intimated to others any explanation of her conduct. How much of the emotion and connecting links of reaction were subconscious it would be difficult to say. With return to her home, defective though it was, came cessation of headaches, and of her delinquencies, and gain of weight.

CHAPTER XI

ABNORMAL SEXUALISM

§ 242. General Considerations.   § 243. Hypersexualism.   § 244. Sexualistic Obsessions and Impulsions.   § 245. Masturbation.   § 246. Early Sex Experiences.   § 247. Sex Perversions.   § 248. Psychoses Accompanied by Abnormal Sexualism.

§ 242. General Considerations.

The words sexualism and sexualistic represent needed additions to our vocabulary and have the same right to existence as the analogous terms criminalism and criminalistic. One may speak of sexualistic crimes, and of abnormal sexualism as a cause of crime.[1] These terms cover a larger field than that discussed in works on pathological sexuality. The latter has been well studied in its legal aspects, but there are several important phases of the relationship of abnormal sexual life to criminalism which are not at all considered by writers on the forensic bearings of pathological sexuality. As students of causes we must include all of these facts. The criterion of abnormality here, we confess, is hard to define when it involves only slight divergence from the normal. It is often necessary to invoke consideration of both social and physiological standards.

In discussing this subject we again follow very practical issues in developing our several headings. Students of the individual offender are concerned with causes, personalities, and types of misdeeds. Each of these has its place in the study of abnormal sexualism. In considering misdeeds in this connection it must be remembered that we have to deal with offenses which are not only directly sexual in nature, but also with those which are instigated by sexualism.

We are not warranted in placing the discussion of abnormal sexualism under the caption of either mental or physiological peculiarities. In some instances the conduct quite clearly is instigated as the result of sheer mental processes. In other cases

---

[1] We avoid the term *erotomania* as we do other words of the same class. It has some value in its practical significance, but it implies a mental lack of balance, which may not be correlated with the hypersexualism.

the physiological basis seems the strongest. Often there is a great admixture of the two elements. It is well recognized that there are several centers in the nervous system from which sex feelings may be generated. As represented in consciousness, the sources of stimulation range all the way from peripheral irritation to mental imagery. Physiological psychology has here a good field for investigation.

We are frequently at a loss to decide what mainly underlies any appearance of abnormal sexualism in the individual, or at least to decide in what proportion various possible causes may have been effective. The mental and the physiological elements are much mixed. Who can tell whether the person who exhibits anti-social sexualistic tendencies is the victim of an excessive output from certain internally secreting glands, or of obsessive mental imagery, or of predisposing anatomical conditions, or of various environmental and physical experiences? Frequently still more difficult is it to decide between innate tendencies as a whole, some of which may be derived from heredity, and the effect of environment. Under the head of heredity, § 144, and in our discussion of the influence of pictures, § 225, and mental imagery, § 233, as well as under abnormalities of development, § 189, § 190, we have shown clearly some of the possible bases of abnormal sexualism. Occasionally one finds a case where some one condition in the physiological or hereditary background, or some one experience seems to account for the whole unfortunate tendency. In many places throughout our work statements of fact will be found which bear upon this matter.

Judges and other court officials, and all those who are concerned in understanding the causes of criminalism, should have a clear conception of not only the technical legal aspects of sex offenses, but also of the physiological relationship which exists between sexualism and crimes which are not overtly sexual. We do not purpose here to go into pathological case histories, nor shall we do more than barely touch on actual abnormal sexualistic practices, or on the explicit content of sexualistic mental imagery. These matters are largely elaborated in other special professional literature (*vide* § 247). It is our business, however, to enumerate specifically the general types of abnormal sexualism. whether as leading to recognized sex crimes or as being the basis of other offenses.

No attempt at discussion of the various sex crimes, as such, is necessary. Rape, incest, various sex perversions, may all be the result of disordered mentality, of environmental conditions, or of hypersexualism in an otherwise normal individual, and so on. To name the crime does not characterize the offender, does not elucidate the prognosis, nor suggest the best treatment. In this field, to be sure, we find some close correlations between types of deeds and types of persons, as in exhibitionism, *vide* § 163, and in certain kinds of sexual violation, *vide* § 244. These cases, however, must be understood as largely standing alone in their peculiar significance.

§ 243. Hypersexualism.

The fact that there are individuals whose sex characteristics show development far beyond the social or physiological norm is patent to every one who studies offenders for courts where they appear on account of their sex delinquencies. We have discussed this from the standpoint of adolescent over-development, § 189, of heredity, § 144, etc. The phenomenon seems sometimes to be a feature of mental life apart from any known physiological factors. It may be that biochemists, who are so industriously nowadays studying the internal secretions of various glands, will sometime be able to throw a great light on this subject. But there is no reason to doubt that early experiences and habits of mental imagery may alone account for many of the cases.

In regard to eroticism being considered primarily a mental peculiarity, we may say that we have had reason to study many cases of extreme show of sexualism in older adolescents with parents who could give us much information. We have yet to see a single case in which the hypersexualism has arisen without the presence either of various physical conditions, such as might readily be responsible, or of unfortunately early sex experiences. To be sure, in males as well as females, at all ages, the part which mental imagery plays in these matters is often great. And that there exist mental peculiarities of susceptibility to the obsession of various imageries is a fact as easily perceived by us as that there are individuals who are eye-minded and those who are ear-minded. Only so far as this do we have any right to go in considering eroticism at all as a mental trait.

The correlation between over-development and sex offenses

402

is clearly shown in the delinquencies of girls, which are so frequently along sex lines and so often involve those of good physique. (*Vide* § 105 and § 190.) It will be noted in our case histories that sex offenses very frequently are combined in these young people with other incidental delinquencies, such as running away from home and stealing. Hypersexualism in males does not often show itself so early. There is no such coloring of life's activities by one dominating impulse as there is among females.

The following represents a type of case of which we have seen scores:

Case 75. — The mother stated that this girl of 15 was crazy about sex matters. Mentally she proved well up to the ordinary in ability and information. Physically she was splendidly developed, possessed a finely-shaped head with broad, high forehead, and intelligent, strong face. She had been long seeking illicit sex relations. She dwelt on the facts without shame. She was now both diseased and pregnant. She rather boasted of having been known as " The Main Street Bum." This attitude she had been assuming for long. In explanation of the genesis of her own career she offered a story of rape, which according to her family had no foundation in fact, but even had it occurred it would not have explained the intense inclinations which she had shown over a long period. In this case, even if we acknowledge the effect of bad environment, we have also to include very definite innate hypersexualistic tendencies.

The overwhelming attraction which negro men occasionally have for white girls and women, directly leading in our social life to delinquency, is to be explained by the hypersexualism of the female attracted. One has seen instances in which the arguments of social ostracism, race antipathy, and religious faith have availed nothing against this extraordinary impulse.

Undoubtedly hypersexualism is a vastly greater cause in early life of other than sex offenses than it is later. The morally disturbing influence would naturally be much more during the years when there is less than normal adult self-control. The older hypersexualistic individual who is mentally normal perceives the necessity of steady behavior and self-control in many ways in order that craving shall be satisfied. For example, if offenses were committed which ended by incarceration, opportunities for satisfaction would be cut off. We may say, then, that hypersexualism in the otherwise normal adult merely leads when uncontrolled to excessive practices. These may be anti-social if they are illicit. The upshot of this whole question is that there are certain individuals of both sexes who by virtue of their own native characteristics, or of desires aroused by experiences, are impelled to seek sexual enjoyment beyond the social norm.

What treatment to recommend depends upon what anti-social habits have been already formed, and what innate characteristics, if any, are at the basis of hypersexualism, upon what powers of self-control are to be relied on, and what reëducation can be carried out. The surgical operations that are often suggested, even by parents, afford little hope, unless they are more thorough than is allowable at the present stage of public opinion on this subject. Minor severings and excisions do not alter predisposed paths of nervous conduction. Of course, actual cases of " satyriasis " and " nymphomania," either one of which may lead to grievous misconduct, are plainly subjects for medical attention. There is very little use in considering moral treatment for such cases as these, which sometimes are based upon definite conditions of the central nervous system or of other organs. The growth of opinion, we feel sure, will be towards greater use of thorough surgery in many of these cases.

Mere repression, such as is undertaken in all sorts of penal institutions, frequently turns the individual from seeking one kind of gratification to another that may be more disastrous mentally. Punishment does not destroy in these sexualistic individuals such deep-set mental and physical inclinations.

It is unfortunate that society must be protected from individuals with hypersexualistic tendencies by methods which do not cure the trouble. In institutions there is frequently an excess of both thought and conversation about sex subjects. When this last fact is faced the greatest effort should be, not to directly combat the inclinations by drawing attention to them, but to supplant them with new interests and new types of mental imagery and new activities of many kinds. What may be successful in one case may not be effective in another. The main hope is to be found in the well-known psychological principle of substitutional mental activities. Forceful new interests sometimes do win the day. Education ánd religion have their place in this treatment.

404

§ 244. Sexualistic Obsessions and Impulsions.

It is probable that in all cases where mental imagery and ideation become obsessional and lead to uncontrolled impulsions, that a neuropathic constitution is in the background. No doubt, however, elements of environmental or physical experience enter into the total result. Very peculiar personal actions and traits may be developed as the result of such impulsions. It is the business of the medico-psychologist to be acquainted with these peculiarities of conduct, many of which do not come within the category of offenses. When the impulsions lead to offenses we have some strange developments; the association between the delinquency and sexualism may not be at all apparent. In the case of exhibitionism, which, however, has psychological aspects not easy to understand, the relation seems obvious. When it comes to certain forms of stealing, which are indulged in under sexualistic impulsions, the meaning of the conduct is not at all to be read on the surface. Abnormal sex impulses may be found active in those who are certainly not to be considered in any way insane, but nevertheless in the actually insane sexualistic impulsions frequently are dominant.

The theft of articles for fetishism, that is for their sexually symbolic purposes, is well known. The whole subject has been satisfactorily dealt with by Binet (341), Krafft-Ebing (188), Havelock Ellis (37), and others. Probably the most common objects stolen are women's handkerchiefs and women's shoes. Gloves and other articles of wear are sometimes found desirable. The theft and cutting of the female hair is undoubtedly an offense done under sexual impulse. The psychological basis of these curious actions has been made the matter of much discussion which we cannot go into here.

The remarkable self-abnegating impulse which leads women to become the abject slaves of men, even to the extent of turning over earnings gained from sex immorality, is of sexualistic origin. The power of the " cadet " over women cannot be understood unless this psychological phase of their relationship is taken into account. Some women find satisfaction in actually suffering at the hands of their masters. This subjection directly gives opportunity for development of sexual vice. Analogous cases of men whose masochistic impulses lead them to desire to be

405

beaten, for instance, by their mistresses, do not so lead to social offenses.

An impulse, the reverse of this last, in which the individual desires to inflict cruelty, perhaps to whip another person, or at least to see the whipping, has been proved to have direct relation to sexualism.

Cases of men who have an impulse to cut or stab women and girls have been exploited in the newspapers and discussed in scientific literature. The offender usually has a preference for some, perhaps non-sexual, part of the body about which imagery has centered. No doubt all of these men are determinably insane. The so-called lust murders are probably always committed by victims of brain disease. The nature of the crime and of the criminal is witnessed to by the strange mutilations and other performances carried out in connection with the deed.

The impulse to insult women in public places is only to be explained upon the basis of abnormal sexualism. Since there is no obvious satisfaction gained, the meaning of the offense has to be sought by psychological analysis. The same type of obsessional impulse may lead to the defilement of woman in various ways, or the cutting of their clothes. Cases of all these types are described in the special literature.

The spying upon persons of the opposite sex, which occasionally is accounted a social offense, is the result of an impulse that is more generally understood and so seems less peculiar. However, it would not be easy for most individuals who engage in this to analyze the nature of their own impulses, or to give clear account of satisfaction received.

The impulse to peculiarly violate little girls, often without rape, is one which unfortunately is not infrequently met with in court work. At the risk of discovery and imprisonment the offense may be repeated over and over, and in this shows the force of an obsessional impulse. We have often used the following example as a text illustrating the inadequacy of ordinary punitive treatment of these cases. We had occasion to know of the career of a man who had served about five years in the penitentiary for immoral conduct with little girls. Within a couple of months after his release he had again repeated his offenses with several children, was reconvicted and sentenced to a longer term. There was no understanding of the nature of this man, or of his impulses, which led to any treatment at the time of his original conviction, or at his release. The result has been the mental defilement of several other young persons.

We know only too well the effects of such practices by older people — the effects upon the mental content and consequent impulses of those who have been so early taught vicious sex practices. We could have safely predicted, even if we had not come to actually know, the miserable results upon the young girls mentioned in the previous paragraph.

The impulse in males to exhibit themselves sexually we have partly dealt with elsewhere, § 163. While most often a phenomenon of old age, younger males with this impulse are occasionally found. Exhibitionism by females, although I have never heard of a case being brought to court, is not at all uncommon, and is certainly an anti-social offense. In girls or women, not prostitutes, the impulse has its roots either in physiological hypersexualism, perhaps only temporary, or in obsessional mental states.

§ 245. Masturbation.

We heartily agree with the judges, police and probation officers, and parents whom we have heard, many of them, insist on the effect of masturbation in causing other delinquencies. We decry exaggeration of this subject because in some ways the habit, like other single factors, is not nearly so important as has been made out. Then, too, our experience in the neurological clinic shows us the truth of what has frequently been observed, namely, that worry about masturbation frequently does more harm than the habit itself. But in our study of young offenders who are well started in careers of delinquency, we have been profoundly impressed with the break-down of will, of physical condition, and of general moral fibre that is correlated with the excessive practice of masturbation. We have found it of the utmost importance as a causative factor in girls as well as in boys. The extent to which it stands out clearly may be seen by our statistics, § 95; in over 10 per cent. the habit was practiced to such a degree that it was to be fairly considered a definite cause. In many other instances the practice may have been a habit, but we did not learn that it was anything of a factor in producing delinquency.

In comparatively few was the practice carried on to the extent that there appeared to be actual mental dulling from it, *vide*

§ 286. It might properly be asked why any weakening influence should cause a tendency to delinquency. We do not think that all weakening influences do, only when together with the dulling of mental activity there comes moral lethargy and consequent establishment of anti-social habits. We have particularly noted in connection with masturbation, such delinquencies as sleeping away from home, unwillingness to go to school or to work, recourse to excess of stimulants, petty stealing, vagrancy, constant giving way to desire for exciting amusement, particularly as afforded by moving picture shows. The cases which go on to develop mental disturbances belong under the category of mental aberrations, § 313.

The connection between masturbation and anti-social offenses seems to be established along the following lines — the effect varying greatly, of course, with environmental circumstances and innate tendencies of the individual. The act in itself is anti-social. The individual feels this, and realizes the stigma which indulgence places upon him. His constant efforts at secrecy in this regard may lead to moral break-down. The sequence is not difficult to understand. First there is weak self-indulgence, then secretiveness and lies, then avoidance of duties and search for stimulation and artificial energy. The effect of masturbation in directly promoting several forms of anti-social behavior among young people is one of the most marked phenomena to be observed in court work.

On account of desire to conceal a habit which is looked down upon, there is great readiness on the part of the offender to ascribe any lassitude or weakness of will to causes other than the habit itself. Boys often allege that their trouble is due to smoking, when the smoking itself is indulged in really to stimulate after the depression caused by this habit. Numerous times we have also found the over-use of tea and coffee to rest on this basis. Superficial judgment about causes thus may readily overlook the more serious factor.

Consideration of the question of treatment involves at once the statement of a very important fact, namely, that with successful treatment of the habit we have seen in some cases a very marked transformation of the individuality, sufficient to prove the point we have been making concerning the effect of this practice in developing criminalistic tendencies. It is true that much the most hopeful time is before puberty. We have seen extrava-

gant cases of bad sex habits in both boys and girls cured when
they have been treated prior to this age. Later the matter is
much more difficult, as might be expected from the fact that
nature has already begun to awaken sex instinct. But even
then we have seen alterations achieved which are quite remarkable — always in cases, however, of normal mental ability, § 286.
It is needless to give long histories.

One girl (*vide* Case 108) of 16, who frequently slept in hallways, ran away from home, engaged in petty stealing, and who
was the picture of mental dullness, a year later became a capable
and self-supporting girl. Her unrecognized trouble had been
extensive indulgence in masturbation. The mother undertook
the treatment in most vigorous fashion and succeeded.

Case 76. — A boy of 14, normal in mental ability, poorly
nourished, with tired look about the eyes, had long been giving
much trouble. He lived with a poverty-stricken mother, who
together with her children had suffered much from the abuse of
her alcoholic husband. When we saw the boy he had run away
from home several times, he had stolen repeatedly, had lied
much, and once had tied himself in a chair to make his mother
believe that burglars had been in the house. This last was done
because he had secreted the little money which she possessed.
We found that this boy had been practicing masturbation for three
or four years, sometimes excessively. His physical appearance and
general manner were very different from that of a younger brother
with whom we could compare him. He did not succeed on probation in his old environment, even after his father deserted the
family, but when placed in a home in the country where his sex
tendencies were watched, he made in a year a wonderful improvement. Our last report of him is that he is strong, healthy, and
as steady as a clock.

It is unnecessary to burden the reader with many other cases
that we could give in which this habit has proved a large factor
in starting delinquent careers. One might go farther and include
the various psychological steps of mental habit and mental
imagery and formation of grudge-like attitudes which are superimposed on indulgence in masturbation, but the general trend
of these points should be obvious.[1]

[1] The comparative results of excessive intercourse and excessive masturbation are often discussed. The review of the subject by G. Stanley Hall (**31,**
Vol. I, p. 440) brings out the essential points.

The treatment of masturbation is very largely an affair of building up new methods of living. The temptation frequently centers about some association; it occurs at the same hour, or in the same place. The old associations should be broken up as much as possible. There is no doubt in my mind but that through the constant supervision of some good person of the same sex, perhaps a member of the family, if the right person can be found, is the best possible means of getting the desired results. The desperate case we spoke of above was handled by the mother remaining with the girl all the time and always sleeping with her. General hygiene should be attended to as well as any local irritative conditions. Treatment is best begun only after a careful medical survey of the individual problem.

§ 246. Early Sex Experiences.

It will be noted in our statistical analysis, § 95, that at least 13 per cent. of our cases had encountered some early sex experience sufficiently serious to be accounted by the student a causative factor of delinquency. In these cases the trouble arose from the teachings of other children and adults of both sexes, as much as from actual bad sex practices with others. In children the unfortunate introduction into sex life came often from persons of the same sex. The effect of immorality on the part of parents, as a causative factor which undermines the whole of moral life, need hardly be mentioned. The incidents of sex life witnessed as the result of crowded housing conditions, and the untoward ideas gained from obscene language heard at home cannot fail to bring about anti-social reactions. When it comes to the actual immoral practices which occasionally spring up in the household the situation is desperate. Incest and other evil practices leave ineradicable stains. It may be contended that early teaching of this kind must fall on fertile ground to produce long enduring vicious results, but there is little doubt that susceptibility exists more or less in all persons. Very many times in our studies of the genetics of a delinquent career we have ascertained that the earliest beginnings were connected with illicit sex practices. There seems to be little reason for the individual pursuing any paths of rectitude when the most intimate relations of life are morally awry.

§ 247. Sex Perversions.

Despite the importance of the subject of sex perversions for all who have to do with offenders, whether in police or court work, or in institutional life, there is no sufficient reason for our discussing it in detail in such a work as this. We grant there has been altogether too much neglect of the subject and too little understanding of the facts by many who should know at least the general phases of unnatural sex conduct, but sources of detailed information are now available in English, and to these we will refer those readers whose business it should be to understand such things. All others should leave the unpleasant subject alone. We are consciously thus producing an incomplete work on the individual offender, feeling that there is no sufficient reason for reiteration of even the general outlines of the subject, nor for recounting any of the many instances which we have studied. Judges and others deeply concerned with this whole problem, which is not easy to understand, should gain a learned outlook upon it. I would counsel study of authors only who deal with the subject thoroughly. The foreign literature is immense; we need not concern ourselves with it here because the masterly works of Krafft-Ebing (188), Havelock Ellis (186), Freud (88), and Moll (339) are now all available in English. These authors cover different parts of the field and take different points of view, no one of which the fair-minded student of the subject can afford to neglect. There is much strife about certain theoretical points, but the facts are all clear. For those who are compelled to deal with the legal aspects of sex perversion the recent translation of Thoinot (338) is a boon.

Nothing, naturally, is of any more interest in the matter of sex perversions than its psychological aspects. It does not do at all, as Naecke (340) points out, to wave aside even the commonest of perversions and say that they simply arise upon a basis of degeneracy. We see clearly from the study of our cases that many types of personalities are involved, and that bad companionship and bad environmental conditions may be the chief, perhaps the sole cause for these socially abnormal practices. While in court work a large number of sex perverts are found to be mentally abnormal, individuals who do not get into court, and those who in institutions and other places where the sexes are segregated

411

practice these vices are frequently entirely sound mentally. The mere practice of sex perversions is a rare cause for the individual being brought into court — that is, rare as compared with the large number of persons who engage in such practices. This fact must not be forgotten when there is attempt to urge reformation upon the individual. Others of his ilk are generally known to him who hold themselves as quite beyond the pale of criminalism. Perhaps the most difficult feature of the situation to combat is the fact, known to many perverts, that people of great ability and of both sexes practice these habits which, because they are anti-social, are called perversions.

Treatment of the tendency to sex perversion is a very difficult matter. Forced repressive discipline in such matters is frequently a farce. We can well understand this in the light of the powers of mental imagery. Study of the authors we have mentioned will show that a great many sex-pervert offenses are instigated by obsessive mental representations, such as are not in the least bettered by ordinary penal treatment. Indeed, life in penal institutions is notorious for inciting to sex practices of many kinds even those who are otherwise not inclined to them. There is much literature bearing on this point.

The importance of sex perversions for criminalistics does not end with consideration of the practices themselves. We have been deeply impressed with the power which the knowledge, to say nothing of the practice, by young people of perversions has for disturbing the general moral equilibrium. In a number of cases we have witnessed secondary effects, stealing, running away, false accusations, etc., arise principally from the morally overwhelming effects of experience with sex-pervert practices. In our chapter on mental conflicts, § 237, and on pathological lying, § 346, may be seen some indications of the facts.

§ 248. Psychoses Accompanied by Abnormal Sexualism.

We have elsewhere dwelled upon the excessive sexualism not infrequently displayed by epileptics, sometimes upon the basis of the early sex development which may accompany the disease. In other conditions where the mind is affected, eroticism may be displayed as one of the chief symptoms, and in such cases the entire social significance of the mental disease may hinge upon this fact. In our chapters on the psychoses will be found some hint of this.

We have seen a number of cases where arrest has been made for sex offenses when the offense itself was merely a symptom of the mental aberration. It is interesting to note that the vast majority of those cases have been females. Males with mental aberrations do occasionally become sex offenders, sometimes of the most violent sort, rapists and perverts, but in much greater measure the conduct of the psychotic girl or woman is imbued with general sex tendencies. A previously moral girl, now the victim of chorea, may begin to show erotic tendencies, and after parental repression, may run away in the full excitement of her disease, and seek experiences with the opposite sex. Many instances of psychoses in adolescents we have witnessed which have been accompanied by signs of eroticism, indeed eroticism itself in some has seemed to be the chief sign of a mild maniacal condition. The possibility of an aberrational mental state being the foundation for such behavior should be kept ever in mind by probation officers and others who come in contact with these markedly sexualistic individuals.

CHAPTER XII

EPILEPSY

§ 249. General Statement. § 250. Varieties of Epilepsy. § 251. Criminalism and Epilepsy. § 252. Our Findings. § 253. Mental Peculiarities of Epileptics. § 254. Physical Peculiarities of Epileptics. § 255. Causes of Epileptic Being an Offender. § 256. Illustrative Cases. § 257. Legal and Other Social Treatment of Epileptic Offenders. § 258. Epileptic Psychoses.

§ 249. **General Statement.** — The amount of space which we shall devote to epilepsy as a genetic factor of criminalism will not be proportionate to the great importance of the subject. The general facts, since the earliest studies of Lombroso published a generation ago, have been well to the foreground in criminology. What is necessary for us to do is to say something of the nature of the epileptic attacks, to refer to our statistical findings while considering certain exaggerations of the subject, to specifically dwell on the mental peculiarities of epileptics which lead them to play so large a part in criminalism, to give two or three typical cases, and to offer some comments on legal aspects. The epileptic psychoses, although difficult at times to distinguish from mere changes in character peculiar to epileptics, are treated below, § 258. (The best professional usage of today is to speak of " the epilepsies," rather than of epilepsy as a single disease. There are several kinds of epilepsy, and probably many etiological factors.) The main facts about the varieties of attacks and the psychical characteristics of epileptics, as set forth below, should be well known to all who deal with offenders.[1]

§ 250. **Varieties of Epilepsy.** — The essential nature of epilepsy as a disease is that its principal manifestations occur in the form of attacks of varying kinds and lengths. Quite apart from the mental states of the epileptic at times other than in the attack, is consideration of the disease itself as expressed in attacks. All students of offenders should be acquainted with the several forms of epilepsy. It is true that the classic division of epilepsy into four principal manifestations is not ultimately satisfactory to

---

[1] The best reference work in English on epilepsy for students of criminalistics is that by Spratling (**26**). This was written from the author's immense experience at the Craig Colony in New York.

professional students of the subject, but for the practical purposes of description this division holds good. It is in general
use even in special institutions for epileptics. Before giving the
divisions we desire the reader to distinctly understand that the
lines between them are not always clear, and that the same person
may suffer from more than one manifestation of the disease.
Often both major and minor attacks are experienced. The main
forms of epilepsy are:

(a) Major epilepsy. *Grand mal.* Attacks in which motor co-
ordination is lost, the patient falls, and there is always unconsciousness. The convulsive seizure is the best known manifestation of major epilepsy.

(b) Minor epilepsy. *Petit mal.* In attacks of this nature consciousness may not be entirely lost, and while there is some
muscular involvement it may not amount to jerking or falling.
There may be merely sudden inability to move, with clouding of
consciousness for a few seconds.

(c) Psychic epilepsy. This is a mental attack leaving the motor
functions undisturbed. There is sudden, temporary loss of the
higher consciousness, of complete apperception, with a pathological loss of memory. These seizures may last for a few seconds
or for hours, and even days. The individual in these states automatically reacts to various perceptions and impulses.

(d) Jacksonian or partial epilepsy consists in spasms of one
set of muscles, or of one part of the body. Often with this there
is no disturbance of the consciousness. It is usually the result
of localized disease of the brain. It has less to do with criminalistics than the other forms of epilepsy.

In addition to the above should be mentioned *epileptic equivalents.* These are curious psycho-physical phenomena due to
paroxysmal disturbances of various nerve centers. They have
been described by Gowers and others. There may be sudden feeling of distress in some organ, or the trouble may take the form
of sensory disturbance, which occasionally amounts to an hallucination, as of smell. Rarely, attacks of this sort may be the only
indication of the epileptic tendency, except that usually there is
a little concomitant disturbance of consciousness. One remarkable case seen by us was that of a boy, repeatedly delinquent,
who showed the characteristic mental deterioration of the epileptic, but who suffered from no seizures other than peculiar
attacks of sweating, accompanied by slight dimming of conscious-

415

ness. Attacks of *violent temper* may be epileptic equivalents according to the opinion of prominent students of the subject. Certainly known epileptics are prone to such emotional disturbances which may seem to take the place of typical seizures. Attacks of bad temper seem also to run in epileptic families, among those who show no regular manifestations of the disease. Further light on this subject may be forthcoming.

The diagnosis, especially the differential diagnosis, of epilepsy, should be left to well-trained specialists. Attacks of other nervous diseases may be wrongly interpreted as epilepsy.

§ 251. **Criminalism and Epilepsy.** — The comprehensive assertion of Lombroso that the criminal is essentially an epileptic, even though he shows none of the ordinary diagnostic signs of the disease, and that epilepsy represents the genus of which criminalism and moral insanity are the species, is not to be taken too seriously. Of course, as Tarde says (**5**, p. 238, ff.), this theory of Lombroso is not without deep significance, even though it be literally untrue. The peculiar ugly temper and outbreaks without provocation, the variable temperament, and the episodic behavior to be observed in some criminals who are not known to be epileptics, form a suspicious chain of resemblances. So far as we ourselves are concerned, with our viewpoint of the practical value of digging deeply into causation in each case by itself, we have not the slightest need for the application of any such general theory. The extent of the relationship between epilepsy and criminality must stand upon its own feet as an ascertainable fact. Many observers working in Germany, France, England, and America have been unable to corroborate Lombroso's theories. Notwithstanding the frequency with which we ourselves have discovered this disease among offenders, we perceive altogether too many sides to the problem of criminalism to have them met in any such one-pointed fashion.

§ 252. **Our Findings.** — Our findings on the appearance of epilepsy as a factor in offenders' careers are that in a straight series of 1000 cases of young repeated offenders 7 per cent. are known to be definitely epileptic and there is a question of doubt in a number of other cases. Our figures are set forth elsewhere, § 107. Our data would seem to be much more complete than could be obtained from observation in penal and other institutions, because of our unusual opportunities for getting in touch with relatives, and hence for learning the story of developmental con-

ditions. Had we not had these antecedent facts many cases of
epilepsy could not have been recognized as such. Thus so far
as the substantiation of any such theory as Lombroso's is concerned we have had an exceptionally good chance.

In making the diagnosis of epilepsy we have not entered at all
into the well-founded modern contentions as to what really constitutes the disease. Medical science is unable yet to declare
itself on this question. We may say, in general, that we have
called those individuals epileptic who have had convulsive attacks
beyond the period of infantile convulsions, or when there has
been first-rate evidence of occurrence of attacks of minor epilepsy.
We have also included cases where spasms or convulsions were
exceedingly frequent during infancy or early childhood, even if
they disappeared later. Convulsions occurring during the course
of infectious diseases, etc. are, of course, not included.

The points in our discussion of this subject for which I should
ask most consideration are those concerned with the mental
peculiarities of epileptics. Those peculiarities merge into the
psychoses, the insanities, but yet in the great majority of epileptic offenders the question of insanity, as ordinarily conceived,
can hardly be brought up. The reader should, however, become
acquainted with the facts concerning the epileptic insanities,
§ 258, as well as the points under consideration.

§ 253. **Mental Peculiarities of Epileptics.** — The mental peculiarities which have special interest for the student of offenders
are (a) the strange variabilities, easily discerned by examination
or observation; (b) the remarkable general characteristics (the
so-called character) typical of the epileptic; (c) the gradual mental deterioration, which is so peculiar to the disease in its well-
marked forms that some specialists say it is one of the principal
points of diagnosis.

In any consideration of the mental life of epileptics as a class
it should be distinctly remembered that very able and wise men
have been sufferers from this disease in mild form. We who see
especially epileptics who are offenders, get a view of correlated
mental peculiarities which does not correspond exactly to the
facts as they exist among non-offenders. Yet we, when grading
according to mental abilities, find variations ranging from fair
or ordinary in ability to feeblemindedness.

(a) First of note among the peculiarities displayed by epileptics is the great variability in their mental functionings. To

417

know the mental capacities of an epileptic today is not to know them tomorrow. We have many times observed that our findings on tests are not duplicated at a second sitting. This is to be quite expected in the light of the wonderful changes which take place in the epileptic's psyche. Not only this, but there is also often great unevenness shown in different mental abilities at one testing. This irregularity in performance has led to the common saying at our clinic that great irregularity in itself suggests the possibility that epilepsy is the correct diagnosis, although those who are mentally dull from depleted physical conditions sometimes show the same phenomena. These variabilities in capacity are less well known than the changeableness of mood and entire disposition. Aschaffenburg (364) has devoted an essay to the important psychological and legal points of fluctuation of disposition. It is especially well shown in one of the cases cited below.

(b) The development of the so-called "epileptic character" is one of the well-recognized psychological peculiarities of this disease. In enumerating rapidly the points to which others have devoted many pages of consideration we have the following: Epileptics are prone to emotionalism, but much inconsistency is shown in their feelings. Some may be subject to constant irritability, but more often there is a sudden showing of anger and vicious conduct entirely without cause. On the other hand, there may be the assumption of an ultra virtuous attitude, with perhaps moralizing and preaching. One of the most cruel epileptic adolescents we have ever studied was a religious enthusiast at times. Periods of sullenness or bad temper may be prodromata of actual attacks, and in some cases it seems certain that ill feelings and their reflection in the mental disposition vicariously replace the attack. Impulsiveness is a very general characteristic.

Another class of epileptic traits, as many observers have noted, centers about their egocentric tendencies. There is a morbid self-love and egocentrism. This leads to self-assertion of all kinds, and to defective appreciation of the rights of others. Excessive obstinacy is frequently seen. In general, the ethical perceptions necessarily play a small part when these other tendencies are active. (The ordinary saying that in epileptics the moral sense is blunted, means merely that they show mental deterioration and overwhelming impulsions.) When there is over-development of the sexual life, as unfortunately there so frequently is, the combination of all these typical characteristics tends to make the epileptic a great offender. The character changes play so large a part in the mentality of the epileptic that it is sometimes said that unprovoked naughtiness is one of the earliest signs of epileptic tendencies in children, but one would have to be careful in drawing such a conclusion. All told, we may not only say that epileptics show many traits which lead in the direction of anti-social behavior, but that they are notoriously incalculable in their moods and impulses.

(c) The remaining class of epileptic mental peculiarities is concerned with general deterioration. Some of the best students go so far as to use this phenomenon as a diagnostic point, and state that without signs of gradual mental deterioration diagnosis of true epilepsy is doubtful. Observers of cases outside of institutions would hardly care to go as far as this. But the fact is that in very many cases there is a slowly progressive tendency towards the loss of mental power. Perceptions and will are affected; the finer ethical discriminations are lost, and the moral inhibitory powers are lowered. On account of just these facts we find the epileptic so frequently becoming an offender. There is much more study to be made of these points, particularly of the fields of mental activity which are involved in the deteriorating process. Thorough psychological study of the mental states of epileptics has yet to be made, but there have been definite starts in this direction.[1]

§ 254. **Physical Peculiarities of Epileptics.** — No consideration of the epileptic's characteristics is complete without taking account of the peculiar fact that this disease is frequently correlated with premature development and over-development, both of the general physique and of sex attributes. In our study of offenders we have seen some astonishing cases of this. We have mentioned it elsewhere, Case 22, and it was one of the main features of Case 79, cited below. I am not aware that any one has offered an explanation of this unexpected correlation.

§ 255. **Causes of Epileptic Being an Offender.** — I would not have it understood that I believe that the innate characteristics of the epileptic are solely responsible for his frequent growth

---

[1] For the student we may refer to Jung's studies on association processes (**365**), to the paper of Rittershaus (**366**) on the Differential Diagnosis of the Forms of Epilepsy by Psychological Studies, and also to the article on the use of tests by Wallin (**28**).

into an offender. The making of the confirmed criminal out of the epileptic is the result partly of his own innate mental and physical tendencies, partly of the formation of mental habits according to the laws of mental life, and is partly due to social conditions. (No small factor in this is the epileptic's continual regarding of himself as an anti-social being, a possible breaker of the laws.) Continuation studies of many an epileptic show clearly the sequence of events. It was, indeed, just this which drew my attention first to the criminological field. As I have elsewhere pointed out (27), the path of the epileptic from the clinic to the bridewell and the penitentiary is astonishingly well worn. Vagrancy and crime are the natural results of social failure, especially when impulses from within surge higher than the powers of inhibition. The young man expressed the point most clearly who came to our court and asked to be sent to a reformatory before he had actually committed the offenses which he felt he was bound ultimately to commit.

§ 256. **Illustrative Cases.** — The following cases have been selected as illustrating a considerable number of the points which typify the antecedents, the individual make-up, and the careers of epileptic offenders.

Case 77. — A young man, now 18 years of age, we have had under frequent observation for three years. The first time we saw him he showed mental hebetude to the extent that he hardly knew his own name and could give very little of his history. In this condition he remained for a number of hours. When seen at another time he proved to be ambitious and a fairly good student, who enlisted sympathy by virtue of his desire to get along well in the world.

This boy is the fourth of eight children, three of whom are dead, two older brothers are steady workers, and one brother is very irregular in his habits and somewhat of a runaway. We hear that this brother, a graduate of the grammar school, has been held in jail in other parts of the country. The father holds a very responsible position, and has been with the same company for 25 years. The mother is a fairly intelligent woman, much worried, neurasthenic and broken down as the result of her troubles. Both father and mother come from large families; they insist that there has been no insanity, feeblemindedness or epilepsy on either side. This is probably a reliable account.

The subject of our study was the result of a normal pregnancy and birth. He was healthy as an infant, but at 2 years began to hold his breath when crying and appear to faint. After that he had occasional attacks of unconsciousness. These have varied in nature from time to time. In the year prior to when we first saw him he had six attacks in which he fell and bit his tongue. He walked and talked early and had no diseases of importance for us. Sometimes he has had attacks in which everything becomes black in front of his eyes, and he would have to sit down until it passed away.

We found him at 15 years to be a well-developed and well-nourished boy. Weight 128 lbs., height 5 ft., 4 1-2 in. Strength good for age. No tremor. Coördination normal. The only stigma was a deep indentation of the lobules of ears. No sensory defect noted. Well-shaped head. We hear from the parents that he has had adult type of sex development for some time. During our acquaintance with this boy he developed still more, and at 18 he is a tall, strong young man with a very deep voice.

His mentality was extremely variable. For hours he might be extremely dull, on other occasions he would talk bravely about the possibility of his becoming a lawyer. Indeed, he had bought books that were recommended as adapted to his beginning such studies and had worked with them. The following is a sample of the result on tests at one sitting. They show remarkable irregularity.

I. 1′ 10″. No trial and error.

II. 1′ 35″. 4 errors.

III. Construction Test A. 18″.

IV. Construction Test B. 54″. Very little trial and error. Decidedly good perception of the relationships of form.

V. Puzzle Box, 6′ 57″. Good perception of the logical relationships of the different steps, but slow procedure.

VII. Reproduction of Geometrical Figures. Very poor result on this simple test. More parts than are necessary in one figure, and entire leaving out of the central part of the second figure.

IX. Cross Line Test A. Correct at 1st trial.

X. Cross Line Test B. Correct at 2d trial, but only in accordance with his own idea of the numbering of spaces, in spite of his having been shown carefully that his own conception of the numbering was wrong.

XII. Memory from Visual Verbal Presentation. 18 of the 20 items given with much verbal accuracy and in correct logical sequence. A very good result.

XVI. Motor Coördination Test. 85 squares at 1st trial. 87 squares at 2d trial. One error only at the 1st trial.

XVII. Writes a fairly good hand. Is curiously erratic in his spelling at times. For instance, "printer" he makes "pritner," but such errors are only occasional.

XVIII. Arithmetic. He tries to do examples in long division and then makes a proof that comes out ridiculously wrong. Shows a strange variability in his mental processes even on such work as attempting to prove an example, which was correctly done at first. At one time he multiplied the divisor by the remainder, and at another time multiplied the quotient by the remainder, and so on.

XXII. In a fragmentary way he knows many facts of history and geography. He has been a great reader. They have a good library of books at home, and he tells us he has been particularly fond of history, yet he says Abraham Lincoln was the first president of the United States, and makes other similar errors. The ordinary items of common scientific interest he knows fairly well, perhaps because his father is an expert mechanic. It is curious to note that his show of information on another occasion was entirely different. He can then tell us who the first president was, but now says the five great lakes are St. Louis, Michigan, Erie, and others which he does not know. Previously he had named them correctly, with the exception of Huron.

This boy had reached 7th grade by the time he was 15 years old, and had on various occasions impressed people with his desire for learning, with his studies in history, and probable ability to become a lawyer. On one of his earliest appearances in court the judge heard that he had an ambition to enter the legal profession, and refused to put any record against him in the hopes that he might change in character. It was said at the time that he was the victim of others who led him on. The first time we saw him he had suffered the previous night a miserable sex-pervert assault. But his delinquencies also involved very different types of behavior. He has stolen from other people as well as from home. At times he quarreled much with his brothers and even threatened their lives. On one occasion he took a check from the family mail box and attempted to get it cashed. Once he was persuaded by a man to go to a house of prostitution, and there acquired a venereal disease.

The worst of his delinquencies, except for a happy circumstance, might well have been train wrecking. One afternoon he was walking in a suburb, but for what purpose he was never able to tell. Indeed, he could never remember how he reached there. Coming to railroad tracks, he inquired when a certain fast train would be coming by. Walking out farther he very cunningly placed some angle irons in such fashion on the track that the train would surely be derailed. Meeting some boys in the vicinity he told them to come on down to the tracks in half an hour, and they would see a good wreck of the Fast Express. Most fortunately, one of the railroad people walking by saw the obstruction and removed it. Inquiry elicited the fact that our boy had given money to some lads to tell him at what time this particular train was due there. The abnormal character of the deed was thoroughly demonstrated by this. The offender was easily apprehended.

I have repeatedly seen this boy in his better moments, when he was always contrite and frank about this railroad affair. He apparently remembers his actions, but cannot give the slightest motive. He saw the track, and thought it would be nice to make a wreck, and then set about his purpose. He had not the slightest cause of grudge against the railroad company or any one in the train. Although he must have been several hours on his way to the suburb, he does not remember any part of that time. He feels that his act was the result of a sudden impulse, and he has no idea why he should have had that.

At other times we have seen him surly, grudgeful, and threatening vengeance on his dearest relatives. Once he told us, " I am better dead than the way I am. Sometimes I feel like killing myself. One day I came near doing it in the bath room, and I had the means there. I am not only making misery for myself." On another occasion, " I 'll never feel on friendly terms with him again. I 'll kill him, if he is my brother. I 'll do it yet." "These things come in my mind, doctor, that 's all there is to it, and I go right away and do them. There ain't no stopping to think. When a thing comes in my mind, I just go right ahead and do it, and I don't know why I do."

As a boy of 14 this lad had a scheme for studying oratory. He read the newspaper account of lawyers' speeches, and made the attempt to commit them to memory. He both wrote and recited them in his efforts at learning. After he left school he never held but one job for any length of time, and, curiously enough, that was for six months as a switch tender on a railroad. The danger of having him in this occupation can well be imagined. At times he has seemed delusional and has told strange stories about hidden treasures and about his acquaintance with girls. The last we heard of this young man was that he had run away to an eastern state and had succeeded in enlisting in the navy.

(Since writing the above we have an inquiry about this young fellow, and learn that after serving with a good record for about a year he, without known cause, deserted. He was then to be tried by court-martial.)

Mentality: Epileptic, great variability.	Case 77.
Delinquencies:	Boy, age 18.
Runaway + +.	
Stealing.	Mental ability:
Attempt to wreck train, etc.	Fair, but variable.

Many a gruesome tale could be told of murder and rape and other offenses of epileptics. We can well afford to leave such studies untold, since many have been recounted by others, particularly by Lombroso, but so many important social and psychological features appear in the following case of a murderer, who was finally hanged, that his history justifies a short recital.

Case 78. — Male 33 years old. I was asked to study as an impartial observer this man who was accused of murder in a small western city. At my disposal were placed the facts known to the lawyers of both sides, those that the police had ascertained, and I also had opportunity to meet the accused at length, and become acquainted with a number of members of his family. There was no question about the murder; the accused acknowledged it. The facts as to his previous history were in many details corroborated by information from different sources. The murder was peculiarly unprovoked. An old woman, who lived in a house by herself, was called up in the middle of the night by this man, who had spent the earlier hours at a party where some drinking had been going on. The woman knew this man slightly, and let him in when he rapped. What occurred afterwards is not altogether known except that the victim was choked, her throat was cut, and her chest and abdomen gashed open. There was some evidence of the viscera having been handled. Then there was search for her possessions. A bag was taken from which on the way home the murderer threw out various letters and some from his own pocket, which gave complete clue to his identity. He went home, prepared breakfast for his children because his wife was still at the party, slept for a time and then went about the town looking for work. On that evening he was calmly sleeping when the police arrived, and quickly went to sleep again after having been placed in the police station. He made no attempt at denial. The bag belonging to the woman was found in his home with no attempt at concealment.

On the physical side we found a very well nourished and heavily

built man. Large neck; rather deep set eyes; overhanging eye-
brows; superciliary ridges very large. Forehead rather retreating, but head fairly well shaped; circumference 57 cm. Regular
profile. Small mouth. Thin lips. Quiet and dull in expression.
General appearance heavy, dull, and rather brutal. No stigma
of importance. Constant fine tremor of outstretched hands.
Coördination tests all done fairly well. No sensory defect noted.
Complains much of hands sweating at intervals. Occasionally
frontal headaches with a feeling of sickness at the times. His trem-
bling and sweating as observed by us could not be counted as evidence of emotion, because he showed none in any other way. At
no time did we see the slightest evidence of excitement or contrition. Always slow pulse. The quiet attitude was said to be
usual with him, even to his being generally downcast. However,
even in jail he could easily be aroused to show humor, emphatically demonstrated by contraction of the orbiculares of the eyes.
Another evidence of the man's general make-up was shown by
the fact that he complained of much sex desire while in jail, in
this respect being as usual.

On the mental side we had before us the question of either aberration or defect. The only signs of aberration were to be found
in a strange emotional lethargy. We could pretty well rule out
postincriminatory disturbance, because his present attitude,
according to his wife and others, was quite usual. The abnormalities which he displayed were all those of a typical defective. He
responded readily to questions, and even had an apparent desire to go into various points of his career, but there was always
much evidence of incomplete memory. He could read only the
shortest words. He had never been able to read an ordinary
passage in a newspaper. He could write his own name, but very
little else, not even a simple letter. In arithmetic he was able
to do only the simplest processes in addition and multiplication.
To tell how much change he should receive from $5 if he bought
7 articles at 5 cents each, was far beyond him. On our Test VIII,
learning symbol associations, although he filled out the practice
part of the work, he utterly failed to remember the associations.
Our easy tests, IX and X, for the powers of mental representation, were also too much for him. Reaction times on association of verbal opposites was extremely slow. He only gave five
correctly, and the average time on these was 5''. His orientation as to time was mainly correct, but he did not know the day

of the month. He knows the president of the United States, and his own politics, but does not know who is the governor of the state. He does not vote. He does not know the names of the Great Lakes nor the lake on which Chicago is, although he has once been there. He knows nothing about the civil war nor the important part played by his native state at that time. All this, other tests given, and his history, showed that we had to do with a feebleminded man, who could converse well in simple fashion, and who had demonstrated the power of earning his living under direction.

He was one of eight children born to honest and temperate parents in a southeastern state. His mother was subject to epilepsy. All the other children have gotten along fairly well, they all gained a moderate education, and none of them developed epilepsy. However, sick headaches, apparently migraine, is a characteristic complaint among them and there has been much severe suffering on this account by several of them.

This boy had epileptic seizures when he was a child. He used to run away from home and stay for two or three days at a time, and act as if he did not know what he was doing, even at times when he did not have a convulsion. In spite of going to school for eight years, and being helped much at home, he never succeeded in learning to read or write. During early adolescence he became a thief. He stole on several occasions, and was finally sent to a reformatory in his home state, but was pardoned soon because he behaved well and *because he was an epileptic*.

This young fellow, shortly after his pardon married the woman who has always been loyal to him. She is neat and trim, and in intelligence far above him. They have two children, 8 and 10 years of age, who are up to their grade in school, and apparently normal in every way. There have been three or four miscarriages artificially produced. The wife has had to work out often, but since she is a very capable woman, there has been no particular financial stress.

His wife tells us that throughout his married life he seemed to be in his right mind as a rule, but he always appeared somewhat queer, inasmuch as he never would care to enter into conversation; he would only speak when urged to talk. Sometimes he would hold his head and say things were black in front of his eyes. At times he would shake and tremble all· over in his sleep, but he has never had any definite convulsions since she has known him.

She knew he had them earlier. Of late years he would walk out of the house and wander off somewhere, perhaps to the next town, and stay away all night. He has always treated her well when he has been sober. Although they live in a prohibition community, he has found it easy enough to get alcoholic beverages. Three or four years previously he was very curiously paralyzed on one side for about a week, but, to the surprise of everybody, he rapidly recovered. She corroborates his statement that he is extremely passionate sexually, and has been so all the time she has known him. Recently he has been even more so. Sometimes he is rough, but never cruel. (Without going into details, I may say that this is one of the most extreme cases of sexual passion that I have known of in medical work.) His memory always seemed to be somewhat poor, but previously he was somewhat brighter than he has been lately. On one occasion he attacked his family, and threw things about the house, and they had to run away until he got quieted down, but, in general, his wife has regarded him as a satisfactory husband.

This man himself frankly tells us all he knows of the murder and of his past history. He remembers the attacks his mother had, and how people told him that he was subject to fits. He tells us of his incarceration at 16 or 17, but cannot remember just how long he was in the reformatory, nor just how old he was. He was married at 18. He lays much stress on his strong sex desires, on his masturbation before marriage, and excessive cohabitation since then. For the last year or two says he has been almost crazy in this way. He has had gonorrhea twice, once before his marriage. Says he was never good at games, and never could shoot anything the way the other boys did. He used to wander off in the woods away from school. Since his marriage he wanders occasionally, and has been on sprees. He has lived steadily with his wife, but has been untrue to her on various occasions. Nearly all his work has been as a farm laborer, but recently he has been a hod carrier's assistant.

This man tells us that he is very changeable in his feelings. He thinks people treat him squarely, but he has not always done what is right. He says he has sometimes spent his wages, and then his wife had to go out to work. He does not think he has had any fits for many years, but something affects his brain at times. Everything gets dark in front of him. He gets weak and has to sit down. Occasionally this comes over him two or three times a day. He has been doing the kind of work where this did not make any difference. He can't recall just the day on which this murder occurred. He had been out of work for three or four days, and the evening before had been drinking a little beer and whiskey. He went to the party that night with his wife, but came away without her. He does not know exactly why he did this, nor does he at all know why he went into the house of the old woman. It was just an impulse that came over him. He thinks he must have cut her after he choked her because other people say so, but he really does not remember doing it. He knows he felt very strange at the time. He thinks perhaps he was angry because she had ordered him out of the house. He denies that he had sex feelings at the time, or that he had sex experiences with her. He was not then particularly hard up for money, and from her bag of belongings, which he discovered, he did not even take the money when he placed it on the shelf at home. He did not change his clothes, on which there were some blood stains, nor did he feel afraid about the affair. He thought perhaps it would not be found out; sometimes such things were not found out. When asked if he had any particular case in mind, he at first said no. (When I heard of the nature of this murder I inquired of the authorities if there had been any similar murders of women in the neighborhood, and I was told of one in a near-by town, and also that this man had been in the company of a dissolute woman at about the time when she was killed, although it was never known that she was murdered.) When I later asked in a general way about this, he said there was a woman who had been murdered under the same circumstances in a nearby country town, and that was never found out. Then I asked him about the other woman who was killed. He said he got to drinking with her down near the railroad tracks and he does not remember what happened. Her body was found much mutilated on account of having been run over by a train. He was found asleep near there. That was a couple of years previously. He says he thinks he would not have committed this murder of the old woman in the cottage had he not previously been drinking, although he certainly did not get drunk. (There is no evidence from the people at the party that he became intoxicated.)

In regard to his connection with the death of the woman on the tracks, his wife verifies the fact that he was found asleep there, but nobody ever ascertained that he knew anything of what had occurred. Concerning the murder of the woman in the neighboring town, she says she believes her husband was away from home on that particular night. Later I asked the man if he thought he had committed that other murder, and the only answer vouchsafed was that he did not know that he had. He very strangely never once denied it. The account of other minor delinquencies, showing his loose way of living, is of no particular importance. He was hanged, as he said he guessed he would be.

In summary: Here was a big, strong man; feebleminded and epileptic; of epileptic heredity; of fair ability in conversation; a satisfactory husband to a woman who was willing to work and help him and his children. He showed very peculiar and aberrational tendencies, but was able in a prohibition community to get plenty of alcoholic stimulants. He perpetrated at least one murder under pathological impulses. His life history, including his early pardon, is a good commentary upon social adjustments which do not take into account psychopathological elements. At no time was there the slightest foresight displayed in the handling of this case.

Mentality: Feebleminded, variable
         epileptic.

  Case 78.
  Man, 32 years.

Abnormal sexualism.

  Heredity: Mother epileptic.
         Much migraine in the family.

    Alcoholism.

Delinquencies:
  Earlier running away.
  Wanderer.
  Stealing.
  Sex abnormality.
  Murder.

An instance where a number of the typical features of the development and career of an epileptic offender are shown in exaggerated form is the following:

Case 79. — A boy of 16 has a long record of delinquency. He has been a frequent runaway from home, and is a thief. He has served one term in a prison for adults. He was in court the first time when he was 11 years old for running away.

Examination showed a young fellow of great size and strength for his years. Weight 155 lbs., height 5 ft. 6 in. Responsive and pleasant expression. No sensory defect. Hutchinsonian teeth suggest congenital syphilis. Very large head; circumference 59, length 21, breadth 15 cm. Sex development very great for his age, already completely adult.

On mental tests we found him irregular, but his abilities in some directions were good.

Heredity was extremely bad on both sides. The father was an excessively immoral man. The maternal grandfather was insane. The mother had miscarriages before this boy was born. The boy himself had scarlet fever and partial paralysis at 2 years of age. He had epileptic attacks until he was 10, and then they entirely ceased. We could not ascertain that he had been having attacks of any kind for several years before we saw him. His general and sex development was extremely precocious. His voice began to change and he developed a slight mustache at 10 years of age. Prior to that time he seemed very dull mentally, but about then began to improve. His school career was made very obnoxious for him on account of his over-development. Even in Sunday School the boys called him grandpa. In the last few years he had been greatly addicted to stimulants — tea, coffee and tobacco.

In this case we found a great mixture of elements, as shown by his causative factor card below. It is very interesting to note that this young man has gradually grown more stable; our last report is that he has been working steadily and behaving himself properly for a long time. Of course the ultimate prognosis depends upon the outcome of his disease.

Mentality: Variable epileptic.	Case 79.
Heredity: Father extremely immoral.	Boy, 16 years.
Maternal grandfather insane.	
Congenital syphilis probable.	
Developmental: Partial paralysis.	
Epileptic attacks.	
Premature puberty extreme.	
Stimulants +.	
Delinquencies:	
Runaway + +.	
Stealing.	

§ 257. **Legal and Other Social Treatment of Epileptic Offenders.**
— Until the nature of the disease or diseases which show themselves in epileptic seizures are known, discussion of the treatment is largely concerned with social measures. On account of
its peculiarities, epilepsy is a disease of great social importance,
and segregation is a measure of precaution and protection that
must be carried out in a large number of cases. The danger of
perpetuating this disease in succeeding generations, since, as
Davenport and Weeks (**367**) and others have shown, it is so
largely hereditary, can only be prevented by segregation or surgical measures. Whether the latter can be carried as far as a
number of parents desire who have been to me with their hearts
full of the horrors which may ensue from their offspring's abnormal sexual tendencies, is a matter to be determined by the
growth of public opinion.

The handling of epileptics under the law presents many
difficulties as laws are now framed. Although it is so well recognized that epilepsy frequently implies mental deterioration
and changes of character, which are part of the manifestations
of the disease, the epileptic, as such, is not recognized as being
an individual who needs peculiar consideration under the law.
A well-considered and forceful opinion rendered not long since
by the Supreme Court of Pennsylvania (**30**) gives the legal
point of view. In a certain case of homicide there were offers of
evidence to show that the defendant, a young man who had passed
his majority, in the early years of his life was subject to frequent
attacks of convulsions or spasms which for the time being rendered him unconscious, that after his 12th year the attacks became
less frequent, much milder in form, never attended with unconsciousness, that he was still subject to these attacks in a modified
form, and that he suffered one as recently as the day before the
crime was committed with which he was charged. It also appeared he had been drinking the afternoon and evening of the
occurrence. The court held that the matter of the intoxication
was irrelevant, inasmuch as no evidence was offered on the point
of the degree of intoxication, if any. Then the court went on and
asserted the following general theories. The unsoundness of
mind that excuses the criminal act must be so great as to control
the will of the subject and deprive him of free moral action. It
may be a physiological fact that one effect of epilepsy is to produce a state of mind easily excited by provocation, but except

as the epilepsy can be shown to have resulted in an unsoundness, which by itself would excuse an act, it cannot become a factor in determining the question of guilt or innocence. The law does not divide men into classes according to temperament or intellect, judging some more favorably than others, but it judges all alike.

If one ponders over the above dictum and the point of view which it represents and compares that with the social significance of the data which we have presented, it will be clearly seen that here the law does not at all strike a fundamental note for bringing about the protection of society which is its own *raison d'être*. As a practical measure there must be legal recognition of the fact that the various deteriorations and impulsive tendencies and emotional disturbances which are so peculiarly a part of the epileptic psyche, quite apart from definitive insanity, are themselves of vast social import. The criminalistic actions of the intelligent young man mentioned above, taken together with his own efforts at introspection, give us a good illustration of this point. While even in his best mental moments he is quite unable to describe his own motives, he himself is very loath to acknowledge his own irresponsibility. His own state of mind at the time of the attempted train wrecking appears to him as if it were under his control. He sometimes thinks that he might have done otherwise had he willed it. But I have heard exactly the same statement from violently insane persons who made a sudden recovery, and, when quite well, insisted that their wildest behavior they can distinctly remember as being definitely willed by themselves.

The basic point for consideration of epilepsy is the fact that this disease presents very peculiar social phenomena, which arise from certain mental and physical characteristics of the epileptic, and from the social dilemma in which he is placed. The limited opportunities offered to an epileptic accentuate his dissatisfaction with the world, times of idleness lead almost inevitably to the habits and the companionship which increase his moral, and perhaps his mental deterioration. Out of this unfortunate combination of circumstances one comes to witness in the life of epileptics almost unparalleled depths of depravity. Not only for what they are in themselves then, but also on account of their social disadvantages, the treatment of epileptics should not be a matter of merely court decision on a single offense, but must, to be effective, include more permanent measures.

§ 258. Epileptic Psychoses.

Quite apart from the epileptic deteriorations of mind and character, which we have elsewhere noted in their correlation to delinquency, § 253, one must consider the mental states connected with epilepsy which amount to actual insanity. Much has been written on this subject and it is hardly necessary to do more than barely mention the phenomena. It must be at once acknowledged, however, that it is frequently difficult to draw a line between the typical mental and moral alterations of epilepsy, and the development of real insanity, such as is demanded for diagnosis before the plea of irresponsibility is legally allowed.

The aberrational mental states connected with epilepsy we may enumerate as follows: According to Spratling (26) there are four paroxysmal epileptic mental conditions;

" (1) *Psychic epilepsy.* A complete morbid entity in itself and wholly destructive of responsibility so long as it is present." *Vide* § 250 (c).

" (2) *Epileptic automatism.* A condition of mental vacuity coexisting with natural bodily activity. This usually follows severe attacks; though it may be induced by those of milder form."

" (3) *Pre- and post-paroxysmal mental disturbances.* These are usually in the form of the most violent and destructive mania, lasting anywhere from a few minutes up to days or weeks, and in rare cases even longer."

" (4) *Paroxysmal or epileptic mania.* This is always destructive and dangerous in character, and in which the mental disturbance coincides with the fit. In cases in which it appears to be a substitute for the fit, it is known as the psychic epileptic equivalent."

(5) Then to these we must add, the slight epileptic dullness of intellect may become much more pronounced just before the seizure, so that it amounts to a thoroughly insane condition in which the individual may perform anti-social deeds.

(6) The well-known epileptic dementia, which may be of all grades, is sometimes disturbed by an excited condition which is possibly the result of an abnormal brain cell discharge. Under these conditions an ordinary sluggish and apathetic individual may be changed into an impulsive madman.

(7) Acute forms of insanity, to be diagnosed along classic lines,

433

are also found in epileptics. There may be occasional confusional states with delusions and hallucinations; there may be melancholias; and manic depressive conditions are met with. Some authors speak in somewhat different terms of the same conditions. Befogged states, conscious deliria, stupor, and epileptic furor are some of the terms used. There is also much mention of the paranoid states which we ourselves have frequently noted among epileptic offenders. Dipsomania is considered by some as a possible manifestation of epilepsy.

With the idea particularly expressed by Spratling (26, p. 476) that "unquestionably the gravest criminalistic result of epilepsy is the commission of assaults and inhuman crimes during the fit, or during the automatic state that immediately follows it," we do not at all agree. His is the standpoint of the institutional authority, while our experience has been with offenders as such, who have been secondarily discovered to be epileptics. Our findings are conclusive that most of the delinquencies of epileptics are committed quite apart from any mental states which could be properly denominated complete insanity. However, there can be no cavilling with the oft-quoted dictum of Clouston that "murder by an epileptic should be looked upon as being as much a symptom of his disease as larceny by a general paretic."

We need not burden our pages with cases showing the different forms of insanity connected with epilepsy. Text books on psychiatry give many such, but one or two instances showing the peculiar social significance of such aberrational states are worth noting.

We have seen a number of instances in which a child, even as young as 6 or 7 years, was designated by relatives and teachers as absolutely incorrigible, cruel, and dangerous, when upon study the case proved to be one of epileptic psychosis. There was hyper-excitability, and lack of self-control, and extreme irritability, connected with other epileptic manifestations, when there was no sign of mental defect or deterioration. Indeed, in some instances superficial brightness was shown by readiness of response and actual reaction to test. The following case remarkably illustrates the psychotic disturbance connected early in life with epilepsy and the growth of definite criminalistic behavior from both inner tendency (the development of the epileptic temperament), and such bad environmental influences as peculiarly beset the epileptic.

Case 80.—Boy 7 years old. Born in Germany. In the United States four years. Was brought in from a German orphanage. They have tried him for a couple of months and cannot tolerate him longer. The uncle, who supports the boy, states that already he has been tried in dozens of places. He has found nobody who will keep him. The complaint is extravagant incorrigibility everywhere. He has already been expelled from schools for kicking the teachers and interfering with the scholars. He is extremely restless and insubordinate, and particularly incalculable — one moment is affectionate and caressing, and the next minute shows violently bad behavior. Extremely talkative and forward. Has not the slightest sense of modesty. One caretaker insists that he is of the born criminal type. He has thrown a knife at some one. Others tell us he will steal anything.

A number of people have commented on his mental peculiarities. On numerous occasions he seemed to imagine he saw things. For instance, asserted that a rat ran past him. Then apparently feels some one touch him at the back, and looks round, he says, to see who it is. Is reported as being utterly self-willed. All united in saying that the boy is mentally bright and perhaps precocious in his abilities. Most notable about him are the variabilities of his emotional and other mental states. In several places he has been observed to have some peculiar attacks. In the orphanage he has been three times unconscious in attacks of convulsions. At other places where he has been observed for only a short time they have seen nothing but his mental peculiarities. Whenever he gets a chance he fairly gorges himself with food. On one occasion he ate a dozen bananas. In one place he developed a very peculiar habit of spitting. There seemed to be the most excessive flow of saliva for a time; the boy would fairly form a little pool on the floor by his continued expectorations.

Physically we found a boy in fairly good general condition. Weight 47 lbs.; height 4 ft. No sensory defects. Very lively attitude and vivacious expression. Bites finger nails. Rather prominent forehead and sharp and prominent occiput. Head; circumference 53.3; length 19.5; breadth 14 cm. He has been circumcised. All other examination negative.

Our psychological examination was readily conducted. The boy was most vivacious and anxious to do anything in the way of tests.

Binet: 1911 series.
4 years, all correct.
5 years, failed only on number 3.
6 years, failed only on number 1.
7 years, 1, 2, failure; 3, 4, 5, correct.
8 years, 1, 2, 3, 5, correct; 4, failure.
9 years, 1, 2, 3, failure; 4, nearly correct; 5, correct.
Of course most of the tests of our series were too difficult for him.
I. All but the triangles done in 3'. Failed on the triangles. Then
he was shown how. He did the whole test later in 1' 28''. The next
day did it without trial and error in 2' 32''.
II. 2' 13''. 8 errors.
IV. Failure in 8'. Was given some help. The next day did it
correctly.

The general apperceptions of this boy were decidedly good.
He talked very well indeed. His capacity for attention at this
time was good, but as observed in the school-room later it seemed
to be decidedly poor. No doubt whatever about this being a boy
of good ability when he is at his best, but he suffers greatly from
epileptic mental variability.

From the uncle we get an intelligent family history. The
father is dead. The boy is one of two children. The older
brother seems to be normal and is doing well in school. The
mother's family not known. In the father's family no insanity,
epilepsy or feeblemindedness known. For some time before this
boy was born the mother was notoriously alcoholic and sexually
immoral. This went on during his pregnancy. Many attempts
at abortion were made. However, he was born at full term and
was a very large baby. The mother deserted the family when
the boy was less than 3 years old. Whereabouts unknown. Outside of the attacks mentioned above, he is not known to have
ever been seriously ill. Never injured.

Since no epileptic colony was open to this boy he had to be
taken care of as best he might by private people who were paid
by this uncle, who himself had no home to give him.

Two years later we again saw the boy after more complaint of
his delinquencies. He had been living in a city environment, being
in a home where there were no other children. He had recently
been expelled from school, even from a special room for defectives. Complaints about him had come in from several sources.
Had been reported several times at the police station. He had
been engaged in obscene behavior and throwing stones at windows. One curious trick of his was to go into some shop or place

of business and refuse to go out, in the meantime swearing at the people who interfered with him. He is known as a great liar.

On examination this time we found him in exceedingly good physical condition. Vivacious and forceful manner. Has much language ability. Repeats long pieces of poetry for us and bears out his general reputation of being a very bright boy. Even a short conversation brings out his erratic tendencies. He weaves fanciful tales, and deals in the most absurd exaggerations. Most unfortunately we hear even from himself that he has been engaged in miserable sex perversions. He has been consorting with a degenerate negro. Nowadays has only occasional attacks, has had no major ones for three months. Very difficult to say whether or not his attacks of temper represent epileptic equivalents.

The outlook for this case is obviously very bad. We may see here the usual interaction between the evil in an ordinary environment and the epileptic type of character. The boy properly needs complete segregation in a colony. Already he has proved expensive as well as troublesome, and is likely to harass society to a much greater extent.

Mentality: Epileptic variability and temperament.	Case 80. Boy, 9 years.
Heredity: Mother bad character.	
Ante-natal conditions: Mother alcoholic and immoral.	
Home conditions: Much changing about.	
Delinquencies: Incorrigibility + +. Violence. Tendency to sex offenses.	Mentality: Psychosis as above.

The violent and even homicidal assaults occasionally perpetrated by epileptics during periods of actual insanity are not necessary for us to dwell on. They are well known as being particularly brutal. The possibilities of criminalism and vice, correlated with aberrational epileptic tendencies are well illustrated by the following typical case:

Case 81. — A young woman, now 20 years old, we have had under observation several years. She is slight in build, of decidedly refined expression, has rather delicate features, speaks in low tones, and is pleasantly responsive. Her good forehead and refined physiognomy entirely belie her record of misdemeanor.

Beginning at 15 years this girl has been the source of much trouble to her family and to the community. She started by running away from home, and was discovered on several occasions in other households working under an assumed name. She always told a fictitious story in great detail to the people for whom she worked. On one occasion she was found through her family advertising for her. Since she would not stay at home, opportunities were found for her to work elsewhere, but she would hold places for only a few days, and then steal and either leave or be discharged. All along she has caused much trouble at times by telling, even to the probation officers who have attempted to befriend her, lies which have sounded very plausible. She always has a very great deal of complaint about the conditions at home or elsewhere. Some serious false accusations were made by her. At times she is in a quite irresponsible condition, wanders about and makes chance acquaintances. During one whole summer she was away from home, and was finally arrested in another county, where she was living on the outskirts of a small town in a shack with a foreign laborer. As a result of that experience she became badly diseased and was treated for long in a hospital. Later she was in court again for forging checks. On another occasion she stole money from her family, again was lost for a couple of weeks and was found in a neighboring town. Once she was placed for some months in an institution for delinquents. She has recently been married (eugenists take notice!) and lives in another state.

On the physical side we never found anything of note, except poor development, poor nutrition and anemia. At our instigation she was treated for a time with much success in a clinic; while under treatment her aberrational conditions and misconduct showed great diminution. It is only fair to say that at one time when she was behaving the worst she had no major epileptic attacks of which we could get any history. We were not sure of minor attacks then because she had grown so unreliable in her statements.

During infancy she had a few convulsions. They have never been very frequent at any period of her life. At one time when we first knew her she had about half a dozen convulsive seizures during the previous year. However, minor manifestations were much more frequent. After a feeling of dizziness she would sleep for hours, even in the daytime, without having any other evidence of an attack. At times she was said to stand and stare for a minute or so without knowing what was said to her. Enuresis continued until she was 16.

The girl is the second of eleven children, two of whom died in infancy. None of the children is thoroughly strong, but we never could get proof that any of them was epileptic. A couple of sisters had rebelled at environmental conditions on account of the peculiarities of the mother, and left home. Before this child was born the father had deserted and the mother was left almost destitute. The child was born prematurely. Both mother and child were in poor condition. It is interesting to note that since then the father, who is not a bad sort of man in general, has lived with the mother and supported her properly. This child was slow in walking and talking and had various infectious diseases, always, however, in mild form. Did not menstruate until she was 17 years old.

The family history is most significant. The father is a healthy and steady man. One of his brothers was subject to very severe attacks of epilepsy, and was totally incapacitated thereby. His sister was a severe sufferer from migraine. The mother is unquestionably mildly insane. At times she has been very neglectful of her family, has been violent, and irresponsibly wanders about the street. Her mental condition evidently varies greatly. No knowledge of her having epilepsy. No more information has been forthcoming about her side of the family.

We had satisfactory evidence from the start that this girl was not feebleminded. She reached 7th grade in school, reads well, does arithmetic through simple fractions, and does well on various tests. These were the results when she was at her best, before she had gone far in the career which we have described above. As time has gone on she has shown more and more unreliability and great mental variation. However, at no time when we have seen her could we actually at that moment denominate her as clearly insane, although every evidence from other observers is that at times she is quite irresponsible mentally.

The social difficulties of dealing with such a case have been illustrated time and again by this girl's career. Her irresponsible behavior might not be shown at all if she came up for examination regarding sanity, and no hope was entertained of her being found insane by the jury methods in vogue in our state. On the other hand, she steadily refused to go to a state hospital voluntarily, and her family, approached at the periods when she was rational and well behaved, were never willing to send her. Her present married state, with its possibilities of defective and poorly cared for offspring we need not dilate on.

The psychic conditions of this young woman have shown variations all the way from the twilight states in which she told foolish and unnecessary lies, and stole money, to quite irresponsible conditions in which she was quite another personality from her refined self, and went on her miserable wanderings, suffering all sorts of vicissitudes.

Mentality: Epileptic psychosis at times.

Case 81.
Girl, 20 years.

Heredity: Insanity, epilepsy, migraine.
Mother mildly insane.

Developmental: Antenatal conditions bad.
Premature birth.

Home conditions: very poor oversight.

Delinquencies:
Running away.
Stealing.
Forging.
False accusations.
Sex.

Mentality:
Epileptic variability
and psychosis.

CHAPTER XIII

Mental Abnormality in General

§ 259. General Considerations.   § 260. Classifications.   § 261. Definitions.

§ 259. **General Considerations.** — Appreciation of the part
which abnormality plays in the production of criminalism is
immensely aided by clear conceptions of what constitutes abnormality in its varieties. It would be well if the outlines of the
subject were definitely understood by all who have to deal with
delinquents. The growth of better social adjustments of offenders
is dependent on such understanding.

So far as definition is concerned, specific names are desirable
when they may safely be applied to characteristics of an individual,
and not otherwise. A point of great interest in this whole matter
is that, while the general fact of abnormality may be certain,
the irregularities of function of that most complex of all phenomena, the human mind, may prevent the abnormality from falling into any of the well-defined specific categories of mental defect
or disease. The inability to apply the name of any definite disease or of any grade of defect to a case should not, however, befog
the practical issue. In court work one sees individuals with mental
abnormality most potent for the production of criminalism, who
cannot be said to be suffering from any of the definitively classified ailments of the text-books. Notwithstanding this there are
plenty of proofs of their abnormality.

It is true that, even in hospitals for the insane, some patients
with major manifestations of psychoses are held to be suffering
from unclassifiable forms of mental disease. A campaign against
too ready naming of mental abnormalities, and indeed, against
the necessity for naming at all except when well-known disease
processes or symptomatic pictures are found, has been carried on
by some of the foremost psychiatrists, particularly Meyer. The
remarkable case we cite in § 306 shows the impossibility of designating according to standard classifications, even after years of
observation. The naming difficulty, so far as the assignment
of a specific mental disease is concerned, is met with even more

441

when the minor psychoses are under consideration. Yet the latter are specially important as actuating criminalism. This stands out clearly in our respective case studies.

In this matter we should not be stampeded in the least by what we are asked for on the witness stand. In regard to mental abnormality the law has its own artificial standard, one that is neither based upon the best that is known in the field of abnormal psychology, nor — which is much more to the point — on studies of the interactive causative factors of delinquency as found in the career of the individual offender.

The main point, for us at least, is whether or not the individual is influenced towards delinquency by any abnormal mental condition, and what is the likelihood for the future. Society has the greatest need of protecting the individual and itself in the light of the prognosis. The idea that the individual should not be held under the law because his act was determinably the result of mental abnormality is unsound from the above standpoint. When it comes to actual prognosis it should be remembered that recurrence of misdeeds is perhaps even more frequent among offenders who cannot be said to be suffering from any named mental disease, although the fact of their abnormality may be patent. Concerning diagnosis of the general fact, steady advance in the ability to scientifically determine mental abnormality is being made by the use of the newer methods of psychological examination, and it is to be hoped the discovery of many corresponding organic conditions will take place.

Under the term of mental abnormality are to be included all types of deviation from the social and racial norms as recognized by common observation of the individual's reactions, or as established by scientific investigation. Abnormality may include unusual activities of normal traits as well as unusual disabilities. In the study of delinquency we are much more concerned with the weakness of mental powers, than we are with the heightening of any abilities, and yet, as may be seen later in our sections on mental peculiarities, the accentuation of some normal traits may be regarded as a direct causative factor of delinquency.

§ 260. **Classifications.** — The main types of mental abnormality are in general terms to be classified either as mental defect, or mental aberration, or mental peculiarity. It is perfectly true that sometimes we cannot sharply divide the lines. The mental defective may have aberrational states superadded;

between mere mental peculiarities and real aberration differentiation at times is often impossible. The main types stand out with great clearness, but indefiniteness for classification besets the border lines. From the less clearly defined regions of mental abnormality arises, however, a full quota of delinquents.

We would also insist that all-inclusiveness is beyond the possibility of definition or the sharp discriminations of a single phrase. The functions of the human mind are too intricate to allow of all their abnormal conditions being characterized in short. Many a psychiatrist has met his Waterloo in attempting a definition merely of insanity. It is partly on account of these inherent difficulties, and partly through the nascence of applied psychology and of the application of its facts to the field of the law, that there are such tremendously loose conceptions of what might be a much more specific terminology. Elsewhere (50) I have given illustrations of the extraordinary contradictions in the use of the terms concerning mental defect, as found in the dictionaries and in legal and medical text books. With the nomenclature adopted now by the American Association for the Study of the Feebleminded there is no further excuse for this.

To make clear the subclasses of mental abnormality is the purpose of the following schedule and related statements:

Mental Abnormality.	Mental Defect.	Feebleminded.	Idiot. Imbecile. Moron.
		Subnormal.	
		Defective only in some special ability.	
	Mental Dullness from Physical Conditions.		permanent. temporary.
	Psychic Constitutional Inferiority.		
	Mental Aberration. (Insanities) (Psychoses) (Psychopathies)	Major types.	chronic. transitory.
		Minor types.	chronic. transitory.
	Mental Peculiarity.		

443

§ 261. **Definitions.** — Under the head of *mental defect* we have to deal with just what the name implies, a definite lack of general mental ability as an irrevocable characteristic. From some cause existing in the germ plasm, or occurring early in the growth of the individual, mental potential never became normal. Full developmental capacity was never present and never can be gained. Mental defect is incurable. The term feeblemindedness (amentia) is improperly used as covering the same ground as mental defect. As we shall see in our case studies, there are minor defects of general mental development, or special mental disabilities, in individuals who are nowise fairly to be denominated feebleminded. For further details on all varieties of mental defect our chapter on that subject is to be consulted.

The recognition of certain other groups of cases most important for studies of the problems of childhood and adolescence, but hardly mentioned in the text books on mental abnormality, depends upon continued observations of the individual. In the examination, especially during the period of development, it is sometimes most difficult to discriminate between those who are innately defective and those who are *mentally dull from poor physical conditions*, or from the indulgence in various debilitating habits. Time, and the betterment of the physical conditions may be necessary for the final classification. But even when the bodily conditions are unalterable, the diagnosis of mental dullness from physical states may often fairly stand. The tentative use of this class offers the chance to group not a few cases which at first it is unsafe to define. We refer the reader to our case studies of this type for more explicit characterization of the group.

Then comes *psychic constitutional inferiority*, which has been particularly designated as standing between feeblemindedness and insanity, perhaps partly invading the territory of each. Largely incapable of social self-control under ordinary environmental conditions, individuals of this class are so on the borderline that they often prove unacceptable to either institutions for the feebleminded or the insane. This is an important group for the student of criminalistics to became acquainted with. For further statements anent this class our specific chapter should be consulted.

Mental aberrations are to be distinguished from mental defects by the fact that they may occur in individuals who are not primarily mental defectives. (Aberrations do also occur in mental defectives. Indeed, it is strange they do not more frequently show them.) The idea of there being such a thing as mental disease comes into play here — given a fairly normal mind, and as the result of various internal or external stresses, or maladjustments, or physical diseases, there may develop a diseased mentality. Then many cases of mental aberration are curable as bodily diseases are curable. The word disease in this connection is only used in its widest interpretation, namely, a wandering from the normal or healthy state. In carrying further the analogy to what we understand as physical disease we meet with much difficulty. The mind cannot be pictured in any way as an object subject to such pathological changes as we recognize in the brain or elsewhere in the body. Then it is altogether a moot question if there be not aberrations caused by internal faults of adjustment, quite apart from any discoverable correlations of physical malfunctionings, or lesions of the brain. The idea that all mental aberrations are due to actual pathological conditions of the brain is only a supposition, perhaps a true one, but which will probably always remain such. Altogether it is better not to use the term mental disease — certainly for our purposes I prefer to speak of mental aberrations.

When we come to the subdivisions of aberrational mental conditions we are at once confronted by the fact that there are numerous temporary, or even permanent, evidences of mental aberration in cases where it is not desirable to apply the term insanity. The whole subject is complex and difficult from the standpoint of hard and fast classification or definition. Various minor mental impairments, which any one would hesitate to denominate insanity, are practically discernible as most important for the student of delinquent causation. By insanity most of us mean mental incapacity which demands segregation and hospital treatment. It is true that some of these minor impairments, such as are associated with nervous disorders like chorea, should have careful treatment, but, while recognizing the temporary irresponsibility of the individual, one would still hesitate to give a certificate of mental unsoundness, such as might redound later to the disadvantage of the individual. This, however, merely serves to show our false social attitude towards the whole question of mental aberration.

For the lay reader we should here emphasize parenthetically that dementia is a totally different thing from primary mental defect or amentia. Dementia implies the previous integrity of a mind which has lost its power, often through preceding mental disease. Dementia may also result from bodily ailments or injuries, including the effect of poisons, such as alcohol.

Our final group under mental abnormality is *mental peculiarity*. It is very clear to all close students of delinquents that repeated offenses may result from some special mental twist, impulse, or even from the over-development of some special capability which is not adequately taken care of by environmental conditions. Such individuals cannot be called aberrational, and yet the peculiarity determines their socially abnormal behavior in their given social settings. Very interesting groups of cases may be subsumed under this heading, as is to be seen in our chapters on the subject.

Once more for the sake of emphasis we must state that there is great overlapping of groups throughout any classification of mental abnormality, and that the border lines between them, even for definition, are not clear. This individual, determinable as showing some mental peculiarity, may later turn out to be an epileptic; this case that shows aberrations after head injury is often one who was primarily a psychopath; this adolescent psychosis may be developed upon an original basis of slight defect; and so on. But it is only when scientific discriminations, which it may be impossible to render, are called for, that there is great difficulty in adjudication of the case according to the best interests of society.

CHAPTER XIV

MENTAL DEFECT

§ 262. General Considerations.   § 263. Nomenclature.   § 264. Definitive Classifications. **Feeblemindedness.**   § 265. Idiots.   § 266. Imbeciles. § 267. Morons. § 268. Treatment of Feeblemindedness. § 269. Treatment of Feebleminded Offenders.

§ 262. **General Considerations.** — The subject of mental defect is of great import in the study of delinquency and its causation. Just what percentage of delinquents are feebleminded appears to be a matter of perennial interest, but well-founded statistics, even if obtained in particular places, may not be applicable to different situations. There can be no doubt that separate reformatory or prison populations if tested would show from 10 to 30 per cent. or even more, to be feebleminded. The numbers which we have found in several years of court work among our somewhat selected group of offenders have been already given, § 103. No essential purpose is subserved by exaggerated statements concerning the proportions which might be found in court work, or in various penal institutions. We might discuss at great length the numbers of mental defectives among offenders from our many notes on the subject; there has been much advance since 1910, when the author was *rapporteur* for this subject at the International Prison Congress and received astonishingly variant statements from different institution people, ranging from the opinion that in certain reformatories none were feebleminded, to the assertion that 40 per cent. or more were defective. But the gist of the situation is that mental defect forms the largest single cause of delinquency to be found by correlating tendency to offend with characteristics of the offender.

Lest there be misapprehension we should here state that even with this clear-cut cause for delinquency, one rarely finds personal characteristics as a sole causative factor of criminalism. Defective offenders, in most cases, upon study prove to be individuals who easily succumb to social temptations, easily learn from vicious examples, easily are stimulated to develop criminalistic trends of thought. In morals they prove themselves wanting in resistance when neglected by their families or by society, so that they have to meet undue temptation and suggestion to immorality.

447

In other words, in these highly representative members of the so-called criminal type one must conclude that the development of criminalism is partially the result of environment as well as of innate tendencies. If one does not believe this, let him study similar defective individuals in the conditions of a good training school for the feebleminded, and see, under appropriate environment, how small an amount of criminalistic tendency is evolved.

Working outside of institutions and with individuals who are not primarily selected according to mental traits, we discover a much greater complexity in the question of mental defect than is set forth in text books on the subject. Authors have developed their conceptions from observation in institutions, and have little or nothing to say about the border-line cases and those in which there are special and peculiar arrangements of mental capabilities and disabilities. Yet these are of the greatest interest for the student of delinquency, because they frequently are most troublesome socially, and because they offer far more hope in the way of adjustment by educational or vocational means than do typical forms of general feeblemindedness.

In our case studies we deal at greater length with the less well known types of mental defect, not because they are numerically more important, but because less has been written about them and because they are not so easily recognized and understood.

§ 263. **Nomenclature.** — The nomenclature to be most recommended is that adopted by the American Association for the Study of the Feebleminded in 1910. This body of experienced scientific workers agreed to use the word feebleminded as a generic term under which there should be the subclasses idiots, imbeciles, and morons (Mωρos, stupid). Heretofore the terms applied to mental defectives have been very loosely used and the definitions of the law are often at variance with medical and psychological usage. It is to be regretted that this whole matter is not clearly set forth in dictionaries and legal text books. Henceforth there can be little excuse for this indefiniteness.

§ 264. **Definitive Classifications.** — There have been many attempts at definitive classification of the feebleminded. Practically all of these until recently have been upon a medical basis: the individual belongs to this or that group because of the etiology of his trouble, or because of the anomalous size of his head, and so on. Sollier began with an attempt at rough psychological classification. For the reason that the old classifications gave little

448

clue to the practical treatment of the case, they have found no place in the scheme of definition adopted by our American Association, or by the British Royal Commission for the Study of the Feebleminded. The report of the British Royal Commission in 1908 made a distinct step in advance. Their well-founded insistence on the social aspects of the feebleminded can never fairly be lost sight of. They define mental defectives, the genus for which we in America have adopted the term feebleminded, as those suffering from a " state of mental defect from birth or from an early age, due to incomplete cerebral development, in consequence of which the person affected is unable to perform his duties as a member of society in the position of life to which he was born."

Under this head the lowest grade, or idiot, is defined as " a person so deeply defective in mind from birth, or from an early age, that he is unable to guard himself against common physical dangers." The middle grade, or imbecile, is " one who, by reason of mental defect existing from birth, or from an early age, is unable to earn his own living, but is capable of guarding himself against common physical dangers." The highest grade, called the feebleminded, but better categorized by the newer term, moron, is defined as " one who is capable of earning a living under favorable circumstances, but is incapable from mental defect, existing from birth, or from an early age, (a) of competing on equal terms with his normal fellows; or (b) of managing himself and his affairs with ordinary prudence."

Nowadays by the application of newer psychological methods we have other helps to both diagnosis and classification. The general scheme of Binet has done much to place our classification upon a rational basis. Binet's method is developed on the idea that the feebleminded individual is one who is best represented as the victim of arrested mental development. This arrest may be measured in terms of psychological norms obtained by the study of young children according to ages. Most of his norms hold good, and we have now at least the skeleton of a measuring scale of defective intelligence.

According to the work of Goddard and others, defectives who are able to get through the Binet test for 12 years are practically never to be found in institutional life. That is to say, individuals of mental ages above 12 are at least in some degree regarded as socially acceptable. Upon the basis of this finding, the limits for distinguishing defectives by mental tests have been scheduled.

The American Association has set forth the following practical scheme of diagnosis: Idiots are those who are able to do the mental tests up to the level of the normal child of 2 years: Imbeciles are able to do the tests performed by a normal child between the ages of 2 and 7 years: Morons are those who equal the mental performance of a child between the age of 7 and 12 years. This makes a very clear-cut formula for diagnosis and definition, and if it were not for the inequalities of mental development which have to do especially with social success, and which will be discussed later, the whole matter of diagnosis might be safely left to the findings of these tests. As it stands, however, there can be no doubt that the safest and most practical definitions for feeblemindedness and its subclasses are to be made by combining the statement of known social disabilities, or special capabilities, with the findings by accredited age tests.

We see difficulties in taking either definition alone because (a) there are some who cannot pass the 12-year tests, partly on account of poor native ability and partly because of lack of schooling, who yet get along normally in some humble sphere, and (b) because there are individuals with various defects who are able to pass the 12-year tests, but who on account of their defects are unable to compete fairly with their fellows.

Our experiences lead us to feel certain that we have the most practical reasons for extending and subdividing the classification of mental defectives according to the possession of certain mental qualifications which have special social bearing, as well as according to the findings by intelligence tests, including the Binet system. A suggestion of this opinion is frequently heard in court work when it is said by the practical onlooker that some given offender cannot be mentally defective because of cunning displayed. The laity particularly emphasize the value of such mental traits as enable the efficient commission of acts — burglary, for instance — and consider the given deed without regard to the tenor of the offender's whole life. Later on we shall give examples where special abilities, such as may be the chief stock-in-trade of a skillful burglar, have been preserved or developed upon a background of general mental disability. We are glad to note that such an experienced penologist as Pollitz (8, p. 132) sees this point clearly. It is such facts as these which enforce upon us the value of more thorough studies of individuals and more classification of them according to their social possibilities or social dangers.

The prognosis, which of course is so vitally important from many points of view and includes even the social outcome, is not afforded by the psychological study or classification taken by itself. There are many medical features which must necessarily enter in, particularly those which have to do with the pathological basis of the mental defect itself, either as found in heredity or in development of the defective himself. Then for our ultimate word on the individual we must depend on a combination of the findings by psychological tests, medical examination, family and developmental histories, and our knowledge of social qualifications of the given defective.

From our own careful studies we have been forced to develop the classification of mental defectives scheduled below. We concur in the sound ideas of the British Commission that defectives are those who suffer from incomplete cerebral development existing from birth or from early age. Thus those who are merely aberrational in type, suffering from what is ordinarily termed a psychosis or mental disease, and those who have become weak in mind secondarily to injury after the first years of life, or to mental disease, or to debilitating physical conditions, are ruled out. We agree also with the general idea of the Binet tests as offering the best method of standardization by psychological classification.

As we suggested above, and have elaborated in the schedule and text below, the classification of defectives, for very practical purposes, has to be extended. We are obliged to deal with a group which ranges above the designated Binet limit of feeblemindedness and who unquestionably yet show subnormality of social importance. These we describe below and term subnormals. Then we have been long interested in a group that one hesitates much to place under the general caption of mental defectives. They are those who are defective in special and limited faculties only, having otherwise normal ability. Individuals belonging to this class frequently are of great significance for the student of criminalistics. We shall deal with them later. Finally we should here make first mention of the group of those who are mentally dull from acquired physical causes, including debilitating habits. These individuals are not always to be differentiated by psychological tests. They are not, properly speaking, mental defectives. Discussion of these also will be taken up in detail.

A practical classification of those who are defective in general or in special mental abilities diagrammatically represented appears thus:

451

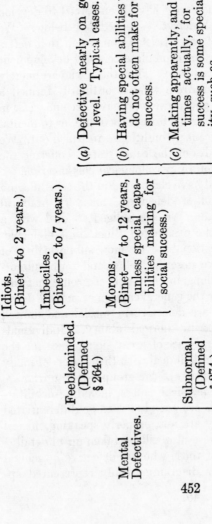

Mental Defectives.

Feebleminded. (Defined § 264.)

Idiots. (Binet—to 2 years.)

Imbeciles. (Binet—2 to 7 years.)

Morons. (Binet—7 to 12 years, unless special capabilities making for social success.)

(a) Defective nearly on general level. Typical cases.

(b) Having special abilities which do not often make for social success.

(c) Making apparently, and sometimes actually, for social success is some special ability, such as

  (a) Good insight into own defect.

  (b) Language ability.

  (c) Motor ability.

Subnormal. (Defined § 274.)

Individuals defective in special and limited abilities only. Otherwise mentally normal.

Defective ability not interfering with social success.

Interfering with social success is some defective ability, such as

  (a) arithmetic.

  (b) language.

  (c) judgment; powers of mental analysis.

  (d) self-control.

The mentality of important types with greatly varying abilities may, in their divergence, be graphically represented as below; many other combinations of abilities, of course, being possible. (*A*) is an individual with special abilities rising high from his general level of mentality, which otherwise approximates the average or normal for his age and race or nationality; (*B*) an individual with special disabilities, but who has otherwise mentality which approximates the average level; (*C*) a typical *idiot savant* with a special ability rising up to normal or even beyond, from a general background of mental defect.

The line drawn in the diagram as representing normal ability is, of course, absolutely arbitrary and may be taken as indicating rather an average for each ability than designating the relative capabilities of any given normal individual. Every one varies in different capacities from any such average. The line indicating those feebleminded who have mental defects ranging nearly on the same level, on the other hand, represents a well-defined, typical relationship to average abilities.

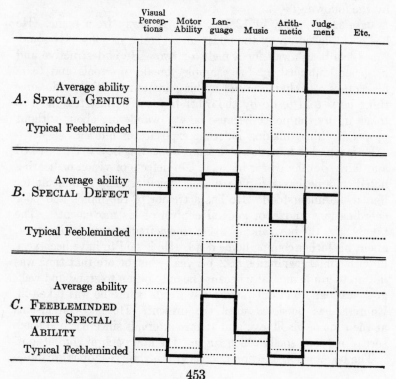

FEEBLEMINDEDNESS.

§ 265. **Idiots.** — The group of individuals properly designated under modern nomenclature as idiots rarely, if ever, are criminals. In practically all cases they are found so intolerable socially on account of their mental defect that they are early segregated and protected.

§ 266. **Imbeciles.** — The middle grade of feebleminded, namely imbeciles, are more frequently encountered in connection with court work, but are not at all numerous. We ourselves have seen less than a dozen cases among 1000 young repeated offenders, but readily concede that in certain institutions where older chronic misdemeanants are sent a larger proportion might be found. It certainly is rare that imbeciles become major offenders. This is because they are very often readily perceived to be socially undesirable, and while young are sent to institutions for the feebleminded. Typical social offenses of this group may be illustrated by the following:

Case 82. — A boy of 13 is a great runaway from home. He has been picked up by the police on several occasions. He sometimes has been away for a night or two. He is destructive and in general unreliable; for example, breaks up tools and tears his clothes. Is characterized by his parents as willing to do anything he is told to do by the other boys. The last time he was taken up by the police because he was wandering about without proper clothing, making indecent exposure of himself.

He is found to be rather a pleasant-appearing boy, well nourished and fairly developed for his age. No defects of vision or hearing noted, but he has a lisping speech which renders it difficult for him to be understood. He has a tremor of the hands and poor coördinations and poor general control of his movements. The family says the boy talks of queer things frequently; for instance, about his father coming home dead. He is said to have been very ill with spinal meningitis at 2 1-2 years, but before that time was not up to grade mentally because he only began to stand and walk at 2 years and had only said a few words before he was taken ill. Enuresis has persisted until the present. He had convulsions at the time of his illness, and at rare intervals since has had some sort of nervous spells which suggest the approach of convulsions. The boy's whole bearing and general mental reactions are indic-

454

ative of his low mentality. When he was given our simple introductory picture form board, Test I, he laid the pieces about
indiscriminately, and even after explanation made no attempt
to put them correctly in place. By the Binet system he is able to
pass none of the 8-year tests, only one of the 7-year, and three
of the 6-year; so clearly the boy belongs to that middle group of
the feebleminded designated imbeciles.

No doubt early illness was a factor in his case, but there is
much evidence of familial degeneracy. Out of nine children no less
than five are known to be defective in some degree, this boy being
the worst, and there is much tendency towards convulsions in
the family without, however, there being any proof of real epilepsy.
Such family history would seem to indicate defective heredity,
but no traces of this are ascertainable. It is the family mentioned in § 146.

The outlook for such a case is, of course, extremely bad from
a social standpoint. The boy might readily acquire a venereal
disease and be led into criminal offenses by those who wished
to use him. He has never got beyond the 1st grade in school.
His parents regret they did not long ago send him to an institution, which they are willing enough to do at present.

Mentality: Imbecile.	Case 82.
Developmental conditions: Meningitis at 2 years.	Boy, 13.
Familial degeneracy.	
Home conditions: Large family, poor control.	
Delinquencies: Runaway +, etc.	

All that is necessary to say about girls of this mental grade is
that unless they are exceedingly well guarded at home or taken
care of in institutions they are almost bound to fall morally by
the wayside.

§ 267. **Morons.** — Of much more importance, so far as criminality is concerned, is the upper grade of the feebleminded, the
class of morons. As we go up in the scale of mentality we naturally find more ability to be an active delinquent. The general
conception of the rôle which the feebleminded play in criminality
is that they are passive, the tool of others. Most unfortunately

455

this is quite untrue, for we know only too well that they may be persuaders and teachers of delinquency, especially in the case where a defective young man or woman influences a younger group. The relation which these upper-grade feebleminded have to delinquency presents no special problem, particularly if the mental arrest of development is spread more or less evenly over all faculties. Out of our scores of cases one or two examples will be sufficient to show the general trend of feeblemindedness in producing delinquency.

A common type of mental defective with rather unusual motor ability is represented in the following case. Here we have an individual learning delinquent ways through lack of proper supervision, and from direct suggestion of others. The lack of satisfactory occupation along other lines is undoubtedly largely responsible in this case for a long record of criminalistic acts.

Case 83. — Mark S. Age 15 years when first seen. Already this boy had been repeatedly in the hands of the police. He had been away from home as many as six days at a time. He had been found in company with vicious people. He often lived by picking up bottles and selling them, and by petty stealing. In the meantime he was staying at cheap hotels. At times he has been engaged in burglaries with other boys, and has been regarded as something of a leader. On at least one occasion he was known to have engaged in wanton destruction when a store was burglarized. He was always troublesome in school and a great truant. The highest grade he ever obtained was the 3d. Towards the last of his school career he was in a room for sub-normals. After being in court numerous times before he was 16, his case always being temporized with on account of his mentality, it was finally necessary to definitely sentence him. The police reported that he was an unusually skillful young burglar.

Mark is the only child of his widowed mother. This unfortunate woman has to work out every day and consequently has been able to give him but slight supervision. When first seen this woman gave a very straightforward account of family and developmental history. As time has gone on, perhaps on account of her hard work and many troubles, she has become rather unbalanced, but has always preserved a vast amount of affection for the boy.

We found him to be well developed and nourished, with no special sense defects. Weight 111 lbs.; height 5 ft. 1 in. Good strength. Heavy, slouchy gait. Rather monotonous voice. Dull expression. Very irregular dentition, pointing to early impaction of teeth in the upper jaw; many now carious. Large, peculiarly shaped head; circumference 57 1-2, length 20, breadth 15 cm. Very prominent occipital protuberance, flat above this to the vertex. All else negative.

On mental tests we found the following:
Binet (1911 series): 8 years, failure on 2 and 4, others correct; 9 years, failure on 1, 2, and 4, others correct; 10 years, failure on all; 12 years, failure on all but the first.
On our own series of tests:
I. 1′ 33″ — trial and error on triangles — no repetitions of impossibilities.
II. 1′ 40″ — 4 errors.
III. 47″ — 12 total moves — 5 impossibilities.
IV. Failure in 10′.
V. 3′ 16″ — steps interspersed with 4 errors.
VI. Full functional account — 4 out of 7 suggestions accepted.
VII. (a) Correct only at 4th exposure.   (b) Correct only at 4th exposure.
VIII. 4 errors in reproduction.
IX. Correct at 4th trial.
X. Correct at 2d trial.
XI. Not given — does not know all the alphabet.
XIII. 11 items — no attempt at verbal accuracy.
XV. 7 errors, 4 failures, average time 3.9″.
XVI. 1st trial 54 squares tapped in 30″; 2d trial 58 squares, no errors.
XVII. Penmanship fair. Jumbles the sentences given.
XVIII. Makes simple combinations by counting.
XIX. Cannot read.
The result of this boy's school education is extremely poor in proportion. He does not spell his own name correctly. Adds simple combinations only by counting them, and even then says that 7 plus 5 are 10, and 2 from 4 leaves the same as 2 from 5. In reading knows only a few words of a 1st grade passage.

Thus we found uneven distribution of abilities. By the Binet system he only graded through the 8-year tests. But he shows considerable power of mental representation and analysis, and also some manipulative skill.

Unfortunately it is impossible to follow up the heredity of this boy on account of immigration; the question of inheritance involves an interesting point. The mother's statement is that both she and the father came from families who were of good ability. No insanity, feeblemindedness or epilepsy on either side.

457

Four weeks before this boy was born the mother came home one day to find her husband and her four other children burned to death in a gasoline explosion. She was in a terrible frame of mind after this, and naturally attributes his deficiency to antenatal conditions. The boy walked and talked early. Said never to have had any convulsions. Started to school at 6 years. Never had a severe illness. The mother has all along known his mental incompetency, but feels quite unable to bear the prolonged separation from him that would be necessary if he went to an institution for the feebleminded. In the meantime she is willing to work her finger ends off to support him, or get him out of trouble. To her he is a child of fate.

From the first it was clear that the outlook for Mark was poor in his old environment. He evidently had much satisfaction in his adept criminalistic offenses. We counselled his segregation as a defective, but it was impossible to carry this out. It was plain to be seen that the boy had ability to be largely self-supporting if he could work under complete direction. The chance of his acquiring vicious practices in cheap city lodging houses seemed very great.

It is of vast interest to us to note the report on this case which we have just obtained. It is that this boy after having been in an institution for delinquents was placed out on a farm. There for about a year he has been entirely satisfied, and has become a good and willing worker, with no desire to reënter city life. The success of his recent treatment is all the more striking in the light of the fact that he had been in court about ten times, and, among other misdeeds, is said to have committed dozens of burglaries.

Mentality: Moron.	Case 83.
Antenatal conditions: Mother terrible experience.	Boy, 17.
Poor home control: Mother works out.	
Bad companions.	
Heredity? Said to be negative.	
Delinquencies: Stealing +. Burglary +. Runaway.	

As an example of other types of delinquency arising on a base of feeblemindedness when the individual is uncared for, the following will serve as illustration.

Case 84. — A girl of 16, very early in life learned sex delinquency which she has practiced most extensively for years. Her family say she was found incorrigible already at 8 years, and even at that age she had been once expelled from school. At times she has been violent, once attacked others with a knife. She will take up with any man or boy. Her mother in insisting on the necessity of putting her in an institution, says that the girl has been bad with scores of men and boys in the small country town in which they live. She has remained away from home all night. Under detention her language was found atrociously bad, and she was a menace even among other girls of the reformatory type because of her sex practices.

Physically she was a strong, but slouchy type. No exceptional development or lack of development of any kind was noted. Puberty remarkably retarded beyond the family average. No gross sensory or physical defect of any kind. Her childish expression and silly manners are indicative of her character.

On mental tests we found the following results.
Binet (1908 series):
Lacks one of grading through the 8-year tests even when credit is given for 2 or 3 of the older tests which she gets right.
On our series:
I.   1′ 40″.
IV. 4′ 18″ — 24 moves.
V.   Failure.
VII. Failure.
VIII. 6 errors in reproduction.
X.   Complete failure.
XI. A ridiculous and imaginative result centered about the correct idea of a fire.
XII. The same type of result.
XIV. Complete failure.
XVII. Writes a fair hand but misspells many of the simplest words.
XVIII. Adds simple combinations.
XIX. Reads 3d-grade passage with good expression and pronounces correctly most of the words.

Thus we found this girl to grade evenly on her abilities and to belong in the lower group of morons.

The family of this young woman are not at all well educated, but the rest of them seem to be fairly normal, and are people of good reputation. She is the last of 10 children; her mother being 45 years of age when she was born. Taking it for what it is worth, we hear from this immigrant family that there has been no epilepsy, insanity or feeblemindedness on either side. She was backward in walking and talking. Is said never to have been very ill, but did.have a few convulsions in infancy. It is reported that there has been no trouble with the other children.

This girl came from an outlying town where there was no juvenile court, no probation officers, or social service work of any kind. The family circumstances precluded active control when she was much younger and needed it badly, as well as more recently. The family make much of her excessive bad sex practices, and it is possible that a certain amount of her present dullness is due to this. In one particular the case is hardly representative, inasmuch as many of the girls who are both mentally deficient and sexually vicious are the victims of physical overdevelopment and early puberty.

The only chance to protect this girl and protect society against her extraordinary bad influences appeared to be segregation, which was carried out.

Mentality: Moron.

Antenatal conditions(?): Mother old.

Case 84.
Girl, age 16.

Home conditions: Large family,
mother old, very poor control.

(Heredity not satisfactorily ruled out.)

Delinquencies:
Sex + + +.

---

§ 268. **Treatment of Feeblemindedness.** — By the very definition of feeblemindedness curative treatment is *nil*. However, various remediable physical conditions and ailments may increase both physical and mental disabilities, so that there is often much reason for professional care. Educational training is a technical matter which is not our province here to discuss. Some general social considerations concerning the treatment of this class, however, we should in short deal with.

It stands out very clearly in our experience that the whole social and educational prognosis for a feebleminded individual of the upper moron grade, at least, varies greatly with the particular capacities of that given individual. It may be it is because we see cases outside of institutions, those who often show much variation from the usual feebleminded types, that we are impressed with varying possibilities. It is plain to us that one cannot at all proceed to give an educational or industrial prognosis according to a mental age classification. General physical capacities, as well as unusual combinations of mental traits, have to be taken into account. Goddard gives a most interesting industrial classification of institutional cases according to Binet age. From this we learn that the feebleminded individual who grades 6 years, for instance, does tasks of short duration, and washes dishes; the mental defective of 8 years runs errands, does light work, makes beds; the one who grades 10 years is a good institutional helper, does good routine work; the one who accomplishes the 12-year test can use machinery, care for animals, can work without supervision, but cannot plan. Exceedingly interesting though this scheme is, we should feel it entirely unsafe to give either a prognosis or to suggest treatment by means of it. Any one who studies the cases which we offer in the next chapter must come to the same conclusion, and if we had this point especially to discuss many more in evidence could be cited. The fact is that much individualization is necessary in looking forward to the social and educational possibilities of many defectives.

With the small proportion of defectives which is now taken care of in institutions, and even with what may be done in the future, there is always bound to be a considerable number of them among us in ordinary life. A generally unsuspected number are taking care of themselves fairly well, and are no special moral menace. With betterment of the earlier treatment of these individuals they could be still more successful — at least those of some industrial capacity.

§ 269. **Treatment of Feebleminded Offenders.** — There are great variations in the tendencies to immorality among the feebleminded. If we considered the sex impulse alone and its basis in physical make-up, or as derived from environmental experiences we can realize how great the differences may be. Other anti-social tendencies may have like conditions in the background. Treatment in these respects must also be individualized. One frequently learns of a steady-going defective without vicious impulses who has created no trouble in a given community over a whole lifetime. Indeed, when considering the possibilities of criminalistic impulses in these cases one must fairly compare them with other offenders who are not mentally defective; and this comparison is not always to the credit of the latter.

One is very frequently asked, even by parents, about surgical treatment of defectives to prevent vicious sex impulses. I feel that in appropriate cases of boys, a thorough-going surgical operation which shall protect them from the habits which so frequently carry them much farther in mental disability, and protect them and society against violent impulses, which sometimes give rise to hideous crimes, is unhesitatingly to be recommended. The smaller operation of vasectomy, which prevents procreation, but not sexual impulse, does the individual himself no good. Parents who have had a defective child operated on in the more thorough way are loud in their praises of its effect upon traits of mind and character. Of course in the case of girls the only protection is through entire segregation or else through complete family espionage. One has known the latter to be very successfully given among careful people of slender means.

We must reiterate here a point we have made in our chapter on alcoholism, namely, that mental defectives should receive the greatest protection from the influence of alcohol. It is now everywhere acknowledged that a considerable share of our worst topers are defectives, and very frequently one comes to know of the disastrous influence which a small amount of alcohol may have upon the life of a feebleminded person, *vide* § 196.

Colonization of the feebleminded with industrial education and employment under supervision is unquestionably the proper solution of the problem of the social treatment of most feebleminded individuals. Properly managed, and with a large percentage of morons, such as is likely under bettered social understanding to be placed in such institutions, the population may be largely self-supporting. But with the features of social and personal treatment mentioned above carried out, it will be found that not a few feebleminded will be safe and useful members of general society.

CHAPTER XV

Mental Defect — *Continued*

Feeblemindedness with Special Abilities.   § 270. Special Abilities Not Socially Significant.   § 271. Special Abilities Socially Significant.   § 272. (a) and (b) Mental Defectives with Normal Insight plus Motor Ability.   § 273. (c) Verbalist Type of Defective.

Feeblemindedness with Special Abilities

§ 270. **Special Abilities Not Socially Significant.** — One does not go very far in the study of feeblemindedness without observing most marked and interesting variations displayed in different mental functions.   Many of these should have much significance for psychologists, but since the interests of this work are not primarily psychological, we deal with such variations as are of special importance for criminalistics.   We have already intimated that we see every reason to include social qualifications as a necessary part of the diagnosis of feeblemindedness, and our observations on the irregularity of mental abilities will make the whole question of social significance clearer than ever.

As before noted, it is a common expression by the laity, heard frequently in court work, that those individuals who show cunning and adeptness cannot be so very subnormal after all.   Such was the remark made by a judge when a watch was displayed in the court room, which I had missed a couple of weeks before, and which had been abstracted from me by one of my young subnormal friends.   This type of argument, however, is essentially weak because the very qualifications which make for success under the social régime of modern civilization includes as a necessity the several higher mental abilities, such as powers of analysis, reasoning and foresight.   Cunning and adeptness might well have been the foremost mental possessions of even our arboreal ancestors.

Some curious examples of the disproportionate growth of certain mental abilities in the feebleminded could be cited from literature or from our own experience.   There is the instance of the great mechanical and constructive genius whom Tredgold (**307,** p. 275) describes at length.   This man produced the most ingenious

463

and complicated mechanical devices. Others have described mentally defective arithmetical geniuses. One of the commonest abilities to be exaggerated above the general level is that of musical talent. A fine instance of this sort was Blind Tom, whose accomplishments on the pianoforte were like a mountain height arising from the plain of his general mental disability. We have ourselves described (Healy, 369) an individual with fairly marvelous powers of recall by methods of visualization, who can perform mental feats quite beyond the abilities of his normal fellows. Through prolonged self-training in the use of his special memory faculties, this low grade moron tells days and dates so rapidly that he has been regarded as a calculating genius. His total ability, however, appears to rest upon his power of recalling occurrences in connection with their dates as observed for many years by the calendar, and recalling them largely by means of mental pictures. Since motor ability has been held by some experienced observers of the feebleminded to be one of the safest criteria for their diagnosis, one might mention the case of a champion right weight prize fighter of a few years back. He was said to be the very surest and swiftest hitter, his motor reactions were always a little quicker than those of his opponent — hence his prowess, although in general mental ability he was well within the limits of feeblemindedness.

Except when exploited under management, none of these special abilities make for social success, and they do not cover up at all the evidences of the general low level of mental ability. For our purposes they require no further consideration.

§ 271. **Special Abilities Socially Significant.** — Arising from a general low level of intelligence there may be special mental abilities which on account of their relationship to social conditions, are of great import. The social demand for mental powers is often satisfied with very limited exertion of certain faculties. However, the types of mental ability which, being present among general mental disability, leave the individual apparently or actually socially acceptable are limited in number. We shall deal with those which have appeared of foremost importance in our observations of criminalistic tendencies. There is (a) the defective individual who has good insight into his own mental limitations, and who on account of the possession of some elements of good judgment, proceeds to avoid as much as possible sources of discouragement or danger, and who limits his occupations to lowly fields where he is successful and comparatively free from temptation. (b) Then there is the individual who perforce of good physical control, so-called motor ability, is able to do good work and perhaps earn well, and who has some powers of judgment, enough at least to keep out of social conflicts, or out of trouble severe enough to prevent his being considered thoroughly undesirable socially. Since insight without industrial ability is not at all likely to help one to hold much of a place in the world, the two types (a) and (b) will best be discussed together. (c) Then there is that most important type of the feebleminded with special abilities, the defective with marked verbal powers. The social, as well as the psychopathological, importance of this type can hardly be over-estimated, and acquaintance with this subspecies should be had by every jurist and criminal lawyer, and by every social worker. We have seen many egregious examples of the troublesomeness of members of this class, who have long passed unrecognized as defectives.

§ 272. (a and b) **Mental Defectives with Normal Insight plus Motor Ability.** — Examples of individuals who by virtue of possession of some insight into their own condition of feeblemindedness and by reason of their having fair motor ability, are able to make their way in the world without being relegated to institutional care, are not very frequently seen by workers such as ourselves who have to deal primarily with social failures. I have little doubt, however, that many such cases exist; many more than institutional people suspect. I should much like to see psychological tests, the Binet system and other tests, tried on large numbers of the most lowly grades of industrial workers, such as railroad section hands and other laborers who work with pick and shovel. One would be inclined to doubt the ability of many of these to pass even the 12-year tests of Binet. Many of them would undoubtedly classify as feebleminded, if we were to go by these tests alone.

Of course I do not mean to say that all these individuals hold their social freedom merely by reason of having good insight into their own mental disabilities. They have ability to perform their assigned motor tasks. In spite of not being definitely on the search for such facts, we have seen numerous examples of individuals feebleminded by tests, who are quite able to maintain their place in the outside world, and indeed to be worthy enough social servants. The fair success of a mental defective who is doing work that is above the lowliest grades is illustrated in the following case, and in this instance, if the home environment were more rational there would have been even less tendency to moral failure.

Case 85. — A boy, now 17 years old, lives in a certain railroad center of Indiana where there is much transfer service by wagon and cab from one station to another. We have had occasion to see him several times, partly on account of his failure to advance in school, and partly because there seemed to be some danger of his becoming thoroughly delinquent. Through a rarely met disinclination on the part of the mother, no reliable data on heredity was obtained, except the following facts which are most significant. The father is a worthless drunkard. The mother for years has vigorously conducted a livery business, on all occasions rounding up her family to work under her auspices. She is a woman with a shrewish tongue, a bad temper, and she defends her family at all hazards. There are five children, the last of whom is this boy. The three eldest graduated from the grammar school at about 13. The first-born has turned out to be a drunkard, but works under his mother fairly well, except occasionally when under the influence of alcohol. The next to the last child reached 6th grade only, at the age of 16 years. There was much trouble with him on account of truancy, but he is said to have turned out to be a nice boy. In regard to our own boy, we have probably a very good developmental history, and we learn that antenatal and natal conditions were normal. He has never been severely ill. No injuries. He walked and talked moderately early, the same as the others, and there is no evidence of causative factors of any kind in the developmental history. Mother and father were each about 35 when he was born.

When seen first at 14 we found this boy to weigh only 77 lbs. Height 4 ft., 10 in. He was fairly nourished and showed no deformity. No defects of special senses. Attitude normal and expression typically boyish. Reflexes normal. Strength good for size. No developmental anomalies. Head good size and well shaped. Teeth in fairly good condition. Normal speech. Very moderate tea and coffee. No evidence of bad sex habits.

At this age he was only in the 4th grade, and was not successful there. His mother says he takes no interest in school work, but is smart in other things. He started to school at 6 or 7. Arithmetic always kept him back. Always been to public school.

He went through the first three grades without being set back. The teachers say he lacks concentration; he sits idle. Mother says that in the last couple of years he will stay away from school at every chance.

Mental tests: Binet, (1908 series). Nine years — 1, 2, 3 correct and very prompt. 4, failure. (5 and 6 inadvertently not given.) Ten years — 1, failure. 2, correct. 3, complete failure. 4, failure. In the latter he says if one has missed a train he should get mad, and if struck by a playmate, who did not mean to do it, he should get angry, and so on. Eleven years — 1, correct. 2, failure. 3, correct, with a good range of abstract words as well as substantives. 4, failure. For instance, absurd misunderstanding of what the word charity, etc., means. 5, failure. Twelve years — all failures, but his memory span for numbers is five digits.

On our own tests he shows the following results:

I. Introduction puzzle done in 2′ 39″, with some repetition of errors on the triangles.

II. School puzzle 1′ 40″, 5 errors.

III. Construction puzzle A done in 58″, with 9 total moves, and only one retrial of an impossibility.

IV. Construction puzzle B was a remarkable failure in 10′ after 56 moves.

V. The work on our puzzle box was practically a failure, since it was only accomplished in 9′ 21″, after interspersing many errors between step one and step two. In fact the latter was done as if by accident.

VII. Reproduction of two geometric figures a failure. The second of the two figures was absurdly inaccurate.

VIII. Rote learning test correctly and promptly done.

IX. Cross line test A failure even at the 4th trial.

X. Cross line test B similarly a failure.

XIV. Done correctly at second trial in 27″.

XV. Antonyms. No less than 6 failures and 2 errors, the latter afterwards corrected. Average time of remainder 3″.

XVII. Writing. He writes a boyish hand, but is able to write from dictation without error, "The printer made some cards."

XIX. Reading. 4th-grade passage slightly halting and a few mispronounced words which he corrected himself. Correct regard for punctuation.

XVIII. Arithmetic. The results were remarkably poor. Adds a simple column of 4 figures correctly, but makes an error when he has to carry. Knows the tables very incompletely and is unable to multiply by 76. Says 7 times 8 are 64; 9 times 8 are 54, etc. Much difficulty in doing an oral sum. Says 8 plus 6 plus 8 minus 3 is 3. On concrete work the boy is very much better. One inquired what the transfer rates on his line were and found they were 25 cents. He then told us very promptly what 13 times 25 cents were and, a little more slowly, how much 28 times 25 cents were.

The boy's range of information was incredibly inaccurate. Says he does not know who the president of the United States is, and that the first president was Rockefeller. Asked who Abraham Lincoln was, he says he is the president now. Knew all the time it was Lincoln, but could not remember his first name. He knows very well the component parts of mortar. Cannot give the names of the Great Lakes. Used to play football, but would much rather work than play.

This boy was tried on a number of tests at intervals of a day or two after the first testing, and corroborative results were obtained. At first it was thought there might be emotional disturbance, but this was ruled out by these later findings.

Altogether we find by testing that this boy comes well within the feebleminded group according to the Binet tests and that he also fails on many of the tests for the higher abilities of mental analysis and powers of mental representation, but he is able to follow instructions, learn by rote, and deals very much better with concrete material, including arithmetic, than with abstractions. Other than this we found him to be normally affectionate, and appreciative of his situation as a defective. His attitude is typically boyish and responsive. Not the slightest indication of vicious disposition. He is reported to be absolutely honest, and quite able to carry on his work as a driver, which he has done for a couple of years after school and in his vacations. It is his enjoyment of occupation in the open air, as well as school-room irritations, which leads him, he says, to prefer his work to school.

His delinquencies consist in very much the type of misdeed that the ordinary truckman gets into — much use of bad language, exhibition of bad temper. He once hit a man with a whip. Formerly he was a great truant, but his irritation at school retardation might account for this. As a matter of fact, he was willing later on to receive special tutoring in arithmetic.

This boy has turned out to be a typical cab and wagon driver, and we hear that he is earning well for his family, that he is quite able to take care of his team and to hold his own in the world. As far as delinquency is concerned it is doubtful if he is as bad as many of his class who are mentally normal.

By the formulae of age tests he is to be regarded as feebleminded, but has other qualifications for getting along fairly well in the world — certainly as well as one could expect when one considers the home conditions with a drunken father and an irascible mother, and in an occupation where men notoriously develop vindictive dispositions and violent ways. Surely no one would allege that the findings on tests in this case formed sufficient grounds for sending this boy to an institution for the feebleminded. Despite the findings on tests we could never make up our minds to call this boy socially feebleminded, and we finally classed him under our caption of subnormality, which, however, is made up almost entirely of those who do vastly better than he on the Binet schedule.

Mentality: Subnormal.
      (By Binet, moron.)

Case 85.
Boy, 14.

   Heredity: Father alcoholic.

      Home conditions: Father and brother alcoholic.

Delinquencies:
   Truancy + +.
   Assault.

Case 86. — Of quite another type is the following case of a boy of 16 who was brought into court from a certain country district where he had been engaged in a number of sex affairs. With the exception of the last occurrence these things were done under much the same circumstances as one might find in many a school community where sex delinquencies are not prevented by careful oversight. The boy had early been taught these things by a certain dissolute girl of the neighborhood, and then he and other boys had sometimes been in bad practices together, and just now he and his brother had tampered with a girl, but had made no real assault. The neighbors testified against him and his brother, but of much longer standing was the court record of the girl who had taught them.

The mother of this boy was found to be an unbalanced woman, aberrational in type, but the diagnosis of her mentality one would hesitate to make upon short acquaintance. The father is a queer-looking man with a battered-up face and a depressed bridge of nose. He is a farm laborer and very poor. Has been in this country about 20 years. They were very affectionate and very much concerned about all the ailments of their family. The mother is temperate. The father is occasionally intoxicated. No reliable hereditary facts were obtained, but we see plainly that the father is a very poor specimen from the physical side and has little mental ability, and that the mother is distinctly

469

aberrational in her mentality. She may have been congenitally
defective. Another fact that bears on heredity is our finding by
examination that the brother is defective mentally. At 12 years
he is only in the 2d grade. Facts of immediate family history
were, as is natural, much more readily obtained and they were
given in voluble account. There have been ten children and two
miscarriages. Only five are now living. The eldest is 19 and said
to be the most promising one of the family. He is a section hand.
Then comes our boy and then the lad of 12 who is subnormal,
and then a very sickly little girl of 6. (Our examination shows
that she has a very severe heart lesion.) Then comes a boy of 5.
The subnormal lad of 12 is said to have been always sickly, and
did not walk until he was 4 years old.

The developmental history of our lad was readily obtained.
The mother gives a long story. Before he was born the
mother was sickly for several months; the diagnosis uncertain.
Birth was normal. As an infant he had " summer complaint
for three summers and was awfully sick. He had typhoid and
brain fever when he was a baby, too. He walked at about 2
years. I did not nurse him because I only had a half a breast.
He can't learn good. He never could." It also appears that
this boy has been very poorly in recent years with tonsilitis and
various fevers. Does not have convulsions or other attacks.
No convulsions in the family.

Our examination showed a jerky, nervous, rat-featured boy
who responded quite nicely when talked to kindly, and was willing to talk freely about his transgressions. He is 16 years old.
Weighs 103 lbs. Height, 5 ft. 1 1-4 in. His frame is comparatively large for his other development. No sensory defects noted.
Strength good for size. Constant tremor of outstretched hands.
Lively knee jerks. Good color. No anomalies of sex development. Moves in notably quick, jerky fashion. Head circumference 54; diameters, anteroposterior 18, biparietal 16 cm.
Shows the following stigmata. Remarkably small chin and
mouth in comparison to cranial size. Wizened type of face.
Head markedly flat at the back with distinct asymmetry. Almost
no occipital protuberance. Very broad proportionately in the
parietal region just above and a little behind the ears. Cranium
then comes sharply to a narrow forehead. Broad uvula. Marked
asymmetry of ears — right upper helix is flattened with a crimp
in it. Nostrils slightly notched near the point of the nose.

Tests showed as follows:

Binet (1911 series). Eight years — 1, 2, 3, correct. 4, failure. 5, correct. Nine years — 1, correct. 2, failure. Said a fork is for hay; a horse is to pull, etc. 3, correct. 4, failure. 5, correct. Ten years — 1, 2, correct. 3, 4, 5, failures. Twelve years — 1, correct. 2, 3, 4, 5, failures. Does not know the meaning of charity or justice.

On our own set of tests were the following results:

I. Introductory picture 2′ 24″. Considerable repetition of error on the triangles.

II. School puzzle 2′ 6″, only 2 errors.

III. Construction puzzle A fairly well done in 1′ 41″. 16 total moves and 3 repetitions of impossibilities.

IV. Construction puzzle B, 2′ 12″, and only 20 moves — the only repetition being on the placing of pieces one and two. Distinct ability to plan was shown in this.

V. Puzzle box in 3′ 13″. Two errors between steps one and two. Otherwise the process was logical.

VI. Aussage test. Scant enumerative account of the details and a good deal of suggestibility shown. No less than 5 out of 7 suggestions accepted. Said he saw the meat in the ice box, bananas on the wall, a cash register and even a cat on the floor.

VII. First one of the two figures correct, but was not able to get the 2d symmetrically drawn until after 4 exposures. Controls his pencil fairly well.

VIII. Arbitrary learning test done slowly with only one final error.

IX. Cross line A correct at 1st trial.

X. Cross line B complete failure at 4th trial.

XII. Visual verbal memory test not given because does not read well enough.

XIII. Auditory verbal memory test only 5 out of 12 items given correctly. Others much jumbled and a totally non-comprehending account.

XV. Antonyms, remarkably poor result. Only 6 correct. Average time 5.7″. 10 errors, 4 failures.

XVI. Motor coördination fair result. 61 and 60 squares at 1st and 2d trials respectively. No errors.

XVII. Can write name, but very little else.

XVIII. Makes simple number combinations by counting fingers.

XIX. Reads only a few of the shortest words. Does not know all the alphabet.

XXIII. Pictorial Completion test 3′ 45″. Four final errors. Studied the test very carefully and finally concludes that everything is in right place. Three of the errors are of the irrational type.

By tests we found that here was a boy who in spite of having been to school more or less regularly for a good many years had not even the elements of the three R's. By the Binet tests he would be ranged about midway in the group of morons. He

471

showed distinct defects in the higher powers of mental representation and analysis and proved himself extremely suggestible. Yet he had power to learn by rote, had moderately good motor control and demonstrated quite fair ability in constructive work. He did as well as many normal persons with the analysis of the mechancial puzzle box. It is quite evident that he works much better with concrete material than with abstract. Beyond this we observed that the boy was very nervous and depressed about his delinquency. Was in great fear of punishment. He met our friendly approach in good spirit, and became quite frank about his various troubles and how they began. This was after a first period of evasion and lying. His own frankness regarding details would seem to indicate his mental calibre, but he showed some feeling of shame. He told of various degenerate sex practices that he had gotten into, probably following the teaching by the dissolute girl.

This boy was reported to be a good worker. He had been employed on a farm at one time. Recently was acting as a janitor in a school building. As observed by one teacher he was found very considerate and responsive in many ways. For instance, he told another boy he must not put the chair against the table because it would make a mark. He makes change correctly. No doubt was expressed by the local officer or by his family of the boy's ability to make his own way in the world.

However undesirable as a member of any community this boy may be considered on account of his bad sex tendencies, and however dangerous he may be socially on account of his hereditary defects as a possible progenitor of his kind, still that is not the point for the moment with us. One could think of surgical measures which would prevent him from becoming the rapist or pervert that he shows signs of becoming. The point that we have here to make is that although the lad by school and Binet tests clearly grades as feebleminded, yet if one undertakes a wider range of observation, one finds him to have certain motor, constructive and industrial capabilities which throw considerable doubt upon his being socially feebleminded, that is being unable to compete on equal terms with his fellows. Indeed, were it not for his immoral proclivities, which may just as fairly be considered acquired as denominated innate, he might well serve as a very useful member of society in doing some of the necessary lowly work of the world.

As a matter of fact, a year or so later the report came that this lad had been doing very well at work on a farm.

Mentality: Moron.	Case 86.
Bad companions: Dissolute girl.	Boy, 16 years.

Heredity: Father and mother both
defective types. Marked stigmata.

Developmental conditions:
Much illness.

Home conditions: Poverty, poor control.

Delinquencies:
Sex +, also perversions.

In considering the question of the insight of mental defectives into their own condition there seems no particular reason why this power should not be found preserved or developed in some cases, just as other faculties may be preserved or developed. The defective who has insight is fortunate. Sources of discouragement and temptation are thereby avoided. More than a few times one has heard from subnormal individuals who make their way in the world without trouble that they realize their own limitations. As we stated before, we have made no special effort to get data on individuals who grade as feebleminded by tests, but who are not to be considered social failures. Our work has brought us directly in contact with the failures. Yet many times we have had indication of the part which insight plays in making these individuals, defective by tests, successful. The outcome in the cases given just previously, as well as in some cited on the following pages, proves well the point.

§ 273. (c) **Verbalist Type of Defective.** — I know of no class of defective or abnormal individuals that is so little understood, or who can give so much social trouble on account of their not being understood, as the mental defectives who have language ability sufficient to make an appearance which deceives the world in general as to their true mental status. It is a type which on account of the legal problems often centering about them should be understood thoroughly by all those who have to deal with human individuals under the law.

On account of their ability to handle language well the members of this group are not properly placed by the ordinary tests of

473

social intercourse. The common method for passing judgment on people is, of course, through conversation. One asks questions and if one gets answers that follow properly, that are consequential and coherent, why then without more ado one infers the answerer to be practically normal. The give-and-take conversational method of the court room may be offered in illustration. Under such conditions this definite class of those who, although mentally deficient, have considerable language ability can slide along undetected among normal people. It seems to be a matter of common-sense observation that those who can talk well must therefore be mentally normal. We ourselves have to confess to being utterly surprised at finding the low mental grade of some members of this class, so ingrained in human judgment is the idea that if an individual can talk well he is, *ipso facto*, of mental normality. It is more generally appreciated that brilliant conversational powers are not incompatible with mental aberrations, including well-defined insanity. Here we may set forth that there is a like combination of affairs to be met with in mental defectives.

If the human mind is thought of in terms of partially separated faculties and abilities, then why should we not recognize the possibility of a language ability overtopping the other mental powers, even when the general level of ability is far below the social par. Other instances of mental unevenness, such as the musical, mechanical and calculating geniuses, we have spoken of above.

A point in connection with these individuals is of much practical interest; it causes many complications. The fact that these people find themselves socially tolerated, and apparently able to meet the world upon its own terms, leads them into a great deal of self-deception. As we have found them, they are markedly lacking in insight into their own disabilities. In this matter they are quite in contrast to the type of case which just previously has been cited. This lack of judgment and apperceptive ability may directly lead to the development of a grudge-like attitude towards the world or towards the individuals under whom they have unsuccessfully served, or with whom they have been in competition and failed. They do not understand the cause of their own failure.

On the other hand, one has also noted a great deal of buoyancy, assertiveness and even ambition among this class. Their very lack of insight prevents them from being depressed by their own failures, while their conversational ability and frequent vivacity lead them to form new associations and acquaintances most readily, and to gain therefrom continually new feelings of power and renewal of sense of importance. They have an abnormally small amount of social modesty or reserve. They are able to ingratiate themselves in public places, and to get new jobs with the greatest facility. Their very vivacity may be a factor in their presenting a prepossessing appearance. They also have other qualities, perhaps not so typical, several of which may be seen in the cases cited below.

Cases of mentally defective verbalists may be of such great legal importance that there is value in citing some instances in detail. I strongly advise all my legal readers to acquaint themselves with this type, and to note upon what common-sense grounds a differential diagnosis can be made. Possible legal complications are only necessary to hint at. To work up the entire gamut of cases of this type we have observed would require a special monograph. We have seen numbers of defectives who were glib talkers even on the witness stand. Since some defective verbalists are great liars it might be supposed they would come under the head of pathological liars, but we have expressed ourselves clearly on this point in our chapter on that subject. The individual who is a liar and defective must be classed primarily as a defective.

The ability of morons who are verbalists to remain at large in society, sometimes regarded simply as immoral or criminal types, is an interesting fact. It is to be noted that in our classification for the moment we are not including cases which get through the Binet 12-year tests. Under the head of mental subnormality, § 276, we have more to say on this point, for the subnormal verbalist is perhaps even a more interesting type. There is, however, only a technical reason for distinguishing between the two; generically both classes are defective. One of the weak points of the Binet system is that it so greatly calls for language responses; those who have good language ability easily grade proportionately higher. We offer somewhat in detail the general findings and some specimens of conversational ability in several cases, the criminalistic trend of which may be clearly seen.

Case 87. — Clara Y., a young Jewish woman, about a year from Russia, was brought to us by a protective agency. We were never quite sure of her age, but she evidently was about 21. She had been getting into difficulties in one way and another, and it was now conceived that perhaps she was not able to take care of herself. She had voluntarily sought the aid of various people at times. The protective agency had attempted to get her properly placed, and had put in a very great deal of time on the case, but somehow, although she seemed to have the best of intentions, she never was able to retain a position; either being discharged or leaving the place herself. It is probable that she did hold one position for three months, but she has had many other places where she has not done well. It is known that she tells many lies, has been morally careless in general, and that she has been sexually delinquent. Her recent action in deliberately asking a man to come and live with her for awhile, which, by the way, he accommodatingly did, seemed altogether too much of a good thing, and there developed the suspicion that the girl was not just right mentally.

Her family is known of through old neighbors; they are said to be intelligent and well-to-do. The results of inquiries make it probable that her people have had much trouble with her, and are glad to be rid of her. She is said to have run away from home with a troupe of actors before she emigrated. Other than this, the family and developmental history is unknown. The girl's own statements in the matter are probably unreliable. She has no relatives in the United States.

We know something of her school history from certificates which she shows from a gymnasium in a small Russian town. The purport of these is that she was the fifth highest pupil when she was in the 4th grade, and had some fair marks at that time in geography, natural history and even arithmetic. She was good in deportment and excellent in penmanship. We do not know the work of the grades, and it may be that geography and natural history were mostly memorizing of language. Clara volunteered the information, whatever it may be worth, that she was not allowed to pass into the 6th grade, and was two years in the 5th. She later told about being in higher grades, but was contradictory on these points, and it is not at all likely.

Clara's delinquencies consist in much lying and misrepresentation, earlier running away from home, and, as time has gone on, gross sex immorality.

Physically we find her to be a vivacious, coquettish type,

small in size, but well developed and nourished and with good color. She has regular features, and with her vivacity might be called rather attractive. Her expression is silly. She laughs and giggles much of the time. It is significant that she is very careless about her personal appearance, a fact most contradictory to her coquettish behavior. No sensory or physical defects of any kind noted.

"Been here a year and four months. Came in July. Worked lots of places, sometimes a month, sometimes a day and sometimes a week. I know that man a couple of weeks, that's all. I met him at the music hall. Had passes to go there. Oh, God, he's a fine man. He said he was married. I told the boarding house keeper about it. He never did anything wrong. Had him because I was starving. Oh, that money I had in the bank? I saved that five months ago. I told lies because people did not believe me anyway. I used to get $8 or $9 a week. Got $16 saved up. Oh, I just told that man I had lots of money. I went eight years to school in the old country — in the gymnasium. I went to the 7th grade. Just in one class two years. God, what funny puzzles you've got here. Believe me, I know French when I want to know it. Sure, I can speak Russian and German and French. All my family are smart. My mother has migraine. She's been to big doctors in St. Petersburg. Sure, they can all read and write. They know lots."

A year later when the girl was in poor condition and she was advised to go to a dispensary, she rattled on as follows: "Were you ever in one of those dispensaries? All the poor dirty people go there and you have to stand in line and take your turn. I would n't do that. I am clean and proud. I don't want you to tell any of those society women where I am — I don't want them giving me anything at all — I am able to earn my own living. You ought to see me on the street. I have a pretty dress and a long black plume, and if those women would see me they would ask me how much it cost and where I got it and everything. They did make trouble for me at one place, and when I got home my landlady said, 'You little liar.' They told her I was a Russian Jew. You know they are dirty and ignorant, and I am not a Russian Jew at all. My right father and mother were French, and when they died it was my misfortune that I should have been given to them. I'm proud and I want to be something."

"My mother has a fine education. My mother was through

477

school higher than me. I faint lots of times when I do hard work like scrubbing. I never did hurt myself then. I would always faint when I did not have right meals."

" I just love music and the theatre. I heard Caruso last week. God, he sings beautiful. I was to grand opera a lot of times this winter. I go to the theatre two or three times a week. Oh, I get passes all right. Maybe some man will take me in. I 'll go and stand in the entrance and look as if I wanted to go in, and maybe some lady would come along and ask me, and I 'd say, ' I just love music,' and she would get me a ticket, and sometimes a man would take me. No, I 'd never know him before."

The girl at this time had been living with different men for a month or two at a time, sometimes having traveled with them. There were the typical results in infections now. She had earned money as a model for artists, and we heard she had been a " living statue " in a cheap theatre.

The above excerpts from her story at different times give some indication of her facility with language, especially when it is remembered she has only been in America a little over a year. On the other hand, they give no idea of her glibness and the rapidity of the flow of her ideas. The latter we considered in the light of an aberrational phenomenon, but after all it was no more than one might hear from many another girl of her stagey tendencies. In our long acquaintance with her this never seemed to vary, nor did she ever grow any more aberrational.

The girl speaks good Russian, the language in which she was educated, speaks, reads and writes fair German, and has picked up enough French to be able to read short sentences and to have a conversational smattering. This, as well as her admiration for the French and desire to be called French, probably came from her early association with French actors in Russia.

Results of mental tests are as follows:
Binet tests (1908 series).
Seven years. — 4, failure, namely, copying a diamond. All the other seven tests correct.
Eight years. — All correct. The two tests, which involve reading and writing, were too difficult for her at first, but later she became able to read and write English quite well.
Nine years. — 1 and 2, correct. 3, the making of change, done with much uncertainty and is a failure. 4, correct. 5 and 6, not given.
Ten years. — All done correctly, even at first testing when she knew less English than later.

Eleven years. — 1 and 2, correct. 3, failure. This was a characteristic result because the girl insisted on giving words in the form of sentences, talking rapidly. We succeeded in getting 29 separate words, but the usual reaction was, "We have breakfast every morning," "We have supper every night." At times she would say, "Don't I talk fast? I can talk much faster than that in Russian. I can make great speeches in Russian." 4, failure on account of lack of knowledge. 5, not given on account of foreign language difficulty.

Twelve years. — 1, failure. Cannot repeat seven numerals. 2, rhyming words correct. 3, repetition of 26 syllables failure. 4, understanding a situation from diverse facts a failure.

Much more significant than even these findings are the results on our own set of tests.

I. 6′. Ridiculous amount of trial and error all the way through. Tried to put in pieces upside down.

II. 2′ 40″. 7 errors.

III. Construction Test A. Failure in 10′. Kept at the job most persistently, but most stupidly. Very many moves tried. After being shown, was able to do it however, extremely rapidly. "Oh, that's easy now."

IV. Construction Test B. For sake of thorough trial was allowed 15′ and even then failed after having made over 100 moves. Entire lack of planfulness and foresight. Trial and error.

VI. "Aussage." Gave a scanty functional account of the picture used. Gave a number of items on cross examination. She showed herself entirely non-suggestible.

VII. Reproduction of Geometric Figures. Entire failure. Striking result for her age.

VIII. Learning Arbitrary Symbol Associations. Worked with apparently good attention. Made three errors, including repetition of the number 2. Seemed to have no idea of working by elimination.

IX. Cross Line Test A. Failure to comprehend the problem.

X. Cross Line Test B. Entire failure. Only learned to draw the model from memory at 5th attempt.

XII. Memory from Visual Verbal presentation. Not given on account of language difficulty.

XIII. Memory from Auditory Verbal presentation. Gave a shorter and simpler passage of 25 words which was repeated with verbal accuracy.

XV. Antonyms. Astonishingly good result considering foreign language factor. No failures. Only one error. Average time 2.2″. Some of the opposites were quickly given in German, and of course counted as correct.

XVI. On this test got remarkable and typical result as verifying the lack of self-control exhibited in other conduct. In tapping the squares Clara would do all right for 20 spaces or so, but then seemed to be unable to keep the task in mind, although she could tell afterwards what was wanted of her. She would even run off the spaces into the margin. At another trial she did 64 squares in 30″ with 12 errors.

XVII. Writing is good in German script. Later on she was able to write a very creditable note in English.

XVIII. Failure for 3d grade multiplication and incorrect even in simple addition. Orally fails to subtract 39 cents from a dollar. Speaks fluently of geometry and algebra, but when given even the simplest formula shows not the slightest comprehension of it.

XIX. Even when seen the first time was able to read slowly a simple passage and to translate it into German.

XXI. The girl's reactions to Sharp's moral questions are quite instructive. Asked about the man who stole bread to give to starving children she responded — "You bet he do right. He did not steal money. He steal bread. If he steal money to get clothes or anything like that it's different. You bet I do the same. That girl in the Mission Home she steal $2 from me. I did not tell no one."

On the 2d of the moral questions about the captain of the besieging village giving up the man to the Indians, "Sure, I see lots of Indians on the stage. They rob people and take all the money. Indians don't shoot. They fight just with knives. I'd give up the man. One man is not so many." When cross-questioned she said, "Well, better kill lots of people for the truth. They've got lots of fight in Russia for the truth. If give up one man the Indians would call for others. The Indians are not educated. They could not understand."

XXII. Has exceedingly small range of information. Does not know who is president, or the largest city. Says she landed at Castle Garden, but is not sure of the name of the city. Remembers the Russian port she came from, and of stopping at Liverpool. She has plenty of information about theatres and grand opera. Last week was five times in the theatre.

This girl was seen several times later and some of the tests retried, with always practically the same results except on language. She speedily instructed herself and became, as mentioned above, able to write a good hand in English and to express herself well. As a vocational test she was given the puzzle box, Test V, with full instructions instead of as a problem. She finally accomplished the task in 5', but only with many variations from what she was told to do. This was significant in the light of the fact of her failure at various occupations.

The significance of this whole case is plain enough from the foregoing. Here is a girl with language ability immensely above her standard of performance in other ways. Her record on the Binet tests is not an indication of the extent of her mental defectiveness because they call for an undue amount of language performance. Much more consonant with her social failure are our findings on other tests. She is clearly feebleminded. On account of her facility with language she has been passed along by all sorts of kind-hearted people and even by social workers as a normal individual, and of course had she appeared in any

480

court on account of her delinquency there would not have been a doubt but that she was well equipped mentally. As a matter of fact, the outlook has all along been outrageously bad, and the welfare of society would demand that she be permanently segregated. On all occasions her tendency to eroticism was most noticeable. She was silly and simpering in her behavior and talked a great deal about the opposite sex. The possibilities of her career as a carrier of disease are not easily measured. The easy way in which she can ingratiate herself into the good will of people is exhibited by her ability to attend grand opera, even when she had no money.

From the first we considered the possibility of this girl being a case of psychosis, but as time has gone on we have seen no mental changes. At any rate if evidence of psychosis should clearly appear it would be on the basis of underlying mental defect, and this diagnosis is the only fair classification for the girl at present. Three years from the time we first saw her, reports would indicate no mental change, but she is said to earn a large share of her living as a *puella publica*.

Mentality: Moron with special
            language ability.

    Heredity? very little known.

      Developmental factors? unknown.

Delinquencies:
  Lying +.
  Sex + +.

Case 87.
Girl, 21 years.

Case 88. — Otto B. A boy now 17 years old came to this country with his family about five years ago. They settled first in an eastern city. Within a year from the time they landed Otto began causing trouble through running away from home and misrepresentation. We saw him first when he was about 14. He had then been in the hands of the police several times in several cities. Then, as now, he appeared to be an aggressive, forceful, healthy boy and he readily made friends everywhere. His family and more than one agency of social service had endeavored to get him sent to some educational institution, but on account of his ability to make a strong appeal before judges, and because of his running away to other places nothing was ever done.

481

Physically we found him active and alert; a nervous, bright-eyed type. He weighed then only 82 lbs., but has since that time been growing. He has always been well nourished and of a healthy appearance. No marked sensory defect. When first seen he was under a good deal of a strain on account of attempting to conceal his true family relationships and was highly nervous. We then noted very active pupillary reactions with marked hippus. As we have seen him since from time to time, we have noted less appearance of nervousness. No other points of significance have ever been revealed by our thorough physical examinations.

Mental tests: On numerous occasions tests have been tried and retried with the idea of discovering variations typical of a psychosis, if there were any. Results have been fairly uniform, except when he had learned how to do the test previously.

Binet tests (1911 series).

Eight years — 1, failure; 2, correct and done promptly; 3, correct, not prompt; 4, correct; 5, correct, but 5 digits was upper limit. Nine years — 1, correct; 2, failure; 3, correct. Counts money rapidly; 4, failure; 5, correct (2 out of 3 answers right at latest trial). Ten years — 1, failure, always one error; 2, failure; 3, half correct; 4, failure. Twelve years — 1, not given, but proved himself non-suggestible on other tests; 2, failure; 3, correct. On this a remarkable result was obtained, for over one hundred words were given in three minutes with a wide range of subjects; 4, ?; 5, ?.

Results on our own series:

I. 5′ 15″. Repetition of errors on the small triangles, which alone took 3′.

II. 3′ 42″, and 5 errors.

III. Construction puzzle A, 2′ 6″. Only 15 moves made, consequently this was done very deliberately.

IV. Construction puzzle B, 9′ 55″, and 67 moves. This is, of course, practically a failure.

V. Puzzle box a failure. Tried this repeatedly on different occasions. Was found at last visit that could do it in 1′ 40″, but even then failed to put it together again.

VI. "Aussage." It is notable that in this test he gives in his free recital eight items, four of which were wrong, a most remarkable result. When reminded of items, however, he got most of them and accepted no suggestions whatever. Said the smooth-faced butcher was old and had a white beard, and that he had ducks in one hand, and so on, but all these imaginative affairs were his voluntary concoctions.

VII. Reproduction of geometric figures; the rectangles correctly, the other a poor failure.

VIII. Learning of arbitrary associations very poor result — five errors out of ten possibilities.

IX. Cross line A, failure even at the fourth trial.

X. Cross line B, similar failure. Does not seem to be able to control his mental representation or analysis of these figures. Been tried many times on these.

XI. Memory from visual verbal presentation. Although he was able to read this passage containing twenty items fairly correctly, most of which are readily comprehended by children ten or twelve years of age, he gave the following incoherent story. " If a man finds a house he has to find a large house and if there is sick people and there has to be a fire and then he takes out the stuff and that's the poor people and the poor girls have the large house."

XIII. Memory from auditory verbal presentation. This was done very much better although still shows incoherency. He gets 9 out of 12 items fairly correct, but intersperses them with three other imaginative or perverted items.

XIV. Recently tried on instruction box. Failed on first two attempts only because his handling of dial was not steady enough. Showed keen effort. Correct third trial in 40″.

XV. Antonyms. Results on this were most curious. Notwithstanding his extensive vocabulary the difficulty seems to be that he lost the idea. The results the first time he was examined were thought to be vitiated by his recent acquirement of English and so they probably were. He was tried later on different sets of words and it was found he could control his associations for a few times and give us correct responses in one or two seconds, but then he would fly off at a tangent. For instance, when asked to give the opposite of the word friend said, " I know my friend is bad to me," and so on.

XVII. Writing. The boy has learned to write a readable hand, but his spelling is atrociously bad, hence his letters are difficult to read.

XVIII. Arithmetic. Has advanced so that he can add up a column of several figures generally correctly, but cannot do much of anything else. Division is an entire failure. It is specially significant that he cannot reason out simple problems concerned with money. For instance tells us that if 4 pencils cost 24 cents, 3 will cost 16 cents. Also fails on other similar tests.

XIX. Reads 3d-grade passage with a number of mispronunciations.

XXII. On the questions of information he says that Lincoln was a great man, he does not know the largest city in America, and so on. He attempts to give an erratic account of electricity.

XXIII. The pictorial completion test showed most irrational apperception processes. He made five final errors out of ten possibilities. He gave a voluble explanation of why he left certain pieces in certain places. He shows much weakness in the perception of the relationship. For instance, where there is a window to be placed in the house, he put in the baby, and says the girl has left the baby indoors and it is crying.

During a year this boy has been seen a number of times and some

483

of the tests have been given over again. He has learned to do the puzzle box and the 2d construction test, but in spite of money offered, which he most desires, he never was able to do the cross line test.

From all this there can be no doubt that we have to do with a feebleminded boy, and not of the highest grade. His range of mental defect is so great that one giving him common-sense tests in almost any way could prove his true mental calibre. But it has seemed to those he met that his forcefulness and volubility indicated anything but the possibility of his being defective. We have thought of this being a case of psychosis, but the boy has grown rather better than worse, and if an aberrant condition develops it will be on top of a primary mental defect. There is at present no indication of any psychosis.

The first time this boy was under observation it was about a week before any track of his family was gained. His stories were so well told they completely covered up his real connections. He was found very talkative and excitable. The diagnosis of his relative abilities and disabilities was readily made. A few excerpts from his rapid-fire conversation will give some indication of his conversational style. At this time he spoke with a typical accent, neither better nor worse than would be expected from the short time he had been in this country.

"I tell you, before my father died, about a month before, I was with my brother. I got a brother as big as I — he's bigger than I. My mother had a fall. She was carrying a baby one month around the street. People took her up. I seen them bring her in. They made an operation right away. The big doctors come and did, and they took out the baby. She kissed me and she could not talk. She liked her so much. Four months a baby and she kissed her goodbye. And we come by her and we catched her dead, and my father had an operation too at the Vanderbilt Hospital. I had an operation. Long time I was sick — great long time — could not tell you how long time it was — long nine years ago. Don't know what I had — I was so sick. We had our own house in Brooklyn. I know we have a house, that's what I know. I don't know why I am arrested. I am going from work. I was in the show. I am singing and dancing and running errands a little. The lady who sings likes black candy to chew. I was going home at half-past twelve. Never saw in my life such policemans as here. Never saw such boys as here," etc.

After his parents were discovered we learned of the complete unreliability of this boy. Even those stories about operations were untrue. They say that Otto is a bad boy in general. He is disobedient at home and does not want to go to school. Is impudent to parents and looks angrily at them. His talk is more like that of an old man than that of a young boy. When he makes money he spends it on shows, he soon began staying away nights and has been found sleeping in five-cent shows. He got his money by peddling papers. His father does not regard him as being mentally incapable, but rather as being a forward type, too " smart and fresh." The boy has long wanted to go to work and before he was 14 had misrepresented his age to get a working certificate. At times he is said to talk incessantly and to be very merry.

The family history is not known altogether satisfactorily from a scientific standpoint, but we have the following main points. The father is a rational man, not well educated, but able to run a small shop successfully. We do not find him entirely reliable about the details concerning the family. The mother seems more intelligent. Otto was the 5th of 8 children, 3 of whom died in their infancy, 2 with tuberculosis and " brain fever." One older brother of 20 went to school in the old country and got to the 4th class, but has turned out to be a loafer here. The next brother is a steady worker and did much better in school. The others seem to be quite normal. There is no history of anything peculiar about the early development of Otto. The birth was normal. At 9 months he had some illness, but it was not very severe. At 8 years he was very sick with typhoid fever and not expected to live. He walked and talked early, as did the others. His schooling in Europe amounted to very little. Both the father and mother were earning their own living and they acknowledged he was neither closely watched nor properly educated. They maintain they did not notice any bad conduct on his part before he came to this country. Now they are much concerned about him. We have never been able to get any history of defective heredity that bears on the boy's abnormalities.

The main trouble with Otto has been his constant tendency to run away from home, and he shows unreliability in other ways. He does not suffer much from his vagrant habits, for his ability to make friends and to concoct plausible stories gain him entrance into places of work and lodging where he can enjoy for a few days good surroundings. His father has a decent home for his class and could give him occupation in the shop. At times he has been successful for a few weeks in helping his father and then has seemed proud of the fact. He has run away so many times that his parents have long since ceased to notify the authorities.

As the parents say, Otto is a tremendous liar, and yet at times he has been able to restrain this tendency for quite a period. His lying itself really amounts to an important delinquency because of the trouble it has given his parents and the authorities. In various places the police and others have spent long and valuable time in endeavoring to place him and trace his family. Otto has at various times obtained money under false pretences. He is not a great thief, but has been willing to help himself sometimes to things not his own, always with the purpose of gain. He once took candy and toys from a shop where he was employed and sold them for a couple of dollars. He has taken things from his father's place. On two occasions he has been known to have a ten-dollar bill in his possession and where he obtained the money has never been discovered.

Otto at one time attempted to start a theatrical career with cheap actors, doing a dance and singing turn, for which, however, he had no ability. He has written many letters calculated to aid and abet his cause in various ways. These have been addressed to teachers and other individuals, but the ones we saw earlier were always too incoherent to be effective. The boy's reaction when confronted with the truth has always been that of showing no penitence whatever, and he has proceeded in a voluble and excited way to make other explanatory statements. When confronted with his parents after denying their existence he behaved in just the fashion he has done on other occasions — telling more falsehoods.

As time has gone on, this boy's facility to handle language has increased wonderfully. (Note the excellent results on the Binet tests which called for sixty words to be given in three minutes.) Specimens of his conversation at later times are as follows:

" Say, doctor, I found $20. I run up to a man who was walking by and he gave me ten of it. It was near 46th Street. Say, doctor, don't that show I never stole a penny. I gave that $10 to my father. What do you think. I spend it! Any pennies I have I always give to my father."

" Oh, today I don't go to school because I told my father I go down to see the doctor. I 'm in the high sixth grade now. My brother and me are going to make a big party when I graduate — have chocolate cake and lots of things."

After he had been working for awhile the following was his style in response to a question as to whether he drove a wagon or not. "Say, doctor, you know what a wagon boy is? Of course we don't drive. There is a driver and he drives and we collect the money. We give it to him and he turns it into the store. We always carry a gun. The other day we had $28. When I was in Germany my family had a big store and we had to deposit money at the bank. Sometimes I went with my mother to the bank and she would give me $1000 to carry. She did not like to carry it herself." Asked why he had lost a certain job he said, " A young fellow came along and hit me over the head just to show people he belonged there. Do you suppose I was going to stay there after that. Good night! My mother did not want me to be a wagon boy because it was so cold in winter, but I showed her I could not get another job. She would not believe it before when I tried it and wanted me to quit after two days. This time I showed her it was the only job I could get. You call $6 good. Well, not for me. Say, what you think I am anyway? Why, I 'm most 17."

He recently turned up after having been away three weeks and says he has a court case on. Tells in the most voluble and circumstantial way the details of the accident. He was wagon boy for a department store. Another wagon ran over a boy when they were standing near, and the boy's mother is suing the department store. Otto is going to give testimony. " See, this is how it is. How can a wagon run over a boy when it is standing still? See, that 's what I 'll say in court. How can you tell me how that is? I called up the mother of that boy that was run over and I says to her, see here, we get $1000 from you because how could we run over a boy when we was standing still. Now you see I get double back pay for time lost, and the driver he was fined too — he 's going to get $150 and a lot of other things are going to come from the woman who is suing."

It is not only the rapid, but also the firm and convincing conversational tone that Otto uses that has often proved persuasive to judges, officers and employers that he is mentally normal, and that he is a typical money maker. As a matter of fact, since he left school he has had many jobs, but has lost them all. It seemed most encouraging when he worked for his father, but home living soon proved tiresome and he began to run away again.

We note with a great deal of interest that as time went on this boy tended to first accuse the officers of misconduct in various ways, such as interfering with his welfare, and then later started for himself in legal proceedings. He was going to testify in one case, and took it upon himself to be most officious in the matter. We especially note this, because we have seen exactly this type of conduct develop in several other individuals, who are of similar mental make-up. Some of these, by virtue of their litigious tendencies and power to carry conviction on first acquaintance have caused a great deal of trouble.

The outlook for this boy developing into a stable member of society was felt by us to be anything but good. Had he had years of training possibly more might have been expected. The handling of such a case without scientific and legal recognition of his special type is clearly most unsatisfactory. It always seemed highly probable that he would continue in his erratic career and finally receive a prison sentence. One point, however, has stood out in his favor; he never did associate much with other delinquents and on account of his arrogance he has never been known to be easily led. Perhaps these qualities have prevented him from getting into serious trouble while he has been floundering about. The last we have heard of him is that he has probably been making his way about from city to city; he has been away from home for a number of months. His earning capacity has not increased with his years.

Mentality: Moron with special abilities.   Case 88.
    School dissatisfaction: Because un-   Boy, 17 years.
        successful.

      Home conditions: Poor control.

Delinquencies:
  Truancy.
  Running away + +.
  Lying +.
  Petty stealing.

Case 89. — We were asked to see a woman of about 40 years of age who had been taken up for vagrancy. Various investigators gave us a good report on her case. The police thought she was mentally defective.

We found a rather good-looking woman, very well nourished, good color, large head and face, and rather good features. No sensory defect noted. She was a woman of quite normal appearance.

On the mental side we soon found we had to do with a low-grade mental defective. She strenuously objected to doing tests, stating in fairly good language it was foolish to ask a woman like her to do them. By much persuasion, however, we got the following significant results. She could not add even simple numbers. Could barely write her own name and read only the simplest words in a newspaper. She did not know the name of the street on which was the institution where she was staying. However, she stated nobody could fool her on money. We then gave her $1.95 which she said was $1.75. A few of the 7- and 8-year-old Binet tests which she was willing to try, she failed on. Our simple Cross line Test, IX, she could not do.

By even common-sense tests, then, this woman was shown to be highly defective mentally, but her ability at language was altogether out of proportion and had undoubtedly kept her going in the world when her other failures would have counted against her. We found her able to string together fairly well her ideas in conversation. She told us she did not know how old she was when she came to this country and acknowledged she has always been " hard in learning," that she has had a couple of husbands, and so on.

" I have not had a home for over a year. My husband is dead. My baby is 17 months, a little over a year old. I am willing to work. I have been out in the country with the baby doing housework. My folks is all in Michigan. I never left home before. My home is everywhere. I was one winter in the English school. My husband has been buried over a year. I had a chance to be married again. I want to get housework. I stayed in the police station because I had no other place to go." Speaking of another man, says, " When we separated we lived on, I can't just tell what street it was on."

Investigators found out that all her adult life this woman had been wandering about, now here and now there, first with one man and then another. Has had several illegitimate children. At the time she was taken up by the police she was living under miserable circumstances in a basement. At times she has been able to get menial work. It seems she has always been able to tell a story that has passed well enough and so has never received the social protection that her mental disability would warrant. In spite of her vagrancy, immorality, and the fact that she has been suspected of infanticide, her normal appearance and language ability have given her the opportunity of going on in her miserable life of vice and misery. Many defectives who range years ahead of her in general intelligence and ability to take care of themselves have not a tithe of her power to make a good presentation of herself.

CHAPTER XVI

Mental Defect — *Continued*

Mental Subnormality. § 274. Definition of Subnormality. § 275. Illustrative Cases. § 276. The Subnormal Verbalist.

MENTAL SUBNORMALITY

§ 274. **Definition of Subnormality.** — In study of individuals who are not brought for examination because they are obviously feebleminded one cannot escape the conclusion that there is a clearly distinguishable group of defectives which stands between feeblemindedness, as defined above, and normality. For lack of a better word we have designated the members of this group as subnormal. Of course all defectives are subnormal, and one hesitates to use this generic term, but unless a new word, such as moron, is invented, the class cannot be better designated. Leaving aside individuals who have specialized mental defects, we have found it advisable to include under the head of subnormals the following:

(*a*) Those who in spite of passing the Binet tests as required, still may be shown to have such lack of mental ability as may prevent their normal success. By tests one may discover very grave incapacities, such as faulty powers of mental representation and analysis, constructive planning, apperception, and so on. These important higher mental powers are not evaluated to any extent by the Binet tests. (One may find a child doing moderately well in his school work and grading about normal by Binet, and yet already showing inability to think out situations and to do constructive planning and the like, which failure is really indicative of some degree of mental defect.)

(*b*) We find some who, notwithstanding they are unable to pass the Binet tests, are socially able to take care of themselves because of certain other abilities not determinable by these tests. For instance, we have found some Binet failures able to do our construction and mechanical tests right well.

(*c*) There is a class which, during school age at least, does not develop normally, but still does not show the three or four years

491

of retardation which in that period is the authoritative qualification for being considered feebleminded. Not all of these are found ultimately to be cases of arrested development.

(d) Then there is need for a class in which to put cases when we are temporarily not sure of anything except the fact that they are not up to normal in mental powers as shown by tests. There is often considerable cause for doubt in the case of a young person as to whether the ultimate diagnosis will be feeblemindedness or not. Sensory disabilities or general physical conditions may perhaps be partly responsible for the poor showing.

Another situation involving the problem of mental subnormality we should parenthetically mention here. It has been a matter of great interest for us to note from time to time that offenders belonging to well-educated circles who have been brought to us with the statement that they were subnormal or even feebleminded have not proved so by our usual range of tests. Yet it was a fundamental social and psychological fact which these parents or friends had in mind. The delinquent was *subnormal for his own social sphere*. Let a boy with barely an ordinary mental equipment be born into a family where all are extraordinarily successful in the use of their mental capacities, and it is obvious that this individual as he grows up will be considered below par. We have studied, for instance, a young man who went through grammar school in the ordinary way, but found a great deal of difficulty in mastering the more advanced studies of a high school course. His relatives were college people, authors, and so on. Their verdict about him was that he was subnormal. The irritation which he experienced in his social sphere was much the same as that which a moron with insight feels in competition with scholars in the grammar grades. The reaction was a usual one; there was development of an anti-social attitude, exhibited, among other ways, in definite delinquency.

§ 275. **Illustrative Cases.** — We may offer in illustration of mental subnormality a few cases from the many which we have seen which seem to fall in this category. Particularly we must offer examples of individuals who grade about normal by Binet, but who are nevertheless defective mentally.

Case 90. — An adopted colored child of 10 years of age, parentage entirely unknown, is reported to be quite possessed by the idea of stealing. It is said that ever since she was old enough she would take pennies. She steals from stores, boarders, school, anywhere. She is quick and cunning. For years she has been taken about the country by her foster mother who is an itinerant character; so the girl has never had a good chance at school. Has only reached 2d grade.

On the physical side we found her fairly developed and nourished with no sensory defects of note. She has an umbilical hernia. Ears imperfectly formed.

Mental tests. Binet (series 1911):
Seven years — 1, 2, 3, 4, 5, correct. Eight years — 1, correct; 2, failure; 3, correct; 4, failure; 5, correct. Nine years, — 1, failure; 2, 3, correct; 4, failure; 5, correct. Ten years — 2, 3, 4, 5, correct.
Our own series:
I. 4' 30''. Spent 3' on triangles, much repetition of errors.
III. Construction test A, 4' 31''. Twenty repetitions of impossibilities.
IV. Construction test B, 1' 52''. The first result was thought to be due largely to chance, and so immediately afterwards she was given the test upside down. She then took 5' 3'' and made 57 moves. This was most significant for the estimation of her mentality.
V. Puzzle box a failure.
VI. "Aussage." She did very well on this and saw many details. Gave them correctly and was not suggestible.
VII. Reproduction of geometric figures. Failure at 1st trial, but correct in each case at 2d trial.
VIII. Learning of arbitrary association symbols. Four errors.
IX. Cross line test A. Complete failure after 4th trial.
X. Cross line test B. Similar failure.
XIII. Memory from auditory verbal presentation; gives, with only a little variation, ten out of twelve items.
XV. Antonyms. Only one error and two failures. Average time 1.9''.
XVI. Motor coördination test done very rapidly but inaccurate. Best she did was 92 squares with 7 errors.
XVII. Writing poor for age, about equal to 2d-grade work. Writes from dictation so that one can read it, "The cat ran away."
XVIII. Arithmetic. Does correctly a few number combinations, but says 3 and 4 are 8.
XIX. Reading. In 2d-grade passage does not pronounce correctly heat, iron, small, etc.

We studied this girl on more than one occasion and found her able to use good sentences and to have a clear understanding of social situations. She had been talked to a great deal by moralizing people, and her apparent insight was perhaps due to parrotlike repetition of words. We found her failing in some very significant tests, although she ranged only about a year

493

behind her age on Binet tests. Her failure at the second trial
on Construction Test B, Test IV, and on the Cross line tests
and other things was most significant. It was not her failure
on the first trial in any of these things which seemed so significant as her lack of ability to profit by experience and to learn
from trial and error. In estimating the girl's capacities for reform,
or in considering the best to be done for her one finds very little
answer in the Binet tests alone. Then, too, her conversational
powers would not lead one to suspect her mental disability. One
saw clearly that she was defective mentally, and yet one could
not classify her as feebleminded.

Mentality: Subnormal.

Heredity: Unknown except that
the child was deserted.

Home conditions: Wandering life.

Stealing + +.

Case 90.
Girl, age 10 years.

Case 91. — A boy of 14 from a neighboring western state,
after having been arrested in Chicago, was seen at length by us.
His fairly intelligent father and mother had come on to get him
and went into all phases of the case at length.

The boy has been a great truant and mischief maker in school.
He has been maliciously destructive and quarrelsome at home.
Is very untruthful at times. Has been in trouble on account of
stealing with boys, and has taken money from home. His
people live in a good community, and the boy goes to private
school where he, evidently by courtesy, is in the 6th grade.

The family history is terrifically bad. Paternal grandmother
and aunt and granduncle insane. Paternal aunt subnormal.
Paternal uncle epileptic. The grandfather on this side and his
sons had a very bad name for sex immorality, and the whole
family were reputed to be alcoholic. The father of the boy was
himself at one time a deserter of his family, but of late years has
been doing well. In the mother's family there is much admin-
istrative genius and wealth.

The boy is 5th of six children, five of them alive. One still-
born. Two older boys somewhat subnormal. They have been
sickly and are still at school — about the 5th or 6th grade. The

oldest and youngest children apparently mentally normal. None had convulsions. This boy's birth and development negative. Never severely sick. Good general habits so far as known.

Physically this boy was fairly developed. Weight, 99 pounds; height 5 ft. Head; circumference 55.8, length 19.3, breadth 15 cm. No sensory defect noted. Strength fair for age. Slightly enlarged thyroid. Eyes bright, but expression rather dull. Tonsils large. Typical Hutchinsonian teeth. No other defects or anomalies found.

Mental tests. Binet (1908 series). Went rapidly up through the 12-year tests.

Results in our own series:

I. 1' 20". Moderate amount of trial and error on the triangles.

II. 2'. 11 errors. Most carelessly done in spite of warnings.

III. Construction test A. Extremely poorly done. 6' 30". 60 total moves. 25 repetitions of impossibilities. Had to be urged to finish test. Wanted to give up this simple job, saying, "That's the best I can do."

IV. Construction test B. 1' 10". Very likely much luck in this through picking up the right pieces first. Compare with result of previous test.

V. Puzzle box. 7'. Made many ludicrous errors in spite of warning to study out the whole situation. Only at 6' was step one done, and the others followed rapidly without errors. Showed in this great lack of planfulness and judgment.

VI. Many details given correctly, but showed himself quite suggestible. Accepted 4 out of 7 suggestions.

VIII. Learning arbitrary symbol associations. Correct and prompt.

IX. Cross line test A. Rapidly correct.

X. Cross line test B. Correct at first trial, after making alterations. He repeatedly represented to himself the figure by making motions in the air.

XI. Code test. In spite of the above success with the component parts of this test, failed to get the idea of the code, and utterly failed in correctness of procedure. This made 9 failures out of 11 possibilities and proceeded in the most painful and slow way. Very difficult for him to concentrate attention.

XII. Memory from visual verbal presentation. Result quite good. 17 out of 20 items were recalled with a good deal of verbal accuracy.

XIV. Instruction box. Failed on the dial on the first two attempts. Did it correctly at the 3d trial — a poor result for a boy of his age.

XVI. Motor coördination test. Showed himself most careless in this work. Much difficulty in self-control. First trial 82 squares tapped with 20 errors. After much warning, next trial 83 squares with 5 errors.

XVII. Writes an irregular hand. Is able to spell simple words.

XVIII. Slowly but correctly adds several columns' of figures correctly. Can do simple multiplication, but fails on division. Does not know the process in simple fractions, and in other simple reasoning arithmetical processes.

XIX. 6th-grade passage read well, fluently and with good expression.

XX. Says he has played checkers a good deal, but when tested showed merely a boyish game with no foresight and the neglect of many chances.

XXII. Information extremely poor considering his age and opportunities at school. Knows little about such boyish interests as electricity and mechanics. Cannot name the five Great Lakes. Thinks Chicago is the largest city in America. Says the Fourth of July is Washington's birthday.

XXIII. Pictorial completion test. The boy's apperceptive powers seemed to be weak. He made 7 final errors, most of them of the irrational type. At another time was given another chance, with the same type of striking results.

We found by our tests that this boy, in spite of rapidly passing the Binet requirements, was distinctly subnormal. He has poor powers of attention, mental analysis and apperception. His results on formal education are decidedly defective, especially in arithmetic. On the other hand his memory processes are good and he can learn well by rote.

The boy has long been dissatisfied with school, but on account of his aptness in reading has not been regarded as subnormal; rather it has been considered that he would not urge himself enough. A curious fact is that he was being specially educated with the idea that he could earn his living in office employment, a style of work for which it is readily seen he was most incompetent. The boy's lack of foresight and planfulness can be observed in his social career as well as in his tests. His conflict with the authorities has induced no attempt at better behavior. The outlook, unless he is placed at an occupation for which he is more suited, is not good.

A very recent report from the parents is that they were not able to make a satisfactory adjustment of this boy's case. A year or so after we first knew him he went around with a gang of young thieves who traveled from town to town. He was apprehended again, but it was recognized that he had been led on by the crowd. His parents then tried him at farm work where he has been more of a success than at anything else he has done.

Mentality: Subnormal.   Case 91.
   Heredity: Insanity, alcoholism,   Boy, age 14.
       epilepsy.
   School irritation: No educational adaptation
       to abilities.
   Developmental: Congenital disease (?)
Truancy.
Lying.
Stealing +.

It will only be necessary to give a single case in illustration of the easily understandable fact mentioned under (*b*) that not all who fail on Binet tests should be graded as feebleminded. In the following instance it is doubtful whether we should ultimately grade the individual as even subnormal.

Case 92. — A boy of nearly 15 has been only 2 years in this country. He has been getting into trouble because he has neither been attending school regularly nor working. Besides that he has been engaged in petty stealing, and is said to be more or less incorrigible at home. However, home conditions have been bad on account of poverty, and at times he has had to work at nights. An older sister has been a disturbing influence on account of her immoral tendencies.

Physically, we find a very small boy for his age. Weight 81 lbs.; height 4 ft. 8 in. Poorly-developed chest and strength not up to normal. In contrast to that is his sex development, which is almost adult in type.

Mental tests:
Binet (1911 series); 9 years, all correct except the second; 10 years, 1, 3, 4, correct; 2, half correct, and 5, failure; 12 years, all failures except the third.
Results on our series:
I. 1′ 39″. Almost no trial and error on the triangles.
III. 2′ 18″. 2 repetitions of impossibilities.
IV. 2′ 28″. 16 moves. Very good record.
IX. Correct at 1st trial.
X. Correct at 3d trial.
XVII. Writes his own name, but almost nothing else.
XVIII. Adds up fairly promptly simple number combinations. Knows how to carry correctly. Can do simple multiplication and reason out small number relationships.
XIX. Reads only the simpler words.

497

XXIII. Pictorial Completion Test done with only two errors, one of these illogical.

Memory span of seven digits.

This short cross-section study illustrates the necessity of adding to the Binet system other inquiries and other testing. It is stated that this boy never went to school in the old country. He shows ability in our performance tests that is on the whole above the grade of subnormality, but temporarily we can include him in this class. As his teachers say, it seems as if he would have done better by this time were he of quite normal mentality.

The other children in the family are all said to be bright. They were brought earlier to the United States and he was left in Europe. He is not known to have had any severe illness. The story of heredity is not forthcoming with accuracy. Part of the boy's lack of success in school has been undoubtedly due to the fact that he was working at night. We recommended he be placed in a certain educational institute and be given special instruction. Another feature back of this boy's present delinquent tendency lies in the fact that he has grown to dwell much on sex affairs and has become hypochondrical concerning them. A definite mental conflict has arisen as the result of suggestions given directly to him by his older sister. He has behaved himself well in these matters, but tells us he has been thrashing them over in his mind.

The boy's whole frank attitude in regard to his trouble, and the finding out of what he was going through mentally, as well as getting the history of his previous lack of educational training, leads us to give a favorable educational and social prognosis.

Lack of educational opportunity (in old country).	Case 92. Boy, age 14.
Family conditions: (Emigration, poverty, influence of immoral sister, etc.)	
Adolescent instability, with disproportionate physical development.	
Mental conflict, over sex affairs.	
Truancy. Incorrigibility. Petty stealing.	Mentality: Temporarily classed as subnormal.

But obviously it would be necessary to have a number of family and school conditions changed.

Case 93. — Interesting, especially from the standpoint of placing in institutions, is the case of a boy of 13 who has for years been engaged in a wide range of delinquencies. He was accused of running away from home, of petty stealing on many occasions, malicious mischief, destructiveness and of some bad treatment of small children. Recently his delinquencies have been carried on in company with two other subnormal children from the same subnormal room, an example of gregariousness which is frequently to be met.

The father entered into the case as fully as he could with us. He is poorly educated, perhaps subnormal, but a very well intentioned man, who is fond of his children and maintains a fairly good home as a laboring man. The parents were first cousins. The mother is dead. She had attacks which probably were epileptic. We could get no other evidence of defective heredity. There were only two children, and these were twins. The sister of this boy is evidently bright and healthy, sharply distinguished from him in both mental and physical ways. The mother used alcohol during pregnancy. Birth was normal.

We get an indefinite history of the boy being very ill and nearly dying when he was a baby. From him we learn of certain dizzy spells and queer appearances in front of his eyes which suggest attacks of minor epilepsy. Says he sometimes sees white and sometimes red which lasts for a couple of minutes before his eyes, and he then gets dizzy and cannot see at all. No evidence of other attacks. His father knew nothing of these. However, the boy as a half-orphan has been in institutions much, and the father really knows little enough about him.

He is rather small for his age, height only 4 ft. 9 in.; weight 86 lbs. Pleasant, but rather dull face. No sensory defects noted. Tonsils enlarged, possibly small adenoids. Although the boy by habit is a mouth breather, he can breathe very readily through his nose.

Mental tests: Binet, 1911 series:
All the 6-year tests done correctly.
Seven-year tests, fails on 2 and 4, others correct.
Eight years — fails only on half of test 4.
Nine years — fails only on test 2.
Ten years — 1, 2, 5, failure, others correct.
Twelve years — 1, correct; 2, failure; 3, correct; 4, failure; 5, failure.

On our own tests:

I. 1′ 8″. Only 13″ of trial and error on the small triangles.

II. 2′ 12″. 3 errors.

III. Construction test A, 2′ 17″. 23 total moves, but only one repetition of impossibility.

IV. Construction test B, 5′ 19″. 61 moves.

V. Puzzle box. 4′ 21″. Many errors interspersed between steps one and two. Other steps followed out logically.

VI. "Aussage." Most items gotten correct either on free recital or on cross-questioning and no sign of suggestibility.

VII. Reproduction of Geometric Figures. Done extremely poorly. Failure.

VIII. Learning arbitrary symbol associations. Promptly and correctly.

IX. Cross line test A. Correct at the 1st trial.

X. Cross line test B. Correct only at 3d trial.

XI. Code test. Could not comprehend the idea, utterly failed on the performance.

XIII. Memory from auditory verbal presentation. Very poorly done. Only 6 out of 12 items recalled.

XV. Antonyms. 4 errors and one failure. Average time 2.7″.

XVII. Writing atrocious and does not spell anything except monosyllables.

XVIII. Knows simple combinations of small numbers and the table of 2's as a series. Nothing beyond this.

XIX. Reading. Fails on a 3d-grade passage and on all the long words such as could, found, etc.

XXIII. Pictorial completion test. Five final errors of the irrational variety.

We found that though he only grades according to Binet a little over 8 years he does comparatively well on tests of performance with material directly given to him. We note a certain amount of variability from day to day, but not sufficient to alter his general standing by tests. It is quite possible that this variability was a phenomenon often observed in epileptics. The immediate problem was concerned with the placing of this boy in an institution. On account of his general ability with concrete material it was decided to try him, under agreement, in an industrial institution where they are very keen to rule out mental defectives.

He was retained the full time, about 18 months, as acceptable in their routine of education, although papers were on file for him to go to the colony for the feebleminded if it seemed desirable. The boy made good educational and moral progress. At present he is giving no trouble in a city environment.

Mentality: Subnormal; unequal abilities;   Case 93.
              possibly epileptic variability.   Boy, age 13.
  Heredity: Mother probably epileptic,
             father subnormal, consanguinity
             of parents.
    Developmental: Severe illness in infancy.
Running away.
Stealing.
Maliciousness.

§ 276. **The Subnormal Verbalist.** — The verbalist type of defective is so important in many ways that emphasis should again be placed on this subject by the citation of a case or two. Even though the grade of mental defect may not be that of feeble-mindedness, yet the disproportion between verbal and other abilities can be so great that anomalous social situations are produced. It is remarkable to what extent these unbalanced people get themselves and others entangled in troublesome matters. The comparative ease with which they use language leads readily to their becoming liars and swindlers.

The strangest feature of this class is the aptitude which verbalists show for using the law. The only explanation I see for this is that, since a large share of the business of the law is carried on merely by the use of language, even superficial acquaintance with legal phraseology goes a considerable distance towards making others believe in the qualifications of the verbalist. A person who has a special ability to use words well is of course likely to get ahead in all those branches of social effort where the usual evidence of good ability is displayed by language.

Case 94. — Sara S. I had the opportunity through a municipal court in a New England town to study this vivacious and fairly good-looking girl of 19. Her delinquencies had consisted in very repeated stealing for a year or more from down-town shops. For some months she had been using a system which she had herself evolved. Off and on she had worked at these stores, and was regarded as a capable young saleswoman. There was no need of her working or of her stealing, because she came from a home where there was plenty of comfort and good cheer.

Sara had never been aware, so far as known, that her supposed parents were really only her foster parents. She was taken into

501

their home from a New York child-placing agency when she was only a year or so old. Her real parentage is quite unknown. The foster parents are very stable people, and except for traveling for a year or two, when the girl had a good deal of healthy experience in the world, they have always lived in this New England town.

As an example of Sara's language facility and her own philosophic sizing up of the world, the following excerpts from her story are well worth reading closely.

"Well, I don't care for house work, and I like to have a little money for myself. Father did not want me to work, but I'm just the same as other girls, and like to have money of my own. I began stealing last year, but they did not catch me. I spent it for gloves and candy. The first time I ever took anything? Well, I was about 8. It was out of my uncle's pants. We all lived in X at the same time. Oh, playmates? Oh, yes, there were a couple of girls around the house then and I knew them best. Yes, they took things, both of them. They were both about the same age. They took money from their family and spent it for candy. I used to share things with them that they bought in this way. They both came from good families and I knew them for many years. When they were little they never went with boys. They began it about 12 years. I am pretty sure it was about that age. They never talked of stealing with me. Probably they did not think I knew about it. One of them turned out awful bad. She went with boys all the time."

"I have known a good many bad girls down town. The worst of all were at M's. Lots of them down there get money that way. Yes, at times I get to thinking about it. Well, I suppose I am sort of dreaming then. I think about all sorts of things. I love to read if I can get good books. My favorite author is Mary J. Holmes, and I like Dickens, too."

"People would come in and say, 'Can't I take this thing out the way it is?' and then I would not hand it in to the inspector and would keep the money. The other day the detective took me into a room, and found $1.80 on me. They saw me take it. I got it from different customers. They scared me terribly. I don't know half of what I said, but 50 cents was the largest sum I ever took. I am always well, but subject to colds. I tell you what I believe. If anything is the matter with you you want to get your mind off that and forget it. I get in the crowd down

town and if my back does ache I don't think any more about it.
You can forget things if you get busy. I saw a detective take a
girl up last summer. She was the only one I knew who took
things that way. Then I was so scared I didn't take anything
for a long time. I saw the other girls there getting money pretty
easy. They would say they made money the night before or
something like that."

" I always got along all right with my teachers. Music was
easy for me. I can play well. Have had music lessons four years.
What I want to do is to go on the stage, but they don't care to
have me. I did not tell my mother about these girls because I
knew she would not let me have gone with them. I am quite
sure I was about 12 when they began to talk so much about
those things and they used to tell me all about it and say, ' Why
don't you do it? ' I was 14 before I knew what it meant. It
was not mother then that told me. It was my Sunday School
teacher. I don't know exactly why I did not go with them."

" I think it is just terrible the way a girl is treated in all these
matters. Just think how she gets the worst of it. If a boy is
under age he can't be arrested, and nothing is done to him for
this. A girl is likely to get into trouble. Now, I don't think
there is much blame about it and I don't think it is so bad. I am
not sure it is as bad as I have done. It is just nature that's all.
If I had done that and got money by it they could not have arrested
me and I think it might have been better if I had instead of stealing. If this gets in the papers I'm a ruined girl and that's all
there is to it. The best thing I can do is to get married to some
nice fellow, and a lot of chance I will get if this gets in the papers.
A fellow will say, ' That's Sara S. whose name was in the paper,
isn't it? ' I don't want any of my girl friends to know it. I go
with girls right now who are fine."

Physically, we found this girl to be in fair general condition,
rather poorly developed; not particularly good looking; notable
is her slouchy attitude (in spite of much training on the part of
her parents); no sensory defects; dental findings very significant
— distinct crescentic erosion of the incisors; expression not
particularly bright, but uses her eyes in affected and stagey
manner.

Results on our own tests:
I. 1' 50". Rapid but no planning. Occasionally tries a piece in
the wrong place.

III. Construction test A. 5′ 15″. 43 total moves. 10 repetitions of impossibilities. Talked in very childish fashion about this and wanted to give up.

IV. Construction test B. 5′ 30″. Good application but very little planning. 46 total moves.

V. Puzzle box. Failure in 10′. Apparently studies it carefully but task is too difficult.

VI. "Aussage." Fair number of details given. Very positive about things not seen and not the slightest evidence of suggestibility.

VII. Reproduction of geometric figures. Very poorly done. Failure.

VIII. Learning arbitrary symbol associations. Very slow performance and three errors.

IX. Cross line test A. In spite of many explanations failed to get the idea at all.

X. Cross line test B. Failed at 4th trial. "I can't think of it or remember it. It's so hard."

XII. Memory from visual verbal presentation. Entire twenty items recalled with the sense correct although many verbal changes.

XIII. Memory from auditory verbal presentation. All items except one small detail recalled and much verbal accuracy included.

XV. Antonyms. No errors. No failures. Average time 1.8″. A remarkable performance in comparison to some of the other work.

XVI. Motor coördination very well done. 75 squares with one error and then she speeded up to 90 squares with no errors.

XVII. Writes a very mature hand and spells all simple words correctly.

XVIII. Long division correctly and has some idea of work with fractions, but fails to carry out the process correctly.

XIX. Reads very fluently with good expression. Has had special training in this.

XXII. Has been a good deal of a reader and knows ordinary items of information to be gathered from newspapers. Simple items correct in geography and history. Quite ignorant of simple scientific information.

Although the Binet tests were not done it is quite clear that Sara's language facility would have carried her well up in the 12-year or even 15-year tests. Her power of mental analysis and her ability to reason out a situation which is presented to her in concrete form is exceedingly poor. In fact she does badly on all of our tests for higher mental power, such as are involved in planning and foresight. Her powers of visual recall of form were also remarkably poor in comparison to her memory for words. She has great conversational ability, and has developed a well-defined and even philosophic attitude towards the world. She carries an air of sophistication and dramatic ability. This, however, may be largely a matter of imitation of the stage, and of the philosophy of her immoral girl friends. We note with the parents that she has a remarkable lack of emotional reaction in regard to her own delinquency, and we also corroborate their opinion that she has very little ability to do anything but talk. There can be no doubt that, though this girl comports herself with such superficial evidence of ability, and was able by virtue of good instruction to do 6th-grade work, and although she proved a very satisfactory saleswoman, still she is mentally subnormal. She did not learn wisdom from family reprimands for stealing, nor through the experience of her thieving shop companion, and in general she shows lack of foresight.

The developmental history as known since one year of age is almost negative. No serious illness. No convulsions. No complaint of headaches. As a little child she seemed bright. Walked and talked at normal age, but after going to school never learned rapidly. Reached the 6th grade without much difficulty, but never went beyond that. Had lack of control of bladder and occasionally of the bowels up to the time she was 6 or 7 years old. Her first teeth were said to have been deficient in enamel. The foster parents speak much about her lack of physical control. They would have been very proud to have had her acquire a fine carriage. In school her deportment was always considered good, but she was thought to have a stubborn will.

It was felt that the exceedingly good home environment of this young woman could be relied on to prevent her from further misconduct. The family suggested that her salvation very likely lay in early marriage. No more delinquencies were reported.

Early sex knowledge with mental conflict   Case 94.
                    about it.   Girl, age 19.
  Bad companions.

  Mentality: Subnormal, verbalist type.

    Antenatal conditions: Probably con-
                        genital syphilis.
  Stealing +.

The following case should be of the greatest interest to all students of human nature and particularly to people of the law. Here we have a young man probably subnormal in various impor-

505

tant mental abilities, who has a facility in language which vastly overtops his other faculties. He is a chronic falsifier and as such belongs in our class of pathological liars except perhaps for the fact that he also is a mental defective. To tell what we know of his career would require many more pages than we can give here, but significant points are offered.

Case 95. — This young man of 20 came to this country with his intelligent and industrious parents from Hamburg when he was 15 years old. I saw him in New York about a year after they had landed, at the request of his father and other interested people. He had recently been in the Tombs, having stated to the authorities that he was over juvenile court age. It was charged that he had been engaged in several swindling operations previously, however, having made such good presentation of his own case that he had not been prosecuted by the parties involved. In the old country his principal delinquency had been truancy. Now the people who wanted the case of this boy studied were interested in him because they conceived a great injustice had all along been done. He appeared to be such an ambitious fellow, he was studying at night to be a lawyer. They thought possibly he was persecuted by the police and not sympathized with by his parents. I studied him then and have seen him at intervals since, and have full reports on his career.

At our first interview we were much inclined to take the view of this boy's recently made friends, and to feel he had been unjustly incarcerated. It appeared that his arrest was immediately due to the fact that he got into a fight in his own family circle and struck his mother and their landlady with a broom stick. The fight came about because his family did not further his interests in giving him clothes satisfactory to himself in which to appear in a court room where there was a case going on in which he was interested.

Part of his first statement runs as follows: " I took a few lessons over in the Y. M. C. A. class and in a law office and I have books at home of every court in New York. I know I got a good chance to work up because I got a good head for the law. My father he won't believe it, that 's the trouble. I know I could stand my own expenses. I said, ' Officer, you wait here a minute. I will explain how this is.' He began stepping on me. He threw me on the floor. I wanted him to go out the back way so nobody would see me, there was a big crowd there, but he kicked me down the front way. Another rough officer pinched my arm. I was in the other court because my father thought I would not work. I was trying to find a position. I was in court by myself in a divorce case. I was interpreter there. The woman paid me three dollars for it. I want to make something out of myself. Labor is all right, but I like office or law work better."

A curiously long record about this boy was obtained from a social service society to which he had applied for assistance some months previously. It seems he has been known all along as a tremendous liar. He persuaded the juvenile court judge to give nearly an hour to his case because the judge hesitated to put on record anything against a boy who desired to be a lawyer.

In the previous year the lad had worked in about 20 different places, getting a job very readily on account of his good powers of self-representation. He had forged various letters and tele-grams about himself. He represented himself as an orphan in a certain newspaper office where they thereupon raised a fund and outfitted him. One or two people who have known him the longest are inclined to think the boy cannot be just right. He has been able to pick up some small law suits, particularly damage cases, and has turned them over to other lawyers after first mak-ing the attempt to handle them himself. Every one reports him as a most ambitious and aggressive type.

Physically we found him to be well developed and nourished, but of a very flabby type of musculature. Regular and rather pleasant features. Expression rather duller than one would expect from the vivacity of his speech. General attitude slouchy; clothes nearly always untidy. Head well shaped; circumfer-ence 54.5; length 18; breadth 15 cm. No sensory defect noted. No complaints of headaches or other physical troubles. Narrow and rather high palate. Low, well-controlled voice. Reflexes normal. Coloration of the irides asymmetrical. Enlargement of the mammae, a marked anomaly. Examination otherwise negative.

Mental tests; our own series:

I. Introductory Form Board Puzzle. 1' 10". Very little trial and error.

II. Not so well done. 55". 4 errors.

III. Construction Test A. 1' 3". No repetition of impossibilities. At a second trial shortly afterwards he did it in 9".

IV. Construction Test B. 4' 25". Done not at all intelligently or planfully, but comparatively few repetitions of impossibilities. A poor showing for his age.

V. Puzzle Box. Failure. Began working with his usual self-confidence, but proceeded without planfulness or evident ability to understand the relation of the different mechanical steps one to another.

VI. "Aussage." Gives a very wordy account of what he sees in the picture, but really recalls very few items. Some of these are imaginative, such as putting words in the mouth of the woman who is buying the sausages, and placing things incorrectly. The total result was poor. Only two suggestions accepted. His main failure was through inability to correctly recall the items, and through his unwarranted use of imaginative details. The general results show a most unusual amount of unreliability.

VII. Reproduction of Geometrical Figures. Failure. Self-confidence shown by his desire to proceed with the reproduction before all of the allotted time was up for observation.

VIII. Learning Arbitrary Symbol Associations. Done promptly with one error, but this was significant inasmuch as it involved placing the same digit in relation to two different symbols and omission of another digit. A thoroughly irrational result.

IX. Cross Line Test A. Done correctly but with considerable effort.

X. Cross Line Test B. Failure. This simple test has been repeatedly tried with this young man during the ensuing years and he has never been able to correctly perform it.

XI. Code Test. This was a failure both on account of his inability to perform the easier task, Cross Line Test B, and because he could not correctly repeat the alphabet either in German or in English.

XII. Memory from Visual Verbal Presentation. An almost perfect result both in regard to sequence and verbal accuracy. An unusually good performance.

XIII. Memory from Auditory Verbal presentation. Similar result. Almost perfect. Only one minor detail missing.

XV. Antonyms. No error, but fails on three, probably because of lack of knowledge of English terms. Average time 2.3″.

XVI. Motor Coördination Test. 75 squares tapped the first trial. 2 errors. 74 squares tapped the second time. 3 errors. This showed poor motor control for his age.

XVII. Writing. Fairly mature and regular hand. Has considerable trouble with spelling, but yet considering that he has only been in this country one year a letter written by him in English is fairly good.

XVIII. Arithmetic. Makes several mistakes in an addition example of several columns. Knows his tables fairly well. Cannot do anything at long division. An interesting observation was made when he was heard to say as he was multiplying, "8 times 4 is 16," and then a minute later, "4 times 8 is 32." A couple of years afterwards he was still unable to do long division in spite of his assertion that he

had learned, and would show us. He did not at all know the
process.

XIX. Reading. The boy all along made a specialty of his reading.
He is very proud of it and of his conquest of the English language. He
reads fluently simple passages and did so when we first saw him. However, after a couple of years, in spite of his boasted ability, we found he
could not read a difficult passage, and could not pronounce and did
not know the meaning of such words as significance, efficiency, physics.
But he has picked up various terms such as jurisprudence, civil engineer and knows in a vague way what these mean. Many legal terms
he has committed to memory and knows the exact meaning of them.

XX. Told us his favorite game was checkers, that he played a
good deal and played a good game. On trial it was found that he
played extremely poorly, and without any foresight. At one time
moved backwards.

XXI. Sharp's questions would seem to give him an opportunity to
display any casuistic ability which he might seem to have. About the
first question of stealing to help a starving woman, he said it would
be right in one way and in another wrong. It was never right to steal,
because if the man was caught he would be sent to the penitentiary,
and have to pay more than the things were worth. Asked if it was not
wrong otherwise he said yes, because a thief would never get along
in the world. On the second question about giving up the man to the
Indians, he said that the white men should battle with the Indians if
the man had done no wrong, but, "I really would rather give up one
man than many. If the chief gets killed himself I rather give this man
up before he put his own life in it." Altogether an incoherent reply.

XXII. Information. Very wordy answers were given to questions,
and whenever he did not know a point he tried to bluff it through.
He knows a good deal about local politics, about the cost of getting
into law schools, he knows some of the ordinary facts of geography,
knows a number of sporting items; knows how the electricity comes
from the power house and makes a motor go in a trolley car, but fails
on other scientific items. Shows much familiarity with newspaper
accounts of notorious law suits, makes much talk about being interested in athletics and about himself being a champion. (He is really
very poor in such things.) His knowledge of German geography, which
he should know well by reason of his long schooling in Hamburg, was
exceedingly faulty. He was unable to spell correctly the name of the
city district in which he used to live. Insisted Paris was a country, etc.

His failure on the above simple tests showed this young man
to be unquestionably subnormal mentally, despite his aptitude
for language. At the end of one year in this country he spoke
English with only a slight accent. His grammar has never been
perfect, but it has gradually improved. However, he makes
up for it by vigor of speech. On numerous occasions he represented
himself as an official interpreter and tried to get a position of this

kind, having cards printed announcing himself as such. There is no doubt but that he can perform such work fairly well when only simple ideas are involved. He had announced to others and told us that he was a graduate of the intermediate school abroad, and had spent some time in a high school. This was quite untrue, but he cited it and his language ability as evidence of his qualifications for becoming a lawyer.

But it was just his record at school which has all along made his father so scornful of the boy's legal pretensions. The fact is that he never got beyond the 3d class of the elementary school, about equivalent to the 3d grade in our grammar school. He went to school for several months when he first came to the United States, but succeeded in advancing only in subjects where language was the chief requisite.

The intelligent parents, in their endeavor to solve the problem of this boy's peculiarities, gave a good family and developmental history. He is the youngest of three children, two of whom are alive. The others were quite bright. The surviving sister is industrious, quiet, and has a good school record. Many in the family have been nervous and excitable, but in general the stock on both sides is said to be quite healthy. A cousin on one side was insane, and a cousin on the other side was probably feeble-minded, but nobody nearer than this was the victim of abnormal mental conditions. Some members of the family have achieved distinct success.

There were two miscarriages just before this boy was born, but his pregnancy and birth were all right. At 3 years he had diphtheria exceedingly severely. He was delirious for a couple of weeks, and following the attack had palatal paralysis for three months. The boy has never seemed normal to his parents since then. Before that he had walked and talked at an early age. His parents remember him as a destructive young child, but outside of that give us no history of peculiarities. He was subject to occasional fevers, and was very sick again at 9 years with scarlet fever. As a young child he was always much inclined to play by himself. Was never known to have bad habits of any kind. A very important point is that up to 14 years this boy suffered from nightly enuresis, with occasional lack of control of bladder and bowels during the daytime.

As time has gone on this young man has sought harder and harder to get himself into legal practice, and has connected him-

510

self with various questionable legal affairs, mainly acting in
some capacity as an assistant. Soon after I first saw him he
was sent for a time to a disciplinary institution. Since then
he has received one definite fine and sentence for attempting to
dispose of property not his own, and another for forging a legal
document. Even at his first appearance before a judge he showed
his typical characteristics in cross-examination of his family and
others in his own defense. Later he had badges made for himself which have represented him to be an officer connected with
a certain official organization. He made complaints to various
authorities about his treatment when in the institutions to which
he has been sent, accused certain individuals of maltreating him
while there, and succeeded on more than one occasion in getting
others interested in the matter. He has shown extremely poor
judgment in much of this, for he brought his own career to notice.

In regard to his use of language we find that he has not proportionately improved as time has gone on. If a subject is developed so that rather complex ideas are dealt with, a certain amount
of incoherency has always been noticeable. But he has accumulated more and more legal terms, with gradual increase of real
understanding of them. His ambitiousness and push still carry
him along so that, in a large city, new business possibilities constantly present themselves, even if many mistakes have earlier
been made. Some excerpts from his conversational reactions
may be instructive.

" You know that Johnny R. and then that K. boy? Judge R.
is going to try them. They are down at the Blank Street Station
and they are going to sign a jury waiver and they can't do that.
They are only 15 years old. I got their ages. It cost me a dollar
to get their ages, and I 'm going to be there when they 're tried.
You ought to see 'em. They look pale. They don't give them
anything but black coffee down there. Who is this attorney?"

" You know I 'm working in three places now. I 'm holding
three jobs. Two days in the week I work for A. and two days
for Mr. B. and then for myself. I make $7 or $8 a week by interpreting. I am saving it up to go to law school. In three years
I graduate. I want to see the judge to get these boys down here
right away before their trial. They are going to hold it up against
them their record, and I 'm going to deny it. It ain't right. I
was talking to the detective that arrested Johnny R. I 'm going
round to see the attorney. I want to represent the case myself."

In the cases referred to, our young man was attempting to get a wrong statement of ages before the judge who was to try them in the adult court and, as usual, was trying to put it on the grounds of seeing that justice was done. He really made quite an investigation in connection with an alleged burglary, and had a speech written up which he wanted to declaim before the judge. On several occasions with unscrupulous lawyers he has attempted to ferret out the situation in various court cases. He has made very little out of it, because even they felt he was not reliable enough to be used for long. He has started damage suits on behalf of members of his family against the neighbors, and has endeavored to get other fellows who have been in jail to commence some cases in the hope of getting some financial returns. In spite of his having been sentenced himself he insists on continuing his legal aspirations. He ingenuously reveals to me the character of some of his business affairs.

"I have a job in the legal department at J's. I get $10 a week. Because my name was so ruined I gave the name of Charles R, and if you would come in and ask for me by my right name there would be no such person there. I'm determined to be a lawyer. Ever since I was a little fellow I have wanted to be. Ever since I have had understanding of what law means. I used to play court with the little ones and talk about law."

At a later time this fellow gave a summary of his recent career which is most significant. "I am general manager for a picture portrait business — you know, enlargements. We have an artist who gets six or seven pictures made in a day. There's money in that, isn't there? I was down in court today. I tell you there was a fellow who got what was coming to him. It was a case before Judge B — assault and battery. He got $10 and costs, in all about $30. Well, it is like this. Well, I had a little dog, and I tell you I have a heart for animals just the same as persons. He kicked the dog, and I told him not to do it and he says, 'You're a liar,' and then he ran downstairs and pushed me along on stones down there. I called the policemen and they did not come for about three quarters of an hour. I put on my clothes and went with them and got out a warrant. Now I'm going to get a complaint out about the boy who lives out there. He lives over my house. Something bad will happen there. He calls my mother all sorts of names and uses bad language. Maybe I was not much of a fellow to praise her, but I could not stand to hear her called those bad names, and if that goes on it will be bad."

"I am studying law. Take the correspondence course. They give you an LL.B. It is a two-years course, and you get all the volumes separately. When I started out I did not know any Latin, but now I tell you I know all the names in it. I studied the first volume, and they send you questions you are to fill out without looking in the books. I would be willing to bet anything I get credits on that."

"Then we have a slander suit. That woman upstairs she called my mother all sorts of dirty names. I'm going to file a $3000 slander suit. I would not let her call names like that. And then she has about $3000 worth of property."

"I have been getting along pretty fine in most ways. Some of the people are down on me. I'm a Scout master. I started with 10 boys, and now I have about 117. We won the championship. We have a great big blue pennant about it. We won in baseball. The boys did everything best. There was an examination on leaves. I had 9 boys up and there were 117 leaves and every boy knew every leaf. Of course I told them or they would not have known."

"Some people are down on the Boy Scouts of America, but I tell them it does them good. I've been through the courts you know, and I made up my mind I'll help other kids. Don't you think that is right? I tell them that judges and officers ain't necessary. 'Sometimes youse kids can be helped by talking to.' They used to smoke and chew and things like that, but they don't any more."

"Then there's me. I won the wrestling championship this year." (At this point I mildly suggest the discrepancies between his statements and the neighborhood fights. He blushed a little and said he was no good at real fighting.) "I'm this kind of a fellow. If you let me alone I'm all right, but if you start monkeying with me then something's going to happen. When you start things don't start it until you are able to carry it through. They were not able to do that."

"I don't know whether I'll file that complaint. I'll give it to the police officer. My time is too valuable. Three times $8 are $24 and that's gone for a week. The boy is dangerous to me as well as my mother. I've got the right of a citizen to protect myself."

513

"A fellow met me and says how long have you been in this country, and when I says four years he says, 'You're a liar.' He says there never was a fellow I ever heard of who got hold of the language and was doing so well in only four years. I go out with my sample case and it's $8. That's get-rich-quick-Wallingford for you!"

It was on the occasion of this interview that the boy had to have his car fare paid, and related an unlikely story about having lost a quarter. Then he also told several other small unnecessary lies besides those which were involved in his boasting. His weak lying has grown to be such a usual phenomenon that it belongs in our pathological class. Our earliest reports from his father and his friends were that he was a tremendous falsifier.

All told, this irregularly subnormal young man with his considerable defect in judgment and his inability to reason or plan well, or to mentally handle abstract material has created a vast deal of trouble and is likely to create still more. By his aggressiveness and fondness for legal situations he has already involved himself in over a dozen court procedures of which we know. He has been a defendant as enumerated above, also he has been a plaintiff in other cases, or instrumental in filing complaints, and these all outside of his experience as office or messenger boy with various law concerns.

(In the last year this young man has been sentenced 3 more times for petty swindling, etc.)

Mentality: Subnormal, verbalist type.	Case 95.
Developmental: Infantile illness with involvement of nervous system.	Man, age 20.

Lying + + +.
Swindling.
Stealing.

CHAPTER XVII

Mental Defect — *Concluded*

Defects in Special Mental Abilities.   § 277. General Statement.   § 278. Language Defect.   § 279. Defect in Arithmetical Ability.   § 280. Defect in Judgment and Foresight.   § 281. Defect in Self-control.

DEFECTS IN SPECIAL MENTAL ABILITIES.

§ 277. **General Statement.** — We now enter upon the discussion of special mental capacities which in an individual of general normal ability fall considerably below the average. It is hardly fair to call persons with defects in a limited sphere mental defectives, although it is proper to include discussion of such phenomena under the head of mental defect. As we have long maintained, we should denominate these individuals as persons with a special defect.

I suppose that practically all people could be discovered to have some portion of their mental abilities below par. We all have localized spots of weakness. But such defects become significant, at least for our present purposes, only when the given comparative disability is of social importance. The vast majority of such defects do not much hinder one's social success, and therefore are not taken much account of. This fact is easily recognized when we remember that many have, for instance, defects in the musical sense which preclude average appreciation or reproduction of music. Now if we were all graded on the basis of musical ability it is obvious that many who now pass for normal would be regarded as defective. But as it is, let an individual have a language or an arithmetical defect and we can see at once that he is likely to be a great social sufferer. We have observed a number of most interesting cases in which a limited mental defect has had a well-marked relation to the causation of delinquency. The irritations which may arise in school life, in employment, or in the individual social circle, as the result of faulty adaptations of ability to environment may be very distressing. The delinquency appears to be a natural reaction. That this latter is not merely a theoretical conjecture on our part

515

is proven by the fact that an alteration of environment and employment has sometimes brought about an entire change of behavior. Indeed the possibility of constructive work with young offenders is emphasized in this field as almost nowhere else.

We have no reason in our present work to deal with all the different varieties of specialized mental defect. We are particularly interested in those defects which have special social importance, and give illustrative cases merely of these.

§ 278. **Language Defect.** — We cannot begin in this place to treat all kinds of language defect. We may, however, give some intimation of the social and educational importance of certain forms of language disability, and the grave need for special adjustment which exists in such cases. (The speech troubles, especially stuttering, which so notoriously are correlated with weakness of character, are discussed in their proper place, § 169.) We have seen several psychological varieties of language defect among delinquents when the defect itself was clearly a causative factor of the delinquency. The variation in the disabilities exhibited is what one might expect from researches on aphasia which demonstrate the great complexity of neural mechanisms that control the powers of perception and reproduction of language.

Case 96. — A boy of 15 was brought to us as presenting both a problem in conduct and education. His parents rather considered his school retardation due to his general delinquent tendencies. We were told that for years he had engaged in a moderate amount of truancy, had occasionally stolen from home, and had been very disobedient. Just now he had run away from home.

From the industrious and well-meaning parents we ascertain that pregnancy and birth were normal, and that the boy was never severely ill. When younger he had headaches with sickness at his stomach and attacks of nausea, but for the last couple of years rarely had anything of the sort. No injuries of any importance. The family have considered him rather hysterical because of his cowardly behavior when punished. No significant information on heredity was obtainable. The mother was only about 17 years old when he was born.

Through early childhood this boy was considered bright. Even in school his teachers gave him this reputation, but said he would not learn. At least one of them worked very hard with him. At 14, in spite of much urging, he had reached only the 5th grade.

His parents are much concerned about him because he cannot read and cannot write a letter. They feel he is going to the dogs on account of his backwardness.

Physically, we find him in rather poor general condition. Round shoulders and narrow chest; weight 100 lbs.; height 5 ft. 3 in.; no sensory defect found; tonsils moderately enlarged. A pleasant and responsive expression. Gives the impression of physical weakness on account of his general attitude and small, narrow face.

Mental tests; our own series:

I. Very rapidly done in 1′ without any trial and error.

IV. Construction test B. 1′ 7″. 29 moves. Rational and fairly rapid performance. Given to him immediately afterward upside down, he did it in 18″ with the minimum possible number of moves.

V. Puzzle box. 2′ 10″. One error interspersed between steps one and two. Put the apparatus together again without error. This latter is a test rarely given because of its difficulties.

VII. Had some difficulty in the reproduction of these geometrical figures. The first time he failed on each, and when he succeeded at the second exposure he stated in response to our inquiry that he said over to himself a sort of verbal description of the figure.

IX. Cross line test A. Correct at first trial.

X. Cross line test B. Correct at first trial.

XI. Code test. Got the idea by himself, but had much difficulty with the reproduction. Made seven errors out of eleven possibilities. Evidently was unable to keep the original represented to himself visually.

XII. Memory from visual verbal presentation. Got the idea much jumbled, although 18 of the 20 items were fairly well recalled. He stated that he accomplished this feat by reading each line and then saying it over to himself.

XIII. Memory from auditory verbal presentation. Recalled nine items, including all the important ones, out of the twelve. Gave them in logical sequence.

XV. Antonyms. One failure and three errors. Average time 1.4″. Many of these opposites were given in remarkably quick time.

XVI. Motor coördination test. Fairly well done. At the first trial he tapped 88 squares with one error, and the second trial tapped 89 squares with 4 errors.

XVII. Writes a fair boyish hand and spells simple words correctly.

XVIII. Does correctly a problem in long division.

XIX. His reading is a most curious performance. Words visually presented, unless they are short and most familiar, seem to have the most haphazard meanings for him. *Crib* is *cab, tunnel* is *turned, cylinders* is *candles,* 60 is 16 and so on. When words are given orally to him to spell he does unexpectedly much better, although with a number of errors on small words. The trouble seems to be in visual recognition of the words.

XXII. Knows most of the common facts of history and geography. Names four of the five Great Lakes correctly. Said that he never read a book — that he never wanted to read, but that his mother used to read to him, and he told the titles of many books she read. He has picked up quite a number of items of scientific information. He knows something of electricity which he has learned by observing the work of a neighbor who is an electrician.

This boy thus proved to have exceedingly good ability in many ways, and did most of the work of his school grade, but he has a pronounced language defect which has been holding him back. In the short time at our disposal for the study of this boy we were unable to completely cover the field for educational diagnosis and recommendations. However, the case is clear-cut, the relationship between the boy's delinquent tendency and his school dissatisfactions being well marked. This is accentuated by the fact that the boy comes from a moral and sympathetic home. His defect is highly specialized, even within the sphere of language ability. Our recommendations were special tutoring in a school where the boy's moral and educational welfare could be looked after in a constructive and not in a repressive way.

Mentality: Special language defect.　　　　　Case 96.
　　Social adaptation faulty: Irritations　　Boy, age 14.
　　　　　　　　　　　both at
　　　　　　　　　　　school and home.
　　　　Physical conditions: Early sick headaches.
　　　　　　　　　　　Now poor general conditions.
Truancy.
Disobedience.
Running away.

The following case in its proved constructive possibilities has much teaching value.

Case 97. — A boy of 15 was reported to the police as a great menace in his neighborhood. It was stated that he showed many immoral tendencies. The specific complaints were extremely bad language, much fighting, molesting of little girls. It was suggested by various friends and observers that he could only be managed by being sent to a reformatory, or perhaps to an institution for defectives. He was in the subnormal room of a city school.

We found the mother to be a pleasant and well-meaning woman who worked out every day. She is much interested in the boy and has no complaint to make about his home behavior. He is obedient and trustworthy. She says he has long been most anxious to go to work. After the father died many years ago, the boy for some time was in an orphanage. The mother speaks very little English. Her son first learned his parents' native language, and they always speak this at home.

This boy was one of twins, each of whom weighed about 4 lbs. at birth. The other died during infancy. There is an older sister who did well at school and is self-supporting. This boy walked and talked early. He was very ill with some disease of the lungs at 4 years of age. Later he had scarlet fever mildly. Had slight injury to his head at about 9 years. All other points about developmental history seem to be negative. Mother knows nothing of her husband's family. On her side there was no mental abnormality or epilepsy. Her people were generally regarded as being quite bright. The boy's father was alcoholic and died early from hard drinking, the doctor said.

Physical examination showed this boy to be in very good general condition, although rather small for his age. Exceptionally well muscled and strong; maintains he can lift one hundred pounds. Height 4 ft. 10 in.; weight 100 lbs. Nutrition and color good. Strong, straight profile, good chin, and large, well-shaped head. His general attitude was of much interest. He seemed quiet and strong, but appeared quite sullen except after much encouragement. When we first knew him he used to speak in a curious whisper, showing great repression in so strong a lad. Development in all ways normal except for the fact that upper lateral incisors absent, said never to have been removed. No sensory defect of importance noted.

Mental tests; our own series:

I. 3′ 5″. No repetition of trial and error on the triangles.

II. 3′ 20″. 13 errors. (The slowness on these early tests is to be accounted for by his sullen attitude at first.)

III. Construction Test A. 3′. His slowness of procedure in this, as well as in the previous one, is shown by the fact that he did only 26 moves in 3′.

IV. Construction Test B. 40″. 11 moves. Remarkably rapid and accurate performance.

519

V. Puzzle Box. Again a remarkably good result. 2′ 30″. Very well planned. Proceeded logically through the performance, except trial of one error between steps one and three.

VI. "Aussage." Full functional account. Practically no evidence of suggestibility.

VIII. Learning Arbitrary Symbol Associations. Done promptly and without error.

IX. Cross Line Test A. Correct at first trial.

X. Cross Line Test B. Correct at third trial.

XIII. Memory Test from Auditory Verbal Presentation. Entire 12 items recalled and logical sequence good, but no attempt at verbal accuracy. The result was given in curious, disjointed manner of speech.

XV. Antonyms. Three failures. Average time 2.7″.

XVI. Motor Coördination Test. First trial 70 squares and no errors. Second trial 77 squares and no errors.

XVII. Normal penmanship, but fails utterly to write the simplest sentence from dictation. Can spell "the," "made," but not "cards," or "printer" or "some." (Although German is largely spoken at home he cannot do any better in that language.)

XVIII. Adds and multiplies correctly simple sums. This work entirely out of proportion to his language defect.

It is hardly necessary to go into the details of this boy's story or his own feelings about his relations to the school and to the world generally. It is enough to say that on the several occasions when we have met him he has always felt certain he did not want to go to school. For years he had wanted to go to work, and after he got to work he was quite satisfied. At our first interview he spoke bitterly of a girl who could do reading, but could not do numbers, "and she got shoved ahead." He said that, on the other hand, he knew his numbers and everything else except reading, but on account of the latter was kept down with the "dippy" ones. He made much of school irritations and how he reacted by fights and bad language, and of how bad the subnormal girls were.

This whole case stands out clearly enough in its various aspects. There was a special mental defect for language. The boy was for a time given a change of environment with plenty of encouragement. With amateur instruction at night he plodded along with his reading and writing. In a few months he was able to read passages containing simple words, and from dictation was able to write, " I see the dog on the street," etc. He also wrote a simple letter. But what was of much greater interest is the fact that his conduct seems to be entirely changed. He has done well in his places of employment from the first. He tried several places, and changed on his own volition until he obtained employment that paid well. As a young man he is doing much to support his mother now. He has also made a big gain in weight and height. The discouragements that came as the result of his school life have been swept away and his capacity to earn well has given him a sense of manliness.

In interpretation of this case it is to be remembered that no definite cause for his special disability was found. It was unfortunate that early he had to strive with two languages, when he had not ability enough for one. But the cause for his bad conduct was successfully diagnosed; after bettered social treatment was offered him, there has been not a single further complaint of delinquency.

Mentality: Special defect for language.   Case 97.
  School irritations: Misfit in educational   Boy, age 15.
          system.
      Poverty: No private tutoring possible.
          Foreign language at home.
General incorrigibility.
Bad sex tendencies.

---

§ 279. **Defect in Arithmetical Ability.** — We need hardly say that just as certain persons may have special talents for arithmetical tasks, so others may have special disabilities in this direction. The following case is especially illustrative of the social significance of such disability.

Case 98. — This is a young man now 20 years old whom we have known for 3 years. He comes of a family of English-speaking immigrants that has done remarkably well, being on the upgrade in every way. He is the youngest of four children, all of whom are alive. The three others have been through school and to business college and have turned out very well indeed. All of them have taken to office work and have marked ability as bookkeepers and the like. The father and mother, as well as the children, are healthy and strong. An undoubtedly good family history has been given, and one hears of no insanity, feeblemindedness or epilepsy on either side. There were aberrant tenden-

cies only in the case of one paternal aunt who was said to be
" soft-hearted and lazy," and a paternal great-aunt who used
to get despondent spells and leave home for awhile and stay with
friends.

The subject of our study has had a developmental history
without a point of significance in it as far as we can learn. His
pregnancy and birth were normal. Always healthy and strong;
no attacks of any kind; his only disease was a slight attack of
measles. He learned bad sex habits early, but never practiced
them sufficiently to interfere with his physical well-being. Recently
has been a moderate user of tea and coffee, and occasionally
lately has taken a few glasses of beer when away from home, as
he frankly tells us. He began to smoke as a young boy, and has
intermittently done so ever since. He was in the juvenile court
two or three times, twice for running away from home. The
only stealing known of was when he took a revolver. His truancy
began as a habit when he was 12 years old, at which time his
mother went back to Europe for a visit. He was once away
from home a whole month, and altogether has run away a number
of times. At home he is obedient and good-hearted, and rather
a quiet fellow. His school record for deportment was good. He
has been disciplined in various ways for his faults, but without
ultimate favorable result. At one time he worked under his
father steadily for half a year.

He went to public school until he was 14, attained 6th grade,
then he attended a good business college for 8 months. Following
that, while he was working, he went for some months to evening
classes in the same school. His family have been doing their
best to push him forward in the line in which they have been
successful, namely, in office work.

Physical examination at 17 years old showed him to be a big,
tall, strong lad, slouchy type. Very pleasant and much smiling.
Well-shaped head. Vision; right 20-25, left 20-40. Nystagmoid
movements on lateral deviation. No anomalies of development.
High Gothic palate; right side of nose totally occluded from a
deflected septum; tonsils much enlarged; hearing about normal.
Good color, much biting of finger nails. Constant fine tremor
of outstretched hands.

Mental tests; our own series:
I. 2' 35". No repetition of errors.
II. 1' 29". Only one error.

III. Construction Test A. 13″. Only 6 moves. Remarkably good result.

IV. Construction Test B. 50″ and 11 moves, the smallest possible number.

V. Puzzle Box. 1′ 20″. Very rapid perception of the steps to be done and quick following them up one after another.

VI. "Aussage." Good account given with a fair number of details. No suggestibility shown.

VII. Reproduction of Geometric Figures. Fairly good result.

VIII. Learning Arbitrary Symbol Associations. Done poorly. Four final errors.

IX. Cross Line Test A. Correct at 3d trial.

X. Cross Line Test B. Done correctly at the first attempt.

XII. Memory from Visual Verbal Presentation. Only three out of twenty items omitted and the rest given in correct logical sequence.

XIII. Memory from Auditory Verbal Presentation. Comparatively poor result. Four out of twelve items omitted, the logical sequence inaccurate, and several alterations of minor details.

XIV. Instruction Box. Done correctly only at the third trial.

XV. Antonym Test. Two failures, two errors and average time slow — 3.3″.

XVI. Motor Coördination Test. 74 and 75 squares tapped respectively at 1st and 2d trials. No errors.

XVII. Writes a childish hand. Uses capitals promiscuously.

XVIII. Arithmetic. Very painfully and slowly adds up a short sum of three columns with one error. Has not the slightest conception of how to go about the multiplication part of a simple example in percentage, although he has had many months of training in the business college.

XIX. Makes such mispronunciations as "man" for "men," and "part" for "party."

XXII. Information is particularly poor. He does not read at all except some of the head-lines of the newspaper, and although he was born in this country he does not know what the Fourth of July celebrates. He cannot name the five Great Lakes. His information on scientific items is very poor. He does not care much for theatres or nickel shows, does not know much about sports. He has worked with tools at home and made various things.

There is much more to be learned about this boy psychologically than is shown by tests. As his parents state, he is a lazy type and has not done nearly so well in school as he might have done, even considering his specialized disability. When under detention he wrote letters to his mother that were full of talk about kisses and caresses, and in court he wept on his mother's shoulder like a little boy, crying so hard that he could not talk. He has had much desire for roving, and has been away on trips out of town. Recently his family attempted to get him into the navy, but he was rejected on account of defective vision. He was very frank with us, altogether pleasant and respectful. He seems like a rather childish, soft and easily led, overgrown boy. He talks about his mother and about girls in the softest kind of way. He feels himself to be a great deal of a failure.

" The first time I ever ran away from home was when I was going to business college. Some other boys were going and I thought I would go with them. We beat it out in a freight to Dwight. Was only there two days and then beat it right home. The second time I was away a month and a week. I was working at a livery stable. I had a thought and I walked off and did not tell any one where I was going. Last time a couple of boys were going and I thought would go with them. We was going to Washington, D. C., but we did not get there. We just got to the gate and that's as far as we got. It was on the Northwestern Railroad. I guess Washington is on the Northwestern — I don't know. These kids work. They were once arrested for a hold-up. They are the kids I mostly go with. That was three years ago. I was here once before for having a gun on me. I stole it from a fellow. It was on top of the desk. I never stole anything before. Once in awhile went with some fellows and some tough girls. First time it was about two years ago. Think that's about the worst of it. I get along in school all right — not so good in business college. I studied book-keeping. I don't think I could get a job of book-keeping — I could not remember it. I like riding on a wagon. I've liked horses ever since I was a kid. Would have liked to go out on a farm. I would be satisfied to get a job out there."

After his second appearance in court this boy was taken home by his parents with the idea of having his physical defects attended to. Their physician began treatment, but the boy ran away from home again. Then he appeared in court once more. At last, with the full understanding of his vocational needs he was placed out on a farm. There he has succeeded admirably ever since. He has done so well that his family go out and spend their vacations at the place where he works.

In summary of this case one sees very clearly that here was a case of very special mental defect. In spite of many years of schooling he was an utter failure at arithmetic. His family, not realizing this, were attempting to force him into an occupation where arithmetic was an indispensable condition of success. They attributed his failure to his general laziness.

There can be no doubt that there were other contributory factors to his delinquent career. There was bad companionship and lack of good parental control at a critical time. There were irritating physical conditions, possibly bad sex habits as a cause of deterioration, and there was adolescent instability and a general tendency to laziness. But it seemed clear that the boy's discouragements in education and occupation were very great, and probably formed the greatest cause of his moral failure. The first step towards success was obviously to try to fit him into his place in the world, and not to keep him in the paths prescribed by his family.

The very good performance which this boy gave on even some of the more difficult of our tests showed him to have considerable ability along certain lines where concrete material might be handled. Some conclusions could also be drawn from the fact that he had never run away when he was working at suitable occupations, and that the last time he was away he had been earning well by working in a livery stable.

If one had been making an educational diagnosis in this instance many features of the case would have to be considered and many studies made. It does not appear that the boy was defective solely in arithmetical ability. His records even in our tests show tendency to other defects, but in nothing like the same proportion, because on arithmetic he had received so many years of special drill. Of course there must have been some general ability, or the boy would not have been carried to 6th grade in spite of his arithmetical failure, and he would not have been able to retain his place in the business college. Intensive study of all his mental aptitudes would have been of great practical value during his school life. Our own work, while so productive of good moral results, was anything but intensive from the standpoint of educational psychology. In other cases, much more thoroughly gone into from the standpoint of the comparative study of mental ability, when arithmetic seemed practically to be the sole source of trouble, we have so far never found an individual defective in arithmetical ability alone, even though it has stood in great contrast to such other capacities as language ability.

The whole case demonstrates by first diagnosis and in its practical outcome the grievous error there may be in trying to fit a square peg in a round hole.

Educational and occupational dissatisfaction.	Case 98.
Mentality: Specialized defect.	Boy, age 17.
Adolescent instability.	
Physical conditions: defective vision, nasal occlusion, etc.	
Truancy.	Mentality:
Runaway +.	Good in some abilities.
Stealing.	Specialized defect.

§ 280. **Defect in Judgment and Foresight.** — Nobody who does even moderately intensive psychological work with delinquents can doubt that there are individuals whose main, if not sole mental defect, is in the realm of certain higher mental capabilities. Perhaps these might be called the higher apperceptions. We would specifically mention the powers of judgment, or reasoning, or foresight, and the ability to make a mental representation and analysis of a given situation. It is easy to see that such defects may have much to do with behavior. A weakness in these qualities is a thing apart from defect in the sphere of the volitions, which we deal with later, § 281.

Many striking cases of the above type of defect are to be found among the criminalistic. The diagnosis is often suggested by conduct itself, but of course, can never be fairly rendered without the use of tests. The following cases, although involving, as most cases do, a number of factors in the production of delinquency, illustrate very well by conduct and by tests the type of defect in the higher mental qualities we have mentioned above.

Case 99. — A boy with a very long record of stealing, truancy, running away, loafing, associating with bad companions and general incorrigibility, in spite of some good opportunities, was studied by us. He was 16 years of age. On account of his orphanage a complete developmental and family history was not obtained, but undoubtedly the major points were correctly given by a sister, who was both intelligent and interested. There is said to have been no trouble in any way with other members of the family, except one brother who drinks. No epilepsy, insanity or feeblemindedness known in the family. Father and mother been dead for years. The boy is the youngest of seven children. All are alive and grown up. The mother was about 30 when he was born. Not known to have had any trouble at time of birth. Walked and talked early. He had spinal meningitis at 2 years of age, which left him partially paralyzed, and he is still somewhat lame from this. A slight attack of pneumonia at 5 years. Had an operation on his throat not long ago. Had enuresis until he was 10 or 11, when he was circumcised. Never any convulsions or any kind of attacks.

He has lived in a number of different homes and in several boarding schools. Was once sent away as a semi-delinquent and has been twice in disciplinary institutions. Reached 5th grade and left school at 14. In spite of his lameness he has been very vigorous about running away from schools and institutions. Not known by his family to have any bad habits except that he chews tobacco a little. He has stolen a number of times from his people, and has even tried to sell the family silver. His truancy began as early as ten years. The boy himself says he began to steal with other boys when he was 12.

From the physical side we found him to be well developed and nourished. Partial atrophy of right leg. Strength only fair for his size. Knee jerks on the right side not obtained. Constant fine tremor of outstreched hands. Fair color. No developmental anomalies. Head fairly large and well shaped. Teeth in good condition. Peculiar, long face. Thick lips. Slouchy and weak attitude. Rather dull expression, mouth breather much of the time. Vision, right 10-40; left, 10-25.

Mental tests; our own series:
I. 1' 15". Very small amount of trial and error on triangles.
II. 2' 30". 6 errors.
III. Construction Test A. Only 6 total moves. 15".
IV. Construction Test B. 1' 15". Only 13 moves. On both of these construction tests the result was extremely good.
V. Puzzle Box. 2' 45". Trial and error moderate until first step was done. After that the steps were done rapidly and without break. No foresight or planning shown in the method of attacking the problem.
VI. "Aussage." Short functional account given at first, but an exceptionally good result given on the cross-examination. Many items given. Two suggestions received, but three rejected.
VII. Learning Arbitrary Symbol Associations. Done rapidly and entirely correctly.
IX. Cross Line Test A. Astonishing amount of difficulty with this,

527

considering age and other mental capabilities. Correct only at the 4th trial after he had drawn the figure from memory three times.

X. Cross Line Test B. Likewise poor result. Correct only at 3d trial. No difficulty whatever in remembering these figures as a whole.

XI. Code Test. An utter failure. Did not succeed in getting the idea and failed in making the necessary mental representations and analyses.

XII. Memory from Visual Verbal Presentation. Logical sequence correct and only three minor details omitted. No attempt at verbal accuracy.

XIII. Memory from Auditory Verbal Presentation. Two out of the twelve items omitted. The others given with correct logical sequence.

XIV. Instruction Box. The only trouble with this was on the close work of the dial. It was finally done rapidly on the 4th trial.

XV. Antonym Test. Two failures, no errors. Average time, 1.3″.

XVI. Motor Coördination Test. 81 squares first trial. No errors. 85 squares second trial. One error.

XVII. Writes a fairly mature hand. Has considerable difficulty with spelling the longer words.

XVIII. Arithmetic. The results very poor for age and school grade. Does not know the process of adding simple fractions. Knows process of long division but makes many errors in subtraction and multiplication. Most trouble seems to be in carrying.

XIX. Reads 5th-grade passage with only one word unknown, namely, cylinders.

XXII. Much jumbled on geography, history and scientific items. Says Abraham Lincoln was the first president; London is the largest city in America; says the moon goes down to the other world in the daytime.

From the results of tests we see that this boy has considerable ability along certain lines, *e.g.*, perceptions and memories. These can carry him quite far in school work and employment. On the other hand he is distinctly defective in the ability to make a mental representation of a situation and analyze it. He handles very poorly anything that savors of abstractions. His judgment seems to be fair only when he is dealing with concrete material. We have evidence proving his poor ability to foresee and plan. He is decidedly pleasant and responsive, but has not the least idea of sizing himself up in his relations to the world. He says his people are good to him, but yet he gives them a tremendous amount of trouble. He is in constant fear of being sent away again to an institution. He dislikes institutions so much that he has more than once run away from them, still he acts in such a way as to make it impossible for him to be kept at home. He does not even know that he has bad eyesight. He has never thought about it, and when asked about an occupation says he would like to be a printer.

" I stole some silver on my sister and tried to sell it and could not do it. I was not working for two or three weeks — I wanted some money — wanted to go to the theatre. I am the youngest. None of the others ever in trouble. I stole first when I was about 10 years old. I was with a bunch of boys. Was not with any crowd this time. Would like to brace up now and go home. I never worked at anything except running errands. I never tried to learn a trade. Never knew about my bad eyesight — nobody told me. I can't tell you what's the matter with me — stealing I guess."

As possible factors in bringing about the boy's delinquency we have his poor physical conditions, the death of his parents, his associating with bad companions; and the mild indulgence in bad sex habits which he tells us about may have been somewhat a source of weakness. But his most extensive and irrational delinquencies, through which he continually gets into situations which he wishes above all things to avoid, and our findings on tests, show the main trouble undoubtedly to be due to defect in the important mental capacities of judgment and foresight.

Mentality: Special defects.

Case 99.

Home conditions: Parents dead. Much changing about.

Boy, age 15 yrs. 8 mos.

Bad companions.

Physical conditions: Defective vision. Sequelæ of nervous disease. Bad sex habits.

Delinquencies:
Truancy +.
Stealing +.
Loafing and incorrigibility.

Mentality:
Many normal abilities, special defect.

A still more convincing case showing special defect in higher mental powers as demonstrated clearly by tests, and as suggested by behavior, is the following:

Case 100. — Amelia R., now 19 years old. This case has been very well studied over a period of about 4 years, and much has been done for her, but in spite of this she has caused a very great deal of trouble to many friends who have tried to help her, and she has frequently appeared in court. The details of her troubles would require long to relate, and we can only give them in part. For our purposes it is enough to show the mental background which overshadows all the other factors as being the main source of her difficulties. Other causes have partly entered into her social failure, but they in their minor relations may be disposed of in a few words.

For some time before we knew her she had been given to times of incorrigible behavior in her family circle. Her parents half maintained she was crazy. With the improvement of her physical conditions these periods of bad behavior have passed away. Later her delinquencies developed the form of persistently going with bad companions, not doing anything to support herself, in disobeying everybody, including the family, probation officers and even the orders of the court. Only by the greatest efforts was she saved from becoming utterly immoral. At one period she repeatedly stayed out very late at night, and at another time engaged in a slight amount of stealing. Her main tendencies to delinquency were centered about the sex impulse. On account of her attractive personality she always had many friends and much was done for her. It has been the wonder of everybody who did not know her innate mental qualities as revealed by tests, that she could not morally and socially succeed.

Amelia is a member of a large family born in this country of immigrant parents. The other children are all more stable and have done better in school than she, but none of them are perhaps as attractive. The one salient fact about heredity is that the father, although well educated for his class, is a most peculiar and erratic individual who shows an insane temper at times and has himself been in conflict with the authorities. He is also said to have been alcoholic at different periods in his life. The girl was born after a very prolonged and hard labor, but without known injury. In infancy she had some severe illness about which we cannot obtain any complete account. She entered puberty very early, but had been a sufferer from general physical weakness for a number of years before we saw her. Largely on account of the latter her school career was intermittent. At 14 she had only reached the 4th grade. The family conditions have never been satisfactory on account of the erratic behavior of the father.

On the physical side she was under close observation for a long period. At 15 years, weight 126 lbs., height 5 ft. 3 in. Vision and hearing about normal. Color fair. Markedly bifurcated uvula. Over-development of sex characteristics for her age. Flabby musculature. Tendency to scoliosis. Occasional frontal headaches.

She was given a course of corrective gymnastics by an expert teacher with the most beneficial results to her carriage and whole general physical condition. Since then her health has been very good and she became exceptionally good looking.

Mental tests. There has been much opportunity for supervision of this girl's mental performance, and she has been tried again and again on many types of tests during three years of observation. The results, unless otherwise stated, were what was obtained at first. They may be shortly summarized as follows:

I. 2' 8''. Much trial and error on triangles.

II. 50''. Three errors.

III. Construction Test A. 1' 27''. No repetition of errors.

IV. Construction Test B. 45''. Only 17 moves. This result seemed suspicious and was thought to be largely a matter of chance. For the purpose of checking up the test it was repeated immediately, as we frequently do, with the board upside down. She then most curiously made a complete failure in 10'. Had made 82 moves and still did not have the pieces inserted correctly.

V. Puzzle Box. 6' 29''. Proceeded by an industrious trial and error method. She tried very many things before she succeeded in getting step one done, but after that went through the different steps with only interspersing one error.

VIII. Learning Arbitrary Symbol Associations. Done promptly and correctly.

IX. Cross Line Test A. Done correctly on first trial on several occasions.

X. Cross Line Test B. Never succeeded in doing this. Many errors at the 4th trial after three times drawing the original figure herself from memory. The same result on several occasions.

XI. Code Test. Complete failure. Did not get the idea.

XII. Memory from Visual Verbal presentation. Very good memory for details. Can recite long and accurate descriptions of stories which she has read.

XIII. Memory from Auditory Verbal presentation. Variable records according to the amount of interest she has in the subject. Can recite comedian's jokes for a whole evening. Two years after having been given our standard Test XIII she remembered it well and recalled it correctly with the exceptions that she introduced two or three dramatic imaginative items, and slightly mixed the logical sequence. Her verbal memory, then, both visual and auditory,

531

is extremely good when her interest is aroused, and her retentive powers are unusual.

XV. Antonym Test. One failure and one error. Average time 1.3″.

XVI. Motor Coördination Test. On this always showed deliberateness but accuracy. The best was 68 squares without an error.

XVII. Writes a fairly good letter, well expressed and with few errors in spelling.

XVIII. Arithmetic. At 15 she knew as far as the smaller multiplications. Adds up correctly small sums. (It was partly on account of her disabilities in this line, and partly on account of much absence from school that she had only reached the 4th grade at 14.)

XXI. On account of her good conversational ability her reactions to Sharp's moral questions are interesting. Her answers were given with much moralizing of a pedantic kind. (*a*) He did right. He did not steal for himself, he stole for some one who needed it more than himself. It is not right to steal, but he could not help them in any other way. He did not do it for himself. It would not have been right for himself. (*b*) The right thing for the captain to do was to give up the innocent man to save the others.

XXII. Information. She has been a great reader of all sorts of books and remembers the plots and details. She has picked up many items of information, but they are most erratically disposed. She tells that the light of the moon is caused by the reflection of the sun, but does not understand at all what reflection means. Of electricity she says Edison got it first. She is very fond of the theatre.

Binet Tests (1911 series):

15 years, 1, correct; 2, failure (?); 3, failure; 4, correct; 5, one-half correct. Adult, 1 and 2, failures; 3, correct. Done very well indeed; 4, correct and well done; 5, correct as evidenced by ability to give resumé of thought in books read, or of Sharp's moral questions. (The difficulty in the Binet passage is in the use of two words, as the center of the thought, which are unknown to even so good a reader as this girl.)

From these interesting results on tests, we are forced to the conclusion that this girl who did right well for her age on the Binet, and on many other tests, has very special defects in her powers of mental representation and analysis. Just the performances which she failed on are accomplished by normal individuals with the greatest ease. Inasmuch as they probably underlie the capacity for foresight they are particularly indispensable for social success under living conditions where good judgment is especially needed. This girl by reason of her early development and physical and even mental attractiveness, was subject to many temptations. The very fact that nobody thought her to be anything but normal mentally led to her being expected

to show strong moral characteristics in difficult situations. But
a well-rounded psychological study would have revealed at any
time that she was not innately equipped for what was asked of
her. It is notable in this case that at no time did Amelia show
such rash actions as are characteristic of those who are lacking
in self-control. (Our studies on the latter subject should be
compared.) Simply stated, it seems as if Amelia never could see
ahead the troubles which she was bound to get into by her conduct. She was not particularly self-willed. She coöperated
partly with those who tried to help her, but she could never be
relied upon to exercise anything like sound judgment at critical
moments. A vast deal of social effort at considerable expense
was placed on this case, which at the last was so much of a failure
that the girl had to be placed in an institution for her self-pro-
tection.

Mentality: Defective in certain higher abilities.   Case 100.

Heredity: Father peculiar.   Girl, age 19.

Home conditions: Family reactions very erratic.

Adolescent instability. Early puberty.

Developmental: Natal conditions bad.
Early severe illness.

Physical conditions: Early weakness,
but overdevelop-
ment of sex char-
acteristics. Very
attractive type.

Incorrigibility.   Mentality:
Petty stealing.   Good in many abilities.
Sex?   Specialized defective.

---

§ 281. **Defect in Self-control.** — A class of individuals very
important for the student of criminalistics is designated by naming their most important characteristic, deficiency in the power
of self-control. It has been very hard for us to decide whether
this characteristic properly belongs under the head of mental
defect. After long consideration of this problem and observation of the outcome in a number of cases it seems clear to us that
a certain number of individuals have a special, definite, innate
defect in the powers of self-control. We would insist that many

533

times the diagnosis cannot with surety be made without pro-longed observation. We have seen remarkable cases in which the lack of the power of self-control has proved to be merely an adolescent phenomenon. We have given a number of examples under the head of Adolescence, § 339. It should also be kept clearly in mind that we are not discussing here those who show defective self-control secondary to, or correlated with feeble-mindedness, insanity, or even with constitutional inferiority. All these are elsewhere discussed. We have seen more than one instance where for a long period the only diagnosis that could be made was that the individual was defective in self-control, and then later a definite psychosis developed. But we can also give a number of cases in which such a first diagnosis, with years of observation, has not been added to in any way. By reason of these findings it seems to us that deficiency in self-control must be reckoned with sometimes as a definite entity, and innate specialized mental defect.[1]

In considering this group we must not lose sight of the follow-ing interesting point. It may well be that some of those whom we call defective in self-control do have far more to contend with, far more to control in their own natures, than many others who have no greater powers of self-discipline. For instance, the phlegmatic type of person may not be called upon to execute as much control over his own characteristics as a nervous individual. The opposition which it is necessary for some persons to make against their own impulses of anger, jealousy, love etc., that they may remain normal in their social behavior, is unquestionably much greater than some other individuals may be called upon to exercise. Of course in our own account of this subject we have attempted to avoid including in this category individuals with such abnormal characteristics that it would require an abnormal amount of will power to overcome them. Some of our studies of particular traits which are given under the head of mental peculiarities, abnormal sexualism, and so on, might be related in this way to questions of self-control.

---

[1] I was much interested during a visit to Elmira Reformatory to have Dr. Christian from his large experience call my attention to the class which they de-nominate there as Control Defectives. This group seems to correspond entirely to the class which we have long recognized and designated by a somewhat similar term. On account of the findings in these cases I am inclined to dislike the term applied to them in Elmira. As stated in the text above they are not defectives in general, and one must not use a term which seems to imply this. It is only fair to say that Dr. Christian is inclined to agree with me on this point.

The following case illustrates well the type of those who are defective in self-control. We acknowledge, however, that it introduces as possibilities the factors of adolescent instability and also of environmental influences. The latter are very difficult to rule out in any case. Frequently one wonders what might have been accomplished with this or that individual if he had received a more adequate and rational discipline during his childhood. In such a case as the following the immediate diagnosis is not in the least in question. But since the individual is not yet an adult every effort should be made to build up both moral and physical stability in the hope that there may be betterment of behavior.

Case 101. — A boy of 17 whom we have known very well for 2 years. He has a court record of 5 years. His delinquencies began with truancy and incorrigibility in school. Since then he has been repeatedly arrested for stealing, carrying a loaded revolver, running away from home, breaking into a freight car and attempting to burn a barn. All his delinquencies have been committed with other boys, and perhaps much that he has been blamed for has been done by others, or at least at the instigation of others. Altogether he has been committed by the courts 4 times, and is at present in a reformatory to stay for a long period.

We have a probably accurate history given by an intelligent and deeply interested mother, whom we have often seen. The father's family is not at all known. He did not marry until he was 60 years old. This would seem to be an important point for us, but the fact that the younger child is healthy and normal in every way shows that probably the father's old age is not the source of the boy's defect. The father was a steady, but never very strong man. He is said to have had angina pectoris, but lived to be over 70. There were 4 pregnancies; the third resulted in a still-birth and the fourth in a miscarriage. On the mother's side all family history is negative except for the fact that one of her brothers became insane in late life.

This boy was born normally after a healthy pregnancy. He was strong and well during infancy. Walked and talked early. Then he had several children's diseases slightly and a severe attack of mumps. At 9 he had scarlet fever severely. Just before this he had had an attack of chorea, and he had a prolonged attack later. No enuresis. No convulsions or any signs of

535

epileptic attacks.   He began to have spasmodic twitchings of the face when he was about 13 years old.

Many people with whom this boy has been in contact are fond of him.   He has many good qualities; is very fond of his family, shows sorrow and repentance and even genuine homesickness. There is no doubt but that he suffers miserably for his bad conduct.   When we first knew him he would weep bitterly over his misdemeanors and assert his desire to do better, but never seemed sure of his ability to carry out his desires.   We noted him as being pleasant, responsive and affectionate.   His school record was from the standpoint of scholarship very satisfactory.

Physically we found him in poor general condition at first, and in these respects he has not materially altered in the two years. His conduct has not given him much of a chance to improve physically.   He is decidedly poorly developed for his age, but fairly well nourished.   At 15 years his height was 5 ft. 1 3-4 in., and weight 100 lbs.   Constant fine tremor of hands, good strength for his size, chest poorly developed, no sensory defect of importance noted.   Mild chronic conjunctivitis for which he has been treated.   No developmental anomalies or stigmata found.   Frequently recurring habit spasms of orbicularis of both eyes.   He ordinarily has a tired, worried expression.

Mental tests; our own series:
I. 2′ 5″.   Only slight trial and error on the triangles.
II. 1′ 50″.   5 errors.
III. Construction Test A.   19″.   Only 7 moves.
IV. Construction Test B.   55″.   Only 19 moves.
V. Puzzle Box.   Very rapid understanding of this problem.   1′ 25″. No errors.
VIII. Learning Arbitrary Symbol Associations.   Done correctly and promptly.
IX. Cross Line Test A.   Correctly and rapidly at 1st trial.
X. Cross Line Test B.   Same good result.
XI. Code Test.   Quickly got the idea and showed good powers of attention.   Only one error.
XII. Memory from Visual Verbal Presentation.   Reads the passage very rapidly to himself.   Every item of importance given correctly and in logical sequence.
XIII. Memory from Auditory Verbal Presentation.   Same type of good result.
XIV. Instruction Box.   Done with great rapidity and every step carefully and accurately.   45″.
XVI. Motor Coördination Test.   86 and 92 squares tapped on successive trials with no errors.

XVII. Writes a good regular hand with no misspelled words in a letter of considerable length.

XVIII. Arithmetic. Handles decimals correctly, but does not know how to work with fractions. Prompt and accurate results as far as he goes.

XIX. Reads difficult passage of poetry correctly and with some expression.

XX. Said he had played checkers much with his brother, but does not play at all a foresighted game. Misses more than three obvious chances.

XXI. In answer to Sharp's second moral problem says, "No, I would have fought as long as the man had not done any wrong. If many had been killed and the village had been burned it would have been better than to have given up an innocent man." Persists in this opinion.

XXII. Knows the ordinary school items of geography and history correctly, but his knowledge of scientific and other things is almost *nil*.

From the above record of tests it is plain that we had here a boy considerably above our average in general ability. He would have been put in our A class, those who are distinctly above the ordinary in information and ability, had it not been for the paucity of his knowledge. He had read but little and, considering his superior abilities, has had a very narrow range of mental interests. If it were not for his distinctly good mental powers, and his otherwise obvious mental normality, one might think of him in terms of constitutional inferiority, but as it stands, there is no justification in the diagnosis of any fundamental cause back of his delinquency other than marked defect in the power of self-control. There is not the slightest evidence of deficiency of judgment, or of powers of mental representation or analysis.

This boy's family are much inclined to blame his behavior entirely to prolonged association with bad companions and to his cigarette smoking. There is no doubt but that both are heavily contributing factors. However the bare fact that they continue to be such factors is proof of his lack of self-control. He began his smoking at 10 or 11 years, but has been kept away from it for long periods when he was in institutions. His people moved away from their old neighborhood in order that this boy might avoid his former associates, but, as they express it, he simply could not keep away from them. A typical example of his weakness in this respect is shown by his own corroborated story of how he repeatedly left home with the best of intentions of going to work and then while on the street car he would pass his old haunts and would jump off and seek out his old companions.

"In trouble with these other kids. They are all kids that I used to go with near our old home. Had worked three days with a telegraph company and had pay coming and was walking down town when got into trouble. Was in court last November and the judge told me to go to school. I did not go. I did not like to go. I got around with the bunch and have been with them. Thought I would like to work, but have not been to work. Don't know why I go with them. Have been running with the same kids about five years. I began to smoke at 10 years. All the kids in the gang smoked. My brother does not. Did not smoke at all in the country. These kids do not run around with girls at all. After the judge told me I did stay away from them for a time. Then went back. Was homesick in the country before. I belong to the boys' club at the settlement. Have belonged one year. Am not much good with athletic sports. Sure, it's going with bad kids that's the matter with me, but they was n't no worse than I was. Don't know why I go with them."

It may be in this case that some fundamental bases for the lack of self-control were never discovered. This is a bit of self-criticism that one can offer in nearly all such instances. But at least the social fact was that the boy could not resist the ordinary temptations of an ordinary environment, and he frequently acknowledged the fact. There seemed to be nothing else to do than to try the disciplinary measures of a reformatory institution, even though he was at heart anything but a vicious character.

Defective in self-control. Moral instability excessive.　　　Case 101. Boy, age 17.

Developmental: Severe chorea. Use of tobacco.

Physical conditions: Poor development, minor nervous disorder.

Bad companions.

Delinquencies:
Truancy.
Running away.
Stealing.

Mentality:
General ability very good.

The phenomenon of the lack of self-control may be correlated with other findings than those of any kind of weakness. Of course it is the commonest finding in insanity, and also may be shown in connection with various neuropathic troubles where the individual cannot at all be fairly denominated insane. Criminal procedure based on the question of responsibility finds here a very delicate problem for solution.

An entirely different type from the first is the following:

Case 102. — We have long had under observation a young man who is now over 20 years old. We have had several conferences with relatives who first drew our attention to him because of their opinion that he was not sound mentally. They simply judged by certain forms of his behavior. The fact that the family is much broken up made it impossible to get the full family history. The boy is of German descent.

Father and mother both dead. The father was a steady worker and died soon after this boy was born. The mother then went out to work and survived the father ten years. This boy is the youngest of nine children, seven of whom are living. Two died in infancy. They had ordinary children's diseases in the family, but it was a matter of pride with the mother that there had never been any serious illness among them. No convulsions or other attacks. The other children have done pretty well. One boy was wild and stole once from his sister, who had him sent to a disciplinary institution. He has turned out well and now thanks his sister for heading off his bad tendencies.

Several uncles and aunts on both sides live in this country and their families are known. It is stated by several persons that in all the family the only individuals who have given trouble are this fellow and his brother.

The subject of our study has throughout his developmental period been normal, so far as known. He has never been very ill. The disciplinary features of his home life have always been most difficult, but principally on account of his own disposition. He started to school at the regular age, and continued with much irregularity on account of truancy and having to be changed around in schools and sent to institutions. He has been in court many times, was sent to one educational institution for dependents and twice to a disciplinary institution, has been put on probation on several occasions, placed on a farm, and so on. Altogether the boy has had many wholesome chances in life, in spite of his earliest home surroundings being defective on account of poverty.

Delinquencies have consisted in early exhibitions of bad temper, much truancy, running away from home, threatening to kill, fighting, associating with bad companions, gambling etc. Notwithstanding this long record of misconduct it must be made plain that this young man is considered by most who know him as no desperate villain. He has many lovable qualities.

On the physical side we have found him to be in good general condition at all times. At 16 years, height 5 ft. 6 in.; weight 135 lbs. Strength good. Chest well shaped. Vision slightly defective in right eye. Tendency to nervousness shown by slight facial habit spasm, and by fine tremor of the outstretched hands. Teeth in good condition. Head — circumference 52.8; length 18 1-2; breadth 14 cm. Color good. No other defect noted except a slight hernia. No developmental anomalies. Strong attitude and pleasant humorous expression. His narrow forehead, narrow chin, large although regularly-shaped ears, his broad nose, and deep-set eyes, far apart, give him a decidedly peculiar, but not at all unpleasant appearance.

Mental Tests; our own series:

I. 45″. Extremely good performance.

II. 1′ 15″. Eight errors. Has a rapid and nervous way of going about things, hence these unnecessary errors.

III. Construction Test A. 1′ 10″. Very intelligent method of proceeding by trial and error. No repetitions of impossibilities.

IV. Construction Test B. 5′ 25″. Although fairly intelligent method pursued, was long in seeing the relative form relationships.

V. Puzzle Box. 6′ 25″. Studied out carefully and slowly, but done with intelligent procedure.

VI. "Aussage." Gave a bare enumeration of all the principal points to be seen in the picture. While he used considerable imagination, for instance, in placing a handkerchief in the hand of the woman at the counter, he showed no suggestibility.

VII. Reproduced Binet's geometrical figures with fidelity.

VIII. Learning Arbitrary Symbol Associations. At first trial reproduced four incorrectly, but wanted to repeat and with a little more learning time reproduced all without error.

IX. Cross Line Test A. Correct at first trial.

X. Cross Line Test B. Correct and prompt at first trial.

XII. Memory from Visual Verbal presentation. Good result with all details given promptly. Sequence not preserved.

XIII. Memory from Auditory Verbal presentation. Out of the 12 details four of the minor ones omitted. Sequence correct.

540

XVI. Motor Coördination Test. Well done. Tapped 84 and 87 squares at first and second trials, respectively, without error.

XVII. Writes a fairly good hand and is able to compose a simple letter about his own interests with few errors in grammar and rare ones in spelling.

XVIII. Does long division fairly rapidly and accurately.

XX. Interesting to note that he plays a careful and fairly fore-sighted game of checkers. As a rule sees a couple of moves ahead.

XXI. On Sharp's ethical question (B) said at first would give up the man to the Indians, but when cross-questioned said no — he would put up a fight even though he knew some of the men would get killed. If there was a fight some of the white people might get free, and any-how if you gave up a man the Indians might take it into their heads to burn the village. If a man was given up they would see that the captain was cowardly and they might demand another man.

XXII. Information on geography items almost *nil*, also on most of the facts of history. Does not care to read books and newspapers and his general line of information and interests is decidedly narrow. Only accurate responses obtained were on sporting items.

It was plain to see that this boy was fair in ability and had fair educational advantages. He had been to 6th or 7th grade, but nowhere had been stimulated to the better type of mental inter-ests. We find not the slightest evidence of any aberrational tendencies. He had insight into the cause of his own troubles in life, and had full realization of his own inability to handle himself, as may be seen in the following paragraphs. His lack of self-control was seen repeatedly by us, when, on a sudden impulse, perhaps he would destroy in a moment the result of much past endeavor to do better. Even in the court room he could not restrain him-self. In anger he became extremely pale and oblivious to all other considerations. His emotional quality was shown when a big, strong boy of 16, by his occasional bursting into tears as he considered his career. After observation of this uncontrolled creature, when he was in the throes of one of his upheavals, one could only feel wonder that he had not done more than he had done in the way of delinquency. An instance will show this boy's innate difficulties. When under detention he was working hard at some problem given him, when a schoolmate brushed past, and struck his arm, probably accidentally. The boy at once became pale with rage, and although his conduct was at that moment a vital point for his escaping sentence, a fight was only narrowly averted by quick action on the part of the teacher.

" Well, when he started to say that in the court room I got mad.

541

He just told a lie, he did. He did not say that he hit me first, and then he said kids put me up to do things. They never did put me up to do things. If they ever told me to do things, I never did 'em, and the things I did, I did because I wanted to. That got me mad. I was bit by a dog when I was a kid, and I guess that's what's the matter with me. My folks and the neighbors say I have a bad temper, and I guess it must be true. They said I was a regular devil when I was small. They said I used to hit kids with a hammer or anything."

" When I was here before, I had been helping a man in his barn, and a kid came along, and told me the boss did not hire me, and he called me a liar, and I went and hit him with a broom. Then I had a fight in a shop with a carpenter. He took me by the neck, and I jerked away and hit him. That's the only fight I've had lately. About a couple of years ago a big feller was going to hit me, and I was going to stab him, but I did n't. I don't get in many fights, but I get in lots of trouble. My sister says the neighbors are sore at me. Some of them are sore because I stole some money off my sister." (Although the boy did not tell us, it seems this was his own money which his sister had saved for him out of his earnings. He had a sudden impulse to get hold of it and spend it.) " I never stole anything in my life before I stole the money from my sister. I never go out with girls, only talk to them. The only trouble with me is my temper."

In respect to the inquiry whether he would like to go to the navy he said, " I was always afraid of the water. I would n't like to go out on the lake in them boats. Maybe they would get in a war."

" Out on the farm they worked you too hard, from early in the morning until late at night, and then I was always afraid to go out there — so far away from your folks — they might kill you or anything. If they did not like anything you did they could hit you or kill you so far away from your own folks. I was always afraid of that."

At another time, " The only trouble I got into since I was here last is what I'm in here for now. One night in front of a nickel show me and a couple of other fellers was making a noise, and the man came out and hit me and threw me around, and then I hit him and threw a brick at him."

We looked frequently for any irritating conditions in this boy's physical make-up which could account for his exacerbations of

542

temper, but found nothing. The reason assigned by his family, namely, that early in life there had been no chance for home control, always seemed quite inadequate to explain his marked defect. On one occasion when he grew turbulent in the court room from hearing the testimony of witnesses, he told the judge that he did not care where he was put or where he was sent; he would be likely to kill somebody some day anyhow. This was in the face of the judge's proposal to put him on probation and find farm work for him.

In making a diagnosis in this case it must be remembered that the misconduct and exhibitions of lack of self-control were always in the nature of reaction to irritating circumstances. There were no episodes and attacks of bad behavior such as are often witnessed in constitutional inferiors.

Defect in self-control, marked case.   Case 102.

    Home conditions: Parents long dead.   Boy, age 20 yrs.
                   Irregular control.

        Physical conditions: Nervous type.

Delinquencies:
    Truancy.
    Violence.
    Gambling.   Mentality:
    Threats to kill.   Fair ability.

We could give many more cases in illustration of our thesis that the fundamental cause of delinquency in some cases is a real defect in self-control. There are great variations to be found in the traits correlated with this defect. A few words about some more cases will show this clearly.

Case 103. — This was a remarkably well-endowed young man of 19 years, who had had every advantage in life except contact with well-balanced parents. Physically he was a splendid specimen. His delinquencies and traits are shown well enough for our purposes in the following causative factor card, but we should add, in considering adolescence as a possible factor in this case, that the young man is pretty well along in that period, and should be showing stability by now. However, even at that, it may be that later on he will develop better powers of self-control as the mere result of increased years. In this instance we also noted a functional defect which in numerous cases we have found correlated with general defect in control. This is enuresis. It was striking to find that so strong and mentally well-equipped an individual had persisted in enuresis until he was 18.

Defect in self-control.

Case 103.
Boy, age 19:

> **Heredity:** Maternal grandmother insane.
> Father erratic, brilliant, neuropathic.
> Mother neuropathic.

> **Home conditions:** Parents separated.
> Poor control.

Adolescence (?)

Delinquencies:
Running away.
Cruelty.
Recklessness.
Violence.

Mentality:
Good ability.

Case 104. — This is the instance of a young man, last seen when he was 18, who was of supernormal mental ability and of good physique except for slightly defective vision. He had unusual mental powers and came from a very intelligent family and had many opportunities, but up to the time we last knew him, his career had for 6 or 7 years centered about a succession of delinquencies. There seemed to be nothing to blame but his own innate characteristics.

Defect in self-control.

Case 104.
Male, age 18 yrs.

> **Heredity:** Mother insane and later suicide.
> Brother criminalistic during adolescence.

Adolescent instability (?)

Delinquencies:
Running away +.
Stealing +.
Burglary.
Intoxication.

Mentality:
Extraordinary ability.

The *prognosis* and *treatment* in cases of defect in self-control are naturally matters of great interest. There can be no doubt that a congenital and innate defect in this direction will show itself more during the period of adolescent instability than it will do later. So, other things being equal, the tendency towards the individual gaining more self-control, or at least being more successful in handling himself because he has less to contend with in his own nature, is better as adult years are reached. But the prognosis undoubtedly depends upon elements in social and other treatment. If the individual, as is sometimes the case, lives with parents or a family who show the same characteristics, then the external irritation is going to tend to increase the innate difficulty. The most stable environment possible is advisable. Then the prognosis also depends very largely upon the individual keeping away from stimulants (alcohol, excessive coffee, tobacco, etc.) which will tend to increase his own nervous or explosive tendencies. Defect in self-control thus ought to be scientifically diagnosed and met by appropriate treatment. The training and steady discipline which is to be found in a few of the best military and industrial schools may unquestionably help the individual to make himself more sociably tolerable. Some individuals with a remarkably good insight have successfully sought to circumvent their own inadequacies of self-control by measures that are personally suited, but this procedure is one that requires high intelligence.

CHAPTER XVIII

MENTAL DULLNESS FROM PHYSICAL CONDITIONS

§ 282. General Statement. § 283. Case Showing Possibilities of Diagnosis and Treatment. § 284. Dullness from General Physical Conditions. § 285. Mental Dullness from Narcotics and Stimulants. § 286. Mental Dullness from Debilitating Sex Habits. § 287. Mental Dullness from Head Injury. § 288. Epileptic Dullness. § 289. Doubtful Cases.

§ 282. **General Statement.** — In cases where defective mental capacity is found in the same individual with acquired physical conditions which may be rationally considered as a possible cause for the mental failure, any correlation of the two should be intimately studied. There can be no more doubt about the possibility of mental dullness arising from physiological causes within the individual than there is of the fact that any of us may suffer from temporary mental hebetude as the result of anemia, weakness or auto-intoxication. Examples of the inability of the mind to work well as the result of such conditions will occur to all. Everybody knows the weakened mental states of exhaustion, of serious illness and of convalescence. Even the mental dullness which supervenes during an attack of jaundice is well recognized. In physiological terms, it is a question of the quality and the quantity of the blood supply to the brain cells which are on duty, and of their present integrity or exhaustion. To be sure, often one finds a combination of congenital mental defects with poor physical conditions, and it is difficult to say whether or not the latter is even a contributory cause of the amentia. This can only be answered by giving the individual the benefits of appropriate treatment and perhaps bettered environment. We frequently find cases where there is to be obtained no history of early lack of mental development, in which at the time of examination mental dullness is present, together with very poor physical conditions. The question at once fairly arises whether the mental dullness, arrest, retardation, or whatever it may be called, is due to the physical trouble. I have no doubt that the majority of cases presenting this dual problem of mental incapacity with defective physical findings ultimately turn out to belong to the category of mental defectives. But such is not always the

546

case, and in the light of that fact it is most unsafe to overlook any instance where therapeutics may be of value. The differential diagnosis of feeblemindedness may be dependent on physical treatment.

Coming to the question of the use of tests for making the differential diagnosis between feeblemindedness and dullness from immediate physical causes, we may say that common sense dictates an answer. We know perfectly well that mental capacities are interfered with by poor physical conditions. All of us who use tests carefully try to be on the lookout for even ephemeral physical disabilities. We get very different results on tests calling for exercise of the powers of attention, will, and even perception, on the person's good days than we do when they are are not feeling well. Even the stimulation of a good meal in a lethargic subject has been known with us to raise the Binet findings over 2 years. We feel very keenly after our years of daily experience, that to judge ultimately of mentality either by what is done on tests, or by what has been learned in school, is a scientifically dangerous procedure if one does not take into account physical conditions. Judgment must occasionally be held long in abeyance.

There are various difficulties, it must be acknowledged, in the solution of this problem, even if one be given time and opportunity for a fair trial of various therapeutic measures. The question, for instance, has not yet been answered as to whether a mind largely unused, by reason of physical or sensory difficulties, may not really lose its capacity for later development. This point has come up in not a few instances. Then again we have frequently seen some of these dull ones who have developed such vicious trends of thought and behavior that it has been found impossible, even when introducing better physical conditions, to get them out of these' habits which militate against their mental development. And when this does occur the question may never be answered whether or not the individual's sensory defects or physical conditions were responsible for the lack of mental development. The last case given in this chapter will illustrate the fact.

§ 283. **Case Showing Possibilities of Diagnosis and Treatment.** — The following case splendidly illustrates the important possibilities of treatment of mental retardation and dullness which is based upon physical causes.

Case 105. — We first saw this boy when he was less than 13 years old and he was then brought to us by a detective as being one of the sharpest and cleverest department store thieves in the city. The social importance of this case must not be minimized; it may perhaps be best appreciated by hearing his own words as they were given at the time when we first became his friends.

" I got caught. The man seen him coming out of the counter. I told him to go and open it — the money drawer. He took the money. He had small change, dollars too, and if we had got out we would divide it. He got caught. The man seen him coming out of the counter. I was watching to see if the man was coming. I was making a fuss, making off as if I was n't with him. I was helping search him. We were going to steal knives instead of to buy them, as we were making off. He says, 'Oh, there 's money there.' I said, 'Go on, take some, we 'll have a good time.' Believe me, I 'll never play with him again. I 'll stay with my father and get a job by him. I always used to call for that boy. When he came around our house my mother would hit him and send him away. First time I was here for kipping." (This is a term used in the youthful underworld for sleeping out at night.) "We slept in a milk wagon. Sometimes used to call for him at night. Three boys slept there about three nights, in a milk wagon, an old wagon. In the day we used to go out and steal. I go in a store and ask for something, a bluff, maybe cream puffs that they have n't got, and we take something and put it in our pockets, so." (Shows me how.) "We used to steal something and sell — balls, fishing things that you turn around. I used to tell the jiggers, give a little whistle, and Mike would go there and steal. We used to sell the things to boys and mens. We sold them some knives in the store where we stole the money. He's got the knives now, he can't sell them. This was long ago, before I was in the first time. When I went around to G. Street, Mike heard the boys call me 'dollar booster,' because I stole a dollar once. But he was a booster himself, he had already stolen. He says, 'You come on, I know a place where we can boost.' We went to S.'s and he got a quarter league 'King of the Field.' And I says, 'Let 's go lots of times,' and we shook hands on it. We went all over, to P.'s and everywhere, and stole all sorts of things, scissors, finger-nail cutter, knives, balls, toys, tennis balls, — there is n't any kind of thing we did n't get. Anything we needed we always got by stealing it. We were always talking about all sorts of things. We always said that we wished that all schools and policemans would n't be. We slept three nights on a boy's roof. We used to go to sleep about 1 o'clock and get up about noon. We stole dese (shows me tennis shoes). We wanted dese because dey did n't make no noise. My mother was always wondering why I wanted dese kind. We stole about three pairs of dese.

" I was to all kind of doctors and they could n't help me and by nurses and everybody. I had lots of sickness when I was little. I was in school three years and could n't do nothing. I went over to the doctor's about five times and lots of them says I can't be cured. I get up in the middle of the night and always get scared. I used to smoke sometimes, but a boy told me I would get consumption and now I am afraid to let it touch my mouth. A boy grabbed a cigarette out of my mouth. He does n't like to see any kid steal or smoke. He has sharp shoes and he gives an awful kick. He used to steal himself. He said if I wanted to boost don't come around here or I will break it for you, my back. First he used to be bad himself, but now he is all right. He says he read in the Bible and sees what bad boys get when they die. When I get out of here I am going to be the same as that boy. If I catch any boys stealing, I will hurt them. These shoes are worn and I won't get any more boosting shoes. When I die I will be going to hell, and I know what I will be getting.

" I can't sit still. Whenever I go to school I 've got to do the things they do. Whenever I see other kids do things (shows me a facial spasm) I do it. Once I did this for about a month. Been to about 300 nickel shows since I 've been in this city, used to sneak in the back. Saw cowboys, and cities, and mountains, and kings, and robbers, and soldiers. I 'd always do the same motions. My mother does n't let me go to shows now. At the Bijou I always used to see the villains and at home I was always playing the villain. What I dream about I think is true. Maybe I dream there is about $2 in my pocket and I look in the morning to see if the money is there. I did n't tell no lie all the morning." (Meaning his account to me.)

We soon obtained full information about environmental conditions, and became on friendly terms with the family. The boy came from a poverty-stricken home. The family were immigrants 7 years previously, and the father had never succeeded in getting along well. The parents were healthy, non-alcoholic, but almost without education on account of poverty in the old country. We obtained a clear denial of insanity, feebleminded-ness or epilepsy on either side. The living conditions were miser-able so far as hygiene was concerned, and the children had very poor food. The boy drank much coffee, and occasionally smoked cigarettes. To bed very late at night. There were four children. A younger sister later became slightly delinquent, but soon mended her ways.

Most important is the history of this boy's developmental conditions. The pregnancy and birth said to be normal. Among other diseases he had scarlet fever when a young baby. Later on he had typhoid fever and was delirious for days with it. He also had diphtheria badly. At 7 years he fell from a second-story window and was unconscious for half an hour. He is said to have talked first at 2 years, and walked at 3 years, but his prior ill-nesses were so severe that they may have entirely accounted for this backwardness. Never any convulsions. During all of his childhood he had been subject to much general nervousness, and at 8 years had a definite attack of "spasms" of the face. Twitch-ing of his facial muscles has been more or less of a habit with him ever since. When we first knew him he was in a subnormal room of a city school. He had been tried in the regular grades, but had not succeeded.

On the physical side there were important findings. When first seen at 12 years of age this active little boy weighed only 62 lbs. and was 4 ft. 6 in. in height. His color was poor. Teeth good condition. No sensory defect noted. Constant, restless, nervous movements, but not of a choreic variety. Tonsils mod-erately large. Complains much of headaches. Expression lively. Occasionally cries and sobs terrifically. Shows much nervous energy and astonishing strength for his size. Well-shaped head; circumference 52.2; length 17.3; breadth 15 cm. After two months in the country we saw him again. Headaches had disappeared. Had now a good color and bright eyes, but not gained in weight.

At 15 years, after having had one year during this time in the country, and living conditions being improved in other ways, he is now found to be 5 ft. 2 in. in height and to weigh 102 lbs. No abnormal movements, and all signs of old nervousness disappeared. He now feels very well. The boy had been steadily gaining.

Mental tests: The tests were done the first time before we had de-veloped some of our apparatus and present methods of scoring. At this time the boy was 12 years and 8 months old.

I. 3' 4". Much trial and error all the way through.

II. 2' 15". 14 errors. Persists in effort to get pieces in wrong place.

III. Construction Test A. Failure at the end of 7'. Made very many repetitions of impossibilities.

IV. Construction Test B. 65". Almost no trial and error. Quickly said, "Oh, I've got it," when he saw how a couple of the pieces went together, then fitted them in very quickly. We noted at the time that this was largely a matter of chance.

V. Puzzle Box. Shows great eagerness and interest. 3' 15".

VI. "Aussage." Gives a full functional account and no suggestibility. A distinctly good result. Much better than expected.

VII. Reproduction of Geometric Figures. Failures on both at first exposure. He showed great nervous hurry and he was allowed to try again when he correctly represented one figure.

VIII. Learning Arbitrary Symbol Associations. Two errors in the learning process and 5 in the reproduction. (In the next few days he was tried twice more on this same work and did not succeed in doing the task.)

IX. Cross Line Test A. Correct at 2d trial after drawing it himself once.

X. Cross Line Test B. Correct and fairly prompt at 1st trial.

XIII. Memory from Auditory Verbal Presentation. Nine out of the twelve items given, but not with accuracy, and in the form of an inconsequential recital. The same result was obtained on other tests of the kind.

XV. Antonyms. Three failures. Average time 2.9".

XVII. Penmanship about normal, but does not know how to spell any but the shortest monosyllables.

XVIII. Does about 2d grade work in arithmetic. Can do small oral sums, such as 12 plus 9 plus 10. Knows the tables up to 6's.

XIX. Reading. Recognizes only a few of the shortest words.

XXII. Information extends to a few contemporary items, but on other subject is almost *nil*.

He was seen a couple of months later, after he had been out in the country, and one then found a distinct improvement as gauged by the tests which he had not succeeded in before.

II. 2' 4".

III. Construction Test A. Now done rapidly in 35". (He had been shown how to do it at the end of the previous sitting.)

IV. Construction Test B. 5' 37". It was as we suspected — the previous result was largely a matter of chance.

VII. Reproduction of Geometric Figures. Correct for both figures, except for some lack of symmetry.

VIII. Learning Arbitrary Symbol Associations. Done without error.

XIII. Memory from Auditory Verbal Presentation. Much better result than formerly. He omitted only one whole item and part of another out of the 12.

XV. Antonyms. One failure and one error. Average time 3.3″.

XVI. Motor Coördination Test. 64 squares with one error.

No other changes were noted. The boy had not been to school in this time.

Six months later when he came in from the country to report he had advanced to the 3d grade. He now promptly did ordinary addition. Showed improvement in both writing and spelling.

Another record is after the boy had been under our observation 2 1-2 years. He was now a little over 15 years old. At the end of a year he had come back to the city and done 4th grade work for some months. Then he stopped school. He had been steadily at work for the last six months.

Unfortunately we did not have any first record of Binet tests that could be fairly offered in comparison with these now obtained, but the general progress of the boy as shown by our other tests, by his school record and his present 'earning capacity and moral behavior is most significant for our main point.

It must be remembered for the interpretation of the following results that it was about two years since any of the tests were given to him. As to his possibly remembering any of them, one must take into account the varying facility with which these different tests may be remembered. For instance, the steps of the Puzzle Box, Test V, may be remembered with ease, while the Arbitrary Associations, Test VIII, would be promptly forgotten.

III. Construction Test A. Done entirely by trial and error method. 4′. 45 moves. 15 repetitions of impossibilities.

IV. Construction Test B. 3′ 20″. 24 moves. Done immediately afterward upside down in 25″. 11 moves.

V. Puzzle Box. 1′ 47″. Steps done consecutively with the introduction of one slight error.

VII. Reproduction of Geometric Figures. Done promptly and correctly.

VIII. Learning Arbitrary Symbol Associations. Promptly and all correct.

IX. Correct as previously.

X. Correct as previously.

XI. Code Test. Fails on this. With difficulty got the idea himself, but could not control his mental processes well enough to get more than two symbols correct.

XII. Memory from Visual Verbal Presentation. He has now learned to read well enough so that this test can be given. Sixteen out of the twenty items given correctly in logical sequence with verbal changes, but with full appreciation of the sense.

XVII. Writes an immature hand. Spells some simple words poorly, and does not use capitals correctly.

XVIII. Adds promptly and correctly. Fails on the tables above 6's. On this point it is to be remembered that he has had very little drill on account of his early backwardness in school life.

XIX. Now reads ordinary newspaper passages understandingly. Mispronounces the difficult words as would naturally be supposed.

XXIII. Pictorial Completion Test. Done fairly rapidly. 3′ 25″, with very few changes and only one final error.

Binet (1911) series:

Ten years — all correct.

Twelve years — 1, 2, 3, correct; 4, failure; 5, correct.

Fifteen years — 1, correct; 2, 3, failures; 4, correct; 5, failure.

This case represents a tremendously satisfactory outcome in its mental, moral and physical aspects. It is well worth earnest attention as being a representative type. The boy was given a moderate amount of individual instruction while in the country and progressed three grades in a year. He came back and held his place in the 4th grade. He soon had to go to work, however, to help support his family. He has become a completely steady worker and moderate earner, a good support to his family, and an entirely changed boy. He may still be regarded as an underling; he is physically not what he should be for his age, and he needs much more instruction in the subjects in which he is deficient. That his mental dullness and retardation was dependent on his physical conditions there can be no doubt from the result which was obtained from building him up on the physical side. The complete moral change has been one of the most gratifying in our experience.

Mentality: Dull from physical conditions.　　　Case 105.
　　Physical conditions: Poor develop-　　Boy, age 13.
　　　　　　　　ment and nutrition.
　　　　　　　　Headaches.
　　　　　　　　Nervousness +.　Anemia.
　　　Stimulants: Coffee.
　　　　Developmental conditions: Many serious
　　　　　　　　　　illnesses.
　　　　　　Home conditions: Poverty.　Lack of
　　　　　　　　　hygiene.　Poor control.
　　　　　　　School irritations: Being in sub-
　　　　　　　　　normal room.
Delinquencies:
　Truancy.
　Stealing + + +.　　　　　　Mentality:
　Running away.　　　　　　As above.

§ 284. **Dullness from General Physical Conditions.** — The following case represents a type occasionally seen in juvenile court work of mental dullness from general physical causes. Unfortunately it also illustrates the fact that parents sometimes cannot be in the least awakened to the fundamental needs of their children.

Case 106. — Boy, 14 years old. Brought in the last time for vagrancy. He had been away from home a week and had been sleeping in alleys down town. Before this on several occasions he had run away from home and had consorted much with bad companions. With them he has been destructive in buildings and has engaged in petty stealing and other misdemeanors. The police have an acquaintance with him on account of his misconduct for over two years. He has been taken up by them time and again.

The father, coming in to see us, tells us the mother is dead. He said she was a drinking woman and probably immoral. Before the boy was born she was healthy and the birth was normal. At about one year of age the child was very ill with summer complaint. He walked early, but was reckoned slow in talking because he used baby language until he was 4 years old. There are only 2 surviving out of 6 children, 4 of whom died early of infectious diseases. The elder is a sickly girl who went to school but little. However, she is bright mentally and doing well now in business life. The mother never had any bad influence over this boy. She has been dead for years and before his birth was never grossly alcoholic. The father has not paid any attention to the physical ailments of his boy as he had not reckoned them of much importance. He always regarded association with bad companions as the cause of all the trouble, and thought his boy did not learn well in school because he did not want to. The highest grade reached was the 4th. For years he has been an excessive drinker of tea. No other bad habits are known.

On examination we found the boy in very poor general condition. Weight 100 lbs. Height 5 ft. Very slouchy attitude. Dull, stupid expression, but is responsive to kindly appreciation. Decidedly anemic. Tonsils large and diseased. Cervical glands enlarged. Extreme phimosis. Vision very defective. Marked case of myopia. Strabismus. Pigeon breast. Upper teeth crowded. Some of the second teeth from lower jaw already lost. Complains of occasional dizziness. Is a restless and fairly active

type.   Notwithstanding poor nutrition, strength is good for his
size.

Mental Tests, Binet (1911 series):
12 years, 1, 2, 3, 4, correct; 5, failure.
15 years, 1, correct and very prompt; 2, 3, correct; 4, half correct; 5, half correct.
Our own series:
I. 2′ 39″. Slow work. No trial and error on the triangles.
II. 3′ 8″. 6 errors.
III. Construction Test A. 32″. 8 moves. Only one repetition of
impossibility.
IV. Construction Test B. 3′ 4″. 27 moves.
V. Puzzle Box. Failure. (Was tried again in about a year later
and this time in a rapid and ridiculous manner by trial and error
method succeeded finally in getting the box open in 6′ 30″. Not any
planfulness; a very irrational procedure.)
VI. "Aussage." Very small amount of free recital. Fair number of
items given on cross-examination. No suggestibility.
VIII. Learning Arbitrary Symbol Associations. Very slow work
and poor results. Four total errors, including duplication of the
same number in different places.
IX. Cross Line Test A. Correct at 1st trial.
X. Cross Line Test B. Correct at 2d trial after drawing the figure
once himself.
XI. Code Test. Failed entirely. Showed much inattentive nervousness. Tried a year later, much the same type of results. Many
errors made. Did not seem to be able to keep his mind on the problem.
XII. Memory from Visual Verbal Presentation. Only ten out of
the twenty items given and these incomplete.
XIII. Memory from Auditory Verbal Presentation. Ten out of the
twelve items given with verbal changes, but logical sequence correct.
XVII. Cannot add up simple columns correctly. Does not know
the tables of 3's or 4's. Tried a year later, he knew most of the tables
up to 8's, and could do little examples in oral arithmetic where four
simple processes, one after another, were given. Fails on simple arithmetical reasoning processes.
XIX. Reads fairly well a 4th-grade passage. All words in it were
known.
XXII. Information of all kinds most scanty.

At first examination we several times had to stop the tests
on account of the boy's general nervousness and inattentiveness.
He needed constant encouragement, and at all times seemed to
have trouble in getting his mind to work. It was clear that his
difficulty was in lack of mental energy and ability to pay attention. It was shown in our own work and also in his school career.
It is noticeable that he ranks a trifle above his age on Binet,

and by his performance on some of our own tests he shows possession of good ability. One cannot deny that the boy may have some special defect for arithmetic, but until he has had a fair chance, no decision on this point can be made. He never had instruction above the 4th grade.

There can be little doubt from a study of this case that the boy's backwardness in school is due to his physical ailments and defects, and perhaps somewhat to his excessive use of tea. Despite our first recommendation to the family, we found, a year afterwards, when the boy was in more trouble, that he had not been helped in any way from the physical standpoint, except that his eyes had been examined and he had received glasses, which he was allowed to go without wearing whenever he wished.

With such a background of poor nutrition, anemia, diseased tonsils, enlarged glands, extremely myopic vision, strabismus, the irritation of defective teeth and extreme phimosis, and the positive findings on mental tests, there can be but little doubt that the boy's mental retardation and dullness, and probably his delinquent career, are dependent upon physical conditions. The amount of neglect in this case had been atrocious and already proven highly expensive to society; through the formation of criminal inclinations it is likely to prove even more costly.

Mentality: Dull from physical conditions.	Case 106.
Physical conditions: Defective vision. Phimosis. Anemia, etc.	Boy, age 14 yrs.
Developmental conditions: Early severe illness. Stimulants, tea + +. Parental neglect and bad companions.	
Delinquencies: Running away. Vagrancy. Stealing, etc.	Mentality: As above.

§ 285. **Mental Dullness from Narcotics and Stimulants.** — The usual result of the overuse of narcotics or stimulants is the development of a neurotic or psychotic disorder. That is, so far as mentality is concerned, the effect is more towards producing aberration than dullness as such. The various dementias secondary to these aberrations we have mentioned elsewhere,

§ 193 ff. We have long been on the lookout for the proof that narcotics and stimulants cause actual mental dullness. Such proof would be most obtainable during youth. The evidence has not been easy to obtain. Excessive use of tea and coffee brings about lack of self-control, not mental lethargy. We have found very few cases of alcoholism among young people, and then the resultant effects were always as mentioned above. On the other hand, a great many children smoke. One can have no doubt that smoking is a harmful habit in many ways, but the proof of any enfeeblement caused directly by it has also been hard to get. Practically all children who smoke excessively also indulge in other bad habits, or are victims of bad methods of living which can rationally be considered as more important in breaking them down mentally and morally than the smoking itself. We have observed this to be the case in many instances which we have studied, but in the following very unusual case we do seem to have some definite evidence that mental debility may be caused by tobacco alone.

Case 107. — This was a girl of 16 who had been much complained of by her own people and the neighbors. She is utterly disobedient. She was formerly a great truant from school. Recently she will not work, stays out late at night, and has repeatedly been a sex delinquent. She comes from a poor and ignorant family. The father is not a drunkard. The mother, now dead, is said to have been a good woman. The general history is very incomplete, but probably correct as far as it goes. The girl walked and talked early. Never been sick. Never any convulsions. She did not do as well in school as her older brothers and sisters who are all said to have been smart. Moreover she is not willing to work regularly as they have all done since they left school. She began to smoke cigarettes when she was 8 years old, and has continued this habit more or less ever since. Her sisters are said not to have smoked.

Physically we find this girl very small for her age. Height 4 ft. 10 in., but she is strong and well built. In development of sex characteristics she is retarded. Has a slight thyroid. Rather defective vision, but since she is accustomed only to coarse work and outdoor life, this probably has been no cause of trouble. She has regular features and very bright eyes. Quiet attitude and rather dull expression. Everything else on the physical side was found negative.

557

Mental tests; our own series:

I. 2′ 51″. Much trial and error on the triangles.

II. 1′ 7″. 3 errors.

III. Construction Test A. 2′ 41″. 45 total moves with only 7 retrials of impossibilities.

IV. Construction Test B. 5′ 32″. 37 moves.

V. Puzzle Box. Failure in 10′. (Succeeded, however, in 12′ after a very slow study and a little trial and error.)

VI. "Aussage." Short enumerative account. Fair result with three suggestions accepted.

VII. Reproduction of Geometric Figures. Done well at the first attempt.

VIII. Learning Arbitrary Symbol Associations. Done slowly and with three final errors.

IX. Cross Line Test A. Failed at the 4th reproduction even after drawing the figure three times herself.

X. Cross Line Test B. Not given.

XII. Memory from Visual Verbal Presentation. Not given because does not read well enough.

XIII. Memory from Auditory Verbal Presentation. Did not comprehend the subject matter. She tried to learn the first phrase without thought of the meaning, reproduced a sentence or two, then stopped and stared vacantly, and no further effort would she make. (It is to be remembered in all these language tests that English is not spoken at home.)

XVI. Motor Coördination Test. Good result. 72 squares at 1st trial and one error. 84 squares at 2d trial and no errors.

XVII. Writes a legible hand, but misspells all but the simplest words.

XVIII. Does not know the tables. Only addition of simple figures done correctly.

XIX. Reading. Hesitates on simple passage. Only one word at a time.

XXII. Information is practically *nil* on all sorts of geographical and historical items.

In estimation of the result of formal education it is to be remembered that this girl has not only been a great truant, but has been to a school where a foreign language is spoken. She has lived in an out-of-the-way place where her school career has not been checked up.

The following is the result of tests done 6 months later, after betterment of her habits:

IX. Cross Line Test A. Correct at 1st trial.

X. Cross Line Test B. Correct at 1st trial.

XI. Code Test. Fails on this as a whole, but succeeds in getting a few of the letters done correctly.

XVIII. Arithmetic. Now does simple multiplication sum with only one error.

This girl tells us that she smokes cigarettes four times a day or so and that she began years ago when a little boy taught her in school. She tells of various sex experiences. She has recently been riding round a good deal with a vegetable peddler. Her teacher at the time we first saw her stated that the girl did not seem to be able to learn, although she attempted to apply herself. She was one whole morning trying to learn to say four lines. She was proportionately better in industrial work.

This delinquent girl was tried in another private home; her people felt that under probation they could not succeed with her. She stopped her smoking, but continued in other bad behavior, keeping company with dissolute men and staying away for several nights. She was then placed in an institution. After 6 months we saw her again. She now seemed much brighter mentally. We obtained, among other evidences of her improvement, the results on tests given last. Some which she failed on before she now did with ease. She had also gained 10 lbs. in weight. We would not have it understood that institutional life offered her better hygienic conditions than she had before, because while living at home she had good nourishment and was out in the open a good deal. The main change in her general trend of living was the cessation of smoking and regular attendance at school during these months. She herself said she guessed she had grown smarter and that in the old days she used to feel not quite well. Her head ached much then, and now she thinks it is because she was smoking so much.

Home conditions: Utter lack of control.

    Mentality: Dull from excessive smoking.

        Smoking +.

Delinquencies:
  Truancy.
  Out nights.
  Sex +.

Case 107.
Girl, age 16.

Mentality:
As above.

---

§ 286. **Mental Dullness from Debilitating Sex Habits.** — Probably no doubt will be expressed about the existence of mental dullness or inefficiency from the effects of excessive indulgence in bad sex habits. The effect is sometimes so marked that the individual in appearance and behavior seems to be genuinely a

mental defective. Unfortunately one who works with delinquents sees numerous cases of this type. They are important
to understand and discriminate because of the possibility of
doing remedial work with them.

In an attempt to do accurate justice to this subject of mental
dullness which may arise from bad sex habits one must carefully
bring to focus on the observed conditions all other likely causes
of physical disability. In doing this we find in many cases other
notable factors also in the background. We are face to face with
the old argument of thoughtful psychiatrists, that those individuals who give way inordinately to self-weakening habits
must in the first place have been defective. We may at once
acknowledge that, as we see them, it is often very hard to determine where cause leaves off and effect begins. In those instances
where one has observed the extremely dragged-out, typical appearance popularly attributed to this trouble, bad sex habits have
almost never been discovered to stand alone as a cause. From
such findings, however, we must not underestimate the importance of these habits, as at least contributory producers of mental
dullness.

But again in this matter it is the practical measures we are
most interested in, namely, what treatment ought to be invoked,
and what are the predictabilities of the case. The only reason
why we are so particular about attributing something like the
correct proportion of mental dullness to these habits is that we
have in mind the predictabilities of given cases in practical
work with delinquents. If these individuals are already weak-
lings through inheritance, or developmental conditions, or anything else, then the outlook is to be stated guardedly, even
though it is possible for them to overcome their habits. This
point, however, must be treated with good judgment, because
it is unquestionably a fact that such habits by themselves may
be a considerable factor in producing delinquency. The latter
fact is treated elsewhere, § 245.

In considering the effect of bad sex habits upon mentality as
evidenced by the results on tests, the type of disability is mainly
to be noted. The common observation of teachers and others
is that the individual shows lack of power to concentrate and to
hold attention. There is easy mental fatigue and quick desire
to change. On tasks of all kinds which are done readily through
bare perceptions and quick associations the response may be

good. Now this is as we find it by the use of tests. The individual does not prove uniformly poor in visualizing ability, or in the exercise of any other given function, but does show the defect by fluctuating attention and easy fatigue.

It has been a matter of great interest to us to find empirically that frequently the trouble at the background of a given career was first suggested by the performance on tests. The results showed mental disability, but this did not conform to any regular type, such as the examination of a feebleminded individual usually shows. The general record may be of the same irregular kind as some epileptics show. This has come to be so well recognized with us that successive workers in our institute have come to feel that they could diagnose a case of this kind, or at least derive valuable suggestions as to the underlying trouble, from tests alone, providing one ruled out epilepsy.

It is a fact that in a study of this kind one finds difficulty in getting definite proof of the cause. Very rarely, in not more than perhaps a half dozen cases in our experience, could we find satisfactory proof of mental dullness produced completely by bad habits. But if shown to exist at all, then it is a factor to be reckoned with, not only where it may be a sole cause, but as a contributory factor. Even in the cases which we have watched develop into definite psychoses, thereby showing other factors at work, one cannot help recognizing the certain amount of deterioration caused by the bad habits. Of this, more in another place, § 313.

We have seen a number of cases in which the delinquency, and perhaps the mental dullness, was caused in part at least by bad sex habits, and in which a most successful mental and moral outcome was obtained through good treatment. In most cases the success was where the individual was below the age of puberty. We have seen very striking results in children of from 6 to 10 years who had become terrifically run down physically, mentally and morally as the result of such habits. In these cases, however, we have not obtained the range of performance on tests which would show the distinctive characteristics of mentality of those who have suffered from these habits. But the good results of treatment would be noted by improved general reactions, school work, appearance, and ordinary behavior.

We have had to see many instances of older individuals, both adolescents and young adults, where there can be no reasonable doubt that at least a large share of dullness displayed was due

561

to the lethargy and lack of general mental strength caused in turn by the habits under discussion. Illustrative cases are the following:

Case 108. — A girl of 16 was brought in by her mother. There had been much complaint of her conduct by others, but not nearly so much as the mother herself offered. The girl had a number of times run away from her home, she then would sleep in hallways. She had been much of a truant, had obtained money by misrepresentation, was an excessive liar, and recently would not hold positions which were obtained for her. Her mother said her actions were so queer that something must be the matter with her head, although she had seemed bright enough in some ways, and in spite of truancy had reached 7th grade at 14 years.

We learned that the girl had never been very sick. She was the twin of a child who never developed normally, either physically or mentally, and who died in early childhood. No convulsions. Walked and talked at the normal age, and everything else about her developmental history is quite negative. Her father was a healthy and bright man and non-alcoholic, but thoroughly immoral, even to the point of committing sex crimes. The mother was married to him when she was very young and these twins were soon born. A younger child is normal in every way. Other facts in heredity said to be entirely negative on the matters we are particularly interested in: no insanity, feeble-mindedness or epilepsy.

Physically we found this girl to be just fairly developed and nourished. Weight 115 lbs., height 5 ft. 4 in. Rather dull, sad expression. Quiet attitude. Compressed lips. Color poor. Vision good in one eye, but very defective in the other, which, however, is not used to any extent. Strabismus.

Mental tests; our own series:

I. 1' 33". Small repetition of error on triangles. Pleased in a childish way at opportunity to do these tests.

II. 2' 25". Two errors.

III. Construction Test A. 2' 38". 35 total moves and 14 repetitions of impossibilities.

IV. Construction Test B. Failure after having made over 100 moves.

V. Puzzle Box. 4' 16". Rapid trial and error method first. Then steps interspersed with errors.

VI. "Aussage." Recital of small amount of details followed by moderately good result on cross-examination and finally 2 out of 5 suggestions accepted.

VII. Reproduction of Geometric Figures. One of the figures done correctly at the 1st trial, but in the other the symmetry was only reproduced after the 3d trial.

IX. Cross Line Test A. Remarkable failure to do this, even after the 4th reproduction, and after having drawn it from memory three times. (It is only fair to say that later in the test the girl asked for the opportunity to retry this one and succeeded at once without trouble.)

X. Cross Line Test B. Correct at 1st trial.

XI. Code Test. Got the idea easily and wrote the phrase correctly with only one error.

XII. Memory from Visual Verbal Presentation. 17 items out of 20 given correctly and in logical sequence.

XIII. Memory from Auditory Verbal Presentation. 11 out of the 12 items given with some verbal changes, but with logical sequence.

XIV. Instruction Box. Correct only at 3d trial. Previously forgot part of it or was inaccurate.

XV. Antonyms. Two errors. One failure. Average time 1.4".

XVII. Writes a fairly good hand.

XVIII. Does long division of decimals correctly. Fails on very simple reasoning process.

XIX. Reads 6th-grade passage fluently and with correct expression.

With a stupid manner and a drawling voice she tells us she runs away because her mother complains, and she sometimes stays out late at night because she is fooling with the girls, and so on. "Was in the 7th grade. Had a hundred jobs since then. Can't keep them because I'm so draggy. They want their money's worth. They want a livelier girl. I don't do the work fast enough for them. My step-father is a good man. Sometimes I dream of things in the daytime. I think I am doing them. Sometimes I stop working to dream. Sometimes dream of things I do, and if I read a good play will dream of that. I feel lonesome and get mad. Don't know why. I feel tired. I just know my mother don't like me. If she did I could please her. I used to go with some bad girls when about 12 years old. They taught me bad things. These girls told me to stay away from school."

The matter was gone into with her mother, and it came out that it was known to the family that the girl was indulging in bad habits when she was 7 years old, but the mother thought that after she had been warned she had stopped it. Much to her surprise it now came out that the girl had been excessively indulging in these ways for years. Recently one of the main sources of her erotic stimulus has been love-making scenes in picture shows.

It is plain to see why this girl seems so dull in her ordinary reactions. Her performance on tests is peculiarly irregular. Some of the simpler things she did extremely poorly, but varied, as we see by the later result on Test IX. It is fair to say that the girl was stimulated to do her best while with us, and undoubtedly felt the necessity of doing so. In this case it was her irregularity on tests that gave us the first suggestion of what was the matter with her. At an earlier interview with her mother the girl denied bad habits, and there was not enough in her appearance alone to make one feel sure that this was the trouble.

As in all cases of this kind, the parent was urged to appreciate the nature of the case and to help. Nothing is so efficient as close friendly companionship and oversight for such cases. Interesting occupations, healthy outdoor life and innocent recreation are all much more valuable than anything in the way of medicines or surgical treatment, unless there be, as there only very rarely is, some definite physical ailments or anomalies. In this case the mother was a vigorous woman. She met firmly the girl's needs. She slept with her and watched over her continually in the most careful way. In a year she had built up her daughter very successfully from the physical, moral and mental standpoints. We did not get a chance to give the tests again, but no better evidence of her improved condition could be had than the fact that she for a period now of over two years has been working steadily in a responsible position where she earns well. Unfortunately it is rare to find a parent who has courage and persistence to so thoroughly essay the treatment of bad habits.

Mentality: Dull from bad habits.

Case 108.
Girl, age 16 yrs.

Physical conditions: Anemic. Defective vision.

Masturbation + +.

Heredity: Father sex offender and criminalistic.

Parental neglect previously.

Delinquencies:
Truancy.
Runaway.
Lying + +.
Teaching bad habits.

Mentality:
As above.

564

Case 109. — A boy almost 16 was the source of much trouble to his family on account of running away from home, sleeping in barns, indulging with others in petty stealing, not holding his jobs, and general indifference to the exhortations of his parents and others.

He is the eldest of seven children, all the others said to be normal. We are assured from a rather intelligent parent that there has never been any insanity, feeblemindedness or epilepsy in either family, but two maternal aunts suffered from chorea. His birth and pregnancy said to have been normal. He walked and talked early and was always regarded as bright. Never enuresis. Never very ill or injured severely. Not known to smoke to any extent; does not drink. Was never a truant, but was mischievous in school. Had a good record for scholarship. Obtained a working certificate at 14, when nearly through 8th grade, and then went to work. He has had a number of jobs since then, but would sometimes quit after working a couple of days. He first stayed away over night once when he was 13, but most of the trouble has been more recent with him. At one time he stayed away for two weeks. His usual trick is to sleep in a barn or even out on the prairie with a crowd of boys. They obtain provisions from their friends or by petty stealing. The father knows nothing of any bad habits.

Physically we found him to be well developed and nourished. Weight 115 lbs., height 5 ft. 4 in. Quiet and strong type. Dull expression and low voice. Fine constant tremor of the outstretched hands. Good color. Teeth in good condition, but very crowded. High Gothic palate. Adherent lobule of ears. Most notable was the fact that at less than 16 he had full adult type of sex development.

Mental tests; our own series:
III. Construction Test A. 33″. Only 7 moves.
IV. Construction Test B. 1′ 4″. 11 moves.
V. Puzzle Box. 5′ 25″. Done entirely by trial and error. Steps all interspersed with errors.
VI. "Aussage." Small amount of free recital and fair result on cross-examination. No suggestibility.
VII. Reproduction of Geometric Figures. Done fairly well, but not with complete accuracy in regard to symmetry.
IX. Cross Line Test A. Correct at the 2d trial.
X. Cross Line Test B. Correct only at 4th trial after having drawn the figure three times for himself.

565

XI. Code Test. Got the idea by himself rapidly, but could not hold his attention long enough to work out the task. Seven out of the eleven items incorrect.

XII. Memory from Visual Verbal Presentation. Fourteen items out of the twenty given correctly and in proper sequence.

XIII. Memory from Auditory Verbal Presentation. Nine of the twelve items given with one error and in logical sequence.

XIV. Instruction Box. Done correctly at the 1st trial. 36″.

XV. Antonyms. One error. Average time 2.2″.

XVII. Writes a very irregular and boyish hand with occasional misspelled words. Can write a long letter in fairly good diction, but is utterly careless about punctuation and general appearance of the production.

XVIII. Arithmetic. Knows the process of calculating interest and the reasoning on other tests, but the accuracy is distinctly poor.

XIX. Reads fluently with correct expression any ordinary passage.

XXI. In reaction to the second moral situation about the white villagers giving up a man to the Indians he is quite sure all through that it is better to take the easier path and give up the man, rather than take chances of having others captured and the village burned.

XXII. Information. Ordinary items of geography correct, but on history much mixed up. Has a pitiably small amount of scientific information in which normal boys are interested.

It is easy to see from the foregoing record that the result from an 8th-grade boy, who had the reputation of being quite bright in school, is distinctly poor on several points, and that all of these are simply such as involve prolonged effort and application. His perceptions are quite good, but where he has to make a careful mental representation of a test, or reason out anything he is utterly at fault.

Of himself he says, "Got in with a bad crowd when about 10 years old. There was one boy who had lots of money and I don't know where he got it from. He went in stores and stole pencils and gave them to me and that's how I got in with him. I was sleeping in a barn a couple of nights ago with a boy. The longest I was ever away from home was a week and a half and then was outside staying around and sleeping on the prairie."

"Once in awhile it gets black in front of my eyes, not every day, and then I walk along and feel kind of light. Don't know what it is. Never smoke much. I like best to be out of doors." Then the boy went on and told me how he had been indulging in bad sex habits for a number of years, and how he felt weak and not like doing anything after those occasions, felt as if he wanted to travel about and not stay long at a job. (It is to be noted that the father explained carefully to us what a downhearted boy this was. He is said to feel things keenly. If his mother scolds him he may stay away for several days.) In his dull way the boy said that what he had told us was at the root of his trouble, and that he would try to do better.

The father and a very competent officer were at once shown the necessities of the case and from that time there was coöperation in the problem. It was necessary to remove the boy from his old neighborhood. He had the inclination to do better, and with the stimulus obtained from these two men has succeeded most admirably. Now, a couple of years afterwards, the boy is doing well in every way. He works regularly and has improved in general appearance.

The behavior and erratic performance on tests by this boy gave rise naturally to a suspicion of psychosis. We have seen other cases in which there was no more primary evidence of mental aberration, that developed later into full-fledged insanity.

Mentality: Dull from sex habits.	Case 109.
Masturbation +.	Boy, age 16 yrs.
Bad companions.	
Over-development, sex.	
Delinquencies:	
Running away +.	Mentality:
Petty stealing.	As above.

The above two cases are selected instances where observed betterment proved our point of the bad sex habits being a causative factor of dull mentality. In cases where there is no betterment it is very hard to say how much of a factor in the total result conditions were which antedate the bad habits. I mean already existing mental and physical defects from any prior cause whatsoever. One has seen in the neurological clinic, and even in our court work, many older individuals who have not succeeded in overcoming these habits and who have developed extreme neurasthenic tendencies. This is a well-recognized after-result of years of masturbation. The question of the relation of this deteriorating influence to the development of a psychosis we have a word on elsewhere, § 313.

§ 287. **Mental Dullness from Head Injury. Traumatic Dementia.** — If from accident or disease the brain is so injured that mental abnormality follows, there may result, aside from any temporary troubles, either an aberrational state, an arrest of development, or a dementia. Since an arrest of development means a loss of potential, it, too, in one sense can be classed as a dementia or loss of power. (Traumatic aberrational states we have discussed elsewhere, § 309.) If violence is done by accident or disease to the cerebral mechanism at birth or near the time of birth, then the resultant mental defect comes properly within the meaning of the term feeblemindedness, as previously defined. Any lesion occurring later than infancy and resulting in mental defect is more properly to be classified as traumatic dementia, or arrested development from injury.

Of course there are various grades of arrest of development. Also, according to the localization of injury to the brain, different functions may be separately involved.

We have seen a considerable number of delinquents who have suffered from head injury, and we deal with the subject in its several relationships elsewhere. But on account of the findings which show mental defect by tests in some cases, this part of the subject is properly discussed here. We shall give only a single case in point, but that is a very straightforward one with most interesting findings tending to show the validity of the Binet tests through their determining arrest of development at the age level of the injury.

Case 110. — This boy, 12 years old at the time of the examination, was seen for a physician in Boston. We again studied his case about a year later.

He comes of an immigrant family in which we are assured there has been no evidence of insanity, feeblemindedness or epilepsy. He is one of five children. The others were not examined by us, but judging from their school records they are normal in ability. They are said to be bright and healthy. This boy walked and talked early. Never had any serious illness. Pregnancy and birth were normal. At 9 years of age he had reached the 3rd grade and was accounted an average scholar. At that time he was run over and terribly injured. One leg was badly broken. He was ruptured and his head was severely hurt. He was unconscious for three days. A little later various operations had to be performed on him, and he was in a hospital for a long time. Since this time the boy has made no advance in school. Indeed, he has had to be put back in his grade work, and has become exceedingly troublesome. He is untruthful, ill-tempered, and a truant much of the time. The family is poor and there has been little home control and the boy has grown steadily worse. Of late he has been in trouble with the authorities on numerous occasions. He was expelled from school. He does not profit at all by warnings given to him.

On the physical side we find a poorly-developed boy. Weight 70 lbs.; height 4 ft. 4 1-2 in. He is slightly lame on account of his injury. Has two immense scars, one on either side of his head, with evidence of much bone involvement at the time of the injury. Vision normal and pupils react normally. Eye movements not defective. No other physical findings of significance except evidences of the accident to his leg and abdomen.

Binet tests (1911 series):
6 years; all correct.
7 years; all correct.
8 years; 1, 2, failures; 3, correct; 4, failure; 5, correct.
9 years; 1, 2, failures; 3, correct; 4, failure; 5, correct.
10 years; 1, correct; all others failures.

It is extremely interesting to note that by the Binet tests this boy gets just through the 8-year series, which corresponds to his age at the time of injury. By tests he classified as a moron and was sent to an institution for the feebleminded. The delinquent tendencies which he had developed made him much of a menace in his environment.

A year later;
Binet tests (1911 series):
7 years, all correct.
8 years, 1, 2, 3, 5, correct; 4, failure.
9 years, 3, 5, correct; 1, 2, 4, failure.
10 years, all failure.
Notable results in our series:
IV. Construction Test B. Done entirely by planning. Pieces put together outside the spaces. No trial and error. 11 moves.
IX. Cross-line Test A. Correct at 1st trial.
X. Cross-line Test B. Failure at 4th trial after drawing as a whole correctly from memory three times.
XIII. Pictorial Completion Test. 8'. 1 logical error only.
Can not read or write more than the simplest words. Adds only simplest combinations.
Memory span, 5 numerals.

The student of tests will find much that is interesting in the above results. The boy is evidently no low-grade moron. His abilities are unequal in ways that the Binet series does not show.

Mentality: Traumatic dementia.   Case 110.
         Moron by tests.   Boy, age 12 yrs.

Head injury, severe.

     Home conditions: Large family.   Poverty.
                  Lack of control.

Delinquencies:
   Truancy.
   Destructiveness.   Mentality:
   Violence.   As above.

Concerning the prognosis in cases of arrested development, it is not to be thought that from diagnosing any given mental level of the individual at any given time that we know what the outcome will be. I should be far from asserting that the above case may not develop further mentally and be more educable than he at present seems. Of course as he gets past the normal educable age for the feebleminded, say 16 or 17 years, the likelihood of his advancing gets less and less.

§ 288. **Epileptic Dullness.** — Mental deterioration or dullness from epilepsy, of which we have seen many cases, should be mentioned here because of the necessity for ruling out epilepsy in every case where mental abnormality exists. Epilepsy in its various mental manifestations and correlated psychical conditions is treated elsewhere, § 249.

§ 289. **Doubtful Cases.** — The following final case is given in illustration of the fact that it is frequently very difficult in the cases of older delinquents, who show mental dullness and physical ailments, to get such physical treatment and educational measures carried out as will prove the point whether or not the dullness was dependent upon the physical conditions.

Case 111. — This girl of 16 has been a great trial to her mother and family on account of extreme incorrigibility. She has persistently stayed out late at night, occasionally even all night. When taken into court she gave no attention to the injunctions of the judge and of her probation officer. She works irregularly. She has had a number of illicit sex experiences during the last few years.

Her mother had to work out during the period when the children were younger, and on that account oversight and control were defective. However, this girl is the third of five children, and none of the others has become delinquent. The father was a periodical drinker, but a steady worker. Before this child was born he was not heavily alcoholic. No other facts of significance in hereditary history were obtained. The pregnancy was normal. The birth with all the children was instrumental, but there was no knowledge of any damage to this child. She was a large fat baby. No convulsions. Healthy infancy. She was slightly backward in walking and talking as compared with the others, but even at that she walked at 18 months and talked at 2 years. She started to school at 6 and at once learned to read. She enjoyed reading little pieces to her mother and was regarded as being bright. Then when she was about 7 she suffered from a severe attack of scarlet fever which left her with defective hearing for a couple of years and with strabismus. After her recovery from the scarlet fever her school progress was slow. She reached only the 4th grade. Since she was 14 she has been working in several places, but has been most of the time in her neat and decent home. Her conduct is by general repute incalculable.

Physically we find fairly good general conditions. No headaches; no evidence obtained of attacks of any kind. Good color and fairly good nutrition; well developed. Weight 108 lbs., height 5 ft. 3 in. She is a mouth breather, has adenoids and large tonsils. Distinctly weak type of face and dull expression. She also has a very high degree of hyperopia and astigmatism, and does not wear glasses. General strength is good. Hearing about normal.

Mental tests; our own series:
I. 6' 18". Used up about 4' in working on the small triangles. Put in one piece correctly and then removed it three times. There is a question, of course, as to whether she saw the picture well enough, but note the findings on the next test.
II. 1' 54" with 12 errors. Much better in proportion than on test I.
III. Construction test A. 4' 19" with 39 total moves and 16 repetitions of impossibilities.
IV. Construction test B. Failure in 9'.
V. Puzzle box. Failure in 5'.
VI. "Aussage." Gave fair enumeration of details and accepted no suggestions.
VII. Reproduced one of these heavily lined geometric figures, but failed on the Roman key design.
VIII. Learning arbitrary symbol association. Two errors.
IX. Cross line A. Correct at the 3d trial.

571

X. Cross line test B. Complete failure.

XII. Memory from visual verbal presentation. A surprisingly good result; 18 out of 20 items given correctly in logical sequence.

XIII. Memory from auditory verbal presentation. 10 out of 12 items given, but not in exact sequence.

XV. Antonyms. Two failures. No errors. Average time 2.2″.

XVII. Writes irregular childish hand.

XVIII. Knows the process of multiplication and long division, but makes a number of errors, some of which are evidently due to poor vision, such as keeping numbers under one another. Outside of this a fair amount of accuracy.

XIX. Reads fluently and with correct expression a 4th-grade passage.

XXII. Information is erratic, and on some things incorrect. Can name the five Great Lakes, but thinks Boston is the largest city, and that the first president was Abraham Lincoln. She has read a few books.

The girl gave a very lucid account of her life, showing good orientation as to her own behavior. "I have been staying out late about a year or a year and a half. Mother would not let me go anywhere. Wanted me to sit in the house and sew every night. I went out nearly every night. I have sisters and brothers. They all don't like me for just that one reason. They go out themselves, but not every evening. You can most generally find them at home. The first time my mother reported to the officer we talked it over with the officer and I promised to stay in at night and be a good girl. Then every time they got mad at me they threw it up to me that I was going to be pinched. When they threw it up to me all the time, I said I did not care, I would do just as I pleased, and I started going out again. I thought I would just dare them to have me arrested."

"The first time I met a couple of fellows on the street and flirted with them and walked along with them a piece, and then I guess he thought he could get the best of me because I was cursing and swearing. I never knew the fellows I went with — would just get to flirting on the street. I have quit though and don't want to do that any more. I got hep to myself. I got wise. I did not want to get into trouble. I did not want to get any disease. I knew some girls who suffered so and wished they had not done it."

The foregoing extracts from a lengthy elaboration of her own life, given at different times, are sufficient to show the clearness of her own understanding about her social relationships. She calmly told the great lengths she had gone with her boy friends.

From the above findings in the way of tests, and the good social apperceptions of the girl it was evident she was not necessarily to be considered feebleminded, but yet was mentally dull. Remembering her great physical defects, the latter might be rationally thought of as sufficient cause for her retardation. It seemed certain that one could not satisfactorily determine whether or not there was any arrest of mental development with the illness at 7 years. Relief of the physical conditions, with attempts at education, could be the only rational way of solving the problem, if it should prove soluble.

Much good work was done by a nurse, by a specialist who became interested in the girl, by a probation officer — all in coöperation with the girl's good mother. Despite all this constructive work and despite the girl's desire to do better, the old ideas of a good time and the old associations proved too much for her mentality, weak in will and in foresight, and after a few months of trial and failure she had to be sent to an institution for delinquents.

We were never able to answer the question of how deep-seated the mental disability was in this case. The girl's behavior stood always in the way of her mental and moral development. Her vicious tendencies were so strongly implanted that she persisted in them even after her physical obstacles to advancement had been largely removed.

Mentality: Dull perhaps from physical   Case 111.
　　　　　　causes.   Girl, age 16 yrs.
　　　　Perhaps subnormal.

　　Physical conditions: Extremely defective vision.
　　　　　　　　Large adenoids and tonsils.

　　Developmental: Severe illness with defective
　　　　　　　hearing, etc., as sequelæ.

　　Home conditions: Poverty. Mother worked
　　　　　　　out, necessitating neglect.

　　Early sex experiences.

　　Heredity: Father alcoholic.

Delinquencies:
Incorrigibility.
Out nights.   Mentality:
Sex +.   As above.

We have unfortunately seen a number of such insoluble cases. Our chief feeling of concern in the matter is in regard to the necessity for such early recognition and correction of physical conditions that mental growth may not be impeded by tendencies to misconduct which have the force of long-continued habit behind them.

CHAPTER XIX

PSYCHIC CONSTITUTIONAL INFERIORITY

§ 290. Definition. § 291. Characteristics. § 292. Illustrative Cases. § 293. Varieties of the Type. § 294. Causations. § 295. Degeneracy. § 296. Treatment.

§ 290. **Definition.** — Psychic constitutional inferiority may be recognized by chronic abnormal social and mental reactions to the ordinary conditions of life, on the part of one who cannot be classified in any of the groups of the insanities, neuroses, or mental defectives. The individual generally shows physical anomalies, either structural or functional.[1]

The terminology of this class of inferiors has been a matter of considerable discussion. The signs and symptoms of their inadequacy are so varied, and socially are so important, that a sharp,

---

[1] For those who wish to go farther in understanding psychic constitutional inferiority, bibliographical references may prove of much worth. One of the first to draw attention to this group was Koch (**177**), whose original contribution gave a definition that is still much depended on, namely, that these constitutional inferiors are primarily those who stand between normality and insanity. Ziehen (**175**) (**178**) has contributed definite statements about various types of the psychopathic constitution. He distinguishes degenerative, hysterical, neurasthenic, traumatic and other types. The most complete recent work is by Stelzner (**179**), a pupil of Ziehen. Under the term, Psychopathic Constitution, she includes Koch's psychopathische Minderwertigkeiten, Kahlbaum's Heboidophrenie, Demoor's moralische Entarte, Weygandt's leicht abnorme Kinder, and the Dégénérés supérieurs of the French school. She has much to say about the criminality of these psychopaths. Scholz (**180**), in his work on Abnormal Children, gives a hundred pages to the discussion of these characters and careers which stand on the boundary between sanity and psychosis. Out of their numerous characteristics he distinguishes a dozen types: the indolent, the depressed, the excited, the periodically varying, the emotional, the impulsive, the unstable, the eccentric or perverse, the fabricators and liars, the obsessional, the morally inferior, the sexually abnormal. In English only fragmentary studies are to be found. To Meyer (**356**) (**357**) we owe the first clear-cut definition of the whole group by exclusion. Of practical import are articles by Wright (**174**), Oberndorf (**181**) (**358**), and Karpas (**182**). The latter emphasizes as a cardinal point the lack of functional mental balance in cases of constitutional inferiority. Variation in the balance between emotion, will, and intelligence produces the special type of personality. The variety of unbalance leading to criminalism, he thinks, is where the volitional powers are not on a par with other mental functions. There are studies devoted to the relationship of psychic constitutional inferiority with criminalism by Trüper (**183**), Staiger (**184**), and Rupprecht (**185**), the state's attorney for juvenile offenders at Munich. This last represents a commendable effort on the part of a lawyer to understand such cases. He sees difficulty of definition, but insists on the easy recognition of the peculiarities, and sure differentiation of this class by negative criteria. Patient education, with understanding of the trouble, he believes has its possibilities.

but yet inclusive characterization of the whole class is imperative. We follow the lead of Adolf Meyer (356) in adopting the
term 'constitutional inferior,' rather than 'psychopathic inferior,'
the favored phrase of the German writers. The latter term hardly
tells the whole story, and, then, psychopathy with us is largely
a synonym for insanity. It must at once definitely be understood
that in this class under discussion a great deal must be included
that has been designated as psychopathic inferiority, psychopathic constitution, psychopathic personality, degeneracy, and
morbid personality.

The facts which we have encountered in the field, showing
the social importance of constitutional inferiority, and particularly its relation to criminalism, are amply corroborated by
numerous statements of other authors. For our purposes we
are not concerned much with the members of this class as seen
after they get into insane asylums. Of course some of them
do eventually become completely unbalanced and many show
episodic mental upsets, but we are particularly interested in the
viewing of them as individuals, not insane, who are unfitted by
reason of inborn mental peculiarities, to lead a law-abiding life.[1]

§ 291. **Characteristics.** The general characteristic of the constitutional inferior is abnormal reaction to some of the ordinary
stimuli of life. Unusual emotional reactions are almost universal
in the members of this class. They are often egocentric, selfish,

---

[1] It is obvious to any specialist in abnormal psychology that careful differentiation should be made of those individuals who have weakened mental
functions from acquired debility, such as may be caused by poor physical
conditions or excess of bad habits. Also psychic constitutional inferiority
should be distinguished from cases of dementia precox. With the development of Abderhalden's methods of diagnosis of certain diseases of the central
nervous system we may look forward to much simpler and surer methods of
differentiating dementia precox and several other psychoses from constitutional inferiority. Wright's (174) helpful distinguishing points are decidedly
worth citing here: (a) The symptoms of constitutional inferiority, perhaps sudden and episodic, are related to external causes. The reactions to environment are such as do not occur in the normal individual, but, however, are not
due to autopsychic disintegration. In dementia precox episodes often occur
in spite of good environment. (b) There is frequent recurrence of upsets, which
subside with removal of the cause and leave no deterioration. (c) The history
of abnormalities in these cases reaches back to an early age, as a rule, contrary to the usual findings in dementia precox. (d) There is no loss or impair-
ment of memory, orientation, or application of previously acquired knowledge.
(e) There is no marked affection in the sensorium. (f) There is no incoherency
or blocking of thought, or dream-like states, etc.

Wright calls attention to the fact that psychoses may, of course, develop
upon a basis of constitutional inferiority as well as upon a basis of mental defect. He also, with others, insists on these individuals requiring special institutional treatment — for they otherwise readily become criminals.

irritable, very suggestible, easily fatigued mentally. Sometimes they are possessed by an abnormal feeling of impotence. They may be slightly defective in intelligence or have light, specialized defects of ability, but very often tests reveal neither defect nor peculiarity. Indeed some members of this class may be regarded as distinctly bright, even geniuses, although weak in power to meet the steady demands of the world. Description of such anomalous personages has often found its place in literature.

Not the least feature of the symptomatology of this class of individuals is the ease with which they fall into anti-social conduct. The attraction towards misdeeds is too much for their weak inhibitory powers in many a case, or their very feeling of social impotence leads to their taking the easiest path. The ranks of vagabondage, tramp life, as may well be imagined, are recruited in considerable part from this class.

From our studies of individuals, we entirely agree with Ziehen (175), that in by far the greater number of cases of psychic constitutional inferiority, distinct bodily abnormalities are to be found. Indeed, I have felt inclined, as I have elsewhere stated, (176), to limit the diagnosis to cases showing signs of both physical and mental inferiority. On the structural side we have discovered poor general development, even dwarfish growth, delayed period of puberty, infantile torso, flabby musculature, irregular and disproportionate growth of parts, and the various so-called stigmata of degeneracy. On the functional side these individuals are notoriously subject to 'general nervousness.' Specifically, we may find tremors, facial or other tics (habit spasms), nystagmoid movements of the eyes, headaches, little attacks of dizziness, enuresis prolonged throughout childhood, and so on. The organs of the special senses are particularly apt to show signs of inferiority; defective vision is very common.

The characteristics that we as students of conduct are specially interested in, the weakness of will, inability to cope with the social demand for self-restraint, the peculiar feeling of impotence, the pathway plentifully sprinkled with good intentions — all these and many more points are included in our case histories.

§ 292. **Illustrative Cases. Case 112.** — Boy, German parentage, 16 years old. His delinquencies consist in truancy, running away from home a number of times, not holding jobs, stealing money from home, and petty thieving elsewhere. These delinquencies have continued over a number of years.

Physically: very poor development and nutrition. 101 lbs., 5 ft. 3. No sensory defects noted. Ears roundish in form, outstanding, parts not well differentiated, and small lobules. Badly deflected nasal septum, with partial occlusion on both sides. Largely a mouth breather. Nose deformity is said to have been caused by an accident. Very narrow, high palate, asymmetrical. Two upper lateral incisors erupted behind middle incisors, and were removed earlier. Voice high and weak for his age. Stammers a little. Backward in signs of puberty. Large and well-shaped head; circumference 53.5; length 19; breadth 15 cm. Good color. Strength poor for age, but good for size. With his thin face, drawn-in lips, and rather prominent eyes, he has a very weak physiognomy.

Mentally: our tests were almost uniformly well done. The boy has quick perceptions, is rapid and dexterous, and of good intelligence. On Construction Test III, he made one of our best records, doing it correctly in 10″, and the next Construction Test IV, he likewise did extremely well — in 29″, and 11 moves. Definite suggestibility was shown. His range of information is decidedly good. He has been a reader of wholesome books. There are no signs whatever of any aberrational qualities that could be designated as a psychosis. Yet he shows the following peculiarities. In a childish, high voice he tells us his story while frequently crying. In spite of apparent frankness he does not tell us all the truth at first. In subsequent interviews he adds much more. He has a very childish attitude of mind. Says that when he steals he spends the money on candy and things to eat and going to shows. He evidently has very little will power. He is led by others easily, and is altogether decidedly suggestible socially. He tells·of many things he would like to do — would like to learn a trade, and so on, but has never done more than make a first start at them. Says again and again, he is going to turn over a new leaf now. He speaks much of being homesick while under detention, although he is so accustomed to running away. In the school-room he is very helpful; and likes to attend to small duties. In general we see that he has very few manly traits, and that he shows no evidence of aggressive viciousness.

The only significant points about heredity and developmental history are as follows. The father is now rather a decrepit old man; 46 when this child was born, while the mother was only

28. She has been dead 6 years. With the exception of one paternal second cousin being insane, no defects in the ancestral stock are known. The father himself seems slow-witted, but has been able to build up a business of his own. He thinks his boy is unbalanced, and that the cause of it was the mother's constant desire for money during the pregnancy. The birth was normal. The child had no convulsions or any other severe illness. A number of years ago he was struck on the nose and later an operation was performed for this trouble. He has been only to the 6th grade. (This is very striking in the light of the boy's good ability, but it may be accounted for by his truancy and his running away.) The father said he always seemed to be a smart boy when he desired to study. There is a brother two years older who turned out well.

This boy's delinquency began when he was very young. Even before his mother died he was showing marked signs of instability. He was only 7 years old when he began to stay out all night. For a time after the mother died there was a housekeeper, but soon the father married and there is a stepmother of whom the boy is very fond. He began stealing before he was 10 years of age. On a couple of occasions he took his mother's savings and took a railroad trip, and on several occasions he has been to distant cities. He is much more prone to run away in the summer, and in fact is never willing to work at that time. He once managed to hold a place in the winter time as long as 3 months. He is not regarded at home as vicious, but weak and easily led by bad companions.

The boy himself tells of his troubles. He says he does not know why he runs away from home. At first he only stayed around his home and he used to sleep in barns. He has no complaint against his family. They have a nice place with a yard and they have pets. Once he rode off with another boy with a horse and buggy and was arrested for that. He used to go with a boy who stole. He remembers how frightened he once was when his brother, with whom there never was any trouble, told his father about some delinquency; that night he slept in a barn. At one time he says he would like to work on a farm, at another, he would like a trade, and so on. Says he thinks the matter with him is that he got into bad sex habits when he was 10 or 12 years old. His stepmother has warned him of the danger of going insane through these things. Says when he has been in the country

579

in the summer, tramps have approached him for these purposes. Whenever we talk with him he cannot get along without crying.

The worker who had charge of this boy states that when he was stimulated to do better after his misbehavior he was willing to go back to school as his father desired, and to the astonishment of the school authorities did admirably, until the warm days came. Then began his truancy, staying out four days at a time, and later again running away from his nice home. The father seems too old to manage the boy, but that is not all the trouble. In a certain interval of four or five days between the time when this boy had made particular promises of better behavior, and his coming to a specialist to report about his nose condition, we were interested to note that he had broken his promises and already gone away from home once over night in company with a boy who had persuaded him to take a ride on a railroad engine. Of course they went farther than they expected. In spite of this, the appointment a week old was kept, but, strangely enough, another appointment made for the next morning for the very same purposes this boy did not keep.

Constitutional Inferiority: Many physical and mental signs. Case 112. Boy, age 16.

(?) **Heredity:** Father poor physically; old when boy born.

Bad sex habits.

Truancy.
Runaway. Mentality:
Stealing. Good ability.
Loafing. Peculiar type.

Case 113. — Boy 14 years old. When he was under detention we were implored to see him by the father, who had taken the trouble to come a long distance from his home town. The father felt that his boy was on the way to becoming a full-fledged criminal.

Physically we find a poorly-developed lad. 85 lbs. 4 ft. 10 in. No sensory defect. Strength is good for age. Well-shaped head. Thin, sharp face with a peculiar, old expression. Formerly some nasal obstruction, which long since was removed by an operation. Fairly good color. No headaches complained of. Reflexes were not abnormal, nor were other signs obtained of abnormal nervous conditions. Teeth very irregular in alignment, irregular

580

imperfections of the enamel of all incisors, distal to a transverse median ridge, but not involving the cutting edge. Nothing significant about pubertal signs. Has a high-pitched, nasal voice.

There was much difficulty in diagnosing him mentally on account of extreme emotionalism — it was one of the most remarkable exhibitions of fear, or simulated fear, and recalcitrancy we have ever seen. Sometimes he did fairly well, then, again, even on simple tests he failed entirely. The negative findings were entirely vitiated by his emotional attitude. We found his information on geography, history and current events to be normal, and he had some little knowledge of scientific events. There were no signs of suggestibility. He showed good powers of comprehension and reasoning in our moral questions, Test XXI. One of the most curious results was in his making no less than 8 errors in the antonyms, Test XV, with a retardation of reaction each time, as if he was considering how to give a somewhat incorrect answer to even the simple words. Altogether, his performance as seen on two or three occasions was most peculiar, and it is quite evident that very often he is not trying to do the work. The following letter, given in his actual spelling and punctuation, gives considerable indication of the mental processes of this peculiar 14-year-old boy. It is written very legibly, in a regular hand.

" Dear Miss X.

Please forgive me for biting and screaming and yelling because I always get thoughs spell. I am not a robber I am a honest boy. I would not been here today only my father did not raise me right. If I was raise right I would not been here. If you learn a habit you cannot get out of it very well. It take a long time to get rid a habit. You know how you used to be when you was small. Its a hard life when you come to think how your father beats you and does not know what have he is doing, I will be willing to repay you back if I did anything or did any harm to you. I think that I am to much in this wide world I dont belong in this world so please Forgive me   Your turly"

The difficulty of diagnosing this case may be seen. Of course he is not feebleminded, his work under favorable conditions shows he has some ability in various directions. He has not gone above 4th grade in school, but there has been excessive changing about. He seems to be on a border line between psychosis and normality.

The father, prematurely grey, bent over, and depressed by his woes, gives us a long story of his family life, which is corroborated by his intelligent second wife, and to a certain extent by the boy. The paternal grandfather was erratic, a drunkard and insane, this last said to have been brought about by a blow on the head. He later recovered and now is living in old age. The father is one of a fraternity of four, all the others having turned out well. He himself was a talented man, of artistic temperament. He led a dissipated life and is now utterly broken down.

The mother of this boy was a thoroughly bad woman. Her parents are good people and are alive in old age. She drank, left home on numerous occasions, was unfaithful, had abortions produced, and so on. Her whole family were undisciplined. One of her brothers is a severe alcoholic. During her pregnancies this woman was a comparatively moderate, but steady drinker. It is not known whether abortion was attempted during this pregnancy, but the mother tried with others, sometimes succeeding and sometimes not. It is strange that the later developmental conditions seem to have been quite good, with the exception of the nasal obstruction which long ago was removed. The boy walked and talked early. He never suffered from convulsions, and never was very ill.

Family affairs have been complicated a good deal by the fact that two older brothers have turned out very badly, thoroughly criminalistic. (Data on their physical and mental conditions are not readily obtainable. They are in other parts of the country. The one most like our boy in temperament is said to be doing well at present under the discipline of an eastern industrial school.) Our boy for a considerable period was brought up in a very lax way on account of the mother's behavior, but of recent years there has been a very good home. He has well nigh ruined it however. In the last two years the family has moved twelve times on account of trouble which he has caused in the neighborhood. The boy is an arrant coward, and gets out of any disciplinary treatment by lying down wherever he may be and screaming, "She is murdering me." "I am ruptured," and so on. His behavior is the same at school as at home, and on account of troublesomeness he has been changed from one school to another, and been refused admittance into some good institutions. During an ordinary physical examination of this boy when with us he suddenly said, "I don't feel right," set

up a tremendous shouting and wanted to fight.   He said he
would throw himself from the window and kill himself.   He persisted in a loud disturbance for a long time, in spite of nothing
having been done to him.   The father, who was present, said he
was very glad to have had this corroboration of his statements,
for now we could see why he was a broken-down man.   On
another occasion when the boy was asked to come and do some
tests he suddenly began screaming in the same way.

Later the boy became quite different in his behavior towards
us, and volunteered information about many things.   As he talked
he showed various nervous signs, picking away at something
and looking about the room.   He talked rapidly, and with normal
emotions.   In jerky fashion he told us much about himself.
We had indication that at least one of his brothers was of the
same type.   He said this brother once fought for an hour and a
half on account of him and that he used to steal a good deal.
Says his mother dances all around with him at home, and they
have all sorts of fun, and he wants to go back there.   Says his
brother got him into thinking of things the way he does.   He
definitely ascribes all of his vicious spells to fear, and readily
makes himself out to be a complete coward.   He makes a few
complaints against his father which easily flatten out.

After prolonged observation of this boy we felt we could not
call him either normal, insane, feebleminded or even hysterical.
We also felt that perhaps much could be done for the building
up of both his mental and moral qualities by prolonged, patient
understanding and consistent disciplinary treatment.

Constitutional Inferiority: Case 113.
               Many mental and   Boy, age 14.
               physical signs.

   Heredity: Grandfather insane.
             Father erratic.
             Mother alcoholic.
             2 brothers criminalistic.

     Developmental: Antenatal, mother alcoholic.

      Lack parental control:

                             Mentality:
Stubbornness.   Poor ability.
Incorrigibility.   Erratic.

The next case, inasmuch as it involves the question of innate tendencies towards sex perversion, must be preceded by a word of explanation, lest unwarranted conclusions be drawn from it. In our work we rule out discussion of the details of sex perversion, *vide* § 247. The present case is cited to show how clearly certain physical and mental peculiarities may make directly for criminalism. Of course, sex perverts are not all of the constitutional inferior type, some of them may even be supernormal individuals. A word on degeneracy in relation to inferiority comes properly after this case history.

Case 114. — This case, very curiously, was brought to our attention first in another city, and then later the mother came to us in Chicago. She is an intelligent woman who immigrated from Germany to marry. During all of her wedded life she has had the hardest of lots, and now at 56 is worn out physically, but most anxious to do something for this wayward 17-year-old boy, her youngest. She has walked the streets day and night looking for him and has begged assistance in her task of attempted reform from many different officials in two cities. The boy seems fond of her, but is continually drawn away by bad influences. We saw him on a number of occasions.

Physically we found a tall, thin, poorly-nourished fellow with a curiously high voice. Strength decidedly poor for his age. Unusually long, delicate hands. Vision very defective in one eye, has glasses. Long, poorly-developed chest; hips appear prominent, largely through his unusual posture. Sex development adult. Pale skin. Thick lips. Decidedly weak facial expression. Many teeth carious. Slight nystagmoid movements of the eyes. As seen during the course of ordinary examination, with no special emotional tension, pulse at times was 149 and varied nervously. Head measurements; circumference 55.3; length 20; breadth 14.5 cm. Occipital protuberance excessive. Complains of occasional marked swelling in one breast. Has supernumerary nipples. Uses his eyes in most peculiar way; drops the lids and snaps them in girlish fashion.

We found a clear and cogent talker. His performance on mental tests showed him to be well up to the ordinary in ability and information. His curious interests and reactions to life must be given in detail. Our knowledge of these comes partly from observation and partly from the story of the mother and son, who on most points strongly corroborate each other.

It seems that much of this boy's earliest remembrances are about his being regarded as a "sissy." He used to cut out paper dolls and play with them. He learned sewing and fancy needle-work. He did not go to school until he was 8 years old, having always stayed close beside his mother. So girlish was he, that he slept with her until he was 14. He had a high soprano voice, and was made much of on account of his singing, his gentleness and good behavior. When other little school boys talked about the girls he never would, and they hit him and called him a "sissy girl." From his earliest years he has been crazy to go on the stage. In the later days of childhood he associated much with women, engaging in their occupations, such as ironing. No bad habits. Never cared in the least for exercise or athletics.

As the boy left childhood he was derided still more for his effeminacy, but with no result on his behavior. After doing pretty well earlier in school, he became truant towards the last. Then he went to work, seeking out positions on the border line of stage life. The men he worked with quickly sized him up, and he quite generally passed by the name of Hattie. He thought much then of impersonating females, and had a dress made by some women friends. He began wearing effeminate types of men's garments, and was once arrested by a policeman who was sure that he was a woman in disguise. About this time he was made acquainted with the most effeminate type of sex perversions, and fell at once in with them. When we first saw him he had been in an eastern city, making his living by female impersona-tions. Before that, while at home, he had grown to be much of a liar, and had obtained money a number of times by misrepre-sentation. His running away had been several times repeated, and even when about home he had often slept in a barn or hall-way, instead of in his own bed.

This enduring of discomfort and suffering seemed very con-tradictory to his delicate type of physique and to his desire for soft occupations, as did also our finding his person and under-wear in a remarkably dirty condition. Drinking or smoking has been all along quite foreign to his tastes. In order to prove that he really had kept much to himself while living in a cheap hotel, and so to prove to his mother that he was not altogether bad, he asked us to go to the proprietor and see the embroidered pillow-cases he had made for his bed.

When seen he weakly lied at first, but later cried and sobbed with his head on the table as he told about his earlier life. There was little emotion about his present mode of living, but he did offer many promises of change. Later he fell on his mother's shoulder and sobbed as she scolded him. He had told many tales of ill treatment, mostly whipping, at home and school, to us, and in earlier years to sympathetic women, who had offered to befriend him from his family. With this excuse he would sometimes spend days at their houses. There has never been any suspicion of his being immoral with women, and he denies it very convincingly, since he frankly admits so much else. The ill treatment turned out to be exaggeration of the scoldings he had received for his extreme effeminacy. This fellow knew the miserable dangers of the life in which he was partially submerged, and, indeed, expatiated on them to us, but we have later heard that after serving a short sentence he went to another city, and was arrested for the most flagrant female impersonations. He was then found to be frightfully diseased.

The incongruous combination of poor general physical conditions, stigmata of degeneracy, delicate bodily organization, effeminacy of mind, dishonesty, show of natural affection, engaging in female occupations by choice, female impersonations, putting up with hardships, lack of care for his own person, plentiful use of good intentions, and absolute weakness of purpose, show him to be a marked type of constitutional inferior.

The only important part of the family history centers about the father. We are told there is no case of epilepsy, feeblemindedness or insanity in either family nearer than a maternal great-great-aunt. Four older children, two daughters and two sons, have turned out well, except that one of the latter drinks occasionally. They despise and scold this lad. The father was accustomed to his "schnapps" in the old country, but was never known then to be intoxicated. He was a man who turned his hand to many occupations. Over 20 years ago he began drinking desperately. For a period of five years between the birth of the older children and this one he frequently deserted home on drinking bouts. His wife refused to live with him, but then he later took the pledge, "religion interfered" and she again took him in. She says of her son, "This is the kind of children a drunkard has. When he came, I was the result of worry, sickness and starvation." This father, before they moved to Chicago several years ago, became the lowest type of drunkard and vagrant, sleeping in alleys, being several times sentenced, and finally died a pauper in a New Orleans hospital.

This child was born at full term, and there was nothing abnormal in his birth or early development known to the mother. No convulsions and never seriously ill. He walked and talked early. No severe accident. He was always regarded as of delicate make-up and was without difficulty closely guarded until he was 13 or 14. He was almost certainly not addicted to bad habits of any kind before this. He had a great amount of religious instruction, and did well in school work up to that time.

Constitutional Inferiority: Case 114.
          Many physical and   Boy, age 17.
          mental signs.

   Heredity: Father excessively alcoholic,
       weak will.

     Developmental: Antenatal conditions bad.

Truancy.
Runaway.   Mental:
Dishonesty.   Good ability,
Sex perversions.   peculiar type.

---

§ 293. **Varieties of the Type.** — We might cite many other cases in illustration of the variations of characteristics of these constitutional inferiors. On the mental side they may range in ability from very high to subnormal. They may have special abilities or special disabilities. They should, if possible, be differentiated from the group of specialized defectives we have elsewhere dealt with. But when a specialized defect in self-control is shown it may be a hard matter to distinguish the two, because the inability of the constitutional inferior to cope with the world seems often to be merely the result of deficient will power. However, other marks of defect are present.

The mental and character instabilities of adolescence must also be kept in mind when rendering either diagnosis or prognosis. Various observers have noted that constitutional inferiors may show increased aberrational tendencies at the time of puberty, however not all pubertal erraticisms are found in cases of inferiority.

The mental characteristics that have to do with balance and

587

evenness of behavior show also much variation among these individuals, which is illustrated in only several main features by the cases given. The tendency to unevenness and impulsions, and bad conduct alternating with remorse and good intentions is not the extent of the episodes. Short attacks of actual depression, even during childhood, with suicidal impulsions, we have also noted. Some cases we have seen have attacks of blurring of eyesight, or of semi-unconsciousness, which may possibly be mild seizures of hysteria or may even partially resemble epilepsy.

The physical signs may include other points than we have mentioned. We have seen premature, as well as backward puberty, enlarged thyroid, signs of congenital syphilis and other antenatal developmental defect, and even deafmutism.

§ 294. **Causations.** — Very interesting is the variation in the possible causation as obtained from family histories. We can see the part that heredity plays; sometimes the child is the counterpart of a constitutionally inferior parent, sometimes it is the product of two lines of partial defectives. Then, diseases of the pregnant mother, syphilis, and alcoholism of the parents, and even morphinism of the pregnant mother figure also as causes. Diseases in early life, such as meningitis, may so leave traces in the growing organism that the individual fitly belongs later to our present category.

§ 295. **Degeneracy.** — The relationship of so-called degeneracy to this class is important. The loose term "degeneracy" seems to cover a good many types of personalities. Even professional people are not very discriminating in the use of the word. It is undoubtedly true that most of these constitutional inferiors may be regarded as degenerates, but many of the so-called degenerates belong to other classes. We ourselves are highly in favor of dropping the term degenerate, and classifying individuals by much more definitive terms.[1]

The notable comparatively small number of female constitutional inferiors found in court work may be best explained, I think, by the greater freedom and restlessness of the male sex.

---

[1] I am often asked for the best available literature on degeneracy, especially on the stigmata of degeneracy, and can offer the following quite satisfactory and easily obtainable list. Talbot's (**197**) work is perhaps the best for the general reader. Good enumerations of the stigmata are given by Meyer (**219**), by Peterson (**198**), and in the government document by Macdonald (**199**). A recent richly illustrated article by A. Marie (**200**) on the stigmata, has appeared in the French international treatise on pathological psychology.

The females of this class become more of the drudge type than offenders. To be sure some yield to temptation and later become, in spite, perhaps, of unattractiveness, members of the low prostitute class. Almost worse for society is the fact that they live in various relationships with a low class of men in camps or shanties, and frequently produce offspring, who, in turn, become problems to society.

§ 296. **Treatment.** — The treatment of the constitutional inferior resolves itself down to very careful oversight and patient education, particularly during the years of adolescence. Permanent colonization is needed for many of them. We have seen very few, indeed, do well ultimately under merely family care, although in very favorable environmental circumstances, such as good country life, this regimen has succeeded. One trouble, as we have seen it, is that these individuals who are brought up amid the stimuli of city life, cannot be satisfied for long with "country dullness." We have noted their return over and over to the dissipations of city sights and sounds. Along the same line is the need which this class feels for the ingestion of stimulants. Early they crave much coffee, tea and tobacco, later many of them take to alcohol. Of course, any stimulants taken in excess markedly increase instability.

One great difficulty which we and others have noted in the disposal of these cases is that their reactions may be satisfactory enough in institutional life, but quite inadequate to meeting the world where they have to assume at least some responsibility. A penal institution may, according to its record of good conduct, find them fit for parole, a hospital for the insane may declare them not out-and-out insane, and so discharge them. Then they return often straight to criminalism.

CHAPTER XX

Mental Aberration

§ 297. General Statement. **Major Psychoses.** § 298. Dementia Precox. § 299. Paresis. § 300. Juvenile Paresis. § 301. Melancholia. § 302. Manic-depressive Insanity. § 303. Epileptic Psychoses. § 304. Dementia. § 305. Paranoia. § 306. Unclassified Major Mental Aberrations.

§ 297. **General Statement.** — At the outset of our discussion of the relation between mental aberration and criminalism it should be understood that we do not consider it necessary to equal a text-book account of mental types. Works on psychiatry are readily accessible. The symptoms of some insanities largely involve anti-social conduct, but the significance of this is so obvious that they need hardly any attention at our hands. If a person easily perceived to be insane runs about naked, or invades the home of another, or assaults somebody, the offense is so readily recognized as the outcome of mental disease that no further words are needed about it from the side of criminalism. On this account we shall deal scantily with the major psychoses; merely giving some facts by way of illustration of the more usual connection of these mental conditions with criminalism. But under the head of minor aberrational conditions we shall introduce much more consideration of certain less clearly distinguished abnormal psychical conditions in their relation to criminalistics than will be found in any of the text books.

In this matter, as ever, we are interested in ascertaining the cause of a delinquent career as near its beginning as possible. Now, early in life mental ailments often have less pronounced signs than later on. We have had reason to see many instances where actual insanity on an organic basis was incipient to the extent that it was not clear to the onlooker, and the individual was merely accounted criminalistic. In other cases the symptoms were so indefinite that the diagnosis of a particular type of insanity was impossible. Some of these later have recovered, others have remained unchanged, and still others have gone on to develop typical forms of psychoses. In working with delinquents there is no need of considering the exact classification of the mental trouble when it exists, except that it may give more positive clue to treatment. The mental findings and the conduct determine the fact of aberration, and that is all that should be necessary for immediate court purposes. Further business of diagnosis should be left to a psychopathic hospital.

Our material, through dealing, as we have done, mostly with adolescents, is peculiarly rich in the history of cases where the mental upset passed off with readjustment of the individual to environmental conditions. In some of these there were recurrences, and in others direct recovery. The discussion of this material is of great importance because these cases are very rarely seen by institutional authorities, and receive altogether inadequate treatment in professional works which emanate from those sources. The favorable mental and moral outcome sometimes observed under treatment proves little of what the evolution of the case might have been without such treatment, yet is highly suggestive of the possibilities of early dealing with mental cases.

I see no better way for our purposes than to classify aberrational mental conditions under major and minor — realizing, however, the impossibility of deciding between the two, even in some important types. The major aberrational conditions are naturally made up of the well-defined insanities, and of other cases which show virulent symptoms although as a whole they may be unclassifiable in any group. Major, as well as minor, aberrations may be either temporary or chronic. The fact that they are either major or minor means very little for criminalistics, inasmuch as many of the most dangerous of our recidivists show aberrational tendencies which cannot be placed under the head of one of the major insanities. Arbitrariness of the division between the two is shown also by the fact that some individuals who are now recognized as being afflicted with some minor mental aberration will later enter the category of major psychoses. The newer methods of diagnosis of dementia precox we look forward to for help in one place where discrimination is important.

The student of offenders is glad to show the arbitrariness of all divisions because of his frequent encounter with the attitude which demands the diagnosis of "some form of insanity" before incompetency is allowed. This point of view is met in institutions for the insane as well as in court. It is particularly impressive to note the repeated crimes committed by markedly aberrational individuals who have not normal powers of social control and who show other signs of mental disturbance, but who

are declared " not insane " because they do not show the symptoms of paranoia, paresis, or other of the main categories of the
psychoses.   The public suffers tremendously from this narrow
conception of the mental aberrations from which it should be
protected.   The medical man as well as the lawyer should be
well apprized of these facts.

Under the caption of minor psychoses we place the aberrant
states which are not so commanding in their general picture.   If
this were a text book on psychiatry very many states could be
enumerated which belong under this heading, but we are only
interested in certain forms of minor aberration which have particularly to do with delinquency, and those we shall specify with
illustrations in the proper place.   Some individuals with only
minor psychoses are easily recognizable as being insane, especially
those cases in which there are marked transitory symptoms.   In
other minor, but chronic aberrations we have to deal with the
typical psychopaths, or semi-responsibles, who are dealt with
to some extent in various modern works on psychiatry.

For dealing with these last groups of cases it has been represented that they should be legally categorized as having attenuated responsibility.   At least for understanding the practical
social situation involved, this partial responsibility must be taken
into account.   On these points our related case histories are
illuminating.

The heading under which to place many cases has been determined along practical lines; there is much overlapping of types
and symptoms.   Minor mental aberrations are frequently most
difficult to classify.   Whether some of them are abortive cases
of the well-distinguished types of mental trouble it is impossible
in the present state of our knowledge to say.   On many accounts
we recommend the student to make a survey of the entire field
of mental aberration in its relation to criminalism, in order to
avoid the dangers of centering interest on only a few of the types.

Major Psychoses.

§ 298. Dementia Precox.

No technical discussion of dementia precox is desirable for this
work.   At present biochemical tests are promised which will
immensely simplify our diagnostic conceptions of this disease.
Here it is sufficient to say that a group of mental symptoms

arising generally during adolescence portends the onset of this primary dementia. The individual is readily recognized as being mentally weak, but yet is not to be classed as feebleminded, both on account of the prominence of aberrations rather than defects, and the fact that at one time he was considered more or less normal. The progress of the disease varies greatly, and there may be remission of symptoms, and even apparent recoveries, but in the majority of the well-recognized cases the symptoms persist. In a small proportion of the instances there is rapid fulmination of the disease, with complete disablement or death.

The disease takes on various forms, and the evidences of actual dementia may not be plain at first. The early signs of this disorder which bring individuals suffering from it so frequently to the notice of police officials, visiting nurses, social workers, etc., are often those of extreme shyness and fear. Sufferers are almost always males. The young man will not go out of doors or meet company. He will not seek a job. He cannot face a prospective employer. He seems utterly ashamed of himself and his own shortcomings, and may hide even from his own family. Many times we have heard the account of just such actions implicating individuals who are serious offenders, perhaps offering violence to their own families or to others, perhaps being thieves and young embezzlers. Variations in the way of excitement, utter dullness, and paranoidal symptoms are seen during the course of this disease. The case of the young boy cited under paranoia (§ 305) may turn out to be dementia precox.

One feature of importance in the evolution of this disease is the practice of masturbation. With astonishing frequency cases of dementia precox indulge excessively in bad sex habits. This is so noticeable that it is often difficult to convince parents that the disease itself is not caused by this practice. There can be little doubt that the debilitating effects of these habits increase the downward tendency, but the excessive indulgence itself is only to be regarded as evidence of lack of balance and self-control. However it is plain that a vicious circle is set up by the combination of disease and bad practices.

The idea of suicide is frequently entertained in cases of dementia precox. Some indication of this may be seen in the single case study we give as a paradigm. In one instance where we could readily determine there was some degree of dementia together with the most excessive amount of masturbation, the boy committed suicide before the family could make up their minds to send him to a state hospital for treatment. This lad was only 15 years old when he took his own life after indulging in perfect orgies of violence and general misbehavior. He had already been sent twice to institutions on account of delinquency. Formerly he had been truant, but had reached 5th grade before he stopped school. He early began excessive use of coffee and occasional indulgence in smoking, while masturbation with him was, according to his own account, a daily matter for years. With bad company he engaged in a long list of petty delinquencies before entering upon the final stages of his career.

In some quarters it has been the tendency to over-estimate the percentage of cases belonging in the dementia precox group which one meets with among young offenders. In going over our own records we find it impossible to be exact in this matter on account of the slow evolution of the disease. Indeed in the cases which we have sent to hospitals for the insane we frequently cannot get exact diagnosis. In the future we hope this may be bettered by new diagnostic methods. But certainly in not more than 25 cases in our 1000 young repeated offenders have the symptoms been interpretable as belonging in any way to dementia precox, and very likely a number of these will prove to be cases of other diseases. The work of Wilmanns (**314**) (**315**), and of Nitsche and Wilmanns (**48**), has been much quoted in this connection, but it must be remarked that their findings are based only on the study of offenders who are already recognized as having some form of mental aberration. Among them the majority was found to be suffering from dementia precox.

A large number of the characteristic symptoms of this disease is to be found in the single case study which we shall offer. The relationship of this primary dementia to criminalism is there made clear, as is also the unfortunate lack of recognition of this disease in ordinary court work.

Case 115. — A young man, almost 19, is brought to us with a long record of delinquency. He has run away from home on numerous occasions. When younger used to go with companions who stole chickens, and coal, and candy. Is said to have had about a hundred different jobs since he left school. Usually holds them only for a day or so. He loafs most of the time, hanging about his own home or getting other people to take him in whenever he can. Often has taken money he has earned

and spent it on prostitutes. Has been in court on several occasions. Was once arrested for making a disturbance in the red
light district. Has already served two terms in the House of
Correction under a charge of disorderly conduct and vagrancy.
Recently the father was about to have him again taken in charge
by the police, but thought he had better see a doctor on account
of the boy's strange behavior.

Physically we found a well-developed and nourished young
man. Weight 134 lbs., height 5 ft. 7 in. Very large head — circumference 57, length 19 1–3, breadth 16 cm. Teeth good condition. Vision practically normal. Reaction of pupils very lively.
Other examination of eyes negative. Physiognomy peculiar.
Poorly balanced profile on account of the large head and small
though not receding chin. Expression rather dull, but pleasant
enough. Considerable asymmetry of action of facial muscles,
with great overuse of the frontalis. Muddy complexion, and
many scars from old acne. Gait very slouchy. Strength of upper
extremities very poor for his size. Coördinations good. Knee
jerks lively; abdominal reflexes extremely lively. Complains
of much headache, and much pain in hands and feet. Voice
deep and rather monotonous. Color poor. Breath offensive.
Sex development plus. Excessive enuresis and some incontinence
of the bladder by day. Has had gonorrhea, and been treated
for it at the House of Correction. In posture the boy is notably
peculiar. Sits or stands in a very stiff fashion. Holds one shoulder
elevated, much higher than the other. Distinctly awkward in
handling the tests. Shows many traces of negativism. It is
with difficulty that one can get him to relax his facial muscles
to look into his mouth. Obeys commands of all kinds very poorly
and with much hesitation.

The mental tests soon showed his aberrations, and it was
impossible to carry them far. He fails to add short columns of
three figures. Does not know the process of long division. Says
$6 \times 8 = 54$; $4 \times 3 = 12$; $8 \times 8 = 64$; $9 \times 7 = 62$; $4 + 4
+ 4 + 8 = 34$. Fails to do even our simple introductory puzzle.
Argues about the impossibility of filling up the triangular space,
insists there is one piece short, and finally gives it up. Fails to
do our Construction Test III. Works at it with one hand for
a long time, jostling the pieces around. Says, " I could not do
this in a hundred years. I can't do it. Try as hard as I can, I
can't do it. In a hundred years I could n't do it." In the Antonym

Test XV, makes 4 failures and 1 error; average times 3.3″, a very slow record. Writes a fairly good hand. Knows correctly the date. Is distinctly talkative.

His moderately intelligent father in describing his mental symptoms tells us he always was a funny kind of a boy. Would not do what the teachers told him. At one time was so severely punished by one of the sisters in his school that the family raised trouble about it. Is a great liar. Says he will drown himself when it has been suggested they put him in the navy. He likes to read joke books. Is crazy for " naked pictures and picture shows, and whenever he gets a half a dollar goes to a theatre." When he would get his wages he would proceed to spend them. He frequently wanders about all day when he is not working, sometimes wet and cold. Often does not get much to eat when away, and comes home tired out. Says to his family, "If nobody cares for me, I don't give a damn for nobody." Is offensive at home on account of various dirty habits, and incontinence of the bladder. At times sits long in a chair, bent over and not doing anything. Sometimes rubs his wrist for long.

From the family we get very little in the way of hereditary or developmental history that throws much light on the problem. The people are ignorant immigrants. Father says they came to this country when the boy was an infant. In the old country there was not any education, and the mother in particular does not care much about it here. Her idea is that "when children get to be 21 they are getting their senses." There are seven others in the family, but there has been no such trouble with any of them. The father is clearly the more intelligent. He tells us that his own father was extremely alcoholic and died of tuberculosis, but outside of that, the family history is practically negative. No one known to be insane, feebleminded or epileptic. In regard to this boy's developmental history, it has been negative. He was born after a healthy pregnancy with a normal delivery. He walked and talked early. Had a healthy infancy and indeed has never been very ill. Five years ago he was injured in the genital region by sliding on a fence, but even for that no physician was called.

The boy's own story is of great significance for us, and one could fairly make the diagnosis from that alone. He tells it readily and talks rapidly. The following is a verbatim sample of his conversation.

596

"For three years I've been sick — not in my right health — I've been in the Bridewell. I told my father I refused to work for his family and everything like that. First time I was arrested I was with a boy. He was throwing potatoes in the windows of the vice district. Then I was given $25 and costs. My father paid one-half of it. Then I was in the Bridewell January and February this year because I would n't work. My father starts an argument, he starts calling me a monkey. I can't help it if I was born that way. So far I feel rotten. I irritate every minute. I don't feel like other men do that come in this world. I'm weak and sick and I ain't fit for work. One man says because I can't do his work I was better to drown myself. He says that. Of course I could n't do that, because I would n't want to suffer. I suffer enough in my house already. Well, my father starts an argument, and hits me, and wishes I'd die and everything. He's got one right way, and I've got my right way. You see I eat in his house and eat his meals. He says lightning should come and strike everybody there. He hit me with a chair this morning and knocked me out of wind. He punches over my eyes and over my face and all over. The doctor said at the Polisinic, 'You are one of those unfortunate fellows that don't seem fit for anything.'"

(When quit school?) "I was about 14 — 14 I was — 5th grade. I was pretty fair. All the rest seem all right, but I'm no good — that's what my father tells. Me? I was working in machine shops. Worked there one week and quit. For two years I feel rotten. Almost worser every day. People make complaint of me. People all stick their finger out at me. I ain't none of these people that can show themselves good, that get along in the world. He was going to send me out there now, but I was crying like everything. Me? I was working in a box factory. Did n't pay much for me and that's why I quit. I could n't get raised up with that job — it was no good for me. The doctor over at the Polisinic he examined my head to see if I was insane. My head is all right, but I've got some sickness and I don't seem fit to work. Read? Why, I read Catholic books and everything. Sure, we've got lots of miscellaneous books at home and everything. Well I don't remember their names, I'd have to think it over. I tell you, doctor, I don't read them five-cent history novels like some boys do. Well, newspapers — I read the News, Journal and every other sort. Well, yesterday I read about the

Mexicans lost in the battle. The United States is going to inter-
vene because they are fighting against the border. No, I never
read any books like that." (*Viz.* Robinson Crusoe.) "I tell you,
doctor, I can tell you about things — Washington was the first
president and things like that."

"Doctor, I tell you about myself. I often have to lay down
and sleep. When people come to the house, instead of going and
talking to them about life and things like that I have to lay down.
That 's no way to make a man out of me."

"I think about good, and bad, and such things. Every man
has his own troubles. Doctor, it is a shame and disgrace to tell
those things, for any fellow to tell them and so I 'm going to say
I never did — I never did any of those things and never went
with a woman and I never did those other things. Doctor, I
want to tell you that I thank you from the bottom of my heart
because I want to make a man out of myself."

"I 'm one of those fellows who never had any luck in the world.
Doctor, I 'll explain you my trouble from A to Z. All my brothers
and sisters are all right, and they get up in the world — people
say they are all right — they are satisfied. My people were going
to get out a warrant at the station and have me sent out to the
Bridewell, but I tell you out there they work you like a horse,
and you get beatings with sticks and things, and the blood runs,
it runs high up on the wall from the beatings. What do you
think about my life? Me? Why, I was going to school and everything. I did n't get plenty of education to get along in the world.
If I 'd got through the 8th grade they would call me a grammar
school graduate, and I can't get good positions in offices because
I ain't worth it. My father has argument every day about it.
If I get a job I would n't go by my father for a hundred years,
but the trouble is I 'm sick and weak and not fit for anything.
Me, I was bad — no, pretty good in school. I could pass 8th
grade if I wanted to. I got in bad company — it spoiled me.
Last year I went with a couple of partners, but they don't come
around me now. I was arrested, and the boy was arrested, but
he 's afraid now. He got scared now. He 's afraid to show his
face. I was bad in school. I did n't read. Oh, I was n't good
in arithmetic, and other miscellaneous things—that 's the reason
I did n't get put down in grades.

"My father 's an old man. He works every night and day.
He 's down on me — he don't see why he should give me meals

for nothing. I did n't get in bad company in school. I was too quick in school. I did n't grow up in the right way — I did n't grow up to be a man. I got in bad company afterwards. I mean I did n't pass the school in the right way. Yes, it was hard to learn. My father was going to send me out to the Navy to make me a manly man, to make a man out of me. They told me I 'm sick and weak, and better go to the doctor to get cured. He says ' We 've got thousands of healthy men waiting to get in, the right kind, too.' I want to be a manly man. I don't want to be a devil. Educational people tell me I ain't right."

At another interview he said, " I 've been feeling no good for half a year straight. Well, now some more confessions. I never smoked or chewed in my whole life. Smell my breath. I ain't the right kind. Lots of fellows on the outside smoke and chew. I can tell a fellow that does by his breath. I don't drink any beer. There 's a lot of fellows that drink beer, but I don't. I can get good and plenty without it. I mean I eat only health food, but I ain't strong the way I should be. I tell you what a man I 'm trying to make out of myself, if I grow up to be 50 or 60 years old what kind of a man will I be? Lots of these old men used to be boys once, and they are lawyers and doctors and so on. I ain't got the chance because I ain't fit. A boy told me once about them bad houses. I asked him where was the houses. He took me. We did n't go in. We got caught — he was throwing potatoes — just possibly for fun. They asked us if this was the place where you get work, and good health, and make a man of yourself. My partner that time he was going to pay 50 cents for me to go and stay with a woman and I said no. I don't go to no shows. Used to. My father refuses now to give me money. He says there must be some reason I stick to the rotten bunch — I must get out in the country, in the fresh air. They always come over and ask me to go there and there with them."

" I have to jump up in that bed and I can't lie. quiet because I have irritations " (He meant urinations). " Any man's life, he 's sorry he don't kill himself. My father says he would take me out on the prairie and shoot five bullets through me — He says you 're good for nothing — I 'm sorry you 're living on this earth. I always had trouble in that way. I always got the bed wet. I get something comes in my eyes and head like that and I feel like killing myself, but I don't make no attempts. I was arrested once and the judge says don't jump in the lake, it 's too

599

cold — and I have n't. But if I had any cause I would. Often have headaches. I have to spit all my food out sometimes. Some people say you eat too quick. My head feels bad, rotten. I was n't injured as long as I live I was n't injured. I was sick a lot of times and everything." (Note denials of father's story. Urged to tell the truth.) "Oh, yes, a long time ago. Of course it was bad. I thought I was going to be dead one time when I fell off the fence. I was about 11 years old. I ain't got no trouble from it. It comes from the stomach, that irritations. We was going in that house in the vice district and we got caught. Because that 's the law of the United States, boys of such age not allowed to go in such places — he can't do as he pleases. The law says his father can feed him until he is 15 years old, or something like that, but the father he can't, he 's got to go and work for his own living. I like to see women in those shows. Pictures, no. He can't feed me all my life. I 've got to go out and work for myself. Let them teach 'em to be correct. That 's what the House of Correction is for, that 's to make people correct and make 'em be good. Naw, you ain't allowed to talk. They watch over you at night. They hit you. If you holler out, gees! they club you to death. They never said a bad word to me. Two times I was there. I don't know for what I am sick. I am weak, worse every day. Jesus Christ, I 'd like to know for what I am weak."

At times this fellow talked much of sex affairs, and, despite negative assertions, showed plainly by his behavior that he indulged in bad habits.

§ 299. Paresis. Dementia Paralytica.

The symptoms of paresis, which in the light of modern knowledge is to be regarded as one of the manifestations of syphilis of the brain, can easily be seen to be conducive to criminality. There are profound disturbances of emotional life, varying from complete satisfaction with all things, to the manifestation of great passion at the most trifling and even imaginary annoyances. There is formation of delusions, which, however, quickly change their character, and the patient is sometimes subject to hallucinations. Now it so happens that the deterioration of mentality which accompanies this disease, fortunately generally interferes with the carrying out in conduct of prolonged vicious impulses. It is generally considered that paresis leads only to

minor offenses, but this is not always true. I know of one case
in which a murderous assault upon a wife was the first indication
to the family of the existence of any real mental disease. The
effect of sudden passions and delusions does sometimes lead to
violence in paresis, but, as a rule, the delinquencies are of a less
startling nature. Petty thieving, even by rich men, the public
use of shameful language, indecencies of conduct, engaging in
orgies of dissipation are more usual forms of offense. The well-
known tendency early in the disease to splurge in business,
and engage in speculation, using for the purpose all the money
possible to lay hands on, becomes under some circumstances a
very grave delinquency. The fact that impulses are very readily
acted on, and suggestions quickly taken, may account for a good
deal of the anti-social conduct.

The disease has well-marked physical as well as mental signs,
and has nothing of the subtlety for the criminologist that marks
a border-line case of paranoia, for instance. It is quite unnecessary
to take space for the citation of examples. The diagnosis ought
to be readily made, but as Bowers (**49**) has recently shown, cases
are sometimes unrecognized and sent to the penitentiary.

§ 300. Juvenile Paresis.

Paresis is usually described as a disease of the prime of life.
It rarely occurs in a juvenile form, but when it does may have
many moral complications.

Case 116. — I was asked to see a boy in whom I should find
the epitome of criminalistic tendencies. If there ever was a
young fellow headed for the penitentiary, and perhaps for the
gallows, this was one. Under the kindest influences he had proved
utterly incorrigible. He stole, lied, ran away, and was violent
and abusive to his mother and others — doing most of these
things in outbursts, with intervals of fairly decent conduct.
This behavior, noted for a couple of years, had made him regarded
as an atrociously anti-social individual. Five minutes of examination, when the complete loss of knee jerks, and the unequal
pupils which failed to react to light were observed, made the
case clear as one of juvenile paresis. Report later from the
hospital on the blood and spinal fluid findings made the case
plain as one of congenital syphilis. The criminal, as such, vanished, and we had left the victim of parental syphilis.

§ 301. Melancholia.

The criminalistic acts committed by sufferers from melancholia are induced not only by their emotional depression, but also by the nature of the delusions and hallucinations from which they may be suffering. The tendency to suicide is very much more common in this mental disease than in any other form. In the endeavor to carry out the suicidal impulses the most extraordinary persistency may be shown, and strange methods may be undertaken. The relationship between the feeling of extreme ill-being, and a desire to die is obvious, but it must be remembered that the attempt at suicide is often carried out, even in melancholia, under an impulse received directly from hallucinatory or delusional sources. There may be a belief that one ought to die because of extreme sinfulness, or voices may be heard commanding that suicide be undertaken. Crimes of violence may rarely be committed by a melancholiac under the same delusional impulses. Murder of near relatives, followed by suicide, is a usual form, and the general impulse to put an end to things connected with one's personality may lead to setting fire to the home. The offenses are thoroughly typical and understandable through the nature of the disease, and need not be gone into further. The disease is very rarely seen before late adolescence.

§ 302. Manic-Depressive Insanity.

Sufferers from the excessive psychomotor exhilaration, always sooner or later followed by abnormal depression, which characterizes the manic phase of manic-depressive insanity, are sometimes criminalistic. Usually their disease is so manifest that they are taken care of comparatively early in institutions, and consequently figure but little in the courts. Quarreling, fighting, running away, unprovoked assault, and attempts to misrepresent, are the types of misdeed ordinarily seen in connection with this disease. Anti-social conduct is so readily seen to be a part of the mental disorder that diagnosis of the cause rarely presents difficulties.

Case 117. — A girl of 12, with the most rapid alternations of exhilaration and mute depression that I have ever seen, running in periods of about twenty days for the former and ten days for the latter, came first under observation on account of collecting money under false pretenses. In her period of excitement she obtained subscriptions ostensibly to help certain sufferers. Prior to this she had been quarrelsome and untruthful. At a later period she ran away from home at night, and on one occasion was caught telephoning to a strange man.

When first seen, the results on test work were most interesting. She could with difficulty hold her mind on even the shortest tasks. Our notes state that she would continually interrupt her work to talk about some unrelated topic. The next time she absolutely refused to speak or approach us, and had not uttered a word for several days. Still later she came running in one day and begged to be allowed to do our interesting tests, saying that she remembered them well, but had not felt like doing anything at all at the previous visit. After several years this girl remains in much the same fluctuating condition, sometimes in the hospital for the insane and sometimes on parole from it.

§ 303. Epileptic Psychoses.

Epileptic manifestations may take the form of major psychoses which, so far as the observer is concerned, may develop apparently out of a clear sky. I once saw a case in which two weeks of excitement, confusion, and disorientation supervened before the fact of earlier epileptic seizures was obtained. No previous psychosis had been observed, and the patient showed only slight mental deterioration. Generally there is a background of dementia on which the psychosis supervenes. The common aggressiveness of the epileptic may lead to dangerous assaults and other offenses during the attack, but, on the whole, on account of the better recognition of the mental state, epileptics who are obviously insane, are to be regarded as less dangerous than those who are not. This whole subject, since both major and minor forms of psychosis are involved, is treated of under the special head of epilepsy.

§ 304. Dementia.

The dementia secondary to psychosis, or brain disease as such, including the involutional conditions of old age, have no large correlation with criminalism. Usually these individuals are taken care of in institutional life and they are not particularly tempted to anti-social conduct. The minor mental peculiarities of old age are treated of by us under the head of senility, § 163.

§ 305. — Paranoia.

This psychosis may be defined best as a chronic, systematized, delusional insanity. The delusions are always egocentric, and center around ideas of personal persecution and of personal grandeur. They are held with great persistency and expand usually into a coherent system of false ideas. The disease occurs as a rule without marked evidences of mental deterioration or disorders of mental activity in other spheres. This latter astonishing peculiarity has led to the psychosis sometimes being called monomania — aberration in only one phase of mental life.

Getting the main characteristics of this psychosis clearly before us serves at once to show the possibilities of aberrant social conduct. Most frequently the individual shows various minor forms of erratic behavior and much complaint of the way he is treated — both being in consonance with the delusions. When the individual believes himself about to be injured in some way, it may seem that something aggressive must be done about it. Or when he believes that the country is being sacrificed by someone whose actions he has been dwelling on, he, seeing the facts so clearly, must be the avenger. Thus it comes about that assaults and homicidal attacks are indulged in with ideas which center about the person of the paranoiac himself, and that occasional important political crimes are committed upon the basis of systematic delusions.

Another type of action characteristic of paranoiacs, not ordinarily classed as delinquency, but sometimes associated with it, and always having great legal importance, is carried out as the result of their well-known tendency to find fault and make formal complaint. I speak of paranoiac litigation, which sometimes assumes large proportions. The same tendencies, based on delusions that others are continually doing wrong to them, which led to the designation by Hitzig of some cases as querulant insanity, bring about litigious monomania. Legal action, on new and old claims, is continually sought with great expenditure of time and money and endeavor. Dr. Glueck, of the Government Hospital for the Insane, tells me that in his department are some individuals who in the course of years had lumbered the courts with hundreds of actions at law before they were officially declared *non compos mentis*.

Any common-sense consideration of the conditions of prison life would lead to belief that delusions of persecution might readily arise in predisposed persons during long incarceration. When retaliation which society has insisted on is the prisoner's main subject of thought it is little wonder if this be conceived in terms of persecution. Whether mental disease ever arises entirely as the result of imprisonment it may be hard to decide, but the fact is that in prisoners not already mentally strong, psychoses do spring up, and one of the best recognized forms of mental trouble arising under those circumstances is paranoia. Nitsche and Wilmanns (48) discuss this condition, and cite the many observations by prison physicians of delusion formation during prison life. It occurs in various psychoses and has characteristically to do with ideas of innocence, of pardon, etc. These delusions may disappear, and return, or become fixed, as in the cases of paranoia. In some of the latter there is also to be observed the development of a litigious tendency, which would seem to be a natural outcome of the legal restraint.

It is true that delusions of persecution arise sometimes on a basis of other mental diseases, so this feature alone is not sufficient for diagnosis. Paranoia itself develops most notably on a background of hereditary mental abnormality of some sort. Preceding the characteristic symptoms there may have been noted distinct mental defect. No doubt the stress of poverty, emotional strain, business reverses, or of a severe illness may be a determining cause in development of the disease.

The whole subject is of great importance, one reason being that the paranoiac often preserves intact many capabilities of a good mind, and another that his delusions may be entirely unsuspected. There are different grades of development of the paranoiac tendency — some may present incompletely developed forms of the disease, and may belong to the more or less harmless class of "cranks." From the clear-cut, classical types of the psychosis, as might be expected in view of the complexities of mental life, there are many variants. A case showing both criminal and litigious tendencies may be shortly summarized as follows.

Case 118. — A strong, healthy-looking German, who emigrated to this country some fifteen years ago, has been appearing in court either as defendant or complainant a large number of times. By his attitude as he sits with his chest thrown out, and his voluble self-assertion one sees at once the egocentric personality. He informs us of his abilities and, notwithstanding these, his failures in business, and tells us at great length of assaults made upon his person, and insults offered, and attempts to destroy his character. All these have emanated from his family. They, all of them, have a grudge against him, and sneer at him, and call him bad names, and incite or even hire others to insult him, and offer him bodily violence. This has been going on for years, with gradual involvement of various members of the family. At times he has perceived, he tells us, impending danger to himself, and has assaulted others, and been arrested for it. On one occasion he did not dare to do anything when his wife called him dirty names, and pounded him with a stick, because his step-son sat in the next room with a shotgun. They have broken him up in business five or six times, and his store has been robbed dozens of times at their instigation.

This man talks well and makes clear statements. He does not always stick to his points, but then he has a tremendous number of them to make; he sometimes counts them off as he proceeds in conversation. He is sure that his wife is unfaithful, that he has been unfairly treated by all, and he discusses in detail the injustices done him by those who have had to do through the courts with his family affairs. He has brought numerous complaints into the courts, and instigated several law suits. He has followed up old records, he says, and done detective work to verify the points which he suspected. He has written very numerous letters, some of them extending over fourteen pages, to various officials and presents affidavits of the truth of his allegations. He continually threatens his present wife, as he did his two previous ones. A characteristic action was shown by his buying a shotgun, and shooting it off early in the morning to let others know that he possessed arms. The neighbors by taking sides with the family have become implicated in his delusions of persecution.

This man has been under observation by court authorities for years and has not shown notable deterioration. His delusions still center about his family, from which he is now parted. He does well at times in a business way, being able to make a good presentation of himself and his wares. The difficulties and dangerous possibilities of such a case are to be readily perceived and need not be enlarged on here.

Case 119. — Occasionally, as in the case of a boy of fourteen years we have studied, paranoidal symptoms may appear in the young. In this instance the individual was subnormal by tests given on numerous occasions, but showed a vast amount of ability and ambition to push himself forward. His forcefulness, as in many a full-fledged paranoiac, made him convincing to many, and his charges of ill treatment against institutions and persons gained much credence. Everybody was unfair to him and to his father, the latter being a man who felt keenly that the world owed him a living, and that he ought not to be put to the trouble of even collecting what was owed. Charges of ill treatment were so continually made by the boy, who gave every indication of being sincere, and who indeed put himself to much physical discomfort in pursuance of his delusions, that their very frequency aroused the suspicion of most of those with whom he had to deal. Nevertheless this type of aggressive character can continually make new friends who will for a time be persuaded of the fairness of the contentions, and who will sympathetically enlist themselves in righting the wrongs. Paranoia is a psychosis of slow evolution, and a mental break-down that definitely forces institutional care may come late or never. The final diagnosis in such an instance as our last cited case must be held in abeyance, but for court purposes the fact was clearly registerable that important aberrational tendencies existed on a basis of mental subnormality.

§ 306. Unclassified Major Mental Aberrations.

For many reasons we are interested to note the cases of undoubted insanity which are held in institutions for the insane as unclassified or unclassifiable. It is clearly acknowledged that individuals with even major manifestations of insanity may not fill the outlines of any set classification. The relation of one such case to criminalism is shown below:

Case 120. — We have long been interested in the career of a woman who was one time under our observation, because of the fact that her mental aberrations have proved so refractory to classification, and because of its several interests for students of criminalistics. At 20 she was a fine-appearing and well-developed young married woman of ordinary grammar school education. Her mental symptoms were first manifested about a year

607

prior to that time, and the cause was attributed to the excitement of religion. She then made a homicidal attack upon her husband under the stimulus of hallucinations, but it was readily thwarted. Later, at a menstrual period, she procured his revolver and shot him so that he permanently carries the bullet at the base of his brain. Then she was treated in a private sanitarium, where she showed no signs of insanity. After this she became pregnant, and during this period was said to be normal. Two or three months after the child was born menstrual signs reappeared, and with them her excitement. This time she dangerously injured her baby. Under observation for some months immediately after this last attack, she was found to be considerably disturbed over religion, but soon became cheerful and talkative and showed marked improvement which continued. Then her husband insisted on taking her home again, and within a year she had taken the life of her second child by burning it in a stove. She then remained under observation in a hospital for over 6 years, and during all this time she only had two or three attacks of excitement during which she was violent and destructive. These were always of short duration. At other times she was very ladylike, agreeable and rational in conversation. It is reported that she showed no mental deterioration. Judgment, reasoning and memory remained about as normal. There was some lack of emotional feeling toward her situation at all times, but perhaps no more than might be seen in many religious people who are living under adversity. Her actions, she explained to us at first, were done under the full feeling that she was carrying out the will of God, and that, indeed, she heard His voice commanding her to do these things. After all these years of observation she remains an unclassified case, though clearly insane at times, and a case of immense importance in the field of criminology.

CHAPTER XXI

MINOR MENTAL ABERRATIONS

§ 307. Hypomania. Constitutional Excitement. § 308. Psychosis of Chorea. § 309. Traumatic Psychoses. § 310. Menstrual Mental Aberrations. § 311. Mental Aberrations of Pregnancy. § 312. Amnesic Fugues. Other Amnesias. § 313. Mental Aberration from Bad Sex Habits. § 314. Hysterical Mental Aberrations. § 315. Transitory Mental Aberrations.

§ 307. Hypomania. Constitutional Excitement.

As representative of a psychiatric group in which there is abnormal excitement and lack of control leading to many delinquencies, the following cases are thoroughly representative. In these instances the mental symptoms were never severe enough for the individual to be committed as insane, and yet the psychotic condition quite precluded normal social behavior.

Case 121. — A girl of 15 has been a repeated sex offender, uses the vilest language, and is altogether incorrigible. She comes of a most ignorant immigrant family. The father was known to the police as an intensely excitable and rough man. He drank much at times, and was a wife beater. He was notorious on account of his great excitability, perhaps he was insane. He had been dead for some years when we saw this girl. The mother was ignorant and dull. She could hardly name her own children. She herself lived in improper relationship with a low-grade foreigner. Of 11 children 5 are dead. One of the remainder is a young man who is a typical loafer and has been under probation from a court. The other children are said to be fairly good. The mother is a scrub woman. The girl's development was quite normal, according to the ignorant mother. Facts about heredity are probably unreliable, but, for what it is worth, the mother's story is that there is no insanity or epilepsy in the family.

On the physical side we found the girl in good general condition. Very strong and active. Much use of the facial muscles. Constant fine tremor of outstretched hands. Pleasant, vivacious and merry expression. Great strength of arm muscles. Good color. Menstruation at 13.

Mental tests: our own series:

I. 1′. Very little trial and error.

II. 1′ 25″. 3 errors.

III. Construction Test A. 41″. No repetition of impossibilities.

IV. Construction Test B. 45″. Twelve moves.

V. Puzzle Box. Done by trial and error method clumsily in just 10′.

VI. "Aussage." Short enumerative account followed by very poor result on cross-examination. Five suggestions taken, and many items incorrectly given.

VII. Reproduction of Geometric Figures. Neither one given correctly.

VIII. Learning Arbitrary Symbol Associations. Done correctly.

IX. Cross Line Test A. Correct at 1st trial.

X. Cross Line Test B. Only correct at 3d reproduction, after two times drawing the figure herself.

XI. Memory from Visual Verbal Presentation. Only eight of the twenty items given correctly. In logical sequence as far as they went.

XII. Memory from Auditory Verbal Presentation. Seven of the twelve items given in order, but without full appreciation of the significance.

XIV. Puzzle Box. Failure even after three trials.

XV. Antonyms. Average time 2.4″. Four errors and one failure. Reactions on words she really knows were very rapid. In other instances she took full 10″ before answering.

XVI. Motor Coördination Test. 76 and 67 squares tapped respectively at 1st and 2d trials without errors.

XVIII. Knows as far as the process of long division. Inaccurate, however, on work.

XIX. Reads ordinary passages correctly.

XXI. Answers to moral questions much mixed up. First says he did right and then he did wrong. Fails to understand the story in the second question.

XXII. Has a complete jumble of information on many subjects. Taft is the president, but Bryan was the president before him. Abraham Lincoln was a bad boy who cut down a cherry tree. Largest city in America is Bohemia, or Chicago, or Illinois or Michigan. Flour is made out of seeds on farms, etc.

Her own story was accompanied by excitable, restless, quick, nervous actions. She spoke very rapidly in a deep, thick, low monotone. "I feel all right but I'm lonesome. Everybody is lonesome for their parents ain't they? I've got three brothers, and I can't think how they look. It is hard to see just how anybody looks." Slams fist down on table and then rubs hands on table. "Where's that woman? She said she would give me a book.

See these scratches? Pins and nails on the floor where we have to scrub. We got three girls sick upstairs. Got twenty girls and three of them sick. Mother she works in the hospital and we got trouble with her. She's sick lots. I hope Wednesday comes soon. What day is today? Today is Friday the tenth. Five days more will be the 15th, Wednesday. I bet you I go. There's girls run away from home upstairs. How's Mr. Y? I hope he's well. I used to go to his church. I love that man. Is Miss M. here? I know her. She had a son. (Who?) Mrs. M. He plays that long thing that goes across your mouth. In my ear it goes like steam. Sometimes it goes like that," etc. etc.

Conversing with the examiner she said, "I can't do that box. There was a lady here yesterday. I could do that box of hers good." (She alluded to the puzzle box.) "Did you ever do that box. She aint come yet." (How far did you get in school?) "Low sixth. Do you know the principal of that school?" (What school?) "T. school. Do you know any of the teachers there? She was mean. I hated her. She would not give you any book. I did not care if I did not have no book. I would have given it away. It ain't right not to give a book to poor people. It ain't her book anyhow. It don't belong to her. It belongs to the school. It belongs to the Board of Education. And when you wanted to stop school she would not let you. Did you graduate from school? You get paid down here, don't you? Have you got parents? Have you got a sister? Does she go to school?"

A reliable policeman who has known the family for years states that this girl has long been most excitable. She differs in this from the other children, who are normally quiet. She seems to take after the excitable father. A social worker confirmed this statement and says the girl talks a great deal and screams sometimes when excited. She seems to show no regret or shame. As observed in school she proved very noisy and excitable and lacking in self-control. Often bursts out into coarse laughter while she is at work. No evidence could be obtained of periods of depression.

Many lay observers had decided that this girl was not right mentally. At the trial of a man who had been sexually delinquent with her, her mental conduct was peculiar and an examination was recommended. However, at no time had there been any complaint of her lack of industry. She was steadily earning her own living by factory work. To call her out-and-out

611

insane seemed unfair. On the other hand, her mental characteristics were certainly largely responsible for her unrestricted sex
delinquencies. There had been many efforts to help her in the
family environment, but she lacked self-control sufficient to take
advantage of these. She was sent to an institution for delinquent girls.

After about a year, during part of which time she had proved
herself very troublesome, she was released. In the 2 years which
have elapsed since then this girl has worked steadily and behaved
herself so well that, considering her environment, her conduct
may be said to be quite normal. All this is good proof of her
mental improvement. We have had no chance recently actually
to observe her ourselves.

Mentality; Constitutional excitement.   Case 121.
    Home conditions: Poverty. Incom-   Girl, age 15.
                    petency.

        Heredity: Father very excitable. Alcoholic.
                    Wife deserter. Mother mentally dull.

        Adolescence ?

Delinquencies: Mentality:
    Sex + +.   Psychosis as above.

Case 122. — This girl of 14 showed abnormal psychomotor
activity, marked enough to be classed as hypomania. She was
a poorly-developed, thoroughly nervous child. Weight 76 lbs;
height 4 ft., 8 in. Teeth excessively crowded in the upper jaw.
Tonsils very large.

Mentally; abilities distinctly above average. Advantages,
through poverty, very poor. She left school by falsification of
age when in 7th grade. A pert, talkative, quickly responsive
girl. An extreme fabricator. Talks incessantly in an airy, but
sure way. No hesitation at all while making up her inventions,
which are clear, connected and plausible. Does the tests brilliantly in regard to rapidity, but is less accurate in proportion.
Much facial expression.

We hear from a parent that the girl comes from a neurotic
family, but no insanity, feeblemindedness or epilepsy is said to
exist in near relatives. Her mother during pregnancy was in
poor condition on account of poverty, sickness and worry. At

birth she weighed only about 5 lbs. and showed poor vitality then. Walked and talked very early. Only one illness of any importance. There is a bad family reaction through displays of nervous ill temper.

For a year or so she has been giving much trouble by her very active delinquencies. She has repeatedly stolen and engaged in misrepresentation. An example of her brazenness was when she stole some goods from a shop, returned them as an undesired purchase, and persuaded the people to refund her the cost price. She has run away from home on several occasions. Once she "beat her way" on the train to a distant city and there, after being in jail, got a place in a nice family through her powers of falsification. She has been written up several times in the newspapers of different places on account of the bright, but untrue, stories she has told, and the activity of her peregrinations. Repeatedly when thoroughly tired she has been known to lie down to sleep under a tree, under a department store counter, or anywhere she happens to be. She has made several trips to a neighboring town, and there has stolen from stores three or four times. When the police get hold of her she quickly invents stories that are not deeply clever, but serve the purpose of the moment. She tells us with much vivacious merriment that she wants to go to other cities; she is tired of the slowness and drudgery of home life. "I am proud of being quick—nothing is too hard for me." Over a period of several months this girl in extraordinarily industrious fashion got into one escapade after another; then we lost sight of her through the family moving to a different state.

The display of activity in this case was, of course, quite abnormal for any girl, and was tremendously out of proportion to her defective physiological conditions. No evidences of mental aberration other than those given above were ever discovered by us.

§ 308. Psychosis of Chorea.

The confusional mental state which frequently accompanies chorea is often mentioned; indeed some authors have gone so far as to say that in all cases there is more or less mental disturbance. The connection between this mental condition and delinquency has been repeatedly forced upon our notice. Truancy, running away from home, extensive lying — sometimes including the very serious delinquency of false accusations — petty stealing, and, above all, the development of immoral sex tendencies in girls, are the types of bad behavior which are to be seen developed as the result of this disease. The sequence may be illustrated by the following cases.

Case 123. — A girl of 14 1-2 years had been creating a great deal of trouble for her family by her excessive lying and general unreliable behavior. On one occasion she stayed out all night. She went to shows and later out on the street. The next day she related a story of kidnapping to the police which led to a lot of fruitless effort. After that, and still more serious, came the girl's false accusations of rape against a distant member of the family.

We found her poorly developed and nourished. Weight 93 lbs., height 4 ft., 9 in. Defective vision for which she has glasses. Exaggerated knee jerks. Palatal-pharyngeal reflexes almost absent. Marked tremor of the hands and very distinct choreic movements in both arms and legs, even when attention distracted. Heart sounds negative.

Reached 7th grade, and has had a good school record. We did very few tests on account of her excited condition; these tended to show her possessed of good mental ability. On the other hand the evidences of her aberrational mental conditions were conclusive, as shown in her own story of her behavior. This was corroborated from several sources.

The account of the girl's heredity and developmental history has many points of significance. Mother has long been dead. The father is excessively alcoholic and a tremendous brute. When a little girl she lived with him. They were at a sort of road house where there were terrific drunken fights in which other members of his family were more or less implicated. On the mother's side the family is quite reputable. The mother was terribly abused by her husband. No evidence of any family disease was obtained. The girl herself has had a number of severe illnesses. Was in a comatose condition when only six weeks old, from scarlet fever and diphtheria. Had measles, whooping cough, etc. For a time she suffered badly from extreme constipation. Walked and talked early. No convulsions. Sometimes severe headache. First menstruated recently. One observer reported that the girl had been subject to slight melancholy in the last year or so. The choreic movements have been present for about a year, but have not been diagnosed as such until recently. During all this time, however, she has been unreliable. In regard to the charge of rape which she made at one time to the police, it was found on examination by the official physician that this had not taken place, nor was there the slightest evidence of an attack of any kind.

The statement which she made to the police and then signed, contained a detailed account of association with bad girls and with men with whom she said she had repeated sexual intercourse. As stated above, she also accused a certain member of her family.

When seen by us the girl was very pleasant and responsive and her story was told directly and coherently. She seemed to have entire memory of her past actions and, in general, of what she said, but the unreliability of her statements is shown in her story, from which the following are excerpts.

" I went away from home by myself. I met a man who looked like a man who had given some money once to another girl and myself on the car when we said we had lost our money. He said, don't you remember when I gave you thirty-five cents to go in the ice cream parlor. He took me to the F theatre. Was there until the show was out. He wanted to bring me home but I would not let him and he gave me a quarter. I went to a nickel show and went to sleep in there and a man told me to get out. A lady saw me and asked me where I was going. It was 4 o'clock in the morning."

" Well, I was telling the first lie, and then I was going to tell the policeman I knew I was telling wrong, but he was so cranky and he said such things to me. He said he knew somebody had done bad things to me and I thought I had to give names and so I gave these names."

This case was readily straightened up when it was explained to the family and to the police that the girl was in a thoroughly unreliable mental condition. It was clear that her misbehavior had only begun within the last year or so. Treatment for her chorea was recommended and carried out, and further delinquency has not been heard of.

Case 124. — A boy of 12, very small for his age, has for long been engaged in various delinquencies. He is a great truant with boys who have been suspended from school. Then he also stays out very late at night. On several occasions did not come home until 2 o'clock in the morning. Has also run away from home. Has stolen sometimes, but on the whole is not considered to be much of a thief. Already he has been tried in one institution and in several private homes, but in the latter places the people would not keep him because of his general disobedience. Shows a good deal of irritability at times, and strikes his brother and sister. He has been taught bad sex habits, but it is doubtful if he is indulging to any extent.

On the physical side we found a very poorly developed and nourished lad. Weight 65 lbs., height 4 ft. 5 1-2 in. No sensory defects noted. Fair color. Small, boyish features. Frank expression. Traces of choreic movements. Pigeon breast. Considerably increased area of cardiac dullness with a roughened systolic sound at the apex and a slight thrill palpable over cardiac region. Diffuse impulse at apex. Complains of getting out of breath easily. Other examination negative.

On the mental side we were particular to do thorough tests because of the fact that the boy is so retarded in school, being only in 2d grade. However, we could account partly for this backwardness by his illnesses, truancy and frequent changes of abode.

Mental tests: our own series:
I. 2′ 13″. Considerable trial and error on triangles.
II. 1′ 18″. Three errors.
IV. Construction Test B. 7′. 33 moves, with much manipulation of pieces, not registered as actual moves. Did this immediately over again, upside down in 32″.
V. Puzzle Box. 4′. Steps interspersed with errors and much use of fingers instead of hook.
VI. "Aussage." Fairly good enumerative account with poor result on cross-examination. Three out of six suggestions accepted.
VII. Reproduction of Geometrical Figures. Extremely poorly done — not recognizable as copies.
VIII. Learning Arbitrary Symbol Associations. Three errors, but these were merely of transposition of the semi-circles.
IX. Cross Line Test A. Correct at 2d reproduction after drawing it himself.
X. Cross Line Test B. Correct at 3d reproduction after drawing it twice himself.
XII. Does not read well enough to do this test.
XIII. Memory from Auditory Verbal Presentation. 11 out of 12 items given in logical sequence.
XIV. Instruction Box. Done correctly only at 3d trial.
XV. Antonyms. 0 failures and 1 error. Average time 2.5″.

XVI. Motor Coördination Test. 37 squares tapped in 30″ with 2 errors. At another trial did about the same. Always proceeded very carefully and deliberately in an attempt to overcome his motor disability.

XVII. Writes his name slowly and painfully, but almost no other words.

XVIII. Arithmetic about equivalent to 2d grade. When asked the half of 24 he slowly evolves 12 as an answer. Said he did it by getting half of 20 as 10 and then half of the remainder as 2 and adding them together.

XIX. Reads only the simplest monosyllables.

Binet Tests (1908 series);

6 years — all done correctly.

7 years — 5, failure; all others correct.

8 years.— 1, 5, failures; others correct.

9 years — 1, 2, correct; 3, 4, 5, failures; 6, not given.

10 years — all four done correctly.

11 years — 1, two-fifths correct; 2, correct; 3, failure, but names 53 words which was almost up to passing mark; 4, 5, failures.

12 years — 1, failure; 2, correct; 3, failure; 4, correct.

This boy was brought to us as being probably feebleminded, but from the results of the above it is clear he was not at all so. There are many irregularities in his work, especially as shown in the Binet tests, but a number of failures in the latter were due to a lack of formal education. For instance, he could not read, and therefore could not do those tests which called for reading ability. In using the Binet 1908 series just this allowance will always have to be made. The other irregularities are significant of his psychotic condition, which is also very well displayed in his own story.

"My step-mother has been boarding me out. Have been in about four homes because I'd be a bad boy. My mother did not want to put me in a Home and she would board me at a lady's house. I used to hit my little sister, and would not do my work right, and besides I'd sass my mother back. My uncle did not like that. And besides I'd stay out all day, and would not see my mother and she'd be looking for me all day. I wanted to go out. I went with bad boys and uncle did not like it and would give me a box on the ear. They were stealing and smoking and swearing and all those bad things. My uncle knew they did that, and he did not let me go with them. The boys I used to play with taught me how to do them bad things. I run away from the reform school. Then I was out at the institution. I stayed

617

there one time for a year and at another time for 5 or 6 months and then went back for about 3 months. When I went first time I was 8 years old. I was home for about 4 or 5 years when I walked away last time. I was 9 or 10 then. It's been about 2 years." (There was no indication that he saw any incongruity in this or in his other curious statements.) "I was lots about the city. You could not tell me any place to go that I could not find it." (Gave me correctly the description of the way to get to various places.) "I go down town and buy my own clothes. I buy clothes for my mother when she is too sick to go. She tells me what color to get and I buy it."

"Sometimes I have hard things to do in school and I get nervous about it, and don't like to go to school that afternoon. There was a boy he was expended (suspended) from school, and me and him we'd play around. My step-mother treats me right, but I don't treat her right. I sass her, and this is the first or second time I run away. One night I come in late. I was up joining the Salvation Army. I heard the singing on the car and I followed it. I joined it. I never was sore at my step-mother. There was a cousin. She was telling me I was not my mother's kid at all. I used to think my mother was dead, and who was my mother right. It was long before I asked her. There was a boy, he taught me all them bad things, and there was a girl, etc."

"I get sometimes — in school — I'd be out at recess and I get excited and I get so I forget everything. Then when I get ready I study good. I had the first attack about 5 years ago. My mother sent me to the doctor. I was in the hospital once. Went about 4 months altogether to school last year."

Very little is known of his heredity, both the father and mother being dead. Father died from an accident. Said to come from a family of big strong people. Mother's family totally unknown. She is said to have died during confinement. The step-mother brought him up since he was 3 years old, at which time he appeared to have developed normally. Never had any severe illness except his numerous attacks of chorea, the first of which occurred when he was only 7 years old. Once was 2 months in a hospital with it. At one time his gait was extremely awkward. He would trip and even fall. Often is irrationally irritable. When a little child was once run over, but not badly hurt.

He went to kindergarten first at 5 years. The kind of moral treatment he has had is suggested by the step-mother's story, who tells us that on one occasion she took him to a police station and down to the cells and showed him the rats and everything. (We hear that she is addicted to alcohol.) For about two months he was good, and then started his misdemeanors all over again. Accounts from other sources as well, made it quite evident that this boy has long been abnormal in his mental, moral and physical conditions.

Rather than in an institution, at least at first, it was recommended that he be placed in the country at a good home. After a couple of months of rest he showed a slight gain in weight and in other ways improved. His heart conditions grew better.

Fundamental features underlying criminalistic behavior were most instructively illustrated by the findings in this case. This treatment of chorea with mental complications by a poor and ignorant family was typically neglectful of causes. On account of his nervous troubles he was not fit for school life. Practically nothing was done to cultivate any other mental interests. He had only the worst of companions with whom to associate, and, of course, most readily learned bad things from them because his mind was not occupied at all with better things.

Mentality: Minor aberrations of chorea.   Case 124.

Physical conditions: Chorea, several   Boy, age 12 yrs.
                  attacks.
                  Organic heart disease.
                  Poor development.

School irritations, on account of nervous trouble.

Home conditions: Parents dead. Irrational
                  treatment by step-mother.

Lack of healthy mental interests.

Delinquencies:
Truancy.   Mentality:
Runaway.   As above.
Stealing.   Fair ability.

---

§ 309. Traumatic Psychoses.

The fact, well known to students of cerebral injuries, that the after effects of a severe injury to the head are frequently shown in change of character, bespeaks the importance which a cranial trauma may have for the production of criminalistic behavior.[1] It has been clearly recognized that the alteration in disposition may take place even without evidences of severe mental damage at the time of the accident, such as unconsciousness or confusion with loss of memory. The so-called post-traumatic disposition or constitution of Meyer (47) forms a clearly recognizable entity. There is instability and irrascibility, there may be feelings of pressure or pain in the head, forgetfulness, etc. For our purposes it is most important to note that the mental changes typically lead to passionate outbreaks and great decrease in the power of self-control and that an easy mental fatiguability creates lack of continuity of purpose. Another point, often observed and of great social importance, is the development of an intolerance for alcohol. A small quantity now upsets the moral poise and induces violence and crime.

Many of the signs of mental disease pass over by easy degrees to mere character peculiarities. In our present subject, as in other instances where erratic conduct is found to have a basis in pathological mental conditions, it may be very difficult to draw the line and make a diagnosis between a real traumatic psychosis and a character change seen reflected in social conduct. The intermittency of many of the mental phenomena in post-traumatic cases, and variations in environmental stress, such as work in overheated places, and in physiological conditions, such as those created by imbibition of alcohol, all lead to great variation in conduct. The individual seen now as a rational and well-behaved human being is at another time an active criminal. There is much hypersusceptibility to minor stresses which do not produce extravagant misconduct in the normal individual.

The outstanding fact in our own findings which bear on this subject, is that among our series of repeated offenders we have found an amount of preceding head injury far greater than that which would be discovered among an average group of individuals. No less than 21 cases out of our 1000 are known to have suffered from some severe head injury. We have not reckoned at all the little accidents which have been so often related by parents, even

---

[1] Many points of importance for students of criminalistics are to be found in Adolf Meyer's study (47) of "The Anatomical Facts and Clinical Varieties of Traumatic Insanity."

when we have heard that the individual was stunned for a short time. In classification of these cases we have rarely had to resort to calling them psychoses, because frequently only an abnormal irritability was ascertained to exist as a possible after-effect. Where there was an actual arrest of development as the result of cerebral traumatism the case belongs under an appropriate heading, § 287.

Here again in the matter of assigning the rôle of a major cause for the delinquent tendencies we are frequently confronted with difficulties. Other possible causes are also nearly always in the background. Often we have gained evidence of a prior neuropathic constitution, or of some grave defect in heredity. Except in a case of arrested development, we can fairly say we have never been able to discern traumatism as the sole assignable factor. We are thus forced to agree with other authors in asserting that injuries to the head are most apt to produce untoward results in already neuropathically predisposed individuals.

Case 125. — A man, age 25 years. In this case we were able to study the individual for only a very short time prior to trial. He was then taken out of our sphere of observation, but we had then and later the opportunity for gaining a most excellent history of him and of his family and developmental background from several reliable people who thoroughly corroborated each other.

This man has been very frequently under arrest. Just now he was in jail for having stolen and pawned some clothes. It is most interesting that he could at the time have taken jewelry and money even more readily. He has stolen in this foolish way previously and engaged in many other erratic misdemeanors, particularly violence.

His personal history, in short, runs as follows. He was a large baby at birth. Walked and talked early. He had no convulsions as a child and did not suffer from enuresis. He went to school at the normal age and seemed to his intelligent family to be quite all right until he was 9 years old. Then he was in the 3rd grade. At this age he had an injury to his head which resulted in a large scalp wound and a rather short period of unconsciousness. The skull was not known to have been fractured. All say that following this his character and mental capacity changed. He complained of not being able to study and became a frequent truant. At 14 he had only reached 5th grade. Beginning with his truancy there was frequent association with bad companions. By the time he was 14 he occasionally drank and used much tobacco. During these years he also ran away, even for a week or two at a time, and stole in petty ways. No desperate characteristics were developed until later. Physically he was strong, but not athletic. He always displayed very acute affections; was extremely kind to stray animals, and often sought to help boys poorer than himself.

By 17 he began to have times of believing that his family were conspiring against him, and was sometimes violent at home. He started regular drinking bouts now, made off from home and returned after a week or two in rags and even bare feet. Enlisted in the navy at 18. He had a bad record for erratic behavior, drinking, and attempted desertion. On one occasion when not drinking he attempted to jump overboard. At 19 he received a second head injury followed by a considerable period of unconsciousness. Again the skull was not known to be fractured. Received a medical discharge.

Since that time he has had long periods of good behavior interspersed with extraordinarily erratic conduct. Marriage brought great jealousy and worry about his wife. His child he hardly looks at and speaks of the fact that he has not normal parental affection. Sometimes talks nearly all night. Once he jumped out of window, and followed an imaginary person. Such actions develop when he is not drinking. He has been in jail at least a dozen times. He was working on a machine recently when he lost control of himself, and his hands were badly smashed.

He occasionally drinks for a short time. These periods are preceded by very erratic behavior when he breaks things at home and rushes out suddenly. He carries prayers about with him. He says that God ought to help him. He gets up in the middle of the night to pray that he may be good. Has threatened suicide if he is not relieved of his erratic tendencies. He has fits of crying. Complains of headaches. For years has been a great reader and occasionally will become so absorbed in a book that he reads all night.

Physically we found him poorly nourished. Our rather incomplete examination revealed nothing of special interest. He complains of severe headache every two or three weeks in the frontal region. He says that if he is tapped on the head there it does not feel solid. We can find no evidence of fracture of the skull.

On the mental side the man seems well oriented. Is rather a talkative type. Is quite sure that at times he is beside himself. Says that he is not and never has been a heavy drinker. Something queer comes over him when he takes even a single glass. He does not allege that he is insane, and does not ask to have his punishment mitigated, he only desires relief.

This whole case is considerably complicated for diagnosis and prognosis by the family history. The paternal grandfather and an uncle were excessively alcoholic. Another paternal uncle was more mildly addicted. The father himself was a periodic drunkard, sexually immoral and finally a deserter of his family. He had attacks, preceded by his crying out, in which his heart beat very fast, and he had to lie down. The grandfather on the other side committed suicide. Out of a large family of children the subject of our study is the only one who has shown aberrant traits. The others are all grown up and are steady and normal. One brother, a successful clerk, has rare attacks, always at night, in which he shakes all over, falls as if dead and acts as if something was choking him. Afterwards he goes right to sleep. No other family history of mental or nervous trouble was known. The antenatal period of our subject's development was much perturbed on account of worry about his father's behavior; abortion was attempted.

Mentality: Post-traumatic minor psychosis.
Perhaps innate neuropath.

Injuries to head at 9 and 18 years.

Heredity: Very defective. See details.

Antenatal conditions defective.

Alcohol, intermittent.

Delinquencies:
Truancy.
Vagrancy.
Stealing.
Violence.

Case 125.
Man, age 25 yrs.

Mentality:
As above.

623

Case 126. — Boy 17 years of age. This lad has a very extensive delinquent record. He has run away from home many times, associated with bad companions and with them engaged in stealing and burglary. The family and others have regarded him as thoroughly incorrigible.

Physically, at 15 years we find a large tall boy. Weight 129 lbs.; height 5 ft. 1 in. Decidedly premature sex development. No special sensory defect. He is a slouchy chap with a dull expression, considering his social advantages. Strong and well muscled. Headaches frequently.

On mental examination we find an extremely pleasant fellow, many of whose social reactions are of the best.

Mental tests: our own series:

I. 1' 1". No trial and error.

III. 2' 13". 7 impossibilities tried and 2 repetitions of impossibilities.

IV. 4' 19". 61 moves.

V. 4' 58". No errors, but was a long time in manipulating with his fingers instead of using the tool. Put the box together with no errors.

VI. Fairly good free recital, many items given on questioning. No suggestions accepted.

VII. Both correct.

IX. Correct on the 3d trial.

X. Correct on the 2d trial.

XI. Got the idea himself and accomplished the task with only 3 errors.

XII. Gave 13 out of the 20 items with fair accuracy and correct sequence.

XIII. Gave 11 out of the 12 items also with fair accuracy.

XIV. Correct at 2d trial.

XV. All given correctly. Average time 1.9".

XVII. Writes a very good hand.

XVIII. Does arithmetic through interest correctly.

XX. Reads fluently an ordinary passage.

XXI. On both of the ethical questions he gave a rational and moral interpretation of the problems involved.

XXII. Has a good range of information and reads many books. Shows interest in healthy subjects.

This boy had reached 7th grade in spite of his severe illness. We classified him as having fair ability. His tests show that he does not have thoroughly good powers of mental representation and analysis. We note also that in his own story of himself and his family there is a lack of cogency and consistent self-realization. All through, both in our tests and in his own account of himself, there is a marked attitude of not having thorough self-control. The question was long before us as to whether the boy had a mild psychosis, but observation of him under quiet conditions gave us no positive evidence of this. However, there was his own story of himself and the account given by others.

The early developmental history of this boy is said to have been entirely negative. He comes of an intelligent German family. There are several other children, some younger, all of whom are doing well. We can get no evidence of defective heredity except that the father, now about 55, has in the last few years developed epilepsy and dementia. No other cases of convulsions or epilepsy are known to exist in the family, and none of the children has suffered from this trouble.

This boy began going with a crowd of bad companions before he was 12 years old. He showed even then a distinct tendency towards unmanageability. His scholarship record was not bad, but he did not apply himself well. When he was almost 13 years old he was struck by a moving train and had a terrific injury to the head. He was unconscious for three days and in bed for several months. No paralysis ensued. The skull was fractured. Since that time the boy has been growing steadily more difficult to manage. He shows great irritability, quarrels much with other members of the household, and seems to the family to be irresponsible, although not actually insane. Since then he at times stays out half the night, and on two occasions has run away to a distant city. He has stolen from members of his family as well as from others.

The boy tells us that the discomfort in his head prevents him from holding any steady job. He has had many good chances, but cannot do inside work. He never had this feeling prior to being injured. He says himself that he has a bad temper, that he is nervous, and that he cannot control himself well. He thinks that his family are unfair to him, and complains that the police get after him for nothing. He spends much of the time in loafing about the streets. At one time he smoked much, but soon stopped.

This boy continued to do very poorly under probation in spite of every effort being made by his family. We advised from the first that he be placed in a quiet environment away entirely from city temptations.

Head injury severe.	Case 126.
Bad companions.	Boy, age 15.
Home control defective.	
Adolescent instability (?)	
Premature sex development (?)	
Heredity (?)	
Delinquencies:	
Running away.	Mentality:
Stealing.	Fair ability, but trau-
Burglary.	matic instability.

The *treatment* of the mental after-effects of cerebral traumatism is a matter of perennial interest because of the frequent claim made by surgeons that through operation there will be relief. Now, as a matter of fact, one can find almost no satisfactorily recorded cases of character changes or other mental cures which have followed operation. It ought to be obvious that brain substance, notoriously incapable of self-restoration, is not going to be regenerated by removing a body which has been for a long time acting unfavorably on it. Not only this, but the most significant damage may have been done in parts of the brain which are not in immediate contiguity with any substance which might be removed. Then at the time of the injury there may have been damage from that vague process known as concussion, or more likely from swelling of the parts.

Of course, if there is any intracranial pressure which can be diagnosed by ordinary neurological methods, operative relief of this may be considered. But it is too much to ask that there should be surgical cure of the more indirect and subtle effects of a severe injury.

Other phases of the treatment of the psychoses and mental peculiarities which follow upon head injury are clearly indicated. There should be absolute avoidance of stimulants, particularly of alcohol, of excessive tea and coffee, and of excessive smoking. Overheating and overwork, too, may prove disastrous. A quiet rural life is most to be desired. We have seen one case where city noises proved extremely irritative, causing a reaction that showed itself largely in anti-social conduct.

§ 310. Menstrual Mental Aberrations.

We discuss here mental disturbances at the menstrual period in women who at other times are accounted normal. Very rarely, as in a case cited, § 306, will there be difficulty in discriminating these cases from the chronic insanities which may show their main manifestations at the menstrual period. As students of criminalistics may see them, the women who have enough mental disturbance at menstrual times to cause anti-social conduct are nearly all victims of a neuropathic tendency. The stress of the periodic auto-intoxication is just enough to carry such individuals a little beyond the bounds where impulses are readily controlled. In connection with the often insoluble problem of responsibility, or in regard to the application of the term insanity to these cases a fine point comes up. To take the typical case of menstrual aberration as seen in the courts, the woman who engages in shop-lifting at her periods (*vide* § 366), we may readily find that the individual knows very well the difference between right and wrong and could even have so discriminated at her menstrual time had she been asked. But she had not the powers of self-control which were hers during the other days of the month. Impulses commanded her which under other conditions would have been resisted. Thus, so far as responsibility is concerned, this person from a standpoint of moral self-control was below normal.

There can be no doubt of the several mental changes which take place in some individuals at menstruation, any more than that many other physical conditions affect the output of mental life.[1] Marx (**305**) in an article on the forensic bearings of menstruation summarizes the facts which several investigators have brought out. Most important is the work done by means of mental tests, giving the unequivocal findings that there is ordinarily mental change at this period. Gaupp (**289**) shows the same statistically by the relation of the menstrual period to suicide. In general, the alterations seem to be that there is an increase of impulsivity and irritability, and that there is less inhibitory

---

[1] A remarkably lucid chapter on this subject is to be found in Krafft-Ebing's text book (**331**). There he says, "If an individual be neuropathic, tainted and bordering upon instability, then the normal process of menstruation may be sufficient in itself to induce disturbance of the central nervous organs, which, depending upon the severity of the taint, expresses itself in all degrees. Actual periodic insanity may result." Also his special work on Menstrual Psychoses (**332**) may be consulted.

control at this time. Aberrational tendencies, as we said before, are shown much more in women who are of the neuropathic or psychopathic type. Gudden (294) states that in all such individuals there are changes in intellectual powers, will, and emotion at this period. Anxiety states, unrest, wandering impulses, dizziness, and temporary stupefaction develop then. All this is well corroborated by observations of other authorities. We particularly introduce these citations in order to show the non-exceptional character of our own cases. Under the head of pathological stealing (§ 366) still other bearings of this subject may be found.

Very well recognized, especially by women themselves who are sufferers from it, is the premenstrual excitement which occurs for two or three days before the monthly period. During this time the tendency towards restlessness and perhaps misconduct, may be just as great or greater, than in the succeeding days. The inclination towards sex misdemeanors is certainly more at this particular time of stress.[1]

A question of practical responsibility would be whether a woman who knew of her own tendency at this period should not be held responsible for going to shops at such times. It is perfectly evident that it takes a combination of three things to arrive at the misdeed itself. There must be the prior tendency, the menstrual period, and the environmental opportunity. We have been peculiarly in position to discover cases of menstrual aberration among adolescents. It might be supposed that the frequently found instabilities of adolescence would in girls be in conjunction with menstrual upsets and add to the latter. On the whole we are surprised at the comparatively small number of cases of this kind we have seen. In the great majority of instances the instabilities of adolescence are not at all centered about the menstrual period.

The following unusually well-observed cases will be quite sufficient to show the type of behavior sometimes developing as a periodic phenomenon.

Case 127. — A girl, age 17, of splendid development and nutrition, a distinctly good-looking girl with a rather sensuous type of face indulges in such bad conduct that her mother insists

---

[1] In order to favor scientific accuracy, the more recent German literature has spoken of ovulation rather than menstruation, in its relations to misconduct. The ripening of the ovum and the menstrual flow are not necessarily quite synchronous. Krafft-Ebing (331) asserts that the mental aberration may occur at a regular period, in absence of menstrual flow.

she must be crazy to do as she does. Others say that she certainly is not mentally normal at times.

As observed by a number of good women, who have tried to help her, as well as according to the testimony of her mother, the girl is restless, independent, obstinate, and utterly willful at times. She leaves home and seeks shelter elsewhere. Even to the women who are her friends she then uses extremely bad language and shows the most violent temper. On several occasions has gone directly to them in a miserable state of intoxication. She has had sex affairs with a number of men or boys, beginning at 15 years, when she ran away from home.

Of her family we know little except that the mother is unquestionably somewhat erratic. Other relatives seem to be quite normal. The story of the girl's developmental history is quite negative. It is only during her adolescence that she has shown bad traits, and it has always been at her monthly periods that she has been so extremely cross and mean.

On the physical side as stated, we find in every way a splendid specimen. Lately there has been an operation for some pelvic infection.

On the mental side the girl proves to have extraordinary abilities in many ways. She did well in school life and on our tests gives some strikingly good results.

Mental tests: our own series:
I. 45″. No trial and error.
II. 1′ 22″. No errors.
III. Construction Test A. 11″. Minimum moves, namely, 5.
IV. Construction Test B. 52″. Minimum moves, namely, 11.
V. Puzzle Box. 3′ 28″. No errors. Steps worked out with keenest perception of logical sequence.
VI. "Aussage." Full functional account. No suggestions accepted.
VII. Reproduction of Geometrical Figures. Correct the first time.
IX. Cross Line Test A. Correct at 1st trial.
X. Cross Line Test B. Correct at 1st trial.
XI. Code Test. Got the idea herself and did the test with only one error.
XII. Memory from Visual Verbal Presentation. Nineteen of the twenty items given correctly in logical sequence.
XIII. Memory from Auditory Verbal Presentation. Eleven out of the twelve items given correctly in logical sequence.
XV. Antonyms. Average time 1″. Only one error.
XVII. Penmanship normal.
XVIII. 6th-grade arithmetic done with accuracy minus.
XIX. Reads fluently.

629

According to tests we should have to classify this girl as somewhat above the ordinary in general ability, although backward in school work. This diagnosis was confirmed by her record at various places where she was employed. Everyone stated she had most extraordinary capabilities.

Concerning herself, the girl says she sometimes gets disgusted at home and feels very cross. Does not know what is the matter. She knows she is particularly cross and obstinate at her monthly periods and perhaps does not do what is right. At these times she does not feel any too well and sometimes does not care what anybody tells her or what becomes of her.

We have attempted to analyze the possible correlation in this case between menstrual periods and bad behavior. It has been noted by several who have known this girl that she was at times ungovernable, obstinate, and that she talked as if she were insane. She herself comes to her friends and reports when doing well. At other times she is as if she were possessed of the worst impulses and quite uncontrolled. She has deliberately sought intoxication several times, and has run away four or five times. She seems then full of hatred towards everybody, including her own mother. Periodicity has been noted by several competent observers. It seems clear that the account of her disturbances occurring at menstrual times is accurate. On a couple of occasions she was so angry that she walked the streets all night, once being arrested then. Once as the reaction to her own bad conduct she made an attempt to commit suicide. She brooded for a time upon the death of a child in the family. We could get no evidence that the pelvic trouble had anything to do with her behavior — there was as much trouble after as before the operative relief. No dysmenorrhea complained of. At times she controlled herself for months, even when under adverse circumstances. It is notable that she did not do her best when apparently most protected from bad environmental influences and apparently when most was done for her in the way of giving her healthy interests. At this time her periodic disturbances happened to be very severe. In this case it is certainly true that bad behavior has occurred at other times besides menstrual periods, but never to anything like the same extent. As she has grown older her tendency has been to do better. For a year or so now there have been no outbreaks of bad behavior. She is now over 19.

This case shows the uncertainty of reckoning on the menstrual factor as the sole cause. However one can but feel that the common-sense observation of parents and other close observers that there is excessive tendency towards misconduct and irrational behavior at menstrual periods is true. The stress of this period belongs in the category of causes sufficient to send over into the border of mental aberration such an individual as the above, who is predisposed by general nature or adolescence towards upsets.

A year later we have another report. An experienced observer, not knowing our study of the case, tells us that the young woman has had great difficulty all along in controlling her impulses at menstrual periods. She did finely for nearly a year in a clerical position. Recently she has shown violent outbreaks of temper, precipitated largely by home mismanagement. These were followed by depression and recourse to drinking. This conduct has led to arrest and probation again. Her pelvic conditions are serious and demand another operation.

Mentality: Minor, menstrual aberration.   Case 127.
  Adolescent instability.   Girl, age 17.

   Physical conditions: Over-development.
           Perhaps pelvic conditions.
   Bad companions.

    Heredity: Mother erratic and not
         intelligent.
Delinquencies:
 Temper.
 Incorrigibility.   Mentality:
 Intoxication.   As above, but
 Sex + +.   very good ability.

Case 128. — A girl tremendously well endowed physically we have seen from time to time over a period of two years, between the ages of 15 and 17. We know her story before that time. She is a strong personality; has a remarkably strong face. Obstinate and rather fiery disposition. Not in the least subjective or introspective. On the mental side she is quite up to the ordinary in ability; shows no deficiencies or peculiarities by tests. Does advanced school work and has held a position that pays well. She comes of an intelligent family. Several brothers and sisters have all turned out well. The family history is all negative with the exception that one maternal great-uncle of the girl was insane, and that the mother herself is more or less a nervous invalid and has attacks of major hysteria, following a period of rapid child-bearing.

Our long account of this girl need not be given in detail. It is sufficient to say that at 13 years she began showing signs of temper, obstinacy, restlessness, and that since that time she very frequently has stolen. Her family insist that these appearances are more or less periodic. On account of the mother's invalidism there has not been careful watch kept upon this daughter in any way. Her delinquencies continued over several years, including the times she was tried in boarding schools. When first seen by us we were unsuccessful in getting at the correct facts about the beginnings of her delinquency. All that we could then obtain was that she had strong impulses to theft, and would steal things she did not want, and suffered much from the consequences. She freely acknowledged bad temper and restlessness, which were inconstant phenomena. She herself thought they had nothing to do with her menstrual periods, and there is no doubt that part of the time her misdemeanors were shown during other periods. She absolutely denied to all any undue knowledge of sex affairs. But when she was 17 years old and had been demonstrating for long an exceeding amount of interest in the opposite sex, and had been flagrantly immoral on a number of occasions, it came out that she had really been first tempted and had succumbed when she was 13 years old. All along she has had much hidden mental life, and many covert experiences.

Now for the purposes of our present discussion it is interesting to note that at times, principally when she was about 15, this girl was under the observation of a very intelligent woman, who had much influence over her. This older friend found the girl perfectly trustworthy at all times except during her monthly periods. Then she was not herself. Just prior to her period she " seemed to be miles away." Then and only then, at this age, did she steal. Her thieving consisted merely of trinkets and perhaps a little money.

In the next two years the girl became quite notorious for stealing and had some sex affairs. Her family still regard her as not being thoroughly vicious and bad, although they have had so much trouble with her. She displays at times most terrible temper. She is said to be fairly crazy about men. She now states frankly to us that the trouble with her all along has been her excessive sex temptation to which she has rarely succumbed. She has repeatedly stolen small sums from places where she has worked.

This case illustrates a point that is well worth considering, namely, whether moral aberrations shown at menstrual periods are not merely temporary excess of a tendency which is present at other times. The lid of inhibitions, which at other times is closed tight over the tendencies, is loosened. The observations of the good friend who, while not knowing the cause of this girl's bad tendencies, was able to control her except at menstrual periods, is of much interest to us. Perhaps the girl on account of inheritance of neuropathic disposition, or on account of poor development of self-control through lack of active parental oversight was not quite up to the normal in inhibitory powers in general, but one may be doubtful on such a point since she seems so strong physically and mentally. The fact is that there was general stress through repressed sex tendencies, and either this stress became excessive, or inhibitions became much lowered at the menstrual period. Reaction in aberrational behavior was sometimes confined to that period.

Early sex experiences. Case 128.
    Physical: Early development. Girl, age 17.
      Mental conflict and repressions.
        Mentality: Menstrual, minor aberrations.
          Heredity: Mother, major hysteria.
            Home conditions: Very poor control.
Delinquencies:
  Stealing +. Mentality:
  Sex. Good ability.

---

§ 311. Mental Aberrations of Pregnancy.

The relation of pregnancy to mental aberrations which in turn may lead to criminalism is well recognized. The physical condition is evident and sympathy is at once aroused on account of it, so that there has been much more recognition of the fact and less trouble in getting the case adjusted than when similar aberrations are caused by less evident conditions. There is no doubt that in some individuals pregnancy has a marked influence upon mental processes. As in menstrual conditions, the psychopaths are prone to suffer worst. There is a great increase of impulsivity, and inhibitory powers are diminished. Many references could be given to literature bearing in some way on this subject, but no satisfactory monograph has yet appeared on it. In many criminal cases it has not been the physical condition alone which has induced the mental aberration, but there have been excessive worries at this period. The most important worries, naturally, are those incident to the bearing of an illegitimate child.

What constitutes sanity or insanity, responsibility or irresponsibility, will here again frequently be a very difficult matter to decide. As Gross (**64**, p. 318) says regarding legal trials, " whoever has before him a pregnant woman with her impressions altered in a thousand different ways, may therefore well be ' up in the air.' " The difficulties surrounding cases can undoubtedly best be solved in accordance with humanitarian ideals after the facts are ascertained. Women during pregnancy are not going to be either incited or deterred to any appreciable extent in criminalistic ways by what has happened under the law to some other women.

Some of the examples from our own experience show many of the questions involved.

Case 129. — A woman of 35 years whom we had reason to study, lived for many years in such connections that we were able to get the most reliable information concerning her character. While not an educated woman, she had been in a position of considerable trust and had proved herself always extremely reliable. She had recently been married and now was pregnant. Her health now and previously had been fairly good. Her husband, a very intelligent man, tells us that early in pregnancy she showed irrational desires which have been causing quite a little trouble on account of the impossibility of his acceding to them. To the great astonishment of her friends and husband she has recently been arrested for shoplifting. With another woman known to have a bad reputation, and who probably had suggested the stealing, she had taken a good many things. A number of these were articles for which she had no use.

The case was very clear in court and this woman was soon

released. As we studied her immediately after the court proceedings it was very clear that she was in a dazed condition concerning the whole affair. She has no idea why she stole, and in
fact is in a confusional state about many things. It seems she
has thought she is going to suffer greatly at the time of her confinement and that worries her much, but worse than all is a feeling of being mixed up, as if she does not know whether all sorts
of things are exactly right or not. Her friends have realized
something of her mental condition, but there was no intimation
that it would lead to bad conduct.

Case 130. — The effect of pregnancy was well marked in another
instance where members of a family were much mixed up in delinquency. A woman of past 40 who had not had a child for over
ten years, was pregnant. Her daughter of 18, under arrest, was
studied by us at this time. She was found to be a case of pathological stealing. Scores of articles had been taken home by this
girl and placed under lock and key. Their value was considerable. The mother had been showing an immense amount of
bad temper and irritability, so that the home for months had
been intolerable to the family. Although this had nothing to do
with the stealing, the father had taken to drinking on account
of home conditions. Previously both he and his wife were of
distinctly good habits. Both came from neuropathic families.
This woman discovered the daughter's hidden stolen property, and
took many of the articles and disposed of them without saying
anything about it. Without doubt her moral attitude was not
at all during this pregnancy what it had been previously or what
it would have been at other times.

Case 131. — A young woman, 20 years old, very well developed and strong; defective vision corrected by glasses; physiognomy suggestive of sensuality; passive, weak type; small
chin and rather flat features.

Mentally: after tests we classify her as having fair mental
ability, but exceedingly poor educational advantages. She has
not been to school since she was 11 years old. We note her
peculiar mental characteristic of great passivity. She shows no
self assertion, does not even inquire as to what is going to be
done with her in any way. Reports about her show that she is
thoroughly a passive type and is easily led or taken care of by
others. There is no evidence whatever of a psychosis at the time
of the examination.

635

This woman has been a great sex delinquent. She has had illicit relations with a number of men and already has had two illegitimate children. One of these she has industriously supported. When the last one was born she attempted infanticide; indeed, she thought she had accomplished this criminal act. At the time of its birth she was doing housework for a family. Her pregnancy was not suspected. When she felt labor pains well established she went out in a rainy night to an old cemetery where she delivered herself. She then wrapped the child up and threw it under an outbuilding. The girl then returned to her room, slept during all the latter part of the night, and next morning prepared breakfast for the family as usual. Early that day some one heard a cry coming from the place where the child was and pulled it out.

There was a great deal of stress upon this girl on account of the coming of this second illegitimate child. She had taken care of the first one until recently, when she had succeeded in having it adopted by a good family. It is notable that this girl had paved the way for explanation, should her absence be noted that night, by saying that she sometimes walked in her sleep. When her absence was noted the family were alarmed, but when she returned they supposed she had been in a somnambulic condition.

We have in this case a girl who is morally colorless about sex affairs, having been brought up amidst surroundings in which illicit relationships and illegitimacy were very common. She always had to work hard, and socially was a menial. Her sex delinquencies could well be accounted for by her sex feelings being all out of proportion to any environmental development of social inhibitions. Her attempted child murder was the result of the mental and social stress of the moment. To cover her shame and disadvantage she was living under the most unfortunate conditions. She was concealing her pregnancy in ways calculated to bring about very abnormal states. It is true she showed premeditation, but the terrible circumstances under which the child was born were enough to account for almost any immediate mental upset. She says she attempted the child-murder because she did not want the people in the house to know she had a baby. She felt later, she said, that it was wrong to do as she did.

Puerperal conditions — mental aberration?	Case 131.
Home conditions: In early life great immorality, etc.	Woman, 20 yrs.
Heredity: Mother mentally subnormal. Mother had illegitimate children.	
Lack of education and other advantages.	
Sex + +. Attempted infanticide.	Mentality: Fair ability. Poor advantages.

The above case illustrates the point made by Marx (**305**) and others, namely, that in studies of criminal abortion or infanticide it is very difficult to evaluate as a factor the mental states peculiar to pregnancy and confinement.[1]

§ 312. Amnesic Fugues. Other Amnesias.

A subject of great interest to scientific students of abnormal psychology is that of transitory amnesia, with or without wandering. In cases where there is a wandering with loss of memory, the phenomenon is called an amnesic fugue. (Fugue means flight or wandering.) In this country, the whole subject seems to have less practical importance — we observed only one case among 1000 young repeated offenders — than it has in Europe where, judging by the literature, not a few vagrants are sufferers from this condition.[2] In our study we naturally should have come across more cases had they been common, because wandering or vagrancy in young people is particularly regarded as an offense.

Irrational journeyings occur as episodes in several pathological mental conditions, particularly in epilepsy, dementia precox and hysteria, and no doubt most cases of pathological wandering are to be properly subsumed under these headings. Indeed, it has been conceived by some authorities, such as Benon and Froissart (**72**), that all cases belong to some one of these

---

[1] For the special student of this subject some very keen observations concerning the bearing of social and mental conditions upon infanticide will be found in a short article by Audiffrent (**373**).

[2] French literature pertaining to the legal aspects of abnormal psychology contain many references to the subject of fugues. Joffroy and Dupouy (**313**) give a thorough survey of the literature. A more recent contribution by Mairet (**317**) covers part of the same ground. More on this same point will be found in our section on vagabondage. Patrick's (**130**) contribution on ambulatory automatism offers for readers of English practical points of much value.

diseases. But it certainly is a fact that one sees instances in which there are no other signs of disease beyond these aberrational tendencies to wander, and so rightly one cannot classify them except by this symptom. This is true both of children and of adults. In the first case that we shall mention, no diagnosis other than that of amnesic fugues seemed in the least justifiable, although one might easily speculate about its ultimate nature. When a more complete diagnosis is possible, such as that of dementia precox, or epilepsy, or hysteria, it is highly important for treatment that it be made.

The existence of other forms of amnesia plays its part in the study of offenders. Every now and again one meets some pathological type or some individual who has reacted in pathological fashion to some upsetting experience, who shows apparent forgetfulness for some period in the past. (We are not here speaking at all of the medico-legal question involved in amnesia arising from traumatism of the head, etc.) When these cases are boiled down they will be mostly found to be instances of hysteria or one of the epilepsies. The application of modern methods of psychological analysis will also clear up the nature of many of these amnesias and of the experiences which have caused them. All who work with this subject should be acquainted with the nature of Ganser's syndrome, in which the patient's desire not to know brings about a state of mind in which he does not know. Cases are recorded in which the forgotten events are recalled under hypnotic and other suggestion, and one has seen cases in which sudden disciplinary shock has brought about the same results. But this type of amnesia is probably quite different from the automatisms with which one deals in rare cases of double personality and in such phenomena as amnesic fugues.

Case 132. — This was the case of a remarkably bright child of 7 years from whose intelligent parents we obtained much detailed information. His physical and mental status can be summarized in a word. He was well developed and apparently entirely normal in all ways. Mentally he was decidedly supernormal, having especially good ability in language. We characterized him as rather a nervous type, but frank, open and agreeable.

This little boy began running away from home when he was 3 years old. At that time he wandered on to a suburban train and went out of town before he was discovered. Since then he has been away frequently, the longest time without discovery has been ten hours. Of late his attacks of wandering have been less frequent, only once in four or five weeks. He is usually fond of being neat, but during these spells is said to change in this and in other ways. His family think they can tell when his attacks are coming on by the change of expression. He is very fond of thoughtful occupations and has never been with bad companions. He never has run away with others. Sometimes he starts early in the morning before his family is up. He wanders without food and thinly clad, even in inclement weather. He does not remember where he has been. His family find him by getting the police to look for him or seeking him themselves. A remarkable feature about the case is the hardship which the boy undergoes in the course of these wanderings.

The antecedents of this boy are remarkable. He is the elder of two children, the other still being very young. The mother is an excitable, neurotic individual who herself has had occasional blank periods with wandering. Also has had several attacks of nervous prostration, etc. She comes from a family in which wandering with amnesia was common. Her father was a very erratic individual. Two of her brothers and one sister were also peculiar. One of the brothers used to journey off during peculiar lapses. Once when he was already a married man with a family, a train stopped near a place where he was resting and he suddenly jumped on and stayed away for a month. Another brother was always a wanderer, and served a term in some penitentiary. Epilepsy in the family is not known, neither is alcoholism. The family has been so broken up that about certain of the fraternity of the boy's mother there is no record available. On the father's side there is also mental peculiarity. His father was nervous and eccentric and exceedingly superstitious. He also had a brother who was somewhat peculiar.

Whence this boy derived his aberrational tendencies it was easy to see, although no ultimate diagnosis could be made, even with the help of his intelligent family. One might well think of psychic epilepsy and hysteria, or the wandering as a peculiar trait of a psychopathic personality. However the only outstanding fact was that he very definitely suffered from a tendency to wander during periods for which his memory was lost, and that this began at an age when anything in the way of simulation was hardly to be thought of.

639

Case 133. — Girl 14 years old. She has been repeatedly taken in by the police or found by her family wandering about the streets away from home. On one occasion she gave herself up to the authorities. Her running away began when she was 8 years old. On the first occasion she was found one morning sleeping on a neighbor's porch. There was no reason known for her going away, nor could she ever give any. Since that time she has been away dozens of times. She has never stolen except perhaps some little things to eat when she was away from home, but she has begged her food and slept in hallways even during inclement weather.

Physically we never found anything significant except somewhat defective vision. She bites her finger nails much. She has a perplexed expression and rather tired look about the eyes, especially after a period of wandering. She complains of little attacks in which things get dark in front of her eyes, especially in connection with headaches. Says first it gets all light and then it gets all dark in her eyes, and then goes away in a little while. Maintains these attacks come two or three times a week. The mother corroborates to the extent of noticing that occasionally the girl's eyes do look staring and queer for a little while, and she does not seem to be herself. Her expression changes in these moments. The girl has fainted a couple of times, but no other attacks are known.

On the mental side we have had very good chance to observe her, and classify her as having fair ability and normal advantages. The results on tests it is not necessary to recapitulate; there is nothing especially significant about them. The girl reached 5th grade in spite of being away from school much, and thinks she would like to be a teacher. We note that she is a sweet, quiet and shy child with a certain amount of repression, but still rather frank. No aberrational tendencies whatever were found at any time by examination, nor have we observed her in any kind of attack. We have many times talked with her about her running away. She is very sad about her behavior, and maintains always that she does not know why she wanders. Insists she does not understand what impulse carries her away, and that she does not remember the first part of the time she is away. Says she sometimes suddenly comes to herself. Says that once it was on the street 2 A. M. when she recovered herself, and she was terribly frightened and sought out a friend's house at once. On other occasions she says she is sort of confused and hardly knows what she is about. She sleeps anywhere she can and sometimes is very cold. Once she was away from home about a week and says she stayed away so long because in the latter part of the time she was so ashamed of herself. Insists there was no cause for her first running away nor for her later doing so. She does not understand what is the trouble, and wishes she could be cured of it.

From the mother, who has been repeatedly seen, we merely get the following facts, but these are most interesting. She has complained of headaches often. Mother is convinced that some sickness does seize her and make her wander away, because there is absolutely no reason otherwise for her going; she is a good girl. Everything at home is all right. Heredity is negative except for the very significant fact that the father himself, who lived in a small town in Europe, and came from fairly well-to-do parents, used himself to run away without any cause whatever until the time when he was about 20 years old. They have discussed this matter often, and he is much ashamed of what the girl does. He thinks it is just the sort of thing he used to do. He would make off from home and sleep anywhere. He says he does not know what made him do it, nor did he know at that time. He would even wander for two or three weeks until his father found him and brought him home. No epilepsy, insanity or feeblemindedness on either side of the family, but most of their relatives are in the old country and not well known. The mother herself is rather a nervous type, but she says it was largely brought on by worry over this girl. Developmental history is entirely negative; early the girl was normal and bright. When first seen, the mother maintained the girl always ran away from home at the same time every month, but our later observations did not corroborate this. The possible epileptic features of the case are only known as given above.

Mentality: Transitory aberrations, probably epileptic. Amnesic fugues.	Case 133. Girl, age 12.
Heredity: Father earlier fugues.	
Delinquencies: Running away.	Mentality: Fair ability.

641

The outcome of this case forms a social lesson. Of course the girl could not be out this way often without falling in with bad companions. The bad reputation which she had gained in her neighborhood would tend to bring this about. In spite of her family doing what they could in their way, the girl has continued at intervals to wander. Now at last she has been mixed up in an illicit sex affair. This, so far as we know, has not occurred while she has been away on her wanderings. Her character has changed a good deal with these experiences, and it is interesting to note that the last time she ran away she did so quite volitionally as a reaction against proposed discipline. She said herself that this was a definite transgression. Institutional life became imperative for her.

§ 313. Mental Aberration from Bad Sex Habits.

We have elsewhere, § 286, attempted to make it very clear that over-indulgence in depleting sex habits causes mental dullness, that is, disinclination for effort and inability to use full mental powers. To what extent these bad habits may cause aberrational conditions is not so sure. Earlier writers spoke of an insanity of masturbation, and even Marro (**273**, p. 764) recently maintains the same point. One is very certain, however, that if masturbation ever does cause insanity it must be extremely rarely. With the development of better diagnostic methods of insanity we shall later learn more on this point, and especially since the symptoms resemble those of dementia precox. We have dealt with some phases of this subject in our chapter on abnormal sexualism.

It is a common supposition among the laity, including police and court officials, that masturbation is the cause of many mental symptoms which lead to social offense. Judges rightly concede much importance to bad sex habits in the causation of delinquency, but how far to ascribe mental symptoms to this cause is not clear. However we have seen now not a few cases in which dullness, and aberration as well, probably rightly were to be ascribed to depleting sex habits since they proved thoroughly amenable to treatment for the latter. The results have been so striking in some cases that I should strongly urge the development of the very best methods of care in these cases, even though this entailed considerable expense. Of course we would not allege that all cases turn out well; we have seen poor physical conditions, mental dullness, erratic behavior, and even suicide follow upon continuance of the habit. The general aspects and behavior of the offender who is given to excessive sex practices are so well known that we need not dwell on the obvious points. A single case and its outcome will show characteristic features and possibilities.

Case 134. — Boy, 16 years old. Physically; tall, well nourished, strong for his age, but pale and unhealthy-looking; 124 lbs.; 5 ft. 5 in.; large, well-shaped head; no sensory defect; sex development already of complete adult type; physiognomy very peculiar, weak profile, small chin, watery, puffy eyes; very evasive expression, stiff and unresponsive. Remarkably untidy for his age, in spite of coming from a very decent family; appears in knickerbockers.

Mental tests: our own series:
I. 1' 55". No trial and error on triangles.
II. 1' 23". 4 errors.
III. 2' 34". 22 total moves. 6 impossibilities tried, and 5 repetitions of impossibilities.
IV. Failure in 10'. For 8' had been trying interchange of 4 pieces in all sorts of impossible situations.
V. 5' 30". Errors occupied 4' 40" and then the steps were done consecutively with one error between.
VI. Gave a very slight account of picture at free recital, but added 20 items upon cross-examination.
VII. One of these figures was reproduced in absurd forms and only correct at 3d trial. The other correct at 1st trial.
VIII. All correct.
IX. Correct at 1st trial.
X. Correct only at 3d trial.
XI. Got the idea by himself and accomplished the task with only two errors — strange contradiction to the preceding test.
XII. Very poor result. Only 8 items out of 20 given correctly.
XIII. Also very poor result. Only 6 items out of 12 given correctly.
XIV. Correct at 2d trial in 34".
XV. Only 1 error. Average time 2.9".
XVI. 73 and 78 squares tapped respectively at 1st and 2d trials, with 3 errors made at last trial.
XVII. Writes a fairly mature hand and composes rather well a long letter, but makes errors in grammar and spelling. (Writes entirely about himself and his own sensations under various conditions.)
XVIII. Does long division correctly with some effort.

643

XIX. Reads a 5th-grade passage correctly except for some long words. Monotonous voice.

XXII. Knows the ordinary items of history and current events. Knows practically nothing about scientific items. Seems to have very little interest in recreations. Has not played ball for 2 years.

During this interview with him we noted the following important features of his behavior. He sits abnormally quiet, except for movements of his face. For instance, for about three-quarters of an hour he sat quite still in a remarkably uncomfortable position — one leg and foot were held inwards and sideways. Facial muscles unusually active, considerable twitching of them. He shows jerky movements of the eyes, and moves his nose somewhat, and even his mouth. Draws the latter down in various peculiar positions. Gaze always averted; never smiles; hair is long and is blown over his eyes. He never pushes it back, but attempts to get it out of the way by tossing his head. In his deep voice he drawls his words in sleepy fashion. He never vouchsafes any information, although he may add a little to what is asked. Although such a big fellow he cries a little, but for the most part is apathetic. As observed under detention in the school-room one morning he refused to do any work at all, but sat quietly. In the afternoon when he was threatened with no dinner he did get to work.

" I don't want to work. There ain't no reason why I should n't. I 'm not sick. There 's nothing the matter with me. I just don't want to. Don't feel like it. It 's too hard. No, I never tried it. I tried chopping wood at the house. That was too hard. My father's mouth is too large. He scolds. No, I don't play no games. I don't get to go out. I have n't been out for about a year. Used to like ball all right, but not any more. No, can't swim. I don't want to, I tell you. That 's all. I don't like to play. Sure, I want to go home. I don't know that I would work. You can't do nothing for me. Don't want nothing done. At home I just sit around — sit quiet — I don't do anything. No, I don't read. I feel all right. I lay awake sometimes. I 'm not happy—I 'm not sad—I 'm not nothing. I get sore at my father. He scolds. I had a fight with my sisters. I never speak to them. Have not spoken to them for about 2 years. Oh, it was about something — I forget. I don't know what 's going to happen. Sure, I was arrested before. Quit school at 14. Have not worked at all. No, no friends. Coffee about 12 cups a day, I guess. I don't feel like working. My sisters work. I don't talk to them. Never go to the parks. No headaches. There 's nothing the matter with me."

This very curious fellow earlier was sent to an institution on account of truancy. Since he left school at 14 he has done no work. Has occasionally been quarrelsome at home, but for the most part simply wants his own way and to be quiet. His father has not even been able to get him down town within the last year to buy a suit of clothes. He is now brought in by his parents on account of his general recalcitrant behavior. His mother maintains he is not right in his head, and wants him sent to an insane asylum. Parents deny any insanity, feeblemindedness or epilepsy in either family. The mother is a nervous and irrational woman, but both she and her husband are well intentioned. This boy is the youngest of four children. Two others are alive and doing well. There has been no trouble whatever at any point of this boy's developmental period. He walked and talked early. Never been very sick in his entire life. It is true, as he says, that he drinks at least 10 or more cups of coffee a day. He sits quietly about the house and sometimes does not speak for a long time. After a time, the boy went fully into the question of his habits with us. He shows no signs of worrying particularly about them, nor did he seem to have much conception that he was suffering from indulgence in them. No sensitiveness in this matter. He told us he had learned masturbation when he was about 9 or 10, and had practiced it very frequently since — at times more than once a day. It came out that the father knew something of this, but not that the case was so bad.

The tentative diagnosis was made that perhaps the aberrational tendency might be due to these excessive habits, and the boy was sent to a certain institution for delinquents where he could have very close watching in this regard. He showed steadily great improvement, and was released after a few months. Since then he has been completely changed in behavior. For more than 2 years he has had a completely good record, has been working steadily, and turning in his money properly at home.

§ 314. Hysterical Mental Aberrations.

The term hysteria represents an abnormal condition of the nervous system which is evidenced by the most numerous and variable signs and symptoms of mind and body that are to be found in any disease. It would be hopeless here to attempt even a review of the findings in their various " complexes." Fortunately, since the individuals suffering from it are particularly hard to handle and difficult for the laity to understand, this ailment has little connection with the major forms of delinquency. The bodily signs of this psycho-neurosis run all the way from epileptoid convulsions and periods of actual blindness to perhaps a loss of feeling in hand or arm. The mental symptoms run through a long category.[1] The etiology of this condition we also cannot enter into for this involves many phases of technical discussion.

Certain manifestations of hysteria are very well known and easily recognized. It is not generally realized that hysteria exists in forms where the individual does not have attacks of excitement. The general impression that it exists only in females is incorrect, although it is much rarer among males. The hysterical individual is correctly conceived as being an individual who is often more or less of a simulator, and who does not carry through delinquent actions which demand considerable exercise of will power. It is a fact that such persons are threateners rather than doers, but yet occasionally their mental condition does lead them much farther than mere intentions. Going over the cases of our hysterical offenders we note that they are guilty of the following offenses: false accusations and other excessive lying, threatening suicide, running away, vagrancy, begging and obtaining money by other false pretensions, petty stealing, notorious obscenity and the more passive sex offenses. As our statistics show, § 92, numerically hysteria does not play a very large part in producing delinquency. Fully realizing the impossibility of covering the varieties of hysteria, about which many volumes have been written, nevertheless giving a short summary of a typical case that has been amply studied, socially and psychologically, seems profitable.

Case 135. — Girl of 18. This girl and her family have given a great deal of trouble to a number of worthy people who have attempted to help them out of their unfortunate circumstances. They have always been most solicitous about receiving aid in many ways, but no one has even been able to get them upon a stable footing. Several factors enter into the family condition, not the least of which is defective heredity. They are immigrants and a thorough knowledge of their antecedents is not to be had, but

---

[1] The student of the mental signs of hysteria can best be referred to the volume by Janet (**197**) on the subject. There the multitudinous forms of the mental manifestations are clearly set forth.

some facts are very well known. The father was a steady worker. The mother was a mental border-line case, a semi-responsible individual of mental capacity in some ways, but said by some specialists to be really insane. Other competent observers have maintained she was merely an excessive case of hysteria. After the father died the family suffered much from poverty although there were certain funds always at their disposal and they had a little property. The family environment was defective, so far as our patient was concerned, through poverty, the mother's erratic control and irrational bickering and complaining, early illicit sex knowledge acquired in the home, and the existence of an hysterical and quarrelsome sister. Her delinquencies have consisted in excessive lying, obtaining help by misrepresentations, failure to hold good positions which have been given her, begging, and petty stealing.

Physically we first found this girl in poor general condition. She was undernourished and anemic. Weak type of face, small mouth held in a queer compressed fashion. She laughed often in a foolish fashion, and did not directly answer a question. (All these conditions, as treatment has been carried out, have vastly improved.) No special sense defect noted. Menstruation appeared normally and is regular. All other examination negative except palatal reflex minus, sensation of pain in the arms distinctly diminished. Complaint of numbness in the fingers, and of peculiar headaches when it hurts her to comb her hair. Distinct dermographism.

On the mental side it was easy to grade her. She was ordinary in ability, considering her advantages. Except for her showing poor psychomotor control on our tapping test, all of her performances were intelligent and quite satisfactory. The results were so uniform there is no need of giving them in detail. (Often hystericals give very irregular results.) She had passed 6th grade in school.

Much more important than the results of tests was the discovery of her peculiar mental attitude. She displayed much indignation against the world, and tried to explain away her delinquencies. Later she was somewhat affected by recounting her offenses, but showed no particular concern for what she had done. She became very friendly, but from time to time showed herself extremely unreliable, even under the better circumstances to which she was introduced. Her main source of worry and mental conflict proved to be about sex affairs, and she said she desired to be cured of bad sex habits which had been somewhat indulged in since she was a child of 4 or 5 years. At times she was obsessed by day-dreams about these affairs, and at night her dreams were fairly saturated with representations of sex matters which were vivid almost to the point of hallucination.

This girl has been most intelligently handled, and her progress during a couple of years has been steadily upward. Whereas she used to give way to attacks of excitement with crying and perhaps wringing of hands, and to times of religious fervor, periods of total moral unreliability, times of muteness and strange fits of giggling and laughing, she now is a fair worker, is much more content and her facial expression is greatly changed for the better. Her friends have helped her to overcome her sex habit and she has stopped excessive drinking of tea to which she was prone previously.

Mentality: Aberrational. Hysteria.	Case 135. Girl, age 18.
Mental conflict — about sex, with repressions. Obsessional thought and dreams.	
Masturbation.	
Heredity: Mother semi-responsible.	
Home conditions: Neglect, poverty, excitement.	
Physical conditions: Poor nourishment, etc.	
Lying +. Unreliability. Begging. Petty stealing.	Mental: Ordinary in ability. Hysterical.

The treatment of hysterical offenders is only properly to be carried out under the auspices of a neurologist who will attempt to get at what there may be in the physical and mental background of the case. It is undoubtedly a fact that many cases of hysteria in girls are straightened out under conditions of regular living, but the exaggerated cases need thorough investigation and treatment of the kind which is undertaken in special private practice.

§ 315. Transitory Mental Aberrations.

Of the existence of transitory mental aberrations there is no more doubt than there is of the fact that the mind of any normal person is not consciously controlled at some moments. Indeed, many of the most stable people can recall short periods when they themselves behaved in some fashion quite out of accord with their general character. Of course, the transitory aberrations which are of importance as producing delinquency occur in individuals whom by temperament we should expect to be upset by stress. There is no need here illustrating the general fact, for under our headings of epilepsy, hysteria, amnesia, menstrual aberration, adolescent conditions, etc., etc., there are numerous instances given of these transitory phenomena. The bearing which the adventitious circumstances of worry, poverty, sorrow, and hardship may have in producing the aberration in predisposed individuals stands out clearly. Zingerle (40) in his study of the subject brings this out clearly. He shows, for instance, (p. 4) in a case that we could hardly parallel in this country, how hunger and sorrow unbalanced a father to the extent of rendering him a murderer of his beloved children.

The student of a case of transitory aberration will do well never to omit thorough consideration of the influence of alcohol or habit-forming drugs. In habitués transitory pathological mental states are often observed quite apart from the moment of actual intoxication. Of course such effects are seen more often in the psychopathically predisposed. Everybody sees the danger which exists, under our present methods of deciding cases according to the theory of responsibility, in giving too much chance for the plea of transitory aberration. But that does not militate against the fact of its existence, one of the best proofs of which is that deeds are enacted which are totally at variance with the desires and impulses of the individual in his normal state. There may be other criteria, but this is a feature of the misconduct which frequently obtains.

Those who examine offenders shortly *after arrest* must not forget the possibility of the existence of a mental condition dependent upon the incrimination and arrest itself. We have seen cases in which we felt it unsafe to pass judgment upon the mental condition for the time being, because of the possibility

of the above factor. Generally, the mental states which supervene partake of the nature of depression, dullness, apathy, immo-
bility, and even negativism. Sommer (**163**) in his work on criminal psychology devotes a chapter to the subject. Risch (**374**)
gives a clear presentation of this group of cases, and calls attention to the fact that the psychogenetic states which may occur as
the result of arrest are often regarded as simulation by the laity
and as dementia precox by the specialist. Of course with the
passage of time the diagnosis is cleared up, but the existence of
such conditions shows the danger of rapidly passing judgment
for court purposes.

CHAPTER XXII

Minor Mental Aberrations — *Concluded*

Adolescent Mental Aberrations. § 316. Diagnostic Considerations. § 317. Illustrative Cases. § 318. Varieties of the Type. § 319. Treatment. **Psychoses from Alcohol.** § 320. Nature of Alcoholic Psychoses. § 321. Alcoholism and Criminality. § 322. Treatment under the Law. § 323. Psychoses of Chronic Alcoholism. § 324. Acute Alcoholic Psychoses. § 325. Alcoholic Psychoses in Adolescents. **Psychoses from Drugs.** § 326. Psychoses from Morphine. § 327. Psychoses from Cocaine. § 328. Psychoses from Other Drugs. § 329. **Other Minor Mental Aberrations.**

ADOLESCENT MENTAL ABERRATIONS.

§ 316. **Diagnostic Considerations.** — In treating the subject of minor mental aberrations which arise during adolescence as distinguished, on the one hand, from the actual insanities, and, on the other hand, from the normal impulsions and peculiarities of this period, we may be at times on ground difficult to maintain. But in some cases the point stands out very clearly that there is at this period an abnormal lack of balance which does not develop into any typical psychosis. We have seen numerous cases that prove this point, and which confirm what we say in discussion of adolescence in general (§ 336), namely, that mental traits during their awakening at this epoch may very readily pass over into abnormality.

The very nature of many of these nascent characteristics, egotism, self-assertion, jealousy, psychic hyperæsthesia, feelings of physical exaltation, and so on, directly suggests lack of balance. The quite normal development of this period includes increase in the power of self-control, reasoning, and development of ideals, but these latter inhibitory forces may come late for the purposes of good mental balance and morality.   Marro (**273**) classifies mental troubles of adolescence as those (*a*) to which the individual has a predisposition, and which merely find in pubertal stress a directly inciting cause; (*b*) mental troubles which are by their nature allied with the evolutionary conditions of puberty; (*c*) mental troubles which are due to imperfect evolution at puberty. Whether his divisions hold or not, at least these theories place the causations of abnormal conditions at this period clearly before us.

Many authors unite in the statement that it is at puberty when the instinctive and moral traits give most trouble in individuals of the degenerate or inferior type. Their powers of self-control are innately too weak to stand the new demands made upon them. It is often also said that at puberty the individual first shows marked evidence of being mentally the offspring of his ancestors. That is, certain hereditary mental traits first tend to show themselves at that period.

There are very few cases of insanity among young children. Even by pubescence cases of psychoses are numerically unimportant. When they do occur then, as Clouston (280) well says, there is an accompanying preponderance of nervous troubles, showing lack of psychomotor control. The duration of the trouble is short, although there may be remissions. But farther along in adolescence the mental ailment stands more by itself, and more often shows typical symptoms belonging to the psychoses. Even when there is not the development of an actual insanity there may be a tendency to maniacal symptoms — this is seen much more often than melancholia — and there may be religious or erotic preoccupation.

As we have noted our cases we should say that the most characteristic symptom of those who showed temporary aberrational troubles in adolescence was that of extreme incalculability, general mental incoherence. The individual frequently seems to be so played upon by varying internal impulses and environmental influences that conduct becomes utterly irrational. It would be impossible to say that the behavior reactions fall at all within the broad lines of any typical psychosis. Any one of the new characteristics, or visionary scheming, or irregularity of temper, peculiar aversions, the general unsettled feelings, the recklessness, may be expressed with enough force to be reckoned a definite mental aberration.

A large number of the cases gradually develop the ability to normally adjust themselves. Rarely under some great stimulus there may be a sudden growth of will power that overcomes the tendency to erraticism. Altogether, the psychiatrist would find much difficulty in placing these cases anywhere in his categories, as named by types of behavior. That so little attention is paid in works on mental troubles to this class can only be due to the fact that nearly all books have been written by men who have relied mostly on institutional experience.[1] To be sure these individuals give considerable trouble, but frequently they are regarded simply as social offenders, and do not receive professional attention. We venture to say that some new chapters in text books would be written if the authors sought extensive experience in juvenile court work, or in institutions for young delinquents.

A strong, complicating feature of many adolescent mental aberrations is found in the debilitating mental and physical effects of bad sex habits, particularly masturbation. Such overstimulation of the nervous system at this period of hyperirritability, greatly predisposes to general erratic conduct. As seen among young offenders there is no other cause of these temporary mental aberrations at all equal to this. The common-sense observations on the subject by many judges and other court officials are true to the facts. We discuss this more properly elsewhere, § 245, § 313.

The difficulty in differential diagnosis of the minor mental troubles of adolescence is often very great. It is often impossible to give any specific name to the type of trouble. When it comes to the question of prognosis, the matter tends to be a little clearer. If the disturbances are grafted upon a basis of mental subnormality or markedly defective hereditary traits, then, of course, the outlook is comparatively poor. One need not be nearly so pessimistic about the outlook as in general psychiatric practice, for the unexpected often happens in the way of cures. Our case histories well illustrate many of the above points. In reading them it should be remembered that these are not the histories of adolescents who could definitely be considered insane to the extent that they need to be sent to a hospital for the insane, or that they need be taken before a court to have the fact of their irresponsibility determined. They belong between the insane and those who are showing only normal adolescent phenomena. So far as their acts are concerned, these are not under the sway of normal powers of self-control, and that is the fact of vital importance for us here.

§ 317. **Illustrative Cases. Case 136.** — A young man of 19 we have had under observation for about 4 years. Earlier he

---

[1] Statistical data, even on insanity among adolescent criminals as given by North (**281**), is worth little for us because they represent the findings on cases that have been actually found insane by courts, or deal with the well-known forms of chronic insanity which happen largely to begin during adolescence.

was repeatedly in trouble with the court, and it was on account of his extensive offenses that he was first called to our attention. He had often stolen, associated with thieving companions, and run away from home. At times he led the life of a typical thief, running down alleys, sleeping out anywhere. So far as known he never stole alone, it was always with other boys. At school he was somewhat of a truant, lazy and inattentive. Although he was given good chances at boys' clubs and the like, he was always extremely changeable, first into one trouble and then another. He broke open a cash register, stole a handbag from a woman, was arrested with other boys in the middle of the night while looting a shop, and twice was committed to semi-penal institutions.

The boy was born in this country from immigrant parents who are on the upgrade financially and socially. The mother is a very intelligent woman for her class and much concerned about the boy. From her and others we probably get very reliable information. He is the fifth of 8 children. None dead and no miscarriages. The other children have done very well indeed in school and in business life. We hear that there is no insanity, feeblemindedness or epilepsy in either family. Developmental history was practically negative. Pregnancy said to have been normal, and birth all right. Walked and talked early, and never been severely ill. Has received intelligent care. Tonsils out at 12 years. It is of much interest to learn that up to within a few months of the time we first saw him at 15 this boy had not grown at all for years.

He only reached the 6th grade at the time he was 14, but this was on account of shifting about in schools, and less perhaps because of his truancy. He began work at 14 and held a number of jobs for very short times. The longest period was 2 1-2 months as a telegraph messenger, until he grew mentally steadier at 17 years.

On the physical side we found him when first seen to be a very well developed and nourished lad. He was then 15 1-2 years. Weight 108 lbs.; height 5 ft. 1 3-4 in. No sensory defects noted. Signs of premature sex development. Voice already changed, mustache appearing. Fairly large head — 54.7 cm. circumference; 19 cm. length; 15 cm. width. Physiognomy somewhat peculiar, more on account of habitual expression than any abnormality of features. Restless facial movements. Lips twisted about much. Most definite, perhaps, is a peculiar quizzical look, which many observers have noted.

In the mental examination it soon became evident that he was up to the ordinary in ability and information, and that his peculiarities did not show in the tests. But in the accounts and our observations of his conduct, and in his own stories about himself, complete proof of aberrational tendencies was obtained.

Results on mental tests are as follows:

Our own series:

I. 1′ 20″. Very little trial and error, even on the triangles.

II. 56″. No errors.

III. Construction Test A. 1′ 15″. No repetition of impossibilities.

IV. Construction Test B. 3′ 14″. Done by method of reasonable trial and error. (This was done before our present method of scoring.)

V. Puzzle Box. 2′ 50″. Steps followed out in logical order, with good perceptions.

VI. "Aussage." Enumerative account, very good in detail. No suggestions accepted.

VII. Reproduction of Geometrical Figures. Correct at 1st trial.

VIII. Learning Arbitrary Symbol Associations. All correctly done.

IX. Cross Line Test A. Correct at 1st trial.

X. Cross Line Test B. Correct at 1st trial.

XI. Code Test. Done promptly and without error.

XV. Antonyms. All words given correctly and rapidly. (Time not scored as later.)

XVI. Motor Coördination Test. Exceedingly good result. 112 and 113 squares tapped respectively at 1st and 2d trials, with only one error on 1st trial.

XVII. Writes a rapid and fairly mature hand.

XVIII. Does long division correctly, but not fractions.

XIX. Reads difficult pieces of poetry fairly fluently.

XX. Plays a foresighted game of checkers.

XXII. Used to read the usual boys' books as taken from the library. Knows the ordinary items of history and geography, but very little about scientific things. Goes to nickel shows practically every night.

From a number of people who have been interested in this boy we hear of his peculiar actions. Various observations run as follows. The report from school was that he was very clownish, lazy and inattentive. With one teacher whom he especially liked he did well for about 6 months, otherwise was troublesome. Many measures have been tried by his mother and others, but he did not respond. Cannot be interested in lectures, or in other subjects of boyish interest. One person said he was not able to hold a job for longer than a week because he could not concentrate his mind. One observer who had long known him, said he was a most peculiar boy. Had visions about what he was going to do, and was always changing from one thing to the other. Notwithstanding his delinquent tendencies, he really was a timid fellow, easily frightened. We note that he is very silly in his talk and actions. At 15 he appears as a large child, not manly.

Among the boys he was regarded as peculiar, and spoken of as "Crazy Jim." A relative, who could give him a place to work, will not have him on account of his foolishness. He answers quickly and pertly. Tries to be smart in a shallow way in whatever is said or done by him. Laughs foolishly in one's face. One teacher, who had had much experience with boys, said she could do nothing with him because he answered so foolishly. On one occasion when under detention he told an attendant he wanted to go to an insane hospital, and suddenly drew from his pocket a clipping from a newspaper which in large letters had the name of the hospital on it. Altogether a number of lay observers were in accord that this boy was irrational and probably insane.

We have seen him very repeatedly over a number of years, and intimately known his development, and his own account of himself at intervals has been of great interest. He has always been on friendly terms with us and told his story directly and cogently. Perhaps at first when he was heavily involved in delinquency, he lied somewhat, but never very much. We have watched his evolution into a completely self-controlled individual. His story, as told at first, ran as follows:

"I'm all right, except my nose which sometimes gets stopped up. Was sent out for 3 1-2 months this last year. Had been stealing. The trouble was I ran around with so much bad company. Ran around with them so much it was hard to keep away from them. This last trouble happened on a Sunday. Me and that other little kid was down on the lake front. We went past a fruit stand where there was a cash register. We began looking at it, and talking about opening it. He went over, and I heard a ring, and I got scared, and ran up an alley. The man caught the little kid, and found 65 cents on him. That was my own money. Father gave it to me. I had on my old clothes and the pockets were full of holes, and I gave it to him to keep. I went home and the detective followed me. I seen him and ran out in the alley. I went down to the boy's house to see what was the matter, and a kid told me he was arrested. I told him I had run away from home, and had no place to sleep. He gave me some carpet to sleep on in his back yard. The man said there was $8 missing. My mother went and paid $4 to him. She did not want to have any trouble. The judge said I ran away, and left the little boy to his fate. Before that I used to go around with another fellow that stole. When I was about 8 years old a kid learned me to go down town and steal. He used to take me around. I never stole alone, always with kids. I get frightened if alone."

"Down there at S. where I was for a week it is mostly iron works. No good kids down there. About the only thing they do is to play cards out in a lot and drink. I was out with them and they kept saying, 'Now you drink,' and passed around a pail. I am not used to it and so I got drunk. That's the first time I was ever that way. My father gave me some spending money down there, and I took it and bought a rifle, and a kid took it and kept it. I did not want my father to know I had it. The next morning the kid would not give it back to me."

"The trouble with me is I do too much thinking. Maybe I begin work and then I get to thinking, and I start to work again, and don't seem to know what I am doing. Maybe I'm reading about something, and then I get to thinking, and put the book aside, and then start reading again. Sometimes I think about boys and sometimes about girls, and sometimes about other things. Sometimes it comes like a picture in my mind. No, I don't remember my dreams. In the daytime I'm thinking I'm doing things, or maybe taking things, and getting caught, or maybe not getting caught, or maybe I'm fighting and all like that. Then comes the capture and a lot of robbers and all strange things like that. It comes many a time like that in my mind. I get to reading, and get to thinking, and I don't know what I'm reading about, and have to read it all over."

At a later time he gave the following account of himself: "Been many places to work lately. I quit or was fired. Was arrested for disorderly conduct. Was out on the street throwing matches lighted into the air. I thought it was fun to throw them up, and the copper arrested me for nothing. I took the matches out of a saloon, and the copper took me in, and the fellow said I was trying to steal cigars. Well, I don't know what is the matter. I think myself it is something like that I am not right. Guess I

657

am kind of luny. I would not like a farm. It is too quiet. I throw money away foolish, out to the Park on shooting gallery or anything. That teacher was down on me because I could not do numbers without talking to myself."

After his second incarceration he looked well, and said he was not going to be so foolish in the future. He constantly regarded himself in the light of a boy who was foolish, or even distinctly queer mentally. Again his good intentions only lasted for a little while, and he was arrested for burglary. At this time in appearance he was queerer than ever. His face had grown thin, his long hair was brushed back in eccentric fashion, his eyes wavered in nystagmoid movements. He looked most strenuous and peculiar. This time constructive measures were urged instead of more incarceration, and when he was placed on probation he asserted, " Now, I will make good."

His behavior from then on, namely, the time when he was 16 1-2 years, has been steady and reliable. He reported regularly to his probation officer, who did much to encourage him, and after a month of good behavior announced that he really did not understand himself, he was doing so well. After that he repeatedly said he wondered why he was doing so well, and what was keeping him straight. It is notable that, following on his own success, he has taken up the idea of helping others straighten out, and has done wonders with a crowd that had become very troublesome about a certain school. He went in for athletics, and, recently seen, he is found to be in very good physical condition, with a much changed expression. The former curious facial movements and quizzical expressions have entirely disappeared. He has worked in one place for a year and developed reliability in every way. He saves up money in business-like fashion, and is anxious to be employed every minute. In looking back upon his old career he still regards himself as having been somewhat crazy over a period of years. Says he was queer then and a little off. Distinctly feels he is an entirely different person now. " I guess I did n't know what I was doing then. I have changed so that I am another fellow now."

The prognosis in this case was long held in abeyance, but in the light of our later experience with cases of this type it should have been more favorable from the start. The boy could control himself quite well at times, as evidenced by tests, and had good ability to size himself up, even when we first saw him. His misbehavior was evidently the result of erratic impulses which were irregularly manifested, and at no time really connoted an essential lack of self-control. The trouble was one of temporary internal maladjustment.

Mentality: Aberrational, probably temporary, adolescent.

Physical. Features of adolescent abnormality. Very rapid growth late.

Stealing + +.
Burglary.
Running away.

Case 136.
Boy, age 17.

Mental:
Good ability,
but aberrational.

Case 137. — Very different manifestations were found in the case of a sweet-appearing little girl of 13 1-2 years who was showing most dangerous delinquent tendencies. The main complaint was that recently at home she had indulged in such threatening and vicious behavior that her family were really terrified. Our information came from different members of the family, so that there could be no question about the truth of what the girl at first denied. While her mother was ill in bed this child threatened to kill her, and made such attempts that she had to be constantly watched. On one occasion she turned on the gas. At another time went with a lighted match to the edge of the bed and said, " No, I won't burn you up — no, not at all." She has thrown milk bottles at the other children, actually pinched pieces of skin off her sister's arm, pinched other children so they were black and blue, and stared and grinned at them in a curious way. Her language has been vile at times, and she would spit at her father and mother. She threw a glass on the floor, and threatened to throw a knife at her mother in bed.

While the above offenses are prominent, still other phases of her conduct give an idea of her mental condition. Her teacher reports that other children tell of the strange things she says to them. She appears melancholy at times in the school-room. At home she locked herself in the clothes closet when other members of her family came. Told her mother that she wanted her to die so she could get a step-mother. Bites her finger nails, pulls her hair, and sometimes lies on the bed and screams. It is notable that she always controls herself when strangers are present, although even then she shows some nervousness. For a time she was sent to a relative's home, and there behaved very well. Her father says she was never anything but the best of girls until a couple of months ago. Since then she swears terribly and uses words that were never known in his house. Even in the presence of other relatives she may whisper bad things to her mother.

The fairly intelligent parents say there is no epilepsy, insanity or feeblemindedness on either side. We have seen several other members of the family, and from them hear the same. This girl is the third of nine children, the rest of whom are doing well, with the exception of a brother who has recently gotten into the court on account of disobedience and getting into bad company. The pregnancy was healthy. Birth was normal, and she never has been very ill. Has had several children's diseases mildly. Passed for 6th grade at 13. Recently on account of mother's illness has had to stay out of school frequently. It may be this girl's mental upset was caused by a fright which she had some time ago. An officer called to arrest her brother for being a member of some crowd that had committed a depredation, and, as the officer came in the front door, the boy ran out the back, and there was much turmoil. It was within a few days of this that she developed her present strange tendencies. She has not yet menstruated.

Physically we found a fairly well developed and nourished girl. Weighed 96 lbs.; 5 ft. in height. A very pleasant expression, innocent-looking and rather pretty child. Complains of headaches, but on account of her unreliability, one is not sure to what extent she has suffered. She has not complained much to her family. Nothing of importance was noted in the entire physical examination except asymmetrical ears, the helix on one side being almost flat.

On the mental side our findings were full of significance. It was quite evident she had a defective remembrance of many of her actions, and that she was not quite well oriented. On tests we found a good deal of irregularity as follows.

Our own series:
I. 2′ 32″. No trial and error on triangles.
II. 1′ 22″. No errors.
III. Construction Test A. 20′. 5 moves.
IV. Construction Test B. 1′ 10″. 11 moves.

660

V. Puzzle Box. Failure in 10'. Says quite sure she can't do this; works quite aimlessly in a half-hearted way.

VI. "Aussage." Very short functional account given. Maintains she did not notice a great many of the details that were asked. No suggestions accepted.

VII. Reproduction of Geometrical Figures. A, correct at first exposure. B, incorrect.

VIII. Learning Arbitrary Symbol Associations. No errors.

IX. Cross Line Test A. Correct only at 4th trial after drawing it three times herself.

X. Cross Line Test B. Failure at 4th trial after drawing it three times herself.

These last two results are very remarkable in comparison to most of her other work.

XII. Memory from Visual Verbal Presentation. Eleven out of the twenty items given in correct logical sequence.

XIII. Memory from Auditory Verbal Presentation. Nine out of the twelve items given in correct logical sequence.

XIV. Instruction Box. Done correctly only at the 3rd trial.

XV. Antonyms. Five errors. Average time, 3.4".

XVI. Motor Coördination Test. 66 and 71 squares tapped respectively at 1st and 2d trials with 3 errors in 1st trial and one in 2nd trial.

XVII. Penmanship normal. Wrote a coherent composition about a farm.

XIX. Reads 5th-grade passage fairly well.

XXII. Information. Is quite inaccurate about the items of geography and history which have been presented to her in school. Some of them given correctly, however. Is very little of a reader. Does not play games and says she likes best to play with a baby.

We feel assured this girl does not talk freely to us although quite pleasantly. Mind does not seem to be altogether on what she is talking about. Seems just a little dazed, then comes to herself, and turns quickly. Answers shortly and in rather an off-hand way, but always pleasantly. Does not express herself at length about anything. Under the circumstances is notably lacking in emotional reaction towards the whole situation, either as being brought to the court, or on account of her bad actions at home. Although she says she wants to go home she does not show any feeling over it. She says she thinks she could control herself now, but steadily maintains she does not remember what she has done. Says she does know that one day her head felt very queer and dizzy. In the presence of one aunt, who corroborates the story of other members of the family, she absolutely denies to us that she has behaved so badly. Later in friendly fashion she gives us her own account of the troubles in the following peculiar way.

" I have pains in my head and sometimes go to bed." (On account of pain?) " No, sir, cause felt kind of tired. My mother says I talk so much, but I don't know anything about it. I don't remember. Mama and papa says I speak foolish. I used to keep on talking, she says. Three weeks about I've been that way. Wasn't in school for three weeks, about two weeks. Was in 5th grade, supposed to pass for 6th, but I didn't have examinations. Started at around 6 years. Born in Chicago. Think I was in 3rd grade for a year and a half and in 5th grade — think two years in 5th grade on account of arithmetic. I usen't to understand, now I understand. Went over to grandmother's two weeks — stayed there two or three days. Went to other grandmother's about a week, stayed about the same days, too. I don't know what was the matter. Mother said I used to bother her and she wanted me to go. Mother is sick with rheumatism. I haven't done things, my mother didn't say I done things. I just spoke all the time. Oh, I've slapped them — sisters, when they done wrong, that's all. I haven't pinched her." (Urged to tell the truth.) " I remember long time ago I pinched her, and she slapped me back. Think it was about three weeks ago. She tried to fight with me — sassed me back. Don't think I remember that I did anything to mama. Said I wouldn't hit her with something I had in my hand — spoon or something. Never took no knife to her. Just happened to say it. Never meant to say it. I remember it was a spoon. Never threw it at her." (More than once?) " Don't know, just once." (The glass?) " Accidentally I threw it down when I was washing dishes, didn't do it on purpose. I wasn't mad. My aunt said I'd shake the bed. If I'd ask something, maybe she'd not hear and be asleep, and I'd just touch it like that."

This little girl says often aside to herself, as if she were trying to persuade herself of something " I don't remember, I don't remember."

" I think what I did do I never meant to. They say I threw a spoon at my mama. Don't remember saying any bad words. Even my mother says I don't remember so well. I don't remember if I used any bad expressions. I feel kind of excited when I talk. I always used to be nervous. If I'd say one thing I'd always keep on talking it — saying if I would hit my mother with this or that — I'd keep on saying something — if I'd say I'd hit my mother with this.   Then I might say something else with different things.   My mother told me I would say she was crazy, and I would forget all about it.   Forget that I had said it.   Once I lit the gas is true, and threw the match down, and I told my sister she would burn her skirt, but I never told anybody I would throw the matches.   She told my father I said I would burn her, but she must not have understood. I don't remember taking any matches to my mama.   Don't remember."

"Been scared many times when anything would happen.   If any one would cut themselves, like my little sister, I used to feel afraid of it.   It was many years ago that I used to feel afraid. Once my father fell off a wagon and I was frightened about it. When my mother was sick I was afraid about that, too.   Because she got up and couldn't move her arms.   Used to feel scared and nervous about it.   Afraid she shouldn't get worse.   Once there was a man hurt, and the ambulance came past and I was scared.   There was man across the street, and he shot himself and his wife.   That was about three months ago.   When my aunt's baby died and they came and told my mother and I felt sorry.   Sometimes at night I would be afraid to go to sleep.   I would hear some noise."   (Urged to tell what frightened her most.   She has not told about her brother.)   "One day a man came in to see if my brother was working, and I was just coming out of my bedroom, and my brother ran and the man ran just as fast as he did, and I didn't know who he was.   He caught him down in our basement.   That's the time he was arrested. I was scared for that, was pretty scared.   It was soon after that I began acting that way.   I would be scared the way he always acted.   He wouldn't work at all.   He never used to behave himself.   Would get up any time he wanted to.   I was always afraid he was going to hit my mother.   My mother fell over the chair as he was going past, I guess he gave the chair a push, she happened to hit him.   Never heard him say bad words. Sometimes he would slap me."

"I remember telling my mother I would spit at her, that's all I remember.   Don't remember ever spitting at father or mother. Must have been when my mother was coming past I spit at her. I didn't scream, but I cried because I acted that way.   I couldn't help myself and I was ashamed of it.   I have never been any

663

place on a vacation. Would like to have some one with me, any one of my relations."

After her first change of environment she stated, "It's very nice. It's very nice out there at the new place — I would like to stay. Mother is better now. She has been once to see me and father twice."

"About that woman in the country — I used to help her with the work. She said things about me that were not true. She said I threw a knife at her. Why she happened to say that was because I left the bread knife on the table. She was reading a book that evening. She said I pinched her too. She told these things behind my back and never gave any proof. I never thought of doing such a thing. I never touched her — it certainly never could be true. Well, my aunt came out and told her little things like that about me, and she wanted some excuse for things. She would not take me places. She tried in the best way to get rid of me. I was afraid to go out in the dark and she would hit me for that." Later she said she did remember having the knife in her hands on that occasion, but could not recollect throwing it.

With the feeling that this girl when first seen was suffering from what proved to be a temporary mental upset it was recommended that she be placed in some private home in the country. At the first place there was much trouble, and the kindly woman who took her became so frightened that the child was soon returned. Things would go well for a week or so, and then she would sneak up behind her hostess and pinch her until she was black and blue, or tensely clinch her own hands and seem desperate. Then she would go out of doors and throw things about and stamp her feet. This was put up with in all kindness until on one occasion when the good woman's back was turned a butcher knife came whizzing past her head. During all this period the girl was in good physical condition and gaining in weight.

Then another place was tried, this time a training school for girls, and there for several months her behavior was quite good. Outside of a little forgetfulness, and the desire to play with younger children, rather than with those of her own age, nothing in particular was noticed about her there. Apparently she became quite normal mentally, and went back to her home where she continued to do well.

About a year afterward this girl again began using bad language and was disobedient. The family, remembering the previous success, asked that she be placed away again for a time. Nothing serious had happened, but prevention was desired. When sent away she began at once to do better.

This case is instructive as showing the possible temporary nature of a mental upset which may take on very serious aspects. It was only by the narrowest good fortune that a tragedy did not occur from this girl's violence. She represents a type of which we have seen numerous examples, usually with less marked inclination to violence, but yet showing many aberrations which lead directly to delinquency. The recklessness and lack of self-control of girls at this period is more frequently expressed in sexual offenses than in other ways, but in this case the aberrational tendency is so clearly set apart from any indulgence in natural desire for pleasure, that it stands out with great significance.

Mentality: Aberrational, adolescent, perhaps temporary.	Case 137. Girl, age 13.
Threatened violence. Bad language, etc.	Mental: Ability fair. Aberrational.

Case 138. — Albert S. Age nearly 17.

The general behavior and the delinquent record of this young fellow convinced a number of people that his mental condition should be investigated. He had already been twice in institutions for delinquents, and was still getting along very poorly. His father is a hard-working, poor man. This boy runs away and sometimes refuses to go home when found. He is not considered exactly vicious by anybody, but he steals and tells a good many lies. He has applied for lodging at a relief organization. In late school life he was a persistent truant. Since leaving school he has been most of the time unwilling to work. He has stolen money from his father and from boarders in the house, once getting away with about $30. Once he burglarized a house, and was later caught in the act of trying to get into the same place. After he has stolen he runs away, even to other states, where he stays for weeks at a time. Some people who became interested in the case found him tractable, and he has proved honest with them.

On the physical side we found rather a curious mixture of conditions. Weight 130 lbs.; height 5 ft. 8 in. Large bones and

665

frame, but poorly-developed chest. Very slouchy carriage. Expression peculiar in its evasiveness. He cries upon the slightest provocation, and at times seems silly and even simpering. Except for an unusually small mouth, his features are good. Broad forehead. Slight facial asymmetry and slight cranial asymmetry in the parietal region. Notably flat occiput. Head; length 17.3; breadth 15.5 cm. Vision about 20/60 R. and L. (Later report from a specialist is that the boy has been constantly undergoing a great deal of eye strain.) He suffers from occasional headaches. All other examination negative. It is interesting that it was the weak and silly expression of this boy in the court room, in spite of his fairly good features, that led directly to his case being further investigated.

On the mental side we also found contradictions. After considerable study we classified him as having fair ability with poor educational advantages, and as suffering from distinct aberrational tendencies. Our diagnosis was based on the following. The boy had attended school from 5 to 14 years but had reached only the 4th grade. The uneducated father could not explain what the trouble was, except that there was considerable complaint from the teachers and the boy was often truant. He has only been to Polish school, and never has learned English well. In the family it was considered that he could not learn well. By tests we found this contradicted as follows;

Our own series:
I. 1′ 26″. Some trial and error on the triangles.

II. 1′ 28″. Only one error.

III. 1′ 23″. 16 moves, but only one repetition of an impossibility.

IV. 2′ 33″. 30 moves.

V. 2′ 51″. Proceeded by trial and error method for a short time only, and then the steps were done consecutively with only one wrong attempt.

VI. Gave only 10 items on free recital, but followed these up with 18 items given correctly on cross-questioning. Accepted 7 out of 8 suggestions.

VII. Both drawn correctly at 2d trial. At the first effort did not get correct conception of geometric figures.

VIII. All correctly and promptly.

IX. Correct at 1st trial.

X. Correct at 1st trial.

XI. Could not do because did not know the alphabet in order.

XII. 11 out of the 20 items given with proper sequence for the ideas presented. It is doubtful if he understood all the words.

XIII. 10 out of the 12 items given correctly in logical sequence. The general sense of the passage well comprehended, but does not understand all the longer words.

XV. 2 failures and 5 errors — all of these very largely on account of trouble with the language. 13 given correctly in average time of 1.2″, a decidedly good performance.

XVII. Writes unexpectedly well. Spells short words correctly, but again there is evidence of trouble with the language.

XVIII. Does long multiplication quite correctly, but stops short there. Does not know the process of long division.

XIX. Reads a 4th-grade passage in a halting way with no mispronunciations.

XXII. Knows correctly the simple facts of geography, of current history, and has a fund of information gained from the newspapers. Thinks he would like to go to Texas and learn to ride a horse. Has enjoyed manual training in the institution for delinquents. Goes much to moving picture shows. Shows great dearth of healthy mental interests.

During our earlier acquaintance with him we repeatedly noted the boy was frank after his confidence was gained, but that he was somewhat hypochondriacal and extremely suggestible. In the school-room of an institution he showed much mental hebetude unless he was definitely stimulated. He will copy the work of others and get any one to do a mental task for him if he possibly can. He has many emotional changes and cries easily.

In the course of his own story of himself he says, " Every time I work in a shop I can't stand it; I can't stay any longer than a couple of days at a time. I get nervous. One day seems like a week. I can't stand it in a factory. I worked two weeks in a box factory, and every evening when I went out of there I was deaf. My father was going to send me to college, but I have n't no mind for it. I can't see good. It would be a long time before I would get through, and then it would not amount to anything. I used to bum from school once or twice a week. The rest of the kids told me to. Whatever they told me to do I would do it."

" This is the third time I was arrested. It was for stealing money. I have not a good mind. My mind is weak. I can't remember nothing. Cigarettes spoiled me, too. I swear to quit and then I can't. I quit only when I 'm locked up. I was locked up in that last place for 6 months. When I got out of there I was looking for a job, and then I looked for three weeks, and I could not find anything, and I got sore and went up into Minnesota and worked in a camp on the railroad. Then I went to St. Paul and did not have a cent. I would go around to the houses and ask ladies for something to eat. I slept in a lodging house. I came back here and I thought I was in a different country. I was all mixed up. I went to a corner down town where I always used to go to nickel shows and I did not know where I was."

"My step-mother she bosses me. Once I hit her on the head and I said, ' You have no business to boss me.' I have headaches every day from ice cream and moving picture shows. I 'm nervous when I write. Things get green before my eyes when I read for an hour or so."

" I tell my story and I don't remember half of it. When I get a job I can't keep it long — something tells me in my mind I can't keep a job. At home I can do work of all kinds. Something in my mind tells me I should quit — I should go stealing, and like that. One thing tells me good, and the other bad. I had it already a year and a half ago. Sometimes I think of my mother and I start to cry. Sometimes I feel happy, and don't care about anything. My father sent me lots of times to the hospital to see whether I 'm well or not. He thought I 'm crazy and like that."

" In my mind things come up, nickel shows and like that, and I think of my mother. She was in the hospital when I got out of that place. I was sorry. She felt bad about me. I play baseball, but not much. I ain't got muscle for doing much. I'd always go by myself — never hang around with kids. I 've got just one partner. He was never arrested. I never went with any gang."

" I can't hold a job — something makes me quit. Sometimes it is all right, and then after ten or fifteen minutes it is different and I quit. Sometimes I feel so happy I jump around and sing, and then in about two minutes I feel as if I was going to be hanged. I feel rotten. The only job I think I like best is on a farm. When I see pictures of farms I get crazy. I wish my father would leave me go. I asked him lots of times. I would like to wash cows and stuff like that in a barn and drive horses."

" Well, it is in my mind to steal. Maybe I would get to doing some work and I would feel like stealing. Something made me take that money on my father. When something gets in my mind I got to do it."

"When I go out in the yard or down in the basement I see things sometimes. I see ghosts. About four weeks ago I had a fight with a ghost and I told my step-mother about it. You bet I was scared. When I went down in the basement with a lamp there was two devils standing there and a ghost, but when I came up near they run off, and gee, that scared me. The first time it happened I was in the toilet room. Something knocked three times on the door. I looked out suddenly and nobody was there. I was afraid to go out in the yard lately. When I look down in the basement I think I can see people standing in the corner. I heard a funny noise down there. It was like a bell going slowly, ding — d-o-n-g."

"When I am at home I can sit in the rocker and rock all day long. My mother says she wishes she could murder the rocker. I don't read any at home."

Further inquiry about his habits brought out that he takes about three or four cups of coffee a day, and rarely a glass of beer away from home. Three or four years ago he began masturbation, which was taught him by other boys. He has indulged altogether too much in this at times. He began smoking cigarettes at about the same period and occasionally would smoke a package in a day. He is quite convinced that both these habits are partly what is the trouble with him, and dwells on them a good deal. He tells us that he has heard that people go crazy from them. (It is to be remembered that during the last 4 years he has twice been for long periods under detention where at least one of these habits could not have been indulged in.)

Gathering up more of his history from available sources, namely, members of the family who are not especially bright, we obtain the following. The mother has been dead a few years. She was healthy formerly. This pregnancy and birth were normal. The other children are mediocre in ability, but certainly not defective. One dead. Albert is the second child. He has never been very sick; measles followed by scarlet fever at 10 years. No enuresis. The father is only a moderate drinker.

No satisfactory family history obtainable, but all main points bearing on this case were declared negative. No other member of the family was regarded as queer. Neither Albert nor any other member of the family had convulsions.

The family thoroughly believe this boy is not right in his head because he acts so strangely. He says queer things to his step-

669

mother about seeing people in the yard when they are not there, and tells stories of ghosts. He also acts in a very silly way. At times he cries a good deal. He does not sit by himself, but mixes with the others at home. He will always pick up money when it is lying around, no matter to whom it belongs. Just recently he has been smoking excessively. They think he is too indolent to work. His conduct at home is good.

It is plain to see from all this that, indefinite though the type of trouble was, there is evidence enough of aberrations. Extremely defective vision very likely caused school dissatisfaction and truancy. Later came the two bad habits we have mentioned. It was clear the boy needed an environment where he could be kept away from these habits, and that he was really quite strong enough to work. It seemed likely that his mental symptoms might pass away.

After his last transgressions the boy entirely refused to go home, saying he was ashamed to do so. He was temporarily placed in another home, but soon ran away. After a little he again turned up, and begged to be placed for a long time in some institution. This was done. Glasses were procured for him, but difficulty was experienced in getting him to wear them.

Mentality: Aberrational, probably   Case 138.
              temporary, adolescent.   Boy, age 17 yrs.
    Adolescence.

    Debilitating habits: At times masturbation
                        and smoking plus.

    Defective vision.

    Poor family control and understanding.

Former truancy.   Mental:
Runaway.   Fair ability, poor
Not working.   advantages.
Stealing. Burglary.   Aberration.

Case 139. —William R. Age 12 years, 9 months.

We saw this boy after getting an admirable account of him and his antecedents from the intelligent mother. He had recently been causing the police much trouble. He was found in a lodging house, and while he was taken for much older than he was, still he was recognized as of juvenile age. He claimed to be a runa-

way from a far western city, but telegraphic communication failed
to establish his connections there. After some days he gave a
city address and his mother was finally found. He had run away
from home about two weeks before, taking a considerable sum
of money which his mother had saved, and made his way to
the part of the country which he later maintained was his
home.

The gist of the story as told by the well-mannered, self-supporting and good mother is as follows: Mother and father both
American. The father has long been thoroughly immoral, but
not alcoholic. He is a big and prosperous-looking individual,
common school education. They have long been separated.
William is the only child. The mother induced miscarriages
prior to his birth. The father's family is not well known, but
there is nothing suspicious ever heard about them. So far as
known, no one on either side was feebleminded, insane or epileptic.
On the mother's side the men were extremely hard drinkers.
Their mentality was normal, but their passion for liquor was
beyond their control. Some of them died early, directly from
alcoholism.

During pregnancy with this child there was much misery. The
father at that time would stay away sometimes all night, and the
mother would walk the floor. Her husband was absolutely without
conscience in money matters, but never did anything to be actually
arrested. During all the pregnancy the mother was on a strain.
Then at this time she had a very severe attack of bronchitis.
The birth was normal. At 6 weeks baby had severe bronchitis
with complications, and it was thought he would die. No convulsions. He was a very fretful baby. Bottle fed. At 7 years
he had an operation for tonsils and adenoids. Walked and talked
at normal age; to school at 6. Had been more or less nervous
since he was 3 or 4 years of age. There has been careful watching for bad habits, but none known to have developed. He
grew rapidly and now he is a very large boy for his age. The last
year or so he jerks his shoulders and face frequently, and gnaws
at his fingers.

He is a bright boy in many ways, but in others a baby. Now
in 7th grade. Has always seemed fond of his mother, and could
not bear to see her suffer. He appeared a very innocent boy
until lately. Reads a good deal; likes to play childish games.
The mother's occupation demands that she live in a crowded

671

portion of the town and he has little chance to be in the open. Some 6 months ago he ran away, but came home the same night. Recently he has been staying out at night, once or twice coming in very late. He has been taking little sums of money from his mother. He talks about Indians and revolvers a good deal. On this last occasion he wrote from out west and his mother forwarded money to him, but when he finally reached his home city he did not go to her. The father has probably had no bad influence over him whatever; he has left the boy very much alone. Naturally, the mother has been terrifically worried about her child.

We found a lad who could easily pass for 16. Weight 116 lbs.; height 5 ft. 3 in. In the first stages of pubescence. General development and nutrition decidedly good. Regular and extremely mobile features; variable expression — pouts nervously at times. Well-shaped head. Vision about normal. Slightly defective hearing in one ear. Bites finger nails excessively. Color good. Heart sounds normal. Knee jerks rather lively. Constant jerkings and twitchings of face and neck, entirely of the purposive type; during examination demonstrates that these are largely controllable. Staccato speech. Good strength. Other examination all negative.

On the mental side many interesting features came out by examination. Comparatively few tests were given on account of the boy's nervousness.

Mental tests: our own series:
IV. 1' 12''. 16 moves.
V. 3' 9''. 3 errors and then the steps done consecutively with only one error.
IX. Correct at 1st trial.
X. Correct at 1st trial.
XI. Got the idea promptly. Made 5 errors out of 11 possibilities.
XII. Gave 12 out of the 20 items, leaving out a whole series of details.
XIII. Gave the entire 12 items in logical sequence with various verbal changes.
XV. Only one failure. Average time 2''.
XVI. 1st trial 75 squares tapped with 12 errors. 2d trial 85 squares tapped with 8 errors. Remarkably bad performance.
XVII. Writes a fair hand.
XVIII. Arithmetic for grade quite accurate.
XIX. Reads well.
XXIII. Pictorial Completion Test. 2' 28''. 2 logical errors.

During the work William behaved very flightily. It was difficult to get him to concentrate at times, and often he would
interrupt his work by suddenly talking on wholly irrelevant
subjects. He has a very jerky way of talking, and shows many
signs of lack of self-control. In conversation it is difficult to hold
him down to anything. He constantly breaks in with a question
or remark about some object in the room. He acts like a nervous
child of 4 or 5 years. Face is in constant motion.

"I'll be 13 in September. Gee, that teacher gets me mad
when she calls me Willie. Anybody ought to be ashamed to lie
the way I did. Gee, I got a habit of twisting my neck. Gee,
do you see how bad it is? Miss D. was making a fool of me — no,
I mean she was joshing me about the pupils of my eyes — they're
so big. Gee, but they say I'm nervous."

"Some kids told me to go on a bum and then my mother told
me the principal wanted to see me. Gee, I was afraid. I thought
she was going to send me to prison for bumming. Are you going
to give me medicine? I heard my mother tell the teacher to put
me under observation. Gee, I got 87 questions to answer in
history. I got so far ahead of the others I guess that is the reason
she gave me that."

"I did not take any pocket book. Sure, I never took any pocket
book." (At this time we asked the boy not to lie to us.) "Well,
I did take it. I bought a ticket to Denver because it was a capital.
I thought it must be a big place. I did not know anything about
it. When I was there I lost $7 someway. I got to Boulder and
these other places and lived in Boulder three days. I just read
about them places on the map and went there. Never heard
of them before. Gee, I got such funny habits. I can run 3 miles.
No, I don't smoke. I never did. Don't take no tea or coffee.
Is that bad for me you think?"

To put down even as connected a story as the above, it was
necessary to overlook his laughing at inappropriate times and
the efforts to get him to withdraw his attention from some object
in the room.

It was easy to make the diagnosis that here we had a boy of
good native ability who was showing very poor control of his
association and psychomotor processes. There was aberrational
trouble on both the physical and mental sides. We recommended
he be placed at once under favorable circumstances in the country, and have his complete fill of outdoor life.

673

Mentality:	Case 139.
Aberration, psychoneurosis.	Boy, age 12½.
Adolescence: Premature puberty.	
Developmental: Antenatal, mother much worried, illness. Sickly infancy. Early nervousness.	
Heredity: F. moral instability. Several maternal male relatives inebriates.	
Runaway.	
Stealing.	Mental:
Misrepresentation.	Normal ability.

§ 318. **Varieties of the Type.** — Many other cases could be cited in detail if it were necessary to show variations on the general theme.

Case 140. — One boy from being implicated at about the time of puberty in the accidental killing of another lad, developed an anxiety psychosis and neurosis. A potent cause of the ensuing psychopathic condition was his repression of knowledge of the affair. In the midst of extreme sensitiveness aroused by all this, he, after forced association with delinquent boys, became definitely a delinquent, mingling with a new type of comrades and engaging in stealing. Then later he showed mild symptoms of exophthalmic goiter. Under good auspices he has become somewhat more stable, but is still a difficult problem.

Case 141. — Another adolescent became so obsessed by religious impulses that he despised his family, who, as a matter of fact, were very good people. His excessive feeling in the matter led to his attacking his mother, breaking furniture, and even to prevarication. It took a long time, and much patience on the part of the family, with periods of living away from home, to get this young man's mental attitude tuned to family living conditions, but with common-sense management it has been accomplished. The boy, at one time, could easily have been adjudged insane, if the incongruity of his violent behavior and expressed beliefs had been emphasized.

Case 142. — In illustration of the fact that the stress at puberty upon an individual who is nervously inferior may be mentally overwhelming is the following. A boy of 15 for three years has

been playing truant and staying away from home sometimes a
week at a time. He has also been stealing in petty ways. At 9
months he had some nervous trouble which left him partially
paralyzed. He was never regarded as backward mentally; he
reached 7th grade. In spite of only partial use of one side, he
gets around well, and occasionally earns his own living by odd
jobs. He began masturbation at 11 or 12. It was evidently
not long after that when he began to have times of looking very
pitiful, so his mother says, and would laugh in a silly way without
answering questions asked him. Periods of depression set in
which would last for several days, following some of which he
would run away. He threatened to commit suicide. His work
on tests shows no indication of defect or abnormality, but his
emotional behavior and his tendencies to misconduct, through
which he himself suffers a great deal, are highly significant. He
is backward in puberty and very poorly developed and nourished.
Weight only 68 lbs.; height 4 ft., 10 in. In such a case personal
attention in a sympathetic country home would usually be best.
If this is not procurable, as it was not in this case, then the proper
kind of a boy's industrial school is to be recommended. This
particular lad has been mentally steadied in a very remarkable
way under the latter treatment, so that now at 16 1-2 he is regarded as quite normal. This is a great success, considering the
desperate nature of the symptoms manifested earlier.

No account of the mental aberrations of adolescence could
pretend to outline the field without doing some justice to the
curious, reckless, vicious, and violent behavior, entirely irrational,
that is frequently observed in adolescent girls. Most striking
in this is the utter neglect often of the first elements of self-
preservation. The demand for self-activity and self-assertion
is quite beyond the mark of ordinary prudence and foresight. Of
course there are as many variations in the cases as there are differences in the physical, mental, and environmental substrata of
the individuals, but the following short summary of a very
long case will serve to show the marked aberrational behavior
of girls who are not, however, to be considered insane.

Case 143. — Jennie S. This girl of just 17 is extraordinarily
well developed. Weight 164 lbs. Height 5 ft. 5 in. Large frame
and very large bones. In age of onset of puberty and in development of sex characteristics she has been rather backward in com-

675

parison. Extremely defective vision for which she has not been willing to wear glasses of late.

On the mental side there was no difficulty in diagnosing her as having fair ability. On some tests she should have done better, but then her eyesight without glasses is atrociously bad. We note that she is a dull, heavy type. When stimulated she always succeeded in doing better at her work; lack of initiative was always present. She is firm and decided in her manner of talking, and has positive opinions about many things. She shows much sense of humor, and quite a little ability in introspection; has developed a definite attitude toward life. Her grudge against her family is largely justified.

After several months of observation and knowledge of her career, to the diagnosis we added that Jennie at times showed a peculiar, unstable mental condition in which she was not at all equal to controlling herself. She made frequent voluntary appeals for moral help, showing herself generally desirous of behaving well, but when much was done for her without committing her to an institution, she did not play fair, or keep her promises. Her delinquencies were of a nature so obviously harmful to herself that their commission seemed highly indicative of mental aberration.

Jennie began at about 14 with recalcitrant behavior at home. Prior to that time she had always been a good girl, and had had a healthy developmental history. One great defect in the environment was the alcoholism of the father; he was a great disturbing influence at home. He comes of a quarrelsome family. Jennie wore glasses during her school period, and got along well to the 7th grade by the time she was 14. At about the period she entered adolescence there were several very upsetting factors, which led to mental conflict spreading out over 2 or 3 years. The abusiveness of her father in the home was one point. Then she worked for a man whom the family respected, but who at a time when he was drunk, attempted to persuade her into bad sex affairs. Then, thirdly, the mother, after enduring some months of Jennie's bad behavior, deceitfully placed her under duress. It was after this that the feeling of grudge, and desire for revenge, and general moral confusion partially unbalanced her. She indulged in much bad language, quarreling, lies and obstinacy. She repeatedly ran away, and failed to do well in a number of places where sympathetic people tried her. Still later she became involved in sex affairs, but never was extensively bad in this direction. She grew steadily more unreliable. She disappeared from all her friends. In numerous places where she was traced she was said to act as if she were insane. Her final arrest was brought about through vagrancy. Being taken to a certain jail she created a great sensation by working up a desperate plot to kill the matron. At this time she had a very furtive and peculiar appearance. Later in court she was perfectly uncontrolled, used extremely bad language, and even made an attempt to strike the judge.

The significant feature of this case is the development of aberrational tendencies under conditions which gave her good chances. Her frequent appeals for moral aid were met by unusual opportunities for reform. In her case there were no adventitious influences such as the use of stimulants, or excessive sex temptations, either personal or environmental. The unfortunate family irritations were greatly diminished by her being placed out. We noted that her aberrational behavior did not center about the menstrual period.

Under restriction in an institution this young woman has finally developed completely stable behavior. From this fact we can offer a further good prognosis if later environmental conditions are reasonably satisfactory. (We are able to add another word: A year has elapsed; the girl is now nearly 19; she has been living quietly at home for several months and is a changed character. She says she has learned to put up with things that used to annoy her bitterly. She is a happy and attractive young woman.)

§ 319. **Treatment.** — The possibility of the successful treatment in an institution for delinquents of a case showing minor mental aberrations of adolescence is of vital importance. That some instances of recovery under the régime of an industrial school do take place we have proof, as illustrated above. The change that has come over the individual with good management and correct hygiene is sometimes most rapid and remarkable. Not every case can be tolerated in these schools, on account of the needs of the other young people, but under the classification possible by the cottage system it is evident, from our experience, that most cases can be taken care of in such an institution. In these adolescent troubles, as so frequently in considering mental disease, environmental stress has to be taken

677

into account. Proper institutional life, affording hygienic mental and physical conditions, reduces this to a minimal irritation in our type of cases, and so at once eliminates a large element of causation.

A very short summary of a typical case, such as we have seen a number of, is the following:

Case 144. — Boy of 14, who earlier had been a truant, and recently had been engaged in stealing and burglary. In the background there was a prolonged serious illness during infancy, premature puberty, and perhaps sex habits. Physically he was poor in development. Weight only 83 lbs.; height 4 ft. 8 in. Notwithstanding this backwardness sex development was almost adult. About his mentality it was very difficult to decide on account of having to work with an interpreter. Tests were done with much irregularity. The parents were sure the boy was not right mentally.

To the judge: "Undoubtedly this boy is mentally peculiar as his mother says, but we can find no reason strong enough for recommending him to any institution for the mentally abnormal. He may be temporarily upset, but is very likely to straighten out under regular conditions of living and education, such as at X."

The report on this boy after a year is that he is getting along famously in the institution and showing great improvement both mentally and physically. He is regarded there as a suitable case for them.

PSYCHOSES FROM ALCOHOL.

§ 320. **Nature of Alcoholic Psychoses.** — For a complete chapter on the intoxication psychoses we must refer to special works on psychiatry. We could not undertake to recount here all the many mental symptoms of acute and chronic alcoholism; the diagnosis frequently demands expert and perhaps prolonged observation.

Some idea of the astonishing variety of psychoses caused by alcohol can be gained from the enumeration of Cramer (**221**), one of the foremost authorities. He distinguishes: (1) the gradual progressive dementia of chronic alcoholism, (2) delirium tremens, (3) alcoholic delusions of jealousy, (4) acute alcoholic paranoid psychosis — the hallucinosis of Bonhoeffer and Wernicke, (5) chronic paranoidal insanity, (6) alcoholic anxiety psychosis, (7) alcoholic paralysis — pseudoparesis, (8) alcoholic epilepsy, (9) the psychosis of intolerance to alcohol, (10) pathological drunkenness, (11) dipsomania, (12) Korssakow's psychosis — a disorder characterized by a peculiar loss of memory and power of orientation.

§ 321. **Alcoholism and Criminality.** — When considering the close connection between alcoholic intoxication in general and criminality [1] we are constrained to exactly agree with Mercier when he insists that acute alcoholic intoxication should be classed as a toxic insanity, usually brief in duration, and having many direct and indirect relationships to criminality. Everybody is acquainted with the crimes against person and property, the acts of cruelty, the ugly deeds of neglect and meanness which are perpetrated in a condition of temporary insanity from alcohol. It seems quite unnecessary to even designate the types of misconduct which are here involved — the subject is so very well known.

However, it is important to note that there is the greatest difference in the predisposition of individuals, and even of certain races or nationalities, to be mentally upset by alcoholic poisons. The whiskey which a Southern gentleman innocently partakes of before breakfast, may in another physiological type incite to murder. All physicians with experience in these matters have known those to whom a glass or two of beer is sufficient to create a topsy-turvy world of moral conditions. In court we see, unfortunately, how the ugliest passions and the most dastardly impulses, ranging from neglect of children to stealing and murder, have been aroused by the imbibition of only a small amount of liquor. Delinquencies are repeated over and over in subsequent attacks of this temporary insanity, and the same type of unlawful behavior may lead the individual to be committed scores of times. The astounding record of Jane Cakebread (*vide* Holmes, **66**), the notorious recidivist in the London courts, with her 280 commitments for " drunk and disorderly," is approached

---

[1] The 1910 Judicial Statistics for England and Wales (**40**, p. 15) show that of a total 168,260 convictions 54,305 involved drunkenness. The report of the French Minister of Justice in 1909 (Journal officiel, **41**) concerned itself largely with the relations between alcoholism and criminality. The statistical results were based upon a system of individual records which were filled out by magistrates, and showed that 22 per cent. of the murders were committed under the influence of alcohol, 33 per cent. of the cases of rape or offenses against decency, and 24 per cent. of the cases of manslaughter. Yvernis (**42**) states that in 1909, 31 per cent. of all those condemned were alcoholics or were intoxicated at the time of the offense.

679

in the careers of other alcoholic delinquents, wife beaters, street brawlers, saloon fighters. Some of these are normal enough socially and mentally when they refrain from drink; they must be sharply distinguished from such as suffer chronically from a psychosis, whether this has resulted directly from the abuse of alcohol, or is merely correlated with it in other than a causal relationship. In passing judgment on this latter point we must ever remember that very many alcoholics are such because of already existing defects or aberrations of mentality.

§ 322. **Treatment under the Law.** — For the practical determination of the actual bearing which alcoholism has in the production of criminality an estimation must be made of the offender's mental status. In undertaking any prediction for court purposes it must never be forgotten that the feebleminded and epileptic have not only less powers of resistance to temptation to drink, but also very frequently are more easily inflamed by alcohol than their better balanced brothers. Although it may not yet be, as stated by the court decision we have cited under the head of epilepsy (§ 257), that the law can safely regard one person as being more readily turned towards crime by liquor than another, nevertheless no fact is better known to even casual observers. This should have much bearing upon the disposition and treatment of those who are thus hypersusceptible.

Taking the general question of alcohol and the criminality it causes through inducing different kinds of mental disturbance, it seems clear that the treatment of the individual case should always be calculated to serve as a warning against further indulgence, and at the same time should look out for the existence of such physical and mental conditions in the offender which make abstinence reasonably possible. Otherwise social treatment becomes totally absurd. Incarceration under will-weakening conditions offers worse chances for improved conduct in the future. Our knowledge of delinquent drunkards leads us to coincide with the opinion of Mercier (**45**): " The usual course of letting him (the drunkard) off with a trifling fine, or a few days imprisonment, has been shown, by the experience of several generations, and of hundreds of thousands of instances, to be utterly futile and ineffective. It has not, apparently, the slightest deterrent effect; and the same offender receives these sentences, hundreds of times repeated, without amending his condition in the least. . . . If every person charged with willful drunkenness, or with offenses committed in a state of willful drunkenness, were to be punished on the first offense with 6 months', or even 3 months', imprisonment, without the option of a fine, charges of drunkenness would be enormously diminished. . . . The drunkard is as much a danger to society as a lunatic at large, which he is; and when he comes to commit an offense in consequence of his drunkenness, he should, in my opinion, be punished, not so much in proportion to the gravity of the offense committed when drunk, as in proportion to the deliberateness of the intentions with which he brought himself into this dangerous state."

§ 323. **Psychoses of Chronic Alcoholism.** — To the student of mental conditions chronic alcoholism presents very definite abnormal psychical features which are as yet little recognized by the law. Cooper (**245**) in his conservative study maintains that all inebriates show in greater or less degree the following peculiarities: (*a*) incapacity to bear physical or mental pain; (*b*) defective moral sense; (*c*) defective sense of responsibility; (*d*) intolerance or tolerance of alcohol beyond the normal; (*e*) defective realization of abnormalities even when the individual is sober; (*f*) defective inhibitions for meeting desires and impulses; (*g*) defective mental equilibrium, shown in deficient powers of concentration and attention, in abnormal emotionalism, etc. Many authors draw attention to the same kind of fact. Crothers (**251**), acutely reviewing the forensic bearings of alcoholism, strongly favors the idea of chronic alcoholics as such being considered not normal mentally. He well calls attention to the fact that testifying physicians get much mixed on the point when they pass judgment according to the theoretical legal conceptions of insanity and responsibility. He rightly insists, moreover, on the fact that there has been altogether too little careful investigation of the actual effects of alcoholism upon various mental powers. The interest in the subject is ahead of our exact knowledge. As Heilbronner (**252**) says in his scholarly review of the subject, the only way to clear the ground is for psychiatrists to stick to their own findings and professional facts, and let legal, theoretical dicta alone.[1]

[1] The literature on the various phases of the relationship between alcoholism, criminality and the law is very rich, and any one who would pass judgment on the individual case, or who would plan for measures of amelioration or prevention should have acquaintance with the best authorities. For such students we offer a selection of some of the best works: A tremendous bibliography covering the whole question of alcohol came out by Abderhalden (**253**) in 1904. A shorter list of the principal books was published in the Jour-

The definite mental disturbances of chronic alcoholism which are particularly related to criminalistic conduct are as follows: there is the progressive *dementia of chronic alcoholism*, which may be accompanied by delusions, hallucinations and uninhibited impulses that incite to misconduct. Sufferers from this weakened mental condition readily find their way into the ranks of criminalism. Their earning capacity is lowered, their social status is poor, their moral inhibitions are largely lost; it is an easy step to vagrancy, petty stealing, and offenses against decency and sex morality. Then there is the so-called acute *alcoholic hallucinosis* (*vide* Bonhoeffer, **9**, and Mitchell, **46**) in which states some of the worst tragedies have been enacted. The condition is mainly characterized by insomnia and irritability accompanied by hallucinations of hearing and vision and depressive delusions. (Delirium tremens is only rarely connected with the commission of crime.) Another important chronic mental state associated with alcoholism is *alcoholic paranoia*. In this there is developed a delusional state marked principally by ideas of persecution and jealousy. A word about a case cited elsewhere, Case 30, will make this point clear, and also demonstrate the importance of the practical recognition of this group. The mother of a family has been sentenced to short terms some scores of times. The reason of her recurrent arrest is that when she gets out she starts housekeeping with her family, very often in a new locality, and then rapidly develops delusions concerning her neighbors. Either with or without drunkenness, she has exacerbations accompanied by violence. She breaks windows and doors, destroys other property, becomes very noisy, and indulges in personal assaults. The cost to the community of this woman's

---

nal of Inebriety (**254**), in 1903. A comprehensive work by Helenius (**255**) appeared in same year. A much quoted study by Baer and Laquer (**256**), which includes the subject of criminality, was published in second edition, in 1907. Perhaps the most valuable general reference work, with citation of numerous authorities, is that by Hoppe (**257**), the eminent German authority, 4th edition in 1912. The same author (**242**) has a special work covering the relationship of alcohol to criminality, and devotes still a third considerable essay (**258**) to the more theoretical legal aspects. Professional people, both legal and medical, will find much of interest and importance in the chapters on the medico-legal connections of alcoholism in Crothers' book (**251**). "The Relation of Alcohol to the Feebleminded" is the title of a work by Potts and others (**259**). Juvenile alcoholism as correlated to criminality is treated at length by Hoppe (**242**), and in its relation to general social pathology by the same author (**257**). For those contemplating the possibilities of institutional work, the various reports of institutions should be consulted; in this country particularly those from Massachusetts, *vide* Neff (**246**).

never having been efficiently treated may be judged by contemplating the history of the family.

§ 324. **Acute Alcoholic Psychoses.** — Leaving aside the brief insanity named intoxication or drunkenness, there are acute alcoholic psychoses especially productive of criminality. Few text books on psychiatry give them. These mental states are seen mostly by those who study offenders as such.[1] Pathological reaction or psychic intolerance to alcohol is seen particularly in neuropathic individuals, in those who have suffered head injuries, and in adolescents. A complete disturbance of the personality may ensue with release of inhibitions of sex impulses, of tendencies to violence and other criminality. In the so-called *pathological intoxication* there may be the most sudden change of emotions, with impulses to violence, or there may be other characteristic signs of insanity such as stereotyped movements. The condition may last from a few minutes to an hour or so. Bonhoeffer divides the forms of this psychosis into delirious and epileptiform, but there is no real line of demarcation. In criminal annals individuals experiencing this psychosis figure as those who suddenly respond to some perception or self-initiated impulse, which is entirely at variance with the individual of the moment before. There is usually an utterly uncalled-for attack upon person or property. German observers have laid much stress for diagnosis upon the fact that the period of pathological intoxication is followed by a terminal sleep, after which the individual usually has no recollection of immediately preceding events.

§ 325. **Alcoholic Psychoses in Adolescents.** — Our special contribution to this subject comes from our observation of still another group of cases in which a pathological reaction to alcohol has extended for days and even over a week or two. Significant bodily signs, such as enlargement of the pupils (*vide* Stapel, **362**), which occurs in pathological intoxication are not found, but the mental aberrations are characteristic and important. There is complete impulsivity which throws all prudence to the winds.

[1] Several German authors have written at length on the topic of pathological intoxication (der pathologische Rausch) and intolerance to alcohol. We would refer particularly to the chapter by Cramer (**221**) on alcoholic psychoses, and to the discussion (**15**) of the same author of the medico-legal bearings of the subject. Bonhoeffer (**9**) still earlier contributed a study on this topic, and Richter (**11**) has a special dissertation on it. Others have given details of cases, one of the best studied in its legal relations being that by Weber (**361**). The type of prolonged pathological reaction to alcohol which we have observed and illustrated above we have found no satisfactory account of in the literature.

There is rapid alteration of the emotions. There is mental rest-lessness, and frequently mild incoherency, inability to pay atten-tion, and perhaps decidedly imperfect memory for recent events. In other words there is a mild clouding of consciousness, confu-sion, excitement and irritability. The effect upon conduct of these psychotic states may well be imagined. In young males we have had particular reason to note a tendency to extravagant violence, entirely prejudicial to their own interests, and in girls reckless abandon to sexual practices which were certainly not called out by any usual desires. The lack of mental control, impulsivity and mild confusion are illustrated in the following cases, where the symptoms in these adolescents have lasted for days, or even a week or two after cessation of drinking.

Case 145. — A boy of 16, very small for his age, when under detention, acted for days in the most violent fashion, directly against his own interests. Even when before the judge he at-tempted viciously to assault first a witness, and then a court attaché. Everybody, including his own parents, thought that he certainly must be mentally disturbed. As observed by us, a few minutes after the court scene, he was an extraordinarily dissipated looking youngster, with swollen eyes and bluish skin. Now, instead of the desperate tough, we had a highly nervous, excitably-talking, friendly boy, who soon began to weep and sob. His only talk was of drinking and smoking, which he said he had been indulging in excessively for some days prior to his arrest, which was about a week previously. Nothing in the way of testing could be done on account of his nervousness, but he was obviously unbalanced. He had been ordered to an institution for delinquents.

The interested parents gave a clear account of a curiously mixed career. This boy is considered the only dull member of a large family of children. His development was normal and he was never seriously ill until he was 8 years old. Then he began having periods of severe headache and vomiting, which would come after a couple of days of queer actions. He had these then for years. He also had typhoid badly at 8 years. He was some-what of a somnambulist, and a great coward always at night. He did very poorly in school, and was at last sent to an institution on account of truancy. Previous to his truancy he had worked hard for over a year, getting up early in the morning to deliver milk before school time. At 14 he was only in the 4th grade.

Then he found a place to work with a big financial concern, braced up and did splendidly for nearly a year, when a craving for country life came over him and he left his good position, where he was well liked, to go on a farm. After he came back from the country he commenced going with one of the toughest gangs in the city. Then followed strange behavior, singing ribald songs at home, jumping out of the window when reproved, staying under the table and looking like a hunted animal when afraid of his father. He even slept on the floor under furniture rather than in his own bed, and at last stayed away from home for days together. His parents say that at times his eyes were glassy and wild, and altogether he appeared most abnormal.

This boy when an infant had one convulsion, none of the other children had any. Nor do they suffer with sick headaches. The father was earlier subject to migraine, later became a hard drinker, but for years had entirely reformed, and was now reliable and respectable. A maternal aunt of the boy was subject to severe headaches, and then later developed epilepsy followed by insanity.

The boy was seen a month later. We found an entirely changed individual, of normal appearance and rather strong type of face. Except for his small size and large adenoids and tonsils we found his physical conditions normal. Mentally, to our great surprise, we found by many tests that his ability was well up to the ordinary. He says he detested school life, deliberately learned as little as possible, and always wanted to live in the open country, which he was never allowed to do. From the story of this now manly appearing boy we hear that for 6 months or so prior to the time we saw him in court, he had been drinking, at least a little beer every day. This is what made him so strange at home, he says. Then what led to his final period of crazy behavior, with burglary, a street robbery, extraordinary defiance of the police, as well as the irrational actions mentioned above, playing a part, was whiskey-drinking with the gang. "I didn't know where I was at in those days."

We never obtained any account of actual intoxication of this boy from any one; the effect of the liquor was simply to create exceedingly erratic and dangerous behavior. The background of neurotic tendency is to be remembered. The best proof of the cause of the trouble was in the total change of his character and condition after a month of abstinence, with no more charges of criminalistic behavior for now several years.

685

Mentality: Psychosis, temporary.   Case 145.
    Stimulants: Whiskey and beer.   Boy, 16 yrs.
           Tobacco + +.
    Neuropathic constitution.
               Earlier attacks resembling migraine.
      Heredity: Father earlier migraine, alcoholic.
           Maternal aunt epileptic and insane.

Earlier truancy.   Mental:
Recently fighting.   Fair ability.
Stealing, etc.   Temporarily aberrational.

One might cite other cases in which an aberrational mental condition persisted, with dangerous social behavior, for a week or two after the cessation of a drinking bout. One could instance the effects of saturnalia engaged in for several days by young toughs, when they shut themselves up in a barn, eat and sleep but little while drinking and smoking excessively. This may bring about a half-dazed condition in which the most vicious impulses have full sway. Offenses, even murder, may be then readily committed. The individual is then quite incapable of listening to reason or appreciating proposals for his own advantage. Neuropathic, defective and adolescent individuals undoubtedly succumb easiest, and are therefore the most dangerous. Perhaps the most vicious young tough we have ever known is a moron in mental grade, a pleasant-faced, dull-minded chap, who with a little liquor becomes utterly irrational and reckless, a wild beast loose in society. A pathological reaction to alcohol is also seen in females, such as the following:

Case 146. — Girl of 17. In this instance a girl, who was held as a witness against some men with whom she had engaged in excessively immoral practices, showed signs of mental disturbance. She was found very difficult to take care of because of her extremely erratic, restless, and reckless behavior, her constant use of the vilest language, and her continual dwelling on sex affairs. In a short time she had managed to pour into the ears of a number of other detained young women the most abject details of low sex practices.

The mother told us that earlier this girl showed unusually good traits. She had a splendid record in school for both scholarship and deportment, and later worked steadily and gave every cent to her mother. The mother had not considered it necessary for the girl to be carefully watched in any way. A couple of months prior she began to stay out late at night and two weeks ago had run away from home entirely. She had now been in custody about a week.

We found on the physical side a very strongly built young woman. No sensory defect. Well-shaped head. Her expression and attitude were remarkable. She was silly, laughing, simpering, slouchy, and nervous.

We soon found that mentally we had to do with a rather bright type of individual who did most of our tests in a nervous way without trouble, but who showed certain peculiarities in the performance.

Mental tests: our own series:

I. 3′ 10″. Very nervous performance on the triangles.

III. 2′. 20 moves. 11 impossibilities, 4 repetitions of impossibilities.

IV. 2′ 13″. 13 moves.

VIII. 1 error, but this was inexcusable for it was a repetition of the same number.

IX. Correct at 1st trial.

X. Correct at 2d trial.

XV. 1 failure and 1 error. Average time 1.3″.

XVI. 88 and 89 with 2 and 4 errors respectively in 1st and 2d trials.

XVII. Writes an ordinary hand. Spells correctly.

XIX. Reads fluently an ordinary passage.

XXIII. Pictorial Completion Test all correct.

Kraepelin subtraction test with simple numbers, as taking 4's from 50, she finds it quite impossible to accomplish correctly.

Nothing further was done at this time on account of the girl's behavior. She would make a diligent effort for a minute or so, and then become nervous, would sigh, and frequently exclaim she wished she had a drink or a smoke to brace her up.

On the next day she still failed to do the subtraction test.

Six days later when this girl was mentally changed, as we state below, she did test I in 36″, test II in the exceedingly swift time of 4″, test IV in 19″. Test XI, the code test, was done with only 3 errors, and the Kraepelin subtraction test on more difficult numbers was done correctly. At this time her behavior was totally different and she said that she felt mentally like a new person.

In the family it is said there has been no insanity, feeblemindedness or epilepsy on either side. The girl's father was a thoroughly bad man, alcoholic and immoral. Earliest development

687

normal, but at 4 years she had "brain fever" severely and was taken to a hospital. Had many other children's diseases lightly. Progress good in school, 7th grade. Never convulsions.

It came out by the girl's story that she had been living a life that the mother knew nothing of. For a year or so, even when a good earner, she had been frequenting wine rooms on the way home in company with young men, and had cultivated a definite taste for alcohol. In the couple of weeks before incarceration she had been drinking hard. She showed some apperception of her own mental condition, even at our first interview.

"I was drinking all last winter, wine and stuff in the saloon. The fellows would buy it for me and then I would duck out. I was wise then. Now, I'm a dummy and they can fool me in everything. I'd believe anything they say. A fellow had a ring and he said it was a diamond ring, and he took my dollar and my gloves for it, and it was only a 10-cent ring. That was the dollar I had from work. If it's a lie or the truth I believe it just the same. I can't subtract them sixes for you, I don't know how to do it. I forget."

All the time at this first interview the narrator was laughing, leering and nervously moving about. When we attempted to get some details of her recent history, especially concerning time, she became confused and incoherent (Korssakow's symptom). Suddenly she jumped up and went to the window. "I want to get out of here, I want to go back to the saloon so I can drink. I like wine. I want a drink now, I'm crazy for it. I used to go with a nice crowd, but they was not wild enough for me after I got started."

Three days later she appeared most unkempt. Says she feels like singing and laughing. When asked to do a simple test insists over and over, "It's too hard for a young girl like me. I can't think the way I used to, it takes me an hour to get anything through my head now. If I could get out now I would start to drink. I love wine, port is the best; gin fizz, that's good."

We note now that her behavior in its negativism suggests some features of dementia precox. She would not allow the physician to see her mouth and throat. Laughs in a silly way. Takes no care of her person.

Four days after this a remarkable change came over her. She wanted to see us and wanted to say that she thanked God an officer had found her before it was too late. She thinks now that her head was not all right the other day, and asked if she said any queer things. She feels much better, but not quite right yet in her mind. Thinks it would be hardly safe for her now to go out, is not sure that she would stay away from saloons. Is sure that previous to drinking hard she used to be much smarter. We note that this girl today looks much cleaner and brighter in expression. Asked if she would do tests, she willingly responds with the good performance we noted above.

Nothing that we observed was any more indicative of mental aberration than the extremely low and reckless behavior which this erstwhile modest girl indulged in after she started her drinking bout away from home. The details that came out in the court were nauseating in the extreme. It seemed incredible that a girl of such previously good reputation could, when in no obviously intoxicated condition, seek out such situations.

She made later still more progress to complete mental normality. It should be remarked that at the time we found this girl showing her marked aberrational symptoms, she had been without alcohol for a week, and that it was after two weeks of custody when her behavior and mental powers became normal.

PSYCHOSES FROM DRUGS.

§ 326. **Psychoses from Morphine.** — On this, as on the following subjects, suitable text books on psychiatry must be consulted for full information about the different psychoses which arise from morphine. We are concerned only with such forms of insanity as are productive of criminality. The general mental and character changes produced by different drugs are discussed elsewhere, § 198 ff.

The long use of morphine brings about dementia, in which moral decrepitude stands out strongly. Thus it comes about that some miserable, demented hag, an old drug habitué, becomes a procurer for houses of prostitution, or engages in illicit distribution of habit-forming drugs. Well known to hospital people are the hallucinatory and delusional states produced by morphine. These latter mental conditions lead to the commission of crimes, but probably no more when they have been produced by morphine than when they arise from other causes. Some of the insane mental states resulting from morphine are only temporary — there may be a sharp recovery from them.

§ 327. **Psychoses from Cocaine.** — We have considered else-where, § 199, the general mental changes produced by cocaine. Definite insanities are also the result of the use of this drug. Whether because cocaine is particularly selected by neuro-pathic individuals, or because of its own peculiar effects, mental aberrations and deterioration much more rapidly ensue than in the case of the overuse of morphine. The chronic excitement of cocainists readily passes off into delirious states. Indeed, there is an acute cocaine hallucinosis which is described in the text books. Individuals suffering from the insanities produced by cocaine are particularly dangerous on account of their maniacal condition. The partially depressed and partially ex-cited state seen after withdrawal of the drug may, too, be provocative of desperate conduct. Both mentally and morally, one of the most unreliable of human beings is the habitual cocaine user.

§ 328. **Psychoses from Other Drugs.** — Insanities produced by chloral, cannabis indica, and other drugs play comparatively little part in criminalism. We confine our remarks to this country, for in the Orient it is a fact that the mental effects of cannabis indica, hasheesh, have long been celebrated as provoking extreme tendencies to violence.

In connection with this subject and, indeed, all the way through our discussion of the effect of stimulants and narcotics upon the mind and character, we should emphasize the relatively powerful effect which drugs have on an individual who is in the more unstable periods of life, such as adolescence. Added to this we should insist on their greater effects also on those of neuro-pathic heredity and constitution. The following case of mental upset caused by excessive use of *tobacco* as *snuff*, in an adoles-cent neuropath, is a most exaggerated instance of the effects of tobacco, but is thoroughly typical of drugs.

Case 147. — A young man of 16 was seen by us after he had been twice in the hands of police authorities. The charges against him were loafing on the streets, not staying at work, getting into street rows brought on by himself, and, worst of all, viciously at-tacking his good mother. On the last occasion when he was taken in charge he was discovered just about to cut off the tail of a cat. He was seated at home in the midst of furniture and dishes which had been broken and strewn about. Even the stove had been taken to pieces. On previous occasions, it had been noted that the boy's mind was much on criminalistic affairs. One could hardly get him to talk of anything but criminals and life at Sing Sing.

We found a pleasant-faced, tall boy, with greatly variable response both as shown by facial expression and mental reaction. Regular features and well-shaped head gave him a thoroughly prepossessing appearance. No sensory defect noted. Knee jerks very lively. Constant fine tremor of the hands. Strength poor for his size. Weight 112 lbs. Height 5 ft. 5 in. Excessive biting of the finger nails and finger tips. Slouchy attitude. Very restless, with peculiar, quick, jerky voluntary motions. Is said to have shown signs of excessive nervousness for years.

His erratic general behavior and great variability made the giving of ordinary tests valueless, except as showing negative results. It was found, however, that in moments of better control he could do our Completion Test, XXIII, correctly. In 3' 50" he said he had finished, although there were two errors. When urged to do better he finally put all the pieces in their right places. One found him to be an excessive liar, to have very deficient memory for certain recent events, and to show in general a tremendous amount of lack of mental control. In conversation every few minutes he would assert, " I can prove it." Although some vague account of his own bad habits was forthcoming, yet in general his own account of himself was quite unreliable.

From the very intelligent father we learn that this is the only living child, that a step-brother by the same mother had epileptic attacks and finally committed suicide while insane. The mother herself had suffered from an attack of melancholia prior to the birth of this child. She later recovered. She was an unusually good woman. Other members of the family are well educated and successful. The pregnancy with this boy was normal. He was very large at birth and instruments were used, but no damage was known to be done. Several convulsions during infancy. Walked and talked early. Had a severe operation for appendicitis at 7 years of age. When in Europe at 10 years learned the use of snuff. The last two years has been taking it regularly. Recently has made an extremely rapid pubertal growth. The family have noted this as being very peculiar. The boy was regarded as bright, but on account of changing residences never advanced well in school. Later he had a good position, and was thought well of by competent business men. He held this position for about a year. His bad conduct began only recently, although before adolescence he was regarded as being nervous.

The connection between the use of snuff and this boy's previous mental condition and bad conduct can only be conjectured. But the last outbreak was so closely under observation that the relationship became clear. After once previously being taken charge of by the authorities he became ill with pneumonia and was placed in a hospital. There he was observed as being nervous and erratic, and when he found that one of the other inmates of the ward had snuff, he gave a great deal of trouble because of his endeavor to get hold of it. Immediately following his illness, and while still in a depleted condition, he went home, and at once indulged in an orgy of snuff using. He used a whole box of it within 24 hours, and as an immediate result began the erratic conduct which again made him complained of. Before becoming violent, his family say he sat and rubbed his hands through his hair, or crawled on his knees over the floor. When we saw him the boy had partially recovered his mental equilibrium. He was frank enough to state that he did not believe he wanted to give up the habit, and that he thought in most public institutions he could use his ingenuity successfully to get hold of snuff.

This is an unusual case, inasmuch as it is rare to see such marked psychic disturbances and misbehavior arising from the use of tobacco in any form — it is to be presumed that the snuff which this boy used, being the usual commercial article, was not any one of the doctored snuffs sometimes obtainable. One would expect to find just such disturbances from cocaine and chloral and hasheesh, but the significant points are all the more valuable when the immediate source of trouble is a less noxious drug. The behavior in this case is almost exactly similar to that of some cocaine users we have seen, and the case will serve with its several factors as a paradigm for the whole group of adolescent drug users. It appears clear from our experience that one may expect the appearance of temporary psychoses with criminalistic behavior in neuropathic individuals, in depleted physical conditions, and particularly during adolescence, when there is indulgence in habit-forming drugs.

692

§ 329. **Other Minor Mental Aberrations.**

For the sake of completeness we must refer under this caption
to the various types of minor mental aberrations, either transitory or permanent, which are discussed by us under the headings
of epilepsy, § 258, senility, § 163, pathological liars, § 344, abnormal sexualism, § 242, and criminalistic mental imagery, § 233.
Under constitutional inferiority, § 290, we mention the characteristic episodes of mental upset which are frequent among
persons of this type. The aberrations of this last group may be
fleeting, but severe while they last. They may arise on a sheer
emotional basis, or from stresses of which alcoholic poisoning
may be reckoned as one. Our idea of the problem of " moral insanity," which may through misconception be regarded as an
aberration, is to be found in a special discussion of the subject,
§ 372.

About the existence of criminalistic *impulsions* or *obsessions*
which cannot be further analyzed and which in some text books
of psychiatry are regarded as minor mental aberrations, we are
not at all sure. After the case is studied for mental defect, mental
aberration, mental conflict, social suggestion, etc., there is apparently extremely rarely anything which is fair to denominate in
any final sense as impulsion. Of course there is an immediate
impulsion, but the explanation of it is to be found in some condition or force back of it. Some idea of the concrete value of
going farther than the mere study of the impulsive tendency is
shown in what we have to say about pathological stealing,
etc., § 366 ff.

CHAPTER XXIII

MENTAL PECULIARITIES

§ 330. General Considerations. **Abnormal Social Suggestibility.** § 331. (a) Abnormal Social Suggestibility of the Individual as a Mental Peculiarity. § 332. (b) Abnormal Social Suggestibility of the Members of a Crowd. § 333. (c) Abnormal Social Suggestibility to the Influence of One Individual. § 334. Hypnotism. § 335. (d) Dual Social Suggestibility.

§ 330. **General Considerations.** — Study of the causation of criminalistic tendencies shows in some instances a special mental trait or peculiarity that is to be regarded as the major factor. By peculiarity I mean some characteristic which cannot be subsumed under the head of either mental defect or aberration. In a considerable proportion of such cases the peculiarity cannot be correlated with any known physical condition, structural or functional, but perhaps extension of our knowledge will some day trace further relationships. Whenever a physical basis for conduct is known I have made it the main consideration for classification. For instance, we do not include here the mental instability of the neuropath, nor the vigorous restlessness of over-development. But there are traits for which no physical correlate or basis is known, and some of these are of high importance in our type of study. Although the comparative number of cases in which mental peculiarity stands out as a major causal factor is not great, each demands skillful attention in order that the individual may be efficiently handled.[1]

We present here findings merely, not theories. We presume that there are mental peculiarities other than the ones we enumerate, tending to produce criminalism, but we must confine ourselves to observed facts. To be sure, part of what we might place in this category has been swallowed up by discussions

[1] One might go far in criminalistics with the discussion of mental peculiarities, as expressed in temperament and character, but profitably we can only here deal with certain of the most important peculiarities recognizable as driving forces. Those wishing to pursue this subject farther can refer to the work of the physician, Krauss (**355**), who a generation ago attempted to build up a psychology of the criminal, largely on studies of temperament. Recently Wulffen (**2**, vol. II) has dealt, mostly in enumerative fashion, with temperamental peculiarities, in a chapter on characterology as applied to offenders.

under other headings. Those, for instance, who show peculiar partial mental defects, even of self-control, have been treated in our chapter on mental defect (§ 281); those obsessed by anti-social grudge are dealt with under mental conflict (§ 237); some temporary mental peculiarities are handled as adolescent phenomena (§ 316); and so on. Transitory adolescent peculiarities, such as the instabilities of this period, offer proof that, just as conservatism is a trait of advanced years, some other peculiarities are largely those of special ages.

Our method of presentation of most types of mental peculiarities concerned in the production of criminalism is, under appropriate heading, simply to call attention to the significance of their bearings. But the cases of abnormal social suggestibility, and extreme love of adventure, have proved of such great importance for the adoption of constructive measures in treatment that they are discussed in much more detail. We know full well, however, that both in enumeration of facts and cases, we have not nearly covered all the points. This part of our study is intended to be practically suggestive, rather than a complete survey of all the manifold variations of human temperament and character.

ABNORMAL SOCIAL SUGGESTIBILITY.

Social suggestibility lies at the very core of social life, and the mere evidences of its existence are to be regarded in nowise as proof of abnormality. The data on abnormal suggestibility which is a factor in criminalism, we may treat by use of the following divisions. (a) Abnormal social suggestibility of the individual as a mental peculiarity. (b) Abnormal social suggestibility of the members of a crowd. (c) Abnormal suggestibility to the influence of one individual. (d) Dual social suggestion.

§ 331. (a) Abnormal Social Suggestibility of the Individual as a Mental Peculiarity.

The immense variation between individuals in their innate liability to social suggestion we have had ample proof of in our case studies. It is a common observation of jurists, especially those who have to deal with offenders in their formative period, that this trait of suggestibility is of high significance for the

establishment of a criminal career. The differences in suggestibility at different periods of life are easy to recognize; we note
the gradual development of self-assertion as the individual ma-
tures. But also at the same period of life there may be discerned essential differences between the characteristics of different
persons in this respect. Knowledge of any tendency to abnormal
suggestibility is essential for correct estimation of the possibilities of moral development under various environmental
conditions.

Although a word on this subject is found here and there in the
literature, we are struck by the inadequacy of its treatment by
writers on criminalistics. We are not surprised that such a fundamental psychological characteristic as suggestibility was not
treated by the fathers of criminology when they were so busy
with their physical data, but the neglect by later writers merely
shows that they have been more occupied with generalities than
detailed study of cases.

Tarde (5), who so brilliantly lays stress upon the preponderance of social causes and points out the influence of individuals
on each other, fails entirely to note the practical point of differences in the social suggestibility of individuals. Mercier (16)
in his discussion of customs, fashions, conformity, reciprocal
conduct, and so on, verges towards our essential point, but never
clearly sees it. Partridge (18), who specifically writes on individual differences in traits, does not at all go into the question of
social suggestibility. Stern (79), whose efforts to develop a
science of differential psychology are second to none, finds no
room, even in the latest edition of his main work, for discussion of
types of individuals showing varying social suggestibility. Sidis
(17), who has given us one of the most original of contributions in his study of social suggestibility, who emphasizes the
fact that man has social suggestibility as an essential characteristic, and who deals with the laws of suggestion, offers no gauge
for estimation of the effect of social suggestion upon any given
type of individual.

Gross (64, p. 492) in a short summary acknowledges the importance of the whole subject of suggestion in criminalism, and makes
a final statement with which we are in thorough accord, namely,
that " we still have too little material, too few observations, and
no scientifically certain inferences." More observational study
and collection of material is needed. We cite the omissions

and weaknesses of the literature in order to show the discrepancy between the previous development of the psychology of criminalistics, and such practical issues as are embodied in the common-sense observations of the many judges who note the significance of suggestibility.

Many relatives also have remarked to us upon the undue suggestibility of some members of their own families. They say, "He can be very easily led," or, "She is altogether too pliable," or, "That's just the way she is. She can be persuaded by anybody to take their views," or, "He will do anything anybody tells him to. If anybody told him to jump into the lake on a cold day I believe he would do it."

The following are typical quotations from offenders' statements: "He told me to," "Somehow I always do what they say," "Like a fool I went back when they called me. They wanted me to go down there and I certainly was a fool," "If I would not go with these boys it would be all right. My mother always told me I would get to this," "If I could go into a convent and keep away from those girls I know I could build up my character."

Should there be the slightest doubt that there is a vast difference in individuals in regard to their susceptibility to suggestion, either as socially observable or as evidenced by tests, one could offer much proof by recounting reactions of diverse types. Any one who will make a study of these qualities can speedily distinguish, not only among children, but also among adults, some individuals who are self-possessed and self-assertive when suggestion is offered, and others who show passive acquiescence. These differences can be observed among normal individuals and defectives as well. I should be far from asserting that extreme social suggestibility is found oftener among delinquents than among others. (We have no norms to compare the two.) But when this trait is observed in offenders it is highly important to recognize it, and adjust conditions with it in mind.

In observing the reactions to suggestion brought out in our "Aussage" test, § 60, § 73, we have found immense differences. Traits of self-assertion, independent judgment, and non-acquiescence to suggestion are found in individuals even prior to adolescence, while the opposite characteristics may be observed in any period of life. However, it must be clearly understood that when distinct traits of suggestibility are shown in social

697

life, sometimes the individual during examination will brace himself up to react with great firmness. The citation of actual cases will serve to make some of these points clearer.

Case 148. — A boy of honest Swedish parents was seen by us at intervals during a couple of years, until at 18 he was shot dead by a policeman. He was attempting escape after having been caught with a companion in a burglary.

We had frequently been consulted by the sympathetic and intelligent mother, and had probably very reliable information about antecedents. The family had immigrated twenty years before. The father was a very steady man, long in the government service. He died when the boy was 8 years old. A good home, however, had always been maintained by the mother. There had been six children, but only two survived, the others having died of various children's diseases. The older sister has grown up to be an unusually nice young woman. We are told there has been no insanity, feeblemindedness, or epilepsy in the near relatives of either family. The pregnancy and birth of this boy were normal. During the nursing period the mother was much worried about the illness of the father, and this child was badly nourished. During his infancy he had whooping cough and several intestinal attacks, once with dropsy. At 15 he had a slight attack of appendicitis, but no operation. Otherwise he has always been well. No convulsions. He has not been accustomed to stimulants. At one time he smoked a little, but later entirely stopped. Walked and talked at normal age, and his development in every way was regular. He was only in the 5th grade at 14, but this was due to much changing about in school life, and especially to interruption on account of delinquency.

Physical: rather well developed; strong and active; 107 lbs., 5 ft. 1 in., no sensory defect noted; good color; well-shaped head; circumference 52.5, length 17, and width 15 cm.; small ears with lobules almost absent give the only suggestion of stigmata.

Mental tests: our own series:

I. 1′ 2″. Small amount of trial and error on triangles.

II. 59″. 2 errors.

III. 3′ 12″. Moderate repetition of errors. (Later method of scoring not then used.)

V. 2′ 15″. Very slight amount of trial and error.

VI. "Aussage." Full functional account given and no suggestions accepted.

VII. Both correct at 1st trial.

VIII. Done promptly and all correctly.

X. Correct at 2d trial.

XIII. The twelve items produced absolutely accurately with the exception of one short phrase omitted.

XV. One error. One failure. Average time 1.4″.

XVI. 68 and 60 squares respectively tapped in 30″ with only one error in the first series.

XVII. Writes a very good hand. Produces a fluent letter, but defective in punctuation. Spells all ordinary words correctly.

XVIII. Does arithmetic up to his grade work. Succeeds with the simple process of fractions.

XIX. Reads rapidly and fluently.

XX. Plays a rather good game of checkers for his age.

XXI. Response to moral questions was (1) The man did wrong. One should not take anything that does not belong to one. Whatever happened the man ought not to have stolen. (2) The white man should not have been given up to the Indians unless he himself was willing to go. He ought not to have been given up because he was innocent.

XXII. He is fond of reading and has many books at home. Says he does not like to read about murders and burglaries in the paper because always dreams of them. Ordinary items of geography and history he gives correctly. Knows very little about scientific items. Has pet animals at home. Is fond of baseball and football. Plays games at home a good deal with his step-father. Would like to be a lawyer.

The diagnosis in this case was easy to make. The boy was in good physical condition, and showed himself to be well up to the ordinary in mental ability. At one time to our knowledge he was doing well at work for a manufacturing firm. Altogether he showed many good mental qualities. In our tests no signs of suggestibility whatever were found.

This unfortunate boy was a great friend of ours, and a favorite with many people. When first seen by us he told us he had been going at times with bad company — a crowd of boys who were nearly all delinquents. His own delinquencies consisted in earlier truancy, for which he was sent to an institution, and later stealing in various ways. He, with others, had stolen bicycles, a horse and buggy, and goods from shops. One of the first times he was caught he was with another lad trying to sell some coal they had stolen.

The boy stated, and it was thoroughly corroborated, that all of his delinquencies occurred while he was with his companions. Sometimes he stayed away from these fellows for months at a time. He says himself that he has a very good home, and sometimes he stays there all of his spare hours reading. He has read 18 books in the last 6 months. He does not smoke. He says the trouble with him is that he has a weak will. When others suggest escapades he forgets that he might get arrested, although he has been in trouble before. When asked about a special delinquency, he tells us that he was one day with a boy some distance from home and they had no car fare. The other boy said, " I 'll show you what we can do," and they went over to where a bicycle was standing and appropriated it.

On one occasion when a trial of himself and companions was pending they were allowed to go home. One of the boys obtained some money and persuaded our friend to go with him to another state — a most foolish trick in the face of his record. They got away a little distance, but soon returned home in much fear.

This boy proved an honest worker, and for 18 months succeeded in getting along without being delinquent by completely staying away from his companions. At home he was always the best of fellows. Frequently he would not go out at all in the evening in order to avoid trouble, for it was well recognized in the family circle that he had neither power nor inclination to resist when any proposal was made to him by his old comrades. Repeatedly at home and with us he showed much contrition and wept bitterly over his own record. After his long period of doing finely with the manufacturing concern, he did not feel well one morning and stayed at home. Later in the day he went out, met one of his old friends who proposed some escapade, and instantly the long good record and unusually good prospects were thrown away.

We urgently advised a new and more sequestered environment, perhaps on a farm, but to our regret this was never acted upon. As is so frequently the case, both the family and the boy felt that in the old environment he somehow would do better. Thus we never were satisfied with the family attempt at constructive work. There was genuine, but not thoroughly intelligent effort to serve him. Our earliest diagnosis was that the boy was abnormally suggestible socially, and he should have been treated as such. It was not long after he had served a short sentence that again with a companion he attempted robbery and was killed.

Mental peculiarity: Social suggestibility +,   Case 148.
                              very marked case.   Boy, age 18.

Bad companions.

Early truancy.   Mentality:
Stealing +.   Ordinary in ability.

To give in detail the stories of other cases of this same sort we have known would hardly add much. The general point is that there are individuals, mentally normal, who succumb with great ease to the suggestions of bad companions. To give the results on tests, even on the "Aussage" test (§ 73), would prove no standard correlation between them and social suggestibility, although it must be confessed that in a few instances our first indication of extreme personal suggestibility was found by the performance on tests. Some variation on the antecedent and environmental conditions are shown in the following cards:

Mental peculiarity: Social suggestibility +.   Case 149.
Home control — defective in interests.   Boy, age 15.
                  Father away much.

    Bad companions +.

       Adolescent instability.

Early truancy.
Running away.
Stealing + +.   Mentality:
                                          Ordinary in ability.

Mental peculiarity: Social suggestibility +.   Case 150.
                        Childish type.   Girl, age 17.

Family conditions. Quarreling at home +.

    Adolescent instability.

                                                Mentality:
Sex +.   Ordinary in ability.

It is almost needless to state that social suggestibility may also be found in abnormal degree among those who are subnormal physically or mentally, but even among such individuals suggestibility is not a standard trait any more than it is among the insane.

701

Some of the latter are practically impervious to suggestion. The constitutional inferiors, who as a class might offhand be considered weak in will power, show no uniformity in this matter. The following case, however, does show these traits.

Constitutional inferiority: Case 151.

  Mental peculiarity: Social suggestibility +.   Boy, age 15.

    Developmental conditions:

        Convulsions very frequent in infancy.

        Backward in development.

        Nose and throat obstruction earlier.

      Heredity.   Paternal uncle subnormal

           and criminalistic.

           Father alcoholic and later

             psychosis.

      Stimulants: Smoking excessive.

        Masturbation +.

        Bad companions.

                              Mentality:

Stealing +.   Dull, perhaps

Violence.   from physical

Attempted arson.   causes.

The *treatment* of abnormal suggestibility should be obvious when once the characteristic is diagnosed and the environmental circumstances are known. The main point to be remembered is that individuals who are abnormally suggestible are suggestible to good as well as bad influences. We have had prolonged experience with a number of cases, and we should earnestly counsel that there be environmental protection as complete as possible, away from bad influences, until the unstable years of adolescence are past. There is no doubt that in general there is a distinct decrease in these weak tendencies as age increases. The phenomenon of extreme suggestibility belongs essentially to the category of childish traits, although there is the greatest variation at corresponding ages. One feels very keenly, after witnessing a series including both failures and successes, that while relapses may occur, treatment which takes the nature of the case thoroughly into account will be successful if there is normal intelligence.

§ 332. (*b*) **Abnormal Social Suggestibility of the Members of a Crowd.**

The several remarkable studies of crowd psychology, particularly those of LeBon (**349**), Sidis (**17**), von Bechterew (**14**), and Sighele (**351**), which have appeared in the last decade or two throw much light upon certain strange phases of human conduct, sometimes involving criminality. Crimes of a crowd, as many criminologists have acknowledged, partake of very different characteristics from offenses which involve only one person. The psychic contagion of a crowd is an unmatched phenomenon, and, as Bechterew says, "stands as an analogous world fact to be compared with pathological contagion." The crowd crimes of a St. Bartholomew's night, or of a modern American lynching, illustrate the fact. Under such circumstances suggestibility is exhibited in its fullest force. The normal moral sense of the individual is for the time uprooted and overthrown. Exactly the same type of social force is at work in lesser degree in the activities of mischievous crowds or gangs which frequently become criminalistic in our crowded centers of civilization.[1]

It is quite beyond the mark to offer any case studies in illustration of the reciprocal influence of members of crowds towards one another in criminalism. The reckoning with companionship as an influence when the individual was a member of a crowd or a gang at the time of commission of a crime is absolutely necessary in any rational consideration of a penalty. Something is said of this in another section of our work. The matter is so patent psychologically that it needs no further elaboration. A very nice point for those who would base the penal system on the fact of responsibility is found in discussion of whether or not the individual as the member of an excited crowd does not by virtue of the fact lose normal self-control. He may have unwittingly joined with the crowd, and later become criminalistically inflamed.

---

[1] We must pass by the many references which could be given to the literature of criminalistic crowds, and which demonstrate the social suggestibility that is the keynote of their activities. Tarde (**5**) summarizes the situation perhaps better than any other. Riis (**350**) has given us the best account of predatory gangs in American cities. From magazines and newspapers we get fairly good accounts of the Camorrists of Italy and the Apaches of Paris. One author, Sighele, has made a specialty of collective criminality. His work on the criminalistic crowd (**351**) is worthy of much attention.

§ 333. (c) Abnormal Suggestibility to the Influence of One Individual.

The person abnormally suggestible is often so well protected that little of social significance comes from the fact, unless influence is brought to bear by some single person so that trouble ensues. In such a combination it is often a balance between the relative strength of the person who imposes his own ideas, and the weakness of the person who succumbs. One can see this just as well at a shop counter, as in criminal affairs. But in still other instances an individual who does not appear in general socially suggestible, may very curiously be swayed by some single other person who apparently is the sole individual who has power over him. Very strange examples of this may be seen. The following is an instance.

Case 152. — A young woman of 17, rather backward in development, but otherwise normal physically, and of good mentality, was under arrest for repeated stealing. She came from an exceedingly good home, and was attending preparatory school. She had met a very commonplace woman, apparently unprepossessing, and quite outside of the girl's own social sphere. This woman had shown her the art of shoplifting and stealing in other ways. On numerous occasions she prevailed upon the girl to get things for her. The source of her influence was inexplicable, even by the girl herself after she had been arrested and was most anxious to break away from the liaison and fathom it. The only other causative factor which could be brought out in the case was that the girl was rather a spoiled child and so had not developed a normal measure of independence; she had retained in mid-adolescence a rather childish type of mind. Very careful attention to the causative factors in this case gave no other insight.

There can be no doubt that in many instances the influence of one person on another rests on a basis of overt or perhaps even unconscious sex relationship. This is true between persons of the same sex as well as the opposite. The strange hold that a bad man or a bad boy occasionally is found to exercise over another individual of the same sex is frequently discovered to be due to secret sex knowledge which is mutually held, or to sex practices between them. The same is true for women or girls. This, we have found, is a highly important fact to remember.

In rarer cases the influence may be the result of a sort of hero worship, in which one of the persons feels himself to be the weaker of the twain, and desires to follow directly in the shadow of the activities of the more aggressive one. In our section on professional criminalism we have mentioned the well-known suggestive influence of a shrewd old-timer upon a neophyte. Occasionally we have found the younger to be the more influential, but always because of superior mental or physical activity.

All this about suggestibility should be kept in mind for the social treatment of the offender. Abnormal suggestibility, even as a reaction to one individual, is an important point to consider, whether the individual is in the penitentiary, is under parole, or is on probation in the environment where a court officer has him in charge. One of the great values of the personal attention to the offender that is planned in the Big Brother movement, has its source in social suggestibility, the influence of one person upon another. This social reaction, so potent for evil, is just as powerful for good. The weakness of institutional treatment is largely due to the impossibility of applying this principle in an ordinary environment.

An interesting point noted by us on a number of occasions is that the individual accused before a judge, or elsewhere, of being readily influenced by others, often strongly resents the statement. The essential weakness implied in the accusation is realized, and the offender insists that he did the deed only because he himself wanted to. We have known this to take place when there was every evidence from parents and officers that the gist of the situation really did lie in the individual's susceptibility to the influence of another offender, or of the gang. The phraseology of such an occasion is, curiously enough, the same as that used by the subjects of post-hypnotic suggestion. The individual who has been definitely influenced to do a certain act, at a later time says he only did it because he desired to.

§ 334. **Hypnotism.** — Discussion of abnormal suggestibility to the influence of one person leads directly to the subject of *hypnotism*. The performance of crime under hypnotic influence has never played anything like the part which was predicted for it a generation ago. The question whether a person could be induced under hypnosis to commit a crime that he was otherwise disinclined to perpetrate, has never been satisfactorily answered. We have never gone beyond the dictum of Delbœuf

705

(363) and James (21, Vol. II, p. 605) concerning the probabilities of this matter. If one attempts to work out the question
by experiment, "the subject surrenders himself good-naturedly
to the performance, stabs with the pasteboard dagger you give
him because he knows what it is, and fires off the pistol because
he knows it has no ball, but for a real murder he would not be
your man." Garofalo (328, p. 289) the jurist, more recently
writing on this subject, is unable to find any authentic proof
that hypnotism has been employed in the commission of crime.
Babinski (359), and after him Meige (360), deny to the hypnotic
state all medico-legal importance. We ourselves have never
seen, nor have we found in the literature a single instance where
the subject has been hypnotized into an offense which was against
his nature to perform.

There is no doubt that occasionally impressionable individuals
may under the influence of an hypnotic state accede to sex advances
which they otherwise might reject. Several authors have maintained this point. (The influence occasionally seen in ordinarily
considered repugnant sex relationships and attributed to hypnotism, may be based on sensualism. In such way is the dominating influence occasionally seen of colored men over white women
and girls to be partly interpreted — *vide* § 243.) Either in
nature or effect, hypnotism exerted over a woman differs so
little from the persuasion of other methods that it is not to be
separated from them as anything unique. Hypnotism used to
produce passivity when rape is committed, if it ever takes place,
hardly belongs to our present field of discussion. The influence
of a man over a weak-willed girl may be semi-hypnotic in the
sense that one person may have the power to entirely over-per-
suade another into vice by bringing about a certain paralysis of
volitional powers. But in such cases the susceptibility of the
person controlled is just as important a factor as the strong will
of the controller. Most authors concede this same point for all
the phenomena of hypnotism. It is indeed doubtful whether
any person of normally strong will power could be hypnotised
against his will.

The border line of hypnotic phenomena may be seen in the
following case.

Case 153. — A young woman of 19, in poor general physical
condition, poorly developed and anemic, was brought by her
mother after misconduct which led to her arrest. She was a

graduate of the common schools and had worked at times. She came of a family which plainly showed distinct physical and mental retrogression through two generations from a previously high standard. Her father is somewhat peculiar and erratic, and her mother a thoroughly weak-willed woman. They are both proud of their family connections, and boast much of the intensely religious upbringing of their children. The girl has long been a religious enthusiast and church worker, but is a colorless character. There was no difficulty in diagnosing her as having ordinary ability and normal emotions.

This young woman had been brought up in the most narrow way, without knowledge or experience in many of the most vital affairs of life. A year or so previously she had met a certain unattractive and coarse-appearing man on a train, and from that time seemed to be entirely under his influence. On this first occasion she went far beyond her destination to travel with him, and clandestinely met him many times afterward. Speaking of her experiences she says, " It seems so funny I can't explain it." She never thought he was particularly good-looking or nice, and yet she felt attracted to him. Of his numerous illicit relations with her, which began almost at once, she says he did not actually force her, but she was always weak-willed in the matter, and always felt him to be her master. She cannot explain it in any way. She never before had any experience with boys or men. He looked at her always in a very strange way, she says, and then she was under his influence.

The first word of the parents was in regard to hypnotism. The man's record was looked up, and it was found he did have some reputation as an amateur hypnotist, but there was not the slightest evidence that he really induced anything more than a passive condition in this girl, which was an ordinary phase of her character. He had used her passivity to bad ends; others had used it for good purposes. It is doubtful from what we learned whether she had been any more influenced by another person on these occasions than she had been hundreds of times before in her life. She was a constitutional inferior, a thoroughly weak character, with defective heredity, who had been brought up amid conditions which had not developed her knowledge or will power. The bad, but strong man, came along and found her easy prey.

§ 335. (d) Dual Social Suggestibility.

Just as the members of a gang will enter into criminalism of which they would have been afraid and would have avoided had they been alone, so two persons may perpetrate an offense which either of them alone would be far from undertaking or even conceiving. This subject has received scholarly treatment at the hands of Sighele (**352**), who gives the history of illustrative crimes. This author founds his conception of dual influence upon the facts of social suggestion. He insists that the mental union of individuals makes a strong force for either good or evil, and that such a dangerous combination as is represented by two persons who develop criminalistic tendencies should be met by much stronger measures than are meted out to single individuals.

There is no doubt that neuropathic personalities are ordinarily in company more led by suggestion than are normal individuals. Two of them, who may be arrant cowards by themselves, as Meyer and Puppe (**353**) suggest in their article on the subject, melt together to act as one in a misdeed. From our extensive list of individuals who have bad companions as a causative factor, we might select many cases which demonstrate the fact that two persons acting together would perform acts which might better be regarded as equal to the product rather than the sum of their separate activities. The following two cases given in a few words illustrate the rather obvious point.

Case 154. — Boy twins, 5 years of age, we were once asked to study because they had together evolved some strangely criminalistic plans to do away with their mother. They were overheard talking about it in their cribs at night. There was no known cause for their disaffection towards her, but the idea grew and grew with them, largely no doubt, as the result of their communications together in the matter.

Case 155. — Sisters, 17 and 15 years old, living with their father, made criminalistic plans which bore fruit in the course of a few months by their running away from home, forging checks and very deliberately engaging in sex affairs. Neither of them was known to be delinquent before then. The mother was an alcoholic, and the family on account of this had long been broken up. They worked up their scheme for a new kind of life by revolving it over with each other.

708

CHAPTER XXIV

Mental Peculiarities — *Continued*

Adolescence. § 336. General Statement. § 337. Characteristics of Puberty. § 338. Adolescence and Misconduct. § 339. Mental Characteristics of Adolescence Causing Delinquency. § 340. Illustrative Cases. § 341. Treatment. § 342. Treatment under the Law. § 343. Preventive Treatment.

ADOLESCENCE.

§ 336. **General Statement.** — The phenomena of puberty and adolescence in their general significance, and also in their psychiatric import, have been made objects of extended study within the last generation. Special data have been acquired on many points, and the entire field has been philosophically approached and summarized, particularly by Marro (**32**) and Stanley Hall (**31**). It is undoubtedly true that there has been a distinct exaggeration of the erratic possibilities of this period and an overdrawing of the facts, which cannot be understood by those whose own adolescent years have been tranquil. But adolescence brings very real peculiarities in many individuals and must be thoroughly reckoned with for the interpretation of some of the careers in which we as students of criminality are concerned.[1]

In this particular place it is our business to deal with the antisocial conduct of puberty and adolescence as met with in those cases where there is neither actual abnormality of physical development nor actual mental aberration. Elsewhere (§ 189, § 190, § 316) we have discussed the more untoward physical and mental conditions which complicate this period. Even in the ordinary case there is an amount of storm and stress accompanying the remarkable new growth and new experiences of puberty which may have strikingly definite connection with the production of moral twists. In a general way the importance of the rapid change from childish to beginning adult type of characteristics has for thousands of years been recognized. The history of religious ceremonies

---

[1] The student will find in recent digests of the literature by B. T. Baldwin (**319**) an invaluable source of information on the progress of the study of adolescence.

proves this point. But studious observations of the phases of adolescence have only begun in the last few years. Something of what is now actually known we can offer in a bare sketch.

§ 337. **Characteristics of Puberty.** — The age of puberty simply means the age of pubescence, that is the appearance of bodily hair. The best observers now agree that only by physical signs can puberty be known. To give average ages, as Crampton (229) says, is likely to be misleading. Diagnosing it in an individual by an age basis is quite unsafe. We have elsewhere (§ 184) in connection with abnormalities of development discussed this point. Speaking of the length of the adolescent period according to average time is open to less objection. We might follow Marro (273), who says that the period of puberty and adolescence covers 5 to 6 years in girls and 8 to 10 years in boys.

The general features of this period it may not be amiss to mention. Marro rather artificially divides the time into three stages; period of preparation, a period of marked acceleration, and a period of perfection. As a whole we may say that there rather suddenly begins an activity of the essential sex organs at the beginning of the pubertal period, with the actual maturing of germ cells. Whether this in turn does not depend upon the internal secretions of certain other glands is not yet satisfactorily determined, but certain pathological conditions of development would indicate a close relation. At the beginning of puberty there is normally a rapid growth of the external sexual parts and of the whole body. The skeletal and muscular structures grow quickly, and the heart shows a peculiar hypertrophy at this time. This acceleration of growth rate means that all of the organs are put under new conditions, which involve an upheaval of the whole being. These physiological features might certainly be considered as cause sufficient for many of the character changes and peculiarities which develop at this time. Stanley Hall says, " Puberty is like a new birth." How to control the new impulses, and to what use to put the new functions and this new strength is the problem that every young individual has to solve. The growth in strength, which frequently amounts to large proportions within a year or so, is alone enough to temporarily interfere with complete balance. The whole time is one of vastly important new adjustments.

On the mental side the changes are no less great. Even normally there is a rapid growth of individuality, of constructive imagination, of the powers of self-control, and of abstract reasoning. At this time, resultantly, conceptions of higher morals are evolved. For us, most important is the fact that during these months or years of passage through new-found activities to complete adaptation to social requirements there may be many stormy places. It is as if the excitation of the physical organism was carried into the mental sphere. As Marro puts it, this is not only the period of development of new desires, aspirations, self-love, jealousy, and so on, but it may also be characterized as the time of psychic hyperæsthesia. It is vastly significant that, since it is only in later adolescence that the higher mental qualities develop, the individual for a long time is receiving impulses which he has not yet the judgment to control. Thus rebellion against authority and the desire for many new experiences arise, which previously have not been even dreamed of. We can easily conceive how various exaltations and depressions and morbid imaginations come about, and the peculiar fault-findings and dissatisfactions with home surroundings that we sometimes find among adolescent offenders. Fortunately many of these peculiarities are temporary.

Looking at the subject in another way, we see from the above considerations that during the pubertal and adolescent period many characteristics develop which may easily, under faulty environmental or poor disciplinary circumstances, make for delinquency. And these are, so far as the practical treatment of behavior is concerned, to be regarded as entirely separated from the affairs of the sexual life which is the mainspring of this developmental epoch. It is true that in the adolescent period there is enough trouble directly on account of actual sex impulses — early, we find, much more commonly among girls than among boys — but taken altogether, the main difficulties arise as the result of what may be termed the secondary characteristics of puberty and adolescence.

The line of demarcation between the normal and the aberrational during the adolescent period is very difficult to maintain. There is hardly a symptom which the psychiatrist names as beginning evidence of adolescent insanities but is to be met with as a temporary condition in many adolescents who never have a psychosis. For instance, Clouston (274), writing on the subject of developmental psychology, notes as morbid changes of adolescence stupidity, lethargy, causeless aversions, incompatibility of temper, visionary schemes, frothy religionism, immoralities, general unsettled conditions, and craving for stimulants. This author also calls attention to the fact that the tendency towards aberration at this period is nearly always along the lines of exaltation. Hardly ever is there depression.

§ 338. **Adolescence and Misconduct.** — It would seem altogether understandable that with these revolutionary physical and mental mutations there should be correlated disorders of conduct. An interesting statistical proof of this is given by Marro (**273**), from the school records of Italian children. He finds that at 11 years six per cent. of the scholars are registered for bad conduct, and at 12 years, ten per cent. There is no particular variation until 16 years is reached, when the number again drops to 7 per cent. and continues at about that figure for the two years more which are enumerated. Thus with the onset of the pubertal epoch there is a distinct change in average conduct tendencies. Many other authors have commented in some way or other on this point.

In our own study of the causative factors of delinquency we have time and again seen every reason to put down adolescent instability as a cause of misconduct. By such instability we mean the exhibition of many of the physical, mental and, particularly, conduct irregularities easily recognizable as belonging peculiarly to that period. In so doing we do not intimate that the individual is suffering from any aberration which could be denominated a psychosis, although as stated before, sometimes it would be very hard to draw the line. Of one thing we may be sure, namely, that these individuals are not up to full powers of self-control, and yet have thrown in upon them impulses which even a strong will might find hard to combat. Whether such individuals are to be considered as persons of lessened responsibility is here again a matter for those who deal with legal principles to decide. For the psychologist there is no difficulty in the question. Any widely experienced student of juvenile delinquency could give many stories of suddenly followed impulses, which were later but vaguely remembered, and for which no satisfactory reason could be adduced. That these were merely momentary and irrational impulses, followed only because of poor inhibitory powers, can be proved by their variance from the rest of the individual's career and the irrationality of the result. Such impulses may run all the way to that of murder. One most remarkable case of homicide by an adolescent whom I studied had apparently as its chief causation the following of a sudden blind impulse. The so-called pubertal ethical defects, as Ziehen (275) maintains, are not due to a lack of power of ethical conception, or of emotional feeling, but rather come from a transitory dropping-out of the capacity for mental resistance. Duprat (33), who devotes an entire work (mostly sociological) to the important relationship between criminality and adolescence, makes much of the peculiar impulses and obsessions frequently found at this period.

The greatest interest for all students of criminology centers about the fact that most frequently the career of the confirmed criminal begins during adolescence. In our opening chapters we have made a special point of emphasizing this. The cause, in turn, is almost altogether to be found in the formative conditions of this epoch, which have such vital significance for the life of the individual that they are equally important for establishing the habits of delinquency or the amenities of spiritual life. Individual growth in the five or six years of first adolescence is strongly centered around new social relationships, whether considered on the physical, instinctive, or intellectual sides. Nothing like it takes place at any other time in the whole of life. The new-grown physical or mental conditions are not nearly so important in themselves for the individual as are the correlated newly-felt needs of social adjustment. The outcome of this adjustment colors all the rest of life.

There have been studies, such as those of Duprat (33), made in the endeavor to discover the peculiar crimes of adolescents. Our own tabulation of the types of delinquencies engaged in during this age shows as characteristic only what might obviously be expected. It is perfectly clear, for instance, that with greater age will come greater skill necessary for committing such crimes as forging, swindling, and so on. The delinquencies of adolescence are, in general, those of impulse. Rough violence is readily indulged in, and there is a recklessness of conduct that is not found later on in life. The behavior that ranks as criminalism partakes of the nature of the other behavior of the period. With the advent of almost full adult strength, and with the retention of immature mental traits, we are not surprised to learn that the maximum age for crimes against the person is between the ages of 18 and 21 years.

§ 339. **Mental Characteristics of Adolescence Causing Delinquency.** — As we look over our adolescent cases, those in which the newly-developed mental characteristics of the period play a considerable part, we find always the admixture of causes which is elsewhere seen. But we can fairly enumerate the main features of mental life which make for delinquency at this epoch: (a) General changeableness or instability of ideas and emotions, and consequently of character. (b) Excessive impulsions, belonging both to the physical and mental spheres. (c) Excessive lack of self-control. (d) Mental and physical lethargy or laziness. (e) The general feeling, perhaps only occasional, of recklessness. (f) Hypersensitiveness, as shown in romanticism, dissatisfactions, hypochondria, etc. (g) Lack of foresight, which is perhaps nothing more than a feature of childish mentality carried over to the time when signs of adult development are showing themselves. (h) Egocentrism. Ambitiousness. These with impulsiveness and lack of experience may lead to unfortunate behavior. Running away to go on the stage is an example.

§ 340. **Illustrative Cases.** — The following case is of great interest because our records carry us through the period of extreme adolescent impulsions to the development of later complete stability.

Case 156. — Annie L. 18 1-2 years. Scotch and American parentage. We saw this girl at the request of her guardians. Her mother, a widow, had been long ill with a chronic disease and had died only a few months previously. Over a considerable period, the exact time being unknown on account of the mother's death, there had been much trouble with Annie. Some nine months previously she had first come in conflict with the authorities, having been reported by a good woman where she had sought shelter. At about this time it was discovered, in spite of the extreme poverty of the family, that the girl had in her possession an unusually fine lot of clothing. When this was discovered Annie told of having kept company with a man who had influenced her a good deal and who wanted to run away with her. At another time she accused a professional man of having ruined her. She maintained that he had given her much money while she was doing office work for him. This was when her mother was in a hospital. When the advisability of pushing the case against these two men was considered, a physical examination revealed that she had not been immoral as she stated.

714

It finally came out that Annie had stolen a considerable sum, about $100, from a woman who had befriended the family. She had spent part of it on clothes and loaned 30 or 40 dollars to the man who, she said, wanted to run away with her. This latter statement proved to be correct. The man was of the swindler type; he was already married.

Within the last two years it seems that Annie has been repeatedly away from her home over night, but when traced she is always found to have been with acquaintances, or to have stayed in a cheap hotel by herself. Her word has long been considered unreliable. On one occasion within the last year she reported herself to the authorities, stating that she ought to be sent to a reform school. When placed in a thoroughly good home her conduct was most irregular. On two or three occasions she has been out all night, but has always accounted for it by saying she was with some other girl. She appears very tired the next day. Notwithstanding appearances being so much against her, the physician's report satisfies every one that she has not been immoral.

Physical: Slight type. Strength good, but slouchy. Pleasant expression. Laughs much, and seems very childish for her age. 110 lbs. 5 ft., 2 in. Broad face with weak type of chin. No sensory defect. Well-shaped head. Good color.

Mentally, we find a girl of quite good ability. She had gone through 7th grade, and says she liked her school work. She writes a very good hand, and is neat and accurate in her work in arithmetic. She does all of our performance tests well. She is quite deft with her fingers, showing in general good psycho-motor control. Perhaps the most interesting result was obtained in the reaction which she gave to our request for analysis of moral situations. She floundered about, and could not get clearly before herself the varying possibilities of the situation. She always advocated a high moral action, but never was sure as to just how it could be carried out. It was very clear that she had difficulty with comprehension of the situation as a whole — much more difficulty than one would suspect from the results on other tests. She has a very narrow range of mental interests, but the information gained from school work she has retained well. She thinks she would like to be a dressmaker because she would like to work with dainty things.

Her family and developmental history was only partially

obtained. Her father is said to have been a bright and well-educated artisan; non-alcoholic. The mother did not have much education, but was a good housekeeper. She had been sickly for many years, had many operations, and been unable to look after her two children properly. Annie has one brother who is a bright boy. She herself had only had one severe illness, and that in her infancy. Menstruation when 13 years old. This has been irregular in the last year or so, with considerable backache. Annie worked for a short time in several places, but has mostly stayed at home looking after her mother until within the last year, when she was placed out in a couple of unusually good private homes.

Annie tells us about herself with much frankness, but some of the details of her story are questionable. She states that she has worked hard to pay back part of the money she stole, and that we know is the truth. But while living in the home where they have given her every chance, she has several times engaged in almost an orgy of misbehavior. She says she has told many lies. " I forget half of what I 'm to say." When she has come back from being away over night and seemed so queer she says it was because she was so excessively tired. Sometimes she had been up all night walking about on the streets. Says everybody keeps her so closely tethered nowadays that when she does get out she is worse than a wild calf. Thinks that if she went out oftener she would not be so bad.

Annie now says she gave that man the money because he threatened her. She used to go out walking with him and grew to be afraid of him. He used to say he would fix her if she would not marry him. She also denies that she ever accused anybody of immorality with her and says she never reported herself as a desirable candidate for the reformatory. (It seemed really doubtful whether she did distinctly remember what she said formerly.) Although she tells us of the money she has stolen, she blushes a great deal when it comes to the question of a watch which she also purloined. She says she does not know why she took it, and that she has been ashamed about all of these things. Maintains that at one time she went out to a suburb and walked about all night long. Complains of being lonesome. Says she has been around with young men whom she met on the streets, but a nurse told her the dangers of disease and pregnancy, and she has been careful of herself.

716

Later we had a very good report from the intelligent people with whom she now lived. They have tried their best to take care of her. They say she acts like a young girl; she likes to play with children. When left alone she stops her work and seems to forget herself. She does fairly well when people are with her. Does not care for reading. She used to be a great prevaricator, but lately hardly lies at all. But they cannot depend on her because she varies so from day to day. Sometimes she seems shrewd and at other times a dunce. She is peculiarly sly at times in little things. For instance, she had been given a dime for car fare, then went to a neighbor several blocks away saying that her people had given her a penny by mistake instead of a dime. She is very good-natured, but seems irresponsible. She went down town with them to buy things and when she got there she claimed to have lost her purse. They advanced her money and searched for days in her room and also in the paths she had crossed. Months later she confessed she had spent the money. She gave them an immense amount of trouble while engaged in the search with them on account of this loss of her savings. Another curious story told by her was of a man being sent by the authorities to test her to see if she was behaving herself.

From these and other facts it seems very clear that this girl has, in the main, wanted to do well. Some of her transgressions represent a silly attempt to avoid condemnation. She gave one kindly officer a great deal of trouble by misrepresenting certain facts when he was trying to help her.

We early offered the opinion, based upon the facts given above, that Annie was in need of light amusement and close companionship, as well as of repressive control, and that after a year or two she was likely to develop much more stable characteristics.

Six months or so later she was again in trouble on account of having stayed away from her guardian's home for several days and nights. Part of the time she had been in the parks with girls and boys. She had been flirting a good deal, but had not been really immoral. She complains to us now of getting very tired of being good for so long. She feels as if she simply " had to go out on a bust." She tells of her experiences with much gusto. She says that this last time she started away with the idea of avoiding the work of the annual housecleaning. We still see evidences of prevarication and note curious contradictions as if she did not think things out at all clearly for herself. Still some

717

months later she was again away for a week. She tells others she has the feeling as if she must go. She is restless and satisfied with nothing. An experienced observer reports to us that Annie speaks as if she were under definite impulsion to do what she does. There is some question as to whether these impulses are not much stronger just before her menstrual period, but the point is not clearly proved. On this last occasion she met a young man she used to know and stayed with him for several nights. She contracted gonorrhea.

After this the record for two years more is that Annie has got hold of herself completely and has become a thoroughly stable person. Prompt medical treatment left her with no permanent ill effects from her infection. She has been much liked by those with whom she has come in contact and has long been a steady-going, self-supporting young woman.

Adolescent instabilities and impulsions.   Case 156.

Home conditions: Parents recently   Girl, age 18 yrs.
                     dead.
                     Earlier lack of control.

Lack of healthy mental interests.

Delinquencies:
  Lying +.
  Stealing.   Mentality:
  Sex.   Good ability.

Another case with very convincing data on adolescent impulsions is the following.

Case 157. — Harold. 16 1-2 yrs. American parentage. The parents asked us to study this case; something strange has come over the boy within the last year. He graduated before he was 14 from the grammar school with the best record for scholarship in his class. After that he worked two years for a financial firm and was particularly well thought of. But the mother's hair is said to have turned gray in the last 6 months over worry with this boy. He has become lazy and listless, but the family are mostly concerned about his stealing. He has been bold and strange about this. Recently he has taken many things from home and he has repeatedly stolen from stores. On one occasion he coolly helped himself to goods in a shop. Once he opened a child's bank to get the money in it. Several times in the last year he has left home and shifted for himself for a week or two at a time. More than once he has spent his whole week's wages in a few hours.

He is a boy well liked by everybody. People in places where he has worked are very fond of him. On leaving home in the morning he promises his mother to behave himself, but fails to get through the day without misconduct. All this trouble has been since he left his previous responsible position. The family have tried to influence him by religion. They have taken him to revival meetings, and there he would pray, but the next day would laugh about it.

The father and mother both come of good stock; we can obtain no history of mental defect, insanity or epilepsy on either side. Harold is one of a large family of children, and all the others have turned out well. Birth was normal. Never injured severely and never been seriously ill.

The physical examination shows a big, strong, and healthy boy. No sensory defects noted. Altogether a satisfactory and normal condition.

A fair opinion of his mentality could not be given from the results on tests. These were surprisingly poor when one considered his past record. But the boy at the time of examination was apathetic, careless and evidently not trying to do himself justice. He said later he did not know what the examination was for and so did not do well. His depression was undoubtedly the result of being brought in contact with the authorities. After the tests he woke up and presented his own case very clearly, expressing himself in decidedly good language, and it was evident that for his age he was really a good thinker. Social apperceptions were surprisingly good and he showed much ability to introspect his own feelings and experiences. One could not doubt from this and his previous remarkably good record that he was quite normal in mental ability. At the same time there was no evidence of any actual psychosis.

He tells us that he is feeling very bad because he is in his present trouble. He worked for the financial house a couple of years and had very responsible work. "Then I got so I did not feel well. Felt dopey and tired most of the time. I worked outside for awhile getting subscriptions, and I seemed to get better right away, but that work is uncertain. It depends on

719

the kind of people you meet and the impression you make. I left the office. I was not fired. I wanted more than they were paying me. Then they got a big man to do the work."

"The last 6 months I have not worked regularly, but have not been out of work more than a couple of days at a time. It was nearly always office work. I always got good positions because I was not afraid to go after them. I could make a good impression, but the work did not last long. I would get tired and stay home a day or so, and of course they would not stand for that."

"The trouble at home was that it stands to reason that when your folks see you work a week and then quit that they think you are not much good. Once when I was away I worked day and night — office work in the daytime and helping about automobiles in the evening, but of course I could not stand that."

"When I was not at home I would steal some. When I took a handful of candy the girls did not say anything. Anyhow I was never caught. I guess I'm pretty clever at it. Perhaps you would not call it exactly clever, but I was quick. People could be looking at me and never see me do it. Anyhow I never stole any money away from home."

"I was always a good boy in school. After that I guess I did not get into quite the right kind of work. I've got a talent for making things. I get nervous just the same as my mother does. It seems to come over us about the same time of year. I get so I can't go out and enjoy myself with my friends. There's a kind of constraint comes over me and I feel I don't belong there. Once when I had been working at that office for a long time, and I was feeling at home all right, I somehow seemed to be a stranger there. I did not belong there. The place seemed strange to me, and when I was told to do something I jumped and ran to do it, and then forgot what I had been told."

The parents had told us they suspected the trouble with this boy was perhaps bad sex habits. He quickly showed he was desirous of talking to us on this subject which had been worrying him. It was a typical case, inasmuch as there was very little to the actual practice of such habits, but there had been a great deal of adolescent worry considering the whole sex subject. He said that a friend had taken him to see a house of prostitution. He entered into a voluble tirade against the existence of such places. "I did not know these places were so public before. They are bad. They are a great detriment to the city. They ought not to allow them to run. I don't see anything in it. It only ruins your health." Of masturbation this boy says he has engaged in it sometimes during the last few months. " I have worried about it. It 's just like an impulse that I can't control. I am like a man that likes drink too well. I have tried to stop it, and I have prayed to God about it. I was afraid to have it get a hold on me. I denied it to my father. It 's such a foolish thing to do. I feel so ashamed because I can't control myself. I had another habit once that they helped me to overcome. From the time I was a baby until I was 8 years old I could not go to sleep without my thumb in my mouth. They put stuff on it and finally broke up the habit."

It is to be noted that this was quite a gentlemanly young fellow who showed neither boastfulness nor undue shyness. He seemed to regard himself in rather an impersonal light. He seemed to be grateful for a chance to have a frank talk. To his parents were recommended closer supervision and more under-standing, and perhaps a trade school if he continued to feel he had special ability.

A couple of years have passed and there has been no further complaint about him.

Adolescent instability and impulsions.	Case 157.
Mental conflict about sex.	Boy, age 16 yrs.
Delinquencies:	
Stealing.	Mentality:
Running away.	Good ability.

We could cite dozens of other cases illustrating the instabili-ties which make for delinquency during adolescence and which pass away with the advance of years.

Case 158. — This was a boy quite normal physically and mentally, who tells us he is of the rough and ready type. He is 16 years old. His people state that they have been having a great deal of trouble with him in the last couple of years. He lies, gambles, and will not work steadily. His father died insane, developing his paresis, however, after this boy's birth. The paternal grandfather also died insane.

This lad tells us he does not like to work at the job his mother wants him to take. He quarrels much at home with her and his older sister. He is playing the part of a young city tough. When we discussed his future he burst into tears and said he would like to stop all his bad behavior and go to work. He says it is the feeling of restraint in his family circle which has made him so irritable. There is a complicating feature of much indulgence in tobacco.

After our study of this case it seemed as if his conduct was a phase which might soon pass over. This opinion was set forth and the boy was placed in the country. He then reacted by a complete change of character. He remained at the same place of employment over a year and there were no further complaints against him.

Adolescent instability.

Home conditions: Lack of under-
　　　　　standing control.

　　Tobacco +.

　　Heredity (?): Father and grandfather
　　　　　insane.

Delinquencies:
　Loafing.
　Quarreling.
　"City tough."

Case 158.
Boy, age 16 yrs.

Mentality:
Fair ability.

Worry about clandestine love affairs may be very upsetting during adolescence, to the point of causing delinquency.

Case 159. — This was a particularly fine, clean-looking, athletic fellow of 16. Previously he had done very well in technical school work. A young married woman, a close friend of the family, had become enamored of this boy. She urged him well to further his professional and other interests, but in the meantime led him along the path of sexual immorality. His reaction was that of complete moral upset. He began truancy, ran away from home, and developed a scheme for obtaining goods by misrepresentation. This was entirely an anomalous reaction, for there was no financial need in the family. As we saw him this young man was utterly depressed. His own behavior seemed inexplicable to himself. It was very interesting to note that the *affaire d'amour* might easily have been carried along as a secret, but the boy was not accustomed to either deceit or immorality.

His newly awakened impulses he reacted to by behavior which would seem to be no logical result of them.

Adolescent impulses.	Case 159.
Illicit love affair.	Boy, age 16.
Delinquencies:	
Running away.	Mentality:
Stealing.	Good ability.

This same type of reaction we have observed when a bright and capable adolescent has met with sex perversion. One striking case was where a remarkably bright young man found himself introduced into these practices with the most sumptuous of accompaniments. Instead of either falling into line or expressing complete opposition and aversion, there was the development of anomalous behavior. It was only after the individual had become delinquent along other lines that the underlying cause of his strange moral break-down was discovered.

Immigration during adolescence may be provocative of delinquency.

Case 160. — This is a boy of 15 who is normal both physically and mentally. He was sent to this country to live with distant relatives because of the extreme poverty of his family in Europe. The change from a quiet and narrow country life in Europe to the conditions of a large American city, especially in the absence of complete family control, proved altogether too much for him. Notwithstanding this boy's proved ability and his expressed desire to lead a steady life, he appears utterly unable to resist his impulses. His relatives tell us the boy seems almost hypnotized at times; he must go out and wander, and then he stays away for nights at a time. A number of people tried to help in this case, and the boy was given thoroughly good chances, but everywhere he showed dissatisfaction with his circumstances. Under close observation no bad habits were discovered. His reputation for behavior before he came to this country was good. His lack of self-control is perhaps shown by the fact that he has occasionally suffered from nocturnal enuresis. He showed great desire for education and was placed in a good school. From this he ran away, and two years afterwards his whereabouts were still unknown.

723

Adolescent instability and impulsions.	Case 160.
Recent immigration.	Boy, age 15 yrs.
Family conditions: Parental control lacking.	
Delinquencies: Running away + +.	Mentality: Fair ability.

Adolescent desire for self-assertion and gaining notice is a large factor in producing delinquency among girls.

Case 161. — It came out sharply in one case where a girl of notably boyish physical contour assumed boy's clothes and went out to work as a young man. There were some irritating circumstances at home, but the girl made no effort to adjust them by well-directed means. Her reactions were typically adolescent. She made of her running away a sensational matter, and kept a diary which gave every detail of her really interesting escapade. Her account is largely exaggerated, showing thereby poor judgment in spite of her assumed mature outlook on life. When she was placed under detention she was very anxious to know if all had seen account of her doings in the newspapers. This girl soon afterwards settled down to completely quiet behavior.

Adolescent impulsions.	Case 161.
Home conditions: Irritations.	Girl, age 17 yrs.
Physical characteristics.	
Delinquencies: Running away. Assuming male disguise.	Mentality: Good ability.

Romanticism may also play a large part in the production of adolescent delinquency.

Case 162. — This was a bright and physically normal young woman of 17. Germanic physical and mental characteristics; *schwärmerisch*. We studied this girl after her two desperate attempts to commit suicide. Her father had objected to a young man of good reputation paying attention to her. Both he and also her most intimate girl friend were of the romantic type. The girl friend had suggested it would be nice to die together. When the father scolded this girl about her lover she swallowed poison which she had kept by her for a couple of years. The occasion of her getting this in the first place was that when she and this girl friend were looking for work they thought if they were not successful they would be scolded, and they contemplated suicide as a response. This girl's emotional life was highly developed in many ways. It was noticed that while in the hospital following her attempt at self-destruction she was frightfully lonely. An older sister is insane and said to have become so from deep grief at the mother's death. An interesting incident in this case followed when the lover, impressed deeply by her loneliness in the hospital, also took poison and himself had to be sent there.

Adolescent impulsions.

Case 162.
Girl, age 17 yrs.

    Peculiar characteristics: Romantic type.

      Companions: Other romantic adolescents.

        Home conditions: Irritating and irrational.

Delinquencies:
    Attempted suicide.

Mentality:
Fair ability.

Adolescent dissatisfaction with family habits or family beliefs has been frequently seen by us as a cause for delinquency.

Case 163. — This was a Jewish girl of 16 who had developed great self-assertiveness which led her to break acutely with her family on the score of their ancient religion and general narrowness in life. Her reaction, however, was excessive, for she took to stage life and sex delinquency.

Case 177. — A Slavish boy found himself here in America so much above the traditions of his people that he could not tolerate the way in which his peasant grandmother cut the bread. As an example of his behavior it may be stated that after frequent appeals to her he grew so enraged one day that he threw the bread at her, seriously hurting her face. On a number of occasions he has grown desperate, as well as exceedingly willful, in his misconduct. But it is notable there has been a growing tendency for him to become steadier as time has elapsed.

We have come to know many other delinquents who find their own home surroundings extremely unsatisfactory and have shown in their reactions such extremely recalcitrant behavior

that they have been led into beginning a career of criminality.
All this is a token of the psychic hyperæsthesia which we have
previously mentioned.

§ 341. **Treatment.** — In considering treatment for any given
unstable adolescent offender full justice should be done to the
peculiarities of the case. Wise observers readily perceive that
slight breaks from discipline do not mean total depravity. The
impulsions, and lack of control, and other special phenomena
of this period may last over a considerable time, and then disappear. A change of environment, even though institutional care is
not invoked, may help. The adolescent offender may be quite
ashamed to show extravagant impulses to strangers, and so do
altogether better away from his own family in the deliberate
cultivation of self-control.

We must not forget that the adolescent is in a peculiar situation in regard to control of his own environment. The adult who
feels himself good for this or that, and who has dissatisfactions,
can find some way of socially adjusting himself, but the young
adolescent has to be satisfied with the environmental circumstances given him. Not that he has the wisdom to choose the
proper environment, but he has nevertheless the dissatisfactions
of not commanding his own surrounding conditions.

Lest we be accused of rendering over-optimistic prognoses in
delinquents whose criminalism begins with the peculiarities of
adolescence, let us say that the above cited cases were selected as
offering scientific requirements. In these the frequent favorable
outcome, as well as the beginning, seemed to prove that adolescent instabilities and impulsions were really the causative factor
which we are always looking for. We grant at once that many
others may have had just this same beginning in adolescence,
and then, through habit formation and the result of other unfortunate conditions, the individual has gone on to develop a career
of criminalism that has extended far beyond the termination of
adolescent years.

§ 342. **Treatment Under the Law.** — The question of age
limits for treating offenders as if they still were in the formative
stage and still were to be practically influenced either for good
or bad by inner and outer conditions is pertinent at this point.
Upon what psychological principles or practical observations a
juvenile court law, for instance, is based that implies a sudden
advent of responsibility and mental stability and general maturity

of moral realizations and control is not at all clear. A purely arbitrary discrimination is made in this matter which is not justified in the least by the facts. It is true that occasionally by 17 or 18 years in some cases mental maturity has been partially reached. The same might be said of occasional cases at 15 or 16 years. But I venture to say from long observation that the vast majority of offenders at 17 or 18 years of age are still in great need of being understood and treated by the methods in vogue in a well-conducted juvenile court where past records with all their showing of factors in environment, personality, opportunities, etc., can be taken into account for further disposition of the case. Many delinquents at the age limit of the juvenile law are still utter children.

It is a matter of practical observation among the best workers with delinquents we have known that the changes of character which apparently result from good influences often take place after they were 17 or 18 years old. Adolescence is supposed to extend from the age of puberty to 22 or 23 years. The adolescence, the formative period, that students of delinquents are so much concerned with, may be reckoned as lasting up to 19 or 20 years, and still be well within the limits that physiologists have set.

§ 343. **Preventive Treatment.** — The best treatment for adolescent troubles is preventive. The preëmption of the field with healthy interests before the age of 13 or 14 forms the best possible safeguard against the development of dangerous social tendencies. The consideration of adolescence as a causative factor of criminalism is no longer a theoretical matter, it is of vast practical import. There is a great social need for carrying the individual safely into this period that during it he may not tend to form bad associations, mental and environmental, which stand in the way of desirable social development. Preventive treatment unquestionably involves the training of proper discipline which gives the basis for self-control, and also equipping the young individual with knowledge which shall forfend development of considerable amount of delinquency which is entered into as the result of ignorance or mental vacuity.

There is little doubt in my mind, as I have elsewhere insisted, that much of the success of institutional work with young delinquents is to be attributed, not so much to the specific activities of the institution, as to the fact that the individual is tided in a stable environment through the adolescent period. The need of just this thing being done appears so assured that to my mind there is no doubt of the value of placing all adolescents showing criminalistic tendencies in some environment that creates healthy interests and is free from stimulation towards misconduct — and this for a considerable share of the formative period of their life. Struggling, for instance, under probation in a bad environment, with adolescents who have deep-set tendencies to misconduct is inviting social failure. That success can be had sometimes by placing the offender in a different home where there is a better range of interests, or where there is less friction, or in country life away from city temptations, as well as by placing in institutions, goes without saying. The success of a variety of therapeutic means may be read from our cited cases.

All through our own studies in adolescent behavior, whether considering what might be called normal outbreaks or distinctly aberrational phenomena, we are impressed by the fact that individuals with defective hereditary background are most prone to suffer. We agree entirely with the many authors who insist that it is the neuropathic and psychopathic types who show the greatest moral, as well as mental upset at puberty and during adolescence. Individuals of this type require for a prolonged period the stablest possible environment, if society is not to suffer later by the development in them of anti-social tendencies.

In attempting moral treatment of the adolescent offender, the peculiar mental characteristics of adolescence must never be forgotten. For instance, the steadiness of purpose or normal desire for self-preservation found in an older person cannot be reckoned on. One comes to have little faith in the efficacy of the cry of danger to many healthy boys and girls during adolescence. At this feckless age the appeal to self-interest will often bring little result. We have noted it fail time and again. The irregularities, impulsions and emotions of this period are all to be considered in their true light as conditions to be struggled with, which with good care may later drop entirely away. Only too often do we hear, even from parents, character tendencies of adolescents interpreted as being the permanent traits of the individual.

728

CHAPTER XXV

Mental Peculiarities — *Continued*

Pathological Lying and Accusation.   § 344. Definition.   § 345. Characteristics.   § 346. Formative Personal Experiences.   § 347. Prognosis. § 348. Illustrative Cases.   § 349. Cases of Self-Accusation.   § 350. Some Cases Prove to be Psychoses.

PATHOLOGICAL LYING AND ACCUSATION.

§ 344. **Definition:** — Pathological lying is falsification entirely disproportionate to any discernible end in view, engaged in by a person who, at the time of observation, cannot definitely be declared insane, feebleminded, or epileptic. Such lying, rarely, if ever, centers about a single event; it manifests itself most frequently over a considerable period of years, or even a lifetime. Various charges against others, and even self-accusations, are sometimes indulged in, which may prove troublesome matters in courts of law.[1] Extensive, very complicated fabrications may be evolved. This has led to the synonyms: mythomania; pseudologia phantastica.

§ 345. **Characteristics.** — For people concerned with court work, the understanding of the peculiar behavior and peculiar personalities discussed under this heading has special importance. The whole subject serves well to illustrate the great value of acquaintance with psychological aspects of legal procedure. A large share of the difficulty, either in court or elsewhere, in dealing with pathological lying arises because the testimony, as judged by ordinary standards, shows little or no antecedent probability of being untruth. Indeed, in some cases, as where a child makes serious charges against a parent without reason for disaffection (*vide* Cases 165, 166), the presumption seems strongly in favor of the testimony being truth.

So far as motives are concerned, it is clear that in many instances advantages to be gained by the lying are not clearly formulated in the individual's mind; there is mere following of an impulse. In

---

[1] The relation of pathological lying to development of a tendency to swindling is easily recognizable; we have seen marked examples of it. As Wulffen (2, Vol. II, p. 131) says, "Die Gabe zu Schwindeln ist eine 'Lust am Fabulieren.'"

other cases the motives are well buried; the connection between design and conduct is only to be traced along hidden and round-about paths. In some, to be sure, the relation of crude lying to a desired end is not difficult to perceive, but the utter disregard of the obvious social disadvantage accruing to a known liar may cause, in the observer's mind, doubt whether the subject knows that he is lying. One great reason for general ignorance of even the existence of this variety of human conduct is due to these incongruities. Pathological lying does not follow the ordinarily conceived standards of misconduct.

For 20 years there has been a slowly accumulating literature [1] on the subject. However, almost nothing has appeared in English, and the legal aspects have not been thoroughly discussed. Here we can only deal with some general phases of pathological lying and a few concrete cases; from our numerous observations a special monograph will be devoted to the subject (202).

The group of pathological liars shows some signs of homogeneity. In other traits besides the peculiar type of lying we find likenesses. Pathological lying seems nearly always to be developed on a mental background from which we might expect, in the light of defective heredity or development, peculiarities to arise. However, there are exceptions, and, occasionally, merely out of some tremendously upsetting personal experience this strange phenomenon shows itself. In addition to those who exhibit no indication of mental or nervous abnormality, we have found pathological lying in persons who are the subjects of rare epileptic attacks, chorea, hysteria, traumatic neurosis, constitutional inferiority, constitutional excitement, mental subnormality. According to our practical diagnosis of mental ability, we have noted individual variations all the way from supernormal ability to subnormality and border-line psychoses. (As stated at first, we have included under our definition no cases of insanity, feeblemindedness or recognizable epilepsy. In these categories, of course, many egregious, fantastic and even notorious cases

---

[1] The pioneer student of pathological lying was Delbrueck (203), whose work has been much quoted by succeeding authors. We may also select for the student the writings of Jörger (205), and Koeppen (204), who further elaborated the subject and added case studies; Stemmermann (206), who collected more cases than any one else. Later Risch (207) contributed a study of several instances of youthful fantastic liars, Vogt (208) made a special study of types of female pathological liars, and Wendt (209) offered the most philosophical discussion of the subject. A long discussion of a single case of much legal importance is by Belletrud and Mercier (210). Rouma (211) gives a valuable psychological and pedagogical analysis of a young boy's pathological lying.

of lying, with or without proved delusions, are to be observed. The notorious lying of drug habitués, which may include even weird self-accusations, is mentioned in another place, § 198 ff.) Pathological lying, then, is only a symptom — the whole diagnosis and the etiology are farther to seek.

§ 346. **Formative Personal Experiences.** — Taking this group in general, passing over the physical and mental differences which may be in the background, it is surprising to observe in how many cases there has been extremely upsetting personal experience, most often involving sex life. The psychic trauma which underlies mental conflict (§ 240) is here frequently met, and indeed in some instances very definite indications of mental conflict itself are discovered.

As practically observed, the types of lying belonging properly to this category are, for the most part, as follows: There may be simple, impulsive making up of stories centered about the relator's own self and experiences. These are often to be easily sized up for what they are worth. There may be indulgence in elaborate fabrications which have no apparent objective end in view, although perhaps some idea of a temporary advantage is conceivable as the aim. It may be that these complicated stories represent dreams of what is desired as experience. We have observed types of lying even more important for the lawyer to become acquainted with — lying that involves false accusations without the motive of grudge, and even false self-accusations. An accusation against those who have done most for the individual, against the nearest members of the family, perhaps mother or father, is everywhere recognized as having antecedent probability of truth, yet some of our most striking cases involve such unnatural accusations falsely made.

Most of our cases have been definitely delinquent over and and beyond the peculiar lying, which, with a few, was in itself as dastardly a delinquency as can be imagined. Most of the offenders have at times run away from home, some have engaged in stealing, and some have indulged in much sex delinquency. In all this there is a striking resemblance to the cases reported in European literature.

§ 347. **Prognosis.** — The outlook for the individual depends not only on what is done in disciplinary or educational ways — due emphasis is always to be placed on these during the formative period of life — but also on the depth of the neurotic constitution, defective inheritance, or whatever else may be a factor. Many of the cases reported abroad have later become clearly insane. In our classification we have attempted to steer clear of all determinable psychoses. While we conceive it likely that a few of our cases will eventually inhabit some hospital for the insane, we have observed some that show signs of recovery by the loss of most of their tendency to prevarication, and we note others remaining unchanged in their main characteristics.

§ 348. **Illustrative Cases.** — We can here afford space only for a few cases illustrating the main phases of pathological lying. The first three involve the phenomenon of false accusations in its most aggravated form, namely, against parents and other members of the same family from whom there has been good treatment.

Case 164. — John S., an undersized boy of 17 years, a pitiable specimen, when under arrest for vagrancy told such a heart-rending story of home conditions with assertions of family immorality, that the judge and others were moved to indignation and an investigation was started.

On the physical side we found a poorly-developed, but fairly-nourished young fellow; plainly of Scandinavian parentage. Only 5 ft. 2 1-2 in. in height, he showed good strength for his age. Stigmata: slight facial asymmetry, ears very long and narrow, dentition very irregular — one upper canine having erupted behind the central incisors. Tattooing on the chest. Vision defective, but how much so was impossible to estimate at present on account of corneal ulcer and general gonorrheal ophthalmia. Gait and attitude very slouchy. In contrast to general poor development, has already full sex development with much hair over body for his age.

On the mental side we find an excitable and talkative young fellow, quite coherent, and giving in no way indication of aberration by the trend of his conversation. He tells us that he reached 6th grade. He willingly works on tests, the results being as follows:

Mental tests: our own series:
I. 1' 11". Triangles put in by trial and error method.
II. 1' 45". 3 errors.
III. 24". 8 moves.
IV. 1' 19". 13 moves.
V. Failed in 15'. Tried a number of errors over and over.

VI. Moderately good free recital. Only a small number of items with errors in color given on cross-examination. Accepted no less than 7 proffered suggestions.

VII. One-half correct.

VIII. Entirely correct.

IX. Correct only at the 3d reproduction.

X. Correct at 2d reproduction.

XI. Made an entire failure because could not get correctly the order of the alphabet.

XII. 16 out of the 20 items given with fair verbal accuracy, all in correct sequence.

XIII. All items given, but with much incorrect sequence.

XV. 4 errors and 2 failures. On the 14 opposites given correctly the average time was 2.1″.

XVII. Writes a very good hand and spells simple words correctly.

XVIII. Does the 4th-grade arithmetic work correctly, but fails on fractions as given in the 5th grade.

XIX. Information on current events is good, but on things learned at school is much mixed up. Says that this country gained its independence from France, that Lincoln was president directly after Washington, that Napoleon Bonaparte was an English nobleman who fought against France and Waterloo, was never defeated, and got sick in England. He has read popular magazines and books from the library. Much of the above was given by the boy following suggestions offered him. For instance, when he spoke of not remembering what country Bonaparte came from, he was asked if it was England, and he immediately seized upon this point.

From all this it will be seen that the boy was extremely poor in school work, much behind what might be expected when we consider other evidences of his ability, or what could be accounted for by defective eyesight. His work on our tests was decidedly irregular. He failed entirely where he was called on for a prolonged mental task, and showed himself in the highest degree suggestible. On account of his present very defective eyesight and general poor condition, a tentative diagnosis of mental dullness from physical conditions was made, with the addition of calling him a possible case of developing psychosis.

Going into his story, as requested, we hear at once that the father has been dead for ten years and that there is a very cruel step-father at home. This man was accustomed to beat the children, and, on occasion, has put the elder sister out of the house. He now has left his wife. Speaking of himself, John says he does n't know what gets into him, but he has run away from home eleven times. He runs away with his wages and stays at a hotel. He has been arrested several times on this account. His mother always telephones to the police about him, and that is why he is here now. He wishes he were at home.

The next day we hear the full horrors which were sketched to the judge. The step-father is a professional thief, and the stolen goods he takes are to be found in their home. John lived with another relative until three years ago. When he returned, this step-father began practicing horrible sex things with him, and John found he was doing these things with the elder sister and a younger brother. This man often leaves home, perhaps taking the mother's wages — she has to work out — and even now is living at a hotel. A doctor said the step-father must be crazy.

Seen later the same day by an assistant, the boy said he wanted to tell the whole story of his family. He tells of the stolen things which may be found there. The step-father blackens the eyes of the sister, and is immoral with her. The latter practices began two months ago. Also perversions began with John two months ago, never before that. The mother is there, and knows about and permits the immoralities. Cross-questioned, after a time the boy says these practices began the night he came home, three years ago, but with his sister it went on before that. He knows, because his mother wrote and told him about it. An uncle responded and told her to put a stop to it, but the step-father follows his mother all the time, and has a revolver.

Talking about Lincoln led to the following story told by John about a celebration at school. "They had it on Lincoln's birthday and on the 4th of July, too. The teacher did not believe that Abraham Lincoln freed the slaves. The children said, oh yes, he did. But she did not believe it. The children all hollered and said yes, he did. Then they all run up on the platform and got to fighting about it. The teachers would not believe that Abraham Lincoln freed the slaves till an old soldier came up there and told them yes, he did do it." I questioned him about this matter, whether it was only playing or were they in earnest. "Oh, all in earnest and they had a fight about it. The teachers would not believe that Abraham Lincoln freed the slaves, and the children all ran up on the platform and had a fight about it."

Home conditions were looked up by a court investigator and found to be very different from what the boy stated. The mother is an honest and hard-working woman who has had much trouble with this boy and has given him many chances. The sister is a girl of thoroughly good reputation. In the meantime we hear of his court record. He has been under arrest several times for vagrancy and petty stealing. The mother and sister, coming to us in much distress, appear to be entirely self-respecting and credible people; quite in accord with their neighborhood reputation. They give us the following story:

Parents Swedish. Father dead 10 years, accident. Both families moderately well known. Significant points in heredity: Mother's sister, insane; cause, "change of life"; father himself a very moderate drinker. He had occasional attacks of epilepsy, not enough to hinder him from working as an artisan. Mother previously healthy, now thinks she has cancer. Has three living children. A number of miscarriages after John was born.

Pregnancy and birth of John normal. Walkèd and talked very early. Never any convulsions. At about 2 years of age was very ill with a great complication of severe diseases. Was sick for 3 months. Later was operated on for rupture. The eye trouble is recent. When he was about 10 years old a teacher told the mother she did not think the boy was right mentally.

There has been an exceeding amount of trouble with this boy. He was a great truant and reached only the 4th grade. When he was living with the uncle there was trouble and he warned her carefully about John. He has run away from home 12 times, stays away perhaps two weeks at a time, and comes home ragged and filthy. He has had many jobs, but stays only a day or two at work. He steals in petty ways, takes money from home when he runs away. He is very lazy, but a great reader, especially of cheap novels.

Among the troubles with this boy is his extremely filthy talk. He has even been discharged on account of this. An aunt caught the boy in bad sex practices several years ago and told the mother. Neighbors, and earlier the school people, warned her that they thought this was what was the matter with him. About a year ago John was found in a room with other boys and a man engaged in bad practices, and the man was sentenced to a long term in the penitentiary on account of it.

Worst of all, the mother says the boy is the most malicious liar she has ever heard of. They have had a frightful time with him on account of this. For over two years John has been telling bad stories about the step-father who recently could not stand it any longer and left the mother. He was a good and rather strict man who took much interest in the children. He tried rewards

735

with John but this was of no avail. She thought it her duty to try further with her own flesh and blood. The boy has destroyed the home. The sister is in utter despair about what John has said concerning her. The younger brother also feels terribly. The boy told these stories all about the neighborhood.

John was sent to an institution. There he was reported to be of a very weak type, would do anything that was suggested to him. No evidences of insanity noted.

Constitutional inferiority: Case 164.
    Stigmata.   Mentality.   Boy, age 17.

Heredity: Father epileptic.
    Maternal aunt insane.

Masturbation +.

Pervert sex experiences.

Developmental: Much early illness.

False accusations +.
Runaway +.   Mentality:
Stealing.   Pathological liar.
Sex perversions.   Dull from physical causes?
Not working.   Beginning psychosis?

Case 165. — A little girl of 9 1-2 years was studied by us at the request of a judge of a criminal court and various relatives and friends interested in the case. Her father, and brother of 18 years had been held in jail some weeks on the charge of incest preferred by this girl, and were now on trial.

We found a bright, pleasant, affectionate child, in fair general physical condition. No sensory defect noted. High, prominent narrow forehead; long diameter of head, 19 cm.; breadth, 13 cm. Slightly asymmetrical frontal bosses. Asymmetry of ears to the extent of .6 cm. difference in length.

The mental findings were, of course, of great importance. She was in the high 3d grade, notwithstanding frequent moving about. She showed no incoherency in her conversation, although from day to day changed somewhat her various stories.

Mental tests: our own series;
I. 1′ 50″. Very little trial and error.
II. 2′ 4″. 4 errors.
III. 37″. 7 moves.

736

IV. 1' 37". 13 moves.

V. 9' 15". The task was quickly understood, but she was awkward with hands.

VI. The result on the "Aussage," or Testimony Test, was, naturally, of special interest. It was done very well. 17 items were given on free recital and 9 added on questioning. 5 out of 7 suggestions were refused, 2 accepted. Only 1 error was made in her statement of details.

VII. All correct.

VIII. 2 errors in reproduction.

IX. Correct at 1st trial.

X. Correct at 2d trial.

XI. This was, as expected, too difficult: 7 errors were made out of 11 possibilities.

XII. 17 out of 20 items on this memory test were given with partial correctness and in proper sequence. With much verbal alteration, the sense was correctly given.

XIII. 10 out of the 12 items were given quite correctly and all in correct sequence.

XV. 17 items given correctly, average time 1.5". The 3 failures were from lack of knowledge.

XVI. At the 1st trial 58 squares were tapped in 30", no errors. At the 2d trial 60 squares tapped in 30", 2 errors.

XVII. Writes a remarkably good hand for age and spells all simple words correctly.

XVIII. Reads 3d-grade passage in a halting manner, and with but one slight error.

XXII. General information is very slight, as one would naturally expect from her social surroundings, but she knows who is president. and who Lincoln was.

We thus found this girl an unusually bright child, easily belonging in our B class, showing no aberrational tendencies, and no disability for testifying.

It is not necessary here to recount all the girl's long story, with its unpleasant details. She showed such intimate knowledge of sex affairs that her story about her father and brother might seem entirely credible, and we did not wonder that a number of good people were stirred to indignation. The mother had long been dead. The father and brother were working people who had no proper home for her, and recently had placed her out with a kindly woman. Before that she had been with other families away from Chicago. The father often visited her in this last place. The woman, observing signs of local irritation, took her to a physician. To him the girl made some statement that caused him to turn the affair over to the police. They and a number of private people pushed the case; the girl stated the charges, and the father and brother were incarcerated. No study and analysis of the case had been made. The judge, in spite of the direct testimony and antecedent probability of its being the truth, since there had been no cause for anything but affection in the family, wisely desired more investigation. We readily found from the child that there was much more to the case than had yet been revealed.

To us she gave an account of her life that seemed entirely contradictory to her appearance. Her pleasant, bright and normal looks and behavior were all in contrast to the experiences she said she had been through. By the time we had had several interviews we heard from this innocent-appearing little girl one of the most miserable recitals of sex practices, including perversions, to which we have ever listened. She maintained that her affairs began before she was 5 years old, and they involved, we counted, at least six girls with whom she had practiced a wide variety of homosexual relations, sometimes herself even soliciting the worst sorts; at least 3 younger boys; and 4 men who had engaged with her in various practices even though, in one case, a wife was in the next room. Beside this she told of a variety of masturbatory habits. Her father and brother have been very kind and good to her. She believes now, she says, as she thinks it over, that perhaps they did not exactly have intercourse with her, although previously she had given complete details. Her story of excessive incest, repeated at first to us, dwindles to certain practices, which she says she herself began. However, she insists that other men long before this did have complete connection, which she describes, and with them she has also engaged in perversions. All this to us, as in the case of others who desired prosecution of the father and brother, was entirely convincing of the most extensive acquaintance with the subject, but times and persons varied in successive accounts.

Later it came out that a couple of years ago, when boarding with other people, the girl made complaint of local trouble and had to be treated for it. Then after being in another home she made charges to her father about the man there. When she came back to her father he obtained salves and injections for her, and used to treat her himself. It was after 6 months of boarding at her last home, away from her father, that, under the conditions mentioned above, she started up charges against both him and her brother.

The local inflammation was found to be of long standing. Whatever the conditions for examination concerning virginity were previously, we cannot say, but now at a careful consultation it was discovered that it was an absolute impossibility that intercourse had ever taken place. The father in custody had earnestly requested the examination for his own defense. The evidence being so completely positive, the father and brother were, of course, released. The girl's own statement of prior affairs was never made in court. Her lying was so extensive that there was no use in pushing a case against anybody. Yet, somewhere she had learned more than most women know.

The extraordinary fact of this child making such grave charges against those of whom she evidently was fond, is not easily explained. The irritating local conditions, which she gave us reason to believe might have been induced by rough masturbation, or perhaps by earlier local disease (no proofs of gonorrhea were found), had long drawn her attention to herself. She probably had seen sexual affairs going on in the houses where she had been placed, and had practiced them with other children. Then, when rooming with her father, there were the improper sights that are the inevitable results of crowded housing conditions. Perhaps the father treating her locally was a factor. We never had a reliable account of family history — the father unmistakably was a poor specimen. The son appeared much above the paternal level, as also did the girl.

Reports a year or so afterward were that this girl's mind was still fairly obsessed by sex affairs.

Early sex experiences and habits atrocious.　　Case 165.
Physical conditions: local irritation.　　Girl, age 9½.

　　Home conditions: With very bad people
　　　　　　　　　in private homes.
　　　　　　　　　Parental　neglect
　　　　　　　　　(through　poverty
　　　　　　　　　and ignorance).
　　　　　　　　　Crowded housing.

　　　Heredity?: F. low type.
　　　　　　　　Stigmata.

False accusations against family.　　　　Mentality:
Sex + +.　　　　　　　　　　　　　　Good ability.

For one more example of the trouble in courts which may be caused by pathological lying, we ask attention to the following summary of a case which covers many pages as worked up by us.

Case 166. — A girl of 16, moderately well developed and nourished, with no sensory defect, and of fair mental ability, was under arrest for prostitution. It was found that within a year she had appeared five times as a witness against her mother and step-father, charging them with having murdered a younger child. She made the statement at the time of the child's death and followed it up through all court stages until the parents were finally acquitted, after having spent four months in jail. The mother was a quiet, frail, tired little woman who looked anything but a murderess. We were glad to be able to solve this strange case.

The dead child was an epileptic and had bruises from falling; these physical signs, as well as the girl's testimony, determined the coroner's jury to hold the parents to the grand jury. But, of course, stronger than anything else was the antecedent improbability of a girl falsely testifying against her mother, with whom she was on good terms. We found that the girl had been a notorious liar for years and had more recently become a sex delinquent. No motive for her false accusations was found, but undoubtedly there was a considerable element of mental conflict. The girl had accumulated a great deal of unfortunate sex knowledge, and the combination of this with the finding out of her illegitimacy seemed to have been overwhelming to her mentally. The heredity was terrifically bad on the father's side. He was alcoholic, a deserter, and perhaps insane. His treatment of this girl's mother was brutal.

During her detention the girl was moved to tell the truth about the whole affair, and gave an account of her own extensive lying which had had so tragic an outcome to the parents.

Mental Conflict +.	Case 166.
Bad companions, including father.	Girl, age 16.
Home conditions: Very bad in early life.	
Heredity: F. alcoholic brute.	
False accusations +.	Mentality:
Stealing +.	Fair ability.
Sex +.	Pathological liar.

The next case is one of pathological lying in general, with constant verging towards the type of behavior of the adventurer whose main stock in trade is duplicity.

Case 167. — A girl of 19, Irish and Scotch parentage, was seen by us in New York at the request of her parents who lived in the West. She had been in that city only a month or so, and had become involved in a peculiar situation at her place of employment. We had ample opportunity at this time and later, when she returned home, to become thoroughly acquainted with her career and traits. Getting into strange sorts of troubles was an old story with her — the problem for us was to get at the nature of the cause, and decipher the outlook.

On the physical side we found a very well developed and nourished young woman, with no sensory defect. She had rather coarse features, broad, deep chest, quiet and strong attitude. No signs whatever of nervous disease. The most notable thing was her varying expression, for at times, when confronted by some of the incongruities of her behavior, she assumed a very peculiar, open-eyed, wondering, dumb expression. On occasions when she was flatly told that her story was a falsehood, she looked one quite straight in the eye and said in a wonderfully demure and half-sorrowful manner, " I am sorry you think so." This expression was well calculated to make even experienced observers half think they themselves must be wrong. Complains of headaches and " quivering " attacks, but can get no corroboration of this from the parents.

On the mental side there are several points of interest to note. After graduating from the grammar school she had been able to get to the second year in high school, and then had stopped because it was said by her physician that she was too nervous to continue successfully. The girl insists that she could not then study as well as she did earlier, and that was why she was nervous. Later she took a commercial course. Her record on tests is significant.

Mental tests: our own series:
III. 18″. 9 moves.
IV. 47″. 12 moves.
VI. Gave seventeen items in free recital with several incorrect additions. On questioning she gave 12 more items correctly, but still more freely invented details. However, she took only one out of 7 suggestions, and that one not important. When asked about one of the persons in the picture she supplied details as her fancy dictated. For instance, she stated the little boy (really a little girl) had his hands

in his pocket, muffler on his neck, a stocking-cap on his head and black shoes and stockings — all of which details are incorrect.

X. Correct at the 1st trial.

XI. Nine of the eleven items done correctly.

XVI. 75 squares tapped in both 1st and 2d trials with 2 errors at the 1st, and none on the 2d trial.

XVII. Writes a fair hand and misspells only the longer words. The composition in a letter is quite coherent.

XVIII. Does ordinary commercial arithmetic.

XXIII. Time on Completion Test 2′ and 2 final logical errors.

The Kraepelin Test, subtraction of 7's from 100, done correctly in 57″.

From this and from her record as a clerk, where we find she is doing fairly satisfactory work, it is clear that she is quite up to the ordinary in ability. The strange discrepancy between the accuracy of her work on other things and in giving testimony on the picture is notable.

In the heredity and personal history, as given by the intelligent parents, there is much of interest. It seems there is a distinct neuropathic or psychopathic tendency on one side of the house, and the parent on the other side has been addicted to narcotics. At about 40 years old this same parent had a definite attack of nervous prostration. A grandmother on the mother's side was an incompetent and unsatisfactory person who was prone to depart from the truth, and she lived in the family when our young woman was a child. However, it is not definitely known that she had any bad influence, although the children were aware of her untruthfulness. There have been sturdy qualities exhibited among the relatives, particularly on the father's side, where some have been successful and learned people. One sister and one brother are university graduates, and are thoroughly stable people.

The early developmental history is peculiarly negative. She was never severely ill, and while she once fell down some steps and was unconscious for a few minutes there were no after-results. The young woman herself complains of many severe headaches, but there was never any evidence at home of these being at all severe. She also gave us some startling accounts of fainting many times, but it seems she only complained of feeling faint and required water to be placed on her forehead, and that was all there was to it. She was never known to have fallen in a faint, as she maintained. She was not taken out of school for any specific nervous trouble, it was merely a matter of general advice given on the strength of her not seeming able to keep up with her studies, and so becoming harassed.

The account of this girl's fabrications would cover many pages. As far as her parents could recollect she began to show this trait at about 12 years. They are certain that as a young child she was never especially imaginative. They then never thought her in any way as different from the rest of the family. Later she has been regarded as the most robust, but has certainly done the poorest in intellectual work, and that has often been a matter of family comment. The others have always been careful truth-tellers. At first she told simple falsehoods, but soon she began to make up little stories, and for the last two or three years has frequently indulged in the most extensive and fantastic lying. Her mother is inclined to think she indulges in this only in the few days preceding menstruation, and maintains she has noticed this with exactness. But as observed by us recently there is no evidence of this periodicity.

Previously she was wont to meet people and give them extravagant accounts of the wealth and importance of her own family. She spread the report that her sister was married and living not far away in a fine dwelling, giving many elaborate details. The untruth was readily disclosed and caused much family discomfiture. By working up the story of an alleged entertainment or party she has been able to fool her own family into getting ready for it. At one time she developed the idea of a young man wanting to marry her and the delicacy of the situation forbade the parents finding out what there really was to it, but at least it was vastly exaggerated. She would argue with her family over many of her stories, maintaining for long that they were really true, even after they had discovered the contrary.

The following story, which we know in detail, will serve as a good example of her fabrications. She had gotten into considerable trouble on account of untruthfulness and entanglement in money matters, and she finally ran away from her home to New York. There, as already stated, she readily obtained employment on account of her apparent sincerity and capability. One day she went to the department manager, and out of whole cloth told him a tale totally uncalled-for by anything in the obvious situation, since she was doing fairly well. She said her father and mother had died in the last year, and then came a long story about her life. When she was about 4 years of age she had been in an accident, and a man had saved her life. Her father, naturally, had always thought very highly of him and pensioned him. This man was old and penniless, and now that her parents were dead she was in a perfect quandary about keeping up her father's obligation. Formerly this pensioner had lived in the country, in the state of New York, but now his family was broken up and he had come to the city. She was earning $8 a week and was able to get along by paying $3 for her own board and $5 for the man's board. She had to take care of him in every way, even to washing his face and dressing him, he was so helpless. She made no demand for any increase of salary, and the story was told evidently without any special intent.

The services of a social worker were enlisted by the firm, and the girl's boarding house was visited. There she was found to be living with distant relatives of her own family, whom she had searched out upon her arrival in New York. They knew she had run away from her home and, indeed, by this time the mother was already present, having been sent for by them. It is to be noted the story told to the firm had been reiterated to this social worker, who might have been expected to look up the facts.

The situation then became still more involved through the girl telling more explanatory details to the social worker and somewhat accusing her own family—altogether making a mess of lies that could with difficulty be unravelled. The story of the man who saved her life was purely an invention from beginning to end. Some time later it was found out that the girl had taken a fancy to a young man whom she had recently met, and who had unfortunately paid her indiscreet attention. She had already begun depositing money to pay for a gold watch for him — a most unwarranted show of generosity.

Later when I saw her she invented a wonderful tale about a young man in her western home to whom she had been engaged, but who turned out to be a defaulter (perhaps this was in deference to my work), and who later died. She maintained it was the shock of this event which caused her to leave home. This was all found to be false. The immediate cause of her running away was her pretending to have a position which she did not have. When pay-day came she had to lie to get out of the situation, and when things were getting too thick to be explained, she took a sufficient sum from her parents and made off to New York.

Later investigation along psychogenetic lines brought out most

interesting points. The girl found herself able to dig up out of
her memory what she stated was her first experience at lying.
Her parents always had high moral standards, and the other
members of the family always lived up to them. She, as a younger
sister, recognized these facts. When she was 12 years old she fell
in with a company of girls who used to lie on the hillside and
discuss sex matters. By them at that time she was thoroughly
instructed in the methods of bringing about self-satisfaction.
Her parents did not know that these girls were in the leastwise
bad, but the dictates of her own conscience led her to tell her
parents that she was going with other girls whom she knew were
better. She kept up this deception, and later had to take special
methods of secret indulgence in the practice she had been taught.
It seems clear it was this habit and the secret concern about it,
which led to her nervousness during school life. However, there
is no sign that she has done herself physical harm by her sex practices, which she states, have not been liberally indulged in. But
she has had to do a great deal of fighting with herself on account
of this, and gives a clear story of much mental conflict. The
mother, who, in spite of her own troubles and weak tendencies,
has been very watchful over her daughters, assures us there
has never been the least suspicion of the girl's knowledge of sex
things. The mother has attempted to meet her on these matters,
but has never grown thoroughly confidential, and the first word
was never said until years after her girl companions had implanted
knowledge.

Great difficulty has been found by the family in handling this
case, particularly on account of the attentions of young men,
of which it has not seemed wise to deprive the girl. She fabri-
cates extensively to her male companions.

Mental conflict.	Case 167.
Early sex experiences and habits.	Girl, age 19.
Home conditions: defective control.	
Heredity: Neuropathic tendencies on both sides.	
Lying + + +.	Mentality:
Runaway.	Fair ability.
Stealing.	Pathological liar.

§ 349. **Cases of Self-Accusation.** — The following case is offered as the sole example of self-accusation which we shall give. It would not be difficult to present mental border-lines cases, types well known to police and penal authorities, who, being accused of one crime, proceed to allege their participation in many others, even to implicating themselves in murders. But it seems more striking to give the case of a young woman falsely accusing herself of immorality.

Case 168. — On the physical side, at 16 years this girl showed several peculiarities. Her general development was just fair, and she was rather attractive-looking, with decidedly pretty eyes. She suffered badly from hypermetropia and astigmatism, but was never willing to wear glasses. Her pupils differed in size, but no signs of organic affection of the nervous system were ever found connected with this. She complained of headaches, and irregularity in menstrual periods, and pains about the heart. The conjunctival and palatopharyngeal reflexes were completely absent. On tests for strength, in characteristic hysterical way makes apparently great effort, but with little result. Distinct analgesia of the arms was found on one occasion. Thyroid slightly enlarged. Eyes bright. Skin clear and color good. She complains much of cold hands. Severe crowding of upper teeth. Other examination negative.

On the mental side we find peculiar reactions, so contradictory at different times that it is not worth while giving the record for tests. At times she clearly demonstrates herself not to be subnormal in ability, but during work on other occasions her mind seems to be wandering and she may need much urging. Extreme variability, then, as shown on different tests at one time, or as shown from time to time, is the rule in her case. Beginning school at 7 1-2 years, and being absent a good deal on account of sickness, she still reached 6th grade. She is fond of such authors as Lytton, Scott, Dickens, and is a great reader of the daily newspapers, dwelling evidently much on accidents and tragedies. Her association and memory processes seem normal. She has a reputation for being able to give very long accounts of sermons which she has heard, but the accuracy of her reports we have not been able to verify. Her psychomotor control is sometimes decidedly defective, for in spite of much urging and several trials on the tapping test, she makes an excessive number of errors. She goes along quite well for a time, and then suddenly starts making errors. When working on the verbal free association test, she would stop for 20″ or so at a time and seemed to be thinking of other things, before she gave another word. Our notes on the case, after having seen her several times, state that every little while some inhibition seems to seize this girl and prevent her from doing her best. Arithmetic for her grade was done promptly and correctly. Besides these main points of irregularity and lack of self-control on other tests, we gained a remarkable record on the testimony test (Test VI). She only gave 6 details in free recital, and was sure that was all she saw. Then on cross-questioning she told 9 more items correctly, but gave 8 other details extensively modified from the truth. There was no main item added, but the result was almost illusional in its incorrectness. She accepted two of the least important of the five suggestions offered, rejecting the others completely.

The developmental history is of great importance. The mother was in excessively poor condition before the birth, probably having malaria. She had convulsions of some kind both before and after confinement. As an infant our subject is said to have been frail, but not to have had any definite sickness or any convulsions, but beginning at about her 5th year there is a long story of illnesses. She was severely afflicted with scarlet fever and also had a number of other children's diseases. She began to have attacks of jerking at 8 years, and these lasted off and on until she was 14. The mother called this chorea, but we have no evidence that it was. Correct diagnosis not ascertainable. The child was once in a hospital for 3 weeks on account of these jerkings. She was always regarded as a very nervous child. She was also a somnambulist until she was about 12. Menstruation began at 15; she is notably nervous for several days before onset, but her periods are regular. Of recent years she has been an excessive user of tea. At times drinks as many as 12 cups in a day.

Heredity is exceedingly defective. Of the maternal family we know almost nothing. The mother has long since died. The father has been twice remarried, the second wife having divorced him. The father really knows very little about his first wife's family, but gives us a long account of his own ancestors. His grandmother, one of his cousins on the same side, and his brother were insane. The last was involved in a desperate tragedy. Two of his aunts are peculiar, nervous, and suffer from attacks of aphonia. He himself is a victim of poor heredity, and could

747

best be denominated a constitutional inferior. He has had numerous fainting attacks of some sort, and at other times is subject to confusion. He has been a litigant, causing much trouble in the courts, and is a notoriety seeker at times. The family has received much aid from charity organizations. The story of his career as obtained from pastors and others would, even in synopsis, cover many pages. Never been excessively alcoholic. His daughter has made accusation of theft against him, but, though his conversation centers much about sex affairs, there was never the slightest suspicion he taught his daughter immorality.

Home conditions, as might well be imagined, have been extremely defective. At times there has been the use of much bad language, but the chief difficulty has been irregularity of discipline and living conditions.

The diagnosis of this case is not difficult. By reason of inheritance and defective development the girl could well have been expected to be a neuropath. Her symptoms are all in accord; she evidently belongs in the category of hystericals. By no stretch would it be possible to call her insane, and she has proved herself not to be subnormal in ability. On account of the peculiarity of her mental make-up she might well be denominated a semi-responsible. More of her mental characteristics are shown in the following story of her own behavior.

She first came to notice after much newspaper notoriety. During the course of revival meetings, at one session of which the scarlet woman was the subject of discussion, she became much excited. A few days later she went to her Sunday-school teacher, and with her to the pastor, and gave a most circumstantial account of her own life as a clandestine prostitute. She gave times and places with apparent accuracy. On the strength of all this detectives set about making a raid upon the secret centers of vice which she named. At the time of the raid she went with the detectives to show them the previously described entrance to a certain house. When they got to this alleged place, it seems to have suddenly vanished, and the girl could not substantiate her story in the slightest detail. Of course, she had thus pronounced herself thoroughly depraved.

Up to this time, by the girl's wishes, the information had been given unknown to the step-mother. The girl was detained in the station as the result of her self-accusation, and when the

748

family appeared it was stated that, notwithstanding her story, she had never been away from home a single evening or night. There was not the slightest reason to believe she had ever been unchaste. It was her first stories as told to the police which got into the newspapers. The family said she came home from the evangelistic meeting, where conditions in the New York slums had been described, in a very hysterical state, and it appeared she had very soon afterward gone to these other people and made astonishing confessions about her own life. Her family stated that her memory was very peculiar. At one time she might repeat much of a long sermon she had just heard, and at another time would seem to be very forgetful of recent events.

In regard to the extent of her lying in the past it was very difficult for us to get accurate information on account of peculiarities of the father, whom we had reason to know from other sources was himself a tremendous liar. But several years of observation of this case have shown us that this young woman is often prone to falsification, and has been able to put up such a front in regard to her lies that many people have been taken in thereby. It is interesting to note that the step-mother says the same thing of the father, and particularly that she herself has been utterly deceived by them both.

The girl later became a runaway from home, and on one occasion stayed with a man in a hotel. She also created a good deal of trouble by lying where she worked. Most of her stories centered about the question of sex. She was taken care of at one time in an industrial school by order of the court, but developed such nervous tendencies it was thought best for her to leave there. She has grown more stable as the years have gone by, and developed into a distinctly nice-looking girl, who has proved very attractive to several boys.

Two years after her first escapade she went to a court official and announced herself to be pregnant, charging some man with the responsibility. In the meantime it was found she was corresponding very affectionately with a certain boy, and after a period of observation it was discovered she was not pregnant and her whole story broke down again. At times she has been able to hold a fairly good position, and to behave herself. Her running away from home, considering conditions there, could hardly be considered a major delinquency. Her associations with young men, though perhaps not actually immoral, have been decidedly discreditable. It was noted by very good people who had given her a home that she was an extreme flirt, and was deceitful in regard to these matters, but that she did not lie to any extent about other things. So far as known she had never been immoral except on the one occasion, three years after her original " confession," when after a dispute at home, she picked up a man on the street, in despair, as she said, and stayed over night with him.

The outlook in this case always was and still is obviously precarious. The young woman is decidedly attractive and is capable of earning a fair living — holding positions well enough until her behavior creates trouble. As she has passed through the earlier years of adolescence she has grown a trifle more stable both mentally and physically. But with her constitutional defects one would always expect that from any stress, such as social conditions, pregnancy, or her own misconduct might throw upon her, she would become still more erratic. There is little doubt but that she will soon be married, and that if she has children, they will in turn be sufferers both from what they inherit and the irrational upbringing they will receive.

Mentality: psychoneurosis, hysteria.　　　　Case 168.
Early sex experiences.　　　　　　　　　Girl, age 19.

    Heredity: much insanity and semi-
        responsibility in family.

      Developmental: antenatal conditions defective,
          later chorea.

        Physical: vision very defective.

        Stimulants: tea + +.

         Home conditions: very defective,
          account of irrationality.

Lying + +.　　　　　　　　　　　Mentality:
Stealing.　　　　　　　　　　Fair ability, but
Runaway.　　　　　　　　　mildly aberrational.
Sex.　　　　　　　　　　　Pathological liar.

---

§ 350. **Some Cases Prove to be Psychoses.** — The following short history illustrates the fact that some cases, at first definable merely as pathological liars, may turn out to be suffering from a mental disease. If it appeared necessary, we could give other examples of excessive lying that have long proved bothersome in courts of justice, in which the individual has finally been found to be suffering from a psychosis.

Case 169. — This boy of 16 or 17 years showed on the physical side no signs of abnormality; he was strong and well built. On the mental side we found the following by tests — the boy having repeatedly asserted to us and others that he had never been to school.

Our own series:
I. 1′ 55″. Trial and error on the triangles.
III. 1′ 4″. 15 moves, 5 impossibilities and 2 repetitions of impossibilities.
IV. 53″. 11 moves.
V. 3′ 16″. Correct steps interspersed with 2 errors. Put the box together, a much harder task, with only 1 error.
VI. 10 simple items on free recital, 16 details correctly on questioning, and adds 3 incorrect items. Accepts 3 out of 6 suggestions.
VII. Correct.
VIII. No errors.
IX. Failure at 4th trial.
X. Correct at 1st trial.
XI. Does not know alphabet in order — did n't get idea.
XIII. 11 out of the 12 items with approximate accuracy.
XV. 18 correct. Average time 3.6″.
XVII. Writes a fair hand and spells most short words correctly.
XVIII. Subtraction correct. Multiplication table correct. Says he is just learning this. (A curious feature observed in his arithmetic is the cheating he indulges in while doing proofs in addition or subtraction — makes the proof come right in any case.)
XIX. Reads a 4th-grade passage fairly well.
XXII. History and geography items partially correct, scientific information *nil*.

Originally we saw this fellow as a vagrant, and otherwise not delinquent. His story was so remarkable that determination of his sanity was requested by the association that was looking after him. We could not in any way find evidence of mental peculiarity, but we did question his story because of its intrinsic improbability. The same story, or with some variation, was told to many people, and the boy proved to be a lengthy letter writer, always dwelling on the theme of his many troubles. He told a history of insanity, murder and other tragedy in the family — all happening in such an obscure place in a western state that no trace of it could be found on maps. He maintained he

751

was the last of his family, had earlier lived about in barns with his sister and brother, had wandered about in half a dozen states, never had a chance to go to school, but had picked up his knowledge while working on a farm, etc., etc. More significant for understanding his case was his complaint of ill-treatment everywhere; one man had defrauded him out of his savings, another had whipped him severely, another waylaid, frightened and beat him at night in a field, the boys at another place had been terribly mean, and so on. Careful questioning elicited the denial of illness, convulsions, fits or anything of the sort.

The boy was found a place in the country. About 6 months afterward he turned up again, having been arrested in the city for carrying a revolver and being in company with a notoriously bad fellow who was, according to our boy's account, planning a street robbery. The stories began again, long letters were written to the judge, winding up with the most gruesome details of how his father became insane, and how he jumped into his mother's grave, when she was buried in the field after being murdered by his uncle. This uncle when she had typhoid fever held her in the watering trough until she drowned, because he said she set the house on fire. This was exactly the same tale the boy had told before. Now there were additions of excessive ill-treatment at the hands of the last farmer, a story of being coaxed away from work here in Chicago by another fellow who persuaded our friend to spend all his money on him. Finally there were long details about just how he was persuaded to hold this robber's gun for him.

This time, as he well knew, there was a chance to trace the facts. The tales of mistreatment in the country were quite untrue. After returning to Chicago he was given a home by a kind-hearted woman. While there he had fits and a physician pronounced them epileptic attacks. The boy denied these altogether at first, but later told us he had had them for years, and he also described other attacks, undoubtedly of *petit mal.*

After serving his sentence it is more than likely this boy resumed his vagrant life. There is no chance to fairly handle such a case as this outside a colony. It is more than likely that he will commit some desperate crime. His lying, so constant, so involved, and largely paranoidal in form, is to be regarded as part of his disease. Until that could be diagnosed he was only to be regarded as a pathological liar.

CHAPTER XXVI

MENTAL PECULIARITIES — *Concluded*

LOVE OF EXCITEMENT AND ADVENTURE.

§ 351. **General Statement.** — The love of adventure is a trait not to be considered lightly in the treatment of young offenders under the law. Perhaps occasionally the causation of adult offenses might be looked at from this standpoint, certainly some of those that belong in the category of " wild west " crimes. The typical cases, however, of those who show this mental peculiarity in full measure are at the time experiencing the instabilities of the adolescent period. Occasionally the trait is strongly shown even younger than this. We shall properly discuss, as love of adventure, the desire for self-expression and for self-activity under unusually stimulating conditions, or apart from the common paths of life. This is to be thought of as quite distinct from the morbid impulse to wander, of which we treat in another place, § 312. Of course here, as elsewhere, there may be border-line cases which are difficult to classify either as normal or abnormal. It behooves one, according to our experience, to rule out carefully the presence of various psychoses, or even physically abnormal states. We have seen more than one instance of undue desire for excitement turn out to be a case of chorea, or of definite mental disease.

This is another subject that has received surprisingly little attention in the literature, even from Stanley Hall and Duprat, who have made a speciality of the adolescent phenomena of conduct. It may be that in this country, where we are accused of allowing our children full play for all their impulses, we should naturally see more delinquency arise from the love of adventure and excitement than in Europe. Apropos of this we have been interested to note some slight discussion abroad on this point. Abels (354), in a paper on rare motives for crime, centers his idea on sport as a motive. He thinks that it is very rare, but that it does occur in the United States. He quotes Naecke, who naïvely says that he, too, has heard of it with us. They are quite right. It certainly is a very real phenomenon in America.

The whole subject has most practical import, because if a certain type of criminalism is direct expression of a desire for activity, normal enough to this given individual, and which well might be satisfied vocationally, or by a different environment, then the treatment should be clear. Besides this, the economic import of the waste of energy and effort, of both the offender and those who try to stop his offenses, should be considered. Why should the state expend moneys for meeting misdeeds by arrest and trials, and for prolonged courses of treatment in reformatories, when the chance for activity of the self in a more open environment, or where there are more manly interests, is all that is needed? The very strength of such impulses should be looked upon as capital not to be wasted. The limitations of city environment in some instances may safely be regarded as sufficient cause for the exhibition of criminalistic deeds.

We could not hope to detail in this chapter all the various bearings of the mental phenomenon which we denominate the love of adventure. In every case it must be a matter of individual study to determine whether or not the love of adventure or excitement belongs in the category of normal or pathological mental conditions, whether it is based on physical conditions, such as over-development, or whether it is the result of environmental influences, such as that of a gang. Only upon the basis of etiology can there be satisfactory answer regarding whether or not the characteristic can be met by the development of other mental interests in the present environment, or by opportunities afforded under freer conditions of living, or whether the impulsions are so powerful that they must be met by repression in an institution.

§ 352. **Types.** — In observing offenders predisposed towards adventure and excitement we can discriminate several distinct types. Their differentiation becomes important as we consider the particular possibilities of treatment. Without presuming to exhaust the field we might enumerate the following:

(a) The restless boy or girl whose mental peculiarities arise largely from the stress of prematurity or of over-development. Of these there are several subclasses, such as we have mentioned in §§ 188 to 192. The tremendous urge, even in a quiet way, that may overpower individuals who are not otherwise aberrational, may be seen in Case 25.

(b) Some individuals, not over-developed or especially strong, are possessed by an overpowering call to action. (It may be that this peculiarity is partially built up from growth of forceful types of mental imagery and mental habit. This would be an interesting problem for psychological study.) Under this category might be found such diversified cases as the individual who in solitary fashion follows his cravings for activity, the offender who loves the excitement of a predatory crowd, or he who finds his greatest joy in personal combat. Certain rough, wild, aggressive natures are unquestionably extremely fond of actual fighting.

(c) The sheer love of wandering, or seeking new scenes without the exercise of any special self-activity, is often found among offenders who are not determinably abnormal. This, as is well known, may be a passing stage of developmental life.

(d) Abnormal craving for externally furnished excitement, such as that obtained from moving pictures, watching games, and particularly as furnished by games of chance. The passion for gambling is a very imperfectly studied and understood phenomenon; certainly in the cases we have seen it has very little to do with any fundamental desire for acquisition.

The last three types are such as may be found in individuals not discernibly tainted by disease or influenced by known physical conditions. A pregnant suggestion is that some professional criminals have the love of adventure as a cardinal cause of their misconduct. Both sexes may show cravings of this order, but females are much limited by physical conditions and social usage. It is true that in all phases of this subject we find ourselves verging towards pathological and border-line offenders. We have the insistent excitability of hypomania, the wanderings of psychic epilepsy and dementia precox, the fugues and craze for excitement of the neuropath. We have also noted many instances in which wandering and excitement are sought as a relief phenomenon where there is mental conflict and repression, § 237 ff. We should warn all students of offenders to attempt to rule this out before assuming that the offenses of adventure are caused merely by innate tendencies. We have sometimes been unable to decide between the two. There is no doubt but that the maximum age of developing powerful desire for exciting adventure is just after the mid-period of adolescence. Thus these manifestations may frequently be regarded as age phenomena, and fortunately in most cases there is later the gaining of steadiness and self-control.

§ 353. **Illustrative Cases.** — Only space for a few examples can be afforded, and these are given with the statement that they represent merely some individual variations of the craving for adventure and exitement. They serve well, however, to show the great driving force which this craving may be towards social offense. That the love of adventure may appear as mental peculiarity apart from any other recognizable abnormality or defect, and that it may show itself as an early trait, is well illustrated in the following case.

Case 170. — After having been in the hands of the police, a boy of 14 was brought to us because his parents had heard that such actions as his were sometimes the result of mental abnormality. They regarded the case in an intelligent light, and were most anxious to get our opinion of it.

The father is a temperate, quiet man, rather quick-tempered. He has held a responsible position for many years. Information in regard to heredity is not complete on account of immigration. The father is self-educated. His family are said to have been rather well endowed mentally, and both they and the mother's family were the kind who " settled down in one place and did pretty well." No feeblemindedness, insanity or epilepsy known to exist on either side. The mother is quite normal and intelligent. This boy is the eldest of 5 children, 3 of whom are living. So far there has not been the slightest trouble with the others. About developmental history only the following points appear of any significance: normal growth of mind and body; one serious illness in early childhood, but without known sequelae. Pregnancy healthy, but during that period the mother was in a western train robbery, and was much frightened because her husband was in another coach. No violence was perpetrated with the robbery, but the mother attributes, in the absence of other known causes, all the boy's peculiar tendencies to this event. Birth normal, but a hard labor. He walked and talked early. The boy drinks 3 cups of coffee a day and smokes a little at times. Otherwise his habits are very good.

On examination one finds an unusually well-developed and nourished boy, with no sensory defects of importance. Very upright in posture and rather more than ordinary strength for his years. Frank expression, boyish, open face.

Mental tests: our own series:

I. 1' 31". Works on the triangles by the trial and error method.

II. 1' 24". 3 errors.

III. Construction Test A. 8' 39". Only ten repetitions of impossibilities. 63 total moves. This is a most peculiar score and not easy to explain, especially in the light of the next two tests.

IV. Construction Test B. 1' 11". 15 moves.

V. Puzzle Box. 2' 24". Steps done without introduction of errors. The only difficulty was with the manipulation.

VI. Fairly good enumerative account with good results on cross-examination, and no suggestibility whatever shown.

VII. Very well done at 1st trial.

VIII. All correct.

IX. Correct at 1st trial.

X. Correct at 1st trial.

XII. 12 out of the 20 items given correctly and in logical sequence. Complete omission of the other items.

XIII. 11 out of the 12 items given correctly, but not in complete logical sequence.

XIV. Done correctly at the 3rd trial. Previous errors simply on manipulation of the dial.

XV. One error. Average time 2".

XVI. 69 and 74 squares tapped at 1st and 2d trials, respectively, with no errors.

XVII. Writes a remarkably graceful and flowing hand for a boy of his age.

XVIII. Does work of fractions rapidly and correctly and knows the beginning processes of square root.

XIX. Plays a fairly foresighted game of checkers for a boy. Misses no easily seen advantageous chances.

XXII. Information is good on ordinary items of geography and history. Knows very little about scientific items.

His chief interest is theatres to which he goes by himself. He has seen a great many plays, both good and bad. Has remarkably mature tastes in this direction. Also goes regularly to the gymnasium and swims well.

This boy is in 8th grade, and has a good report for scholarship. There has been some complaint of his behavior in school, but only on account of ordinary mischief. Except on one occasion, he has been truant only when on his travels. His emotions are normal. Once when we saw him he was highly indignant for having been arrested when away from home because he was

loafing about, something that had never happened previously
on his wanderings. Most noticeable about him is his extreme
independence, self-reliance and feeling of ability to meet the
world upon its own terms. When he was held by the police a few
days among a tough crowd of boys, he remarked it did not matter
because he was quite able to hold his own anywhere. He has a
quick temper and may be quite mischievous on occasion. Self-
orientation is good, he has his own philosophy of life and only
shows partial boyish naïveté. His own nature and inclinations
seem clearly to present themselves to him as irrevocable, and
in response to questions, he recounts his adventures without
concealment and without boasting. There is thus every reason
to diagnose his mental ability as good.

In general he is honest, although shortly after the time when
we first knew him he committed a little theft. He does not even
take the household money, and is otherwise a good boy at home.
His principal misdemeanor is causing distress to his family by
leaving home in search of adventure. This began before he was
8 years of age, when they lived in the suburbs of a large city. At
that time he would start off by himself and wander about the
city in search of what might interest him. Particularly he liked
to go to shows. Speaking of himself, he says that even then he
liked to ride — " ride all the time — on a freight — on ice boxes —
anywhere." Since that time, in spite of his having enjoyed school
work pretty well and kept up to his grade, and having normal
home interests — such as playing games with his father — he
has on many occasions run away. His longest stay has been a
month. He has visited numerous towns on his wanderings, and
made his own way everywhere by working at various jobs.

It is a tribute to his capacity that he has so readily found work
and good wages. Of course he often has to suffer hardship.
Sometimes he runs away alone, but occasionally he persuades
companions to accompany him. Frequently when he makes
an excursion to the large city from the outlying suburb where he
lives, he manages to get back for the night, and when he goes
farther he returns, as a rule, on Saturday. For such a young boy
his travelings have been extensive. On one trip he went to
various places in Ohio, and worked for awhile in a glass factory.
Sometimes he has secured employment with farmers. At another
time he went to Pittsburg, Baltimore and Philadelphia. He has
been to nearer cities many times. Most of his traveling is done

on freight trains. He himself says he does not exactly know why
he goes away — " I guess it 's just for the fun of it." Sometimes
he writes home when he is away. He has only one other time
been taken up by the police, and that was for looking on at a
game of dice, he says, and then he was quickly let go. He thinks
his mother does not worry much about him any more, because he
is well able to take care of himself. He has the idea that he
would like to be a dentist when he grows up, or something like
that.

Case 171. — Fred R. Age 18. We have known this young
fellow for 5 years. He is strong and active both physically and
mentally, but shows no over-developments or abnormalities in any
direction. Nor were mental defects found by tests. He is well
up to the ordinary in mental ability.

The reading of this boy has been significant. As a little fellow
he always sought out such works as " Treasure Island " and the
" Life of Daniel Boone." He has been known to sit up all night
to read. In his home life he has had an unusual supply of healthy
interests, but never enough to satisfy his intense desire for exciting experiences. When younger he was even taken on short
hunting trips — only with the result of adding fuel to the fire of
his cravings.

Fred comes from an excellent family where his traits are frankly
recognized in their psychological import, although they have
never been adequately faced. His father and mother are very
quiet and stable people. They have lately moved away from a
large city in Ohio, where I first saw them, on account of the unpleasant experiences of frequently having to deal with the police. The
latter, however, have been exceedingly lenient in this case. There
is a young daughter who is quite normal in conduct. There is said
to be no insanity, feeblemindedness or epilepsy in any of the
near relatives. Several are notably intelligent people. One
grandfather was a very active man physically; adventuresome,
and a great roamer. The other apparently was a distinctly
neuropathic type, at one time dissipated and at another exceedingly religious. Fred himself has been dealt with by a mixture
of about one-third attempt at repression by punishment, one-
third occasional supply of sufficient interests, and one-third
laissez-faire. There has been much financial drain in settling for
his misdeeds. At 15 he was sent to a private school where he
managed to hold himself within bounds for a couple of school

years, always breaking loose again, however, during vacation. Lately he has escaped from a reformatory institution, has been through an extraordinary series of wildly exciting escapades, and has landed once more in jail.

We have had reason to know about the police record of this boy in more than one city. It has been authoritatively stated that as a boy of 13 or 14 he was one of the most skillful young burglars on record. He carried on his adventures in the evening, after properly attending to his school duties during the day. When he was only 10 years old he ran away from home and camped with other boys on a river bank for a couple of weeks, his family not knowing where he was. On another occasion, at about the same age, he traveled to a point some hundreds of miles from home, and then went himself to the police and asked to be returned. For the most part, however, the boy remained at his home in the city until he was 15, and sought his pleasures in the excitement of skilled burglary.

His own attitude towards his career has always been a matter of great interest to us. We may quote a few of his own words. " I don't know why I do it. I'm excited. About stealing that gun — I just got kind of excited after I saw it first. I saw a man pointing with it — saw it through the window, and we joked about it — a boy was with me. About three days afterward I went back by myself, crawled in and took the shotgun. Had not thought anything about it until I was walking by, and I was thinking I would like to have it. I used to have a rifle and a revolver. I bought them. Father broke up the rifle. I don't know why he took it away."

" I like football and baseball best. I can hit clay pipes at the shooting gallery nearly every time. I would like to live out West. Would like to shoot and ride good. I get excited when I think of how I want to go out — to Texas or Wyoming. I like to fish better than I do to hunt. I told my mother when I ran away and camped, but did not tell her where I was going because my father would come out after me."

" Why do I get into houses? Well, I think I'm a darn fool. Oh, I just love excitement. When I see fire I just want to be right up there on top of the house with an axe in my hand. I don't think I would ever rob from poor people. These others could afford to lose it. I have a partner mostly. We don't have to go out very often for what we want. We get it easily.

We never carried revolvers. We figured the fellow in the house would be just as scared as we would be. We never stayed out late. One night we looked in an open window, and my partner wanted to see if there was anybody in the house. I boosted him, and then he called me in. We got eight watches and rings and things. It is not so much fun doing it — all the time you are afraid you are going to get caught. But, gee, it 's exciting when you know people are in the next room — you just ought to hear your heart going pit-a-pat. I like excitement of any kind. I never was discovered in a house."

If we went over the whole case as we have known it during these years, pages would reveal nothing more to the point than the above statements offer. Fred turned from burglary when he was less than 15, but later has sought adventuresome excitement in other directions, much to the discomfiture of numerous people whose automobiles have been stolen and wrecked, and much to the depletion of his father's pocketbook. He still says, "It 's just that crazy habit of mine; wanting to do something exciting." There has been desperate speeding of stolen machines, and occasionally a street robbery has varied the program. Thoroughly characteristic of this young man's whole career is his most recent adventure. We have the details from reliable police and other sources. He went back to his Ohio home town. There he picked up two or three other fellows and started in a stolen automobile on an excursion of adventure to New York. After running a couple of hundred miles the machine was wrecked. They returned, our young man produced another machine, and they started off again. This time they got as far as a Pennsylvania town when their funds gave out. Our fellow, in true desperado fashion, proceeded to "hold up" by threatening with a revolver, the cashier in a shop. He was caught before they left the town.

Concerning the treatment of this case: at the start we insisted that the boy's aptitudes and desires were all in line with the life that he might lawfully experience on the mountains, or plains, or sea. The fact that his school course was unfinished militated against anything that we could say, and at no time has he ever been placed in what we conceived to be a suitable environment. The lesson of his failure is just as convincing as in cases where success has been established by environmental modifications. The fact that there is good mental ability in this instance has

761

always made his reform seem imminent to those most vitally concerned, and I have little doubt but that it will eventuate.

Case 172. — The following card gives the main facts in a case where no observable physical conditions had any bearing. The boy was only moderately well developed for his age. His tendencies showed before adolescence.

Mental peculiarity: Immense love of excitement   Case 172.
and adventure.   Boy, age 15.

  Home conditions: Father away much on business.

   Lack of healthy interests for his needs.

    Bad companions.

Stealing.   Mentality:
Rowdyism.   Ordinary in ability.

Case 173. This is an instance of indomitable aggressiveness long displayed, in spite of his having been sentenced three times.

Mental peculiarity: Wild, aggressive, undisci-   Case 173.
plined nature.   Boy, 16 yrs.
Physically strong
(not over-developed).

  Bad companions: Street robbers and others.

   Heredity: Mother extremely aggressive type.
Brother subnormal.

    Home conditions: Father dead.
Mother blind.
Terrific quarreling.
No discipline.

   Adolescence.

Early truancy.   Mentality:
Stealing + +.   Ordinary in ability.
Violence.

The above cases represent a few of those which seem merely to have innate love of adventure and excitement as the main cause for their offenses. When we come to the instances of girls showing these tendencies we nearly always have marked physical over-development. In both sexes there may be a distinct neuro-pathic tendency as the basis for the love of exciting adventure. An example of a border-line case is the following:

Mental peculiarity: Extreme love of excitement. Case 174.
                        Much imagery of adventure. Boy, age 15.

    Neuropathic type: Nervous. Unstable.

      Developmental conditions: Antenatal.
                         Mother in poor health
                           and old.
                         Brain fever and frequent
                           spasms in infancy.
                         Excess of opiates given.

         Home conditions: Spoiled child.

           Motion pictures.

Truancy in school.
Stealing.   Mentality:
Runaway + +.   Ordinary in ability.

We have seen several cases where the desire for excitement of some definite kind was overwhelming. Particularly in young boys and girls one may observe the craving for motion pictures, which latterly have taken the place of the old exciting cheap novel. In older adolescent boys we may note the love of gambling, particularly of throwing dice. The passion for gambling as met with in men, and occasionally in women, is well recognized, and we need not give space for it here.

§ 354. **Desire for Travel.** — The desire to wander or to travel, "*die Wanderlust*," is only one phase of our whole subject. It has received in other places (§ 312, § 369) considerable attention at our hands. The desire may be shown astonishingly early in life, and may be only a passing trait, or it may be preserved for a lifetime. We have had the chance to study many cases of peculiar interest, showing in various combinations the typical causative factors we have spoken of. It is not easy to say at first sight of a case what there may be in the background.

Case 175. — One little boy, very poorly developed, began running away from home within a few days after landing in America, an utter stranger. Over years he kept up his wanderings at intervals, until he was placed in the reformatory institution where he now is. This would seem to be a marked case of the outbreak of innate tendencies, but we were never able to persuade ourselves of this, because of the probability of there being strong mental conflict concerning the unfortunate circumstances of his illegitimate birth of which he at about that time first became aware.

The often mentioned relationship in vagrants between the wandering impulse and laziness, when boiled down, as we have shown under the heading of vagabondage, § 369, turns out largely to be the relationship between wandering and physical or mental disease and defect.

§ 355. **Explosions of Desire for Excitement.** — The craving for excitement is always more or less intermittent. We note that some criminalistic individuals are able to maintain themselves on a normal basis for long periods, and then the urgent desire for explosion becomes overpowering. In one most intelligent young woman whom we knew for years there would come periods when she simply would have to " break loose." The urgency of this desire is to be fairly compared with dipsomania. Indeed the whole phenomenon, with its periodic lack of self-control and throwing away of advantages, which amounts to temporary loss of the sense of self-preservation, savors highly of the pathological. Outbursts of temper, of flagrant sex indulgence, of carousing, of rowdyism, and of adventuresome stealing are characteristic. The strangeness of the impulse is well recognized by some offenders themselves. We have often heard them comment on it. Ellis (**124**, p. 168 ff.) gives interesting illustrations on this point. That any individual under the monotonous conditions of prison life may desire occasionally to " break loose " is most natural.

The phenomenon of intermittent explosions of emotion is a common feature of every-day life. But the individual who feels the necessity to break over the traces to the extent that he jeopardizes his own welfare and liberty is most frequently a distinct neuropath. It has been well suggested that further investigation of these explosive features of criminalistic conduct should be carried on in connection with studies of epileptic variations, as found in the families of the offenders. There is much room for research in this line.

§ 356. **Desire for the Stage.** — An intense desire to enter theatrical life, the impulse of the " stage-struck " girl, which may definitely lead to delinquency, upon analysis seems to be little else than love of excitement and adventure. The glamour of the footlights may appear to arouse dramatic instinct and desire for self-expression, and perhaps it does to a certain extent, but the arousal of such desire does not imply any special dramatic talent. It must be rare indeed, judging from our experience, that the " stage-struck " impulse is based on any especial ability for dramatics. The possession of real talent, then, has here little or nothing to do with development of waywardness.

§ 357. **Treatment.** — The treatment of the abnormal love of excitement and adventure is, as may be seen from the above cases, a highly individual matter, but when properly undertaken frequently yields immensely good results. It cannot be supposed that suppression of these dominant characteristics is going to evoke anything but dissatisfaction and further recalcitrancy. Some sort of an outlet must be afforded. In our civilization we are not doing as well in this matter as we did a hundred years ago, when pioneer and sea life offered opportunities for the satisfaction of many of these cravings. As it is now, each case must be sized up for itself in relation to physical background and other things, and families must be convinced of the practical necessities of the situation.

OTHER PECULIARITIES.

§ 358. **Racial Characteristics.** — We have occasionally said that an offender represented in character the essence or prototype of his racial characteristics. For instance, a negro was so lazy, shiftless, sensuous, immoral, and talkative that it seemed as if he gathered within himself all the unfortunate and perhaps aboriginal traits of his race. Or the offender with Indian blood was so taciturn, cruel, and roving that he represented the worst qualities of his people. In the same way we observe Southern Italians, or Sicilians, who are easily angered and prone to quick violence with weapons; one feels that they show strongly a national characteristic. Thus in occasional cases one does feel justified in diagnosing the mental characteristics of the individual as those peculiar to his race. It may be possible to analyze the general character into its constituent parts, but for the purposes of direct expression and understanding, the use of the term racial characteristics is often valuable in explanation of the peculiarities which lead to social offense.

§ 359. **Contrary Suggestibility.** — A marked and easily recognized human trait is obstinacy. In some this is so dominant that general conduct may be measured in its terms. The obstinate person is supposed to represent the very antithesis of social suggestibility, and yet in some the tendency to opposition and perversity is as clearly set along definite lines by way of reaction as when the positive forms of suggestibility are shown. It is the old story of the individual who is so against everything, that he is ready to do the opposite of whatever he is told. This would hardly seem to have direct connection with delinquency, but yet I am constrained to believe upon the basis of several experiences that excessive, contrary self-assertion may be a real driving force towards social offense. One must agree with McDougall (20) in his highly original essay on the subject, that in certain individuals this "negative reaction to suggestion appears as a permanent and temperamental attitude."

The high-spirited action of adolescence when there is a breaking away from family restriction and the disobeying of parental admonitions may be a considerable cause of delinquency during that period. The tendency to contrary reaction may thus appear as a phenomenon belonging to the mental growth of a particular age.

General obstinacy no doubt is frequently part of a temperamental attitude, but often there is a chronically aggravating cause, such as results from some untoward experience. A case which we originally wrote up for this section of our work was apparently one of the best possible illustrations of a spiteful and obstinate reaction on the part of a young woman physically and mentally very well endowed. Her behavior for a number of years had been the most glaring example of reaction by contraries. Exhortation to better behavior was to her a challenge to do the opposite. Further study of this remarkable case brought out, however, that the young woman had been undergoing an experience which no one knew about. That she was an individual with some innate tendency to react obstinately no one could doubt, but the major incitement towards such reaction was unquestionably the unfortunate experience which she had been for years hiding.

We might philosophically assume with McDougall that the function of contrary suggestibility is the enrichment and organization of experience. At least this is true of the self-assertion and contrary suggestibility shown during adolescence. But when it comes to the setting of one's face against the social order, only a stage of development is represented in which the crude material of rational action has not been successfully coördinated. The obstinate temperament thus may be taken partly into account in considering the treatment of offenders, but as nothing final. The next step for the student of the individual is to find out why obstinacy is the dominant activity.

§ 360. **Revengefulness.** — A stubbornly persistent form of self-assertion is the desire for revenge. Within limits it is one of the most naturally expressed emotional reactions, but it may follow upon anger as an obsessional phenomenon, and be as much a sign of the lack of self-control as anger itself is. The desire for revenge plays a considerable part in the production of criminal-istic deeds of violence. As such it must be reckoned with alone, although in the cases where it is exhibited to the degree that the individual endangers himself, there is very frequently an abnormal basis. Many of these individuals, as we have noted them, are deficient in self-control, in reasoning power, or are clearly aber-rational. Further study of them after the recognition that they possessed a revengeful disposition has always elucidated these other facts. So it comes about that the term " revengeful dis-position," although frequently offered in superficial judgment of the facts, has found no place in our category of explanatory causes.

Of course one might discuss this topic of revenge at much greater length, but to little more purpose as far as diagnosis is concerned of the causative factors in the individual case. The spirit of revenge, sometimes a thoroughly dominating cause, occasionally is to be considered under the head of social sugges-tion inasmuch as it may be entirely inculcated by the species of education or the contagion of ideals resulting from life among certain associations and in certain communities, such as those of Sicily or the Kentucky mountains.

§ 361. **Excessive Irritability.** — Although irritability is fre-quently spoken of as a mental trait, and much understanding of the individual is gained through use of the term, yet we have failed to find excessive irritability without some physical cause for it. It would be well if all workers with offenders would remem-ber this, because of the added possibilities of treatment. In cases reported as having excessive irritability we have discovered poor general development, various nervous ailments (such as chorea or traumatic neuroses), under-feeding, overuse of stimulants, alcoholism, sex over-indulgence, incipient tuberculosis, signs of over-work, and other physical conditions in the background. On account of finding these conditions so frequently we have become more and more convinced of the value of looking for them in all cases. We studied one very irritable boy at intervals for a long time without understanding him until he was placed under careful observation. Then it was found that he indulged greatly in sex practices, which he had always, although apparently frank, denied to us.

Mental peculiarity: Extremely irritable. Fiery disposition. Melancholy at times.	Case 176. Boy, 15 yrs.
Physical conditions: Poorly nourished for long. Depletion from masturbation.	
Family conditions: Poverty from much tuberculosis in family; lack of proper control.	
Violence. Stabbing. Threatening.	Mentality: Dull probably from physical conditions.

§ 362. **Special Abilities.** — In a few instances of adolescent offenders we have seen much proof of the fact that the possession of unusual general ability, or of some special ability, which would not fit in with the environment was apparently a considerable factor towards developing criminalism. We have already spoken under the head of professionalism, § 227, of individuals who had motor dexterity which readily led them, in a defective environment, to become skilled offenders. We noted in the case of one vigorous, independent boy, who was a truant and a thief, that there was a great deal of school dissatisfaction based on the fact, it came out, that he was not in the least a book-minded young person. We have seen instances of children with extraordinary ability born in an environment where their capacities were not only unappreciated, but held down by poverty and non-understanding. The reaction to this anomalous situation easily tends towards delinquency. The possession of strong imaginative and dramatic powers has also started children in social offenses. In one particularly difficult case of a boy of 12, who was a great wanderer from home, and a little thief, it seemed very sure that the love of the dramatic held full sway over him. The poor home gave him no opportunities whatever for satisfying his innate desires.

§ 363. **Restlessness.** — Whether or not restlessness is a mental peculiarity that may be separated from physical conditions is not quite clear. It can be a great factor making for delinquency. It is sometimes observed in cases where there is decidedly good physical strength and good mental powers. In nearly all cases that we have observed the characteristic has been found apparently to rest on some sort of a physical basis, perhaps inherited, as in Cases 1 and 2.

§ 364. **Stupidity.** — We deplore the use of this term as employed by some authors to denote a mental peculiarity. Of course many offenders show stupidity as a secondary characteristic, but when their mental assets are tabulated very definite defects are found, and they may be more fundamentally diagnosed. They are either high-grade feebleminded, or individuals with special defects, lacking perhaps foresight and powers of mental representation, or they may be dull from physical causes.

CHAPTER XXVII

Pathological Stealing — "Kleptomania." Pathological Arson — "Pyromania." Suicide. Vagabondage. Simulation. "Born Criminals." "Moral Imbecility"

§ 365. General Considerations. § 366. Pathological Stealing — "Kleptomania." § 367. Pathological Arson — "Pyromania." § 368. Suicide. § 369. Vagabondage — Tramp Life. § 370. Simulation. § 371. "Born Criminals." § 372. "Moral Imbecility" — "Moral Insanity."

§ 365. **General Considerations.** — A number of remaining points need discussion either because they are moot questions in the field of criminology, or because the widespread use of some term has determined the way in which a related group of facts is generally viewed. Nothing is so catching as a name, and frequently, as shown below, appellation counterfeits explanation. While these names represent subjects frequently considered under criminology, they do not properly belong under the head either of types of individuals or types of causes, such as make up the divisions in Book II.

As we have endeavored previously to show in § 122, the classification by deeds means little for us. Murders may be committed with a range of intent varying from that of Charlotte Corday to that of a Jack-the-ripper. A few definite types of offense tend to be committed by certain types of offenders, then the correlation is valuable. Our standpoint in slurring these matters, although opposed to much in the literature, is justified by the considerations which appear in many places throughout this work. Such parts of the following discussion as center about special delinquencies bring out interesting facts anent this question of subdividing criminalistics according to crimes.

§ 366. **Pathological Stealing** — "**Kleptomania.**"

In common with many authors we are much averse to using the term "kleptomania."[1] This is because of the loose way in

---

[1] "*La kleptomanie est un mot, et c'est une explication qu'on demande*" (Dubuisson, **330**, p. 16). Peculiarly offensive is the common employment of the term, *kleptomaniac*, inasmuch as it pretends to tell something of the personal qualities of the offender and yet does not.

which the word is used — the variety of connotations leading away from anything like scientific accuracy and clear meaning. Like "pyromania," it has been seized upon with avidity for journalistic and general purposes. Often it seems to mean merely excessive stealing, and hence has no particular significance for us. Then on the other hand, as used by some psychiatrists, it betokens a form of impulsive insanity. We find that limitation too narrow, for just the same form of offense is indulged in by individuals who are not insane. The general phenomenon we are interested in is a peculiar kind of thieving, which can best be designated as pathological stealing. As thus used, the term is consonant with pathological lying — the latter being a designation that is already clearly defined (*vide* § 344), and widely used.

The definition of pathological stealing is similar to that of pathological lying. The criterion of both is the fact that the misconduct is disproportionate to any discernible end in view. In spite of risk, the stealing is indulged in, as it were, for its own sake, and not because the objects in themselves are needed or intrinsically desired. It is important to apply this gauge, because otherwise cases of excessive stealing which arise from cupidity or development of a habit might be included. Pathological stealing, even if we do not go so far as the dictum of Kraepelin, and accept it as evidence of insanity of impulsion, is obviously to be regarded as abnormally conditioned action.

The types of causation which lead to pathological stealing and the types of individuals who engage in it are found described under other headings. For these reasons it is not necessary to dwell on pathological stealing as the central fact in case studies. We have discussed the relationship of mental conflicts, and of the minor psychical aberrations of menstruation (§ 310), and of pregnancy (§ 311), to pathological stealing. It is clear that mental defectives may have the habit of stealing for the sake of stealing, although here the distinction is difficult. One case of so-called "kleptomania," was that of a feebleminded boy who frequently stole watches, even when he had some, but the lad was partly following out a sort of collecting impulse, and partly wanted the watches to pull them to pieces. In his exaggeration of a normal boyish instinct he succeeded in stealing many. But it was hardly a case of pathological stealing any more than lying indulged in by a feebleminded person is pathological lying. The epileptic, during twilight or automatic states, may steal things

771

which are not in themselves desired, and thus engage in pathological stealing. But this is an individual with a brain disease that causes temporary insanity, who automatically steals. Such cases are rare and belong in their special categories. The vast majority of all instances of pathological stealing are those in which individuals, not determinably insane, give way to an abnormally conditioned impulse to steal.

The interpretation of the causes of this impulse to steal is of great interest. We have shown in our chapter on mental conflicts how it may be a sort of relief phenomenon for repressed elements in mental life. The repression is found often to center about sex affairs. Such basis for the stealing impulse is found by analysing the underlying subconscious motives. Janet (306) has very cleverly shown this relief activity in a case of recurrent melancholia he has studied. He found that his patient overcame her tendency to depression by extensive purloining of small articles from shops. He avers that this illustrates a general fact. Such an impulse gets its force from the need of excitement, occurring, in his case, during the course of intense depression through the feeling of incompleteness which the depression brings about.

The correlation of the stealing impulse to the menstrual or premenstrual period in woman leads us to much the same conclusion. Gudden (294), who seems to have made the most careful of studies of the connection between the two phenomena, maintains that practically all cases of shoplifters whom he has examined, were, at the time of their offense, in or near their period of menstruation. Most of them were properly to be regarded as hysterical individuals. They gave way to some strong impulse which suddenly came to them while they were in the shops. Their actions were planless. In other words, a tendency was subconsciously present and relief was sought in action.[1]

_____

[1] The principal conclusions of this careful student, Gudden (294), are worth citing in this connection on account of his considerable experience with department store thieving. He states that 99 per cent. of shoplifters are women; that very few of these are country people; that practically none are intoxicated; that in two-thirds of the cases no special motive or need was present; that the criterion of the pathological action is found in the stealing of unusable goods; that nearly all cases were at the period of menstruation; that a few were pregnant; that the deed was planless and really done half consciously; that many had shown a tendency to aberrational states before the stealing. He thinks the exhibition of goods offers the opportunity for these women to give vent to their impulses by simply stretching out their hands. The fact that goods are frequently returned anonymously shows the lack of intent. He saw some of these women at a later menstrual period, and found evidences of excitation then. As far as they go these observations fall in line with the

From such observations as those of Gudden it would be supposed that practically all pathological stealing was connected with menstruation, but as we have shown in our chapter on mental conflict (§ 235), some of the most extravagant cases of pathological stealing occur years before the onset of menstruation, or may occur in boys and young men. Instances of such stealing which occurs during pregnancy (§ 311) are well known. We studied the case of a woman of prior unblemished reputation, who suddenly during pregnancy gave way to an impulse to steal in a shop. She seemed afterward to be in a state of stupefaction in regard to the event. She was shocked by what she had done, and could hardly remember doing it. This woman had been for many years in a position of great trust, and pregnancy, it seems, brought about an impulse that was, as far as ascertainable, foreign to her whole previous nature. The statement that the impulse to steal may come on first at the menopause we have not had opportunity to corroborate. Those, e. g. Stekel (**143**), who are wedded to the view that "kleptomania" type of stealing is always due to the repression of the elements of sex life will, of course, find no reason to be less convinced by Gudden's findings that so many of these cases occur about the time when sex excitement is often increased.[1]

In discriminating cases of actual pathological stealing one must be careful to rule out those who steal for the sake of adventure, for the love of excitement plus possession. Other forms of stealing, for example, of objects of fetishism, may in a sense be termed pathological stealing, but yet here the objects taken are,

experience of other observers, and with our own, but by no means all the field of pathological stealing is covered by a study of its correlation with the menstrual period. Some of our most marked instances of excessive impulse to steal have been in young children; one who upon analysis was found to have a very striking conflict about sex affairs was only six years old.

[1] The thousand and one other references which could be given to items in the literature on this topic would bring forth no different point of view, nor really any better collection of facts. Considering the frequent use of the word "kleptomania," there is astonishingly little record of well studied cases. Some authors, e. g., Wulffen (**2**, Vol. I, p. 120) demonstrate in this matter the danger of making a classification. Once more, it is deep analysis, rather than the application of a terminology, that we need for understanding the subject. Kaufmann (**81**, p. 154), in his being forced, as he says, to confess that in "kleptomania" there is evidence of pure monomania, because of a case he observed, illustrates clearly our point. One wonders what his case would have revealed had it been analytically studied for subconscious motivation. Dubuisson (**330**) in his analysis of 111 cases, says that 33 were victims of some definite brain abnormality, 26 belonged to the neurasthenic category, 37 were hysterical, and 15 merely suffered from sex conditions, menstruation, pregnancy and the menopause. His analysis of possible stress is incomplete.

desired for themselves. Merely symbols of curious esoteric ideas and imageries, they are desired as such. A word more about this can be found under the head of Abnormal Sexualism (§ 244).

§ 367. Pathological Arson — "Pyromania."

" Pyromania " has often proved an inviting topic for lay writers, but in professional works there has also been loose usage of this term. The setting of fires, arson, even when indulged in repeatedly, may or may not be due to the impulse of an insane or otherwise abnormal person. Thus the word " pyromania," applied to fire-setting, as such, with its connotation of mental aberration is often unwarrantably employed. This affords another good example of the impossibility of classifying either the offender or the cause by the character of the deed. For the abnormally motivated fire-setting we offer, again, as a matter of consonant usage, the term, pathological arson.

Under the conditions of modern insurance arson may be engaged in for profit, and even, through conspiracy, as a business. It also has long been practiced as one of the easiest methods of revenge. On occasion it offers a chance of enjoyable excitement. A number of cases have been reported abroad where homesickness or desire to get away has been the cause. Among our offenders we have seen some who show this last background for the offense. An individual unwillingly kept in an institution, sets fire to it, perhaps with the idea of creating a commotion during which escape will be possible, or perhaps with the idea of getting even with society, and with the institution in particular. In mental conflict cases (§ 240), a reactive outlet has been sought in the deed. Also feebleminded individuals have delighted themselves by starting fires in houses. In other words, there are manifold reasons for arson, and many types of individuals may be implicated. The discussion of pyromania as given under the head of impulsive insanity in works on psychiatry is extremely unsatisfactory. A much wider view of the subject must be taken.

Cases showing peculiar causes for arson have been frequently reported in the literature.[1] The only large and important study

[1] If the student wishes reports of special cases, a number can be found scattered through Gross' "Archiv für Kriminalistik" during the last ten years. Monkemoeller's article mentioned in the text cites many other cases and authors.

is that by Monkemoeller (**304**). This author thoroughly summarizes the literature and gathers many cases for analysis. He finds, as every experienced investigator must, that the impulse to burn arises from many normal and pathological motives. Statistical studies of the type of offenders show nothing of great importance, except, of course, that the defectives and epileptics are proportionately more involved in this transgression. It is true that puberty shows great rise in the tendency, but that is only in accord with findings on other delinquencies. Immediately following this period of life, girls more than boys show increase in tendency towards fire-setting. The total significance of all research on the subject is that there is the greatest need for the individual study of every person who sets fires. Even if mental aberration is not shown, there is every reason for unearthing the cause of the impulse. Pathological arson is fire-setting under an abnormally conditioned impulse by a person not determinably insane.

§ 368. Suicide.

Suicide, or attempt at suicide, is an act which stands at the border-line of criminalism. Certainly it is, in our civilization, to be regarded as anti-social conduct. For the criminologist it has always been a subject of considerable interest because of its frequent relation to other criminalistic tendencies and deeds, and because of the possibility of correlating it with various personal peculiarities, or mental diseases, or with external influences. There are very many reasons for committing suicide, and very many types of individuals who attempt the act, but, even so, much more scientific generalization on these points is possible than in, for instance, murder. Correlation of one form of insanity, melancholia, with suicide demonstrates this point. For our purposes we need not dwell long on this topic.[1]   The

[1] For the student who would go further in getting at the several points of general interest in the problem of suicide, we may recommend the following important studies. Stelzner (**288**) analyzed 200 cases and studied the subject from the standpoint of the prognosis of cases in which there are mental disturbances connected with suicidal thoughts. Perhaps the best general study of the subject in its many phases is that of Gaupp (**289**). A very interesting official report on the suicide of school children in Prussia appeared by the statistician, Behla (**290**). Condensed summaries of 169 cases are given by Wassermeyer (**291**). This author shows that of the men who were not insane, one-half were chronic alcoholics. Among the women who were not insane, the majority were hysterical. But these are studies only of attempted suicide. In his analysis of 1000 consecutive cases of attempt, East (**292**) lays the same stress on alcoholic impulse. This author brings forward also a number of

bearings of definite causations on the suicidal tendency is nearly always clear, and special case studies are here unnecessary.

Statistical investigations of the subject have proved fascinating for many scientific writers. The safest of their conclusions are as follows: Of all mental troubles, melancholia stands in much the closest relationship to self-destruction. As East (**292**) points out, the suicidal attempt very frequently arises as an alcoholic impulse. In children under 15 it is rare, but shortly after the appearance of puberty the tendency in the female develops rapidly. It occurs oftener in childless marriages, and is more frequent in the widowed and separated. The notórious extent of suicide among school children in Germanic countries has been shown to be largely due to the mental disturbances, major and minor, which arise about the time of puberty. Pathological development of the fear impulse at this period is shown to have important bearing. In our own case studies (Cases 60, 162) of various types, some bases of the tendency to suicidal impulses are clearly shown. We thoroughly agree with the students of the subject, such as Gaupp (**289**), who have remarked that statistics do not offer causes for this phenomenon, but only stimulate further seeking. It need hardly be said that the most experienced authorities do not allege that suicide is by itself any sign of insanity. A point to be taken some account of as possibly bearing on statistics, is that the causative background is, naturally, easier to ascertain in cases of merely attempted suicide than when the deed is carried out.

§ 369. Vagabondage — Tramp Life.

Considerable interest in the last decade or two has been centered about the phenomenon of tramp life. The anti-social conduct exhibited by those who refuse to take up a fixed abode, and who prefer the many hardships which they endure to the greater comforts which could be obtained with the exercise of only a moderate amount of occupational stability, is certainly most curious. Many have insisted that this manner of life is proof in itself that the individual is not normal. However, here

other important conclusions. The viewpoint of deeper analysis of the suicidal impulse is to be found in a symposium (**293**) by Freud, Adler and several others. This is a study that should not be neglected by those who desire to go thoroughly into the subject. Terman (**371**) offers a short study of "Recent Literature on Juvenile Suicides."

again we are in the presence of conduct which may have several reasons for its existence. The delights of " the open road " are very appealing, even to those of poetic temperament. A period of real *Wanderlust*, at least in the *Wanderjahre*, is no sign of aberration. We have seen vagabondage in cases of feeblemind-edness, epilepsy, dementia precox, but we have also seen the same behavior in normal boys who had conceived a grudge, with or without good reason, against home conditions. Again, we have observed normal lads who have been seeking larger experi-ences in this way. Sometimes other causes may be at work, such as the suggestion and influence of a crowd, or of another individual; and bad behavior, particularly sex perversions, may give the start towards tramp life.

When vagabondage is continued past the unstable years of adolescence, generalizations on the character of individuals concerned are more likely to be correct. But even here the only chance of adequate conception of the relationship between behavior and the type of individual who engages in it is to be found in personal study of him. What is found true in one country or locality might be quite different from that in another. Already there is a considerable literature on the subject, but in this country the field has seemed more fruitful to the journalist than to the scientific investigator.

Psychopathologists abroad have undertaken serious research on vagabondage.[1] It is because such a large percentage of tramps are abnormal personalities that the subject has proven so invit-ing to students of abnormal psychology. In our discussion of certain minor mental aberrations, viz., fugues, we are upon the same ground that many European writers have taken when discussing vagabondage in general. But there are many types of individuals, who on account of their peculiarities, become

---

[1] Here, again, for the student we may offer the results of our experience with the literature. There is a wealth to choose from. The scholarly volume by Joffroy and Dupouy (**313**), while devoted mainly to the fugue impulse, surveys other parts of the field. The work by Marie and Meunier (**309**), men-tioned above, contains the conclusions of deep students. Wilmanns (**314, 315**), a much quoted investigator, has made detailed studies of tramps with definite psychoses. He especially affirms the presence of much dementia precox among them. Pagnier (**316**) offers some notable figures on the social importance of vagabondage in France. Mairet (**317**), in a well-considered monograph, with much reference to the literature, discussed various types of abnormal impulse which led to wandering. Again we may refer to the works of Flynt mentioned in the text. There is every reason to consider this whole subject in connection with fugues proper (§ **312**), as most French authors have done.

wanderers. The main pathological types who form the vagrant class are constitutional inferiors, epileptics, the high-grade feeble-minded (morons), and cases of dementia precox. Bonhoeffer (**308**) found from his study of four hundred vagrants that at least 70 per cent. would have been declared unfit for the usual German compulsory military service. Not all, of course, were mentally abnormal, but the majority presented incontestable signs of psychical defect or aberration. From the immense French literature we may best excerpt, with slight changes, the following instructive classification of modern vagabondage from Marie and Meunier (**309**):

A. Wanderers from economic or social reasons.
1. Legitimate wanderers.
    (*a*) Laborers without work.
    (*b*) Exiles.
    (*c*) Workers whose occupation is ambulatory.
2. Delinquent wanderers.
    (*a*) Those who are avoiding the scene of offenses, and recidivists.
    (*b*) Simulators of mental or other disease, and degenerate types.
    B. Vagabondage of pathological origin.
1. Physical troubles.
    (*a*) Temporary, such as convalescents and those with chronic ailments who can only work at times.
    (*b*) Permanent cases of weakness, or physical defect.
2. Mental troubles.
    (*a*) Neurasthenic types.
    (*b*) Hysterical types.
    (*c*) Epileptics.
    (*d*) Degenerates (constitutional inferiors), with eccentricities.
    (*e*) Manic-depressive types with remittent symptoms.
    (*f*) The persecuted and mystical types — apostles and prophets, (paranoiacs).
    (*g*) Vagabondage as the result of alcoholism, etc.
    (*h*) Demented types, including dementia precox, senility, etc.

Further space in the text can hardly be afforded for more reference to the literature, with one exception. No American student of this subject should forego acquaintance with the works (**310, 311**) of our countryman, who was both litterateur and tramp, Josiah Flynt. Flynt has much to teach criminologists, although occasionally his conclusions are found distinctly wanting in knowledge of the details of psychopathology. He himself, brilliant though he was, offered one of the best illustrations of the

career of a constitutional inferior who had definite impulsions
to wandering, which amounted in his childhood days to fugues.
The power of abnormal impulsions in a family where some members had ability to control them, and others not, is given a classic
place in the literature of human experience by this author.

Running away and truancy in childhood, although so frequently
made light of, has been found by ourselves, and many other
investigators, to be a distinctly serious matter. There is not
only the worry caused by it to any careful family, but there is
also the accompanying secretiveness, lying, association with bad
characters of all sorts, and indulgence in bad habits, all of which
tend directly to an anti-social career. Youthful vagabondage,
truancy, is well called the kindergarten of crime.

Not least among the evils of tramp life in general is the well-
recognized tendency under these conditions to homosexual perversions. Flynt (**312**) from his social standpoint has written on
this matter and many medical men have commented on it.

Prevention of vagabondage demands nothing more or less
than individual study of the particular person with a tendency
to tramp life, and social adjustment of his characteristic needs.
Any colony established for tramps, as such, will have to reckon
definitely with the difference in personalities, just the same as a
reform school or asylum for inebriates must, in order to be successful. We have given examples in several chapters of various
types showing a tendency towards wandering.

§ 370. Simulation.

Since simulation of either mental or physical disease, as a
social offense, is not a fact of any great moment in this country,
we can dispense with it in a few words. With the development
of insurance against disabilities, malingering in Germany has
become an important delinquency. There fine discriminations
have to be made and whole volumes on different forms of simulation have already been written.

With us there is occasional simulation of injury in order that
damages may be recovered. This type of swindling is so obvious
that it need hardly be mentioned. A more subtle form of pretense is found where the winning of sympathy for some supposed
trouble opens the way to stealing or to obtaining money by
false representation. Frequently the simulators are physical or

mental underlings who take advantage of the disabilities which they have and show appearance of exaggerated suffering. One man with a bad heart lesion used to appear overcome in the neighborhood of some physician's residence. He would, of course, be taken in by kindly people who quickly sent for the doctor. The latter would find the apparent cause of the trouble, and all would join in helping the afflicted one. It was always found that assistance was needed to help the sufferer get to his home in a neighboring state. The several dollars required usually were rapidly subscribed. The performance could be repeated in different localities on the same day.

One of the most notorious criminals in this country is a woman called "fainting Bertha," who comes from a criminalistic family. She has been a real sufferer from attacks, which are either epilepsy or hysteria. She also simulates her attacks to perfection, falls against some likely person, who in all kindness helps her to some neighboring house or shop. Later he finds his pockets have been deftly picked. The amusing but highly profitable method of the boy who simulated distress by voluntarily weeping as he sold chewing gum, we have recounted elsewhere, § 165. Simulation by beggars is not nearly so frequent here as it is in Europe.

He who deals with delinquents after indictment meets occasionally with simulation of epilepsy and insanity. Detection of the simulation of epilepsy presents very little difficulty to an experienced person. I remember one case in a detention home where a boy, who had a friend who was an epileptic offender, pretended to have a fit so that he might not have to appear before the judge. Some drops of water allowed to fall upon his eyelids and upon his abdomen quickly produced reflexes which, although the individual still simulated unconsciousness, gave sufficient proof of the facts.

The successful simulation of insanity, as has well been said, is almost beyond the powers of any one who is not already a psychopathic individual. Very few cases have been recorded which have given any trouble over long periods of observation, although an opinion based upon a single interview may be quite unsafe in the case of skillful simulators. The almost universal tendency, as we have many times observed, is for both offenders and their families to be vastly more willing to acknowledge delinquency than either epilepsy or insanity. We have never studied a case which gave us any ultimate trouble in this matter. (I am here speaking of mental abnormality, and not of "legal insanity," an opinion upon which is demanded by lawyers according to their artificial standards of responsibility.)

White (73), who has had an immense experience in the legal phases of insanity says, "In all my experience I have never known of but one case in which a sane man escaped punishment on a plea of insanity. In this case it was evident that the accused was not insane, but the jury wanted to free him." Sommer (163, p. 223) feels so sure of the above phase of simulation of insanity, as well as of the fact that it is mostly undertaken by those who are already abnormal individuals, that he specifically insists that the diagnosis of simulation should be made with the greatest care.

In considering some cases of possible simulation, transitory mental aberrations (*vide* § 315) should be taken into account.

§ 371. "Born Criminals."

The subject of born criminals, which found a main place in a criminology which discussed offenders by putting them in large general classes, can be disposed of by us in a few words. When we come to study cases more fully, we see no reason for maintaining any general notion that there is a class properly designated as born criminals. Of course, mental defectives and epileptics and others, especially if brought up in bad environments, may be regarded as having secondarily criminal dispositions, but placing them in such a category tells us nothing of worth concerning them. In spite of the denial of the value of this terminology by many authors, it still happens that the picturesque is sought, and cases are described as belonging to this class. There are several arguments against the use of this term at all: one is that the use of it does not scientifically place individuals in their proper primary category. Second, it would be a matter difficult to demonstrate that these criminalistic individuals were not such as the result of environmental defects added to innate mental weaknesses. We have much reason for believing the environment to be a big factor, because of the observations on non-criminalistic lives of the same types of individuals brought up under better environmental conditions. Third, this theory presupposes that it is possible to have a moral defect apart from

781

all other evidences of intellectual weakness. This has not been proven, and, if it does occur, must be extremely rare (§ 372). A fourth reason for discouraging the use of the term is the fact that if we are satisfied with such a general characterization of the individual we have really gained no clue to the practical disposition of him. This is one of the greatest objections.

The gist of the whole situation concerning "born criminals" is that they are individuals who definitely belong in the scientific categories of mental defect and mental aberration. They show, by reason of early teaching, of environmental opportunities, of developed habit of mind, or such physical conditions as abnormal sexuality, a very definite tendency to criminalism. They are primarily mentally abnormal, and secondly, criminalistic. Nothing is gained by loose generalization on the subject. There is much food for thought in Devon's keen statement that "the criminal is born and made just as the policeman is born and made." Certain mental and physical qualities lead in certain definite directions of behavior if society allows the chance.

§ 372. "Moral Imbecility" — "Moral Insanity."

The equivalent of many volumes has been written upon the subject of moral insanity and moral imbecility since the first use of the former term by Prichard (**298**) in 1835. The largest share of this discussion has hinged upon the fact that different authors have been talking about different things. It behooves us at once, then, to define our terms. We, first of all, desire to make it absolutely clear that we can see no reason for leaving the definition open for loose construction. Cases of insanity or mental defect with a tendency towards anti-social conduct, perhaps as the result of innate tendencies, and perhaps more often the effect of environmental experiences, we would at once rule out. In this procedure we are at one with many students who have given the subject careful consideration. ("Moral insanity" sometimes signifies immoral tendencies developing on a basis of mental disorders — in that sense it is misleading. Oftener it covers the same ground as the other term, moral imbecility. Our discussion, after this explanation, will gain clarity by its avoidance.) The use of the term, moral imbecile, by Barr (**299**), Tredgold (**307**), and others, in their categories of feeble-mindedness, is highly confusing for the issues of moral conduct which confront the student of criminalistics. If an individual is mentally defective or insane, it is desirable to primarily classify him as such. It is often desirable to state that here is such and such a type of abnormal person with special trend towards bad conduct, but the larger fact should first of all be made clear.[1] The field is then open for consideration of our real problem, namely, abnormality of such mental functions as have to do with the moral life.

This brings us at once to the question whether there is any such thing as a separate ethical department of mental life. A "moral sense" seems to have appeared first in philosophical psychology with Locke, Shaftesbury and Hutcheson in the 17th and 18th centuries. In the last two generations of philosophical thought there has been a decided falling away from this conception. It is now clearly perceived that our notions of right and wrong are inextricably mixed up with social judgments, and with the evolution of social relationships. Not only does learning and experience in these matters come into play, but also native intelligence as well. One could almost say that the person who failed to appreciate his moral duties was the person who had not intelligence enough to realize what was best for even himself as a social being. Indeed, such definitely was the trend of Aristotelian thought.[2]

The results of our experience, and our main conclusion in this whole matter would better at once be set forth; discussion may then follow. When we began our work there was no point on which we expected more positive data than on moral imbecility. But our findings have turned out to be negative. We have been constantly on the look-out for a moral imbecile, that is, a person not subnormal and otherwise intact in mental powers, who shows himself devoid of moral feeling. We have not found one. Many cases have been brought to us as moral imbeciles, but they have always turned out somehow mentally defective or aberrational; or to be the victims of environmental conditions or mental conflict, and not at all devoid of moral feeling. Superficially the individual frequently has seemed to be mentally normal, as in the cases where there was great development of language

---

[1] Some writers do see this point. For instance, W. E. Fernald speaks, not of the moral imbecile, but of the imbecile with criminal instincts (**344**).

[2] For a clear-cut discussion of the problem of the existence of a "moral sense" we would refer the reader to the masterly text book on Ethics by Dewey and Tufts (**372**).

ability (§§ 273, 276), but in every single instance a well-rounded investigation has shown distinct abnormality in some other field than the moral sense, or, in a few cases of children,[1] further growth has carried the individual past a stage of anti-social conduct.

In the light of our practical findings we have considered carefully many opinions expressed in the literature. There has been so much thoughtful attention paid to the subject that a judicious attitude towards it is demanded. We may neglect the many authors who uphold our point of view (*vide* Anton's summary of the literature mentioned below). We find at once that the great probable source of difference of opinions is in the extensive theorizing, and the lack of careful statement either of definition or of the results of survey of all investigatable elements of mental life. The self-contradictions which are to be found in some authors would hardly be possible if a graphic setting forth of mental abilities and disabilities was undertaken in cases of so-called moral imbecility. For example, Mercier's statement (**148**, p. 201) regarding the absence of intellectual defect in moral imbecility could hardly have been made and there been a profound view of the case which he himself pictures on a preceding page by way of illustration — the case of the Afghan thief who, even after his hand had been cut off and he had been threatened with execution, publicly stole an article useless to him. If the fact that this man took no pains to avoid detection when he was certain of his fate is not in itself a sign of intellectual defect or aberration, then what in the world would indicate it? Just so with another case this same author gives. The point is lost by the very statement of it.

The instances of moral feeblemindedness (fundamentally incorrigibles) given by Kraepelin (**343**, p. 285 ff.) as types, will not stand the application of his own measuring rod. One man with insanity in his heredity, who had been discharged from the army as mentally defective, who had, both before and after this time, shown many criminalistic tendencies, and who had already been in three insane asylums is given as an example. " If you only look at the knowledge, memory, and natural manner of our patient," says Kraepelin, " and the continuity of his course

---

[1] In these otherwise unexplained cases of children, I think it highly probable that had we done better work, psychogenetic or experiential elements back of the morbid behavior would have been discovered, as they were in many other instances.

of thought — that is, at those features which first and most obviously come under consideration, you will hardly suppose that you have to deal with a morbid personality here." Later it is acknowledged that this patient had always presented instability of will power, was irritable, sometimes had fainting fits, etc. If all this and the utter lack of judgment, foresight, and apperceptive ability which this patient displayed is not convincing of mental abnormality outside the sphere of ethical perceptions then it is hard to say what would be convincing. The fact that the man while in an asylum had learned mathematics and other things which enabled him to get employment for which he had occasionally been well paid does not prove his normality. As a matter of fact, Kraepelin acknowledges in a footnote that eighteen months later this example of moral imbecility still remained in an asylum, and showed depression at intervals resembling the phenomena seen in epileptics.

In a recent argument for recognition of the moral sense as an entity based even on cerebral localization (a supposition of which physiological psychology knows nothing), Steen (**342**) mentions as sole evidence of the fact, a case under observation in a hospital which was said to show nothing but moral defect, such as was expressed in the actions which had brought him there. Here again we may be permitted the query, based both on common sense and psychology; if judgment and will were really intact in this individual how can one account for his getting himself into such undesirable circumstances? Separation of the moral from other elements of mental life certainly is not satisfactorily demonstrated here.

One writer, Berze (**301**), who attempts to clear the ground for judicial procedure admirably succeeds. He also emphasizes the correlation of uneducability with "moral insanity," but allows for the bare possibility of its occurrence without disturbance of intellection, even as regards perception of moral relationships. He says that even if it is impossible to deny the existence of moral defect arising from degeneration of the feelings alone, at least in such cases we need not be concerned about the question of lessened responsibility. The latter is to be connected only with intellectual defect. Berze insists upon the changing intellectual and emotional conditions characteristic of degenerates, and would introduce variability of moral perception into the main question.

785

One cannot read far into this subject without perceiving its importance, not only for the student of criminalistics, but also for philosophical ethics, psychology and psychopathology. Its interesting bearings are well brought out in a recent thoughtful article by Gudden (300), who relegates research in this problem to students of comparative psychology. Moral imbecility, he thinks, is ordinary among aborigines, and is based on physiological conditions, namely, the lack of brain development. Among civilized nations it is to be regarded as a pathological condition. The very best way to gauge the presence of moral imbecility is by evaluating educability. Let the various character accompaniments of moral defect be what they may — boundless self-seeking, vanity, superficiality of reasoning, or what not — the crowning and absolute sign of the trouble is to be found in the individual's uneducability in those higher powers which make for practice of the best social sanctions. He thinks there will not be much difficulty in recognizing the mental defects of the so-called moral imbecile if systematic testing of the learning ability is carried out. He warns that the responsibility of such individuals cannot be considered any higher than their ability to perceive the differences between right and wrong, but this latter must not be measured merely by verbal responses.

An extensive and interesting discussion on moral imbecility is offered in a forty-eight page chapter on "Moral Deviates" by Arthur Holmes (141). This author reviews many opinions and finds them contradictory; compares several theories of ethics and discovers irreconcilable differences in the viewpoint; inclines to the view that the moral sense may be absent without other mental defect; and then proceeds to class all "moral deviates" according to corrigibility and incorrigibility. The second class alone contains the moral imbeciles. These latter he then proceeds to subclassify, and out of his entire argument we get simply the practical findings of Barr that moral imbeciles are mental defectives. Even the highest grade has not reasoning power enough to understand that his actions will deprive him of the privileges he covets. The single case of "true moral imbecility" cited by Holmes is that of an idiot who, insensible himself to pain, frequently slashes others. Thus at the end of his long survey of the subject, we come back to just our own standpoint, namely, that probably all moral imbeciles are primarily mentally abnormal.

No student of this subject can afford to neglect the short monograph of Anton (**302**) which treats the literature in the form of a symposium. This author collects the opinions of 80 years and endeavors to clarify them. He shows that the majority of authors maintain that "moral insanity" is always accompanied by some degree of intellectual weakness. Others, however, take the contrary point of view. Without going further into the separate parts of his summary we may give his final conclusions: although the term "moral insanity" betokens very many forms of trouble, yet it remains as the signal for a definite clinical fact, namely, that there are conditions of disease and abnormal development which disproportionately affect feelings and moods, and consequently influence the conduct which springs from these sources. Anton, in verging towards the notion of an ethical department of mental life separate from other mental activities, offers not a single case which tends to establish his view.

The elaborate work of Mairet and Euziere (**303**) on "moral invalids " touches on many types of individuals who are pathologically anti-social, but the detailed citation of them shows all to be mentally abnormal, either having congenital defects or acquired pathological states.

Hermann (**345**) attacks this whole matter from another point of view, namely, that of the moral comprehension of the feeble-minded, and the degenerate types of criminals. He finds that in mental defectives the development of moral comprehension does not run parallel to various other powers of mental representation. (Of course we should not expect this, any more than we should expect the parallel development of language ability.) In instances of moral imbecility where defect of intelligence has not been shown, this author asks if it is not due entirely to a fault of method. Various psychiatrists have suggested this. He concludes that the problem in criminalistics is not at all whether there exists separate pathological deficiency alone of the higher moral comprehension. He maintains that, on the contrary, our business is to so size up the individual that we may know what fairly to expect from him in social life; that is, has the person intellectual defect, or disturbance of the affective and impulsive life, which causes him to be incapable of leading an average social existence? He specifically condemns the phrases "moral imbecility" and "moral insanity" as positively unserviceable for modern clinical use.

One might in this way deal long with expressed opinions of

many authors.   (Ellis (**124**, p. 141 and 284 ff.) presents a particularly readable survey of this subject.)   However, the main trends
of opinion are already shown.

Our own conclusion, to repeat, is simply, that if the " moral
imbecile " exists who is free from all other forms of intellectual
defect, he must indeed be a *rara avis*.   We see clearly the differences that varying innate characteristics and varying experiences may create in inner moral reactions, but for the individual
to be without the possibility of developing such moral reactions
is another thing.   As some suggest, the individual who is imbecile
on the moral side alone would be educable in social ways.   Steen
says he might learn to respect what others respect, just as a
color-blind person learns to say that the grass is green.   But in
the meantime, until well-studied cases prove the main point, we
need not concern ourselves with side topics.   The fact is that
approximately, and perhaps entirely, all individuals who react
to moral situations as imbeciles belong in very definite pathological
categories.   There is no reason for using terms, then, which
lead to confusion of practical issues.

APPENDICES

APPENDIX A

BIBLIOGRAPHY

253. ABDERHALDEN, E., "Bibliographie: Alkohol und Alkoholismus." Berlin, Urban & Schwarzenberg, 1904, pp. 504.

354. ABELS, A., "Seltene Verbrechens-Motive." Gross' Archiv für Kriminalistik. 1912, 49, p. 218.

231. ADDAMS, JANE, "The Spirit of Youth and the City Streets." Macmillan, New York, 1909.

158. ALLFELD, PHILIPP, "Der Einfluss der Gesinnung des Verbrechers auf die Bestrafung." Leipzig, Engelmann, 1909.

68. American Institute of Criminal Law and Criminology: Journal of, July, 1910. "A System for Recording Data Concerning Criminals." Report by William Healy. Also published as Bulletin No. 2. Dec., 1909, pp. 15.

69. —— Bulletin No. 12. April, 1913. "Further Development of a System for Recording Data Concerning Criminals." Report by William Healy, pp. 17.

335. ANGELL, J. R., "Psychology." Holt, New York, 1908. pp. 468.

302. ANTON, G., "Ueber krankhafte moralische Abartung im Kindesalter." Halle a. S., Marhold, 1910, pp. 30.

1. ASCHAFFENBURG, GUSTAV, "Das Verbrechen und seine Bekämpfung." 1st edition, Berlin, 1903, 2d edition, 1906. English edition, "Crime and Its Repression." Boston, Little, Brown and Co., 1913, pp. 331.

263. —— "Zur Psychologie der Sittlichkeitsverbrecher." Monatschrift für Kriminal-psychologie. Bd. II, p. 404.

364. —— "Ueber die Stimmungschwankungen der Epileptiker." Halle, 1906.

373. AUDIFFRENT, "Quelques considérations sur l'infanticide." Archives Anthropologie criminelle. 1900, pp. 1-9.

359. BABINSKI, J., "Comment concevoir l'hypnotism," etc. Paris, Semaine Médicale, 1910. July 7, pp. 349-360.

256. BAER, A. AND LAQUER, B., "Trunksucht und ihre Abwehr." 2d ed. 1907. Berlin. Urban & Schwarzenberg, pp. 242.

62. BAHNSEN, "Beiträge zur Charakterologie." Leipzig, 1862.

319. BALDWIN, BIRD T., "Adolescence." Psychological Bulletin. Oct. 1911, Oct. 1913.

321. BARNES, EARL, "Studies in Education." Vol. II, p. 144.

299. BARR, MARTIN W., "Mental Defectives." Philadelphia. Blakiston's, 1904, pp. 368.

63. VON BECHTEREW, W., "La Psychologie objective appliquée à l'étude de la Criminalité." Arch. d'Anthrop. Crimin. Mch. 15, 1910.

14. VON BECHTEREW, W., "Die Bedeutung der Suggestion im sozialen Leben." Wiesbaden, Bergmann, 1905, pp. 142.

159. BEGBIE, HAROLD, "Twice-Born Men. A Clinic in Regeneration." New York, F. H. Revell Co., 1909, pp. 280.

290. BEHLA, "Report on Suicide among School Pupils in Prussia." Medizinische Reform, 1909. Abstract in Journal Amer. Med. Assoc'n. Feb. 5, 1910.

210. BELLETRUD AND MERCIER, "Un cas de mythomanie." L'Encéphale, June, 1910, p. 677.

72. BENON AND FROISSART, Journal de Psychologie, normale et path. July, 1909, No. 4.

301. BERZE, JOSEF, "Ueber die sogennante 'Moral Insanity' und ihre forensische Bedeutung." Gross' Archiv für Kriminalistik, 1908, Bd. 30, pp. 123–151.

276. BIANCHI, "Text Book of Psychiatry." Chapter on Delinquency. English edition, Ballière, London, 1906.

341. BINET, A., "du Fetischisme dans l'amour." Revue philosophique. 1887. Also volume of essays by same title. Paris, Doin, 1891.

74. —— "L'Année Psychologique." 1905, 1908, 1911, etc.

100. —— "La Suggestibilité." Paris, Schleicher, 1900, pp. 391.

101. —— "La Suggestibilité au point de vue de la psychologie individuelle." L'Année Psychologique, V, 1899, p. 82.

85. BINET, ALFRED AND SIMON, TH., "L'Année Psychologique." 1905, 1908, 1911. (The last article was entitled "Nouvelle Recherches sur la Mesure du Niveau intellectuel chez les Enfants d'Ecole," in the above publication and also "La Mesure du Developpement de l'Intelligence chez jeunes Enfants," in the Bulletin de la Société libre pour l'Etude psychologique de l'Enfant.) Paris, 1911.

115. BINET AND HENRI, "La Psychologie Individuelle." L'Année Psychologique, 1895–1896.

129. BOAS, FRANZ, "Changes in Bodily Form of Descendents of Immigrants." Washington. Government Printing Office, 1910.

237. BOAS, KURT, W. F., "Alkohol und Verbrechen nach neueren Statistiken." Gross' Archiv für Kriminalistik. 1908, Vol. 29, p. 66.

286. BOIES, H. M., "The Science of Penology." p. 10. New York, Putnam, 1901, pp. 459.

308. BONHOEFFER, "Mendicants and vagabonds in the cities." Allg. Zeitschrift für Psychiatrie. 1900, p. 570.

9. —— "Die akute Geisteskrankheiten der Gewohnheitstrinker." Jena, Fischer, 1901.

49. BOWERS, P. E., "Paretic Patients Sent to Prison." Journal Amer. Medical Assoc'n. Mch. 16, 1912.

318. BRECKINRIDGE AND ABBOTT, "The Delinquent Child and the Home." New York, Charities Publication Committee, 1912, pp. 355.

266. BRESLER, JOH., "Greisenalter und Criminalität." Juristisch-psychiatrische Grenzfragen. Bd. V, Heft 2, 3, pp. 58. Halle a. S., Marhold.

138. BRILL, A. A., "Psychanalysis — Its Theories and Practical Application." Philadelphia, Saunders, 1912, pp. 337.

333. BROCKWAY, Z. R., "The Reformatory System in the United States." 1900.

322. BURK, CAROLINE FREAR, "The Collecting Instinct." Pedagogical Seminary. July, 1900, pp. 179–207.

189. BURK, FREDERIC, "Growth of Children in Height and Weight." Amer. Jour. of Psychology. April, 1898, pp. 253–326.

53. BYRNE, "Professional Criminals of America."

128. CHANNING, W. AND WISSLER, C., "The Hard Palate in Normal and Feebleminded Individuals." New York, Papers American Museum of Natural History. Aug. 1908.

150. CHURCHILL AND BRITTON, "Medical Work of Juvenile Court, Chicago." Archives of Pediatrics, Feby., 1910.

274. CLOUSTON, T. S., "Unsoundness of Mind," Chap. XX, London, Methuen, 1911, pp. 360.

280. —— "The Neuroses of Development." London, 1891, also *vide* (274).

215. CONRADI, EDWARD, "Speech Defects and Intellectual Progress." Journal of Educational Psychology. Jan. 1912, pp. 35–38.

285. CONTI, UGO, "Comments on the American Prison System." Journal of Criminal Law and Criminology. July, 1911, p. 207.

370. CONYNGTON, MARY, "Relation Between Occupation and Criminality of Women." Vol. XV of Report on Woman and child wage earners in the United States. Washington, Government Printing Office.

245. COOPER, J. W. ASTLEY, "Pathological Inebriety; its causes and treatment." Ballière, London, 1913, pp. 151.

15. CRAMER, "Gerichtliche Psychiatrie." 1908, 4th ed. Jena, G. Fischer.

221. —— "Chapter on alcoholic psychoses," in Lehrbuch der Psychiatrie by Cramer, Hoche, *et al.* Jena, Fischer. 3d ed. 1911, p. 412.

229. CRAMPTON, C. WARD, "Psychological Age — A Fundamental Principle." Pamphlet, pp. 56. Reprinted from American Physical Educational Review. Nos. 3 to 6 inclusive, 1908.

232. —— "The Significance of Physiological Age in Education." Proceedings of 15th International Congress on Hygiene and Demography.

233. —— "The Influence of Physiological Age on Scholarship." Psychological Clinic. Vol. I, p. 115.

251. CROTHERS, T. D., "Inebriety — A clinical treatise." (Includes medico-legal relations.) Cincinnati, Harvey Publishing Co. 1911, pp. 365.

260. CROTHERS, T. D., "Morphinism and Narcomanias From Other Drugs." (Includes medico-legal relations.) Philadelphia, Saunders and Co., 1902, pp. 351.

261. —— "Criminality and Morphinism." N. Y. Medical Journal. Jan. 27, 1912, p. 163.

262. —— "Cocainism." Journal of Inebriety. 1910, p. 78.

6. DEVON, J., "The Criminal and the Community." London, Lane. 1912, pp. 348.

277. DAVENPORT, C. B., "The Trait Book." Bulletin No. 6, Eugenics Record Office, Cold Spring Harbor, N. Y., Feb. 1912.

367. DAVENPORT AND WEEKS, "Inheritance of Epilepsy." Jour. Nervous and Mental Diseases. Nov. 1911, pp. 641–670.

363. DELBOEUF, J., "On Criminal Suggestion," The Monist, Vol. II, pp. 363–385.

203. DELBRUECK, A., "Die pathologischen Lüge und die psychisch abnormen Schwindler." Stuttgart, 1891, pp. 131. (Now out of print.)

121. DE QUIROS, C. B., "Las nuevas teorias de la criminalidad." Madrid, 1898. Eng. edition, "Modern Theories of Criminality," Boston, Little, Brown and Co., 1911.

372. DEWEY AND TUFTS, "Text Book of Ethics." New York, Holt, 1908, pp. 618. Section on the Moral Sense, pp. 317–322.

168. VAN DIJCK, "Bijdragen tot de Psychologie can den Misdadiger." Te Groningen, Van der Klei, 1906, pp. 275.

330. DUBUISSON, PAUL, "Les Voleuses des Grands Magazins." Archives d'Anthropologie Criminelle, 1901, p. 1 and p. 341.

220. DUDLEY, E. C., "Hypertrophy of Prepuce. Adherent Prepuce." Principles and Practice of Gynecology. Philadelphia, Lea Bros. 4th ed. p. 512.

33. DUPRAT, G. L., "La Criminalité dans l'Adolescence." Paris, Alcan, 1909, pp. 260.

292. EAST, E. NORWOOD, "Attempted Suicide, with an Analysis of 1000 Consecutive Cases." Jour. of Mental Science, 1913, p. 428.

105. EBBINGHAUS, H., "Ueber eine neue Methode zur Prüfung geistiger Fähigkeiten." (Especially "Ergänzungsmethode.") Zeitschrift für Psychologie; 13, 1897.

124. ELLIS, HAVELOCK, "The Criminal." 3d edition. London, Scott Co., 1907. pp. 419.

186. —— "Studies in the Psychology of Sex." Six volumes, 1900, and later. Philadelphia, F. A. Davis and Co.

226. ENGELEN, O., "Behandlung der sogenannten vermindert Zurechnungsfähigen." Juristisch-psychiatrische Grenzfragen. Bd. IX, Heft 1.

34. ENGLEMANN, G. J., New York Medical Journal. Feb. 8 and 15, 1902.

172. FEISENBERGER, "Vergiftung aus Rachsucht und Heimweh." Archiv für Kriminalanthropologie, 1905, No. 21.

295. FENTON, FRANCES, "The Influence of Newspaper Presentations upon the Growth of Crime." Thesis. University of Chicago Press. 1911, pp. 96.

109. FERNALD, GUY C., American Journal of Insanity. 1912.

104. —— "An Achievement Capacity Test: a preliminary report." Journal of Educational Psychology. June, 1912.

344. FERNALD, W. E., "Imbecile with Criminal Instincts." Amer. Journal of Insanity. April, 1909.

312. FLYNT, JOSIAH, Chapter on sex perversions among tramps in "Studies in the Psychology of Sex" by Havelock Ellis. Philadelphia, Davis and Co., 1900.

311. —— "My Life." New York, Outing Publishing Co. 1908, pp. 365.

310. —— "Tramping with Tramps." New York, Century Co. 1901, pp. 398.

60. FOLSOM, CHAS. F., "Studies of Criminal Responsibility." The Case of Jesse Pomeroy. Privately printed, 1909.

234. FOSTER, F. L., "Psychological Age as a Basis for Classification of Pupils." Psychological Clinic. May, 1910.

84. FRANZ, SHEPHERD I., "Handbook of Mental Examination Methods." New York, Journal of Nervous and Mental Diseases, Monograph, No. 10. 1912, pp. 165.

293. FREUD, ADLER, FRIEDJUNG et al. "Ueber den Selbstmord, insbesondere den Schuler-Selbstmord." Beiträge, 1910. Wiesbaden, Bergmann.

187. FREUD, SIGMUND, "Drei Abhandlungen zur Sexualtheorie," 1909. English translation, "Three Contributions to the Sexual Theory." New York, Journal of Mental and Nervous Diseases. 1910, Monograph, pp. 91.

135. —— "Ueber Psychoanalyse; Deuticke" Vienna, 1910. English translation: "The Origin and Development of Psychoanalysis"; American Journal of Psychology. April, 1910.

155. GANT, SAMUEL G., "Diseases of the Rectum and Anus." 2d ed. 1903, Philadelphia, F. A. Davis Co.

328. GAROFALO, R., "Criminology." English edition, Boston, Little, Brown and Co., 1914, pp. 478.

10. —— In Lombroso's "L'Homo Delinquente." Vol. 3., and in Ferrero's "Lombroso's Criminal Man." p. 210. New York, Putnam, 1911.

289. GAUPP, ROBERT, "Ueber den Selbstmord." 2d ed. 1910. München, Gmelin.

326. GAUTIER, EMILE, "Le monde des prisons." Archives de l'Anthropologie criminelle. 1888, p. 541.

283. GLUECK, BERNARD, "The Mentally Defective Immigrant." New York Medical Journal. Oct. 18, 1913.

75. GODDARD, H. H., "Measuring Scale of Intelligence." Vineland, New Jersey. The Training School. Jan. 1910.

80. —— "Standard Method of Scoring Binet Tests." Vineland, New Jersey. The Training School. April, 1913.

795

86. GODDARD, H. H., "The Binet and Simon Tests." 1905 Series. Vineland, New Jersey. The Training School. Dec. 1908. "A Measuring Scale for Intelligence." (1908 Series.) Same Publication, Jan. 1910.

88. ——— "Revision of the Binet-Simon Scale." Vineland, New Jersey. The Training School. 1911.

151. ——— "Responsibility of Children in the Juvenile Court." Vineland, New Jersey. The Training School. Sept. 1912.

152. GODDARD AND GIFFORD, "Defective Children in the Juvenile Court." Vineland, New Jersey. Training School. Jan. 1912.

160. GORING, CHARLES, "The English Convict, a Statistical Study," pp. 440. London, Wyman & Sons, 1913.

375. GOTTSCHALK, ALFRED, "Materialen zur Lehre von der verminderten Zurechnungsfähigkeit." Berlin, Guttentag, 1904.

25. GRASSET, J., "Les Demi-Fous." In Eng. "The Semi-Responsibles." Trans. by Jelliffe. New York, Funk & Wagnalls, 1907, pp. 415.

83. GREGOR, ADALBERT, "Leitfaden der Experimentellen Psychopathologie." Berlin, Karger, 1910, pp. 222.

64. GROSS, HANS, "Criminal Psychology." English Translation, Boston, Little, Brown & Co. 1911, pp. 514.

147. GRUHLE, HANS W., "Die Ursachen der jugendlichen Verwahrlosung und Kriminalität." Heidelberger Abhandlungen. Heft I. Berlin, Springer, 1912, pp. 451.

294. GUDDEN, HANS, "Die Zurechnungsfähigkeit bei Warenhausdiebstähler." Vierteljahrschrift für gerichtliche Medizin, XXXIII. 1907, Suppl. Heft, pp. 64.

300. ——— "Das Wesen des moralischen Schwachsinns." Archiv für Psychiatrie. 1908. Bd. 44. pp. 376–91.

201. GULICK AND AYERS, "Medical Inspection of Schools." Chap. XII. Retardation and Physical Defects. New York, Charities Publication Committee. 1908.

218. GUTZMANN, A., "Das Stottern." 6th ed. Berlin, 1910.

376. GWYN, M. K., "Mental Tests." New York, Medical Record, Jan. 31, 1914.

31. HALL, STANLEY, "Adolescence." Two vols., pp. 589 and 784. New York, Appleton, 1904.

320. ——— Pedagogical Seminary. Vol. I, p. 234.

112. HAMILTON, G. V., "A study of trial and error in mammals." Journal of Animal Behavior. Jan.–Feb., 1911.

250. HANNES, W., "Zur Frage der Beziehungen zwischen asphyxtischer und schwere Geburt und nachhaltigen psychisch und nervösen Störungen." Zeitschrift für Geburtshilfe und Gynäkologie. 1911, 68, p. 712.

325. HAYFORD, LESLIE, "Immigration and Crime." Report of the Immigration Commission. Washington, Government Ptg. Office, 1911, pp. 449.

24. HEALY, WILLIAM, Vide American Institute of Criminal Law, etc. (68).

27. HEALY, WILLIAM, "Epilepsy and Crime." Illinois Medical Journal. Feb. 1913.

29. ——— *Vide* American Institute of Criminal Law, etc. (69).

50. ——— "Mental Defectives and the Courts." Journal of Psycho-Asthenics. Vol. XV. Oct. 1910.

176. ——— Chapter on "Delinquency and Crime in Relation to Mental Defect or Disorder." p. 233. Vol. I, Modern Treatment of Mental and Nervous Diseases, edited by White and Jelliffe. Philadelphia, Lea & Febiger, 1913.

202. ——— Pathological Liars, Accusers, and Swindlers. To appear later.

369. ——— "A Feebleminded Genius," by Geo. Mogridge and William Healy. Journal of Psychasthenics. March, 1912, pp. 93–102.

378. ——— A Pictorial Completion Test. The Psychological Review. May, 1914.

70. HEALY, WILLIAM AND FERNALD, GRACE M., "Tests for Practical Mental Classification." Psychological Monograph, No. 54, March, 1911. Princeton, New Jersey. Psychological Review Publishing Co., Princeton University.

252. HEILBRONNER, "Trunkenheitsdelikte und Strafrecht." Muenchener medizinische Wochenschrift. 1908, March 31.

255. HELENIUS, MATTI, "Die Alkoholfrage." Jena, 1903.

12. HELLER, E., Zeitschrift für die gesamte Strafrechtswissenschaft. Bd. 31. Heft. 6. Reviewed by William Healy in Journal of Criminal Law and Criminology. 1911, p. 282.

296. HELLWIG, ALBERT, "Die Beziehungen zwischen Schundliteratur, Schundfilms und Verbrechen." Gross' Archiv für Kriminalistik, 1913. Bd. 51, pp. 1–32.

345. HERMANN, "Das moralische Fühlen und Begreifen bei Imbezillen und bei Kriminellen Degenerierten." Halle a. S., Marhold, 1912, pp. 90.

137. HITSCHMANN, E., "Freud's Theories of the Neuroses." English translation by C. R. Payne. New York, Journal of Nervous and Mental Diseases Publishing Co. 1913, pp. 154.

265. HOCH, AUGUST, AND AMSDEN, G. S., "A Guide to the Descriptive Study of Personality." Review of Neurology and Psychiatry. Nov. 1913, pp. 577–587.

270. HOCHSINGER, "After-history of children with congenital syphilis." Wiener Klinische Wochenschrift. June 23, 1910.

241. HOEGEL, Address at International Statistical Institute, Vienna, 1913. Quoted U. S. Brewers' Association Year Book, 1913, pp. 278 *ff*.

216. HOEPFNER, TH., "Ueber die Disposition der Stotterer-Psyche zu asozialer Entwicklung." Gross' Archiv für Kriminalistik. 1912. Vol. 49, pp. 149–173.

141. HOLMES, ARTHUR, "Conservation of the Child." Philadelphia, Lippincott, 1912, p. 342.

214. HOLMES, ARTHUR, "Can Impacted Teeth Cause Delinquency?" Psychological Clinic. Mch. 1910, p. 19.

66. HOLMES, THOMAS, "London Police Courts." Nelson & Sons, 1900, pp. 384.

242. HOPPE, HUGO, "Alkohol und Kriminalität in allen ihren Beziehungen." Wiesbaden, Bergmann, 1906, pp. 208.

257. —— "Die Tatsachen über den Alkohol." München, Reinhardt, 4th ed. 1912, pp. 746.

258. —— "Der Alkohol im gegenwärtigen und zukünftigen Strafrecht." Juristisch-psychiatrische Grenzfragen. 1907, Bd. V, Heft 4 and 5, pp. 78.

323. HOWE, ELIZABETH, "Can the Collecting Instinct be Utilized in Teaching?" Elementary School Teacher. Vol. VI. May, 1906.

329. HOWARD, JOHN, "The State of Prisons in England and Wales with Preliminary Observations, and an Account of some Foreign Prisons." 1777.

131. INGEGNIEROS, "Nuevos rumbas de la Antropologia criminal," Archivos de Psiquiatria y Criminalogia. 1907. For readers of English this classification will be found on page 55 of "Modern Theories of Criminology," by De Quiros (121).

346. Internationale Kriminalistische Vereinigung. Mitteilungen der Inter. Krim. Ver., VI. p. 582, 1897. Or vide Aschaffenburg (1) p. 206.

21. JAMES, WILLIAM, "Psychology." 2 vols. New York, Holt, 1893.

334. —— "Habit." Chap. IV in Vol. I. "The Principles of Psychology." New York, Holt, 1893, also Popular Science Monthly, Feb. 1887.

197. JANET, PIERRE, "The Mental State of Hystericals," translated by Corson. New York, Putnams. 1901, pp. 535.

306. JANET, "Kleptomania and Mental Depression." Journal die Psychologie normale et pathologique. No. 2, March–April, 1911.

169. JASPERS, K., "Heimweh und Verbrechen." Leipzig, Vogel, 1909. See also Gross' Archiv für Kriminalanthropologie. 1909. No. 35.

313. JOFFROY AND DUPOUY, "Fugues et Vagabondage." Paris, Alcan, 1909, pp. 368.

139. JONES, ERNEST, "Psychoanalysis and Education." Journal of Educational Psychology. May, 1912. "Rationalization in Every-day Life." Journal of Abnormal Psychology. Aug. 1908, etc.

192. JONES, ROBERT, "Dementia in Relation to Responsibility" (and discussion). Journal of Mental Science. July, 1912.

205. JÖRGER, J., "Beitrag zur Kenntnis der Pseudologia phantastica." Vierteljahrschrift für gerichtliche Medizin. 1904, XXVII, 3. Folge, Suppl. Heft, pp. 189–242.

41. Journal officiel. 1909, Report of Minister of Justice in regard

to crime in 1907. Summary of report. Journal American Medical Ass'n. Paris letter. Nov. 30, 1909.

254. Journal of Inebriety, Boston. 1903. Reference list of works on alcoholism, etc.

40. Judicial Statistics, England and Wales, 1910. Published by Home Office. 1912. pp. 185. London, Eyre & Spottiswoode.

365. JUNG, C. G., "Analyse der Assoziationen eines Epileptikers." Jour. für Psychol. und Neurologie. Bd. V, 1905, p. 73.

142. —— "Diagnostischen Associations-Studien." Barth, Leipzig. 1906. The Association Method. Amer. Jour. of Psychology. April, 1910.

227. KAHL, WILHELM, "Der Stand der europäischen Gesetzgebung über verminderte Zurechnungsfähigkeit." Juristisch-psychiatrische Grenzfragen. Bd. IX, Heft 1.

182. KARPAS, M. J., "Psychic Constitutional Inferiority." New York Medical Journal. March 21, 1913, p. 594.

81. KAUFFMANN, MAX, "Die Psychologie des Verbrechens." Berlin, J. Springer, 1912, pp. 344.

127. KELLOR, FRANCES A., "Experimental Sociology; Delinquents." New York, Macmillan, 1901, pp. 316.

52. KINBERG, OLAF, "Ueber das strafprozessuale Verfahren in Schweden." Halle a. S., Marhold, 1913, pp. 152.

161. —— "Obligatory Psychiatric Examination." A paper read before the Seventh International Congress for Criminal Anthropology. Translation, Journal of American Institute of Criminal Law and Criminology. March, 1912.

235. KING, IRVING, "Physiological Age and School Standing." Psychological Clinic. Jan. 1914.

164. KNECHT, "Ueber die Verbreitung physikalen Degeneration bei Verbrechern." Allgemeine Zeitschrift für Psychiatrie. Band 55, Heft 5.

324. KNEELAND, GEO. J., "Commercialized Prostitution in New York City." New York, Century Co., 1913.

377. KNOX, H. A., "Scale for Estimating Mental Defect." Journal Amer. Medical Assoc'n. Mar. 7, 1914. p. 741; also Journal of Heredity, Mar. 1914, p. 122.

177. KOCH, J. L. A., "Die psychopathischen Minderwertigkeiten." Ravensburg, Maier, 1891, pp. 427.

157. KOEHLER, AUG., "Der Vergeltungsgedanke und seine Praktische Bedeutung." Leipzig, Engelmann, 1909, pp. 285.

204. KOEPPEN, "Ueber die pathologische Lügner." Charite-Annalen. 1898. XXIII, pp. 674–719.

343. KRAEPELIN, E., "Lectures on Clinical Psychiatry." English translation. New York, Wood, 1904.

188. VON KRAFFT-EBING, R., "Psychopathia Sexualis; A Medico-Legal Study." English translation. Philadelphia, Davis & Co., 1901, pp. 436.

267. —— "Lehrbuch der Gerichtlichen psychopathologie." 3d ed. 1892, p. 170.

331. VON KRAFFT-EBING, R., "Text Book on Insanity." English edition translated by Chaddock. Philadelphia, Davis, 1905. pp. 638.

332. —— "Psychosis Menstrualis." Stuttgart, 1902.

355. KRAUSS, A., "Psychologie des Verbrechens." Tübingen, 1884.

145. Kritische Beiträge zur Strafrechtsreform; Herausgegeben von Birkmeyer und Nayler. Leipzig, Engelmann, 1911. (14 volumes have appeared.)

89. KUHLMANN, F., "A Revision of the Binet-Simon System for Measuring the Intelligence of Children." Monograph Supplement to Journal of Psycho-Asthenics. Faribault, Minnesota, Sept. 1912.

91. —— Journal of Psycho-Asthenics. Vol. XV. Nos. 3, 4. 1911.

244. LADAME, P.-L., "Alcohol et Exhibitionistes." Archives d'anthropologie criminelle. April, 1913, pp. 266–272.

349. LE BON, GUSTAV, "Psychologie des foules," Paris, Alcan. "The Crowd — A Study of the Popular Mind." London, Unwin, 1897, pp. 219.

102. LIPMANN, O., "Die Wirkung von Suggestionfragen." Leipzig, Barth, 1909. Also in Zeitschrift für angewandte Psychologie, 1, 2; 1908.

23. LOMBROSO, CESARE, "L'homme criminel." Vol. II. pp. 50–201. "Criminal Man According to Lombroso," by Madame Ferrero. New York, Putnams, 1911, pp. 58, 69, 72. "Crime: Its Causes and Remedies." Little, Brown & Co., Introduction, p. XXIII.

230. —— "La Donna Delinquente," Turin, 1903. English translation, "The Female Offender." New York, Appleton, 1909.

239. —— English edition, "Crime, Its Causes and Remedies." Boston, Little, Brown & Co., 1911, pp. 471.

238. MACDONALD, ARTHUR, "Statistics of Alcoholism and Inebriety." Journal of Inebriety. Boston. Autumn, 1909, pp. 18.

199. —— "Juvenile Crime. — Stigmata of Degeneration." Washington, Government Printing Office, 1908, pp. 339.

20. MACDOUGALL, ROBERT, The Journal of Abnormal Psychology. Vol. VI. No. 5, p. 368.

303. MAIRET AND EUZIÈRE, "Les Invalides Moraux. Coulet," Montpellier, 1910. pp. 282.

317. MAIRET, "Le Vagabondage constitutionnel des Dégénéres." Annales medicopsychologique. Continued article, 1911 and 1912.

282. MANTEGAZZA, P., "Physiognomy and Expression." London, Scott, 1906. pp. 327.

200. MARIE, A., "Psychiatrical Anthropology," (Stigmata), pp. 160; 189 illustrations. in "Traité International de Psychologie Pathologique." Tome I. Paris, F. Alcan, 1910.

309. MARIE AND MEUNIER, "Les vagabonds." Paris, 1908.
273. MARRO, "Evolution Psychologique Humaine à l'école Pubère."
     Traité International de Psychologie Pathologique. Tome
     I. pp. 710–814. Paris, Alcan, 1910.
 32. ———— "La Puberté." Paris, Schleicher, 1901.
170. MARTIN, E., "Brandstiftung aus Heimweh." Archiv für
     Kriminalanthropologie und Kriminalistik. 1905. No. 20.
305. MARX, HUGO. "Ovulation und Schwangerschaft in ihrer Be-
     deutung für die forensische Psychiatrie." Berliner Klin.
     Wochenschrift. 1908. No. 39. Sept. 28, p. 1776.
 56. MATZ, "Unsere Jugendlichen." Monatschrift für Kriminal-
     psychologie, Vol. V.
191. McCONNELL, R. M., "Criminal Responsibility and Social
     Constraint." New York, Scribners, 1912, pp. 337.
360. MEIGE, H., "Comment concevoir l'hypnotisme," etc. Revue
     Neurologique. Jan. 15, 1911, p. 12.
  3. MERCIER, C. A., "Conduct and Its Disorders." London, Mac-
     millan, 1911, pp. 377.
 45. ———— "Crime and Insanity." New York, Holt, pp. 254.
148. ———— "Criminal Responsibility." Oxford, Clarendon Press,
     1905, pp. 232.
 47. MEYER, ADOLF, "The Anatomical Facts and Clinical Varieties
     of Traumatic Insanity," American Journal of Insanity.
     1904, No. 3, LX, pp. 373–441.
 67. ———— "Scheme for Examination of Cases." Printed for
     New York State Pathological Institute.
153. ———— "A Discussion of some Fundamental Issues in Freud's
     Psychoanalysis." New York State Hospitals Bulletin. March,
     1910, pp. 22.
219. ———— "A review of the signs of degeneration and of methods
     of registration." American Journal of Insanity. 1895–1896.
     LII, p. 344.
356. ———— p. 20, Report of New York State Pathological Insti-
     tute. 1904–1905.
357. ———— p. 823, State Hospitals Bulletin. March, 1910. New
     York State Commission in Lunacy.
337. MEYER, MAX, "The Fundamental Laws of Human Behavior."
     Boston, Badger, 1911, pp. 241.
353. MEYER AND PUPPE, "Ueber gegenseitige Anziehung und
     Beeinflussung psychopathischer Personlichkeiten" Viertel-
     jahrschrift für gerichtliche Medizin, 1912. Bd. 43, p. 84–
     116.
228. MEZGER, E., "Die Klippe des Zurechnungsproblems." Juris-
     tisch-psychiatrische Grenzfragen. Bd. IX., Heft 1.
 46. MITCHELL, "Types of Alcoholic Insanity." American Journal
     of Insanity, Oct. 1904, and Diefendorf, "Clinical Psychiatry."
     1907, p. 189.
339. MOLL, ALBERT, "The Sexual Life of the Child." Translated by
     Paul. New York, Macmillan, 1912, pp. 339.

304. MONKEMOELLER, "Zur Psychopathologie des Brandstifters." Gross' Archiv für Kriminalistik. Bd. 48; Heft 3 and 4, pp. 193–310.

287. MOORE, FRANK, Thirteenth Annual Report of New Jersey State Reformatory, p. 15. Rahway, New Jersey, 1913.

347. MOORE, LANGDON W., "His Own Story of His Eventful Life." Published by Himself. 1893, pp. 700. Many illustrations. Gambler, burglar, safe-blower, etc. Many Prison Experiences.

54. MORRISON, W. D., "Crime and Its Causes." Swan, Sonnenschein & Co. 1891.

223. ———— "Juvenile Offenders." Appleton & Co. 1900, pp. 317.

95. MÜNSTERBURG, HUGO, "On the Witness Stand." New York, 1908, pp. 309.

111. ———— "Psychology and Industrial Efficiency." Boston, Houghton, Mifflin Co., 1913, p. 86.

340. NAECKE, P., "Homosexuality and Psychosis." Allgemeine Zeitschrift für Psychiatrie. 1911. Heft 3.

246. NEFF, I. H., Foxborough State Hospital Report. "Drunkenness in Massachusetts, conditions and remedies." 1910. pp. 70.

368. ———— "Treatment of Inebriety," etc. Boston Medical and Surg. Journal. June 16, 1910. p. 809, and Jan. 26, 1911, p. 112.

48. NITSCHE AND WILMANNS, "History of the Prison Psychoses." Translated by Barnes and Glueck. New York, Journal of Nervous and Mental Diseases Publishing Co. 1912. pp. 84.

99. NORSWORTHY, NAOMI, "The Psychology of Mentally Deficient Children." New York, Columbia University, Nov. 1906. Monograph, pp. 111.

281. NORTH, C. H., "Insanity Among Adolescent Criminals." Amer. Jour. Insanity. Apr. 1911. p. 677.

51. OBA, SHIGEMA, "Unverbesserliche Verbrecher and ihre Behandlung." Berlin, Bahr, 1908. pp. 83.

181. OBERNDORF, C. P., "Constitutional Inferiority and Its Psychosis." Jour. Amer. Medical Association. Jan. 27, 1912. p. 249.

358. ———— "Constitutional Abnormality." New York State Hospitals Bulletin. March, 1910, p. 814.

39. OTTOLENGHI, Archivio di Psichiatria. Fasc. II–III. Vol. XVIII. 1897.

316. PAGNIER, A., "Le vagabond." Paris, Vigot frères, 1910, pp. 244.

190. PARSON, P. A., "Responsibility for Crime." Columbia University Studies, pp. 200.

18. PARTRIDGE, G. E., "An Outline of Individual Study." New York, Sturgis & Walton, 1910, pp. 240.

247. ———— "Studies in the Psychology of Intemperance." New York, Sturgis & Walton, 1913, pp. 275.

130. PATRICK, H. T., "Ambulatory Automatism." New York, Journal of Nervous and Mental Diseases. June, 1907.

240. PEARSON AND ELDERTON, Eugenics Laboratory Memoirs XIII. London, Dulan & Co., 1910. "A Second Study of the Influence of Parental Alcoholism," etc.

269. PEISER, J., "Prognosis of Congenital Syphilis." Berlin, Therapeutische Monatshefte. April, 1909. Bd. 23, Heft 4, pp. 185–240.

268. PERCY, J. F., "Phrenitis prostatica." Jour. Amer. Med. Ass'n. July 2, 1910, p. 19. Also Illinois Med. Jour. Nov. 1908.

198. PETERSON, FREDERICK, "Nervous and Mental Diseases." Church and Peterson. 4th ed. pp. 690–712. Philadelphia, Saunders & Co.

249. PETTER, GEO. E., "Chronic Alcoholism." Journal Amer. Med. Ass'n., Nov. 25, 1911.

140. PFISTER, OSKAR, "Die psychanalytische Methode." Vol. I of Meumann and Messmer's Paedagogium. Leipzig, Klinkhardt, 1913, pp. 490.

8. POLLITZ, P., "Die Psychologie des Verbrechers." Leipzig, Teubner, 1909, pp. 148.

259. POTTS, W. A., et al., "The Relation of Alcohol to the Feebleminded." British Jour. of Inebriety. 1909, pp. 135–149.

298. PRICHARD, "A treatise on Insanity." London, 1835.

132. Psychanalytical Review, Edited by W. A. White and S. E. Jelliffe. New York, Jour. of Nervous and Mental Diseases Publishing Co.

136. PUTNAM, J. J., "Comments on Sex Issues from the Freudian Standpoint. Paper read before the New York Academy of Medicine, April 4, 1912. New York Medical Jour., June 15 and 22, 1912.

133. ———— "Etiology and Treatment of the Psychoneuroses:" a Paper Read Before the Canadian Medical Association, 1910. Boston Medical and Surgical Journal, July 21, 1910.

149. QUINTON, R. F., "Crime and Criminals." New York, Longmans, 1910. pp. 259.

171. REICHEL, HANS, "Brandstiftung aus Heimweh." Archiv für Kriminalanthropologie und Kriminalistik. No. 36, 1910.

71. RIBOT, T. H., "Sur la valeur des questionnaires en psychologie." Journal de Psychologie normale et path. I, 1904.

11. RICHTER, "Ueber pathologische Rauschzustände." Inaugural Dissertation, Berlin, 1909.

350. RIIS, JACOB, "How the Other Half Lives," 1890.

374. RISCH, B., "Ueber die Verkennung psychogener Symptomkomplexe der frischen Haft." Monatsschrift f. Psychiatrie u. Neurologie. April, 1909, p. 281.

207. ———— "Ueber die phantastiche Form des degenerativen Irresseins." Allgemeine Zeitschrift für Psychiatrie, 1908, 65, Heft 4, pp. 576–639.

366. RITTERSHAUS, "Zur psychologischen Differentialdiagnose der einzelnen Epilepsieformen." Archiv für Psychiatrie u. Nervenkr, Bd. 46, Heft 1 and 2.

278. ROSSOLIMO, G., "Die Psychologische Prophile. Zur Methodik der quantitativen Untersuchungen der psychischen Vorgänge." Klinik für psychische u. nervöse Krankheiten, 1911. Vol. VI, Nos. 3–4.

211. ROUMA, G., "Un cas de Mythomanie." Arch. de Psych., 1908, pp. 259–282.

185. RUPPRECHT, "Straffällige Jugend und psychopathische Minderwertigkeit." Münchener medizinische Wochenschrift, No. 14. 1911, p. 742.

55. RYLANDS, G. GORDON, "Crime: Its Causes and Remedies." London, Unwin, 1899.

123. SALEILLES, R., "L'individualisation de la peine." English edition. "The Individualization of Punishment." Boston, Little, Brown & Co., 1911.

180. SCHOLZ, L., "Anomale Kinder." Berlin, Karger, 1912, pp. 442.

217. SCRIPTURE, E. W., "Stuttering and Lisping." pp. 251. London, Macmillan Co. 1912.

195. SERNOFF, "Die Lehre Lombroso's und ihre anatomischen Grundlagen im Lichte moderner Forschung." Biologisches Zentralblatt, XIV, p. 305.

110. SHARP, F. C., "Study of the Influence of Custom on the Moral Judgment." University of Wisconsin. Bulletin 236, June, 1908, pp. 144.

194. SIBENALER, P. C. A., "L'age du discernement consideré sur la responsibilité de l'enfance coupable." Bordeaux, Cadoret, 1906, p. 108.

17. SIDIS, BORIS, "Psychology of Suggestion." New York, Appleton, 1899. pp. 386.

145. ——— "The Causation of Psychopathic Maladies." Monthly Cyclopedia and Medical Bulletin, March and April, 1912. "The Pathology and Diagnosis of Psychoneuroses." Same Jour., May and June, 1910, etc.

297. SIGHELE, "Litterature et Criminalité." Paris, Giard et Briere, 1908, pp. 222.

351. ——— "La Foule criminelle." Paris, Alcan.

352. ——— "Le Crime à Deux." Paris, Giard, 1910.

196. SLEYSTER, R., "The Physical Bases of Crime." Bulletin, Amer. Academy of Medicine, Dec. 1913. "The Criminal Physique." Jour. Amer. Medical Assoc'n. May 3, 1913.

92. SMEDLEY, F., Report of Child Study Department, Chicago Public Schools. 1900, 1901.

82. SOMMER, R., "Lehrbuch der psychopathologische Untersuchungs-Methoden." Berlin, Urban & Schwarzenberg, 1899.

163. ——— "Kriminalpsychologie." Leipzig, Barth, 1904, pp. 388.

162. SPAULDING, EDITH R., AND HEALY, WILLIAM, "Inheritance as a Factor in Criminality." Bulletin of the Amer. Academy of Medicine. Feby. 1914, pp. 24.

222. SPAULDING, E. R., "The Wasserman test for Inmates of Penal Institutions." Jour. Amer. Inst. of Crim. Law and Criminology. Jan. 1914, p. 712.

26. SPRATLING, W. P., "Epilepsy." Philadelphia, Saunders, 1904, p. 522.

184. STAIGER, "Die Behandlung psychopathischen minderwertiger Strafgefangener." Allg. Zeitsch. für Psychiatrie. Bd. 69, Heft 4, June, 1912, p. 458.

362. STAPEL, "Das Verhältnis der Pupillen bei der akuten Alkoholintoxication." Monatschrift für Psychiatrie, 1911.

4. STARKE, "Verbrechen und Verbrecher in Preussen 1854–1878." Berlin, Enslin, 1884, pp. 240.

342. STEEN, R. H., "Moral Insanity." Journal of Mental Science, July, 1913, p. 478.

143. STEKEL, W., "Die sexuelle Wurzel der Kleptomanie." Zeitschrift für Sexualwissenschaft. 1908, pp. 588–600.

179. STELZNER, HELENEFRIEDERIKE, "Die psychopathischen Konstitutionen und ihre sociologische Bedeutung." Berlin, Karger, 1910, pp. 249.

288. —— "Analyse von 200 Selbstmordfälle." Berlin, Karger, 1906. Pamphlet, pp. 124.

206. STEMMERMANN, ANNA, "Beiträge zur Kenntnis und Kasuistik der Pseudologia phantastica." Berlin, Reimer, 1906, pp. 102.

79. STERN, WILLIAM, "Differentielle Psychologie in ihren methodischen Grundlagen." Leipzig, Barth, 1911, pp. 503.

93. —— editor, Beiträge zur Psychologie der Aussage. Leipzig, Barth.

264. STOCKARD, CHARLES R., "Alcoholic injuries to germ cells." American Naturalist. Nov. 1913. Also Journal of Heredity, Feb. 1914.

30. Supreme Court of Pennsylvania in the Case of Commonwealth vs. Snyder. (73 Atl. R., 910.)

166. TALBOT, EUGENE S., "Stigmata of Degeneracy among American Criminal Youth." Journal American Medical Association. April 9, 1898.

167. —— "Degeneracy: its Causes, Signs, and Results." pp. 374. New York, Scribners, 1904.

5. TARDE, GABRIEL, "Philosophie pénale," 1st edition, 1890, 4th edition, Paris, 1903; English edition, "Penal Philosophy." Boston, Little, Brown & Co., 1912, pp. 581.

165. TARNOWSKY, PAULINE, "Études Anthropométriques sur les Prostituées."

90. TERMAN, L. M., AND CHILDS, H. G., "A Tentative Revision and Extension of the Binet-Simon Measuring Scale of Intelligence." Baltimore, Journal of Educational Psychology, Feb. to May, 1912.

106. TERMAN, L. M., Pedagogical Seminary, Sept. 1906; and with increased material in Journal of Educational Psychology. April, 1912.

371. —— "Recent Literature on Juvenile Suicides." Jour. Abnormal Psychology. April–May, 1914, pp. 61–66.

113. —— Journal of Educational Psychology. April, 1912.

118. —— Pedagogical Seminary. 1906.

379. "Testing Intelligence by Means of Jokes." Allgemeine Zeitschrift für Psychiatrie. Bd. 64. Heft. 6. 1908.

338. THOINOT, L., "Medicolegal Aspects of Moral Offenses." English translation by Weysse. Philadelphia, Davis, 1911, pp. 486.

224. THOMPSON, J. A., "Heredity." New York, Putnams, 1908. Section on Maternal Impressions, p. 161.

272. THOMSEN, BOAS, et al., "Investigation of Mental Deficiency, etc., with Wassermann's Test for Syphilis." Berliner Klinische Wochenschrift, 1911. Bd. 48, p. 891.

336. THORNDIKE, E. L., "Elements of Psychology."

87. TOWN, CLARA H., Translation: "A Method of Measuring Development of the Intelligence of Young Children." Chicago Medical Book Co. 1913, pp. 82 and illustrations.

307. TREDGOLD, A. F., "Mental Deficiency." New York, Wood, 1908, pp. 391.

183. TRÜPER, JOHANNES, "Psychopathische Minderwertigkeiten als Ursache Gesetzverletzungen Jugendlicher." Beiträge zur Kinderforschung, 1904, Heft 8, pp. 57.

213. UPSON, HENRY S., "Insomnia and Nerve Strain." New York, Putnams, 1908.

271. VAS, J., "Later development of children with inherited syphilis." Berlin, Jahrbuch für Kinderheilkunde. April, 1912. Bd. 75, No. 4, pp. 403–532.

243. Vice Commission of Chicago, A Study and Report by the Municipal Vice Commission. 1911, pp. 399.

208. VOGT, "Jugendliche Lügnerinnen. Zeitschrift für die Erforsch. d. jugend. Schwachsinns." 1910, Bd. 3, Heft 5, p. 405.

193. WAGNER VON JAUREGG, "Ueber Krankhafte Triebhandlungen." Wiener Klinische Wochenschrift, XXV, No. 11, pp. 404–438.

28. WALLIN, J. E. W., "Experimental Studies of Mental Defectives" (Epileptics), Baltimore, Warwick & York. 1912.

212. —— "Experimental Oral Euthenics." Dental Cosmos. April, May, 1912.

291. WASSERMEYER, "Ueber Selbstmord." Archiv für Psychiatrie. Bd. 50 Heft 1, 1912.

361. WEBER, "Einfache Betrunkenheit oder pathologisch Rausch." Klinik für psych. u. nervöse Krankheiten, Bd. IV, Heft 3, pp. 195–211, 1908.

209. WENDT, E., "Zur Kasuistik der Pseudologia phantastica," Allgemeine Ztsch. für Psychiatrie. Bd. 68, Heft 4, pp. 482–500.

225. WEST, MRS. MAX, "Prenatal Care." Publication No. 4, Children's Bureau, pp. 41. Washington, Government Printing Office, 1913.

78. WHIPPLE, G. M., "Manual of Mental and Physical Tests." Baltimore, Warwick & York, 1910, pp. 534. New edition, two vols., 1914.

96. ——— Manual of Tests. 1910. pp. 286–311. Psychological Bulletin. May 15, 1909, and July 15, 1912. Journal American Institute of Criminal Law and Criminology. Nov. 1912.

119. ——— "A Range of Information Test." Psychological Review, No. 16, 1909, p. 347. See also his "Manual," p. 465.

348. WHITE, GEORGE M., "From Boniface to Bank Burglar." Bellows Falls, Vermont, Truax Printing Co. 1905, pp. 495.

73. WHITE, W. A., Jour. of Criminal Law and Criminology. May, 1913, p. 109.

134. ——— "Mental Mechanisms." New York, Journal of Nervous and Mental Disease Publishing Co. 1911, pp. 151.

156. WHITMAN, JOHN L., "Importance of an Up-to-Date Medical Department in a Penal Institution." Proceedings, American Prison Association. 1913.

327. WIDEN, L. E., "Young Criminals in the Nebraska State Penitentiary." Abstract of a study. The Survey. Nov. 18, 1911, pp. 1221–1224.

107. WIERSMA, E., Zeitschrift für Psychologie, 30, 1902.

97. WIGMORE, J. H., "Münsterberg on the Psychology of Evidence." Illinois Law Review, Feb. 1909.

248. WILLIAMS, TOM A., "The Psychological Bases of Inebriety." New York Medical Jour. April, 1909.

35. WILLIAMS, W. R., British Gynecological Journal, May, 1902.

314. WILMANNS, KARL, "Psychoses among Tramps." Centralblatt für Nervenheilkunde, Dec., 1902.

315. ——— "Zur Psychopathologie des Landstreichers." Leipzig, Barth, 1906, pp. 418.

173. ——— "Heimweh oder impulsives Irresein." Monatsschrift für Kriminalpsychologie, 1907, No. 3, 136.

142. WITMER, LIGHTNER, See many places in his journal, The Psychological Clinic, Philadelphia.

279. WOODS, F. A., "Mental and Moral Heredity in Royalty." A Statistical Study in History and Psychology. New York, Holt, 1906, pp. 312.

174. WRIGHT, H. W., "A Consideration of Constitutional Inferiority." New York Medical Journ., Dec. 26, 1908.

2. WULFFEN, ERICH, "Psychologie des Verbrechens." Langenscheidt, Gross-Lichterfelde, 1908, 2 vols. pp. 448 and 546.

98. ——— "Gauner und Verbrechertypen." Berlin, Langenscheidt, 1912.

284. YERKES, ROBERT M., "Introduction to Psychology." New York, Holt, 1911, pp. 28.

42. YVERNIS, MAURICE, "L'alcoolisme et la criminalité." Archives d'anthropologie criminelle, 1912. Vol. 27, pp. 5–35.

114. ZIEHEN, TH., "Die Prinzipien und Methoden der Intelligenzprüfung. Berlin, Karger, 1909.

175. ———"Zur Lehre von dem psychopathischen Konstitution." Charité Annalen, Vols. XXIX, XXX, 1911.

178. ——— "Die Erkennung der psychopathischen Konstitutionen und die öffentliche Fürsorge für psychopathisch veranlagte Kinder." Berlin, Karger, 1912, pp. 34.

275. ——— "Ethische Defektszustände in der Pubertät." Allg. Zeitschrift für Psychiatrie, 1910, 67, p. 481.

40. ZINGERLE, H., "Ueber transitorische Geistesstörungen und deren forensische Beurteilung." Halle a. S., Marhold, 1912, pp. 52.

APPENDIX B

ORGANIZATION OF THE JUVENILE PSYCHOPATHIC INSTITUTE

The Juvenile Psychopathic Institute was organized in March, 1909, with an endowment for five years, provided through the public-spirited generosity of Mrs. W. F. Dummer. The organization represented an effort in practical research which, as the result of several preliminary observations, had been for some time deemed highly promising. The plan of organization is due to Miss Lathrop, now Chief of the Children's Bureau, Washington. The activities were at once placed entirely in the hands of the director, who at all times has been free to be guided only by professional needs and professional counsel. Those of the advisory council whose activities have led them to be specially interested have given freely of their advice. We must also acknowledge indebtedness to a considerable number of other persons — judges, psychologists, medical specialists, officers of institutions — who have felt the importance of the work enough to give counsel.

The Institute was incorporated and the official organization made up as follows:

OFFICERS

Miss Julia C. Lathrop . . . . *President*
Mrs. George R. Dean . . . . *Secretary*
Mrs. W. F. Dummer . . . . *Treasurer*

Director

William Healy, M.D.

ADVISORY COUNCIL

Prof. James R. Angell   Dr. Adolf Meyer
Judge E. O. Brown   Horace K. Tenney
Dr. H. B. Favill   Henry W. Thurston
Judge Julian W. Mack   John H. Wigmore
Prof. George H. Mead   Judge M. W. Pinckney
Judge Harry Olson

EXECUTIVE COMMITTEE

Jane Addams   Julia C. Lathrop
Mrs. W. F. Dummer   Dr. Hugh T. Patrick
Dr. Frank S. Churchill   Mrs. Geo. R. Dean
Allen T. Burns   Dr. Graham Taylor

809

The office of Psychologist has been successively filled by Grace M. Fernald, Ph.D., Mary H. S. Hayes, Ph.D., Jean Weidensell, Ph.D., Clara Schmitt, Ph.D., Mary W. Chapin, Augusta F. Bronner, Ph.D.

Special researches have been carried out by Dr. Anne Burnet, Frances Porter, and Dr. Edith R. Spaulding.

The efficient secretary to the director for four years has been Emily Deane Macmillan.

In April, 1914, under an appropriation from the Board of County Commissioners, the Juvenile Court of Cook County, Merritt W. Pinckney, Judge, established the Psychopathic Institute as a new department. The director remains the same, with Dr. Augusta F. Bronner as assistant director.

Recently Dr. Frank Perkins, Miss Josephine T. Thomas, and Miss Frances Porter have been actively assisting in the Institute.

INDEX

INDEX

[References are to pages]

A

Aberrational types, analysis of, in our group, 132.

Abilities as distinguished from desires, 101.

Abilities, classification according to, 113; special, of the feebleminded, 463; tests for, 100; varieties of, 101.

Abnormal developmental conditions, discussion of, 234.

Abnormal psychology of fugues, literature on, 637.

Abnormal sexualism among epileptics, 424 ff.

Aboriginal moral imbecility, 786.

Abortion, attempted, as causing defect in offspring, 206.

Accusation of self, case of, 746.

Accusations, false, cases of, 732 ff.; pathological, definition of, 729.

Achievement capacity test, 96.

Action, impulse to, excessive in certain individuals, 755.

Adenoids as a factor, 219.

Adolescence and immigration causing criminalism, case of, 723.

Adolescence as related to defect in self-control, 534.

Adolescence, general considerations on, 709; mental growth during, 710 ff.; related to premature puberty, 248; stages of, 710; time of influence by stories, 306.

Adolescent aberration complicated by bad sex habits, 653.

Adolescent age limits as related to juvenile court law, 726.

Adolescent characteristics leading to criminality, cases of, 714 ff.

Adolescent dissatisfaction with parents, 725.

Adolescent hypersensitiveness related to psychosis and criminalism, cases of, 674 ff.

Adolescent hypersusceptibility in the home, 290.

Adolescent impulses and love of excitement, 753.

Adolescent instability as a cause of misconduct, 712; as related to love of adventure, 756; in relation to defective heredity, 728; reaction of at home, 290.

Adolescent mental aberrations of girls, 675 ff.; treatment of, 677.

Adolescent mental peculiarities, literature on, 709 ff.

Adolescent misconduct, treatment of, necessity for individualism in, 726.

Adolescent over-development, 243.

Adolescent pathological lying, cases of, 732, 740 ff.

Adolescent period, tiding through, by institutional treatment, 727.

Adolescent psychoses, 651; leading to criminalism, 653 ff.; varieties of, 674.

Adolescent romanticism leading to suicidal impulses, 724.

Adolescent self-assertion and obstinacy, 766.

Adolescent tendencies to misconduct, treatment of, 726.

Adolescent types of criminality, 713.

Adolescents, alcoholic psychoses of, 683; characteristics of, leading to aberration, 651; effect of alcohol upon, 267.

Adventure, abnormal love of, treatment of, 765; and excitement, predisposition toward, types of, 754; love of, general considerations concerning, 753.

Adventurous type of behavior related to pathological lying, 741.

Age levels discriminated by tests, 79 ff.

Age limits of juvenile court procedure, reform necessary in, 726.

Age norms, developmental, 237.

Age-weight statistics, 144.

Ailments, physical, enumerated for our group, 135.

Alcohol, affecting mental defectives, 269; affecting responsibility for crime, 273; and delinquency, 262 ff.; and individual susceptibility, 679; and mental defectiveness, 462; and

813

procreation, 264; as a factor in defective heredity, 263; in vice, 267; as indulged in by our group of cases, 138; causing exhibitionism, 271; creating its own need, 269.

Alcohol, effect of, on adolescent girls, 686 ff.; on adolescents, 267; use of, relationship to criminalism, 262.

Alcoholic hallucinosis, 682.

Alcoholic paranoia, cases of, 682.

Alcoholic parents, cases of, 286.

Alcoholic psychoses, varieties of, 678.

Alcoholics, classification of, 272.

Alcoholism and crime, 23; and criminalism, statistics on, 262; and criminality, literature on, 681; and defective environment, 264; and development of children, 264; and suicide, 775 n., 776; chronic psychoses of, 681; complications of, case of, 273; creating defective environment, details of, 266; in homes, cases of, 286; literature on, 262 n., 681; of delinquents, in our cases, 267; of parents of offenders in our group, 152; of pregnant mother in relation to delinquency of offspring, 204; treatment of, 271; typical family history of, 265.

Algometer, 58.

Ambitiousness of adolescence, 714.

American Institute of Criminal Law, Committee A of, 52.

American love of adventure, 754.

Amnesias, 637.

Amnesic fugues, cases of, 638.

Analgesia in criminals, 17, n.

Analysis of visual perceptions, tests for, 91.

Analysis, psychological, 115.

Antecedent probability as applied in cases of pathological lying, 729.

Antenatal conditions, defective, enumerated for our group, 137.

Antenatal history, schedule for, 55.

Anthropometry, limitations of, 57.

Anthropometry, schedule for data of, 57.

Anti-social attitude as the result of mental conflict, case of, 376.

Anti-social conduct arising from custodial experiences, 310; developed from newspaper reading, 301.

Anti-social tendencies caused by school irritations, 295.

Antonym test, norms on, 110.

Apperceptive powers, tests for, 96.

Applied psychology, newness of, 104.

Arithmetical ability defective, as related to criminalism, 521; importance of, 90.

Arrest of mental development from injury, 568.

Arson, pathological, 774.

Asphyxia neonatorum, as cause of defect, 208.

Association processes, mental, tests for, 86.

Association reactions, 118.

Attitude, an understanding, necessary for testing, 49; necessary in examination, 47; of examiner, 35; of relatives, 46; towards offender influences him, 171.

Attention, tests for, 85.

Attenuated responsibility of psychopaths, 592.

Auditory memory, tests for, 83.

"Aussage" Picture Test, norms on, 108.

"Aussage" Test, literature on, 84; on socially suggestible offenders, 95; picture for, 84.

Austrian Imperial Criminalistic Institute, 173 n.

B

Bad companions as a factor in our group of cases, 135; teaching of, leading to mental conflict, cases of, 357 ff.

Bad homes and recidivists, 285.

Big Brother Movement, necessity of studying individual for success in, 178; value of social suggestibility for, 705.

Binet tests, 79; critique on, 79 ff.; for classification of feebleminded, 449 ff.; literature on, 79.

Biographical material in criminology, 186 n.

Biological defect, familial, case of, 198.

Birth abnormal, statistics on results of, 208.

Birth, data concerning, schedule for, 55; difficult, as cause of defect, 208.

Bladder, lack of control of, as a factor in delinquency, 227.

Blood-and-thunder literature causing criminalism, 305.

Blue Book, *vide* Judicial Statistics of England (**40**), 10.

"Born criminal," the 17, 781.

C

"Cadet's" power over women, psychology of, 405.

Capital punishment, not evaluated by us, 166 n.

Card system of record of causative

Crowd companionship, influence of, 703.

Crowd psychology, literature on, 703.

Custodial experiences creating delinquency, 310.

D

Dance halls, relation of, to criminalism, 295.

Data concerning delinquents, schedule of, 53; our, availability of, 184.

Deafmutism as a factor, 222.

Deceit in treatment, dangers of, 172.

Deceitfulness and mental conflicts, 356.

Deception in tests, 105.

Defect in arithmetical ability as related to criminalism, 521; in language ability as related to criminalism, 516; in self-control, as related to criminalism, 533; in self-control leads to enuresis, 226.

Defective environment created by alcoholism, 264 ff.

Defective mental capacity, caused by physical conditions, 546.

Defective special mental abilities, 515.

Defective types, enumeration of in our group, 131.

Defective vision as a factor, 217.

Defectives, mental, as distinguished from aberrational individuals, 444; verbalist type of, 473.

Degeneracy, literature on, 588 n.; statistics of, 146.

Degenerate murderer, epileptic, case of, 424.

Delayed puberty, case of, 240.

Deliberate choice, cases of, 332; definition of, 331; of criminal career from mental conflict, cases of, 393.

Delinquencies of males and females compared, 144; of our repeated offenders, 140.

Delinquency as caused by excess of physical vigor, 231; related to pathological lying, 731; related to restlessness, 769; the result of mental conflict, cases of, 357 ff.; caused by adolescent self-assertion, 724; bad language at home, 284; characteristics of adolescents, cases of, 714 ff.; defect in self-control, cases of, 535 ff.; desire for stage life, 764; amnesic fugues, cases of, 640; incompetent parental control, 289; masturbation, case of, 409; unsatisfactory vocation, 296; excess of tobacco, 280; indirectly caused by excess of tea and coffee, 278; by hypersexuality, 403;

by masturbation, 407; instigated by sexualism, 400; interpretation of, effect upon the offender of, 172; record of, 61; relation of undernourishment to, 230; special bases of enumerated, 32.

Delinquent careers, determinants of in youth, 11; early influences on, 12.

Delinquent girls and physical overdevelopment, 246.

Delinquents, not all abnormal, 4; numbers in families of, 148; understanding of, 6; treatment of, in youth, 12; study of, advantage of early, 38; age for, 12; best opportunities for, 40; each case different, 38; equipment for, 44, 45; follow-up work necessary for, 19; for treatment, 8; in institutions, 41; in relation to the trial, 41; laboratory for, 40, 44, 45; lack of practical literature on, 3; length of time for, 42; necessity for thorough, 43; to whom should appeal, 6; when ingenuous, 12.

Dementia, 603; as distinguished from mental defect, 445.

Dementia paralytica, 600.

Dementia precox, 592; and masturbation, 642; proportion of among offenders, 594; suicide, case of, 593.

Desire for social advancement thwarted causing delinquency, 290.

Detention experiences creating bad results, 311.

Deterioration of the offender caused by incarceration, 311.

Deterrency of idea of punishment, 166, 167.

Development, abnormal, general discussion of, 234; mental and moral, schedule for data concerning, 56.

Developmental anomalies and adolescence, 235; our statistical findings on, 236.

Developmental anthropometry, schedule for data of, 57.

Developmental conditions, defective, enumerated for our group, 137; as causative factors of delinquency, critique on, 201; importance of knowledge of, 11.

Diagnostic summary, 61.

Differential psychology, definition of, 74.

Discipline of children, lack of, related to impulses of excitement, 753.

Discrimination, mental, Ziehen test for, 92; tests for, 92.

Disposition in relation to physical conditions, 228; revengeful, as related to delinquency, 767.

Dissatisfaction, adolescent, with family causing delinquency, 725.

Disturbing conditions in mental tests to be recognized, 105.

Drinking among children, 264.

Drug habitués, lying and self-accusation of, 731.

Drugs, psychoses from, 689.

Drunkards often feebleminded, 23.

Drunkenness and procreation, 264; failure of treatment of in England, 23.

Dual social suggestibility, literature on, 708.

Dullness from physical causes, case showing result of treatment of, 547; in classification, 114.

E

Ear ailments as a factor, 218.

Early treatment, advantage of beginning, 172.

Education among our group of offenders, 151.

Educational neglect causing delinquency, 300.

Educational tests, critique on, 81; interpretation of, 81.

Effeminacy in males leading to delinquency, case of, 241.

Egocentrism of adolescence, 714.

Emotional condition in offenders studied, 69, 70.

Emotional life of offenders, subject for study, 70; schedule for history of, 71.

Energy, cases of inheritance of excess of, 189.

Enuresis and sex habits, 227; in delinquents, 226.

Environment and so-called "born criminals," 781; as a cause vs. personality, 283; balanced with other factors as a cause of delinquency, 283; effect of upon body measurements, 17 n.; physical differentiated from psychical, 284; schedule for data concerning, 56; treatment of in cases of delinquency, 176.

Environmental factors, general statement concerning, 282; only to be interpreted through psychical effects, 284; treatment of, 285.

Environmental influences surrounding the epileptic, cases illustrating, 434 ff.

Epilepsy among young repeated offenders, 416 n.; and criminalism, literature on, 414 n.; pathological lying, case of, 751; as a factor in

criminalism, 414; related to amnesia 638; in criminalism, Lombroso on, 416; of pregnant mother in relation to delinquency of offspring, 203; our criterion of the disease, 417; prematurity, and sex delinquency, case of, 250; principal manifestations of, 415; simulation of, 780; statistics of in our group, 147; unfortunate environmental tendencies of, cases illustrating, 434 ff.; varieties of, 414.

Epileptic aberrational mental states, 433.

Epileptic automatism, 433.

Epileptic career of girls, typical case of, 437.

Epileptic character, the, 418.

Epileptic equivalents, 415.

Epileptic fugues, cases of, 640.

Epileptic mania, 433.

Epileptic murder, typical case of, 424.

Epileptic psychoses, 603; in children, cases of, 434 ff.; effect of alcohol on, 270, 271; mental deterioration caused by, 419.

Epileptics as offenders, cases of, 419, 420 ff.; mental conditions of, during criminalism, 434; mental functionings of, 417; mental peculiarities of, 417; psychological studies on, 419 n.; physical peculiarities of, 419; violent assaults of, 437.

Ergograph, 58.

Eroticism, bases of, 402.

Erotomania an undesirable term, 400 n.

Ethical defects of puberty, 713.

Ethical discrimination, tests for, 99; weakened in senility, 212.

Ethics, philosophical conceptions of, and the "moral sense," 783.

Examination, length of continuation of, 48; medical, schedule for, 58; persons present at, 48, 49 n.; proper attitude for, 69; stenographic report of, 48.

Examiner, assistants to, 46; necessary previous training of, 36; selection of, 34; tactful attitude of, 47; temperament and attitude of, 34.

Examiners, women as, 36.

Excitement, abnormal love of, treatment of, 765; desire for, explosions of, 764; love of, general considerations concerning, 753.

Exciting literature, habit of reading, 305.

Exhibitionism compared in the sexes, 407; relation of alcohol to, 271; sexualistic impulsion, 405.

Experience, ability to profit by, tests

linquency, 293; immoral, 288; irritation in, 288; want of, causing delinquency, 292.

Home, conditions as cause of delinquency, critically considered, 282; defective, enumeration of in our group, 134.

Home life, lack of healthy interests in, causing delinquency, 298.

Homesickness and criminality, 356 n. causing arson, 774; mental conflict, 357; mental conflict and delinquency, case of, 398.

Housing conditions causing delinquency, 291; misconduct, 410.

Hungarian Law for study of delinquents, 173, 331.

Hutchinsonian teeth, statistics of, 146.

Hypersensitiveness of adolescents, 714.

Hypersexual tendencies, cases of inheritance of, 192.

Hypersexualism a disturbing influence during adolescence, 403; dominating influence, case of, 403; discussion of, 231; inadequacy of repressive treatment, 404; nature and causes of, 402; of epileptics, cases of, 424 ff.; operations for, 231; treatment of, 404.

Hypnotism, 705; border line of, in misconduct, case of, 706.

Hypomania, 609.

Hysteria and criminalism, 645; as related to amnesia, 638.

I

Idiots, 454.

Idiot savants, cases of, 463 ff.; type, 453.

Illegitimacy, in our group, 149; and aberration of pregnancy, case of, 635.

Illness, early, effect of, 209.

Imagery and empty minds, development of, 341; and hallucinations, 340; motor consequences of, 340; of criminalistic conduct, 339; producing misconduct, cases of, 341; types of visual, related to criminalism, 307.

Imbeciles, 454.

Imbecilic offenders, cases of, 454.

Immigration during adolescence causing criminalism, 723.

Immoral families causing delinquency, cases of, 288.

Immorality, self-accusation of, case of, 746.

Impaction of teeth as a factor, 220.

Imprisonment, the physical and mental effects of, 312.

Improper language as an environmental factor, 284.

Impulses, abnormal, leading to wandering, 779.

Impulses, adolescent, leading to criminalism, cases of, 714 ff.

Impulsions, sexualistic, 405.

Incrimination, mental aberration from 649.

Individual, abnormal, proper study of, 29; as center of criminalistic problem, 22; practical value of study of, 22; study of, growth of idea of, 24; to include all factors, 24.

Individual study, importance of, 5; recent development of, 18.

Industrial classification of feebleminded, 461.

Infancy and childhood, data concerning, schedule for, 55.

Infanticide, case of, 635.

Influence of older criminals, 705.

Information, evaluation of sources of, 50; from relatives, 39; general, inquiry into, 102; skepticism about, 39; sources of, 40.

Inheritance of physical traits, case of, 198.

Injury, criminalistic simulation of, 779.

Insanities, enumeration of in our group, 132; some unclassifiable, 441.

Insanity as distinguished from minor mental aberrations, 445; of masturbation, 642; of pregnant mother in relation to delinquency of offspring, 203; in heredity of our offenders, 156; simulation of, 780.

Instability, adolescent, general considerations of, 712.

Institutional life of offenders previously, in our group, 151.

Institutional treatment of delinquents, individualization in, 176; of offenders, general ideas about, 176.

Instruction-box Test, norms on, 110.

Instructions, 100.

Instrumental delivery, as cause of defect, 208.

Intent as guide to penalty, 20.

Intoxication creating irresponsibility, 273; of adolescents leading to criminalism, cases of, 684 ff.; pathological, 683.

Introduction puzzle, Test I, norms on, 106.

Introspection, the method of psychoanalysis, 117.

Investigation, sympathetic, necessity of, 34.

Irritability and criminalism arising from bad sex habits, 768; as related

Mental traits, schedule of study of, 71, also *note*.

Mental types, varieties in, diagram showing, 453.

Mental vacuity during prison life, 170, 314.

Mentally subnormal offenders, cases of, 492.

Method of presentation of cases, 185; of psychological inquiry, critique of, 68.

Methodology, our outlook on, 18.

Methods of medical examination, 65; of study, general conclusions about, 159.

Mill, J. Stuart, on the aim of punishment, 8.

Misconduct in children based on epilepsy, 434 ff.; peculiar to adolescence, 712; result of mental life, 28.

Monomania, 604.

Moral comprehension of the feebleminded, 787.

Moral contagion arising from bad companions, 293; during incarceration, 169, 313.

Moral danger during custody, 168.

"Moral feeblemindedness," 782.

"Moral imbecility," 782.

"Moral insanity," 782; literature on, 782 ff.

"Moral invalids," 787.

Moral judgment, tests for, 98; tests for, critique on, 99.

Moral Questions Tests, norms on, 110.

"Moral sense," philosophical conceptions of, 783.

Moral traits during adolescence, 652.

Morons as offenders, cases of, 455 ff.; definition of, 450.

Morphine addiction causing criminality, 275; mental results of addiction to, 275; psychoses from, 689.

Morphinism of pregnant mother in relation to delinquency of offspring, 204.

Morphinist, mental states of, 276; responsibility of, 275.

Motor coördination, norms on, 110; tests for, 86.

Motor functioning, desirable data concerning, 58.

Moving pictures creating a craving, 309; environment of, creating delinquency, 308; psychology of, related to criminalism, 306; stimulating to sex instinct, 308.

Moving picture shows and mental imagery, cases showing relation of, 341 ff.

Murders, possible range of intent in, 770.

Mutes, delinquent, cases of, 222.

Mythomania, *see* PATHOLOGICAL LYING, 729.

N

Narcotics causing mental dullness, cases of, 556.

Natal conditions defective, enumerated for our group, 137.

Nationality, of our offenders as compared to general population, 149, 150; of parents of our offenders, 150.

Neglect of parents causing delinquency, 292.

Negro men, attraction of, caused by hypersexualism, 403.

Nervous disorders, cases of in delinquents, 224; minor, as a factor in delinquency, 223.

Neuropathic foundations of menstrual aberrations, 628; mental aberrations during pregnancy, 634.

Newspaper influence in criminalism, researches on, 302.

Newspaper notoriety desired by delinquents, 304.

Newspapers, influence of, in creating criminalism, 301.

Nomenclature concerning feeblemindedness, 448.

Norms of age-weight records, 145; on puberty and menstruation, 237.

Nose obstructions as a factor, 219.

Nymphomania, treatment for, 404.

O

Obscenity in old age, 212.

Obsessions, sexualistic, 405.

Obstinacy and self-assertion as related to prior experiences, 766; as a trait leading to misconduct, 766.

Occasional criminalism, 316.

Occupational activities, lack of, causing delinquency, case of, 298 ff.

Offenders, emotional condition of under study, 70; harmed by punishment, 168; predisposed toward adventure, types of, 754.

Offenses, as compared with actual court charges, 144; of old age, peculiarities of, statistics on, 210; of our repeated offenders, 140.

Office force, 46.

Ohio law for study of offenders, 173, 331.

Old age, offenses of, 209; of parents at

conception, as a factor in delinquency of offspring, 206.

Opposites Test, norms on, 110.

Otitis media as a factor, 219.

Outbursts of temper, misconduct, etc., 764.

Over-development, general, related to sex characteristics, 244; of boys, related to delinquency, 255; physical, case of, 242.

P

Pain, diminished sensation of in criminals, 17 *n.*

Paranoia, 604.

Pardons of epileptic offenders, 426.

Parentage, uncertainty about causing mental conflicts, 356.

Parental control, incompetent, causing delinquency, 289.

Parental immorality, neglect, etc., enumerated for our group, 134.

Parental lack of comprehension causing delinquency, 292.

Parental separation causing delinquency, 290.

Parental severity causing delinquency, 289.

Parents, alcoholism of, creating defective environment, 266.

Parents, alcoholism of, diseases of, etc., schedule for recording, 54.

Parents, immorality of, causing misconduct, 291, 410.

Parents of our offenders, alcoholism of, 152, 286.

Parents separated, in our group, 149.

Parents' neglect of sex teaching, 354.

Paresis, 600; caused by syphilis, 229.

Paris institut de medicine légale, 173 *n.*

Pathological arson, 774; in case of mental conflict, 384; literature on, 774.

Pathological intoxication, 683.

Pathological lying, cases of, 732 ff.; characteristics of, 729 ff.; definition of, 771; prognoses in cases of, 731; in its relation to psychoses, 750; Kraepelin's idea of, 771; literature on, 729.

Pathological stealing, 770; during menstrual period, 772; during pregnancy, 773; from mental conflict, cases of, 360 ff.; and mental conflict, case of, 374; types of, causation leading to, 771; typical case of, 374.

Pathological wandering, 776.

Peculiar mental types, enumeration of in our group, 132.

Peculiarities, individual, too complex for criminological systems, 18.

Penal institutions, sex perversions in, 412.

Penal philosophy in relation to responsibility, Tarde on, 20.

Perceptions, analysis of, tests for, 91.

Perception of form and color relationships, 87.

Performance tests, development of, 78.

Personality made up of past and present factors, 25.

Persuasion as related to suggestibility, 93.

Phimosis, as a factor, 225; definition and importance of, 225; in girls, 226.

Photography, value of, 58.

Physical anomalies, chronological, 235.

Physical causes of delinquency, treatment of, 174; of irritability, 767.

Physical characteristics, cases of, inheritance of early development of, 193.

Physical conditions, abnormal enumerated for our group of cases, 135; creating mental dullness, 546; leading to poor social opportunities, case of, 238 ff.

Physical development, cases of inheritance of, excess of, 189.

Physical examination of wayward girls, 65.

Physical inferiority of offenders, 238.

Physical irritations, causing character tendencies, 228.

Physical maturity, 245.

Physical over-development and prematurity of epileptics, cases of, 420 ff.; case of, 242, 244; related to premature puberty, 248.

Physical sex characteristics, over-development of, 245.

Physical traits, inheritance of as causative factor, 198.

Physical vigor, excess of, as cause of delinquency, 231.

Physician as examiner, 36 ff.; prison, qualifications for, 36 *n.*

Physiognomy, changes in, resulting from prison experiences, 311; criminal characteristics in, 58.

Physiological age, as related to mentality, 250 *n.*

Physique of adult criminals, 215; of boys and girls compared according to age, 145; of female offenders, 242.

Pictorial Completion Test, 97; norms on, 111.

Picture, Testimony Test, norms on, 108.

Psychological standpoint, limitations of, 31.

Psychological view of conduct, practical value of, 27.

Psychologist as examiner, 36 ff.; practical problem of, in studying offenders, 76.

Psychology, applied, field of, 31 *n.*; cf adolescent aberrations, 651 ff.; of "the criminal" literature of, 30 *n.*

Psychomotor activity of constitutional excitement, case of, 612.

Psychoneurotic delinquent, case of a, 224.

Psychopathic constitution, synonyms and literature of, 575.

Psychopaths: constitutional inferiors, literature on, 575.

Psychoses and pathological lying, 750; enumeration of in our group, 132; epileptic, 433; from alcohol, 678; from cerebral injuries, 619; major and minor, distinction between, 591; of acute alcoholism, 683; of alcohol among adolescents, 683; of chronic alcoholism, characteristics of, 681; some unclassifiable, 441.

Psychosis caused by excess of snuff, 281, 690.

Pubertal characteristics, 710.

Puberty and mental aberrations, *vide* adolescent psychoses, 651; average age of, statistics on, 237; delayed, case of, 240; premature, in relation to adolescent aberration, cases of, 653 ff.; premature, without overdevelopment, 256; premature, with poor development, case of, 258; premature, related to general over-development, 248; schedule for data concerning, 57.

Punishment, necessity of, 166.

Punitive necessities, 166.

Puzzle-box Test, norms on, 108.

"Pyromania," 774.

Q

Quarreling in families as result of alcoholism, 264.

Quarrelsome parents, as causative factors, 288.

R

Racial characteristics, 765.

Range of Information Test, 102.

Recidivism, Oba's method of dealing with, 25; of alcoholic offenders, 679.

Recidivists coming from bad homes,

285; importance of, 10; statistics on, 10; moral feeling of, 319.

Records as made during examination, 73; character of, 47; extent of, 49; form of, 50, 51; making of, 43; of delinquently inclined, 61; of follow-up work, 62; of psychological tests, 60; subsidiary, 62.

Recreation, relation of to prevention of delinquency, 247.

Recreational centers may be cause of delinquency, 284.

Recreational interests, paucity of, causing delinquency, case of, 298 ff.

Reform in age limits of juvenile court procedure, 726; of prison conditions dependent upon psychological considerations, 315.

Released prisoners, environment of, 286.

Religion among our group of offenders, 151; as substitute for sex impulses, 247.

Religious treatment of delinquency, 175.

Repeated offender, definition of, 14.

Repeated offenders, our group of one thousand, 127; *vide* also RECIDIVISTS.

Research, criminalistic, motives for, 15.

Responsibility for crime while under liquor, 273; of epileptics, 431; legal, 19; difficulty of, 20; insolubility of, 20; problem of, not necessary to face, 20; lessened, of abnormal types 30; recent literature on, 19 *n.*

Restlessness as a characteristic, 769; of adolescence, 714.

Retardation, mental, caused by physical conditions, 547.

Retentive memory, test for, 84.

Rewards and disciplines, the value of in penology, 167.

Revengefulness as leading to delinquency, 767.

Ringworm causing expulsion from school, case of, 232.

Romanticism, adolescent causing suicidal impulses, 724.

S

Sadistic impulses, 406.

Satyriasis, treatment for, 404.

Scheme of classification according to abilities, 113.

School children, physical ailments among, statistics on, 219.

School companions causing delinquency, 293.

School history, schedule for data concerning, 56.

School irritation causing anti-social tendencies, 295.

School work, tests for, 81.

Scientific studies necessary for proper treatment, 178.

Secondary dementia, 603.

Scolding leading to mental conflict, case of, 394.

Seasonal crimes, validity of theory of, 23.

Seduction by males as compared to seduction by females, 144.

Self-accusation of drug habitués, 731; of morphinists, 277; case of, 746.

Self-assertion, adolescent, causing delinquency in girls; 724; as an excessive phenomenon leading toward social offense, 766.

Self-control defective, causing criminalism, 533; no excuse for legal fredom, 167.

Self-control, defects in during adolescence, 714; treatment of, 545; lack of, periodic, 764.

Semi-responsibles, 592.

Senile criminality caused by alcohol, 271.

Senile delinquents, as first offenders, 211; mental conditions of, 211.

Senile dementia and delinquency, 210.

Senile offenders, local physical conditions in, 212.

Senile sex offenses, relation of enlarged prostate to, 228.

Senility in relation to delinquency, 209; of parents at conception, as a factor, 206.

Sensitiveness, lack of, caused by mental defect, 76.

Sensory illusion tests, 93.

Sensory judgment, tests for, 92.

Separation of parents causing delinquency, 290; in our families, 149.

Setting fires, 774.

Severity of parents causing delinquency, 289.

Sex characteristics undeveloped after puberty, 240.

Sex crimes as related to individual peculiarities, 402.

Sex delinquency of feebleminded girls, case illustrating, 459; in girls, as prevented by marriage, 248; relation of to early maturity, 253.

Sex experiences, early, causing other misconduct, 410; improper, enumerated for our group, 134.

Sex habits causing mental dullness,

559; excessive, 409 n.; in prison life, 313.

Sex impulses excessive, cases of inheritance of, 192; treatment of by segregation, 247.

Sex life, abnormal, causing mental dullness, 559; and mental conflicts, 356.

Sex offenses, relation of hypnotism to, 706; and over-development in girls, 246.

Sex organs, irritation of, 227.

Sex over-development, cases of inheritance of, 193 ff.

Sex perversions among vagrants, 779; as related to pathological lying, cases of, 732 ff.; experiences with, causing reaction towards criminalism in adolescents, 723; importance of, 411; in penal institutions, 412; literature on, 411; psychological aspects of, 411; relationship of effeminacy to, 241; treatment of, 412.

Sex pervert and constitutional inferior, case of, 584.

Sex precocity related to delinquency, cases of, 244, 248, 256, 258.

Sex prematurity of epileptics, cases of, 429 ff.

Sex relationship causing susceptibility to influence of another, 704.

Sex teaching, neglect by parents, 354.

Sexual abnormality, criterion of, 400.

Sexual fetishism, thieving to gratify, 405.

Sexualism, abnormal, 400; as distinguished from sexual criminalism, 400; related to epilepsy, 412; related to psychoses, 412; relation of to stabbing women, etc., 406; underlying conditions of, 401.

Sexuality, pathological, field of, 400.

Sexual offenses of old age, 210 ff.

Sexual vice, arising from housing conditions, 291; caused by self-abnegation of women, 405; of epileptic women, case illustrating, 437; of mental defectives, treatment of, 462.

Sex vigor, excessive, case of in epilepsy 231.

Shoplifting during menstruation, 634. during pregnancy, 634 ff.; studies on, 772 ff.

Short term punishments, folly of, 171.

Simulation of epilepsy, 780; insanity, 780; mental or physical disease, 779.

Snuff, [tobacco], excess of, creating psychosis, 281; psychosis from overuse of, 690.

Social basis of mental classification, 114.

Social importance of dementia precox, 593.

Social requirements in relation to mental subnormality, 492.

Social suggestibility, abnormal, 695; cases of, 698 ff.; dual, 708; individual variations of, 697; in relation to tests, 93 ff.; of members of a crowd, 703; resentment of idea of by offenders, 705; treatment of, 702.

Social service for ex-prisoners, 286.

Social treatment of epileptics, 431.

Socially important abilities of the feebleminded, 463 ff.

Socially suggestible individuals, results of tests on, 94.

Special abilities leading to adolescent dissatisfaction and criminalism, 768; tests for, 100.

Special capacities, tests for, 82.

Special genius of feebleminded individuals, 463 ff.

Special picture puzzle, norms on, 107.

Speech defects as a factor, 220.

Sphincter, lack of control of, in delinquents, 227.

Sphincter, tight, relationship to delinquency, 228.

Stage life, desire for, 764; relation of to criminalism, 295.

Statistical methods, application of, 6; as extremely applied, 24 n.

Statistical summary of causative factors in our group, 130.

Statistics, critique on the basis of, 126; interpretation of our, 129; of children in families of delinquents, 148; of birthplaces, of our offenders, 149; of parents of our offenders, 150; on alcoholism and criminality, 679; criminalistics, causative factors necessary for, 15; suicide, 775 n.; our group of cases for, 127.

Stealing as a result of mental imagery, cases of, 341 ff.; result of picture shows, cases of, 341 ff.; the result of mental conflict, cases of, 357 ff.; at the menstrual period, 628; during pregnancy, 634 ff.; for fetishism, 773; for the sake of adventure, 773; pathological, 770.

Stealing impulse, interpretation of causes of, 772; relation of to menstrual period, 772.

Step-parents, of our offenders, 149.

Stigmata, desirable data concerning, 58; of degeneracy, statistics of, 146; of degeneracy in normal compared with abnormal, 17 n.; of degeneracy in feebleminded, 17.

Stimulants and narcotics, as indulged in by members of our group, 138; causing mental dullness, cases of, 556; the use of, with relation to masturbation, 408.

Stories, pernicious, causing criminalism, 304.

Study, of case causing cure, 14 n.; of delinquents, economic value of, 15.

Stuttering, as a factor, 221.

Stupidity, as a trait, 769.

St. Vitus dance, mental conditions of, 613 ff.

Subconscious mental life, 116 ff.; controlling conduct, 26, 27.

Subnormality, mental, definition of, 491.

Substitution, after psychoanalysis, 121.

Substitution phenomena in mental conflict, case of, 367.

Suggestibility, abnormal, social, 695.

Suggestibility by tests as compared to lawyer's examination, 94; contrary, 766; social, as related to tests, 93 ff.; social, paucity of literature on, 696; tests for, 93, 697; to one individual, 704.

Suggestible individuals, socially, results of tests on, 94.

Suggestion, hypnotic, to criminalism, literature on, 706; to criminalism arising from newspaper reading, 303.

Suicidal impulses from adolescent romanticism, 724; from imagery of picture shows, case of, 347.

Suicide, 775; and dementia precox, 593; and insanity, 776; and melancholia, 602; and psychoanalysis, 776 n.; as an adolescent impulse, 776; at the menstrual period, 627; in heredity of our offenders, 156; literature and statistics on, 775.

Summary, diagnostic, 61, 122.

Surgery for hypersexualism, 404.

Surgical operation for hypersexualism, 231.

Swindling, pathological, case of in subnormal verbalist, 506.

Syphilis, blood tests for, 205; congenital, 137, 138; after-effect of, statistics on, 205 n.; in relation to later delinquency, 205; mental deficiency in sufferers from, 206; moral development in sufferers from, 206; statistics of, 146; relation to criminalism, 229.

System, card, for statistical purposes, 52; for recording data, 53; of records 51.

encies, 341; related to criminalism, 307.

Visual memory for form, test for, 84; norms on, 108.

Visual verbal memory, test for, 83.

Vocabulary, test for, 103.

Vocational dissatisfaction causing delinquency, 296.

Vocational diagnosis, value of this approach, 47.

Vocational judgment test, 92.

Vocational tests, hints on, 100.

Volitional powers, tests of, 95.

Volubility of cocainists, 278.

W

Wanderers, classification of, 778; homosexual perversions among, 779; physical condition of, 778.

Wandering, as aberrational impulse, 777; related to desire for excitement, 755; result of sex perversions, 777; in cases of feeblemindedness, 777; literature on, 777 n.; pathological, 776; tendency to from constitutional excitement, case of, 612; with loss of memory, 637 ff.

Wanderlust, Die, 763, 777; and mental conflict, 764.

Weight correlated with age, 144.

Will, tests for, 95; critique on, 96.

"Wild West" crimes, 753.

Women, self-abnegation impulses of leading to immorality, 405.

Working methods and statement of, 33.

Z

Ziehen's judgment tests, 92.

PATTERSON SMITH REPRINT SERIES IN
CRIMINOLOGY, LAW ENFORCEMENT, AND SOCIAL PROBLEMS

1. Lewis: *The Development of American Prisons and Prison Customs, 1776-1845*
2. Carpenter: *Reformatory Prison Discipline*
3. Brace: *The Dangerous Classes of New York*
4. Dix: *Remarks on Prisons and Prison Discipline in the United States*
5. Bruce *et al: The Workings of the Indeterminate-Sentence Law and the Parole System in Illinois*
6. Wickersham Commission: *Complete Reports, Including the Mooney-Billings Report.* 14 Vols.
7. Livingston: *Complete Works on Criminal Jurisprudence.* 2 Vols.
8. Cleveland Foundation: *Criminal Justice in Cleveland*
9. Illinois Association for Criminal Justice: *The Illinois Crime Survey*
10. Missouri Association for Criminal Justice: *The Missouri Crime Survey*
11. Aschaffenburg: *Crime and Its Repression*
12. Garofalo: *Criminology*
13. Gross: *Criminal Psychology*
14. Lombroso: *Crime, Its Causes and Remedies*
15. Saleilles: *The Individualization of Punishment*
16. Tarde: *Penal Philosophy*
17. McKelvey: *American Prisons*
18. Sanders: *Negro Child Welfare in North Carolina*
19. Pike: *A History of Crime in England.* 2 Vols.
20. Herring: *Welfare Work in Mill Villages*
21. Barnes: *The Evolution of Penology in Pennsylvania*
22. Puckett: *Folk Beliefs of the Southern Negro*
23. Fernald *et al: A Study of Women Delinquents in New York State*
24. Wines: *The State of the Prisons and of Child-Saving Institutions*
25. Raper: *The Tragedy of Lynching*
26. Thomas: *The Unadjusted Girl*
27. Jorns: *The Quakers as Pioneers in Social Work*
28. Owings: *Women Police*
29. Woolston: *Prostitution in the United States*
30. Flexner: *Prostitution in Europe*
31. Kelso: *The History of Public Poor Relief in Massachusetts: 1820-1920*
32. Spivak: *Georgia Nigger*
33. Earle: *Curious Punishments of Bygone Days*
34. Bonger: *Race and Crime*
35. Fishman: *Crucibles of Crime*
36. Brearley: *Homicide in the United States*
37. Graper: *American Police Administration*
38. Hichborn: *"The System"*
39. Steiner & Brown: *The North Carolina Chain Gang*
40. Cherrington: *The Evolution of Prohibition in the United States of America*
41. Colquhoun: *A Treatise on the Commerce and Police of the River Thames*
42. Colquhoun: *A Treatise on the Police of the Metropolis*
43. Abrahamsen: *Crime and the Human Mind*
44. Schneider: *The History of Public Welfare in New York State: 1609-1866*
45. Schneider & Deutsch: *The History of Public Welfare in New York State: 1867-1940*
46. Crapsey: *The Nether Side of New York*
47. Young: *Social Treatment in Probation and Delinquency*
48. Quinn: *Gambling and Gambling Devices*
49. McCord & McCord: *Origins of Crime*
50. Worthington & Topping: *Specialized Courts Dealing with Sex Delinquency*